READINGS IN CHILD BEHAVIOR AND DEVELOPMENT

Third Edition

Readings
in
Child
Behavior
and
Development

THIRD EDITION

CELIA STENDLER LAVATELLI
University of Illinois

FAITH STENDLER
Massachusetts Mental Health Center

HARCOURT BRACE JOVANOVICH, INC.
New York   Chicago   San Francisco   Atlanta

PHOTOGRAPH CREDITS

Cover: David Attie
Part 1 (facing page 1): Ken Heyman
Part 2 (page 70): Oscar Buitrago
Part 3 (page 138): David Attie
Part 4 (page 210): Science Curriculum Improvement Study
Part 5 (page 308): Berne Green
Part 6 (page 416): Ken Heyman

ISBN: 0-15-575805-5

Library of Congress Catalog Card Number: 74-184120

Printed in the United States of America

PREFACE

The Third Edition of *Readings in Child Behavior and Development* was both easier and more difficult to prepare than its predecessors. The structure of the anthology was not hard to establish; it was dictated by the concerns of the field. Choosing the papers was more difficult, because of the exponential expansion of the literature. We favored papers that presented important concepts, that illustrated a variety of methodological approaches, and that would seem relevant to today's students.

The book is divided into six parts, each with a detailed introduction that serves as a brief summary of what is important in the various domains of child development. The first part, "The Grand Systems," is intended to give the reader a solid theoretical foundation with which he can approach the individual papers. We identify the "grand systems," or major schools, as the psychoanalytic, the behaviorist, and the interactionist, and we include papers by authors closely identified with each system. The psychoanalytic school is represented by Erik Erikson and Anna Freud; the behaviorist by B. F. Skinner; and the interactionist by Heinz Werner and Jean Piaget as well as by Eckhard Hess on the ethologist's contribution to child study. This section acquaints the reader with concepts and terms he will meet in later selections, such as *object permanence* (derived from Piaget), *latency* (of Freudian origin), *attachment behavior* (from the psychoanalytic and ethological schools), and *behavior modification* (derived from behaviorism). Each of the papers in the five parts that follow ("The Culture and the Child"; "Infancy"; "Perceptual and Cognitive Development"; "Socialization Processes"; "Socializing Agents") reflects one of the theoretical approaches introduced in Part 1.

The field of child development is in constant flux. Research findings are changing our perspectives, new hypotheses are being tested, and new conclusions are constantly being drawn. The selections included here reflect some of the major changes that have influenced the field since the Second Edition appeared. We have of course included some classic papers, such as Erikson's "Eight Ages of Man," Anna Freud and Sophie Dann's "An Experiment in Group Upbringing," and Berta

Bornstein's "On Latency," but the majority of the articles were published within the last six years, and all but four of the selections are new to this edition.

This edition differs from the second in its organization. As already noted, there is a separate section for theoretical orientation, whereas theory was not made so explicit in the last edition. Also, there is no separate section on the determinants of behavior (including biological factors) as there was in the Second Edition. It seemed to us that the field of child development is now sufficiently sophisticated to assume the biological as the foundation for each theoretical school. Implicit in the interactionist theory of Piaget and Werner, as well as in psychoanalytic and behaviorist theory, is the notion that man is a biological system and that nature as well as nurture must be acknowledged. John Bowlby's paper on the development of attachment is a good illustration of this new sophistication. He discusses attachment behaviors in several species as forms of instinctive behavior that in man gradually become modified in organism-environment interaction.

Because we felt that conceptually the research studies on the disadvantaged included here differed so greatly from one another, we decided to place these studies in the sections dealing with the specific problems they treat rather than to have a separate section dealing only with the disadvantaged. Lee Rainwater's classic study of black families, William Labov and Paul Cohen's paper on Black English, Herbert Birch on health and educational problems of the poor, Lawrence Kohlberg on compensatory education, Gerald Lesser *et al.* on special cognitive abilities of various ethnic groups, Robert Hess and Virginia Shipman on social-class differences in language training—all make a special contribution to some aspect of how children grow and develop as well as to our understanding of the problems of the disadvantaged.

New to this edition is a separate section on infancy. We felt that the numerous studies on the infant's visual behavior, attention, and attachment behavior, all revealing a far more competent organism than had previously been suspected, warranted special treatment.

Cognition has been one of the dominant themes of developmental research in the last decade, and this edition reflects the strong interest and advances in this area. The material on Piaget, strong in the Second Edition, has been expanded here. The introduction to Part 1 includes a lengthy and, we hope, clear explanation of Piaget's developmental theory, with a paper by Piaget, "Development and Learning," included as a follow-up. In addition, Part 4, "Perceptual and Cognitive Development," includes two papers that deal with the difficult problem of fostering equilibration in the Piagetian sense, and that offer positive guidelines, in contrast to the negative results of the earlier research that is reviewed in the introduction to Part 4. Moreover, the papers in Part 2, "The Culture and the Child," are cognitively oriented. Whereas formerly anthropologists were concerned with the cultural foundations of personality, many are now doing cross-cultural studies of cognitive problems.

Choosing papers on language development was difficult, because there are so many of high quality available. We finally opted in favor of papers by Carol Chomsky, Labov and Cohen, and Hess and Shipman. Chomsky's study of how children master one of the many complexities of syntactic structure is valuable for two reasons: it introduces the student to the fascinating intricacies of linguistics, and it is one of the few available studies of syntax acquisition beyond the preschool level. Labov and Cohen's paper also sheds light on language structure, in this case differences between Black English and Standard English. The Hess-Shipman paper, in Part 6, is one of the few laboratory studies of how black mothers use language in interacting with their children. These three papers, together with the discussion of language in the introduction to Part 4 and some of the sources cited in the references for that section, should provide a valuable introduction to an important area of developmental psychology.

Social learning theory and behavior modification receive a great deal more attention in this edition than in the earlier ones. Albert Bandura and his students have been actively researching the role of imitation and modeling in socialization, and Donald Baer has been one of the major researchers on modifying behavior by the use of Skinnerian techniques. Papers presenting their points of view are included in Parts 5 and 6.

Students who take courses in child development or developmental psychology often do so for very personal reasons. They seek knowledge not only about the child, but about themselves. We believe that one of the aims of child study courses should be to meet this need. In the introduction to Part 1 there is a detailed explanation of development from a psychoanalytic point of view. Erik Erikson's "Eight Ages of Man," which for more than twenty years has been helping students increase their sense of self-awareness, is our opening selection. Papers by Anna Freud, Berta Bornstein, and Samuel Waldfogel *et al.* also contribute valuable insights into the dynamics of personality. And Kenneth Keniston's analysis of student dissent may have special significance for many readers.

The aim of this anthology is not only to educate the student about the concerns of developmental psychology but to familiarize him with the various methods and techniques of research. The papers reporting empirical research represent a wide range of such methods and techniques. Many of the selections have been abridged to remove material that seemed overly technical or peripheral, but the basic methodology has been preserved in each case. There are papers that are normative in character, describing aspects of development in a natural setting, such as Carol Chomsky's paper on language development. Those papers that are normative-explanatory, like Lawrence Kohlberg and Edward Zigler's on sex-typing, seek to analyze the normative in terms of a deeper behavioral structure. Other empirical studies (for example, Silvia Bell's paper on the development of the concept of object) attempt to find causal relations among, or antecedents for, particular behaviors. And finally, there is the research methodology of the experimentalist, who, in addition to using experimental methods, works directly on observable behaviors, such as infant sucking. Whereas the investigator working on socialization problems must often infer from overt behavior the existence of the particular trait that interests him, the "pure" experimentalist is interested only in highly predictable behaviors that can be observed directly under laboratory conditions. The Philip Salapatek and Lewis Lipsitt articles in the "Infancy" section are examples of particularly valuable research of this type.

Our view of the child has changed in the eighteen years since the First Edition appeared. We now see the infant as actively regulating his own development, and we can spell out in far greater detail than was possible earlier the factors involved in that self-regulation. We are also wiser—though sadder—about the impact of American culture, particularly on middle-class youth and the poor. We have seen the passive college-age generation of the 1950's give way to the rebellious generation of the 1960's—a generation demanding radical changes in a materialistic, war-dominated culture—and this in turn give way to a quieter, but still concerned, generation. Many students have rejected careers in science because they want to be involved with human beings. Concerned about the effect of society on the child, they are choosing to work with children as teachers, psychologists, guidance counselors, social workers, and researchers. They enter developmental psychology or child development courses often to seek self-understanding as well as an understanding of children. We hope that these readings will help give these students a view of the child that is rooted not only in scientific inquiry but in the humanities as well.

We want to acknowledge the editorial help, intelligent and supportive, of Judith Greissman and Ronne Peltzman of Harcourt Brace Jovanovich; the unfailingly reliable and competent secretarial assistance of Mildred Goff; the cheerful, capable assistance of Bridget Lamont Later, librarian; and the discerning comments of the reader-critics who reviewed preliminary outlines and drafts: Eugene S. Gollin (University of Colorado); Wilbur A. Hass (Shimer College); Martin L. Hoffman (University of Michigan); Freda G. Rebelsky (Boston University); Harold W. Stevenson (University of Michigan); and, especially, Jerome Kagan (Harvard University) and Barry Silverstein (The William Paterson College of New Jersey).

Celia Stendler Lavatelli
Faith Stendler

CONTENTS

Part Three INFANCY

Part Four PERCEPTUAL AND COGNITIVE
              DEVELOPMENT

Part Five SOCIALIZATION PROCESSES

Part Six   SOCIALIZING AGENTS: THE HOME, THE SCHOOL, AND THE PEER GROUP

THE GRAND SYSTEMS

INTRODUCTION

Developmental psychologists are interested in studying and explaining the behavior of children. Such studies and explanations, while they may be carried on empirically, are rooted in a theory of how growth and development take place. Three theories or grand systems predominate: *psychoanalytic theory,* stemming from Freud and revised and extended by post-Freudians, notably Erikson; *Piagetian theory,* based on the equilibration or interaction principle; and *behaviorism,* developed by Pavlov, Hull, Skinner, and others. Although each of the grand systems is complete in itself—that is, each in its own way has the potential to shed light on any aspect of psychological development—there is some specialization with regard to the kinds of problems to which they are applied. Freudian psychoanalytic theory is usually applied to character and personality problems, and Piagetian theory to problems in cognition. It is only recently that relationships between affectivity and the intellect, between Freud and Piaget, have begun to be explored. Behaviorism, with its offshoots in S-R theory and social learning theory, has had a longer history of application to separate problems of personality dynamics and learning, but it has not been used to explain relationships between the two areas.

PSYCHOANALYTIC THEORY

Psychoanalytic theory is a scientific theory originally developed by Sigmund Freud to explain human personality and behavior. Central to this theory is the concept of the unconscious, the belief that much of what motivates human beings is determined by memories, thoughts, or wishes of which we are not consciously aware. Closely allied with the concept of the unconscious is the principle of psychic determinism, which maintains that each psychic event is predetermined by previous psychic events of which we may not be consciously aware.

Memories, thoughts, wishes, or other mental phenomena are excluded from conscious awareness when they are in some way objectionable or painful to the conscious self. They are not, however, completely pushed aside but are expressed in some disguised manner. An obvious example is that of the do-gooder who feels he is protecting the morality of the public by reviewing obscene books or movies for censorship but is simultaneously hiding from himself the tremendous unconscious gratification obtained in the course of his duties as public censor. Similarly, the man who is so angry at his boss that he wants to give him a good punch develops a hysterical paralysis of his right arm so as to protect himself against the fulfillment of the objectionable impulse. The phenomenon of excluding from consciousness an objectionable thought, wish, or idea is termed *repression*. The individual represses what is unacceptable and rationalizes what he has done by attributing it to reality. The girl who criticizes her friend's taste in clothes represses her real motivation— envy for her friend's clothes and hatred of her for the admiration she arouses—and rationalizes her statements by the conviction that the clothes "really are ugly."

Before we elaborate on the content of psychoanalytic theory, it is important to comment on the methodology of psychoanalysis. The empirical data on which the theory is based came primarily from Freud's clinical observations of himself and others, not from controlled laboratory studies. The patient was asked to relax and to repeat his thoughts as they came to mind, ignoring any logical contradictions or tendencies toward self-criticism. The idea was that the patient would be guided by his own thoughts or free associations. With this technique, Freud was able to discover the existence of repressed wishes and memories that stemmed from infantile emotional experiences which were not otherwise accessible to conscious awareness. By this method, Freud was able to explain how adult personality traits and characteristic ways of reacting were originally shaped by childhood experiences. For example, the man who becomes violently angry at his boss for not granting a desired special expense account may be angry at him not only because of the reality of the financial hardship but also because the boss represents his harsh and depriving father. His boss's refusal to grant a privilege also represents the frustration of his wish to be "special" in his relationship to his father. In short, this man may be overreacting to the reality of the situation because of the predetermination of his character by his early childhood experiences. Thus psychoanalytic theory holds that fantasies and wishes we had as children are repressed but persist in the unconscious and make their influence felt on the adult personality.

Psychoanalytic theory is a theory based on instincts, or drives. The two most important instincts are the sexual (libidinal) and aggressive drives. Unfortunately the psychoanalytic theory of aggression is not yet well elaborated in the literature, so we shall restrict ourselves here to a discussion of the development of libidinous strivings and the theory of infantile sexuality. From analysis of the free associations of his patients, Freud discovered that, contrary to popular opinion, sexuality does not begin in adolescence but that sexual impulses are present during the first years of life. The term *sexuality* is not restricted to adult sexual intercourse but is used in a broader sense to include love between friends of the same sex, parent-child relationships, and pleasant bodily sensations deriving from the three principal erotogenic zones—the mouth, the anus, and the genital organs—and from the skin. The infant experiences interest in his bodily organs and gains sensual or sexual gratification from this interest. Early sexual experiences differ from adult genital desires in that they are independent of the need to love another person. Hence they are autoerotic.

The first zone to be utilized for sexual purposes is the *oral* zone. The infant uses his mouth not only for obtaining nourishment but for pleasurable stimulation as well. This is evidenced by the fact that the infant will suck his thumb when the bottle or the breast is not available. Taking in with the mouth is equated with getting love and affection. With the eruption of teeth the oral receptivity (sucking) becomes more aggressive and there is more active taking in. Ideas of being eaten or eating up represent a way of uniting with another person or object and hence are a primitive form of relating to objects. Experiencing satiation is equated with feeling loved; deprivation and hunger are equivalent to a state of being unloved. At first, however, the infant does not differentiate between himself and other objects or persons. Other objects are valuable to him only insofar as they satisfy his own needs and tensions. These needs and tensions are not always taken care of immediately—the baby is allowed to go hungry and experiences the feeling of frustration. In his frustration, he comes to realize that it is only through external persons that his needs get satisfied. Thus he comes to differentiate the self from the not-self.

The infant's experience in this oral period must not be too frustrating or too gratifying lest he become fixated at this level. Fixation means that the predominant ways of relating to objects—the taking in of objects in an orally aggressive way and the attitude that objects exist only for one's satisfaction—persist beyond the first year of life. Adults who failed to successfully resolve this period characteristically relate to others in a demanding, voracious "I could eat you up" way. They are also noted for their predominantly narcissistic orientation, that is, an urge to satisfy their own needs for emotional supplies without consideration of their objects. The orally fixated individual wants love but is unable to return it.

About the second year of life the *anal* phase begins and the anus becomes the primary erotogenous zone. The enjoyment of pleasurable sensations through excretion and retention of feces becomes paramount. The first anal strivings are autoerotic but later become object-directed as the child becomes involved in toilet training with the mother. The retention of feces as well as the violent expulsion of them gives opportunity for hostile as well as sexual gratification; the child can now exercise power over the mother by giving or not giving the feces. If the toilet training is too strict the child may retaliate by being messy, extravagant, disorderly, and irresponsible. Alternatively, he may defend against such tendencies by being excessively neat, clean, frugal, fastidious, and preoccupied with time and money.

The next stage of psychosexual development is the *phallic* phase. Here, for the first time, we must consider the development of boys and girls separately. In boys, the penis becomes the dominant zone for sensual pleasure. The little boy takes pride in urination and in displaying his penis to little girls. However, the pride he takes in it is still autoerotic and is not aimed at giving pleasure to another individual. At the same time, the little boy has to deal with the blow to his self-esteem of not being quite grown up and having a penis as big as his father's. (We call this blow to self-esteem a *narcissistic injury.*) The little boy also has to deal with *castration anxiety.* Because he does not differentiate between males and females, but instead thinks in terms of castrated and not castrated individuals, the little boy assumes that girls have lost their penises and fears that something may happen to his prized organ as well.

During this time the boy's love for his mother becomes more intense. He wants to possess his mother exclusively and sees his father as his rival. The aggression he feels for his father—the wish to kill him off and replace him—is at least as significant as the sexual urges he has for his mother. This set of feelings is known as the *Oedipus complex*. The little boy realizes that he cannot have his mother in the same way that his father has her. He realizes that his intense wish to possess her is prohibited, and he fears that he will be castrated for his desires. The fear of castration and the recognition that he cannot have his mother act as the impetus for him to repress his love for her and identify with his father. In short, he says to himself that he will become like daddy and someday when he grows up he can have someone like mommy.

The phallic phase in girls is quite different from that of boys because of the anatomical difference. Freud contended that the clitoris is the female's counterpart to the penis, and that initially it serves the same function. According to Freud, there is pleasure associated with being like the father and enjoyment of clitoral sensations. When the little girl discovers that boys have more prominent organs, she develops intense *penis envy*. She sees the male as having opportunities for sexual gratification that she does not have, feelings of inferiority and inadequacy develop, and she blames her mother for her deprivation. As the initial tie to the mother is weakened, the little girl develops an intense desire for her father. She deals with the narcissistic injury resulting from not having a penis by developing a wish to have a baby by her father. Most often it is a male baby she wishes to have, a wish that is interpreted as a compensation for the lack of the male sexual organ.

The development of the Oedipus complex in girls is complicated, for it involves a change in object from the pre-Oedipal mother to the father. The girl wants the father, but like the boy realizes that she cannot have the opposite-sexed parent. Her relationship with her mother is not solely one of hatred but rather is ambivalent; she feels rivalry and hostility toward her mother, but she also loves her mother very much and realizes that she needs her. She fears that her wish to possess daddy will enrage mother, and it is this fear of loss of love, as well as the realization that her wish cannot be attained, that impels her to renounce her sexual desires for her father and identify with her mother. The incentive to renounce the Oedipal strivings is less intense in girls since there is no anxiety over castration.

Failure to resolve the Oedipal struggle is seen as the basis for all neuroses. Certain situations and conditions make it difficult for the child to work through his Oedipal conflict. One such condition is seductiveness on the part of the parents. The seduction may be subtle and not overt; instances of actual seduction are rare. Parents do not engage in intercourse with their children, but they often seduce children without being aware of it. They may, for example, take a child into bed with them under the guise of his being sick, overstimulate the child through too intense tickling games, dress and undress in front of him, and generally fail to set limits. If parents are generally too permissive, the child comes to believe that if they cannot say "no" to any of his demands, the parents cannot say "no" to his sexual desires. Seductive behavior on the part of the parents increases the intensity of these desires and makes the child feel helpless to control his impulses. This is frightening for the child.

Seduction may stimulate regression to an earlier mode of relating, such as the anal or oral stage. For example, the boy whose mother is seductive may regress to a homosexual object choice. He sees all relations with women as being as frightening as the original experience with his mother and so turns to men for his love objects. A woman, unable to renounce her love for her father and disappointed in her search for her father in all relationships, seeks out situations to reenact the relationship with the pre-Oedipal mother.

Psychoanalytic theory describes not only a theory of personality development and its dynamics, but also the organization of personality. Thus it has its structural as well as its developmental and dynamic components. The human personality is divided into three categories. The first is the *id,* the basis for instinctual drives, most of which are unconscious. The id is primitive and unorganized, and it follows primary process thinking to the exclusion of such processes as logical reasoning and the consideration of reality. The id operates on the pleasure principle—it wants what it wants and it wants it immediately. It seeks gratification, regardless of the consequences in reality.

An individual who is guided purely by his id has not adapted well to reality. Impulsive behavior may actually result in less gratification—stealing, for example, may result in being locked up. To make a successful adaptation to life, one must consider reality and negotiate with the environment. To do this a new structure is required, the *ego.* In the well-adjusted personality, the ego is the executive of the personality and controls the id. It can say to the id "wait!" and postpone gratification until the conditions in reality are ripe. Through thought and reason—secondary processes—the individual can develop a plan of action that best accomplishes what he wants. The ego can test reality, can try out various solutions until it finds one that works.

Defense Mechanisms

As the individual learns that he cannot seek immediate gratification of his impulses but must conform to both the demands of reality and the demands of morality, the ego develops a set of defensive maneuvers, or *defense mechanisms,* against the id. The ego fears the consequences of unchecked instinctual gratification, either from the outside world or from his conscience. As a result, anxiety develops and sets in motion the defense process. We cannot present here a complete account of all of the different defense mechanisms, but a few of the most common ones will be reviewed.

One of the most important defense mechanisms of the ego is *repression.* The ego excludes from conscious awareness objectionable instinctual demands or their derivatives in the form of memories, emotions, or desires. Repression is the key defense in normal or neurotic individuals. For example, most individuals are not aware of the incestuous fantasies they have for their parents; these are repressed. A young woman may seek to fulfill the fantasy by marrying someone who is "like daddy," but her real motivation in seeking such a mate is not accessible to conscious awareness. Before repression takes place, Oedipal fantasies may be very much on the surface. Thus it is not unusual to hear a small child talk of how he wants to marry mommy so he can be a daddy to her. In adulthood, these fantasies are repressed, except in serious emotional disturbances.

In the psychoses, there is failure of repression. The ego of the psychotic individual may be flooded with all sorts of incestuous or homosexual fantasies that the neurotic is able to keep from consciousness. It is this flooding of the ego that leads to the "crazy" behavior of the psychotic; the socially unacceptable, bizarre fantasies may find some kind of expression in real life. Similarly, in alcoholic or drug intoxications repression is weakened and the ego is unable to defend against libidinal or aggressive impulses. The defense mechanism of repression can be very useful in helping an individual get along in the world. Sexual impulses that have been repressed are expressed in the form of acceptable flirtatious behavior; aggressive impulses are expressed through doing one's work and getting ahead in the world. With the passing of the Oedipus complex, these acceptable behaviors are what the child must learn. Later, the coming of adolescence brings a heightening of instinctual drives, and the defensive structure of the individual is taxed again. Once again he must struggle to maintain the repression of his drives. When these impulses are successfully repressed and channeled into socially acceptable behavior, the additional defense process involved is *sublimation:* the individual redirects the energy of his instinctual drives into the performance of socially useful tasks.

Reaction formation is another defense mechanism of the ego used both by neurotics and by normal individuals. In this defense, the ego covers up the existence of an impulse by assuming the opposite attitude. Hate is replaced by love, cruelty by gentleness, dirtiness by cleanliness, and so on. The case of a child who always has to be good and never mischievous is an example of a situation where this defense is important. The excessive rigidity with which these obsequious attitudes are adhered to betrays their defensive quality.

Isolation is a defensive maneuver that is similar to repression. The difference is that instead of forgetting the fantasy connected with a wish or a crucial memory, the individual forgets only its emotional significance. Often the painful effects associated with a past experience are dealt with by isolation. A child, for example, may acknowledge the death of a loved one, but he will bar from his consciousness the sadness associated with the loss, thus making the loss more bearable. This defense mechanism is commonly used in the obsessive-compulsive neuroses.

Regression may also be considered a defense mechanism. It most commonly occurs in connection with Oedipal strivings. In the face of severe conflicts in this phase of instinctual development, the child may regress to an earlier phase of his instinctual life which he remembers to be more gratifying. The disappointments of the Oedipal period—the frustration of not being able to exclusively possess mommy or daddy—may be dealt with by regressing to the pre-Oedipal object choice. The little girl, instead of moving forward in her latency tasks, such as growing more independent of her mother or mastering tasks demanded by the school, may attempt to reenact the earlier mother-child relationship. In an attempt to re-create the exclusive relationship she had with her mother as an infant, she may, for example, withdraw from her peers or refuse to go to school.

Denial and *projection* are defensive maneuvers used commonly in childhood. Denial involves treating an intolerable reality or instinct as if it did not exist. It is used extensively in play and fantasy. The child who moves to another neighborhood and loses a friend denies the loss by inventing an imaginary companion. Similarly, the child may deny his own smallness and weakness in comparison to his father by playing at being Superman. As one can see from these examples, denial involves a serious impairment of reality-testing and is indicative of a serious disturbance if it persists or is used extensively in adulthood. Thus we are amused by the child's imaginary companion or his being Superman, but we regard the grandiose delusions that the psychotically ill person has about being someone important or famous as quite "crazy" and bizarre.

Similarly, projection plays its greatest role in early life. Projection involves attributing a wish or an impulse of one's own to someone or something outside oneself. Thus the individual denies his hostility for another person and projects it onto that person. He says, in effect, "I don't hate him; he hates me." This is a common phenomenon in early childhood. The child who is scolded and told he is naughty says to his parent, "No, it's not me who's naughty; it's my brother." Projection, like denial, involves a serious disturbance of reality-testing. If projection is used extensively, boundaries between self and not-self become unclear, for there is confusion as to which impulses are one's own and which can in fact be attributed to others. It is thus considered a defense originating in the first year of life, before the differentiation between self and not-self has been made. It is used to some extent by neurotic individuals, but it is most blatant in paranoid schizophrenia, where the patient may, for example, project his violent impulses and feel that he is being followed by people who intend to kill him.

An object, which may be any person or thing toward whom sexual energy is directed, may be incorporated, a process in which a substitute for the object may be built up within the self. This mechanism is termed *introjection* and can be considered a defensive maneuver. For example, the child may feel rage at his mother for leaving him. But because he dares not outwardly express the rage he feels toward her, he instead incorporates her image and then takes his anger out on himself as though she were part of him. It is a primitive defense, for it implies the unconscious union with another, such as that enjoyed prenatally or during early infancy. It is most commonly used in dealing with loss; the lost object is incorporated and the relationship with the lost object is then continued on an intrapsychic level. The self-degradation, self-reproaches, and feelings of guilt of the depressed patient are indications that the struggle with the ambivalently held object is being repeated within the personality, with the rage aroused by the loss of the object now directed toward the self. The individual himself becomes the victim of the rage that the lost object once received.

Identification is a defense mechanism that is related to introjection, but which can be considered less primitive. While introjection involves complete incorporation, identification involves the taking on of only certain aspects or attitudes of another person, and in a more abstract, less self-punitive way. The little boy identifies with the strength and competence of his father. Because he identifies with what the father can do well and wishes to emulate him, he learns tasks crucial to making a successful adjustment to life. He does not devour the father, as in introjection, but internalizes only certain characteristics of the father. Identification is thus a process important to healthy development; introjection is a more pathological process in which the total object is incorporated. The extent to which we use these processes determines to a large extent the way we relate to others. We are all threatened by the individual who uses introjection, since none of us wishes to be "devoured." The depressed patient tries to do just that and betrays himself by the hungry, demanding way in which he relates to others. On the other hand, we are flattered by the individual who would identify with us; instead of wishing to devour us, he only takes on certain traits or attitudes that are ours.

The paper by Anna Freud included here illustrates how intricate the workings of defense mechanisms can be when two or more mechanisms combine or when the same mechanism is used against both an external and an internal force. The phenomenon of *identification with the aggressor* (the title of her paper) is a classic example of defense mechanisms at work. Identification with the aggressor is a way of dealing with the frightening and threatening feelings stirred up in the child when he is the victim of aggression. Instead of assuming the position of the person being threatened, he becomes like the person making the threat. Thus his stance changes from a passive one to an active one.

The third structure of the personality, in addition to the id and the ego, is the *superego*. The superego consists of internalizations of parental prohibitions, standards, and morality. A primitive superego is present at around age two, when the child recognizes he must conform to parental standards, but it is mainly formed as part of the resolution of the Oedipus complex. Although the superego contains elements of identification with both parents, the definitive identification is with the parent who is the source of the decisive frustrations. Usually this is the father, but in our matriarchal society it may be the mother. The superego consists of two subsystems: the *ego ideal* and the *conscience*. The ego ideal is what the child feels his parents consider good; the conscience is the child's concept of what the parents feel is bad.

The superego is idealistic and perfectionistic, rather than realistic, and passes judgment on what the ego does. In studying for an exam it is the superego that says "You have worked hard enough" or reprimands the ego "You have been bad. You have not done your work." Most healthy people have some degree of conscious guilt. We feel guilty when we have done something inappropriate. In healthy people the superego is integrated into the personality and prevents them from making transgressions for which their superego will reproach them. An overly harsh, primitive superego, however, creates difficulties for an individual. This kind of superego can give no praise or reward. The result is low self-esteem, for the individual is constantly criticized and degraded by his conscience. Often if the superego is unduly harsh and primitive, the individual cannot tolerate conscious awareness of it. He rebels against it and acts out of a sense of guilt. Individuals who are constantly getting into trouble with society often use this mechanism. By doing wrong they seek punishment from an externalized superego, the society.

The strength of the superego derives from the intensity of the instinctual drives —the stronger the impulses, the greater the need for control and the more severe the superego. For this reason, it is important for adults to help children to control their impulses. If parental controls are lacking, the child often internalizes a set of prohibitions that are much harsher than any real parent would impose.

Modifications of Freudian Theory

Neo-Freudians have long been critical of certain aspects of Freudian theory and have attempted to modify it. One tendency (represented here by Erikson's paper) has been to emphasize the role of cultural factors in personality development. More recently, the Women's Liberation movement has attacked Freudian theory because it relegates women to an inferior role. The concept of penis envy is particularly objectionable to these critics. However, neo-Freudians, some of whom are women, would argue that the wish does exist, unconsciously, and is resolved in the healthy woman by the development of her feminine narcissism. That is, the woman comes to feel that she is attractive and appealing as a woman and derives satisfaction from the realization that she can bear children. She can also have a career outside the home; with the development of feelings of being worthwhile and valuable as a woman, she no longer feels rivalry and competitiveness toward men. Furthermore, there are men, they point out, who are envious of the female capacity to bear children. And, while Freudian theory pictures the female conscience as less demanding than that of the male, one *might* interpret this to mean that the female is thereby more inclined to make allowances, to see the gray as well as the black and white, to be less inclined toward authoritarianism, and to be more compassionate and sympathetic. (Perhaps this is just the bias of two female editors!) And, the argument concludes, even if Freud personally relegated women to an inferior role, one need not throw out the baby with the bath water.

Freudian theory seeks to explain character and personality development largely in terms of innate instinctual drives that manifest themselves during the first five years of life. Erikson's paper, included here as an example of psychoanalytic theory, differs from classical Freudian theory in several significant respects. While Freudian emphasis was on the biological and instinctual, Erikson places more emphasis on the development of the ego. His stages of psychosocial development roughly parallel Freud's stages of libidinal development. However, he places more emphasis on the development of the ego and its adaptation to reality. More emphasis is also placed on the human social environment and the way in which the culture shapes the individual. His theory also spans the whole life cycle, dividing adulthood into different phases and showing how there is opportunity to work through infantile conflicts at each phase. Erikson thus shows, in contrast to Freud, how human beings continue to develop beyond the resolution of the Oedipus complex.

PIAGET'S DEVELOPMENTAL THEORY[1]

Piaget's theory is a *developmental* one. Thinking processes change during childhood, and the thinking of a four-year-old is *qualitatively* very different from the thinking of a fourteen-year-old. It isn't simply that the older child *knows* more; he

---

[1] From C. Lavatelli, *Piaget's Theory Applied to an Early Childhood Curriculum* (Boston: American Science and Engineering, 1970), pp. 27–29, 33. © Center for Media Development, Inc. Reprinted by permission.

does different things with what he knows. Piaget describes the changes in stages that are age-related, but not age-determined.

The Sensorimotor Stage

The origins of intelligence are to be found in what Piaget calls the *sensorimotor* stage, which begins at birth (Piaget, 1952). The infant comes into the world with two kinds of reflexes: those, like the knee jerk, that are not altered by experience, and others, like grasping and sucking, that are modified as the infant exercises them. The modification occurs through assimilation and accommodation. For example, the infant accommodates the grasping reflex to the shape of the object to be grasped, curving the fingers in one way for a long, narrow object, and in a different way for a plastic play ring. Later, looking and grasping become coordinated; the infant can put out his hand and grasp what he sees. Each newly discovered experience brings with it a need to repeat the experience; activity begets activity. And as the infant operates upon the physical world with his sensorimotor system, he acquires notions of objects, space, time, and causality. Ask a ten-month-old baby, "Where's Mommy?" and he looks toward the door through which Mommy has just disappeared; he "thinks" about the concepts of time and objects with his motor system, that is, Mommy was here but is not now. However, she still exists. Objects have a permanence and do not cease to exist when out of sight.

The Preoperational Stage

Gradually, his actions become internalized; the child can represent in thought processes that which was first developed in the sensorimotor system. This second stage begins at eighteen months and extends to seven years of age (roughly). The stage is called *preoperational,* for logical operations have not yet appeared. During the early part of this stage (eighteen months to four years), language is developing at a fantastically rapid pace. Furthermore, thought and language are becoming interrelated; from thinking only in images, the child moves to thinking in words. He can express his ideas in words and can understand the communications of others.

We do not know very much about the early part of this stage, for it has not been studied systematically, but Piaget has contributed enormously to our knowledge of development from the age of four years onward. He and his colleagues at Geneva employ what they call the *clinical method* to study development. The examiner presents the child with one of the many cognitive tasks used at Geneva to study the development of intelligence. The examiner is interested in finding out how the child thinks about the problem in order to determine how mental processes essential to logical thinking are developing. Therefore the child is asked not only to perform a task but to explain what he is doing and why he is doing it. In questioning the child, the examiner does not employ an interview schedule with every question worked out in advance. Rather, succeeding questions must be phrased in terms of what the child has already said, much as any clinical interview would be conducted. From an analysis of responses, the characteristics of children at each stage of development become known. For example, the child at the preoperational level (before logical operations have emerged) is likely to think that an object weighs more if its shape has changed. If one of two identical balls of clay is elongated while the child looks on, he thinks that the elongated shape now has more "stuff" in it and weighs more. He judges in terms of how things look to him and centers on *one* variable, length, because length stands out more than does thickness. The child lacks the ability to carry on a mental operation that Piaget calls *reversibility*—reversing a process mentally to compare what is now with what was.

The thinking of the child at the preoperational level (four to seven years), may be described as follows:

1. The child is perceptually oriented; he makes judgments in terms of how things *look* to him. Piaget has shown that perceptual judgment enters into the child's thinking about matter, space, time, number, and causality. For example, the child at the preoperational level is likely to think that the number of objects in a set changes if the objects are bunched together rather than spread out.

2. The child *centers* on one variable only, usually the variable that stands out visually. He lacks the ability to coordinate variables. In the clay problem described above, length stands out more than does thickness, and the child fails to coordinate the change in length with the change in thickness.

3. The child has difficulty in realizing that an object can possess more than one property and thus can belong to several classes at the same time. A long red pencil can belong to the class of pencils, to the class of red objects, to the class of long objects, to the class of writing tools, and so on. One can live in Chicago and in Illinois at the same time. This property of a class is referred to as *multiplicative* classification, or sometimes, more simply, as *multiple* classification.

The Stage of Concrete Operations

The child's thinking processes change, however, as he continues to interact with the physical world. After about six or seven years of age, we begin to see the emergence of logical operations. The child becomes able to reverse a process; mentally he can restore the sausage of clay to its original shape and thus see that the amount of clay is conserved. (Later he will recognize conservation of weight.) He can combine subclasses into a supraclass and take the supraclass apart, so he knows that if all the birds in the world died, there would be no ducks left, but that if all the ducks died, there would still be some birds. Or he may use an identity operation to arrive at a logical conclusion; he may say of the area left when barns are scattered on one field of grass, "Just line both sides up and you'll see the grass is the same." (See Figure 1.) And, finally, there is the operation of associativity; we can combine $3 + (4 + 2)$ to make 9, or we can combine $(3 + 4) + 2$ and get the same result. The same goal can be reached by different paths.

The model that Piaget believes mirrors the thought of the child is a grouplike structure, or *groupement*. Piaget uses the term *groupement* in the Poincaré sense of the word *groupe,* to refer to a system of displacements. The child can shift the data around mentally in the four different ways described above as he tests reality. Note that at this stage the child is using concrete data to make the displacements; he is not able to think abstractly about a problem. Adults often do the same thing. If we

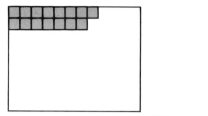 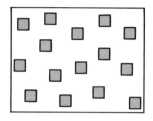

FIGURE 1

A Piaget Task: Given two pieces of cardboard of equal size to represent fields, and fifteen 1-inch cubes, representing grass, placed on each field as shown above, would a cow have more grass to eat on one of the fields, or would the amount of grass be the same in both fields?

forget a formula which is an abstraction, we may mentally reconstruct a specific situation, work out the relationship of one variable to another, and arrive at the solution to the problem at the level of a concrete operation.

The Stage of Formal Thinking

Roughly at about eleven or twelve years of age, Piaget again finds changes commencing in the child's thought processes. Now thought is decreasingly tied to the concrete; the adolescent becomes more and more capable of abstract reasoning. This is the stage of *formal thinking.* He reasons in terms of propositions, and he can make logical combinations of these propositions. He can compare by conjunction, as when he says, "Both A and B make a difference." He can combine by disjunction, as when he says, "It's got to be this or that." He can combine by implication, "If it's this, then that happens." Or he can combine by incompatibility, "When this happens, then that doesn't." His thinking is in terms of possible combinations and not with objects or events directly.

Each of these combinations can then be transformed by identity, negation, reciprocation, and correlation. For example, one can start with a conjunctive statement, "Both p and q make a difference," and perform an identity transformation by substituting equivalent factors for either p or q, or both. Or one might negate both factors by hypothesizing that neither one will make a difference. Or one might transform the conjunction by reciprocation, that is, by hypothesizing that either p is what it seems to be and q has no effect, or that p has an effect and q is not what it seems to be. And lastly, a transformation by correlation can be made, as when the subject states a positive correspondence between p and q.

The reader with some knowledge of symbolic logic will understand more fully the Piaget model of adolescent thinking, for Piaget uses the language and symbols of logic. For such a reader, Inhelder and Piaget (1958) describe the formal structure of thought and offer an example of the sixteen binary operations (pp. 103–04). If one uses all possible combinations and transformations, one will have stated sixteen different hypotheses to explain a phenomenon where there are two propositions.

Piaget's Equilibration Model[2]

The key word in Piaget's definition of intelligence is *equilibration*. Piaget was a biologist before becoming a psychologist and epistemologist, so it is not hard to understand that his conception of intelligence is couched in a biological framework, as a basic tendency toward equilibrium in mental structures. There is such a basic homeostatic tendency in other systems of the body; when there is a disturbance to any system, various mechanisms go to work automatically to restore equilibrium to that system. If, for example, the body becomes overheated, automatic mechanisms act to induce sweating, dilate blood vessels, and carry on other bodily changes that will lower temperature and restore temperature equilibrium. These are biological adaptations.

Piaget finds adaptation in mental processes as well, but of a superior form. When equilibrium in mental structures is upset, there is a basic tendency to restore it. However, in this case, adjustment is not automatic; the individual exercises some control over the operations of intelligence. Furthermore, mental structures are actually changed in the equilibration process.

Two mechanisms are important in equilibration: *assimilation* and *accommodation*. There is assimilation each time an individual incorporates into his own mental framework the data from an experience. However, to assimilate an object or a situation, one must act upon it and transform it in some way. New objects or events then become incorporated in intelligence as a scheme or concept that can be repeated and applied in different situations.

Piaget (1952b) distinguishes three types of assimilation: *reproductive* assimilation, where one reproduces an action in cognitive activity; *recognitive* assimilation, by which one screens objects that can be assimilated into a particular scheme; and *generative* assimilation, which permits the enlargement of a scheme to encompass a wider range of objects or events to be assimilated. The reader may recognize these three types in his own mental activity.

The simplest form, reproductive assimilation, is to repeat an idea to oneself; for example, one might say: "Piaget says that self-activity of a mental nature is essential to the act of knowing." In cognitive assimilation, one might say, "If I simply repeat the idea from memory without 'thinking' about it, without trying to understand what Piaget says about the necessity for self-activity, can I really 'know' what Piaget is talking about?" Here, one is screening a particular idea to see if it will fit a particular scheme. Assimilation of a generative sort is what one does when one says, "What I am doing now is carrying on mental activity in order to understand what Piaget means by self-activity. I'm really acting on and extending the idea." In other words, one is enlarging the scheme to be assimilated. In each case, the reader is doing something with the data, though his thought processes become more complex as he goes from simple reproductive to more complex generative assimilation.

The transformation of data by the subject finds its counterpart in modification of the existing framework of thought. This modification is accomplished through the

[2] From Lavatelli, *op. cit.*, pp. 36–39.

process of accommodation. Accommodation consists of refining and modifying the framework in order to incorporate the data one has assimilated. In accommodation, one "makes up one's mind" about what one believes or accepts as true. The changes in framework are not submitted to passively by the subject; like assimilation, accommodation is an active and an orienting process. There is no accommodation, no change in the framework of thought if the learner is content merely to state the inadequacy of the existing framework; he must take a stand, or make up his mind, about the new data.

Accommodation presupposes effort and initiative on the part of the learner; he must make a "choice," as Piaget puts it. Let us suppose that a child is exposed to data that challenge some previously held notion. He may see a demonstration or carry on an experiment in which he finds that a cylinder of lead will raise the level of water in a glass to exactly the same height as a cylinder of aluminum of equal volume. His previously held notion was that the heavier cylinder would raise the water level higher. What does he do with the data that he has assimilated? He can think, "Oh, there's something queer going on, but I'm not going to bother about it," or he can think, "Maybe there's something funny about these two particular cylinders. I'll try two others the same overall size, one heavy and one light, and see what happens." He may continue his experimentation, varying volume of cylinders next, and assimilating data from each experiment until he convinces himself that some factor other than weight is the cause of the phenomenon he is witnessing. He must take a stand, "It's not weight; it must be something else," and with continued assimilation from his next experiments, he may eventually discover that cylinders of equal volume will displace equal amounts of water, regardless of their weight.

Through progressive assimilations and accommodations, equilibration proceeds and equilibrium is achieved at a higher level. Equilibrium is not a static state; it is, rather, a dynamic compensation resulting from activity of the subject in response to exterior disturbances at a given point in time. Piaget (1964) speaks of a stable state in an open system; the state does not attain a final form but continues to change as new factors enter the system, leading to successive refinements both in knowledge and in the instruments of thought.

There are, of course, individual differences in the age at which certain structures of logical intelligence appear in children. Are these differences inherited, perhaps as differences in rates of maturation? Are they attributable to the fact that some children have been taught certain ways of thinking, or have been exposed to certain kinds of experiences? Can the onset of a particular stage be accelerated? Possible factors contributing to answers to these questions are discussed by Piaget in the paper included here.

Piaget continues to be a giant in developmental psychology. There have been literally hundreds of follow-up studies, most of which support his theory. Perhaps the chief area of conflict is that involving the question of training. We return to this issue in Part 4, where papers by Wallach and Smith dealing with the problem are included.

THEORIES STEMMING FROM BEHAVIORISM

Under the umbrella of "behaviorism" one can find many schools of thought differing in certain respects, but all having in common an emphasis on stimulus-response and the conditions under which a stimulus and a response become connected. All assume that the more complex problem-solving behaviors can be broken down into discrete S-R units for study. All derive their methods from the natural sciences and rely more on laboratory methods for data collection than on clinical or naturalistic observation.

Pavlov's discovery of conditioned responses may be taken as a beginning. His classic experiment with dogs showed how, through repeated simultaneous exposure to the stimulus (S) of a light followed by food, a given response (R) of salivation could be produced by turning on the light alone. In this country, J. B. Watson, the father of behaviorism, expanded on Pavlov's work by demonstrating that a given stimulus could produce a certain response in human beings as well as in animals. His famous experiment based on Pavlovian theory (Watson and Rayner, 1920) demonstrated emotional conditioning in an infant boy. Albert was deliberately frightened by a loud sound while happily playing with a white rat. He subsequently showed fear not only of rats but also of other furry objects, including a Santa Claus beard. (For the worried reader, Albert was reconditioned in a later experiment by being exposed to a pleasant stimulus, food, while the rat was kept at a gradually narrowing distance.) Clark Hull of Yale University took a major step forward by deriving principles to explain more complex habit formation and laws of reinforcement, while his students, notably Kenneth Spence and Neal Miller, continued to elaborate and expand learning theory. From this school of thought have been derived explanations of how such secondary drives as dependency and achievement are learned, as well as principles to predict what would happen under given schedules of reinforcement (intermittent as compared with continuous reinforcement, for example). With emphasis on S-R and response learning as well as on conditioning, this body of thought came to be known as *S-R theory, reinforcement theory,* or *learning theory.* We will use these terms interchangeably here.

In developmental psychology, the influence of learning theory has been evident in both the procedures used and the problems studied. With respect to procedures, the emphasis has been on small-scale experiments using animals as well as human beings, and rigorously controlled variables. While cognitive psychologists also study behavior under experimental laboratory conditions, they are likely to be more daring and therefore less "pure." They disagree with the assumption of the S-R school that complex behaviors can be broken down and understood in terms of basic units, arguing that the basic fallacy of the theory lies in such simplistic assumptions. They point out, too, that the S-R school is indeed able to exercise tight control over variables in the laboratory, but that in so doing, the investigators frequently create an artificial situation, for they divorce a subject from his environment.

White (1970) lists six categories of problems studied by learning theorists; these illustrate the great diversity of expression that exists within this school of thought:

1. Problems of operant analysis and methodology, concerned with the functional analysis of child behavior. The work of Bijou and Baer (1960) is an example.

2. Investigations relating to assumptions or variables in the work of Hull and Spence (timing of reinforcement, for example, or intermittent versus continuous reinforcement). Spiker's (1963) work illustrates this type of study.

3. Studies analyzing procedures of classical conditioning, instrumental learning, verbal learning, and so on, for regularities in such procedures, as illustrated by Lipsitt (1967).

4. Studies of social reinforcement (Gewirtz, 1967), imitation (Bandura and Walters, 1963), and the analysis of conscience (Aronfreed, 1964), in which an attempt is made to translate social interaction into stimulus-response terms and to study it experimentally. *Social learning theory* is the term usually applied to the theoretical basis for these studies.

5. Investigations applying stimulus-response analysis to the study of verbal behavior, curiosity, mediation, stimulus generalization, transposition, and discrimination learning. Kendler and Kendler (1967) are active here.

6. Problems in behavioral engineering, in which operant conditioning techniques are used to shape behavior, following the principles outlined by Skinner (1953) and further elaborated by Bijou and Baer (1967).

Learning theory is not epigenetic theory; theorists pose no developmental stages through which all children pass in a predictable sequence. Investigators may discover and describe changes that occur with age, but these are described within the framework of S-R theory. Thus S-R investigators, like Piagetians, find radical changes in thinking processes around seven years of age, but they seek to explain them in terms of cumulative, identifiable S-R bonds rather than by an equilibration model, as Piaget does.

White (1970) maintains that the learning theory tradition is waning, and he is probably right. As one searches the developmental literature, one finds many investigators who might formerly have described themselves as "learning theorists" but who would now probably prefer the designation "experimental child psychologists." Experimental child psychology, however, is not based on a unified body of theory about how children grow and develop. Some experimental child psychologists work within Piaget's framework, attempting to test parts of his theory under rigorous experimental conditions. Some work within the framework of social learning theory and attempt to study the social development of personality in terms of antecedents and consequences. And some are behavioral engineers who use operant techniques to change behavior. But all share to a greater or lesser degree a belief that the S-R bond is the basic unit in behavior, and that reinforcement is the critical factor.

ETHOLOGY AND CHILD DEVELOPMENT

The reader will find in many of the papers in this volume assumptions about development that derive from *ethology,* the science of animal behavior. Concepts such as "critical period," originating in embryology but widely used by ethologists;

"imprinting"; and, more recently, "attachment behavior" have been borrowed by developmental psychologists to explain human behavior. Sometimes the concepts are "tried on for size," so to speak, and then modified or abandoned. The notions of *critical period* and *imprinting* are examples of such concepts. "Critical period" in embryology refers to the special period in the prenatal timetable for the development of each organ, in which a growth disturbance (some viral infections, for example) can affect the development of that organ irreversibly. In ethology, the concept has been applied to "imprinting," a process of object-fixation with respect to a single behavior that occurs in many animals. Lambs, for example, become fixated or imprinted to the mother sheep soon after birth, as exemplified by the "following-the-mother response," and thereafter follow her "like sheep." Substituting a different object for them to follow results in imprinting on that object; apparently, the stimulus that sets off the "following" response can be any moving object. Specific stimuli which elicit the "following" response have been identified for a number of animals.

Developmental psychologists have found such concepts useful, particularly in studying early development, in determining whether there are critical periods for the acquisition of certain motor, social, and cognitive behaviors. However, man turns out to be quite a flexible creature, and no one at this point is prepared to say unequivocally that there is a critical period for most areas of postnatal development ("critical" in the sense of damage being irreversible). The exceptions may be damage to the nervous system caused by malnutrition or disease in infancy, and a severe disturbance to the hormonal system that may interfere with growth during the pre-adolescent growth spurt.

The concept of *sensitive period,* however, or *optimal period* for development is one that has had wide acceptance. The term has proved particularly useful in the areas of cognition and social development, and today a tremendous volume of research is being devoted to specifying the exact time periods when intervention in early development will be most helpful. Should cognitive training for disadvantaged infants begin before language emerges? Or does the sensitive period extend from about eighteen months to five years?

Even more important to the study of the child are such ethological concepts as *releasers,* or innate releasing mechanisms. What sets off a particular response in the newborn of any species? What sets in motion the herring gull chick's pecking at its parent's bill tip, for example? It turns out that the releasers of each response are very narrowly defined. In the herring gull, it is *any* red spot on an object. In the lamb, the "following" response is "released" or activated by a moving object that is not necessarily the mother. Color, special markings, movement, odor, or sound can all be releasers. The mechanism has adaptive value; in the spring, color changes in birds release courting behaviors essential for mating and preservation of the species. The reader will find further discussion of releasers and other ethological borrowings in the Infancy section.

Perhaps the greatest influence of the ethologists has been in helping to move child development investigators from a position where they argued over the relative importance for development of heredity and environment, nature and nurture, maturation and learning, to a position emphasizing interaction between the two forces. Ethologists have not been alone, of course. Piaget's description of the modification of certain reflex behaviors through the activity of the infant (pp. 168–169) is an example of a great theorist's conception of interaction. And as Silverstein (1971) has pointed out, both Piaget and Werner, whose paper is included here, utilize concepts derived from biology, that is, assimilation and accommodation, differentiation and hierarchic integration. Silverstein goes on to say, "To my mind, the concepts of differentiation and hierarchic integration are crucial to the understanding of developmental phenomena. If Piaget emphasizes adaptation, Werner emphasizes organization which, as Piaget himself argues, are two sides of the same coin. Adaptation depends upon organization but also leads toward increasing organization" (personal communication).

REFERENCES

Aronfreed, J., "The origin of self-criticism." *Psychological Review,* 1964, 71, 193–218.

Bandura, A., and Walters, R. H., *Social learning and personality development* (New York: Holt, Rinehart and Winston, 1963).

Bijou, S. W., and Baer, D. M., *Child development: readings in experimental analysis* (New York: Appleton-Century-Crofts, 1967).

———, "The laboratory-experimental study of child behavior." In P. H. Mussen, ed., *Handbook of Research Methods in Child Development* (New York: Wiley, 1960).

Gewirtz, J. L., "Deprivation and satiation of social stimuli as determinants of their reinforcing efficacy." In J. P. Hill, ed., *Minnesota Symposium on Child Psychology,* vol. I (Minneapolis: University of Minnesota Press, 1967).

Inhelder, B., and Piaget, J., *The growth of logical thinking from childhood to adolescence: an essay on the construction of formal operational structures,* trans. by A. Parsons and S. Milgram (New York: Basic Books, 1958).

Kendler, T. S., and Kendler, H. H. "Experimental analysis of inferential behavior in children." In L. P. Lipsitt and C. C. Spiker, eds., *Advances in Child Development and Behavior,* vol. III (New York: Academic Press, 1967).

Lipsitt, L. P., "Learning in the human infant." In H. W. Stevenson, E. H. Hess,

and H. L. Rheingold, eds., *Early Behavior: Comparative and Developmental Approaches* (New York: Wiley, 1967).

Piaget, J., *The child's conception of number* (London: Routledge & Kegan Paul, 1952).

———, *Les mécanismes perceptifs* (Paris: Presses Universitaires de France, 1961).

———, *The origins of intelligence in children* (New York: International Universities Press, 1952).

———, Three lectures in R. E. Ripple and V. N. Rockcastle, eds., *Piaget rediscovered* (Ithaca, N.Y.: Cornell University, 1964).

Silverstein, B., The William Paterson College of New Jersey. Personal communication.

Skinner, B. F., *Science and human behavior* (New York: Macmillan, 1953).

Spiker, C. C., "The hypothesis of stimulus interaction and an explanation of stimulus compounding." In L. P. Lipsitt and C. C. Spiker, eds., *Advances in Child Development and Behavior,* vol. I (New York: Academic Press, 1963).

Watson, J. B., and Rayner, R., "Conditioned emotional reactions." *Journal of Experimental Psychology,* 1920, 3, 1–14.

White, S. H., "The learning theory and tradition of child psychology." In P. H. Mussen, ed., *Carmichael's Manual of Child Psychology,* vol. I (New York: Wiley, 1970).

EIGHT AGES OF MAN

ERIK H. ERIKSON

1. BASIC TRUST vs. BASIC MISTRUST

The first demonstration of social trust in the baby is the ease of his feeding, the depth of his sleep, the relaxation of his bowels. The experience of a mutual regulation of his increasingly receptive capacities with the maternal techniques of provision gradually helps him to balance the discomfort caused by the immaturity of homeostasis with which he was born. In his gradually increasing waking hours he finds that more and more adventures of the senses arouse a feeling of familiarity, of having coincided with a feeling of inner goodness. Forms of comfort, and people associated with them, become as familiar as the gnawing discomfort of the bowels. The infant's first social achievement, then, is his willingness to let the mother out of sight without undue anxiety or rage, because she has become an inner certainty as well as an outer predictability. Such consistency, continuity, and sameness of experience provide a rudimentary sense of ego identity which depends, I think, on the recognition that there is an inner population of remembered and anticipated sensations and images which are firmly correlated with the outer population of familiar and predictable things and people.

What we here call trust coincides with what Therese Benedek has called confidence. If I prefer the word "trust," it is because there is more naïveté and more mutuality in it: an infant can be said to be trusting where it would go too far to say that he has confidence. The general state of trust, furthermore, implies not only that one has learned to rely on the sameness and con-

Reprinted with abridgment from pp. 247–73 of *Childhood and Society*, Second Edition, Revised, by Erik H. Erikson. By permission of W. W. Norton & Company, Inc. Copyright 1950, © 1963 by W. W. Norton & Company, Inc. Reprinted also by permission of Chatto and Windus, Ltd., London.

tinuity of the outer providers, but also that one may trust oneself and the capacity of one's own organs to cope with urges; and that one is able to consider oneself trustworthy enough so that the providers will not need to be on guard lest they be nipped.

The constant tasting and testing of the relationship between inside and outside meets its crucial test during the rages of the biting stage, when the teeth cause pain from within and when outer friends either prove of no avail or withdraw from the only action which promises relief: biting. Not that teething itself seems to cause all the dire consequences sometimes ascribed to it. As outlined earlier, the infant now is driven to "grasp" more, but he is apt to find desired presences elusive: nipple and breast, and the mother's focused attention and care. Teething seems to have a prototypal significance and may well be the model for the masochistic tendency to assure cruel comfort by enjoying one's hurt whenever one is unable to prevent a significant loss.

In psychopathology the absence of basic trust can best be studied in infantile schizophrenia, while lifelong underlying weakness of such trust is apparent in adult personalities in whom withdrawal into schizoid and depressive states is habitual. The re-establishment of a state of trust has been found to be the basic requirement for therapy in these cases. For no matter what conditions may have caused a psychotic break, the bizarreness and withdrawal in the behavior of many very sick individuals hide an attempt to recover social mutuality by a testing of the borderlines between senses and physical reality, between words and social meanings.

Psychoanalysis assumes the early process of differentiation between inside and outside to be the origin of projection and introjection which remain some of our deepest and most danger- ous defense mechanisms. In introjection we feel and act as if an outer goodness had become an inner certainty. In projection, we experience an inner harm as an outer one: we endow sig- nificant people with the evil which actually is in us. These two mechanisms, then, projection and introjection, are assumed to be modeled after whatever goes on in infants when they would like to externalize pain and internalize pleasure, an intent which must yield to the testimony of the maturing senses and ulti- mately of reason. These mechanisms are, more or less normally, reinstated in acute crises of love, trust, and faith in adulthood and can characterize irrational attitudes toward adver- saries and enemies in masses of "mature" indi- viduals.

The firm establishment of enduring patterns for the solution of the nuclear conflict of basic trust versus basic mistrust in mere existence is the first task of the ego, and thus first of all a task for maternal care. But let it be said here that the amount of trust derived from earliest infantile experience does not seem to depend on absolute quantities of food or demonstra- tions of love, but rather on the quality of the maternal relationship. Mothers create a sense of trust in their children by that kind of ad- ministration which in its quality combines sensi- tive care of the baby's individual needs and a firm sense of personal trustworthiness within the trusted framework of their culture's life style. This forms the basis in the child for a sense of identity which will later combine a sense of being "all right," of being oneself, and of becoming what other people trust one will become. There are, therefore (within certain limits previously defined as the "musts" of child care), few frustrations in either this or the fol- lowing stages which the growing child cannot endure if the frustration leads to the ever-re- newed experience of greater sameness and stronger continuity of development, toward a final integration of the individual life cycle with some meaningful wider belongingness. Parents must not only have certain ways of guiding by prohibition and permission; they must also be able to represent to the child a deep, an almost somatic conviction that there is a mean- ing to what they are doing. Ultimately, children

become neurotic not from frustrations, but from the lack or loss of societal meaning in these frustrations.

But even under the most favorable circum- stances, this stage seems to introduce into psychic life (and become prototypical for) a sense of inner division and universal nostalgia for a paradise forfeited. It is against this power- ful combination of a sense of having been de- prived, of having been divided, and of having been abandoned—that basic trust must main- tain itself throughout life.

Each successive stage and crisis has a special relation to one of the basic elements of society, and this for the simple reason that the human life cycle and man's institutions have evolved together. In this chapter we can do little more than mention, after the description of each stage, what basic element of social organization is related to it. This relation is twofold: man brings to these institutions the remnants of his infantile mentality and his youthful fervor, and he receives from them—as long as they manage to maintain their actuality—a reinforcement of his infantile gains.

The parental faith which supports the trust emerging in the newborn, has throughout his- tory sought its institutional safeguard (and, on occasion, found its greatest enemy) in or- ganized religion. Trust born of care is, in fact, the touchstone of the *actuality* of a given re- ligion. All religions have in common the period- ical childlike surrender to a Provider or pro- viders who dispense earthly fortune as well as spiritual health; some demonstration of man's smallness by way of reduced posture and hum- ble gesture; the admission in prayer and song of misdeeds, of misthoughts, and of evil inten- tions; fervent appeal for inner unification by divine guidance; and finally, the insight that individual trust must become a common faith, individual mistrust a commonly formulated evil, while the individual's restoration must become part of the ritual practice of many, and must become a sign of trustworthiness in the community.[1] We have illustrated how tribes dealing with one segment of nature develop a

---

[1] This is the communal and psychosocial side of religion. Its often paradoxical relation to the spirituality of the individual is a matter not to be treated briefly and in passing (see *Young Man Luther*). (E.H.E.)

collective magic which seems to treat the Super-
natural Providers of food and fortune as if they
were angry and must be appeased by prayer
and self-torture. Primitive religions, the most
primitive layer in all religions, and the religious
layer in each individual, abound with efforts at
atonement which try to make up for vague
deeds against a maternal matrix and try to restore faith in the goodness of one's strivings
and in the kindness of the powers of the universe.

Each society and each age must find the institutionalized form of reverence which derives
vitality from its world-image—from predestina-
tion to indeterminacy. The clinician can only
observe that many are proud to be without
religion whose children cannot afford their
being without it. On the other hand, there are
many who seem to derive a vital faith from
social action or scientific pursuit. And again,
there are many who profess faith, yet in practice breathe mistrust both of life and man.

2. AUTONOMY vs. SHAME AND DOUBT

In describing the growth and the crises of
the human person as a series of alternative
basic attitudes such as trust vs. mistrust, we
take recourse to the term a "sense of," although, like a "sense of health," or a "sense of
being unwell," such "senses" pervade surface
and depth, consciousness and the unconscious.
They are, then, at the same time, ways of *experiencing* accessible to introspection; ways of
behaving, observable by others; and unconscious *inner states* determinable by test and
analysis. It is important to keep these three
dimensions in mind, as we proceed.

Muscular maturation sets the stage for experimentation with two simultaneous sets of
social modalities: holding on and letting go. As
is the case with all of these modalities, their
basic conflicts can lead in the end to either
hostile or benign expectations and attitudes.
Thus, to hold can become a destructive and
cruel retaining or restraining, and it can become a pattern of care: to have and to hold.
To let go, too, can turn into an inimical letting
loose of destructive forces, or it can become
a relaxed "to let pass" and "to let be."

Outer control at this stage, therefore, must
be firmly reassuring. The infant must come to
feel that the basic faith in existence, which is
the lasting treasure saved from the rages of
the oral stage, will not be jeopardized by this
about-face of his, this sudden violent wish to
have a choice, to appropriate demandingly,
and to eliminate stubbornly. Firmness must protect him against the potential anarchy of his as
yet untrained sense of discrimination, his inability to hold on and to let go with discretion.
As his environment encourages him to "stand
on his own feet," it must protect him against
meaningless and arbitrary experiences of shame
and of early doubt.

The latter danger is the one best known to
us. For if denied the gradual and well-guided
experience of the autonomy of free choice (or
if, indeed, weakened by an initial loss of trust)
the child will turn against himself all his urge
to discriminate and to manipulate. He will
overmanipulate himself, he will develop a precocious conscience. Instead of taking possession
of things in order to test them by purposeful
repetition, he will become obsessed by his own
repetitiveness. By such obsessiveness, of course,
he then learns to repossess the environment and
to gain power by stubborn and minute control,
where he could not find large-scale mutual regulation. Such hollow victory is the infantile
model for a compulsion neurosis. It is also the
infantile source of later attempts in adult life
to govern by the letter, rather than by the spirit.

Shame is an emotion insufficiently studied,
because in our civilization it is so early and
easily absorbed by guilt. Shame supposes that
one in completely exposed and conscious of
being looked at: in one word, self-conscious.
One is visible and not ready to be visible; which
is why we dream of shame as a situation in
which we are stared at in a condition of incomplete dress, in night attire, "with one's pants
down." Shame is early expressed in an impulse
to bury one's face, or to sink, right then and
there, into the ground. But this, I think, is
essentially rage turned against the self. He who
is ashamed would like to force the world not
to look at him, not to notice his exposure. He
would like to destroy the eyes of the world.
Instead he must wish for his own invisibility.
This potentiality is abundantly used in the edu-

cational method of "shaming" used so exclusively by some primitive peoples. Visual shame precedes auditory guilt, which is a sense of badness to be had all by oneself when nobody watches and when everything is quiet—except the voice of the superego. Such shaming exploits an increasing sense of being small, which can develop only as the child stands up and as his awareness permits him to note the relative measures of size and power.

Too much shaming does not lead to genuine propriety but to a secret determination to try to get away with things, unseen—if, indeed, it does not result in defiant shamelessness. There is an impressive American ballad in which a murderer to be hanged on the gallows before the eyes of the community, instead of feeling duly chastened, begins to berate the onlookers, ending every salvo of defiance with the words, "God damn your eyes." Many a small child, shamed beyond endurance, may be in a chronic mood (although not in possession of either the courage or the words) to express defiance in similar terms. What I mean by this sinister reference is that there is a limit to a child's and an adult's endurance in the face of demands to consider himself, his body, and his wishes as evil and dirty, and to his belief in the infallibility of those who pass such judgment. He may be apt to turn things around, and to consider as evil only the fact that they exist: his chance will come when they are gone, or when he will go from them.

Doubt is the brother of shame. Where shame is dependent on the consciousness of being upright and exposed, doubt, so clinical observation leads me to believe, has much to do with a consciousness of having a front and a back—and especially a "behind." For this reverse area of the body, with its aggressive and libidinal focus in the sphincters and in the buttocks, cannot be seen by the child, and yet it can be dominated by the will of others. The "behind" is the small being's dark continent, an area of the body which can be magically dominated and effectively invaded by those who would attack one's power of autonomy and who would designate as evil those products of the bowels which were felt to be all right when they were being passed. This basic sense of doubt in whatever one has left behind forms a sub-

stratum for later and more verbal forms of compulsive doubting; this finds its adult expression in paranoiac fears concerning hidden persecutors and secret persecutions threatening from behind (and from within the behind).

This stage, therefore, becomes decisive for the ratio of love and hate, cooperation and willfulness, freedom of self-expression and its suppression. From a sense of self-control without loss of self-esteem comes a lasting sense of good will and pride; from a sense of loss of self-control and of foreign overcontrol comes a lasting propensity for doubt and shame.

If, to some reader, the "negative" potentialities of our stages seem overstated throughout, we must remind him that this is not only the result of a preoccupation with clinical data. Adults, and seemingly mature and unneurotic ones, display a sensitivity concerning a possible shameful "loss of face" and fear of being attacked "from behind" which is not only highly irrational and in contrast to the knowledge available to them, but can be of fateful import if related sentiments influence, for example, interracial and international policies.

We have related basic trust to the institution of religion. The lasting need of the individual to have his will reaffirmed and delineated within an adult order of things which at the same time reaffirms and delineates the will of others has an institutional safeguard in the *principle of law and order*. In daily life as well as in the high courts of law—domestic and international—this principle apportions to each his privileges and his limitations, his obligations and his rights. A sense of rightful dignity and lawful independence on the part of adults around him gives to the child of good will the confident expectation that the kind of autonomy fostered in childhood will not lead to undue doubt or shame in later life. Thus the sense of autonomy fostered in the child and modified as life progresses, serves (and is served by) the preservation in economic and political life of a sense of justice.

3. INITIATIVE vs. GUILT

There is in every child at every stage a new miracle of vigorous unfolding, which constitutes a new hope and a new responsibility for all. Such is the sense and the pervading quality of initiative. The criteria for all these senses and qualities are the same: a crisis, more or less beset with fumbling and fear, is resolved, in that the child suddenly seems to "grow together" both in his person and in his body. He appears "more himself," more loving, relaxed and brighter in his judgment, more activated and activating. He is in free possession of a surplus of energy which permits him to forget failures quickly and to approach what seems desirable (even if it also seems uncertain and even dangerous) with undiminished and more accurate direction. Initiative adds to autonomy the quality of undertaking, planning and "attacking" a task for the sake of being active and on the move, where before self-will, more often than not, inspired acts of defiance or, at any rate, protested independence.

I know that the very word "initiative" to many, has an American, and industrial connotation. Yet, initiative is a necessary part of every act, and man needs a sense of initiative for whatever he learns and does, from fruit-gathering to a system of enterprise.

The ambulatory stage and that of infantile genitality add to the inventory of basic social modalities that of "making," first in the sense of "being on the make." There is no simpler, stronger word for it; it suggests pleasure in attack and conquest. In the boy, the emphasis remains on phallic-intrusive modes; in the girl it turns to modes of "catching" in more aggressive forms of snatching or in the milder form of making oneself attractive and endearing.

The danger of this stage is a sense of guilt over the goals contemplated and the acts initiated in one's exuberant enjoyment of new locomotor and mental power: acts of aggressive manipulation and coercion which soon go far beyond the executive capacity of organism and mind and therefore call for an energetic halt on one's contemplated initiative. While autonomy concentrates on keeping potential rivals out, and therefore can lead to jealous rage most often directed against encroachments by younger siblings, initiative brings with it anticipatory rivalry with those who have been there first and may, therefore, occupy with their superior equipment the field toward which one's initiative is directed. Infantile jealousy and rivalry, those often embittered and yet essentially futile attempts at demarcating a sphere of unquestioned privilege, now come to a climax in a final contest for a favored position with the mother; the usual failure leads to resignation, guilt, and anxiety. The child indulges in fantasies of being a giant and a tiger, but in his dreams he runs in terror for dear life. This, then, is the stage of the "castration complex"; the fear of having the (now energetically eroticized) genitals harmed as a punishment for the fantasies attached to their excitement becomes intensified.

Infantile sexuality and incest taboo, castration complex and superego all unite here to bring about that specifically human crisis during which the child must turn from an exclusive, pregenital attachment to his parents to the slow process of becoming a parent, a carrier of tradition. Here the most fateful split and transformation in the emotional powerhouse occurs, a split between potential human glory and potential total destruction. For here the child becomes forever divided in himself. The instinct fragments which before had enhanced the growth of his infantile body and mind now become divided into an infantile set which perpetuates the exuberance of growth potentials, and a parental set which supports and increases self-observation, self-guidance, and self-punishment.

The problem, again, is one of mutual regulation. Where the child, now so ready to over-manipulate himself, can gradually develop a sense of moral responsibility, where he can gain some insight into the institutions, functions, and roles which will permit his responsible participation, he will find pleasurable accomplishment in wielding tools and weapons, in manipulating meaningful toys—and in caring for younger children.

Naturally, the parental set is at first infantile in nature: the fact that human conscience remains partially infantile throughout life is the core of human tragedy. For the superego of the child can be primitive, cruel, and uncompromising, as may be observed in instances where children overcontrol and overconstrict themselves to the point of self-obliteration; where they develop an over-obedience more literal than the one the parent has wished to exact;

or where they develop deep regressions and lasting resentments because the parents themselves do not seem to live up to the new conscience. One of the deepest conflicts in life is the hate for a parent who served as the model and the executor of the superego, but who (in some form) was found trying to get away with the very transgressions which the child can no longer tolerate in himself. The suspiciousness and evasiveness which is thus mixed in with the all-or-nothing quality of the superego, this organ of moral tradition, makes moral (in the sense of moralistic) man a great potential danger to his own ego—and to that of his fellow men.

In adult pathology, the residual conflict over initiative is expressed either in hysterical denial, which causes the repression of the wish or the abrogation of its executive organ by paralysis, inhibition, or impotence; or in overcompensatory showing off, in which the scared individual, so eager to "duck," instead "sticks his neck out." Then also a plunge into psychosomatic disease is now common. It is as if the culture had made a man overadvertise himself and so identify with his own advertisement that only disease can offer him escape.

But here, again, we must not think only of individual psychopathology, but of the inner powerhouse of rage which must be submerged at this stage, as some of the fondest hopes and the wildest phantasies are repressed and inhibited. The resulting self-righteousness—often the principal reward for goodness—can later be most intolerantly turned against others in the form of persistent moralistic surveillance, so that the prohibition rather than the guidance of initiative becomes the dominant endeavor. On the other hand, even moral man's initiative is apt to burst the boundaries of self-restriction, permitting him to do to others, in his or in other lands, what he would neither do nor tolerate being done in his own home.

In view of the dangerous potentials of man's long childhood, it is well to look back at the blueprint of the life-stages and to the possibilities of guiding the young of the race while they are young. And here we note that according to the wisdom of the ground plan the child is at no time more ready to learn quickly and

avidly, to become bigger in the sense of sharing obligation and performance than during this period of his development. He is eager and able to make things cooperatively, to combine with other children for the purpose of constructing and planning, and he is willing to profit from teachers and to emulate ideal prototypes. He remains, of course, identified with the parent of the same sex, but for the present he looks for opportunities where work-identification seems to promise a field of initiative without too much infantile conflict or Oedipal guilt and a more realistic identification based on a spirit of equality experienced in doing things together. At any rate, the "Oedipal" stage results not only in the oppressive establishment of a moral sense restricting the horizon of the permissible; it also sets the direction toward the possible and the tangible which permits the dreams of early childhood to be attached to the goals of an active adult life. Social institutions, therefore, offer children of this age an *economic ethos,* in the form of ideal adults recognizable by their uniforms and their functions, and fascinating enough to replace, the heroes of picture book and fairy tale.

4. INDUSTRY vs. INFERIORITY

Thus the inner stage seems all set for "entrance into life," except that life must first be school life, whether school is field or jungle or classroom. The child must forget past hopes and wishes, while his exuberant imagination is tamed and harnessed to the laws of impersonal things—even the three R's. For before the child, psychologically already a rudimentary parent, can become a biological parent, he must begin to be a worker and potential provider. With the oncoming latency period, the normally advanced child forgets, or rather sublimates, the necessity to "make" people by direct attack or to become papa and mama in a hurry: he now learns to win recognition by producing things. He has mastered the ambulatory field and the organ modes. He has experienced a sense of finality regarding the fact that there is no workable future within the womb of his family, and thus becomes ready to apply himself to given skills and tasks, which go far beyond the mere playful expression of his organ modes or the pleasure in the function of his limbs. He develops a sense of industry—i.e., he adjusts himself to the inorganic laws of the tool world. He can become an eager and absorbed unit of a productive situation. To bring a productive situation to completion is an aim which gradually supersedes the whims and wishes of play. His ego boundaries include his tools and skills: the work principle (Ives Hendrick) teaches him the pleasure of work completion by steady attention and persevering diligence. In all cultures, at this stage, children receive some *systematic instruction,* although . . . it is by no means always in the kind of school which literate people must organize around special teachers who have learned how to teach literacy. In preliterate people and in nonliterate pursuits much is learned from adults who become teachers by dint of gift and inclination rather than by appointment, and perhaps the greatest amount is learned from older children. Thus the *fundamentals of technology* are developed, as the child becomes ready to handle the utensils, the tools, and the weapons used by the big people. Literate people, with more specialized careers, must prepare the child by teaching him things which first of all make him literate, the widest possible basic education for the greatest number of possible careers. The more confusing specialization becomes, however, the more indistinct are the eventual goals of initiative; and the more complicated social reality, the vaguer are the father's and mother's role in it. School seems to be a culture all by itself, with its own goals and limits, its achievements and disappointments.

The child's danger, at this stage, lies in a sense of inadequacy and inferiority. If he despairs of his tools and skills or of his status among his tool partners, he may be discouraged from identification with them and with a section of the tool world. To lose the hope of such "industrial" association may pull him back to the more isolated, less tool-conscious familial rivalry of the Oedipal time. The child despairs of his equipment in the tool world and in anatomy, and considers himself doomed to mediocrity or inadequacy. It is at this point

that wider society becomes significant in its ways of admitting the child to an understanding of meaningful roles in its technology and economy. Many a child's development is disrupted when family life has failed to prepare him for school life, or when school life fails to sustain the promises of earlier stages.

Regarding the period of a developing sense of industry, I have referred to *outer and inner hindrances* in the use of new capacities but not to aggravations of new human drives, nor to submerged rages resulting from their frustration. This stage differs from the earlier ones in that it is not a swing from an inner upheaval to a new mastery. Freud calls it the latency stage because violent drives are normally dormant. But it is only a lull before the storm of puberty, when all the earlier drives reemerge in a new combination, to be brought under the dominance of genitality.

On the other hand, this is socially a most decisive stage: since industry involves doing things beside and with others, a first sense of division of labor and of differential opportunity, that is, a sense of the *technological ethos* of a culture, develops at this time. We have pointed in the last section to the danger threatening individual and society where the schoolchild begins to feel that the color of his skin, the background of his parents, or the fashion of his clothes rather than his wish and his will to learn will decide his worth as an apprentice, and thus his sense of *identity*—to which we must now turn. But there is another, more fundamental danger, namely man's restriction of himself and constriction of his horizons to include only his work to which, so the Book says, he has been sentenced after his expulsion from paradise. If he accepts work as his only obligation, and "what works" as his own criterion of worthwhileness, he may become the conformist and thoughtless slave of his technology and of those who are in a position to exploit it.

5. IDENTITY vs. ROLE CONFUSION

With the establishment of a good initial relationship to the world of skills and tools, and with the advent of puberty, childhood proper comes to an end. Youth begins. But in puberty and adolescence all sameness and continuities relied on earlier are more or less questioned again, because of a rapidity of body growth which equals that of early childhood and because of the new addition of genital maturity. The growing and developing youths, faced with this physiological revolution within them, and with tangible adult tasks ahead of them are now primarily concerned with what they appear to be in the eyes of others as compared with what they feel they are, and with the question of how to connect the roles and skills cultivated earlier with the occupational prototypes of the day. In their search for a new sense of continuity and sameness, adolescents have to refight many of the battles of earlier years, even though to do so they must artificially appoint perfectly well-meaning people to play the roles of adversaries; and they are ever ready to install lasting idols and ideals as guardians of a final identity.

The integration now taking place in the form of ego identity is, as pointed out, more than the sum of the childhood identifications. It is the accrued experience of the ego's ability to integrate all identifications with the vicissitudes of the libido, with the aptitudes developed out of endowment, and with the opportunities offered in social roles. The sense of ego identity, then, is the accrued confidence that the inner sameness and continuity prepared in the past are matched by the sameness and continuity of one's meaning for others, as evidenced in the tangible promise of a "career."

The danger of this stage is role confusion. Where this is based on a strong previous doubt as to one's sexual identity, delinquent and outright psychotic episodes are not uncommon. If diagnosed and treated correctly, these incidents do not have the same fatal significance which they have at other ages. In most instances, however, it is the inability to settle on an occupational identity which disturbs individual young people. To keep themselves together they temporarily overidentify, to the point of apparent complete loss of identity, with the heroes of cliques and crowds. This initiates the stage of "falling in love," which is by no means entirely, or even primarily, a sexual matter—except where the mores demand it. To a consider-

able extent adolescent love is an attempt to arrive at a definition of one's identity by projecting one's diffused ego image on another and by seeing it thus reflected and gradually clarified. This is why so much of young love is conversation.

Young people can also be remarkably clannish, and cruel in their exclusion of all those who are "different," in skin color or cultural background, in tastes and gifts, and often in such petty aspects of dress and gesture as have been temporarily selected as *the* signs of an in-grouper or out-grouper. It is important to understand (which does not mean condone or participate in) such intolerance as a defense against a sense of identity confusion. For adolescents not only help one another temporarily through much discomfort by forming cliques and by stereotyping themselves, their ideals, and their enemies; they also perversely test each other's capacity to pledge fidelity. The readiness for such testing also explains the appeal which simple and cruel totalitarian doctrines have on the minds of the youth of such countries and classes as have lost or are losing their group identities (feudal, agrarian, tribal, national) and face worldwide industrialization, emancipation, and wider communication.

The adolescent mind is essentially a mind of the *moratorium,* a psychosocial stage between childhood and adulthood, and between the morality learned by the child, and the ethics to be developed by the adult. It is an ideological mind—and, indeed, it is the ideological outlook of a society that speaks most clearly to the adolescent who is eager to be affirmed by his peers, and is ready to be confirmed by rituals, creeds, and programs which at the same time define what is evil, uncanny, and inimical. In searching for the social values which guide identity, one therefore confronts the problems of *ideology* and *aristocracy,* both in their widest possible sense which connotes that within a defined world image and a predestined course of history, the best people will come to rule and rule develops the best in people. In order not to become cynically or apathetically lost, young people must somehow be able to convince themselves that those who succeed in their anticipated adult world thereby shoulder the obligation of being the best. . . .

6. INTIMACY vs. ISOLATION

The strength acquired at any stage is tested by the necessity to transcend it in such a way that the individual can take chances in the next stage with what was most vulnerably precious in the previous one. Thus, the young adult, emerging from the search for and the insistence on identity, is eager and willing to fuse his identity with that of others. He is ready for intimacy, that is, the capacity to commit himself to concrete affiliations and partnerships and to develop the ethical strength to abide by such commitments, even though they may call for significant sacrifices and compromises. Body and ego must now be masters of the organ modes and of the nuclear conflicts, in order to be able to face the fear of ego loss in situations which call for self-abandon: in the solidarity of close affiliations, in orgasms and sexual unions, in close friendships and in physical combat, in experiences of inspiration by teachers and of intuition from the recesses of the self. The avoidance of such experiences because of a fear of ego loss may lead to a deep sense of isolation and consequent self-absorption.

The counterpart of intimacy is distantiation: the readiness to isolate and, if necessary, to destroy those forces and people whose essence seems dangerous to one's own, and whose "territory" seems to encroach on the extent of one's intimate relations. Prejudices thus developed (and utilized and exploited in politics and in war) are a more mature outgrowth of the blinder repudiations which during the struggle for identity differentiate sharply and cruelly between the familiar and the foreign. The danger of this stage is that intimate, competitive, and combative relations are experienced with and against the selfsame people. But as the areas of adult duty are delineated, and as the competitive encounter, and the sexual embrace, are differentiated, they eventually become subject to that *ethical sense* which is the mark of the adult. . . .

The danger of this stage is isolation, that is the avoidance of contacts which commit to intimacy. In psychopathology, this disturbance can lead to severe "character-problems." On the other hand, there are partnerships which amount to an isolation à deux, protecting both partners from the necessity to face the next critical development—that of generativity.

7. GENERATIVITY vs. STAGNATION

In this book the emphasis is on the childhood stages, otherwise the section on generativity would of necessity be the central one, for this term encompasses the evolutionary development which has made man the teaching and instituting as well as the learning animal. The fashionable insistence on dramatizing the dependence of children on adults often blinds us to the dependence of the older generation on the younger one. Mature man needs to be needed, and maturity needs guidance as well as encouragement from what has been produced and must be taken care of.

Generativity, then, is primarily the concern in establishing and guiding the next generation, although there are individuals who, through misfortune or because of special and genuine gifts in other directions, do not apply this drive to their own offspring. And indeed, the concept generativity is meant to include such more popular synonyms as *productivity* and *creativity,* which, however, cannot replace it.

It has taken psychoanalysis some time to realize that the ability to lose oneself in the meeting of bodies and minds leads to a gradual expansion of ego-interests and to a libidinal investment in that which is being generated. Generativity thus is an essential stage on the psychosexual as well as on the psychosocial schedule. Where such enrichment fails altogether, regression to an obsessive need for pseudo-intimacy takes place, often with a pervading sense of stagnation and personal impoverishment. Individuals, then, often begin to indulge themselves as if they were their own— or one another's—one and only child; and where conditions favor it, early invalidism, physical or psychological, becomes the vehicle of self-concern. The mere fact of having or even wanting children, however, does not "achieve" generativity. In fact, some young parents suffer, it seems, from the retardation of the ability to develop this stage. The reasons are often to be found in early childhood impressions; in excessive self-love based on a too strenuously self-made personality; and finally (and here we return to the beginnings) in the lack of some faith, some "belief in the species," which would make a child appear to be a welcome trust of the community.

As to the institutions which safeguard and reinforce generativity, one can only say that all institutions codify the ethics of generative succession. Even where philosophical and spiritual tradition suggests the renunciation of the right to procreate or to produce, such early turn to "ultimate concerns," wherever instituted in monastic movements, strives to settle at the same time the matter of its relationship to the Care for the creatures of this world and to the Charity which is felt to transcend it. . . .

8. EGO INTEGRITY vs. DESPAIR

Only in him who in some way has taken care of things and people and has adapted himself to the triumphs and disappointments adherent to being, the originator of others or the generator of products and ideas—only in him may gradually ripen the fruit of these seven stages. I know no better word for it than ego integrity. Lacking a clear definition, I shall point to a few constituents of this state of mind. It is the ego's accrued assurance of its proclivity for order and meaning. It is a post-narcissistic love of the human ego—not of the self—as an experience which conveys some world order and spiritual sense, no matter how dearly paid for. It is the acceptance of one's one and only life cycle as something that had to be and that, by necessity, permitted of no substitutions: it thus means a new, a different love of one's parents. It is a comradeship with the ordering ways of distant times and different pursuits, as expressed in the simple products and sayings of such times and pursuits. Although aware of the relativity of all the various life styles which have given meaning to human striving, the possessor of integrity is ready to defend the dignity of his own life style against all physical and economic threats. For he knows that an individual life is the accidental coincidence of but one life cycle with but one segment of his-

tory; and that for him all human integrity stands or falls with the one style of integrity of which he partakes. The style of integrity developed by his culture or civilization thus becomes the "patrimony of his soul," the seal of his moral paternity of himself (". . . pero el honor/Es patrimonio del alma": Calderón). In such final consolidation, death loses its sting.

The lack or loss of this accrued ego integration is signified by fear of death: the one and only life cycle is not accepted as the ultimate of life. Despair expresses the feeling that the time is now short, too short for the attempt to start another life and to try out alternate roads to integrity. Disgust hides despair, if often only in the form of "a thousand little disgusts" which do not add up to one big remorse: *mille petits dégôuts de soi, dont le total ne fait pas un remords, mais un gêne obscure."* (Rostand)

Each individual, to become a mature adult, must to a sufficient degree develop all the ego qualities mentioned, so that a wise Indian, a true gentleman, and a mature peasant share and recognize in one another the final stage of integrity. But each cultural entity, to develop the particular style of integrity suggested by its historical place, utilizes a particular combination of these conflicts, along with specific provocations and prohibitions of infantile sexuality. Infantile conflicts become creative only if sustained by the firm support of cultural institutions and of the special leader classes representing them. In order to approach or experience integrity, the individual must know how to be a follower of image bearers in religion and in politics, in the economic order and in technology, in aristocratic living and in the arts and sciences. Ego integrity, therefore, implies an emotional integration which permits participation by followership as well as acceptance of the responsibility of leadership.

Webster's Dictionary is kind enough to help us complete this outline in a circular fashion. Trust (the first of our ego values) is here defined as "the assured reliance on another's integrity," the last of our values. I suspect that Webster had business in mind rather than babies, credit rather than faith. But the formulation stands. And it seems possible to further paraphrase the relation of adult integrity and infantile trust by saying that healthy children will not fear life if their elders have integrity enough not to fear death.

9. AN EPIGENETIC CHART

In this book the emphasis is on the childhood stages. The foregoing conception of the life cycle, however, awaits systematic treatment. To prepare this, I shall conclude this chapter with a diagram. In this, as in the diagram of pregenital zones and modes, the diagonal represents the normative sequence of psychosocial gains made as at each stage one more nuclear conflict adds a new ego quality, a new criterion of accruing human strength. Below the diagonal there is space for the precursors of each of these solutions, all of which begin with the beginning; above the diagonal there is space for the designation of the derivatives of these gains and their transformations in the maturing and the mature personality.

The underlying assumptions for such charting are (1) that the human personality in principle develops according to steps predetermined in the growing person's readiness to be driven toward, to be aware of, and to interact with, a widening social radius; and (2) that society, in principle, tends to be so constituted as to meet and invite this succession of potentialities for interaction and attempts to safeguard and to encourage the proper rate and the proper sequence of their enfolding. This is the "maintenance of the human world."

But a chart is only a tool to think with, and cannot aspire to be a prescription to abide by, whether in the practice of child-training, in psychotherapy, or in the methodology of child study. In the presentation of the psychosocial stages in the form of an *epigenetic chart* analogous to the one employed . . . for an analysis of Freud's psychosexual stages, we have definite and delimited methodological steps in mind. It is one purpose of this work to facilitate the comparison of the stages first discerned by Freud as sexual to other schedules of development (physical, cognitive). But any one chart delimits one schedule only, and it must not be imputed that our outline of the psychosocial schedule is intended to imply obscure generalities concerning other aspects of

development—or, indeed, of existence. If the chart, for example, lists a series of conflicts or crises, we do not consider all development a series of crises: we claim only that psychosocial development proceeds by critical steps—"critical" being a characteristic of turning points, of moments of decision between progress and regression, integration and retardation.

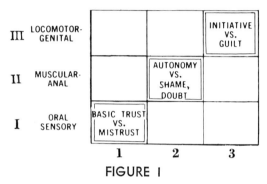

FIGURE I

It may be useful at this point to spell out the methodological implications of an epigenetic matrix. The more heavily-lined squares of the diagonal signify both a sequence of stages and a gradual development of component parts: in other words, the chart formalizes a progression through time of a differentiation of parts. This indicates (1) that each critical item of psychosocial strength discussed here is systematically related to all others, and that they all depend on the proper development in the proper sequence of each item; and (2) that each item exists in some form before its critical time normally arrives.

If I say, for example, that a favorable ratio of basic trust over basic mistrust is the first step in psychosocial adaptation, a favorable ratio of autonomous will over shame and doubt, the second, the corresponding diagrammatic statement expresses a number of fundamental relations that exist between the two steps, as well as some facts fundamental to each. Each comes to its ascendance, meets its crisis, and finds its lasting solution during the stage indicated. But they all must exist from the beginning in some form, for every act calls for an integration of all. Also, an infant may show something like "autonomy" from the beginning in the particular way in which he angrily tries to wriggle himself free when tightly held. How-

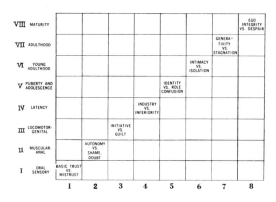

FIGURE 2

ever, under normal conditions, it is not until the second year that he begins to experience the whole *critical opposition of being an autonomous creature and being a dependent one;* and it is not until then that he is ready for a decisive encounter with his environment, an environment which, in turn, feels called upon to convey to him its particular ideas and concepts of autonomy and coercion in ways decisively contributing to the character and the health of his personality in his culture. It is this encounter, together with the resulting crisis, that we have tentatively described for each stage. As to the progression from one stage to the next, the diagonal indicates the sequence to be followed. However, it also makes room for variations in tempo and intensity. An individual, or a culture, may linger excessively over trust and proceed

from I 1 over I 2 to II 2, or an accelerated progression may move from I 1 over II 1 to II 2. Each such acceleration or (relative) retardation, however, is assumed to have a modifying influence on all later stages.

An epigenetic diagram thus lists a system of stages dependent on each other; and while individual stages may have been explored more or less thoroughly or named more or less fittingly, the diagram suggests that their study be pursued always with the total configuration of stages in mind. The diagram invites, then, a thinking through of all its empty boxes: if we have entered Basic Trust in I 1 and Integrity in VIII 8, we leave the question open, as to what trust might have become in a stage dominated by the need for integrity even as we have left open what it may look like and, indeed, be called in the stage dominated by a striving for autonomy (II 1). All we mean to emphasize is that trust must have developed in its own right, before it becomes something more in the critical encounter in which autonomy develops —and so on, up the vertical. If, in the last stage (VIII 8), we would expect trust to have developed into the most mature *faith* that an aging person can muster in his cultural setting and historical period, the chart permits the consideration not only of what old age can be, but also what its preparatory stages must have been. All of this should make it clear that a chart of epigenesis suggests a global form of thinking and rethinking which leaves details of methodology and terminology to further study.

A CASE HISTORY IN SCIENTIFIC METHOD

B. F. SKINNER

It has been said that college teaching is the only profession for which there is no professional training, and it is commonly argued that this is because our graduate schools train scholars and scientists rather than teachers. We are more concerned with the discovery of knowledge than with its dissemination. But can we justify ourselves quite so easily? It is a bold thing to say that we know how to train a man to be a scientist. Scientific thinking is the most complex and probably the most subtle of all human activities. Do we actually know how to shape up such behavior, or do we simply mean that some of the people who attend our graduate schools eventually become scientists?

Except for a laboratory course which acquaints the student with standard apparatus and standard procedures, the only explicit training in scientific method generally received by a young psychologist is a course in statistics—not the introductory course, which is often required of so many kinds of students that it is scarcely scientific at all, but an advanced course which includes "model building," "theory construction," and "experimental design." But it is a mistake to identify scientific practice with the formalized constructions of statistics and scientific method. These disciplines have their place, but it does not coincide with the place of scientific research. They offer *a* method of science but not, as is so often implied, *the* method. . . .

. . . So far as I can see, I began [my activities as research psychologist] simply by looking for lawful processes in the behavior of the intact organism [while carrying on my thesis research]. Pavlov had shown the way; but I could not then, as I cannot now, move without a jolt

Reprinted with abridgment by permission of the author and the American Psychological Association from *American Psychologist*, 1956, **11**, 221–33.

from salivary reflexes to the important business of the organism in everyday life. Sherrington and Magnus had found order in surgical segments of the organism. Could not something of the same sort be found, to use Loeb's phrase, in "the organism as a whole"? I had the clue from Pavlov: control your conditions and you will see order.

It is not surprising that my first gadget was a silent release box, operated by compressed air and designed to eliminate disturbances when introducing a rat into an apparatus. I used this first in studying the way a rat adapted to a novel stimulus. I built a soundproofed box containing a specially structured space. A rat was released, pneumatically, at the far end of a darkened tunnel from which it emerged in exploratory fashion into a well-lighted area. To accentuate its progress and to facilitate recording, the tunnel was placed at the top of a flight of steps, something like a functional Parthenon (Figure 1). The rat would peek out

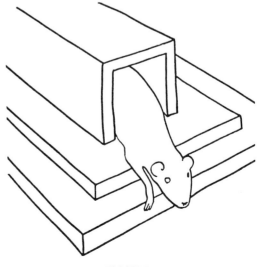

FIGURE I

from the tunnel, perhaps glancing suspiciously at the one-way window through which I was watching it, then stretch itself cautiously down the steps. A soft click (carefully calibrated, of course) would cause it to pull back into the tunnel and remain there for some time. But repeated clicks had less and less of an effect. I recorded the rat's advances and retreats by moving a pen back and forth across a moving paper tape.

The major result of this experiment was that some of my rats had babies. I began to watch young rats. I saw them right themselves and crawl about very much like the decerebrate or thalamic cats and rabbits of Magnus. So I set about studying the postural reflexes of young rats. Here was a first principle not formally recognized by scientific methodologists: When you run onto something interesting, drop everything else and study it. I tore up the Parthenon and started over.

If you hold a young rat on one hand and pull it gently by the tail, it will resist you by pulling forward and then, with a sudden sharp spring which usually disengages its tail, it will leap out into space. . . .

. . . I decided to study this behavior quantitatively. I built a light platform covered with cloth and mounted it on tightly stretched piano wires (Figure 2). Here was a version of Sherrington's torsion-wire myograph, originally de-

signed to record the isometric contraction of the *tibialis anticus* of a cat, but here adapted to the response of a whole organism. When the tail of the young rat was gently pulled, the rat clung to the cloth floor and tugged forward. By amplifying the fine movements of the platform, it was possible to get a good kymograph record of the tremor in this motion and then, as the pull against the tail was increased, of the desperate spring into the air.

Now, baby rats have very little future, except as adult rats. Their behavior is literally infantile and cannot be usefully extrapolated to everyday life. But if this technique would work with a baby, why not try it on a mature rat? To avoid attaching anything to the rat, it should be possible to record, not a pull against the substrate, but the ballistic thrust exerted as the rat runs forward or suddenly stops in response to my calibrated click. So, invoking the first principle of scientific practice again, I threw away the piano-wire platform, and built a runway, eight feet long. This was constructed of light wood, in the form of a U girder, mounted rigidly on vertical glass plates, the elasticity of which permitted a very slight longitudinal movement. The runway became the floor of a long tunnel, not shown, at one end of which I placed my soundless release box and at the other end myself, prepared to reinforce the rat for coming down the runway by giving it a bit of wet mash, to sound a click from time to time when it had reached the middle of the runway, and to harvest kymograph records of the vibrations of the substrate.

Now for a second unformalized principle of scientific practice: Some ways of doing research are easier than others. I got tired of carrying the rat back to the other end of the runway. A back alley was therefore added (Figure 3). Now the rat could eat a bit of mash at point C, go down the back alley A, around the end as shown, and back home by runway B. The experimenter at E could collect records from the kymograph at D in comfort. In this way a great many records were made of the forces exerted against the substratum as rats ran down the alley and occasionally stopped dead in their tracks as a click sounded.

There was one annoying detail, however. The rat would often wait an inordinately long

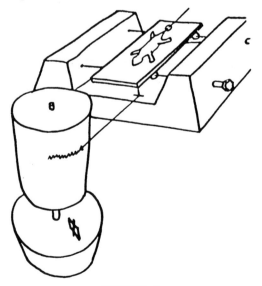

FIGURE 2

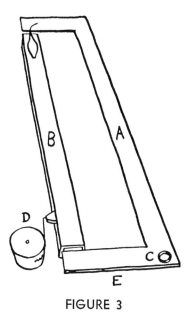

FIGURE 3

time at C before starting down the back alley on the next run. There seemed to be no explanation for this. When I timed these delays with a stop watch, however, and plotted them, they seemed to show orderly changes. This was, of course, the kind of thing I was looking for. I forgot all about the movements of the substratum and began to run rats for the sake of the delay measurements alone. But there was now no reason why the runway had to be eight feet long and, the second principle came into play again, I saw no reason why the rat could not deliver its own reinforcement.

A new apparatus was built. In Figure 4 we

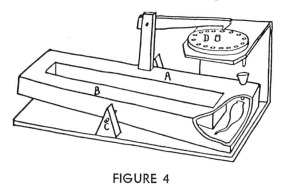

FIGURE 4

see the rat eating a piece of food just after completing a run. It produced the food by its own

action. As it ran down the back alley A to the far end of the rectangular runway, its weight caused the whole runway to tilt slightly on the axis C and this movement turned the wooden disc D, permitting a piece of food in one of the holes around its perimeter to drop through a funnel into a food dish. The food was pearly barley, the only kind I could find in the grocery stores in reasonably uniform pieces. The rat had only to complete its journey by coming down the home stretch B to enjoy its reward. The experimenter was able to enjoy *his* reward at the same time, for he had only to load the magazine, put in a rat, and relax. Each tilt was recorded on a slowly moving kymograph.

A third unformalized principle of scientific practice: Some people are lucky. The disc of wood from which I had fashioned the food magazine was taken from a store room of discarded apparatus. It happened to have a central spindle, which fortunately I had not bothered to cut off. One day it occurred to me that if I wound a string around the spindle and allowed it to unwind as the magazine was emptied, I would get a different kind of record. Instead of a mere report of the up-and-down movement of the runway, as a series of pips as in a polygraph, I would get a *curve*. And I knew that science made great use of curves, although, so far as I could discover, very little of pips on a polygram. The difference between the old type of record at A (Figure 5) and the new at

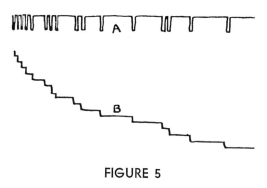

FIGURE 5

B may not seem great, but as it turned out the curve revealed things in the rate of responding, and in changes in that rate, which would certainly otherwise have been missed. By allowing the string to unwind rather than to wind, I had got my curve in an awkward Cartesian quadrant, but that was easily remedied. Psychologists have adopted cumulative curves only very slowly, but I think it is fair to say that they have become an indispensable tool for certain purposes of analysis.

Eventually, of course, the runway was seen to be unnecessary. The rat could simply reach into a covered tray for pieces of food, and each movement of the cover could operate a solenoid to move a pen one step in a cumulative curve. The first major change in rate observed in this way was due to ingestion. Curves showing how the rate of eating declined with the time of eating comprised the other part of my thesis. But a refinement was needed. The behavior of the rat in pushing open the door was not a normal part of the ingestive behavior of *Rattus rattus*. The act was obviously learned but its status as part of the final performance was not clear. It seemed wise to add an initial conditioned response connected with ingestion in a quite arbitrary way. I chose the first device which came to hand—a horizontal bar or lever placed where it could be conveniently depressed by the rat to close a switch which operated a magnetic magazine. Ingestion curves obtained with this initial response in the chain were found to have the same properties as those without it.

Now, as soon as you begin to complicate an apparatus, you necessarily invoke a fourth principle of scientific practice: Apparatuses sometimes break down. I had only to wait for the food magazine to jam to get an extinction curve. At first I treated this as a defect and hastened to remedy the difficulty. But eventually, of course, I deliberately disconnected the magazine. I can easily recall the excitement of that first complete extinction curve (Figure 6). I had made contact with Pavlov at last! Here was a curve uncorrupted by the physiological process of ingestion. It was an orderly change due to nothing more than a special contingency of reinforcement. It was pure behavior! I am not saying that I would not have got around to extinction curves without a breakdown in the apparatus; Pavlov had given too strong a lead in that direction. But it is still no exaggeration to say that some of the most interesting and surprising results have turned up first because of similar accidents. Foolproof apparatus is no doubt highly desirable, but Charles Ferster and I in recently reviewing the data from a five-year program of research found many occasions to congratulate ourselves on the fallibility of relays and vacuum tubes.

I then built four soundproofed ventilated boxes, each containing a lever and a food magazine and supplied with a cumulative recorder, and was on my way to an intensive study of conditioned reflexes in skeletal behavior. I would reinforce every response for several days and then extinguish for a day or two, varying the number of reinforcements, the amount of previous magazine training, and so on.

At this point I made my first use of the deductive method. I had long since given up pearl barley as too unbalanced a diet for steady use. A neighborhood druggist had shown me his pill machine, and I had had one made along the same lines. It consisted of a fluted brass bed across which one laid a long cylinder of stiff paste (in my case a MacCollum formula for an adequate rat diet). A similarly fluted cutter was then lowered onto the cylinder and rolled slowly back and forth, converting the paste into about a dozen spherical pellets. These were dried for a day or so before use. The procedure was painstaking and laborious. Eight rats eating a hundred pellets each per day could easily keep up with production. One pleasant Saturday afternoon I surveyed my supply of dry pellets, and, appealing to certain elemental theorems in arithmetic, deduced that unless I spent the rest of that afternoon and evening at the pill machine, the supply would be exhausted by ten-thirty Monday morning.

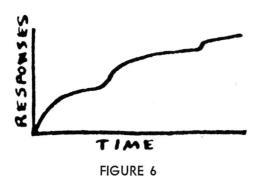

FIGURE 6

Since I do not wish to deprecate the hypothetico-deductive method, I am glad to testify here to its usefulness. It led me to apply our second principle of unformalized scientific method and to ask myself why *every* press of the lever had to be reinforced. I was not then aware of what had happened at the Brown laboratories, as Harold Schlosberg later told the story. A graduate student had been given the task of running a cat through a difficult discrimination experiment. One Sunday the student found the supply of cat food exhausted. The stores were closed and so, with a beautiful faith in the frequency-theory of learning, he ran the cat as usual and took it back to its living cage unrewarded. Schlosberg reports that the cat howled its protest continuously for nearly forty-eight hours. Unaware of this I decided to reinforce a response only once every minute and to allow all other responses to go unreinforced. There were two results: (*a*) my supply of pellets lasted almost indefinitely and (*b*) each rat stabilized at a fairly constant rate of responding.

Now, a steady state was something I was familiar with from physical chemistry, and I therefore embarked upon the study of periodic reinforcement. I soon found that the constant rate at which the rat stabilized depended upon how hungry it was. Hungry rat, high rate; less hungry rat, lower rate. At that time I was bothered by the practical problem of controlling food deprivation. I was working half time at the Medical School (on chronaxie of subordination!) and could not maintain a good schedule in working with the rats. The rate of responding under periodic reinforcement suggested a scheme for keeping a rat at a constant level of deprivation. The argument went like this: Suppose you reinforce the rat, not at the end of a given period, but when it has completed the number of responses ordinarily emitted in that period. And suppose you use substantial pellets of food and give the rat continuous access to the lever. Then, except for periods when the rat sleeps, it should operate the lever at a constant rate around the clock. For, whenever it grows slightly hungrier, it will work faster, get food faster, and become less hungry, while whenever it grows slightly less hungry, it will respond at a lower rate, get less food, and grow

hungrier. By setting the reinforcement at a given number of responses it should even be possible to hold the rat at any given level of deprivation. I visualized a machine with a dial which one could set to make available, at any time of day or night, a rat in a given state of deprivation. Of course, nothing of the sort happens. This is "fixed-ratio" rather than "fixed-interval" reinforcement and, as I soon found out, it produces a very different type of performance. This is an example of a fifth unformalized principle of scientific practice, but one which has at least been named. Walter Cannon described it with a word invented by Horace Walpole: *serendipity*—the art of finding one thing while looking for something else.

This account of my scientific behavior up to the point at which I published my results in a book called *The Behavior of Organisms* is as exact in letter and spirit as I can now make it. The notes, data, and publications which I have examined do not show that I ever behaved in the manner of Man Thinking as described by John Stuart Mill or John Dewey or in reconstructions of scientific behavior by other philosophers of science. I never faced a Problem which was more than the eternal problem of finding order. I never attacked a problem by constructing a Hypothesis. I never deduced Theorems or submitted them to Experimental Check. So far as I can see, I had no preconceived Model of behavior—certainly not a physiological or mentalistic one, and, I believe, not a conceptual one. The "reflex reserve" was an abortive, though operational, concept which was retracted a year or so after publication in a paper at the Philadelphia meeting of the APA. It lived up to my opinion of theories in general by proving utterly worthless in suggesting further experiments. Of course, I was working on a basic Assumption—that there was order in behavior if I could only discover it—but such an assumption is not to be confused with the hypotheses of deductive theory. It is also true that I exercised a certain Selection of Facts but not because of relevance to theory but because one fact was more orderly than another. If I engaged in Experimental Design at all, it was simply to complete or extend some evidence of order already observed.

Most of the experiments described in *The*

Behavior of Organisms were done with groups of four rats. A fairly common reaction to the book was that such groups were too small. How did I know that other groups of four rats would do the same thing? Keller, in defending the book, countered with the charge that groups of four were too *big*. Unfortunately, however, I allowed myself to be persuaded of the contrary. This was due in part to my association at the University of Minnesota with W. T. Heron. Through him I came into close contact for the first time with traditional animal psychology. Heron was interested in inherited maze behavior, inherited activity, and certain drugs—the effects of which could then be detected only through the use of fairly large groups. We did an experiment together on the effect of starvation on the rate of pressing a lever and started the new era with a group of sixteen rats. But we had only four boxes, and this was so inconvenient that Heron applied for a grant and built a battery of twenty-four lever-boxes and cumulative recorders. I supplied an attachment which would record, not only the mean performance of all twenty-four rats in a single averaged curve, but mean curves for four subgroups of twelve rats each and four subgroups of six rats each. We thus provided for the design of experiments according to the principles of R. A. Fisher, which were then coming into vogue. We had, so to speak, mechanized the latin square.

With this apparatus Heron and I published a study of extinction in maze-bright and maze-dull rats using *ninety-five* subjects. Later I published mean extinction curves for groups of twenty-four, and W. K. Estes and I did our work on anxiety with groups of the same size. But although Heron and I could properly voice the hope that "the possibility of using large groups of animals greatly improves upon the method as previously reported, since tests of significance are provided for and properties of behavior not apparent in single cases may be more easily detected," in actual practice that is not what happened. The experiments I have just mentioned are almost all we have to show for this elaborate battery of boxes. Undoubtedly more work could be done with it and would have its place, but something had happened to the natural growth of the method. You cannot easily make a change in the conditions of an experiment when twenty-four apparatuses have to be altered. Any gain in rigor is more than matched by a loss in flexibility. We were forced to confine ourselves to processes which could be studied with the baselines already developed in earlier work. We could not move on to the discovery of other processes or even to a more refined analysis of those we were working with. No matter how significant might be the relations we actually demonstrated, our statistical Leviathan had swum aground. The art of the method had stuck at a particular stage of its development. . . .

I think it can be said that a functional analysis proved adequate in its technological application. Manipulation of environmental conditions alone made possible a wholly unexpected practical control. Behavior could be shaped up according to specifications and maintained indefinitely almost at will. One behavioral technologist who worked with me at the time (Keller Breland) is now specializing in the production of behavior as a salable commodity and has described this new profession in the *American Psychologist*. . . .

The effect of a behavioral technology on scientific practice is the issue here. Faced with practical problems in behavior, you necessarily emphasize the refinement of *experimental* variables. As a result, some of the standard procedures of statistics appear to be circumvented. Let me illustrate. Suppose that measurements have been made on two groups of subjects differing in some detail of experimental treatment. Means and standard deviations for the two groups are determined, and any difference due to the treatment is evaluated. If the difference is in the expected direction but is not statistically significant, the almost universal recommendation would be to study larger groups. But our experience with practical control suggests that we may reduce the troublesome variability by changing the conditions of the experiment. By discovering, elaborating, and fully exploiting every relevant variable, we may eliminate *in advance of measurement* the individual differences which obscure the difference under analysis. This will achieve the same result as increasing the size of groups, and it will almost certainly yield a bonus in the discovery of new variables which would not have been identified in the statistical treatment.

The same may be said of smooth curves. In our study of anxiety, Estes and I published several curves, the reasonable smoothness of which was obtained by averaging the performances of 12 rats for each curve. The individual curves published at that time show that the mean curves do not faithfully represent the behavior of any one rat. They show a certain tendency toward a change in slope which supported the point we were making, and they may have appeared to justify averaging for that reason.

But an alternative method would have been to explore the individual case until an equally smooth curve could be obtained. This would have meant, not only rejecting the temptation to produce smoothness by averaging cases, but manipulating all relevant conditions as we later learned to manipulate them for practical purposes. The individual curves which we published at that time do not point to the need for larger groups but for improvement in experimental technique. . . . In a single organism, three different schedules of reinforcement are yielding corresponding performances with great uniformity under appropriate stimuli alternating at random. One does not reach this kind of order through the application of statistical methods.

In *The Behavior of Organisms* I was content to deal with the over-all slopes and curvature of cumulative curves and could make only a rough classification of the properties of behavior shown by the finer grain. The grain has now been improved. The resolving power of the microscope has been increased manyfold, and we can see fundamental processes of behavior in sharper and sharper detail. In choosing rate of responding as a basic datum and in recording this conveniently in a cumulative curve, we make important temporal aspects of behavior *visible*. Once this has happened, our scientific practice is reduced to simple looking. A new world is opened to inspection.

It is perhaps natural that psychologists should awaken only slowly to the possibility that behavioral processes may be directly observed, or that they should only gradually put the older statistical and theoretical techniques in their proper perspective. But it is time to insist that science does not progress by carefully designed steps called "experiments" each of which has a well-defined beginning and end. Science is a continuous and often a disorderly and accidental process. We shall not do the young psychologist any favor if we agree to reconstruct our practices to fit the pattern demanded by current scientific methodology. What the statistician means by the design of experiments is design which yields the kind of data to which *his* techniques are applicable. He does not mean the behavior of the scientist in his laboratory devising research for his own immediate and possibly inscrutable purposes. . . .

REFERENCES

Breland, K., and Breland, Marion. A field of applied animal psychology. *Amer. Psychologist,* 1951, 6, 202–204.

Heron, W. T., and Skinner, B. F. An apparatus for the study of behavior. *Psychol. Rec.,* 1939, 3, 166–176.

DEVELOPMENT AND LEARNING

JEAN PIAGET

First I would like to make clear the difference between two problems: the problem of *development* in general, and the problem of *learning*. I think these problems are very different, although some people do not make this distinction.

The development of knowledge is a spontaneous process, tied to the whole process of embryogenesis. Embryogenesis concerns the development of the body, but it concerns as well the development of the nervous system, and the development of mental functions. In the case of the development of knowledge in children, embryogenesis ends only in adulthood. It is a total developmental process which we must re-situate in its general biological and psychological context. In other words, development is a process which concerns the totality of the structures of knowledge.

Learning presents the opposite case. In general, learning is provoked by situations—provoked by a psychological experimenter; or by a teacher, with respect to some didactic point; or by an external situation. It is provoked, in general, as opposed to spontaneous. In addition, it is a limited process—limited to a single problem, or to a single structure.

So I think that development explains learning, and this opinion is contrary to the widely held opinion that development is a sum of discrete learning experiences. For some psychologists development is reduced to a series of specific learned items, and development is thus the sum, the cumulation of this series of specific items. I think this is an atomistic view which deforms the real state of things. In reality, development is the essential process and each

Reprinted by permission of the author and editors from pp. 7–19 of *Piaget Rediscovered*, edited by R. Ripple and V. Rockcastle, Cornell University, 1964.

element of learning occurs as a function of total development, rather than being an element which explains development. I shall begin, then, with a first part dealing with development, and I shall talk about learning in the second part.

To understand the development of knowledge, we must start with an idea which seems central to me—the idea of an *operation*. Knowledge is not a copy of reality. To know an object, to know an event, is not simply to look at it and make a mental copy, or image, of it. To know an object is to act on it. To know is to modify, to transform the object, and to understand the process of this transformation, and as a consequence to understand the way the object is constructed. An operation is thus the essence of knowledge; it is an interiorized action which modifies the object of knowledge. For instance, an operation would consist of joining objects in a class, to construct a classification. Or an operation would consist of ordering, or putting things in a series. Or an operation would consist of counting, or of measuring. In other words, it is a set of actions modifying the object, and enabling the knower to get at the structures of the transformation.

An operation is an interiorized action. But in addition, it is a reversible action; that is, it can take place in both directions, for instance, adding or subtracting, joining or separating. So it is a particular type of action which makes up logical structures.

Above all, an operation is never isolated. It is always linked to other operations, and as a result it is always a part of a total structure. For instance, a logical class does not exist in isolation; what exists is the total structure of classification. An asymmetrical relation does not exist in isolation. Seriation is the natural, basic operational structure. A number does not exist in isolation. What exists is the series of numbers, which constitute a structure, an exceedingly rich structure whose various properties have been revealed by mathematicians.

These operational structures are what seem to me to constitute the basis of knowledge, the natural psychological reality, in terms of which we must understand the development of knowledge. And the central problem of development is to understand the formation, elaboration, organization, and functioning of these structures.

I should like to review the stages of development of these structures, not in any detail, but simply as a reminder. I shall distinguish four main stages. The first is a sensory-motor, pre-verbal stage, lasting approximately the first 18 months of life. During this stage is developed the practical knowledge which constitutes the substructure of later representational knowledge. An example is the construction of the schema of the permanent object. For an infant, during the first months, an object has no permanence. When it disappears from the perceptual field it no longer exists. No attempt is made to find it again. Later, the infant will try to find it, and he will find it by localizing it spatially. Consequently, along with the construction of the permanent object there comes the construction of practical, or sensory-motor, space. There is similarly the construction of temporal succession, and of elementary sensory-motor causality. In other words, there is a series of structures which are indispensable for the structures of later representational thought.

In a second stage, we have pre-operational representation—the beginnings of language, of the symbolic function, and therefore of thought, or representation. But at the level of representational thought, there must now be a reconstruction of all that was developed on the sensory-motor level. That is, the sensory-motor actions are not immediately translated into operations. In fact, during all this second period of pre-operational representations, there are as yet no operations as I defined this term a moment ago. Specifically, there is as yet no conservation which is the psychological criterion of the presence of reversible operations. For example, if we pour liquid from one glass to another of a different shape, the pre-operational child will think there is more in one than in the other. In

the absence of operational reversibility, there is no conservation of quantity.

In a third stage the first operations appear, but I call these concrete operations because they operate on objects, and not yet on verbally expressed hypotheses. For example, there are the operations of classification, ordering, the construction of the idea of number, spatial and temporal operations, and all the fundamental operations of elementary logic of classes and relations, of elementary mathematics, of elementary geometry and even of elementary physics.

Finally, in the fourth stage, these operations are surpassed as the child reaches the level of what I call formal or hypothetic-deductive operations; that is, he can now reason on hypotheses, and not only on objects. He constructs new operations, operations of propositional logic, and not simply the operations of classes, relations, and numbers. He attains new structures which are on the one hand combinatorial, corresponding to what mathematicians call lattices; on the other hand, more complicated group structures. At the level of concrete operations, the operations apply within an immediate neighborhood: for instance, classification by successive inclusions. At the level of the combinatorial, however, the groups are much more mobile. These, then, are the four stages which we identify, whose formation we shall now attempt to explain.

What factors can be called upon to explain the development from one set of structures to another? It seems to me that there are four main factors: first of all, *maturation,* in the sense of Gesell, since this development is a continuation of the embryogenesis; second, the role of *experience* of the effects of the physical environment on the structures of intelligence; third, *social transmission* in the broad sense (linguistic transmission, education, etc.); and fourth, a factor which is too often neglected but one which seems to me fundamental and even the principal factor. I shall call this the factor of *equilibration* or, if you prefer it, of self-regulation.

Let us start with the first factor, maturation. One might think that these stages are simply a reflection of an interior maturation of the nervous system, following the hypotheses of Gesell, for example. Well, maturation certainly does play an indispensable role and must not be ignored. It certainly takes part in every transformation that takes place during a child's development. However, this first factor is insufficient in itself. First of all, we know practically nothing about the maturation of the nervous system beyond the first months of the child's existence. We know a little bit about it during the first two years but we know very little following this time. But above all, maturation doesn't explain everything, because the average ages at which these stages appear (the average chronological ages) vary a great deal from one society to another. The ordering of these stages is constant and has been found in all the societies studied. It has been found in various countries where psychologists in universities have redone the experiments but it has also been found in African peoples, for example, in the children of the Bushmen, and in Iran, both in the villages and in the cities. However, although the order of succession is constant, the chronological ages of these stages varies a great deal. For instance, the ages which we have found in Geneva are not necessarily the ages which you would find in the United States. In Iran, furthermore, in the city of Teheran, they found approximately the same ages as we found in Geneva, but there is a systematic delay of two years in the children in the country. Canadian psychologists who redid our experiments, Monique Laurendeau and Father Adrien Penard, found once again about the same ages in Montreal. But when they redid the experiments in Martinique, they found a delay of four years in all the experiments and this in spite of the fact that the children in Martinique go to a school set up according to the French system and the French curriculum and attain at the end of this elementary school a certificate of higher primary education. There is then a delay of four years, that is, there are the same stages, but systematically delayed. So you see that these age variations show that maturation does not explain everything.

I shall go on now to the role played by experience. Experience of objects, of physical reality, is obviously a basic factor in the development of cognitive structures. But once again this factor does not explain everything. I can give two reasons for this. The first reason is that some of the concepts which appear at the beginning of the stage of concrete operations are such that I cannot see how they could be drawn from experience. As an example, let us take the conservation of the substance in the case of changing the shape of a ball of plasticene. We give this ball of plasticene to a child who changes its shape into a sausage form and we ask him if there is the same amount of matter, that is, the same amount of substance as there was before. We also ask him if it now has the same weight and thirdly if it now has the same volume. The volume is measured by the displacement of water when we put the ball or the sausage into a glass of water. The findings, which have been the same every time this experiment has been done, show us that first of all there is conservation of the amount of substance. At about eight years old a child will say, "There is the same amount of plasticene." Only later does the child assert that the weight is conserved and still later that the volume is conserved. So I would ask you where the idea of the conservation of substance can come from. What is a constant and invariant substance when it doesn't yet have a constant weight or a constant volume? Through perception you can get at the weight of the ball or the volume of the ball but perception cannot give you an idea of the amount of substance. No experiment, no experience, can show the child that there is the same amount of substance. He can weigh the ball and that would lead to the conservation of weight. He can immerse it in water and that would lead to the conservation of volume. But the notion of substance is attained before either weight or volume. This conservation of substance is simply a logical necessity. The child now understands that when there is a transformation something must be conserved because by reversing the transformation you can come back to the point of departure and once again have the ball. He knows that something is conserved but he doesn't know what. It is not yet the weight, it is not yet the volume; it is simply a logical form—a logical necessity. There, it seems to me, is an example of a progress in knowledge, a logical necessity for something to be conserved even though no experience can have led to this notion.

My second objection to the sufficiency of experience as an explanatory factor is that this notion of experience is a very equivocal one. There are, in fact, two kinds of experience which are psychologically very different and this difference is very important from the pedagogical point of view. It is because of the pedagogical importance that I emphasize this distinction. First of all, there is what I shall call physical experience, and secondly, what I shall call logical-mathematical experience.

Physical experience consists of acting upon objects and drawing some knowledge about the objects by abstraction from the objects. For example, to discover that this pipe is heavier than this watch, the child will weigh them both and find the difference in the objects themselves. This is experience in the usual sense of the term—in the sense used by empiricists. But there is a second type of experience which I shall call logical-mathematical experience where the knowledge is not drawn from the objects, but it is drawn by the actions effected upon the objects. This is not the same thing. When one acts upon objects, the objects are indeed there, but there is also the set of actions which modify the objects.

I shall give you an example of this type of experience. It is a nice example because we have verified it many times in small children under seven years of age, but it is also an example which one of my mathematician friends has related to me about his own childhood, and he dates his mathematical career from this experience. When he was four or five years old —I don't know exactly how old, but a small child—he was seated on the ground in his garden and he was counting pebbles. Now to count these pebbles he put them in a row and he counted them one, two, three, up to ten. Then he finished counting them and started to count them in the other direction. He began by the end and once again he found ten. He found this marvelous that there were ten in one direction and ten in the other direction. So he put them in a circle and counted them that way and found ten once again. Then he counted them in the other direction and found ten once more. So he put them in some other direction and found ten once more. So he put them in some other arrangement and kept counting them and

kept finding ten. There was the discovery that he made.

Now what indeed did he discover? He did not discover a property of pebbles; he discovered a property of the action of ordering. The pebbles had no order. It was his action which introduced a linear order or a cyclical order, or any kind of an order. He discovered that the sum was independent of the order. The order was the action which he introduced among the pebbles. For the sum the same principle applied. The pebbles had no sum; they were simply in a pile. To make a sum, action was necessary—the operation of putting together and counting. He found that the sum was independent of the order, in other words, that the action of putting together is independent of the action of ordering. He discovered a property of actions and not a property of pebbles. You may say that it is in the nature of pebbles to let this be done to them and this is true. But it could have been drops of water, and drops of water would not have let this be done to them because two drops of water and two drops of water do not make four drops of water as you know very well. Drops of water then would not let this be done to them, we agree to that.

So it is not the physical property of pebbles which the experience uncovered. It is the properties of the actions carried out on the pebbles and this is quite another form of experience. It is the point of departure of mathematical deduction. The subsequent deduction will consist of interiorizing these actions and then of combining them without needing any pebbles. The mathematician no longer needs his pebbles. He can combine his operations simply with symbols and the point of departure of this mathematical deduction is logical-mathematical experience and this is not at all experience in the sense of the empiricists. It is the beginning of the coordination of actions, but this coordination of actions before the stage of operations needs to be supported by concrete material. Later, this coordination of actions leads to the logical-mathematical structures. I believe that logic is not a derivative of language. The source of logic is much more profound. It is the total coordination of actions, actions of joining things together, or ordering things, etc. This is what logical-mathematical experience is. It is an experience of the actions of the subject, and not an experience of objects themselves. It is an experience which is necessary before there can be operations. Once the operations have been attained this experience is no longer needed and the coordinations of actions can take place by themselves in the form of deduction and construction for abstract structures.

The third factor is social transmission—linguistic transmission or educational transmission. This factor, once again, is fundamental. I do not deny the role of any one of these factors; they all play a part. But this factor is insufficient because the child can receive valuable information via language or via education directed by an adult only if he is in a state where he can understand this information. That is, to receive the information he must have a structure which enables him to assimilate this information. This is why you cannot teach higher mathematics to a five-year old. He does not yet have structures which enable him to understand.

I shall take a much simpler example, an example of linguistic transmission. As my very first work in the realm of child psychology, I spent a long time studying the relation between a part and a whole in concrete experience and in language. For example, I used Burt's test employing the sentence, "Some of my flowers are buttercups." The child knows that all buttercups are yellow, so there are three possible conclusions: the whole bouquet is yellow, or part of the bouquet is yellow, or none of the flowers in the bouquet is yellow. I found that up until nine years of age (and this was in Paris, so the children certainly did understand the French language) they replied, "The whole bouquet is yellow or some of my flowers are yellow." Both of those mean the same thing. They did not understand the expression, "some *of* my flowers." They did not understand this *of* as a partitive genitive, as the inclusion of some flowers in my flowers. They understood some of my flowers to be my several flowers as if the several flowers and the flowers were confused as one and the same class. So there you have children who until nine years of age heard every day a linguistic structure which implied

the inclusion of a sub-class in a class and yet did not understand this structure. It is only when they themselves are in firm possession of this logical structure, when they have constructed it for themselves according to the developmental laws which we shall discuss, that they succeed in understanding correctly the linguistic expression.

I come now to the fourth factor which is added to the three preceding ones but which seems to me to be the fundamental one. This is what I call the factor of equilibration. Since there are already three factors, they must somehow be equilibrated among themselves. That is one reason for bringing in the factor of equilibration. There is a second reason, however, which seems to me to be fundamental. It is that in the act of knowing, the subject is active, and consequently, faced with an external disturbance, he will react in order to compensate and consequently he will tend towards equilibrium. Equilibrium, defined by active compensation, leads to reversibility. Operational reversibility is a model of an equilibrated system where a transformation in one direction is compensated by a transformation in the other direction. Equilibration, as I understand it, is thus an active process. It's a process of self-regulation. I think that this self-regulation is a fundamental factor in development. I use this term in the sense in which it is used in cybernetics, that is, in the sense of processes with feedback and with feedforward, of processes which regulate themselves by a progressive compensation of systems. This process of equilibration takes the form of a succession of levels of equilibrium, of levels which have a certain probability which I shall call a sequential probability, that is, the probabilities are not established a priori. There is a sequence of levels. It is not possible to reach the second level unless equilibrium has been reached at the first level, and the equilibrium of the third level only becomes possible when the equilibrium of the second level has been reached, and so forth. That is, each level is determined as the most probable given that the preceding level has been reached. It is not the most probable at the beginning, but it is the most probable once the preceding level has been reached.

As an example, let us take the development of the idea of conservation in the transformation of the ball of plasticene into the sausage shape. Here you can discern four levels. The most probable at the beginning is for the child to think of only one dimension. Suppose that there is a probability of 0.8, for instance, that the child will focus on the length, and that the width has a probability of 0.2. This would mean that of ten children, eight will focus on the length alone without paying any attention to the width, and two will focus on the width without paying any attention to the length. They will focus only on one dimension or the other. Since the two dimensions are independent at this stage, focusing on both at once would have a probability of only 0.16. That is less than either one of the two. In other words, the most probable in the beginning is to focus only on one dimension and in fact the child will say, "It's longer, so there's more in the sausage." Once he has reached this first level, if you continue to elongate the sausage, there comes a moment when he will say, "No, now it's too thin, so there's less." Now he is thinking about the width, but he forgets the length, so you have come to a second level which becomes the most probable after the first level, but which is not the most probable at the point of departure. Once he has focused on the width, he will come back sooner or later to focus on the length. Here you will have a third level where he will oscillate between width and length and where he will discover that the two are related. When you elongate you make it more thin, and when you make it shorter, you make it thicker. He discovers that the two are solidly related and in discovering this relationship, he will start to think in terms of the transformation and not only in terms of the final configuration. Now he will say that when it gets longer it gets thinner, so it's the same thing. There is more of it in length but less of it in width. When you make it shorter it gets thicker; there's less in length and more in width, so there is compensation—compensation which defines equilibrium in the sense in which I defined it a moment ago. Consequently, you have operations and conservation. In other words, in the course of these developments you will al-

ways find a process of self-regulation which I call equilibration and which seems to me the fundamental factor in the acquisition of logical-mathematical knowledge.

I shall go on now to the second part of my lecture, that is, to deal with the topic of learning. Classically, learning is based on the stimulus-response schema. I think the stimulus-response schema, while I won't say it is false, is in any case entirely incapable of explaining cognitive learning. Why? Because when you think of a stimulus-response schema, you think usually that first of all there is a stimulus and then a response is set off by this stimulus. For my part, I am convinced that the response was there first, if I can express myself in this way. A stimulus is a stimulus only to the extent that it is significant and it becomes significant only to the extent that there is a structure which permits its assimilation, a structure which can integrate this stimulus but which at the same time sets off the response. In other words, I would propose that the stimulus-response schema be written in the circular form—in the form of a schema or of a structure which is not simply one way. I would propose that above all, between the stimulus and the response there is the organism, the organism and its structures. The stimulus is really a stimulus only when it is assimilated into a structure and it is this structure which sets off the response. Consequently, it is not an exaggeration to say that the response is there first, or if you wish at the beginning there is the structure. Of course we would want to understand how this structure comes to be. I tried to do this earlier by presenting a model of equilibration or self-regulation. Once there is a structure, the stimulus will set off a response, but only by the intermediary of this structure.

I should like to present some facts. We have facts in great number. I shall choose only one or two and I shall choose some facts which our colleague, Smedslund, has gathered. (Smedslund is currently at the Harvard Center for Cognitive Studies.) Smedslund arrived in Geneva a few years ago convinced (he had published this in one of his papers) that the development of the ideas of conservation could be indefinitely accelerated through learning of a stimulus-response type. I invited Smedslund to come to spend a year in Geneva to show us this, to show us that he could accelerate the development of operational conservation. I shall relate only one of his experiments.

During the year that he spent in Geneva he chose to work on the conservation of weight. The conservation of weight is, in fact, easy to study since there is a possible external reinforcement, that is, simply weighing the ball and the sausage on a balance. Then you can study the child's reactions to these external results. Smedslund studied the conservation of weight on the one hand, and on the other hand, he studied the transitivity of weights, that is, the transitivity of equalities if $A = B$ and $B = C$, then $A = C$, or the transitivity of the equalities if A is less than B, and B is less than C, then A is less than C.

As far as conservation is concerned, Smedslund succeeded very easily with five- and six-year-old children in getting them to generalize that weight is conserved when the ball is transformed into a different shape. The child sees the ball transformed into a sausage or into little pieces or into a pancake or into any other form, he weighs it, and he sees that it is always the same thing. He will affirm it will be the same thing, no matter what you do to it; it will come out to be the same weight. Thus Smedslund very easily achieved the conservation of weight by this sort of external reinforcement.

In contrast to this, however, the same method did not succeed in teaching transitivity. The children resisted the notion of transitivity. A child would predict correctly in certain cases but he would make his prediction as a possibility or a probability and not as a certainty. There was never this generalized certainty in the case of transitivity.

So there is the first example, which seems to me very instructive, because in this problem in the conservation of weight there are two aspects. There is the physical aspect and there is the logical-mathematical aspect. Note that Smedslund started his study by establishing that there was a correlation between conservation and transitivity. He began by making a statistical study on the relationships between

the spontaneous responses to the questions about conservation and the spontaneous responses to the questions about transitivity, and he found a very significant correlation. But in the learning experiment, he obtained a learning of conservation and not of transitivity. Consequently, he was successful in obtaining learning of what I called earlier physical experience (This is not surprising; it is simply a question of noting facts about objects.) but he was not successful in obtaining a learning in the construction of the logical structure. This doesn't surprise me either, since the logical structure is not the result of physical experience. It cannot be obtained by external reinforcement. The logical structure is reached only through internal equilibration, by self-regulation, and the external reinforcement of seeing the balance did not suffice to establish this logical structure of transitivity.

I could give many other comparable examples, but it seems to me useless to insist upon these negative examples. Now I should like to show that learning is possible in the case of these logical-mathematical structures, but on one condition—that is, that the structure which you want to teach to the subjects can be supported by simpler, more elementary, logical-mathematical structures. I shall give you an example. It is the example of the conservation of number in the case of one-to-one correspondence. If you give a child seven blue tokens and ask him to put down as many red tokens, there is a preoperational stage where he will put one red one opposite each blue one. But when you spread out the red ones, making them into a longer row, he will say to you, "Now, there are more red ones than there are blue ones."

Now how can we accelerate, if you want to accelerate, the acquisition of this conservation of number? Well, you can imagine an analogous structure but in a simpler, more elementary, situation. For example, with Mlle. Inhelder, we have been studying recently the notion of one-to-one correspondence by giving the child two glasses of the same shape and a big pile of beads. The child puts a bead into one glass with one hand and at the same time a bead into the other glass with the other hand.

Time after time he repeats this action, a bead into one glass with one hand and at the same time a bead into the other glass with the other hand and he sees that there is always the same amount on each side. Then you hide one of the glasses. You cover it up. He no longer sees this glass but he continues to put one bead into it while putting at the same time one bead into the other glass which he can see. Then you ask him whether the equality has been conserved, whether there is still the same amount in one glass as in the other. Now you will find that very small children, about four years old, don't want to make a prediction. They will say, "So far, it has been the same amount, but now I don't know. I can't see anymore, so I don't know." They do not want to generalize. But the generalization is made from the age of about five and one-half years.

This is in contrast to the case of the red and blue tokens with one row spread out, where it isn't until seven or eight years of age that children will say there are the same number in the two rows. As one example of this generalization, I recall a little boy of five years and nine months who had been adding the beads to the glasses for a little while. Then we asked him whether, if he continued to do this all day and all night and all the next day, there would always be the same amount in the two glasses. The little boy gave this admirable reply, "Once you know, you know for always." In other words, this was recursive reasoning. So here the child does acquire the structure in this specific case. The number is a synthesis of class inclusion and ordering. This synthesis is being favored by the child's own actions. You have set up a situation where there is an iteration of one same action which continues and which is therefore ordered while at the same time being inclusive. You have, so to speak, a localized synthesis of inclusion and ordering which facilitates the construction of the idea of number in this specific case, and there you can find, in effect, an influence of this experience on the other experience. However, this influence is not immediate. We study the generalization from this recursive situation to the other situation where the tokens are laid on the table in rows, and it is not an immediate generalization but it is

made possible through intermediaries. In other words, you can find some learning of this structure if you base the learning on simpler structures.

In this same area of the development of numerical structures, the psychologist Joachim Wohlwill, who spent a year at our Institute at Geneva, has also shown that this acquisition can be accelerated through introducing additive operations, which is what we introduced also in the experiment which I just described. Wohlwill introduced them in a different way but he too was able to obtain a certain learning effect. In other words, learning is possible if you base the more complex structure on simpler structures, that is, when there is a natural relationship and development of structures and not simply an external reinforcement.

Now I would like to take a few minutes to conclude what I was saying. My first conclusion is that learning of structures seems to obey the same laws as the natural development of these structures. In other words, learning is subordinated to development and not vice-versa as I said in the introduction. No doubt you will object that some investigators have succeeded in teaching operational structures. But, when I am faced with these facts, I always have three questions which I want to have answered before I am convinced.

The first question is, "Is this learning lasting? What remains two weeks or a month later?" If a structure develops spontaneously, once it has reached a state of equilibrium, it is lasting, it will continue throughout the child's entire life. When you achieve the learning by external reinforcement, is the result lasting or not and what are the conditions necessary for it to be lasting?

The second question is, "How much generalization is possible?" What makes learning interesting is the possibility of transfer of a generalization. When you have brought about some learning, you can always ask whether this is an isolated piece in the midst of the child's mental life, or if it is really a dynamic structure which can lead to generalizations.

Then there is the third question, "In the case of each learning experience what was the operational level of the subject before the experience and what more complex structures has this learning succeeded in achieving?" In other words, we must look at each specific learning experience from the point of view of the spontaneous operations which were present at the outset and the operational level which has been achieved after the learning experience.

My second conclusion is that the fundamental relation involved in all development and all learning is not the relation of association. In the stimulus-response schema, the relation between the response and the stimulus is understood to be one of association. In contrast to this, I think that the fundamental relation is one of assimilation. Assimilation is not the same as association. I shall define assimilation as the integration of any sort of reality into a structure, and it is this assimilation which seems to me fundamental in learning, and which seems to me the fundamental relation from the point of view of pedagogical or didactic applications. All of my remarks today represent the child and the learning subject as active. An operation is an activity. Learning is possible only when there is active assimilation. It is this activity on the part of the subject which seems to me underplayed in the stimulus-response schema. The presentation which I propose puts the emphasis on the idea of self-regulation, on assimilation. All the emphasis is placed on the activity of the subject himself, and I think that without this activity there is no possible didactic or pedagogy which significantly transforms the subject.

Finally, and this will be my last concluding remark, I would like to comment on an excellent publication by the psychologist Berlyne. Berlyne spent a year with us in Geneva during which he intended to translate our results on the development of operations into stimulus-response language, specifically into Hull's learning theory. Berlyne published in our series of studies of genetic epistemology a very good article on this comparison between the results of Geneva and Hull's theory. In the same volume, I published a commentary on Berlyne's results. Now the essence of Berlyne's results is this: our findings can very well be translated into Hullian language, but only on condition that two modifications are introduced. Berlyne himself found these modifications quite considerable, but they seemed to him to concern more the conceptualization than the Hullian theory itself. I'm not so sure about that. The two modifications are these. First of all, Berlyne wants to distinguish two sorts of responses in the S-R schema. First, responses in the ordinary, classical sense, which I shall call "copy responses," and secondly, what Berlyne called "transformation responses." Transformation responses consist of transforming one response of the first type into another response of the first type. These transformation responses are what I call operations, and you can see right away that this is a rather serious modification of Hull's conceptualization because here you are introducing an element of transformation and thus of assimilation and no longer the simple association of stimulus-response theory.

The second modification which Berlyne introduces into the stimulus-response language is the introduction of what he calls internal reinforcements. What are these internal reinforcements? They are what I call equilibration or self-regulation. The internal reinforcements are what enable the subject to eliminate contradictions, incompatibilities, and conflicts. All development is composed of momentary conflicts and incompatibilities which must be overcome to reach a higher level of equilibrium. Berlyne calls this elimination of incompatibilities internal reinforcements.

So you see that it is indeed a stimulus-response theory, if you will, but first you add operations and then you add equilibration. That's all we want!

THE CONCEPT OF DEVELOPMENT
FROM A COMPARATIVE AND ORGANISMIC
POINT OF VIEW

HEINZ WERNER

The field of developmental psychology, as it is conceived here, transcends the boundaries within which the concept of development is frequently applied: development is here apprehended as a concept not merely applicable to delimited areas such as child growth or comparative behavior of animals, but as a concept that proposes a certain manner of viewing behavior in its manifold manifestations. Such a developmental approach to behavior rests on one basic assumption, namely, that wherever there is life there is growth and development, that is, formation in terms of systematic, orderly sequence. This basic assumption, then, entails the view that developmental conceptualization is applicable to the various areas of life science, and is potentially useful in interrelating the many fields of psychology. . . .

THE ORTHOGENETIC PRINCIPLE
OF DEVELOPMENT

Developmental psychology postulates one regulative principle of development; it is an orthogenetic principle which states that wherever development occurs it proceeds from a state of relative globality and lack of differentiation to a state of increasing differentiation, articulation, and hierarchic integration. This principle has the status of an heuristic definition. Though itself not subject to empirical test,

Reprinted with abridgment by permission of the editor from pp. 125–46 of Heinz Werner, "The Concept of Development from a Comparative and Organismic Point of View," from *The Concept of Development*, edited by Dale B. Harris, University of Minnesota Press, Minneapolis © 1957 University of Minnesota.

it is valuable to developmental psychologists in leading to a determination of the actual range of applicability of developmental concepts to the behavior of organisms.

We may offer several illustrations of how this orthogenetic principle is applied in the interpretation and ordering of psychological phenomena.

According to this principle, a state involving a relative lack of differentiation between subject and object is developmentally prior to one in which there is a polarity of subject and object. Thus the young child's acceptance of dreams as external to himself, the lack of differentiation between what one dreams and what one sees, as is found in psychosis, or in some nonliterate societies, the breakdown of boundaries of the self in mescaline intoxication and in states of depersonalization—all of these betoken a relative condition of genetic primordiality compared to the polarity between subject and object found in reflective thinking. This increasing subject-object differentiation involves the corollary that the organism becomes increasingly less dominated by the immediate concrete situation; the person is less stimulus-bound and less impelled by his own affective states. A consequence of this freedom is the clearer understanding of goals, the possibility of employing substitutive means and alternative ends. There is hence a greater capacity for delay and planned action. The person is better able to exercise choice and willfully rearrange a situation. In short, he can manipulate the environment rather than passively respond to the environment. This freedom from the domination of the immediate situation also permits a more accurate assessment of others. The adult is more able than the child to distinguish between the motivational dynamics and the overt behavior of personalities. At developmentally higher levels, therefore, there is less of a tendency for the world to be interpreted solely in terms of one's own needs and an increasing appreciation of the needs of others and of group goals.

Turning to another illustration, one pertaining to concept formation, we find that modes of classification that involve a relative lack of differentiation between concept and perceptual context are genetically prior to modes of classification of properties relatively independent of specific objects. Thus, a color classification that employs color terms such as "gall-like" for a combination of green and blue, or "young leaves" for a combination of yellow and green, is genetically prior to a conceptual color system independent of objects such as gall or young leaves.

It may be opportune to use this last example as an illustration of the comparative character of the developmental approach. That the color classification attached to specific objects involves a mode of cognition genetically prior to a classification independent of specific objects is, of course, consistent with the main theoretical principle of development. In regard to the comparative character of our discipline, however, it does not suffice for us merely to find this type of classification more typical of the man of lower civilization than of the man of higher. The anthropological data point up the necessity of determining whether there is a greater prevalence of such primitive color conceptualization in areas where cognition can be readily observed in terms of lower developmental levels, e.g., in the early phases of ontogenesis. Experimental studies on young children have demonstrated the greater prevalence of concrete (context-bound) conceptualization with regard not only to color but to many other phenomena as well. Again, to take organic neuropathology as an example, in brain-injured persons we find, as Goldstein, Head, and others have stressed, a concretization of color conceptualization symptomatic of their psychopathology; similar observations have been made on schizophrenics.

At this point we should like to state that a comprehensive comparative psychology of development cannot be achieved without the aid of a general experimental psychology broadened through the inclusion of developmental methodology and developmental constructs. There have appeared on the scene of general psychology beginnings of an extremely significant trend toward the studying of perception, learning, and thinking, not as final products but as developing processes, as temporal events divisible into successive stages. Such "event psychology," as one may call it, introduces the dimension of time as an intrinsic property into all experimental data. It stands thus in contrast to approaches, like that of classical psychophysics, in which the treating of successive trials as repetitive responses eliminates as far as possible sequential effects. European psychologists, particularly in Germany and Austria, have turned to the direct study of emergent and developing mental phenomena. For instance, using a tachistoscope, we may study the developmental changes in perception which occur when the time of exposure is increased from trial to trial. In studies of this sort, such developmental changes, or "microgenesis," of percepts are predictable from a developmental theory of the ontogenesis of perception. Some of the ensuing parallels between microgenesis and ontogenesis might be summarized as follows: In both microgenesis and ontogenesis the formation of percepts seems, in general, to go through an orderly sequence of stages. Perception is first global; whole-qualities are dominant. The next stage might be called analytic; perception is selectively directed toward parts. The final stage might be called synthetic; parts become integrated with respect to the whole. Initially perception is predominantly "physiognomic." The physiognomic quality of an object is experienced prior to any details. At this level, feeling and perceiving are little differentiated. Again, in the early stages of development imaging and perceiving are not definitely separated. . . .

UNIFORMITY VERSUS MULTIFORMITY OF DEVELOPMENT

The orthogenetic law, being a formal regulative principle, is not designed to predict developmental courses in their specificity. To illustrate, it cannot decide the well-known controversy between Coghill's and Windle's conceptions concerning ontogenesis of motor behavior. According to Coghill, who studied the larval salamander, behavior develops through the progressive expansion of a perfectly integrated total pattern, and the individuation within of partial patterns that acquire varying degrees of discreteness. Windle's conception, derived from the study of placental mammals, is that the first responses of the embryo are circumscribed, stereotyped reflexes subsequently combined into complex patterns. It may be possible to reconcile, under the general developmental law, both viewpoints as follows: The development of motor behavior may, depending on the species or on the type of activity, involve either the differentiation of partial patterns from a global whole and their integration within a developing locomotor activity (Coghill) or the integration of originally juxtaposed, relatively isolated global units which now become differentiated parts of a newly formed locomotor pattern (Windle). In both cases there are differentiation and hierarchic integration, although the specific manifestations differ.

Now, it is precisely this polarity between the uniformity of a general regulative principle and the multiformity of specific developmental changes that makes the study of development necessarily a comparative discipline. If we were merely to seek the ordering of changes of behavior in terms of a universal developmental principle, developmental theory might still be of interest to the philosophy of science and theoretical psychology, but it would be of far lesser value to empirical psychology.

In order to get a clearer picture of what is involved here, it might be advantageous to refer to one of our studies, namely, that of the development of the acquisition of meaning, by the use of a word-context test (Werner, 1952).

In this experiment eight- to thirteen-year-old children had the task of finding the meaning of an artificial word which was embedded successively in six verbal contexts. For instance, one such artificial word was "corplum." After each of these six sentences the child was interrogated concerning the meaning of the artificial word.

The six sentences in which "corplum" (correct translation: "stick" or "piece of wood")

appears, are as follows: (1) A corplum may be used for support. (2) Corplums may be used to close off an open place. (3) A corplum may be long or short, thick or thin, strong or weak. (4) A wet corplum does not burn. (5) You can make a corplum smooth with sandpaper. (6) The painter used a corplum to mix his paints.

Now, the task confronting the subjects in the word-context test is essentially the synthesis of the cues from a set of six contexts for the purpose of forming a general meaning of the word, that is, a meaning applicable to all six sentences. The success of such an operation is reflected in two kinds of results. The first shows a steady and continuous increase in the achievement of a correct solution with increasing age. The second reflects changes in the underlying patterns of operation. As to the first point, there is a developmental increase in achievement which signifies the increasing capacity for hierarchization, that is, for integrating the various cues within a common name. However, the finding concerning a steady rise in achievement of correctness was, for us, not the most important result. Our main aim was to study the processes underlying such achievement. We were far more concerned with detecting the fact that conceptual synthesis is not achieved by a unitary pattern of operations, but that there are various sorts of processes of synthesis which differ from each other developmentally. The lower forms were found to emerge, to increase, and then to decrease during intellectual growth, yielding finally to more advanced forms of generalization.

Studies of this sort inform us that the workings of the orthogenetic law as a uniform, regulative principle have to be specified through the ordering and interpretation of the multiform operations. Such a view implies the rejection of a tacit assumption made by many child psychologists that the measured achievement always reflects unequivocally the underlying operations, or that overt achievement is necessarily a true gauge of the developmental stage. This assumption is untenable; the same achievement may be reached by operations genetically quite different. An analysis of types of operations rather than measurement merely in terms of accuracy of performance often reveals the truer developmental picture. In fact, a greater accuracy in certain circumstances may even signify a lower developmental level, as in the case of a decorticate frog who shows greater accuracy in catching flies than the normal frog. Gottschaldt presented normal and mentally deficient eight-year-old children with the task of constructing squares or rectangles from the irregular pieces into which these figures had been cut. The normal children had difficulties with the test because they tried to relate the figuratively unrelated pieces to the end form. Operating on a purely mechanical level, the mentally deficient children matched the edges of the same length and thus performed quicker and with fewer errors. Again, a thinker oriented toward and capable of highly abstract thought may be at a disadvantage in certain concrete tasks of concept formation, compared with a concretely thinking person.

CONTINUITY VERSUS DISCONTINUITY OF DEVELOPMENT

The orthogenetic principle of increase in differentiation and hierarchic integration is not meant to imply continuous progress as the exclusive characteristic of developmental change. A good deal of the controversy centering in the continuity-discontinuity problem appears to be due to a lack in clarification of these terms. In particular, there has been considerable confusion about two different aspects of change. One is the quantitative aspect of change. Here the problem of continuity versus discontinuity is related to the measurement—in terms of gradual or abrupt increase with time—of magnitude, of efficiency, of frequency of occurrence of a newly acquired operation in an individual or in a group. The other aspect concerns the qualitative nature of changes. Here the problem of continuity versus discontinuity centers in the question of the reducibility of later to earlier forms—emergence—and the transition between later and earlier forms—intermediacy.

It seems that discontinuity in terms of qualitative changes can be best defined by two characteristics: "emergence," i.e., the irreducibility of a later stage to an earlier; and "gappiness," i.e., the lack of intermediate stages between earlier and later forms. Quantitative

discontinuity on the other hand, appears to be sufficiently defined by the second characteristic.

Now it seems that in many discussions, particularly among psychologists, the quantitative and qualitative forms of continuity and discontinuity have not been clearly kept apart. Thus, a change may be discontinuous in terms of quality but may become distinguishable (e.g., measurable) only gradually; i.e., there may be a continuous quantitative increase, such as in frequency of occurrence or in magnitude. For instance, the attempt of the young child to walk on two legs is discontinuous with four-limb locomotion, though the successive actual attempts may show gradual progress toward precision and success. In accordance with our definition given above, two-legged locomotion cannot be reduced to four-limbed locomotion, and, furthermore, there is limitation in regard to intermediate steps.

Another related mistake is that of accepting smallness of change, whether qualitative or quantitative, as an indicator of continuity. For instance, the genetic changes termed "mutation" may be very slight, but there has to be "discontinuity inasmuch as there are no intermediate forms between the unchanged and the changed." This significant fact in mutation, namely, discontinuity, says Schroedinger, "reminds a physicist of quantum theory: no intermediate energies occurring between two neighboring energy levels. He would be inclined to call de Vries's mutation theory . . . the quantum theory of biology." Because of the smallness of change, in developmental psychology as well as in developmental biology, one often will find it possible to argue for discontinuity only on the basis of extensive data accumulated in extensive temporal sequences; discontinuity in change may then be concluded after a trait has become sufficiently distinct in terms of frequency, permanency, and magnitude.

Other factors that are often not clearly recognized for their importance in determining sequences as either continuous or discontinuous are (a) the handling of the data and (b) the nature of the universe of discourse.

Concerning the first factor, it should be realized that discontinuous process changes typical in individual development may be obscured by averaging developmental achievement scores of individuals to secure a composite curve for a group which then suggests continuous growth.

Another fallacy in deriving continuity of behavioral development from group scores has been most recently discussed by Lashley in regard to a particular feature of the usual mental tests, namely, the heterogeneity (discontinuity) of the items which the test patterns comprise. Lashley's criticism implies that discontinuity of processes may be obscured by interpreting developmental data on the assumption that variations in achievement can be based only on variations in a single underlying process. As noted before, the achievement of correctness on our word-context test shows a steady increase with age, whereas underlying processes give a picture of the rise and decline of more or less primitive operations and the abrupt rise of an adult type of generalization around ten or eleven years of age. Reference should be made here to the important study by Nancy Bayley (1933) concerning mental development during the first three years. She could show that in terms of accumulated scores there was a steady increase with age; however, a further analysis of the test items in terms of underlying operations revealed a shift from one type of function ("sensorimotor") to a qualitatively different type ("adaptive") occurring at approximately nine months of age.

Secondly, it should be recognized that it is the universe of discourse, the interpretational frame within which the material is grasped, that often determines the ordering in terms of continuity or discontinuity. To illustrate by an analogy, one may represent the relation between color hues in physical terms, i.e., wave length, that change continuously within the range of visibility. Within the psychological frame of reference, however, there is discontinuity. The gradual variation from blue to green is discontinuous with the gradual variation from green to yellow, which, in turn, is discontinuous with the gradual variation from yellow to red.

There is no logical necessity for a concordance in terms of continuity between the quantitative and qualitative aspects of any developmental series. A discontinuous (epigenetic) qualitative change may become distinct gradually; that is, it does not need to be "saltatory"

in a quantitative sense, if by that word is meant that a new form or function becomes suddenly overt. Nor does unevenness—spurt versus depression—of any growth curve necessarily point to novel process formation. However, though we have to beware of confusing quantitative discontinuity-continuity with qualitative discontinuity-continuity, quantitative unevenness may, possibly more often than not, point to qualitative discontinuity or emergent evolution. We may illustrate this from Paul Weiss's discussion on embryonic growth: "An obstacle to simple mathematical treatment of growth is its lack of continuity; for embryonic growth advances unevenly, in spurts and jumps, with intermittent depressions. These depressions correspond to phases of intensive histological differentiation." Furthermore, if embryonic growth curves in terms of weight are compared with progress in terms of differentiation and morphogenesis, one finds that both kinds of progressions advance unevenly, but, that "maxima of differentiation coincide with minima of growth." From this, Weiss concludes that "acceleration of differentiating activity is attended by retardation of growth activity, or in other words, that there is some antagonism between differentiation and growth." . . .

Quite possibly there are analogies to this vicarious correspondence between quantitative growth and qualitative development on the level of psychological behavior. To illustrate, one such analogy might be found in a frequent observation concerning certain phases of speech development. There appears to occur between the stage of babbling and that of naming, a period during which vocalizing is depressed. It seems plausible to interpret this period as one during which the awareness of sound patterns as verbal symbols emerges. Once this novel operation has emerged, the child bursts forth with naming, increasing its vocabulary at a swiftly accelerating rate.

In conclusion, it seems to me, that development cannot be comprehended without the polar conceptualization of continuity and discontinuity. Within the "universe of discourse" in which the orthogenetic law is conceived, development, insofar as it is defined as increase in differentiation and hierarchization is, ideally, continuous. Underlying the increase in differentiation and integration are the forms and processes which undergo two main kinds of changes: (a) quantitative changes which are either gradual or abrupt, and (b) qualitative changes which, by their very nature, are discontinuous.

UNILINEARITY VERSUS MULTILINEARITY OF DEVELOPMENT

The orthogenetic law, by its very nature, is an expression of unilinearity of development. But, as is true of the other polarities discussed here, the ideal unilinear sequence signified by the universal developmental law does not conflict with the multiplicity of actual developmental forms. As implied in the conclusion of the preceding section, coexistence of unilinearity and multiplicity of individual developments must be recognized for psychological just as it is for biological evolution. In regard to human behavior in particular, this polarity opens the way for a developmental study of behavior not only in terms of universal sequence, but also in terms of individual variations, that is, in terms of growth viewed as a branching-out process of specialization or aberration.

To illustrate, "physiognomic" perception appears to be a developmentally early form of viewing the world, based on the relative lack of distinction between properties of persons and properties of inanimate things. But the fact that in our culture physiognomic perception, developmentally, is superseded by logical, realistic, and technical conceptualization, poses some paradoxical problems, such as, What genetic standing has adult aesthetic experience? Is it to be considered a "primitive" experience left behind in a continuous process of advancing logification, and allowed to emerge only in sporadic hours of regressive relaxation? Such an inference seems unsound; it probably errs in conceiving human growth in terms of a simple developmental series rather than as a diversity of individual formations, all conforming to the abstract and general developmental conceptualization. Though physiognomic experience is a primordial manner of perceiving, it grows, in certain individuals such as artists, to a level not below but on a par with that of "geometric-technical" perception and logical discourse.

FIXITY VERSUS MOBILITY OF DEVELOPMENTAL LEVEL OF OPERATION

The assumption that all organisms normally operate upon a relatively fixed and rather sharply circumscribed developmental level appears to be tacitly accepted by many psychologists. A contrary view is that all higher organisms manifest a certain range of genetically different operations. This means, for instance, that a child of a certain age or an adult, depending on the task or on inner circumstances, may, qua normal, perform at genetically different levels. Furthermore, there is, so to speak, not only "horizontal" differentiation but also "vertical" differentiation; that is, the more mature compared with the less mature individual has at his disposal a greater number of developmentally different operations.

It should be recognized that these views are not necessarily antagonistic; i.e., fixity as well as mobility of levels of operation coexist as polar principles of development. The principle of fixity is implied in, or can be inferred from, the intrinsic trend of any evolution toward an end stage of maximum stability. Such maximum stability, as the end stage of a developmental sequence, implies the ceasing of growth; that is, implies the permanency, for instance, of specialized reaction patterns, or automatization of response. But the principle of fixity would finally lead to rigidity of behavior if not counterbalanced by the polar principle of mobility. As most generally conceived, mobility implies "becoming" in contrast to "being"; it implies that an organism, having attained highly stabilized structures and operations may or may not progress further, but if it does, this will be accomplished through partial return to a genetically earlier, less stable level. One has to regress in order to progress. The intimate relation of regression to progression appears succinctly expressed in the statement of one of the early evolutionists, Richard Owen. On interpreting the resemblance of the embryo to the phylogenetic ancestry, Owen said: "We perceive a return to the archetype in the early embryological phases of development of the highest existing species, or ought rather to say that development starts from the old point."

An impressive illustration of the relation between renewed development and regression on the biological level can be found in the processes of regeneration. Such regeneration, as extensively studied at the amphibian level, consists of two phases, regressive as well as progressive. The progressive phase—analogous to normal embryonic development—starts with the formation of the "blastema" or regenerative bud. But prior to progression there is regression. The regressive phase involves de-differentiation of already specialized cells. Another probable source for blastema formation is reserve cells, that is, cells that have remained at a low state of differentiation. It is noteworthy that power of regeneration, being associated with capacity to de-differentiate is, in general, inversely correlated with the organism's ontogenetic or phylogenetic status of differentiatedness.

In speculating by analogy from biological events of this sort to human behavior one might argue that in creative reorganization, psychological regression involves two kinds of operations: one is the de-differentiation (dissolution) of existing, schematized or automatized behavior patterns; the other consists in the activation of primitive levels of behavior from which undifferentiated (little-formulated) phenomena emerge.

The polar conceptualization of normal levels of operation in terms of fixity-mobility appears thus closely linked to another polar distinction, namely, that involved in the relation between lower and higher levels of operation. In regard to this relation, one particular problem among many has aroused considerable interest. It concerns the degree of fixity or mobility of an operation emerging at a certain level, in relation to developmentally later forms of operation.

As mentioned before, development, whether it concerns single functions, complex performances, or the totality of personality, tends toward stabilization. Once a certain stable level of integration is reached, the possibility of further development must depend on whether or not the behavioral patterns have become so automatized that they cannot take part in reorganization. We may refer here to Rapaport's concept of "apparatus" or to Piaget's concept of "schema." The individual, for instance, builds up sensorimotor schemata, such as grasping, opening a box, and linguistic patterns; these are the goal of early learning at first, but later on become instruments or apparatuses for handling the environment. Since no two situations in which an organism finds itself are alike, the usefulness of these schemata in adaptive behavior will depend on their stability as well as on their pliability (a paradoxical "stable flexibility").

Furthermore, if one assumes that the emergence of higher levels of operations involves hierarchic integration, it follows that lower-level operations will have to be reorganized in terms of their functional nature so that they become subservient to higher functioning. A clear example of this is the change of the functional nature of imagery from a stage where images serve only memory, fantasy, and concrete conceptualization, to a stage where images have been transformed to schematic symbols of abstract concepts and thought.

DIFFERENTIAL VERSUS GENERAL DEVELOPMENTAL PSYCHOLOGY: INDIVIDUALITY AS A PROBLEM OF DEVELOPMENTAL PSYCHOLOGY

At Clark University we are becoming increasingly impressed with the fruitfulness of the developmental frame of reference for the study of group and individual differences. We may illustrate this approach to the many problems which are in need of investigation by referring to a few studies on cognitive organization.

One problem concerns the over-all maturity status of the individual, that is, his cognitive level of operation under optimal conditions, and the stability of this level under varying internal and external conditions. Friedman, Phillips, and their co-workers at Worcester State Hospital and at Clark University have constructed a genetic scoring system of the Rorschach test founded on developmental theory, and standardized through an ontogenetic study of children. The scoring system is based essentially on the occurrence and frequency of "genetically low" and "genetically high" scores. Restricting ourselves here mainly to the various whole and detail responses, genetically low responses are those which indicate amorphous, diffuse, or confabulatory percepts where little attention is given to part relations and to perception of contours. The genetically high percepts are reflected in the responses whereby the percept is that of a precisely formed unit with integrated parts, where the whole is composed of relatively independent sub-wholes brought together in an integrated fashion. Applying this developmental scoring analysis to the responses of 160 children of from three to eleven years of age, Hemmendinger found the basic principle of development confirmed. That is, with age there is a decrease of the undifferentiated diffuse whole and detail responses along with an increase of the highly articulated, well-integrated whole and detail responses. There is further an interesting shift from the early whole responses toward small detail responses between the ages of about six and eight; later on there is a decline in favor of the integrated whole responses.

We may add at this point that for the study of individual differences in their developmental aspects, experimental methods other than those based on ontogenesis have become available. Among these, probably the most promising method is that of "microgenesis." This method, already mentioned above, is based on the assumption that activity patterns, percepts, thoughts, are not merely products but processes that, whether they take seconds, or hours, or days, unfold in terms of developmental sequence. . . .

Another developmental aspect of individuality that is in need of experimental and clinical study concerns what one might call the genetic stratification or the developmental heterogeneity of a person. Developmental stratification means that a person is structured into spheres of operations which differ in regard to developmental level. Still another aspect concerns the flexibility of a person to operate at different levels depending on the requirements of a situation.

In a particular way, it seems to us, this aspect of flexibility is connected with a further problem of individuality, namely, that of creativity. Now creativity, in its most general meaning, is an essential feature of emergent evolution, and this, in turn, implies progression through reorganization. Since we assume that such progress through reorganization cannot be achieved without "starting anew," that is, without regression, it follows that a person's capacity for creativity presupposes mobility in terms of regression and progression. The hypothesis would then be that the more creative the person, the wider his range of operations in terms of developmental level, or in other words, the greater his capacity to utilize primitive as well as advanced operations.

It might also be possible to study persons at the other extreme end of mobility, that is, those who, because of their excessive yearning for security, are coping with the environment in terms of rigidly formalized behavior. In this regard the work by the Swedish psychologist Ulf Krogh seems very suggestive. He studied the microgenesis of complex pictures with various groups of people. Among other results he found that persons such as the compulsion-neurotics, whose reaction patterns to the environment are inordinately formalized, are lacking in microgenetic mobility, that is, they are lacking the intermediate steps that are normally present during the unfolding of percepts.

We should like, then, to conclude with this observation: The original aim of developmental theory, directed toward the study of universal genetic changes, is still one of its main concerns; but side by side with this concern, the conviction has been growing in recent years that developmental conceptualization, in order to reaffirm its truly organismic character, has to expand its orbit of interest to include as a central problem the study of individuality.

REFERENCES

Bayley, N., "Mental Growth during the First Three Years," *Genet. Psychol. Monogr.,* Vol. 14 (1933), No. 1, p. 92.

Werner, H., "The Acquisition of Word Meanings: A Developmental Study," *Monogr. Soc. Res. Child Developm.,* Vol. 15 (1952), No. 1, p. 120.

IDENTIFICATION WITH THE AGGRESSOR

ANNA FREUD

It is comparatively easy to discover the defence-mechanisms to which the ego habitually resorts, so long as each is employed separately and only in conflict with some specific danger. When we find denial, we know that it is a reaction to external danger; when repression takes place, the ego is struggling with instinctual stimuli. The strong outward resemblance between inhibition and ego-restriction makes it less certain whether these processes are part of an external or an internal conflict. The matter is still more intricate when defensive measures are combined or when the same mechanism is employed sometimes against an internal and sometimes against an external force. We have an excellent illustration of both these complications in the process of identification. Since it is one of the factors in the development of the super-ego, it contributes to the mastery of instinct. But, as I hope to show in what follows, there are occasions when it combines with other mechanisms to form one of the ego's most potent weapons in its dealings with external objects which arouse its anxiety.

August Aichhorn relates that, when he was giving advice on a Child Guidance Committee, he had to deal with the case of a boy at an elementary school, who was brought to him because of a habit of making faces. The master complained that the boy's behaviour, if he were blamed or reproved, was quite abnormal. On such occasions he made faces which caused the whole class to burst out laughing. The master's view was that either the boy was consciously making fun of him or else the twitching of his face must be due to some kind of tic. His report was at once corroborated, for the boy be-

gan to make faces during the consultation, but, when master, pupil and psychologist were together, the situation was explained. Observing the two attentively, Aichhorn saw that the boy's grimaces were simply a caricature of the angry expression of the teacher and that, when he had to face a scolding by the latter, he tried to master his anxiety by involuntarily imitating him. The boy identified himself with the teacher's anger and copied his expression as he spoke, though the imitation was not recognized. Through his grimaces he was assimilating himself to or identifying himself with the dreaded external object.

My readers will remember the case of the little girl who tried by means of magic gestures to get over the mortification associated with her penis-envy. This child was purposely and consciously making use of a mechanism to which the boy resorted involuntarily. At home she was afraid to cross the hall in the dark, because she had a dread of seeing ghosts. Suddenly, however, she hit on a device which enabled her to do it: she would run across the hall, making all sorts of peculiar gestures as she went. Before long, she triumphantly told her little brother the secret of how she had got over her anxiety. 'There's no need to be afraid in the hall,' she said, 'you just have to pretend that you're the ghost who might meet you.' This shows that her magic gestures represented the movements which she imagined that ghosts would make.

We might be inclined to regard this kind of conduct as an idiosyncrasy in the two children whose cases I have quoted, but it is really one of the most natural and widespread modes of behaviour on the part of the primitive ego and has long been familiar to those who have made a study of primitive methods of invoking and exorcising spirits and of primitive religious

Reprinted from pp. 109–31 of *The Ego and the Mechanisms of Defense* by Anna Freud, by permission of the author and International Universities Press, Inc. Copyright © 1966 by International Universities Press, Inc.

ceremonies. Moreover there are many children's games in which through the metamorphosis of the subject into a dreaded object anxiety is converted into pleasurable security. Here is another angle from which to study the games of impersonation which children love to play.

Now the physical imitation of an antagonist represents the assimilation of only one part of a composite anxiety-experience. We learn from observation that the other elements have also to be mastered.

The six-year-old patient to whom I have several times alluded had to pay a series of visits to a dentist. At first everything went splendidly; the treatment did not hurt him and he was triumphant and made merry over the idea of anyone's being afraid of the dentist. But there came a time when my little patient arrived at my house in an extremely bad temper. The dentist had just hurt him. He was cross and unfriendly and vented his feelings on the things in my room. His first victim was a piece of indiarubber. He wanted me to give it to him and, when I refused, he took a knife and tried to cut it in half. Next, he coveted a large ball of string. He wanted me to give him that too and painted me a vivid picture of what a good lead it would make for his animals. When I refused to give him the whole ball, he took the knife again and secured a large piece of the string. But he did not use it; instead, he began after a few minutes to cut it into tiny pieces. Finally he threw away the string too, turned his attention to some pencils and went on indefatigably sharpening them, breaking off the points and sharpening them again. It would not be correct to say that he was playing at 'dentists.' There was no actual impersonation of the dentist. The child was identifying himself not with the person of the aggressor but with his aggression.

On another occasion this little boy came to me just after he had had a slight accident. He had been joining in an outdoor game at school and had run full tilt against the fist of the games-master, which the latter happened to be holding up in front of him. My little patient's lip was bleeding and his face tear-stained, and he tried to conceal both facts by putting up his hand as a screen. I endeavoured to comfort and reassure him. He was in a woe-begone condition when he left me, but next day he appeared holding himself very erect and dressed in full armour. On his head he wore a military cap and he had a toy sword at his side and a pistol in his hand. When he saw my surprise at this transformation, he simply said, 'I just wanted to have these things on when I was playing with you.' He did not, however, play; instead, he sat down and wrote a letter to his mother: 'Dear Mummy, please, please, please, please send me the pocket-knife you promised me and don't wait till Easter!' Here again we cannot say that, in order to master the anxiety-experience of the previous day, he was impersonating the teacher with whom he had collided. Nor, in this instance, was he imitating the latter's aggression. The weapons and armour, being manly attributes, evidently symbolized the teacher's strength and, like the attributes of the father in the animal-phantasies, helped the child to identify himself with the masculinity of the adult and so to defend himself against narcissistic mortification or actual mishaps.

The examples which I have so far cited illustrate a process with which we are quite familiar. A child introjects some characteristic of an anxiety-object and so assimilates an anxiety-experience which he has just undergone. Here, the mechanism of identification or introjection is combined with a second important mechanism. By impersonating the aggressor, assuming his attributes or imitating his aggression, the child transforms himself from the person threatened into the person who makes the threat. In *Beyond the Pleasure Principle* the significance of this change from the passive to the active rôle as a means of assimilating unpleasant or traumatic experiences in infancy is discussed in detail. 'If a doctor examines a child's throat or performs a small operation, the alarming experience will quite certainly be made the subject of the next game, but in this the pleasure gain from another source cannot be overlooked. In passing from the passivity of experience to the activity of play the child applies to his playfellow the unpleasant occurrence that befell himself and so avenges himself on the person of this proxy.'[1] What is true of

---

[1] *Beyond the Pleasure Principle*, pp. 15–16.

play is equally true of other behaviour in children. In the case of the boy who made faces and the little girl who practised magic it is not clear what finally became of the threat with which they identified themselves, but in the other little boy's ill-temper the aggression taken over from the dentist and the games-master was directed against the world at large.

This process of transformation strikes us as more curious when the anxiety relates not to some event in the past but to something expected in the future. I have told elsewhere of a boy who had the habit of furiously pealing the bell of the Children's Home where he lived. As soon as the door was opened, he would scold the housemaid loudly for being so slow and not listening for the bell. In the interval between pulling the bell and flying into a rage he experienced anxiety lest he should be reproved for his lack of consideration in ringing so loudly. He upbraided the servant before she had time to complain of his conduct. The vehemence with which he scolded her—a prophylactic measure—indicated the intensity of his anxiety. The aggressiveness which he assumed was turned against the actual person from whom he expected aggression and not against some substitute. The reversal of the rôles of attacker and attacked was in this case carried to its logical conclusion.

Jenny Wälder has given a vivid picture of this process in a five-year-old boy whom she treated.[2] When his analysis was about to touch on the material connected with masturbation and the phantasies associated with it, this little boy, who was usually shy and inhibited, became fiercely aggressive. His habitually passive attitude disappeared and there was no trace left of his feminine characteristics. In the analytic hour he pretended to be a roaring lion and attacked the analyst. He carried a rod about with him and played at 'Krampus,'[3] i.e. he laid about him with it on the stairs, in his own house and in my room. His grandmother and mother complained that he tried to strike them in the face. His mother's uneasiness reached its climax when he took to brandishing kitchen knives.

Analysis showed that the child's aggressiveness could not be construed as indicating that some inhibition on his instinctual impulses had been lifted. The release of his masculine tendencies was still a long way off. He was simply suffering from anxiety. The bringing into consciousness and the necessary confession of his former and recent sexual activities aroused in him the expectation of punishment. According to his experience, grown-up people were angry when they discovered a child indulging in such practices. They shouted at him, checked him sharply with a box on the ears or beat him with a rod; perhaps they would even cut off some part of him with a knife. When my little patient assumed the active rôle, roaring like a lion and laying about him with the rod and the knife, he was dramatizing and forestalling the punishment which he feared. He had introjected the aggression of the adults in whose eyes he felt guilty and, having exchanged the passive for the active part, he directed his own aggressive acts against those same people. Every time that he found himself on the verge of communicating to me what he regarded as dangerous material, his aggressiveness increased. But directly his forbidden thoughts and feelings broke through and had been discussed and interpreted, he felt no further need of the 'Krampus' rod, which till then he had constantly carried about with him, and he left it at my house. His compulsion to beat other people disappeared simultaneously with his anxious expectation of being beaten himself.

In 'identification with the aggressor' we recognize a by no means uncommon stage in the normal development of the super-ego. When the two boys whose cases I have just described identified themselves with their elders' threats of punishment, they were taking an important step towards the formation of that institution: they were internalizing other people's criticisms of their behaviour. When a child constantly repeats this process of internalization and introjects the qualities of those responsible for his upbringing, making their characteristics and opinions his own, he is all the time providing material from which the super-ego may take shape. But at this point children are not quite whole-hearted in acknowledging that institution. The internalized criticism is not as yet immedi-

---

[2] From a verbal communication made in the Vienna Seminar on the treatment of children.

[3] A devil who accompanied St. Nicholas and punished naughty children.—*Translator's note.*

ately transformed into self-criticism. As we have seen in the examples which I have given, it is dissociated from the child's own reprehensible activity and turned back on the outside world. By means of a new defensive process identification with the aggressor is succeeded by an active assault on the outside world.

Here is a more complicated example, which will perhaps throw light on this new development in the defensive process. A certain boy, when his Œdipus complex was at its height, employed this particular mechanism to master his fixation to his mother. His happy relations with her were disturbed by outbursts of resentment. He would upbraid her passionately and on all sorts of grounds, but one mysterious accusation invariably recurred: he persistently complained of her curiosity. It is easy to see the first step in the working-over of his prohibited affects. In his phantasy his mother knew of his libidinal feeling for her and indignantly rejected his advances. Her indignation was actively reproduced in his own fits of resentment against her. In contrast to Jenny Wälder's patient, however, he did not reproach her on general grounds but on the specific ground of curiosity. Analysis showed that this curiosity was an element not in his mother's instinctual life but in his own. Of all the component instincts which entered into his relation with her his scopophilic impulse was the most difficult to master. The reversal of rôles was complete. He assumed his mother's indignation and, in exchange, ascribed to her his own curiosity.

In certain phases of resistance a young patient used bitterly to reproach her analyst with being secretive. She complained that the analyst was too reserved and she would torment her with questions on personal matters and be miserable when she received no answer. Then the reproaches would cease, only to begin again after a short time, always in the same stereotyped and, as it seemed, automatic fashion. In this case again we can detect two phases in the psychic process. From time to time, because of a certain inhibition which prevented her speaking out, the patient herself consciously suppressed some very private material. She knew that she was thereby breaking the fundamental rule of analysis and she expected the analyst to rebuke her. She introjected the phantasied rebuke and, adopting the active rôle, applied the accusation to the analyst. Her phases of aggression exactly coincided in time with her phases of secretiveness. She criticized the analyst for the very fault of which she herself was guilty. Her own secretive behaviour was perceived as reprehensible conduct on the analyst's part.

Another young patient used periodically to have fits of violent aggressiveness. I myself, her parents and other people in less close relation with her were almost equally the objects of her resentment. There were two things in particular of which she constantly complained. First, during these phases she always had the feeling that people were keeping from her some secret which everybody knew but herself, and she was tormented by the desire to find out what it was. Secondly, she felt deeply disappointed by the shortcomings of all her friends. Just as, in the case which I last quoted, the periods in which the patient kept back material coincided with those in which she complained of secretiveness in the analyst, so this patient's aggressive phases set in automatically whenever her repressed masturbation-phantasies, of which she herself was unaware, were about to emerge into consciousness. Her strictures on her love-objects corresponded to the blame which she expected from them because of her masturbation in childhood. She identified herself fully with this condemnation and turned it back upon the outside world. The secret which everybody kept from her was the secret of her own masturbation, which she kept not only from others but from herself. Here again, the patient's aggressiveness corresponded to that of other people and their 'secret' was a reflection of her own repression.

These three examples have given us some idea of the origin of this particular phase in the development of the function of the superego. Even when the external criticism has been introjected, the threat of punishment and the offence committed have not as yet been connected up in the patient's mind. The moment the criticism is internalized, the offence is externalized. This means that the mechanism of identification with the aggressor is supplemented by another defensive measure, namely, the projection of guilt.

An ego which with the aid of the defence-mechanism of projection develops along this particular line introjects the authorities to whose criticism it is exposed and incorporates them in the super-ego. It is then able to project its prohibited impulses outwards. Its intolerance of other people is prior to its severity towards itself. It learns what is regarded as blameworthy but protects itself by means of this defence-mechanism from unpleasant self-criticism. Vehement indignation at someone else's wrong-doing is the precursor of and substitute for guilty feelings on its own account. Its indignation increases automatically when the perception of its own guilt is imminent. This stage in the development of the super-ego is a kind of preliminary phase of morality. True morality begins when the internalized criticism, now embodied in the standard exacted by the super-ego, coincides with the ego's perception of its own fault. From that moment, the severity of the super-ego is turned inwards instead of outwards and the subject becomes less intolerant of other people. But, when once it has reached this stage in its development, the ego has to endure the more acute 'pain' occasioned by self-criticism and the sense of guilt.

It is possible that a number of people remain arrested at the intermediate stage in the development of the super-ego and never quite complete the internalization of the critical process. Although perceiving their own guilt, they continue to be peculiarly aggressive in their attitude to other people. In such cases the behaviour of the super-ego towards others is as ruthless as that of the super-ego towards the patient's own ego in melancholia. Perhaps when the evolution of the super-ego is thus inhibited it indicates an abortive beginning of the development of melancholic states.

'Identification with the aggressor' represents on the one hand a preliminary phase of super-ego development and, on the other, an intermediate stage in the development of paranoia. It resembles the former in the mechanism of identification and the latter in that of projection. At the same time, identification and projection are normal activities of the ego and their results vary greatly according to the material upon which they are employed.

The particular combination of introjection and projection to which we have applied the term 'identification with the aggressor' can be regarded as normal only so long as the ego employs it in his conflict with authority, i.e. in its efforts to deal with anxiety-objects. It is a defensive process which ceases to be innocuous and becomes pathological when it is carried over into the love-life. When a husband displaces on to his wife his own impulses to be unfaithful and then reproaches her passionately with unfaithfulness, he is really introjecting her reproaches and projecting part of his own id.[4] His intention, however, is to protect himself not against aggression from without but against the shattering of his positive libidinal fixation to her by disturbing forces from within. Accordingly the result is different. Instead of an aggressive attitude towards some former external assailants the patient develops an obsessional fixation to his wife, which takes the form of projected jealousy.

When the mechanism of projection is employed as a defence against homosexual love-impulses, it is combined with yet other mechanisms. Reversal (in this case the reversal of love into hate) completes what introjection and projection have begun and the result is the development of paranoid delusions. In either case —defence against heterosexual or against homosexual love-impulses—the projection is no longer arbitrary. The ego's choice of a billet for its own unconscious impulses is determined by the material at hand (*Wahrnehmungsmaterial*), 'by which the unconscious impulses of the partner are likewise betrayed.'[5]

From the theoretical standpoint, analysis of the process of 'identification with the aggressor' assists us to differentiate the various modes in which the specific defence-mechanisms are employed; in practice, it enables us to distinguish in the transference anxiety-attacks from outbursts of aggression. When analysis brings into the patient's consciousness genuine, unconscious, aggressive impulses, the dammed-up affect will seek relief through abreaction in the transference. But, if his aggression is due to his identifying himself with what he supposed to be

---

[4] Cf. 'Certain Neurotic Mechanisms in Jealousy, Paranoia and Homosexuality.' Freud, *Collected Papers*, vol. ii, p. 232.

[5] Loc. cit., p. 233.

our criticism, it will not be in the least affected by his 'giving it practical expression' and 'abreacting' it. As long as the unconscious impulses are prohibited, it increases, and it vanishes, as in the case of the little boy who confessed his masturbation, only when the dread of punishment and of the super-ego has been dissipated.

THE VALUE OF ETHOLOGY
TO THE STUDY OF HUMAN BEHAVIOR

ECKHARD H. HESS

Fundamentally, it is the ethological *attitude* which is most valuable in the analysis of human behavior, rather than merely the use of the particular *terms* used by ethologists. An investigator does not need to be an ethologist or even to have had any direct contact with ethology to make behavior analyses which are congruent with ethological thinking. He merely must approach his subject with a concern for the *complete* context in which observed behaviors occur, including biological bases and adaptive function.

Ethologists have made a great many speculations on human behavior, and there have been several actual experimental investigations. For example, von Holst demonstrated that relative coordination of movement occurs in man just as it does in other animals: if two arms are moving at different speeds, one twice as fast as the other, the faster arm will make alternate long and short sweeps in coincidence with the down and up strokes of the slower arm. And, of course, psychologists have known for some time that locomotion matures in human beings just as it does in animals.

Lorenz has described a relatively stereotyped motor response which occurs in humans. The touch stimuli from an insect crawling on the skin release the action of throwing it off quickly with the hand. There is both a fixed pattern component and an orientation component in this reaction. Hence it is not simply a reflex. Tinbergen has suggested that this action, though maturing relatively late, is probably innate.

Reprinted by permission of the author and editor from Chapter 1, "Ethology and Developmental Psychology," pp. 24–32 of *Carmichael's Manual of Child Psychology*, Vol. I, edited by Paul H. Mussen, published by John Wiley & Sons, Inc., 1970.

The application of ethological concepts appears particularly apropos to problems of human development in both the ontogenetic and phylogenetic sense. The behavior stereotypies of captive animals, for example, have been observed to be akin to the behavior stereotypies that can be seen in orphaned children, as reported by Klimpfinger. The reiteration or perseveration of certain movements by hospitalized children can also be seen in home-reared children whose mother has no child care helper and is very busy with her housework or her profession. Maternal deprivation thus appears as a factor in the etiology of this behavior in children, just as social deprivation appears in the etiology of the cage stereotypies of captive animals.

Several ethological concepts currently are becoming increasingly important in application to human development. One such concept is that of "sensitive periods." The notion of sensitive periods in development has been utilized since 1900 by Europeans in many different fields. Even before this there were several beginnings of the sensitive period notion in the work of the early embryologists, notably Geoffroy-St. Hilaire (1822) and Dareste (1869, 1877). In biology, the Dutchman de Vries applied it to the growth of plants. He found that there was a time during which environmental conditions could influence the form taken by poppy flowers of a particular variety; after this particular developmentally linked sensitive period had passed, such environmental conditions could no longer influence subsequent morphological development, even though the development in question had not yet even occurred. In fact, de Vries himself used the term "sensitive period" to denote this phenomenon, which he also observed in the development of many other plants.

In the beginning of the development of psychoanalysis Sigmund Freud stated the notion that there are sensitive periods in the early development of children. Freud postulated that injurious events during these periods had relatively lasting effects on adult behavior. In education, the Italian Maria Montessori applied the concept of sensitive periods fully to the mental development of children. At the same time Lorenz, an Austrian, applied the notion to the imprinting phenomenon in the social behavior of precocial birds.

Lorenz observed the behavior of newly hatched geese, both in the company of the natural parents and when he presented himself to the young animals as a parental object before they had an opportunity to associate with their own parents. Because the latter animals later in life treated other human beings as fellow species members and the former animals remained with their own species as a result of having first associated with their own parents, Lorenz concluded that species recognition was "imprinted" (*Prägung*) onto the nervous system of these young during the first period of exposure after hatching.

Under natural conditions imprinting serves its purpose quite well: the first object seen is, of course, the natural parent. Furthermore, the rapid attachment of the young to the parent is necessary for the survival of the young animal. During the first days of life, the parent broods the young, protects it from predators, leads it away from dangerous situations, and takes it to food objects in the environment.

Since the early 1950s imprinting has been extensively studied in the laboratory, particularly in the United States. This work has been reviewed in papers by Moltz, by Hess, by Sluckin, and by Bateson. The results of laboratory investigation on imprinting carried out by Hess can be stated in five main points, each of which appears to make imprinting a phenomenon quite different from the association learning commonly studied by experimental psychologists.

1. In waterfowls there was a sharp and distinct critical period found by Hess. In the case of wild mallard ducks there is a peak of sensitivity to the imprinting process at about 16 hours after hatching in socially isolated birds, after which time the sensitivity drops rapidly. By 32 or 48 hours of age the increased fear response of the young animal appears to interfere with further imprinting capability. Similar critical periods have been found for imprinting in other birds as well. Although they are not necessarily within the first day, all of them are in the very early life of the organism.

2. The use of certain drugs, particularly muscle relaxants, interferes completely with the acquisition of the imprinting effect. These same drugs do not interfere at all with the normal acquisition of a discrimination habit such as would be experimentally studied in a psychology laboratory.

3. Massed practice is more effective than spaced practice. In addition, Hess discovered the *law of effort,* which states that the strength of imprinting is positively related to the amount of energy expended by the precocial hatchling bird in going to or in attempting to go to the imprinting object.

4. Primacy and recency work in a way completely different from association learning. In imprinting it is clearly the first thing that is "learned" which is retained, whereas in association learning a primacy-recency experiment will show that the animal tends to respond to the last meaningful stimulus.

5. The effect of punishment, or painful stimulation, is the opposite of what occurs in an association learning situation. This notion is of particular interest in the field of child psychology and in psychiatry. A study on this phenomenon was published by Kovack and Hess.

In Kovach and Hess's investigation there are data on groups of chicks at an age close to the critical period peak of 13–16 hours after hatching, 18 hours, and at an age well beyond the critical period for imprinting, 48 hours. At each age the experimental animals were given electrical shocks while in an imprinting apparatus with a model (a "parent" object), while others received no shock in this situation. However, the animals that were shocked during the optimum period for imprinting actually followed the parent model significantly more than the control animals that did not receive any shock. The reverse was true for the chicks exposed at the age of 48 hours.

Although these results would be perplexing from the standpoint of association learning, they are not unreasonable from the standpoint of instinctive behavior and the normal survival value of such behavior, in ethological terms. If, for example, in the natural situation the young animal were to be stepped on by the parent before it leaves the nest, it would not be biologically useful to have the young avoid the parent, leave the nest, and die. If anything, there seems to be an overcompensation for any punishment associated with the parental object since the animals receiving shock did follow better than the control animals when the initial exposure occurred during the critical period. Anthropomorphically, it is as though the animal in a painful situation depends at that moment on the parent to a tremendous degree insofar as survival is concerned, and will then seek to get even closer to the parent object.

At least one paper published in the psychiatric literature seems to tie this phenomenon to behavior in young children. Menaker relates submissive behavior in a child with an unloving, powerful, exploitative, and dominating mother to innate mechanisms of submission which prevent species members from killing each other. However, it would appear that, in the light of the research involving imprinting and shock, the child who is in an essentially punishing relationship with the parent and reacts by idealizing the parent and picturing this parent as all-powerful and loving is doing much the same thing that a chick does during the critical period when it follows a model even more closely when punished in its presence. The motor patterns involved in the two cases, of course, are different and therefore not in any sense homologous. It is not impossible that both submission and intensified affiliation can operate in the human child and be vital to survival. Just as there is a selection pressure for a chick or a duckling to stay with the parent under the most adverse conditions, a similar selection pressure must operate with the human child who obviously could not survive alone.

The fact that most modern societies have made provisions to give children adequate physical care may obscure the functioning of a mechanism which would bind the child to the parent during his period of dependency even when he is physically punished. As Polt suggests, it almost seems as though the normal parent-child relationship implicitly assumes that something of this sort operates. Whereas association learning would predict that when a child is chastised by the parent for an undesirable act, the child will associate the punishment with the parent as the agent of the punishment, the child in fact associates the punishment with the misdemeanor.

Numerous theoretical papers have attempted to delineate the relationship between socialization in human infants and the imprinting phenomenon. Bowlby, for example, has pointed out several congruent features between the ethological findings regarding imprinting and psychoanalytic principles on the development of social attachments in human babies: the innate drive to make a "love" relationship with a parent figure, the strong influence of the individual's early love object on the selection of a love object (both sexual and parental) in adult life (a process which in abnormal cases in human beings may be carried to the point of pathological fixation), and the critical or sensitive phases of development with reference to both the organization of the motor patterns adopted and the nature of the object selected.

With regard to the notion of sensitive periods for the establishment of emotional bonds between mother and infant, several writers have postulated specific ages for primary social development to occur. Gray proposed the period of six weeks to six months, Hess the first five and one-half months of age, Rollman-Branch the first six months, and Ambrose the age period from five to twelve weeks.

Ambrose has contended that there are good grounds for drawing an analogy between social imprinting and primary socialization in humans. On the basis of his own earlier research with the smiling response, he suggested that the sensitive period for supra-individual learning of the human face starts at approximately the fifth week of life and ends at approximately 12 weeks of age for family-reared infants and at approximately 18 weeks of age for institutionalized infants. The postulation by Ambrose that the location of the sensitive period depends upon the nature of the caretaking to which the child has been exposed is congruent with the idea that the end of the sensitive period for social imprinting is delayed when the sensory-social input to the organism is below normal, a notion found in some other studies of social imprinting. The supra-individual learning of the human face, furthermore, was proposed by Ambrose as the human analogue of supra-individual learning of the species in precocial birds.

The question of whether social imprinting exists in man has been a perennial one. This issue is certainly difficult and complex. One of the principal difficulties is that the baby cannot actually follow the parent at an early age, as is the case with precocial species which have demonstrated imprinting in primary socialization. Furthermore, it appears to many writers that primary socialization occurs in the human child before it is able to crawl.

Gray has suggested that the smiling response is homologous to the following response of young precocial birds, particularly since it ends when a fear response to strangers appears, as we mentioned earlier. The comparison between the fear response of young infants to strangers and that shown by young birds has also been made by Freedman. However, it certainly is not permissible to *homologize* between avian and human species: the motor patterns of following and smiling are not the same. Besides, there is an insufficiency of cases of social imprinting in intermediate species. Also, just because there is a period of positive responsiveness and positive attachment followed by the fear reaction, this does not establish the existence of a social imprinting phenomenon in human beings, as Ambrose has rightly contended. The distress behavior evident in young chicks or ducklings already imprinted to their siblings or to another parent object may possibly reflect a searching for the lost companionship rather than fear of the new situation per se. Thus, while fear may cause incompatible response in birds which have been completely isolated socially since hatching, this may not be the case in socially maintained ones.

Other comparisons between social imprinting in birds and primary socialization in humans,

however, have been suggested by Ambrose. He pointed out the broad similarity between the nature of the innate releasing situations for smiling in babies and following in chicks and ducks, which are both releasing situations that involve mother objects. Not only are there close similarities in causation, in his opinion, but there is also a close similarity in function. This function is keeping the young organism close to the mother object. Whereas the young chick or duckling can follow, the human infant is utterly incapable of doing so for several months. However, the human baby's crying normally does serve to bring his mother to him from a distance and his smiling serves to keep her present when she is already nearby. Ambrose also pointed out that another similarity between smiling in human babies and following in chicks and ducks is that both gain in response strength in the period of supra-individual learning of the species without any conventional reward such as food.

Lastly, Ambrose also postulated that the time at which fixation upon an object is possible is a better criterion for the beginning of social imprinting and the beginning of supra-individual learning of the species in human babies than is the time when learning is first evident, which Gray had proposed. This is because, as Ambrose pointed out, a bird cannot learn its parent unless it can follow, and following of the parent is impossible unless the young bird can keep it fixated. Thus commencement of visual learning, he suggested, is conditional upon the achievement of the ability to fixate an object. In line with this notion Ambrose suggested that the mother's eyes are the first object to consistently elicit visual fixation by the infant, particularly since the studies of Ahrens and others have indicated that the smiling response is initially elicited by the eyes alone. It is of interest that Caldwell has also suggested that *visual pursuit* constitutes the "following" of the parent figure by the infant.

However, the existence of these several similarities does not necessarily force the conclusion that there is actually a phylogenetic connection between the imprinting phenomenon in birds and filial attachments to parents in human infants, as Hinde has pointed out. The synapsid and diapsid reptiles, from which mammals and birds arose, have been distinct since at least the Permian period of the Paleozoic era. Therefore parental care and infant-to-mother attachment behaviors probably have evolved independently in the two groups. Hence the similarities would more accurately indicate that these behaviors constitute analogies rather than homologies, and they originate from similar selective forces in the evolutionary process.

Hinde is undoubtedly correct with respect to the development of social attachment. However, it must be pointed out that if *imprinting* is a type of learning process which, as Hess has proposed, can be applied to a variety of situations in which specific behavior patterns are attached to a class of stimulus objects, such as food imprinting in chicks and turtles, maternal imprinting in goats, or environmental imprinting in a variety of species (as reviewed by Hess, in preparation), then imprinting is a genetically programmed learning mechanism which probably is very old phylogenetically. Indeed it seems likely that the imprinting process could have been independently seized upon by both mammals and birds for use in the development of social behavior systems, as well as in other object-response relationships. Therefore the homology, if it exists at all, would be through the phylogenetic transmission of the imprinting phenomenon and not through the phylogenetic transmission of parental care and filial attachment systems.

It can be seen that the implications regarding the effect of environmental influences during early life on the later behavior of an animal are now, and will become, increasingly important in the study of human development. Certainly the notion of stages or phases in psychological development in human beings is a very old one. The stages of babyhood, childhood, adolescence, adulthood, and old age have been enumerated for centuries. Froebel (1826) long ago declared that events in each of these stages had consequences very important for succeeding ones, a notion which has assumed since then considerable importance in the investigation of the ontogeny of behavior. To date very many sensitive periods have been suggested in the literature (reviewed by Hess, in preparation), particularly in the spheres of social-emotional behaviors and intellectual activities. The

very variety of these proposed sensitive periods shows that this will continue to be a fertile field of investigation for several decades to come.

The concept of displacement activity, an extremely widespread phenomenon in the animal kingdom, has proven to be another notion of considerable interest to psychiatrists and other scholars in the area of human behavior and development. The ethological concepts of ambivalent behavior and redirected activity have already been foreshadowed for some time in the case of human behavior. Freud clearly enunciated the concept of ambivalent motivation in normal and disturbed persons. Simultaneous love and hate is the best known case of such ambivalence. Redirected behavior, particularly in the form of scapegoating, has indeed been folklore. Banging tables or desks in anger and throwing crockery are some of the most common instances of this, as is also kicking the dog or scolding the wife after a harrowing day at the office. Lorenz has described several specific examples of scapegoating as instances of redirected aggression.

Still other indications regarding displacement activities in human behavior may be found in remarks by Tinbergen and Morris. Tinbergen noted that learned activities as well as innate ones can function in this context. Examples of such learned activities include cigarette lighting and handling of handkerchief or keys; examples of innate activities having this function include head scratching and preening, often manifested in mild conflict situations. Women, for example, can often be seen adjusting nonexistent disorder in their coiffure, while men handle their beards and mustaches or cheeks and chins if clean shaven. Morris has added to this list of human displacement activities drinking, eating, nose scratching, nose picking, ear lobe pulling, lip licking, and hand rubbing.

Makkink some time ago discovered sleep functioning as a displacement activity in the avocet when in a conflict between aggression and escape. It has since then been found in several wading birds. It is interesting in this connection that there is a widespread belief among many people, including college counselors, that fatigue commonly occurs as a response to frustration, anxiety, or boredom, rather than solely as a consequence of overexertion. Tinbergen pointed out that yawning is a low intensity manifestation of sleep and is very commonly seen in moderate conflict conditions. Yawning, as most of us know from personal observation, is "catching" and it is rather amusing to find that the same phenomenon should occur in the ostrich, as reported by Sauer.

Contemporary psychiatrists have used the displacement activity concept in at least three ways as a tool for approaching human behavior. Although each approach is somewhat different, each seems to provide a valid working *hypothesis* at the human level. Naturally, these comparisons between human and animal behaviors, just as with any comparison between different animal species, must be tested by appropriate means. This is the case even when behavior phenomena are as ubiquitous as are displacement activities: considerable caution must be taken in regarding the human examples as actual cases of displacement activities.

The fact that many displacement activities at the animal level do not serve to maximize the survival of the individual or the species has been emphasized by Weigert. She has related displacement activity to neurotic anxiety, which Freud considered to be the result of a frustrated libidinal impulse and which is, of course, basically detrimental to the individual. This interpretation of displacement activity emphasizes the nonfunctional aspect of neurotic behavior. At the same time it should be kept in mind that the conflict situation experienced by the individual may, under certain circumstances, result in the sublimation of libidinal energy into activities condoned by society, a point which was strongly made by Freud.

Another way of viewing displacement activity is that taken by Ostow. After drawing some parallels between the psychoanalytic and ethological concepts of instinct, he used displacement activity as an illustration of a logical progression of development in man. Taking only the sexual instincts as an example, Ostow has hypothesized that the gratification of these instincts takes different forms during different periods of development and that the mechanism which leads from one form to another functions in the same way that displacement activity functions in lower animals. As one mode of

gratification is inhibited, the instinct accepts another mode of gratification. In this way Ostow traced the sexual aims in the psychic development of humans through oral, anal, phallic, and genital stages.

The third view is that of Kaufman, who suggested, on the basis of his study of ethology, that in addition to the sexual and aggressive instincts in man, there might also be an instinct for flight. Kaufman has drawn heavily on work with displacement activities since many of them are the result of a conflict between aggression and fear. He pointed out that with most infrahuman animals components of sexual behavior, aggression, and flight are all built-in tendencies and that the same is likely to be true of man. Further, he has advanced the notion of the usefulness of this theoretical paradigm in the treatment of patients where shyness and timidity would not have to be construed as a reaction to hostile or sexual impulses, but as a drive in its own right, that is, as a low intensity manifestation of a flight tendency.

Whereas the members of the human species have generally considered intraspecific aggression among themselves as antisocial and undesirable since it can be highly destructive, Lorenz has taken the position that it has the same positive functions as it does in infrahuman animal species and, in fact, has had an important role in the formation of human society from the beginning of mankind's existence. "Aggression, far from being the diabolical, destructive principle that classical psychoanalysis makes it out to be, is really an essential part of the life-preserving organization of instinct. Though by accident it may function in the wrong way and cause destruction, the same is true of practically any functional part of any system."

The observation of the various means by which aggression is dealt with in animal behavior during interactions between congeners (members of the same species) prompted Lorenz to point out the existence of several similarities in human behavior. The aggression drive, being primarily a species-preserving instinct, arises spontaneously in the organism and is subject to the same building up of specific energy and discharge that we discussed earlier for other instincts. The very same process can be seen in human beings, and Lorenz cited several instances of it. Redirection of the aggression to other objects, superstitions, and ritual ceremonies are all among the means utilized by both lower animals and human beings to deal with intra-specific aggression. Culturally derived "manners," Lorenz pointed out, have an aggression-appeasement function which immediately becomes apparent through the reaction of hostility when a person fails to observe them. This can readily occur when people from different countries or even from different regions of the same country come into contact and are unaware that there are differences in what are considered "good manners." Similar observations have been made by a sociologist, Hall.

Our discussions of aggression, smiling behavior, responses to babyishness, pupil responses (as indicators of differences between males and females in biological reaction to specific pictorial stimuli, of personality differences, and as social-communicative signals in specific situations), and displacement activities have covered only a small range of ethology's great potential in making theoretical and substantive contribution to the study of normal and abnormal human behavior. The large body of experimental data on the effects of early experience and imprinting has made it possible to draw parallels, though with considerable caution, and, in at least some respects, to test hypotheses generated by the animal work in relation to human early behavior.

Of considerable importance is the application of the methods and techniques developed by ethologists to the analysis of human behavior. For example, knowledge of the normal behavior and the normal development of behavior are cases in point. The use of schematic representations to determine whether or not sign stimuli or releasers are operating at the human level, such as in the case of the smiling response to schematic representations of the human face, allows us to come to grips with certain aspects of early human behavior.

The use of still other techniques which do not involve verbal responses may allow us to gain information regarding the development of attitudes and perceptions in the infant and growing child, either before verbal responses may be obtained or where verbal responses may not be trustworthy. Two examples of

such techniques are the recording of changes in the size of the eye pupil, which has been used in a preliminary study of psychosexual development in boys and girls from the age of 5 to 8 years by Bernick and the recording of the length of visual fixation of different objects by human infants. Both of these techniques are clearly ethological methods.

In the same vein, several studies on proxemic behavior by sociologists and anthropologists bear strong similarities to the ethological method of behavior study. Both emphasize the communicative (but nonverbal) function of such behavior, that is, the reaction of other individuals to specific actions that are performed. The use of space and the effects of population density are also allied to the ethological approach. In fact, Leyhausen, an ethologist, is studying the effects of population density on behavior.

However, it is not only the ethological tradition of objectivity in behavior study that has importance for the study of human development. Of even greater importance are the twin concepts of the phylogenetic context of human behavior and the biological bases of this behavior. There are now many cases in which these have been or currently are applied to human behavior.

One such is the investigation of actions expressive of emotions. Indeed, Darwin was among the first to investigate this from a phylogenetic viewpoint. Other investigators, ethologists or not, have studied the form and function of expressive actions in human beings from a functional and objective viewpoint, and this area of investigation has considerable promise. Scheflen, a psychiatrist, has observed the existence of various "quasi-courtship" gestures functioning as communicative signals in interactions with others and apparently on an unconscious level. These gestures were discovered through the objective recording of the motor actions and body postures of participants in interpersonal situations and not through introspection or verbal interviewing. Leg crossing, preening movements, sitting back or leaning forward, and arm folding were found to be among such movements and to be useful in establishing rapport and communication in psychotherapeutic situations. Blurton Jones has studied three- to five-year-old nursery school children with respect to facial and bodily motor expressions and the specific responses which these elicit from others. Wickler has made a preliminary comparison of sociosexual signals in man and other primates.

A frankly biological approach to human behavior may be found in genetics. This is a very young field that promises to become extremely fertile, particularly when the ethological premise of the biological bases of behavior is accepted without racist handicaps. In my own unpublished research I have found a strong and highly consistent correlation between eye color and modes of perception and personality. Blue eyes were associated with form dominance in perception and a scientific attitude, whereas brown eyes were associated with color dominance in perception and a nonscientific attitude. The genetic bases of this obviously could be studied.

The significance of the phylogenetic viewpoint in the consideration of human behavior is highly apparent in Lorenz's *On Aggression:* "all specifically human faculties, the power of speech, cultural tradition, moral responsibility, could have evolved only in a being which, before the very dawn of conceptual thinking, lived in well-organized communities. Our prehuman ancestor was indubitably as true a friend to his friend as a chimpanzee or even a dog, as tender and solicitous to the young of his community and as self-sacrificing in its defense, aeons before he developed conceptual thought and became aware of the consequences of his action." Also, Lorenz asserted, "if, in the Greylag Goose and in man, highly complex norms of behavior, such as falling in love, strife for ranking order, jealousy, grieving, etc., are not only similar but down to the most absurd details the same, we can be sure that every one of these instincts has a very special survival value, in each case almost or quite the same in the Greylag and in man. Only in this way can the conformity of behavior have developed." These similar behaviors in the Greylag Goose and in man, Lorenz emphatically stressed, arose through convergence and not through common inheritance. Such convergence supports even more strongly the notion that these behaviors have highly important species-survival functions.

In closing, it would seem that the most significant contribution of ethology to the study of human development, in both the phylogenetic and ontogenetic senses, is the recognition that man is a biological organism, and that he has an evolutionary history. The present-day members of the species of man have an ancient repertoire of behaviors. From the ethological point of view, the human infant is not a completely naïve being, but possesses a legacy of potential behavior patterns which at one time assured the survival of the organism even without the aid of social learning or customs. Some of these innate behavior patterns involve elements of sexual behavior, aggressive behavior, and innate social responses. Recognition of these as part of our heritage is important because, in terms of man's evolutionary history, we are not at all far from the time when there were no widespread cultural influences upon our behavior. Without our built-in behaviors, we, as a species, simply could not have managed to survive for a million years.

Indeed, as Desmond Morris has suggested, man needs to face up to the accumulated genetic legacy of his whole evolutionary past, and as a result he may be "less worried and more fulfilled." It is the realization that these potential, genetically programmed behaviors are present and that many of them must be channeled into quite different directions in our present-day civilized world, which may make the greatest contribution toward an approach to the problems of the human species and may have a tremendous impact on the search for mental health as well as a fuller understanding of human behavioral development. In this connection Morris, in stating that basic biological changes rather than simply acculturation have been primarily responsible for the development of uniquely human behavior from its original primate form (one example is the incest taboo), has stressed his belief that "our unbelievably complicated civilizations will be able to prosper only if we design them in such a way that they do not clash with or tend to suppress our basic animal demands."

This, of course, presupposes that we actually

do succeed in knowing just what our basic animal needs are. To assume, for example, that aggression is solely the result of bad training and environment is to close one's eyes to the evolutionary usefulness and possible biological survival value of aggression, factors which surely must have a place in the make-up of man, as they do in all other animal organisms.

If in this case alone the theoretical viewpoint becomes one in which aggression, when properly directed, is recognized as a useful biological consequence of man's inherent constitution, it would seem that ethology will have made a major contribution to the field of human behavior.

PART TWO

THE CULTURE AND THE CHILD: CROSS-CULTURAL, CLASS, AND ETHNIC DIFFERENCES

First, a word about why this volume contains a separate section on cross-cultural studies. There are at least two ways of organizing readings in child development. One is to include one or more cross-cultural studies under appropriate sections: for example, the section on infancy might include a paper on infant care in Japan. The other way, used here, is to have a separate section for cross-cultural studies, even though each study deals with one of the issues treated in the other sections of the book. This way, the impact of culture on various aspects of development is likely to impress the reader more strongly. We are very likely to have "cultural blinders," to assume that what is true for, say, child perception or cognition in any one culture is true universally. Hopefully, a concentrated consideration of cross-cultural influences may serve as a corrective.

One purpose of cross-cultural studies is to provide data that shed light on the heredity-environment controversy or at least raise questions about the issue. One such study is that of Meredith (1969) on body size of contemporary groups of eight-year-old children in different parts of the world. Data on ninety-eight groups were reported in the complete study, and a graph showing height in relation to weight in these groups is included here. It is interesting to note nature's tendency to maintain a constant proportion between height and weight—only a few groups are unusually heavy or light for their height. Disparities in weight among the ethnic groups studied is much greater than disparity in height. The heaviest children weigh twenty-two pounds more than the lightest, while the tallest are only five inches taller than the shortest. The data provide a valuable background for further research into the interaction of cultural habits, nutrition, and genes.

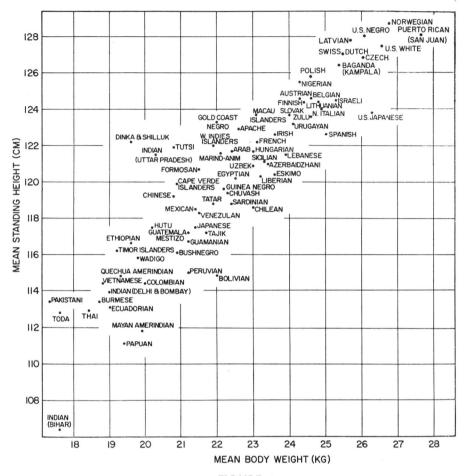

FIGURE I

The relation of mean standing height and mean body weight among contemporary groups of 8-year-old children.

From Howard V. Meredith, "Body Size of Contemporary Groups of Eight-Year-Old Children Studied in Different Parts of the World." Reprinted by permission of the author and The Society for Research in Child Development from *Monographs of The Society for Research in Child Development*, 1969, **34,** Ser. no. 125, 48. © 1969 by The Society for Research in Child Development, Inc. All rights reserved.

STUDIES OF NON-AMERICAN CULTURES

The Caudill-Weinstein report of infant and maternal behavior in Japanese and American families included here also illuminates impact of environment on maturation. The investigators found that Japanese three- and four-month-old infants differed from American babies with respect to physical activity, "happy vocalization," and exploration of toys and hands, with American babies being more active. They also found differences in maternal behavior between Japanese and American mothers that could conceivably explain the differences in physical activity. Similarly, the degree of motor precocity of Ganda infants in comparison with Western norms, first noted by Géber (1957) and later confirmed by Ainsworth (1967), is attributed by both investigators to environmental factors—to the postural adjustments babies make in the first year as they are carried about and to the babies' freedom to move. The Ganda babies crawled two and one-half months earlier than Western ones and walked at eleven rather than fourteen months. Dennis (1960) made a study of institutionalized children in Iran. In one of the institutions studied, less than 50 percent of babies between 1.0 and 1.9 years old could sit alone, and none could walk alone. Dennis attributes the retardation to paucity of handling, including the failure of attendants to place children in a sitting position. However, while a given environment can support or depress motor development, we must not lose sight of genetic differences. Uganda infants, for example, are precocious even in reflex behaviors during the first month of life, and black Americans are more accelerated than whites in physical development.

The contemporary approach to cross-cultural research in child development differs markedly from earlier approaches. Two decades ago, much of the emphasis was on the impact of culture on personality. Usually, investigators described a particular society's child-rearing practices and its values system as reflected in cultural mores; they then speculated on the relationship between such factors and the adult personality. Thus, the Hopi baby, for example, was pictured as being raised with much love and affection but also under pressure of fear of *Kachinas,* who might come to punish him; of the spider woman; and of *powabas,* or owls and gods and famine and drought. Investigators also pointed out the terrifying impact of white schools, where the child, torn from his parents, was exposed to a culture that held in contempt the customs he had learned as an Indian and scorned the things he considered sacred. These, along with other pressures, produced, according to earlier analyses, a kind, generous, and gentle people, who regarded both competition and physical aggression as being in bad taste but who also argued endlessly over tribal matters, gossiped a good deal, mistrusted one another, and were fearful of spirits.

More recent research, while still directed toward exploring cross-cultural factors in personality differences, is being carried out to test specific hypotheses regarding differences in child-rearing practices and subsequent differences in personality. One large cooperative project, involving social scientists from Harvard, Yale, and Cornell, is testing hypothetical relationships between such factors as aggression and dependency in six different countries—Kenya, India, Japan, Mexico, the Philippines, and the United States. An example of the hypotheses being tested is: "Indulgence in infancy, a large number of nurturing agents, and mild transition from infantile indulgence into childhood will produce: (1) a trustful attitude toward others, (2) general optimism, and (3) sociability." (The reader will find the theoretical roots for such a hypothetical relationship in Erikson's description of the first three stages of man.) The first volume, *Six Cultures: Studies of Child Rearing* (Whiting, 1963), reported on the cultural material that will be used for hypothesis-testing. Whiting notes:

> Implicit in the research design is a general concept of the relation of personality to culture, which may be presented as follows: The ecology of the area determines the maintenance systems, which include basic economy and the

most elementary variables of social structure. In other words, the type of crops grown, the presence or absence of herding, fishing, and so on, depend on the nature of the terrain, the amount of rainfall, the location of the area vis-à-vis centers of invention and diffusion. These basic economic conditions determine in part the arrangement of people in space, the type of houses, and household composition. These in turn set the stage for child-rearing practices [p. 4].

The chart below shows the conceptual background for the research design:

IMPACT OF ECOLOGY AND MAINTENANCE SYSTEMS ON ADULT BEHAVIOR

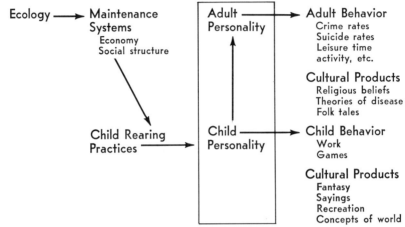

Reproduced by permission of the editor from B. B. Whiting, ed., *Six Cultures: Studies of Child Rearing*, p. 5. Copyright © 1963 by John Wiley & Sons, Inc.

In line with the trend to test specific hypotheses about child development in cultures other than our own are current studies in cognition. In recent years there have been far more cross-cultural cognitive studies than before. One avenue pursued by some anthropologists has been the study of the effect of cultural values and expectations on IQ scores. Typically, an intelligence test like the Draw-A-Man Test, which does not depend on content derived from Western culture, is used in testing non-Western unschooled populations. In one such study, included here, Johnson, Johnson, and Price-Williams found that among Guatemalan children, Indian girls scored lower than Ladino girls, and both scored lower than boys. Such a finding reverses the sex difference usually found in the United States, where girls score higher than boys. The investigators attribute the low scores of the Indian girls to the social expectations prevailing in their culture. The girls are accustomed to learning passively, to repeating answers they have memorized, and they are not prepared for a situation in which they are asked to do something original, like drawing a man.

Zigler and Butterfield (1968) have noted a similar phenomenon among black preschool children in this country. These investigators argue that the low IQ scores of disadvantaged children may be due in part to personality variables, such as motivation. The child may know the answers to the questions asked by the examiner, but he will answer "I don't know" because, fearful of the examiner, he wants to end the testing as soon as possible. When an optimal testing procedure was set up, it was found that increases in IQ were due to the child's ability to perform better in the standard testing situation rather than to an actual increase in cognitive factors. Like those of the Guatemalan Indian girls, scores of the culturally deprived in our own country may be affected by cultural factors not necessarily in the cognitive area but rather in the affective.

A different type of cross-cultural research investigates the relationship between culture and logic. Are the logical processes of preliterate people different from the logic of Western man? Gay and Cole (1971) have carried out some interesting experiments on this problem. They presented two types of verbal logical problems to Kpelle adults in Liberia. The typical Kpelle adult could solve syllogisms where the conclusion was given (e.g., "Everybody in the town eats rice. The chief is in the town. Therefore the chief eats rice."); subjects had more difficulty with syllogisms for which they had to draw conclusions (e.g., "Flumo and Yakpalo always drink cane juice together. Flumo is drinking cane juice. Is Yakpalo drinking cane juice?"). Here answers depended on the particular verbal context; subjects were likely to say that Yakpalo was not drinking cane juice because he happened to go to the farm that day, or to suggest that the investigator ask Yakpalo! Ability to make logical judgments, however, depends on education as well as on the way in which the problem is posed. Westernized, literate Kpelle adults responded more or less like educated Americans to verbal problems like those above.

STUDIES OF AMERICAN SUBCULTURES

The impact of culture on child development is being studied extensively in non-Western societies, but even more so in American society. Both black culture and youth culture are being described and analyzed in a profusion of publications. Two papers on these subcultures are included in this volume: one on the black family and the other on the psychology of youth. Rainwater's paper on the black family was selected because it appears to correct many of the misconceptions about black family life, and Keniston's paper performs the same service for the youth culture.

The subject of the black family has been a controversial one ever since the publication of the Moynihan Report in 1964. Moynihan was commissioned by President Johnson to draw up recommendations for changing federal civil-rights policies to emphasize liberty rather than equality. From government data and social-science studies, Moynihan concluded that the chief obstacle to achieving equality was the deterioration of the black family, especially the low-income family. He described the families as unstable: almost a quarter of black women are divorced or separated, almost a quarter of black births are illegitimate, almost a quarter of all black families are headed by a woman. Moynihan quite properly traces the beginnings of family instability to the conditions of slavery, which denied marriage to slaves, made it impossible to establish two-parent families, and placed the burden of child-rearing on the female. Many males have never had a real chance to learn to be good fathers. Economic conditions maintained by racism since the end of slavery have made it particularly difficult for black males to find jobs paying enough to support a family. Moynihan's data show that pathological family life has a particularly strong impact on boys, who more frequently turn to crime and drugs in order to escape conditions they cannot change.

While liberals do not quarrel with the statistics or with the history behind the statistics, they are dismayed that right-wing groups use these statistics to support their claims that blacks are immoral and not worthy of government aid. Critics of the report also point out that families may be broken for various reasons, and breaking up a family need not have pathological results. Also, say the critics, it would be better to place the emphasis on improving the economic lot of blacks than on changing black family structure. The Rainwater article deals with the culture of black lower-class life and in many ways acts as a corrective to the Moynihan Report.

Other subcultures in the United States have been somewhat less subject to research than the blacks: Mexican-Americans (Chicanos), Chinese-Americans, Puerto Rican–Americans, and American Indians are some of the ethnic groups with distinctive cultural patterns who have experienced discrimination from majority-group Americans. Family studies of these groups are not as numerous as those of black families. Where they exist, however, the message is the same: values like the work ethic, independence, initiative, and aggressiveness are not emphasized in other subcultures as they are among the white–Anglo-Saxon–Protestant groups. These differences, together with discriminatory attitudes, result in assigning many minority-group members to the lower class and keeping them there. As Keniston points out, white middle-class youth is increasingly rejecting traditional middle-class values, and perhaps some changes in our values system will come out of the various revolutionary struggles in which America is presently engaged.

Student dissent will undoubtedly change in the 1970s. However, Keniston's social and psychological insights into college youth are not likely to be quickly dated. Writers like Eisenberg (1970) and Bettelheim (1970) find the prolongation of adolescence in part responsible for adolescent rebellion, a social condition not easily changed in a technological society. The biological and social roots of rebellion persist and are likely to produce some form of dissent until the energy, idealism, and intelligence of youth are utilized in the mainstream of national life.

REFERENCES

Ainsworth, M. D., *Infancy in Uganda: infant care and growth of love* (Baltimore: The Johns Hopkins Press, 1967).

Bettelheim, B., *Obsolete youth: towards a psychograph of adolescent rebellion* (San Francisco: San Francisco Press, 1970).

Dennis, W., "Causes of retardation among institutional children: Iran." *Journal of genetic psychology,* 1960, 64, 47–59.

Eisenberg, L., "Student unrest: sources and consequences." *Science,* 1970, 167, 1688–92.

Gay, J., and Cole, M., *The cultural context of learning and thinking* (New York: Basic Books, 1971).

Géber, M., and Dean, R. F. A., "Gesell tests on African children." *Pediatrics,* 1957, 30, 1055–65.

Kendler, T. S., "Verbalization and optional reversal shifts among kindergarten children." *Journal of Verbal Learning and Verbal Behavior,* 1964, 3, 428–36.

Le Vine, R. A., "Cross-cultural study in child psychology." In P. H. Mussen, ed., *Carmichael's Manual of Child Psychology,* vol. II (New York: Wiley, 1970).

Meredith, H. V., "Body size of contemporary groups of eight-year-old children studied in different parts of the world."

Monographs of the Society for Research in Child Development, 1969, 34, Ser. No. 125.

Moynihan, D., *The Negro family: the case for national action* (Washington, D.C.: Office of Policy Planning and Research, U.S. Department of Labor, 1965).

Whiting, B. B., ed., *Six cultures: studies of child rearing* (New York: Wiley, 1963).

Zigler, E., and Butterfield, E. C., "Motivation aspects of changes in IQ test performance of culturally deprived nursery school children." *Child Development,* 1968, 39, 1–14.

MATERNAL CARE AND INFANT BEHAVIOR
IN JAPAN AND AMERICA

WILLIAM CAUDILL   HELEN WEINSTEIN

Human behavior can be distinguished, in one sense, from that of other animals in the degree to which it is influenced by culture—that is, influenced by shared patterns of action, belief, feeling, and thinking that are transmitted knowingly and unknowingly from one generation to the next through learning. The influence of culture is universal in that in some respects a man learns to become like all men; and it is particular in that a man who is reared in one society learns to become in some respects like all men of his society and not like those of others. A general question underlying the investigation reported here concerns the degree of importance of particular cultural differences, as a variable in the understanding of human behavior.

We began the present longitudinal study of children over the first six years of life in Japan and America because we wished to explore how early in the lives of infants, and in what ways, cultural differences become manifest in behavior. Our focus on culture as a variable is in no way meant to deny the great, and inter-related, importance of other major sources of variation, such as genetic endowment and physiological functioning of the infant, psychological characteristics of the parents, and position of the family in the social structure. Rather, by either controlling for or randomizing the effect of these other sources of variation, we wished to estimate more clearly the amount of the total variance in our sample of human behavior which may be attributed to cultural differences.

In the present study, we selected a matched sample of 30 Japanese and 30 American three-

Reprinted with abridgment by permission of William Caudill from *Psychiatry*, 1969, **32**, 12–43.

to-four-month-old infants—equally divided by sex, all firstborn, and all from intact middle-class families living in urban settings—and carried out an observational study in the homes of these infants during 1961–64. This article gives the results of that study. Subsequently, we made observations in the homes of the first 20 of these same children in each culture at the time they became two-and-a-half years of age, and again when they became six years of age, but these data have not as yet been analyzed.

Earlier studies by ourselves and others in Japan and America have indicated meaningful cultural differences in values, interpersonal relations, and personality characteristics. On the basis of this previous work we predicted that our Japanese mothers would spend more time with their infants, would emphasize physical contact over verbal interaction, and would have as a goal a passive and contented baby. We predicted that our American mothers would spend less time with their infants, would emphasize verbal interaction rather than physical contact, and would have as a goal an active and self-assertive baby. Underlying these predictions is the assumption that much cultural learning takes place out of the awareness of the participants, and although the Japanese mother does not consciously teach her infant specifically to become a Japanese baby, nor does the American mother specifically teach her infant to become an American baby, such a process does take place. We therefore also expected that by three-to-four months of age, infants in the two cultures would behave differently in certain important ways.

Our hypotheses were generally confirmed, although there were some surprises, and we conclude that, largely because of different patterns of interaction with their mothers in the two countries, infants have learned to behave in different and culturally appropriate ways by three-to-four months of age. Moreover, these differences in infant behavior are in line with preferred patterns of social interaction at later ages as the child grows to be an adult in Japan and America.

BACKGROUND AND HYPOTHESES

Before we began our study we thought a good deal, in a conceptual and theoretical sense, about the sources of the wide variation that we expected to find in any of the dependent variables in our observations of the behavior of Japanese and American infants and their caretakers.

We planned to do our observations in the natural setting of the home and because of this we knew, of course, that chance events would contribute to the variation in the data. The main systematic sources of variation, however, we believed would arise from biological, psychological, social, and cultural dimensions of human behavior. Although all of these dimensions are interrelated in actual behavior, each is sufficiently distinct to be thought of as a separate system (Caudill, 1958). In the biological dimension we decided to control on birth order, age, and sex of our infants. We expected that the influence on behavior of *individual* differences in genetic endowment and physiological functioning among the Japanese and American infants would be randomly distributed in the two samples. We do not, however, know of any *group* genetic or physiological differences between Japanese and American populations that would meaningfully exert an influence on the behavior of infants. In the psychological dimension, also, we expected the influence of individual differences in the personalities of the mothers and the infants to be randomly distributed in the two samples. . . .

In the world at present, we believe that each of [the] dimensions—the cultural and the social —exerts a relatively independent influence on human behavior, and that both dimensions need serious consideration in any cross-national

study. There is considerable empirical evidence in the literature, from our own work and that of others, to support these ideas.

For the foregoing reasons we decided in our study to control on social class in the selection of the sample of infants, and thus reduce the variation in our data that might be expected if the families came from differing positions in the social structure. As noted, all families in our sample are middle-class, but we did divide the sample in each country into two groups: (1) the father is the owner or employee of a small, established, independent business; (2) the father is a white-collar, salaried employee in a large business or in government. This distinction between an entrepreneurial and a bureaucratic occupation, and its ramifications in family life, is an important one in Japan, and we expected to find some differences in the behavior of mothers and infants in the two types of families.[1] . . .

In the light of the sources of variation we expected, and the controls we decided to use, in the biological, psychological, and social dimensions of infant and caretaker behavior, we emerged, by design, with the cultural dimension as the main independent variable.

On the basis of our previous work in Japan over the past fourteen years, coupled with a study of the literature, we have come to feel that the following differing emphases on what is valued in behavior are important when life in Japan is compared with life in America. These differing emphases seem to be particularly sharp in the areas of family life and general interpersonal relations with which we are most directly concerned here, and perhaps to be somewhat less evident in other areas of life such as business, the professions, or politics. Japanese are more "group" oriented and interdependent in their relations with others, while Americans are more "individual" oriented and independent. Going along with this, Japanese are more self-effacing and passive in contrast to Americans, who appear more self-assertive

[1] We predicted that the Japanese mother in the small-business family would spend more time with her infant, would carry him more, and in general would be more attentive than the Japanese mother in the salaried family; and, because of the greater attention, we believed that the infant in the small-business family would be more responsive than the infant in the salaried family. . . .

and aggressive. In matters requiring a decision, Japanese are more likely to rely on emotional feeling and intuition, whereas Americans will go to some pains to emphasize what they believe are the rational reasons for their action. And finally, Japanese are more sensitive to, and make conscious use of, many forms of nonverbal communication in human relations through the medium of gestures and physical proximity in comparison with Americans, who predominantly use verbal communication within a context of physical separateness. One particularly pertinent example of the latter point is that a Japanese child can expect to co-sleep with his parents until he is ten years of age, and that in general a person in Japan can expect to co-sleep in a two-generation group, first as a child and later as a parent and grandparent, over half of his life span; to sleep alone is considered somewhat pitiful because a person would, therefore, be lonely.[2] In this regard, things are quite different in America, and the generations are usually separated in sleeping arrangements shortly after birth and remain so throughout the life cycle of the individual.

In summary, in normal family life in Japan there is an emphasis on interdependence and reliance on others, while in America the emphasis is on independence and self-assertion. The conception of the infant would seem to be somewhat different in the two cultures. In Japan, the infant is seen more as a separate biological organism who from the beginning, in order to develop, needs to be drawn into increasingly interdependent relations with others. In America, the infant is seen more as a dependent biological organism who, in order to develop, needs to be made increasingly independent of others. Our more specific hypotheses in this study came from this general background of family life and interpersonal relations in the two cultures.

As indicated earlier, we expected that our Japanese mothers would spend more time with their infants, would emphasize physical contact over verbal interaction, and would treat them as objects to be acted upon rather than as objects to be interacted with. But, more than this, we expected the quality of the interaction to be differently patterned in the two cultures, and in Japan for it to be a mutually dependent, even symbiotic, relation in which there was a blurring of the boundaries between mother and child. In contrast, we expected that our American mothers would spend less time with their infants, would encourage their physical activity and chat with them more, and would treat them more as separate objects to be interacted with. And we expected the interaction in America to give evidence of the self-assertion of the child and his budding awareness of separateness from his mother.

By focusing on the contrasts in the behavior of mothers and infants in the cultural dimension, we do not mean to imply that we thought of child rearing as completely different in the two countries; we anticipated that we would find many similarities centering around the basic biological needs of the infant and the necessity for the mother to care for these needs. The differences we expected refer more to the "style" of caretaking and its effect upon the child. Equally, we do not mean to imply that one style of caretaking is "better" or "worse" than the other. An individual mother can do a good or a poor job of caretaking within either style. Our emphasis, rather, is upon the effect of differences in behavior as these are repeated day after day in the simple routine of life. . . .

---

[2] These patterns of sleeping are not a function of "overcrowding" in the Japanese home, but rather are a matter of choice, as is shown in Caudill and Plath. Much the same point can be made concerning bathing. Starting at approximately the beginning of the second month of life, the Japanese infant is held in the arms of the mother or another adult while they bathe together in the deep bathtub (*furo*) at home or at the neighborhood public bath (*sento*), and this pattern of shared bathing will continue for a Japanese child until he is about ten years of age, and often much longer. In contrast, the American mother seldom bathes with an infant; rather, she gives him a bath from outside of the tub, and she communicates with him verbally and by positioning his body.

Although Japan is at one extreme in the length of time spent co-sleeping in a two-generation group, America is probably at the other extreme in this, and in many matters concerned with child rearing. Indeed, compared with the rest of the world, family life in the United States is in many ways rather peculiar.

DESIGN AND METHOD

The design of our study called for 30 Japanese and 30 American normal infants, who at the time of observation would be between three and four months of age and would be matched

TABLE I

Distribution of Cases in Terms of Independent Variables

	Japanese (30 cases) Father's Occupation		American (30 cases) Father's Occupation	
Sex of Infant	*Salaried*	*Independent*	*Salaried*	*Independent*
Male	9	9	10	5
Female	6	6	10	5

as previously described. Our plan was to gather data on the Japanese infants during 1961–62, and then to match the Japanese sample as closely as possible on all characteristics with an American sample that was to be studied during 1962–64. We were able to carry out this plan, although with some variation in the number of cases in each cell. The number and distribution of cases in the final sample used in the analysis of data are given in Table 1.

The Japanese families are of solely Japanese ancestry, and the American families are white and at least second-generation families of European ancestry. All of the Japanese families are nominally Buddhist, and the American families are divided among Protestant (18 cases), Catholic (9 cases), and Jewish (3 cases) affiliation. . . .

Japanese mothers in the sample are somewhat older on the average (26.6 years) at the time of birth of their first child than the American mothers (23.7 years). Similarly, Japanese fathers are somewhat older on the average (29.7 years) than American fathers (26.7 years). These differences are in line with the reality in the middle class in the two countries concerning the age of marriage.

All of our families are intact, and the largest number of households (15 Japanese and 25 American) in both samples consists of father, mother, and new baby—that is, the nuclear family. For the Japanese, those households with additional members (usually the father's parents) are mainly independent business families.

All of the families are residents of large cities. In the Japanese sample, we selected 20 cases from Tokyo and 10 from Kyoto because we wished also to take a look at the differences,

if any, in child rearing in the two cities. The general way of life in Tokyo is thought of as more modern, and in Kyoto as more traditional. We did not find any significant differences between the two cities as measured by the dependent variables for infant and caretaker behavior, and have combined the cases from the two cities. In the American sample, all cases were selected from the metropolitan area of Washington, D.C.

All of the families are middle class as measured by the occupation and education of the father, and the education of the mother. Although the Japanese sample is equally divided into 15 salaried and 15 independent business families, the American sample contains 20 salaried families and 10 independent business families because we had trouble in locating American cases in which the father was engaged in a small independent business. . . .

In making the observations we used a time-sampling procedure adapted from that originally developed by Rheingold. In this method, one observation of approximately one second in duration is made every fifteenth second in terms of a set of predetermined variables concerning the behavior of the infant and the caretaker. We designed an observation sheet that listed the variables down the side of the page, and provided columns for 40 observations across the page. For each observation, a decision was made for all variables as to their occurrence or nonoccurrence, although only occurrences received a check mark on the observation sheet. Four observations were made each minute, and thus a single observation sheet covered a period of ten minutes, or 40 observations. Upon completion of an observa-

TABLE 2

Adjusted Mean Frequencies, in Total Observations, of Infant Behavior: By Culture, Father's Occupation, and Sex of Infant

	Adjusted Mean Frequencies								
	Culture			*Father's Occupation*			*Sex of Infant*		
Categories of Infant Behavior	Japa-nese	Ameri-can	Corre-lation	Sala-ried	Inde-pendent	Corre-lation	Male	Female	Corre-lation
Infant Awake	494	493	.01	474	521	.20	498	488	.04
Breast or Bottle	66	55	.11	59	62	.03	63	57	.06
All Food	68	74	.06	71	71	.00	74	68	.06
Finger or Pacifier	69	172	.44**	116	127	.06	124	116	.04
Total Vocal	94	116	.25	100	112	.13	108	102	.07
Unhappy	66	45	.33	50	64	.21	55	57	.03
Happy	30	59	.51**	45	44	.02	48	41	.14
Active	51	95	.45**	73	74	.02	73	73	.00
Baby Plays	83	170	.50**	129	124	.03	133	119	.09
Toy	48	82	.28	66	64	.01	76	52	.21
Hand	14	27	.33	21	20	.01	21	20	.01
Other Object	22	57	.47**	41	38	.04	34	46	.18
Total Cases	30	30		35	25		33	27	

One asterisk (*) indicates $p < 0.01$, two asterisks (**) indicate $p < 0.001$.

tion sheet, the observer took a five-minute break during which she clarified, if necessary, the data recorded on the completed sheet, and also wrote descriptive notes concerning the context of the behavior that had just occurred. At the end of this five-minute break, another sheet of 40 observations was begun.

On the first day, observations were made from 9:30 a.m. until noon, and on the second day, from 1:30 p.m. until 4:00 p.m. Thus, 10 sheets, or 400 observations are available for each day, resulting in a total of 800 observations per case for the two days. This is a key number to be kept in mind because it forms the basis upon which the statistical analysis of the data is carried out. . . . [There is a detailed discussion in the original paper at this point of the dependent variables selected for study: twelve variables for infant behavior and fifteen for caretaker behavior. These appear in Tables 2 and 3. The authors also report on reliability; in only two instances was reliability poor: 49 percent agreement on "positions" and 61 percent on "affections." (Ed.)]

RESULTS

Total Observations

The results of the analyses of the main effects of the independent variables over the total 800 observations in each case are given in Tables 2 and 3. A general inspection of the tables will quickly indicate that culture is by far the most important variable in accounting for the differences in infant and caretaker behavior. Before turning to a detailed examination of the results by culture, however, let us dispose of the findings for the other two independent variables.

As can be seen in Tables 2 and 3, there are no findings by sex of infant for the behavior of either the infant or the caretaker. Equally, an examination of the intra-Japanese and intra-American analyses reveals no significant findings by sex of infant.

Father's occupation does not produce any findings for infant behavior, but it does produce an interesting pattern of findings for caretaker behavior. As can be seen in Table 3, mothers in small independent business families

TABLE 3

Adjusted Mean Frequencies, in Total Observations, of Caretaker Behavior: By Culture, Father's Occupation, and Sex of Infant

Categories of Caretaker Behavior	Adjusted Mean Frequencies								
	Culture			Father's Occupation			Sex of Infant		
	Japa-nese	Ameri-can	Corre-lation	Sala-ried	Inde-pendent	Corre-lation	Male	Female	Corre-lation
Caretaker Present	541	421	.37*	437	543	.33	471	494	.08
Feeds	74	71	.03	71	74	.04	78	65	.13
Diapers	23	17	.24	19	21	.08	20	20	.02
Dresses	12	13	.03	12	14	.11	13	12	.05
Positions	8	19	.49**	13	14	.02	15	12	.17
Pats or Touches	34	47	.23	38	43	.08	41	39	.04
Other Care	17	23	.15	21	19	.05	19	22	.10
Plays with	39	24	.25	29	35	.10	34	28	.10
Affections	7	9	.09	7	10	.17	9	7	.20
Looks at	242	299	.27	247	302	.26	278	260	.09
Talks to	101	123	.21	101	127	.24	116	107	.09
Chats	79	120	.42**	94	108	.25	102	96	.06
Lulls	22	3	.44**	8	20	.28	14	11	.09
In Arms	197	139	.27	133	217	.36*	163	175	.06
Rocks	46	20	.35*	22	47	.34	39	25	.19
Total Cases	30	30		35	25		33	27	

One asterisk (*) indicates $p < 0.01$, two asterisks (**) indicate $p < 0.001$.

are present more, and lull, carry, and rock their infants more than mothers in salaried families. When, however, we look at the separate intra-cultural analyses, there are no significant findings by father's occupation in the American data. In the Japanese data, on the other hand, all of the findings in Table 3 are significant in the same manner, and in addition there are two further findings in the same direction on "infant awake" and caretaker "talks to" baby. Thus, the pattern of findings in the intra-Japanese analysis is that in the small independent business family the baby is awake more, and the caretaker is present more and doing more talking to, lulling, carrying, and rocking of the baby than is the case in the salaried family. It seems evident, therefore, that as a minor theme, occupational style of life does make a difference in Japanese culture, but not—at least in our data—in American culture.

Let us look now at the results of the analyses by culture in more detail. We will consider the areas of similarity in behavior before turning to the areas of difference.

As can be seen in Table 2, the types of infant behavior in which there are no differences between the two cultures are those clearly concerned with biological needs. Thus, there are no significant differences in the amount of time awake, sucking on breast or bottle, or intake of all food. Technically, there also is no difference in the amount of total vocalization, but the correlation is .25, which is just short of being significant.

For the caretakers in the two cultures, most of the areas of similarity indicated in Table 3 are concerned with basic functions involved in caring for the infant's biological needs for nutrition, elimination, and physical comfort. Thus, there are no significant differences in "feeds," "diapers," "dresses," "pats or touches," and "other care." Also, there is no difference in the overall amount of talking to the infant, but the manner in which this talking is done is clearly different. Affectionate behavior toward the infant may or may not be a requirement of basic caretaking, depending on one's point of view, but, in any event, there is no difference in such behavior between the two cultures. Finally, playing with the baby, which is not a requirement of basic caretaking, shows no difference in a technical sense, but the finding has a correlation of .25, on the borderline of signficance.

To generalize, the areas of similarity in both cultures point to the expression of biological needs by all of the infants, and the necessity for all of the mothers to care for these needs. Beyond this, however, the differences lie in the styles in which infants and mothers behave in the two cultures.

The American baby appears to be more physically active and happily vocal, and more involved in the exploration of his body and his environment than is the Japanese baby, who, in contrast, seems more subdued in all these respects. These differences can be seen in Table 2, which shows the American infant as more active, more happily vocal (and quite possibly more totally vocal, as indicated earlier), more exploring of his body by greater sucking on his fingers (or by putting other parts of his body and objects into his mouth), and more exploring of his environment in playing with toys, hands, and other objects. The Japanese infant, on the other hand, is only greater in unhappy vocalization. . . .

The differences in styles of caretaking in the two cultures appear to be equally pronounced. The American mother seems to have a more lively and stimulating approach to her baby, as indicated in Table 3, which shows the American caretaker as positioning the infant's body more, and looking at and chatting to the infant more. The Japanese mother, in contrast, is present more with the baby, in general, and seems to have a more soothing and quieting approach, as indicated by greater lulling, and by more carrying in arms, and rocking.

It may also be that the Japanese mother plays with her baby more, but of even greater interest is the very different pattern of intercorrelations for this variable in the two cultures. The Japanese mother's playing with baby is negatively correlated with "hand" (−.39), and "other object" (−.36), and positively correlated with "caretaker present" (.48), "affections" (.63), "looks at" (.53), "talks to" (.77), "chats" (.65), "lulls" (.66), "in arms" (.76),

and "rocks" (.61). At the least, this pattern means that those Japanese mothers who play more with their babies also do more soothing of their babies. In contrast, the American mother's playing with baby is correlated with "positions" (.36), "pats or touches" (.57), "talks to" (.47), and "chats" (.47). There is no suggestion in the American pattern that a mother who plays more with her baby is also likely to do more soothing.

The key link between the infant and mother in the American culture seems to us to show up in the pattern of correlations with infant's "happy vocal." For the American infant "happy vocal" is correlated negatively with "finger or pacifier" (−.41), and is positively correlated with "total vocal" (.92), "active" (.80), "baby plays" (.55), "toy" (.48), "hand" (.39), "caretaker present" (.48), "affections" (.37), "looks at" (.39), "talks to" (.39), "chats" (.39), and "rocks" (.38). We feel that the link between baby's happy vocalizations and caretaker's chatting with baby is especially important, as it indicates a major type of communication between the American infant and his mother that is not found in the Japanese data. For the Japanese infant, "happy vocal" is correlated only with the following: negatively with "rocks" (−.36), and positively with "active" (.43) and "other care" (.48).

In summary, then, of the analyses by culture of the total observations, the expression of the infant's biological needs, and the mother's basic caretaking of these needs, are the same in both cultures; but beyond this, the styles of the infant's behavior and the mother's care are different. The Japanese baby seems passive, and he lies quietly with occasional unhappy vocalizations, while his mother, in her care, does more lulling, carrying, and rocking of her baby. She seems to try to soothe and quiet the child, and to communicate with him physically rather than verbally. On the other hand, the American infant is more active, happily vocal, and exploring of his environment, and his mother in her care does more looking at and chatting to her baby. She seems to stimulate the baby to activity and to vocal response. It is as if the American mother wanted to have a vocal, active baby, and the Japanese mother wanted to have a quiet, contented baby. In terms of the styles of caretaking of the mothers in the two cultures, they seem to get what they apparently want. That these two patterns do, indeed, discriminate between the cultures is indicated by the significant . . . correlations for infant behavior (.80) and for caretaker behavior (.79). . . .

[At this point in the original paper the investigators analyze their data in terms of what infant and caretaker are each doing during waking and sleeping states with caretaker present or absent. Results showed interesting cultural differences in caretaking: The Japanese mother, for example, chats with her infant to soothe him when he is fussy, whereas the American mother vocalizes also to stimulate the baby. (Eds.)]

DISCUSSION

We feel that the most parsimonious explanation of our findings is that a great deal of cultural learning has taken place by three-to-four months of age, and that our babies have learned by this time to be Japanese and American babies in relation to the expectations of their mothers concerning their behavior. Nevertheless, we are aware that some of our findings might be thought of as due to group genetic differences, or to group differences in rates of physiological development. These questions cannot be answered with finality within the limits of our sample, but we did what checking we could on biological dimensions in our data that might be related to the infant's physical activity and total vocalization, as these are two central areas of difference between the cultures. A thorough check of the data (by Spearman's rank-order correlation) for the variables of "active" and "total vocal," both in terms of all 60 cases and of the 30 cases in each culture considered separately, did not reveal any significant differences in the relation of either variable to the independent variables of birth weight of infant, age in days of infant at time of observation, age of mother at time of birth of infant, or type of feeding of infant (in terms of breast, bottle, or mixed feeding).

There is considerable experimental and observational evidence, on the other hand, that

supports our conclusion that infants have learned by three-to-four months of age to respond in culturally appropriate ways. For example, Weisberg has shown experimentally that the vocalizing rate of three-month-old American infants can be increased (operantly conditioned) by the social consequences provided by the experimenter (briefly touching the infant's chin, smiling, and talking to him), but not by nonsocial consequences (the ringing of a door chime), nor by the mere presence of an inactive adult. This experimental result closely approximates the results obtained in the comparison of the observed behavior of American and Japanese caretakers in our study.

Our results on activity, playing, and vocalizing are also reflected in a study by Rubenstein of maternal attentiveness and exploratory behavior in American infants. In her study, maternal attentiveness (as defined by the number of times the mother was observed to look at, touch, hold, or talk to her baby) was time-sampled in the homes of 44 five-month-old infants who were later examined at six months for exploratory behavior. Three groups of babies were distinguished at five months of age as receiving high, low, or medium attentiveness. At six months of age, the high-attentiveness group significantly exceeded the low-attentiveness group in looking at, manipulating, and vocalizing to a novel stimulus presented alone, and the high-attentiveness group exceeded both other groups in looking at and manipulating novel stimuli in preference to familiar ones. Rubenstein interprets her data as suggesting that maternal attentiveness facilitates exploratory behavior in the infant. We would agree on the basis of our results, if we conceive of attentiveness mainly in terms of stimulating the infant to activity, play, and vocalization, as appears to be the pattern for the American mothers in contrast to the Japanese mothers.

The observational study by Moss in the homes of 30 firstborn American infants equally divided by sex, at one and three months of age, is, in its latter phase, almost exactly the same as ours. Using a series of dependent variables for infant and caretaker behaviors, he made observations by a time-sampling procedure, using a unit of one minute in which behavior could occur or not occur, over eight hours, resulting in a total of 480 observations per case. Many of the variables used by Moss were defined in almost exactly the same way as ours, and by converting his data and our American data to percentages of total observations, a direct comparison is possible. When this is done, either for the total samples, or separately by sex, the results of the comparisons (by means of a Mann-Whitney U test) show no significant differences for the infant behaviors of "awake," "finger or pacifier," "active," or "unhappy vocal." The data for the infants in the Moss study on his variable of "vocalizes" (which includes our variable of "happy vocal" plus "neutral" vocalizations such as grunts) significantly exceed those for our variable of "happy vocal." Equally, for caretaker behaviors, there are no differences in the two studies on the variables of "feeds," "looks at," "talks to," "in arms," and "rocks." It is therefore fairly obvious that much the same results would be achieved in a comparison of infant or caretaker behaviors in America and Japan whether we used our American data or used the data from the Moss study.

Finally, we wish to draw attention to the detailed study by Arai, Ishikawa, and Toshima of the development of Japanese children from one month to 36 months of age, as measured by the Gesell norms established on American children. The Japanese investigators used a sample of 776 children in the Tōhoku area (the northern part of the main island of Japan near the city of Sendai), equally divided across the age range of one to 36 months. In the areas of motor development and language development, which are closest to the variables in our study of physical activity and total vocalization, the findings of the Japanese study were that the Japanese infants matched the American norms in both respects in the age period from 4 to 16 weeks, but after that there was a steady decline from the norms in the Japanese scores for both motor and language development from 4 months to 36 months of age. In general across the entire age range, Arai, Ishikawa, and Toshima say: "For children having a developmental quotient between 90–119, . . . motor behavior is 71.5 percent of the norms, social behavior is 70.4 percent, and language aptitude (the weakest behavior) is 66.0 percent."

It seems likely from the results of this study in the Tōhoku area of Japan that there are no differences in motor or verbal behavior of Japanese and American infants during the first several months of life. If this is so, it strongly supports our contention that these are learned more than genetic or maturational differences.

CONCLUSION

In this report of work with Japanese and American middle-class mothers and their first-born, three-to-four-month-old infants, our analysis quickly revealed that of the three independent variables considered, culture is by far the most important source of difference in the behavior of these infants and caretakers. This is followed by father's occupation, which is important in the Japanese situation but not in the American. Sex of infant, at least at three-to-four months of age, is of little relevance.

Reviewing our findings in reverse order of importance, there is a hint, stemming from the intra-cultural analyses, that American mothers may give somewhat more attention, particularly of an affectionate sort, to their boy babies, but this is a tenuous finding in the American data, and there are no findings by sex of infant in the Japanese data.

The analysis by father's occupation produced more results, but all of these, upon further examination, proved to be important only for the Japanese data. In the Japanese independent business families the infant is awake more, and the caretaker is present more, and talks to, lulls, carries, and rocks the infant more than in the salaried families. In contrast, the caretaker in the salaried families is only greater in looking at the infant when compared with the caretaker in the independent business families.

In the single matter of looking at her infant more frequently, the mother in the salaried Japanese family seems more like the American mother, who, in the general cross-cultural analysis, looks at her infant more often. But the American mother also chats with her infant frequently, whereas the Japanese salaried mother is more silent than the Japanese independent business mother. If, as is reasonable, we consider the salaried mother in Japan to be more "modern," then, in her move toward modernity, she seems to have subtracted from traditional ways of caretaking rather than to have added anything new. If anything, the independent business mother in Japan is closer to the American mother in the extent of her direct involvement with her infant. Thus, with regard to the relation of child care to social change, there would not seem to be any simple connection between a move toward modernity for the family in general and a shift toward Western patterns of child care.

The preceding findings, although of interest, become pale in the light of the strong findings of cultural differences. American infants are more happily vocal, more active, and more exploratory of their bodies and their physical environment, than are Japanese infants. Directly related to these findings, the American mother is in greater vocal interaction with her infant, and stimulates him to greater physical activity and exploration. The Japanese mother, in contrast, is in greater bodily contact with her infant, and soothes him toward physical quiescence and passivity with regard to his environment. Moreover, these patterns of behavior, so early learned by the infant, are in line with the differing expectations for later behavior in the two cultures as the child grows to be an adult.

For now, we believe we have arrived at distinctive patterns of learned behavior for infants in Japan and America. Analysis of our data for the first 20 of the same cases in each culture at two-and-a-half and six years of age will establish whether these patterns persist and jell in the behavior of the children we are studying. Our prediction is that this will happen, because of the strong external pressures for conformity and the strong internal pressures toward being accepted favorably by one's fellows, in any culture.

If these distinctive patterns of behavior are well on the way to being learned by three-to-four months of age, and if they continue over the life span of the person, then there are very likely to be important areas of difference in emotional response in people in one culture when compared with those in another. Such differences are not easily subject to conscious control and, largely out of awareness, they accent and color human behavior. These differences add a zest to life and interpersonal encounters, but they can also add to bewilderment and antagonism when people try to communicate across the emotional barriers of cultures.

We hope that our analysis helps to illuminate the reasons for some of these difficulties in cross-cultural communication despite the seeming increase in similarity between countries in the modern world. One may wish, on moral and practical grounds, for greater real understanding by people of each other across cultures, but it is a moot point whether the world would be a better place in which to live if such cultural differences were to be obliterated.

REFERENCES

Arai, S., Ishikawa, J., and Toshima, K. "Développement Psychomoteur des Enfants Japonais." *La Revue de Neuropsychiatrie Infantile et d'Hygiène Mentale de l'Enfance* (1958) 6:262–269.

Caudill, William. *Effects of Social and Cultural Systems in Reactions to Stress;* New York, Social Science Research Council, Pamphlet 14, 1958.

Caudill, William, and Plath, David W. "Who Sleeps by Whom? Parent-Child Involvement in Urban Japanese Families," *Psychiatry* (1966) 29:344–366.

Moss, Howard A. "Sex, Age, and State as Determinants of Mother-Infant Interaction," *Merrill-Palmer Quart.* (1967) 13:19–36.

Rheingold, Harriet L. "The Measurement of Maternal Care," *Child Development* (1960) 31: 565–575.

Rubenstein, Judith. "Maternal Attentiveness and Subsequent Exploratory Behavior in the Infant," *Child Development* (1967) 38:1089–1100.

Weisberg, Paul. "Social and Non-Social Conditioning of Infant Vocalizations," in Yvonne Brackbill and George G. Thompson (Eds.), *Behavior in Infancy and Early Childhood;* Free Press, 1967.

THE DRAW-A-MAN TEST AND RAVEN PROGRESSIVE MATRICES PERFORMANCE OF GUATEMALAN MAYA AND LADINO CHILDREN

DALE L. JOHNSON   CARMEN A. JOHNSON   DOUGLASS PRICE-WILLIAMS

A comparative psychology of mental development requires the careful examination of children of various ages, and of adults, from a variety of different cultures. We are in the position at the present time of knowing something about intelligence testing and the influence of certain environmental factors. But we are still unable to explain why persons who identify with a particular culture differ in their testing performance from persons who identify with a different culture.

To be able to explain such cultural variations we require two general kinds of information about how individuals in various cultures respond to our standardized tests. First, we must document the full range of variation in human intellectual development under all possible cultural conditions. Second, we must examine the way the testing situation is understood by the subjects themselves, in order to evaluate the significance of the testing performance for the behavior of the individual.

The crucial nature of the latter requirement was recognized as early as 1913 by Rouma working with the Quechua and Aymara Indians of South America (cited by Goodenough and Harris, 1950). He reported, for example, that his instructions involving the term 'up' were misconstrued by his subjects to mean toward the sky, rather than toward the top of the page. In the present study assumptions concerning such matters as privacy, task orientation, and relation to the investigator had to be carefully

Reprinted with abridgment by permission of the authors and *Revista Interamericana de Psicologia* from *Revista Interamericana de Psicologia*, 1967, **1**, 143–56.

reexamined in order to adequately understand the obtained results.

Research Objectives

The purposes of the present research were threefold: 1) to assess the intellectual status of two ethnic groups among Guatemalan children, utilizing standard measuring instruments, thus allowing both comparison with results from other cultures and comparison with results from other tests with the same Guatemalan children; 2) to advance a comparative psychology of mental development, including exploration of universal or constant factors, and locally variable factors, along the lines visualized by Werner (1948), Dennis (1957), and others; 3) to explore testing methods in non-Western cultures.

Subjects

The subjects of the present study were children enrolled in a public school located in the department of Totonicapan in the Central Highlands of Guatemala. The school was situated in a town of approximately 14,000 inhabitants and was accessible by bus from two large cities.

The town served as a cabecera, or local government center, in a densely populated area. It boasted a beautiful and important church to which delegations of Indians from the surrounding villages came on holy days. There was available in the town a potable water service, electricity, and radio-telegraph communication with the national and international world.

In spite of these advantages, the town was predominantly rural. With the exception of a few Ladino business families, the citizens of the town were commuting farmers, agricultural workers, or part-time farmers who supplemented their incomes with weaving, carpentering, butchering and other skills. Modern health services consisted of monthly or bi-monthly visits by one medical doctor. Sewer service was unavailable.

The significance of the distinction between the Indian and Ladino ethnic groups was borne out in all measures of social and economic variables. Indians had lower incomes, were less well-educated, less well-fed, and received little or no medical care (Whetten, 1961). The ethnic affiliations of the public school students, as indicated by their teachers, followed the definition based on style of life as developed by Adams (1957).

Ladinos appeared with greater frequency in our subject group than in the general population. In the department of Totonicapan 3.2 per cent of the inhabitants were reported as Ladino in the 1950 census. In our school population approximately 35 per cent of the students were identified by their teachers as Ladino. We surmise that our 40 Ladino boys were from lower income families who were pressed by economic circumstances to seek an education at an inferior local school. Ladino girls, by contrast, were apt to be kept near home to go to school regardless of the family resources, since education for them was clearly frosting on the cake and not a serious undertaking. In the case of the 112 Indian boys, it is likely that we encountered some of the most capable youngsters, since Indians have scant opportunities to send their children to a better school in the city. The 52 Indian girls, like their 52 Ladino counterparts, apparently were not seriously prepared for any life outside of the traditional Indian way.

The department of Totonicapan reported 90 percent illiteracy in rural areas in 1950. In the research town this rate was undoubtedly lower because of the presence of the school. Nevertheless, the illiteracy rate, high daily absenteeism, and the presence of a Catholic school in the town, probably functioned to bias our sample toward the medium income Indian

group and the lower income Ladino children.

Our subjects ranged in age from six to sixteen years and constituted about three-fourths of the total student load in the six grades of public school. In all, 152 boys and 104 girls were tested.

PROCEDURE

Instruments selected for this portion of the research were the Draw-A-Man Test (DAMT), the Raven Progressive Matrices (RPM), and teacher ratings of pupil intelligence. The DAMT and RPM were chosen because of the largely non-verbal nature of the required responses. The RPM test appeared, superficially at least, to resemble the complex designs of the native fabrics of the research town. Since the children of weaving families helped with the work from a very young age, we were interested in exploring the nature of the cognitive problems presented by such a situation through a standard test which seemed to present a similar task.

The DAMT had the advantage of a large cross-cultural literature against which to compare results. Since two excellent reviews are readily available (Goodenough and Harris, 1950; Harris, 1963) we shall direct attention here to some of the trends which have emerged from cross-cultural applications of this test.

Research previous to 1940 generally reported mean IQs below 100 for American Indians, Mexican-Americans and other North American minority groups. However, during and after the 1940s research with Indian populations began quite consistently to report IQs above 100. Other minority groups continued to score below the usual IQ level.

The relatively high American Indian scores have been explained on the basis of a cultural emphasis placed on the graphic arts by Indians (Russell, 1943; Dennis, 1942). Conversely, the low scores obtained by children in the Near East have been partially explained as a function of the sanctions against human figure drawing by the Moslem religion (Dennis, 1957). A summary of selected cross-cultural DAMT studies is presented in Table 1. . . .

TABLE I

Results of Selected DAMT Studies from 1926 to 1962

Investigator	Year	Ethnic Group	Number of Subjects	Mean IQ
Goodenough	1926	Hoopa	79	85.6
		Anglo-Amer.	396	100 to 107
Manuel and Hughes	1932	Mexican-Amer.	440	90 to 94
Telford	1932	Sioux	225	88.6
		Chippewa		
Eels	1933	Eskimo	364	89.6
		Aleut	105	93.6
		Indian	58	91.6
Dennis	1942	Hopi	152	108.3
Russell	1943	Zuni	41	105.7
Havighurst	1946	Hopi (Oraibi)	46	110.5
Gunther		Hopi (1st Mesa)	32	117.1
Pratt		Zuni	42	111.7
		Zia	32	109.6
		Navajo	47	109.7
		Papago (I)	49	108.5
		Papago (II)	25	103.6
		Sioux (Pine Ridge)	23	102.0
		Sioux (Kyle)	30	113.6
Carney and		Midwest (Anglo)	66	101.2
Trowbridge	1962	Fox	36	114.9

RESULTS

As may be seen by referring to Table 2, the DAMT responses, considered as a whole, obtained a mean IQ of 85.08. Scores ranged from 56 to 146. Sex differences were striking. Boys obtained a mean IQ of 89.94, but the girls' scores reached a mean of only 77.98. Differences between boys and girls mean IQs reached significance at the .001 level.

Ethnic differences considered for the group as a whole were not significant. However, when the groups were separated by sex, it can be seen in Table 2 that this was largely due to the more or less equal performances of Indian and Ladino boys. Ethnic differences were especially severe for the girls. Ladino girls obtained a mean IQ of 82.00 as against a mean IQ of only 73.96 for Indian girls.

Many recent studies of intelligence involving "culturally disadvantaged" children have noted lower IQs for older children. The possibility that this might be true of the population in the present study was checked. The DAMT results analyzed by age appear in Table 3. In order to make a clear distinction between younger and older children a cut-off point was arbitrarily set at age ten. Younger children were those between six and ten years of age inclusive. Older children were designated as those eleven years of age and older. Age differences significant at the five percent level were revealed by this procedure. Older Indian boys scored lower on the DAMT than younger Indian boys. The same age difference was evident for older and younger Ladino boys and older and younger Ladino girls. Indian girls, however, scored uniformly low in both older and younger age groups.

Correlations of the teacher ratings with the DAMT scores presented a varied picture (see Table 4). Correlations of .71, .04, and .50 were obtained with Third, Fifth, and Sixth grade teacher ratings respectively. The mean of the three correlations was .41. This is approximately the expected relationship between this type of test and teacher ratings of pupil intelligence.

Considering now the RPM responses as a group, we can observe that they indicate uniformly low intellectual capacity. The median

TABLE 2

Sex and Ethnic Group Differences in Draw-A-Man Test IQ's

	N	Mean	S.D.	t	p
All Subjects	256	85.08	13.88		
Total Boys	152	89.94	12.97	9.13	<.001
Total Girls	104	77.98	11.95		
Total Indian	164	85.12	14.40	Not Significant	
Total Ladino	92	85.02	12.87		
Boys					
Indian	112	90.29	12.81	Not Significant	
Ladino	40	88.95	13.37		
Girls					
Indian	52	73.96	10.85	3.61	<.001
Ladino	52	82.00	11.59		
Indian					
Boys	112	90.25	12.81	7.89	<.001
Girls	52	73.96	10.85		
Ladino					
Boys	40	88.95	13.37	2.63	<.01
Girls	52	82.00	11.59		

TABLE 3

Draw-A-Man Test IQ's by Age, Sex and Ethnic Group

	Boys				Girls			
	N	Mean	N	Mean	N	Mean	N	Mean
Age	Indian		Ladino		Indian		Ladino	
6	1	146.0		....	1	107.0		....
7	7	92.9	3	97.7		....	3	88.0
8	12	94.3	4	85.5	5	73.4	12	85.3
9	22	92.7	8	99.0	7	74.4	11	84.6
10	16	88.3	2	87.0	17	78.4	7	73.1
11	17	88.7	6	86.7	8	71.5	7	80.1
12	9	87.0	7	83.7	10	67.1	3	85.7
13	13	90.7	3	91.3	4	68.8	4	71.0
14	4	78.5	5	85.2		....	2	62.0
15–16	9	86.9	2	77.0		....	1	76.0

	Ages					
	6–10		11–16			
	N	Mean	N	Mean	t-test	p
Boys						
Indian	58	92.72	52	87.79	2.03	<.05
Ladino	17	94.17	23	85.22	2.71	<.05
Girls					Not Significant	
Indian	30	77.60	22	69.00		<
Ladino	37	84.57	17	76.59	2.36	<.05

TABLE 4

Intercorrelations of Draw-A-Man Test, Raven's Progressive Matrices and Teacher Ratings

Draw-A-Man Test Scores vs. Raven Progressive Matrices Raw Score	N = 34	r = .59
Draw-A-Man Test IQ vs. Teacher Ratings		
Third Grade	N = 17	r = .71
Fifth Grade	N = 20	r = .04
Sixth Grade	N = 34	r = .50
Raven Progressive Matrices Percentile vs. Teacher Ratings (Sixth Grade)	N = 31	r = .49
Raven Progressive Matrices Raw Score vs. Teacher Ratings (Sixth Grade)	N = 31	r = .53

percentile achieved by the Guatemalan children was the 5th, with a range of from below the fifth percentile to the thirtieth percentile according to Raven's British norms (1956). An item analysis was prepared using the boys' results in an attempt to explain these unusually low scores. . . .

. . . Guatemalan responses to all four sets exhibit a similar pattern. The first problem of each set elicited a high proportion of correct responses, indicating that the boys were relating appropriately to the materials and the investigator. The attitude of the children was one of interest and delighted cooperation throughout. Following their initial success, however, the proportion of correct responses fell precipitously until only two or three sixth grade boys could respond correctly to the final problems of sets B, C, and D.

Although some recovery in number to correct responses was indicated after the low point of each set, it is evident that, with a few exceptions, the group as a whole was not able to understand the logic of the matrices test design.

DISCUSSION

Intellectual Status

The results indicated a remarkably low intellectual performance for the subject group as a whole. On the DAMT the mean IQ was 85.08 compared with a mean of 102 to 117 for the North American Indian children. The RPM

scores which rated at only the 5th percentile were even lower than the DAMT scores.

An explanation of these low scores calls for an analysis of relevant factors in the subjects' developmental background. Three explanations offer themselves from the cross-cultural literature on intellectual functioning: a) it is likely that sub-standard conditions of nutrition and health function to depress the general intelligence level; b) it has been suggested for other cultures that the value placed upon graphic arts may affect performance on a test in which the single response is one of drawing a human figure; and c) the formal educational experience of the subjects may have prepared them for the testing experience in a manner which varied from that expected by North American investigators. Each of these explanations will be reviewed in turn.

a) Research evidence advanced by Pasamanick and Knobloch (1966) and Knobloch and Pasamanick (1966) has demonstrated a link between sociological, physiological, and psychological variables. On the very lowest socioeconomic levels, prenatal and maternal care is poor and nutrition is inadequate. This leads directly to high indices of prematurity and complications of pregnancy, and these in turn are associated with high proportions of infant brain-damage. One outcome of this sequence of events is lowered intelligence. Other results are cerebral palsy, epilepsy, and learning disorders.

In 1950 an INCAP survey in the department of Totonicapan reported that 84 percent of all children examined had intestinal parasites. Endemic goiter was present in 46 percent of all cases examined. Probably the most important finding of the nutritional survey in regard to intellectual functioning was the evidence of a widespread deficiency of Vitamin A. Clinical observations of this deficient condition have repeatedly pointed out sluggish mental activity (Whetten, 1961). Such information indicates that explanation (a) deserves serious consideration in explaining the unusually low test results.

One difficulty in accepting the Pasamanick-Knobloch line of explanation, as sufficient in itself, however, arises from the DAMT literature on North American Indian children. These North American youngsters have grown up under comparably poor economic, nutritional, and medical conditions, but obtain higher DAMT IQs than our Guatemalan subjects. One other discrepancy is the significant sex difference in our Guatemalan results. Prenatal nutritional deficiencies would be expected to affect both boys and girls with equal seriousness, yet the girls in our sample scored significantly lower than the boys.

An alternative explanation in view of this cross-cultural evidence is, (b) that the positive evaluation placed on graphic arts by North American Indians was reflected in a general drawing ability on this particular task, which would be absent or mitigated in the case of our Guatemalan subjects. Unfortunately, the DAMT literature does not provide estimates of intellectual functioning utilizing variously valued tasks in order to assess the weight which should be accorded this explanation.

However, in the case of our Guatemalan subjects, we can say that the moderately high correlations between the DAMT, which depended upon drawing ability, and the RPM which did not, as well as the primitive correlation with the ratings by classroom teachers who were familiar with students' daily performance, suggest that in this case at least, the difficulty did not lie in a general cultural devaluation of artistic expression. At the very least we can state that this argument is inadequate to explain the present results.

We observed the weaving procedure in order to evaluate the similarity between the cognitive problems presented by the native task and those presented by our imported foreign task.

The intricately patterned fabrics of the research town are produced by the following method. The purchased yarn is tied or wrapped by one or more women in a series of knots which is repeated over and over until the end of the skein is reached. Different types of sequences of knots have individual names. Once the skein has been dipped in a purchased dye, dried and rolled into a ball, the ball receives the name of the knot sequence. Even very little children are taught to recognize and name on sight the type of knot sequence for each ball.

For the weaver the cognitive task is to memorize the names of individual balls in the order in which they occur in a band of the traditional pattern. Whereas a certain amount of innovation was evident in the use of materials, i.e. silk as well as cotton and wool thread, for the individual weaver the task is one of rote memorization. In a series of observations in different parts of the town, not a single incident of problem solving as required by the matrices appeared in the weaving sequence.

It thus appears that while the complex weaving designs seemed to be similar in construction to the Progressive Matrices designs, the complexity in the case of the weaving was located in the social organization, particularly in the intercorrelation of specialized skills which contributed to the fineness of the finished product. The matrices on the other hand required a single individual, working alone and without advice, to distinguish and utilize the logic of the unfamiliar matrix presented to him.

A third possible explanation (c) of the low test scores may be found in the contrast between the formal educational experience of the children and the task presented by our foreign tests. During the DAMT administration, attempts to trace from the backs of school books were fairly frequent, especially among the girls. These children were demonstrating the fact that they were never asked for an original solution to a problem. Ordinarily, classroom questions came supplied with ready-made answers. The children, especially the girls, expected to be told what the answer was, and then to memorize it. Children were not expected to take any initiative in the ongoing educational enterprise. Every question already had its answer, based on authority and tradition.

In the case of the Indian girls passive learning was so much the order of the day that a Ladino girl would occasionally burst into the testing room, take the pencil from the Indian girl's hand, and attempt to make her drawing or to answer questions for her. Indians were more passive learners than Ladinos, and Indian girls were the most passive of the four groups.

One final observation of the formal educational situation needs to be cited. It is that the primary grade classrooms were overwhelmed by sheer numbers of children. There were more than 100 children enrolled in the first grade alone, in a school where the total enrollment was but 400. Furthermore, attendance was most irregular. Passive learning, overcrowding and high absenteeism no doubt contributed to the inhibition of intellectual development.

Sex Differences

According to Harris (1963) North American girls usually obtain higher DAMT scores than boys. Our finding that Guatemalan boys scored significantly higher than girls suggests an important difference between North American and Guatemalan cultures. Girls in highland Guatemala live relatively sheltered lives; they are expected to defer to others, to be passive, and to avoid the appearance of intellectual ambitions. It is possible that where appropriate sex role behavior is narrowly defined, the kind of problems posed by the psychological tests and testing situation could be construed as more appropriate for boys than for girls, thus prejudicing the results in favor of the boys.

Age Differences

Our results showing older children to have lower DAMT IQs than younger children, were consistent with other studies of educationally disadvantaged children which indicate that IQs go down as children grow older if they do not live in an intellectually challenging environment (Wheeler, 1942). While it is possible that this is a valid interpretation of the present results, there are reasons for caution. The most troubling problem is that of sample representativeness. Many students drop out of school after a few years. We do not know whether the able or the inept students drop out more often. The second difficulty has to do with a peculiarity of the DAMT. Its value as a test of intellectual functioning declines during adolescence because normally there is very little improvement in drawings from age 13 and on (Harris, 1963). In fact, the adolescent's self-consciousness regarding such things as artistic productions often inhibits his drawing performance and lowers the scores obtained.

Cross-Cultural Testing

One objective of this research was to explore the suitability of various cognitive tasks for cross-cultural research. The wider range of functioning elicited by the DAMT as compared with the RPM suggested that the DAMT provided a superior measure of intellectual level. Although the RPM results correlated favorably with the teacher ratings, the range of scores elicited was extremely narrow since few of the children were able to make the required shift from simple to complex problem-solving. The teacher ratings provided a check for the results of the foreign tasks against the observations of students' daily performance. Ideally, however, an accurate survey of intellectual functioning should indicate the language abilities of the subject population as well as a realistic appraisal along the entire continuum of cognition which exists in the subject population.

REFERENCES

Adams, R. N. Cultural surveys of Panama, Nicaragua, Guatemala, El Salvador, Honduras. Washington: Pan American Sanitary Bureau, Regional Office of the World Health Organization, 1957.

Carney, R. E. & Trowbridge, Norma. "Intelligence test performance of Indian children as a function of type of test and age," *Perceptual and Motor Skills,* 1962, 14, 511–514.

Dennis, W. "The performance of Hopi children on the Goodenough Draw-A-Man Test," *Journal of Comparative Psychology,* 1942, 34, 341–348.

Dennis, W. "Performance of Near Eastern children on the Draw-A-Man Test," *Child Development,* 1957, 28, 427–430.

Eels, W. C. "Mental ability of the native races of Alaska," *Journal of Applied Psychology,* 1933, 17, 417–438.

Goodenough, Florence. "Racial differences in the intelligence of school children," *Journal of Experimental Psychology,* 1926, 9, 388–397.

Goodenough, Florence & Harris, H B. "Studies in the psychology of children's drawings: II, 1928–1949," *Psychological Bulletin,* 1950, 47, 370–433.

Harris, D. B. "A note on some ability correlates of the Raven Progressive Matrices (1947) in the kindergarten," *Journal of Educational Psychology,* 1959, 50, 228–229.

Harris, D. B. *Children's Drawings as Measures of Intellectual Maturity,* New York: Harcourt, Brace & World, 1963.

Havighurst, R. J., Gunther, Minna, & Pratt, Inez. "Environment and the Draw-A-Man Test: the performance of Indian children," *Journal of Abnormal and Social Psychology,* 1946, 41, 50–63.

Knobloch, Hilda & Pasamanick, B. "Prospective studies on the epidemiology of reproductive casuality: methods, findings, and implications," *Merrill-Palmer Quarterly,* 1966, 12, 27–44.

Manuel, H. T. & Hughes, Lois S. "The intelligence and drawing ability of young Mexican children," *Journal of Applied Psychology,* 1932, 16, 382–387.

Pasamanick, B. & Knobloch, Hilda. "Retrospective studies on the epidemiology of reproductive casuality: old and new," *Merrill-Palmer Quarterly,* 1966, 12, 7–26.

Raven, J. C. *Guide to the Standard Progressive Matrices,* London: H. K. Lewis & Co., 1956.

Russell, R. W. "The spontaneous and instructed drawings of Zuni children," *Journal of Comparative Psychology,* 1943, 35, 11–15.

Telford, C. W. "Test performance of full and mixed-blood North Dakota Indians," *Journal of Comparative Psychology,* 1932, 14, 123–145.

Werner, H. *Comparative Psychology of Mental Development,* N.Y.: Science Editions (1948), 1961.

Wheeler, L. R. "A comparative study of the intelligence of East Tennessee mountain children," *Journal of Educational Psychology,* 1942, 30, 321–334.

Whetten, N. L. Guatemala: *The Land and the People,* New Haven: Yale University Press, 1961.

TEMNE AND ESKIMO PERCEPTUAL SKILLS

JOHN W. BERRY

The nature of the relationship between perception and culture is merely part of the larger problem of psychological differences between groups of people who are living under varying geographic, economic, social and cultural conditions. Biesheuvel (1963) has noted that, "it is generally accepted that there are psychological differences between ethnic groups which are at different stages of development." However different ethnic groups do not necessarily follow the same developmental paths since their particular goals and requirements may be different. With Biesheuvel (1959), it is considered that, "through the medium of educational practices and other social pressures, a culture produces the kind of personalities that are adapted to its requirements." This paper, however, will not be concerned with "personality," nor with the study of "culture and personality"; it will, though, attempt to demonstrate a relationship between the cultural and ecological characteristics of a society and the perceptual skills developed by members of that society. The hypothesis guiding the study was that differences in visual perceptual skills would exist between societies with differing ecological and cultural characteristics and that these perceptual differences would not be random in kind or degree, but might be predicted from an analysis of the ecological requirements and cultural practices of each group. In order to test this hypothesis, two societies with contrasting cultural and ecological characteristics were administered a battery of perceptual tests, standard for both societies, and the resulting test differences were examined in the light of the specific hypotheses concerning the different ecological requirements and cultural practices of each society.

Reprinted with abridgment from the *International Journal of Psychology*, 1966, **1**, 207–229, by permission of the author and the International Union of Psychological Science and Dunod, Publisher, France.

CULTURE AND SAMPLE DESCRIPTION

The two societies chosen for study were the Temne of Sierra Leone and the Eskimo of Baffin Island. A reference group of Scots was also tested so that the cross-cultural data might be related, through the Scots, to the accumulated mass of Western psychological findings.

Culture Description of the Temne

The Temne inhabit an area of about 10,000 square miles in central and coastal Sierra Leone and number close to 500,000 individuals (McCulloch, 1950). Most live in small villages, but towns are growing, especially where wage employment is becoming available. Most Temne are rice farmers, but they also cultivate groundnuts and hot peppers for cash. There is only one crop each year; frequently too much rice is sold at market after harvest, and in the following September, the rural areas experience their "hungry season." Very few people hunt; the little meat available is usually caught in traps hidden in fences surrounding the upland rice farms. The Temne are polygynous and the wives do much of the routine farmwork while carrying the youngest child on their backs. Both male and female children are welcomed and treated kindly up to the age of weaning (2 to 2½ years). Thereafter, however, discipline is harsh, with frequent beatings. Women, as well as the children, are strictly controlled, and infractions of marital laws are heavily punished. The secret societies have been the main source of formal education among the Temne: the Poro Society for the boys and the Bundu Society for the girls. Traditional skills and roles are learned during the months in the bush, after which initiation takes place. Many Temne youths also attend dawn and evening

Arabic schools where they learn Koranic texts by rote and occasionally become fully literate. In the rural areas, the Christian Mission schools teach in both Temne and English. For the first two or three years, there is little difference between these mission schools and the Arabic ones; the main concern in both is learning religious texts and prayers, and becoming familiar with the rules of the classroom—sitting still, paying attention and responding to questions. In the urban areas, education is mainly in English and secondary school graduation may be attained.

Culture Description of the Eskimo

The Canadian Eskimo number only 12,000 persons and are spread across a 3,000 mile expanse of Arctic coast. Most live in family-sized hunting camps dotted along the coast from administrative and trading settlements, but like the Temne, some have begun to settle in towns where wage employment is available. Their land is harsh and generally barren of vegetation; an expanse of rocks, and snow or lichens, depending upon the season, covers most of the land area. Most Eskimo men are hunters; even many of those who have taken wage employment still hunt on the weekends using motorized toboggans to take them to fresh grounds. In the more traditional camps, seals are hunted from the ice in winter and from boats in summer, while on the land, caribou are hunted and white fox are trapped for trading. The Eskimo are now monogamous, but have practised both polygyny and polyandry in the past. Some marriages are still contracted by traditional agreement, but most are now formalized by the missionaries. Children are welcomed and are treated with great kindness and consideration; punishment is rarely seen and much freedom is allowed their offspring. Very little control is exercised over their women as well as their children. Traditionally education has been given in the family. The boys learn on the hunt through close contact with their fathers from the age of nine or ten on; girls are instructed in the home skills and crafts by their mothers. A syllabic script for writing has generally been available since the 1930's, and has been transmitted to the children by their parents. This script plays much the same role in Eskimo society as does the Arabic script among the Temne. Schools, teaching in English, in the isolated areas can provide little more than the basic skills, but a child who shows promise may be sent to a larger centre where secondary schooling is available. Since those people in the isolated areas rely upon hunting for their livelihood, all cannot come to live near a school. The government has recently provided hostels, each run by an Eskimo family, to house those children who are voluntarily sent in to the schools in the settlements. They are not compelled to stay, however, and frequently return to the camps for hunting, during which time traditional skills are maintained. . . .

ECOLOGICAL
AND CULTURAL DIFFERENCES

It is the usual concern in cross-cultural psychological research to construct "culture-free," "culture-fair," or "culture-reduced" tests in order to reduce or eliminate cultural bias. In the case of the present study, however, no attempt has been made to avoid the bias of the tests. Indeed, the opposite has been the case; cultural and ecological differences have been investigated, isolated and utilized in selecting and constructing tests for presentation to the various societies. By working with these differences, rather than attempting to eliminate them, it was considered that their effects upon perception might be observed and gauged. In the next section, a number of specific hypotheses will be presented concerning perceptual differences between the Temne and the Eskimo. In each case, the hypotheses will be derived from the following discussion of the ecological and cultural differences existing between the two societies.

Ecological Requirements

We have seen that the Temne and the Eskimo visual environments differ greatly. The Temne land is covered with bush and other vegetation providing a wealth of varied visual stimulation. Colour is also abundant; trees and grasses vary from dark to light green, and flowers, fruits and berries provide splashes of the brighter colours. On the other hand, the Eskimo environment is bleak at any time of the year; in winter the whiteness of the land merges with the frozen sea while in the few short weeks of summer, moss and lichen cover the rocks and sand giving the land a uniform grey-brown tone. A few flowers and heathers bloom in the summer, but these are scarce and short-lived. It is apparent then even from these short descriptions, that the Eskimo, when compared to the Temne, inhabit a world of uniform visual stimulation. We have also seen that the Temne and the Eskimo differ markedly in their economies; the Temne are farmers who work land near their villages and rarely have to leave the numerous paths through the bush. The Eskimo, on the other hand, are hunters who must travel widely on the sea and land, and far along the coasts in search of game and trap animals.

It is evident that the Eskimo must develop certain perceptual skills, merely to survive in their situation, which the Temne are not called upon to do. 1. He must first of all in order to hunt effectively develop the ability to isolate slight variation in visual stimulation from a relatively featureless array; he must learn to be aware of minute detail. 2. Secondly, in order to navigate effectively in this environment he must learn to organize these small details into a spatial awareness, an awareness of his present location in relation to objects around him. The fact that the Eskimo hunt effectively and range far over unknown territory suggests that he has been able to develop these two skills to some degree. But the fact that the land requires these skills is no guarantee that they will be developed automatically, solely in response to ecological requirements, for migration to less demanding territory or extinction are both logical alternatives to the development of these skills. It was considered that other factors had contributed to the emergence of these required skills; three of these were investigated to discover how they might have promoted the development of the perceptual skills required by the land.

Cultural Aids

LANGUAGE   It is reasonable to expect that the content of a person's language will reflect the type of experience he usually faces and the type of discrimination he finds it useful to make. To discover whether the Temne and the Eskimo possess systems of geometrical-spatial terms consistent with the requirements of their respective lands, analyses were made of these terms in both languages. One hundred English geometrical-spatial terms were arbitrarily chosen for translation, where possible, into Temne and Eskimo. The terms were translated in a single session by two literate native speakers of the language. . . .

[Analysis revealed] that the Temne find it necessary to make only about one third as many geometrical-spatial distinctions in their language as the Scots do and the Eskimo somewhat more than half. More important though for the present discussion, is that the Eskimo make, at least linguistically, 28 more distinctions of this type without borrowing from English. The seven Temne borrowings from English suggest that the Temne are beginning to need these concepts, while the lack of Eskimo borrowings suggests that the Eskimo find their own system adequate. From a less ethnocentric point of view, an attempt was made to discover any Temne geometrical-spatial terms not found in English; none were found. But Gagné (personal communication), a linguist working with the Canadian Department of Northern Affairs, has discovered that the Eskimo possess an intricate system of words, termed "localizers," which aid in the location of objects in space. These localizers form an integral part of the word; the use of them, and hence the distinction, is obligatory. These distinctions are not normally required of users of English, and so it is possible that the Eskimo possess a geometrical-spatial term system as complex as that of Western technical man. It is apparent, then, that the Eskimo, when compared to the Temne, have available a fairly complete system of words which aid in the dissection of, and communication about, the space around them. It is also apparent that the Eskimo will find it easier than the Temne to pass on more of these distinctions and concepts to their offspring.

ARTS AND CRAFTS   Practice of graphics, sculpture and the decorative arts provides considerable opportunity for the development of observational and spatial skills. A survey of the arts and crafts of the Temne and the Eskimo reveals another aspect of their cultures where they show marked differences. The Eskimo is world-renowned for his fine soapstone carving and, more recently, for his efforts in stencil and block printing. Both clothing and tools are intricately ornamented with embroidery or etchings, and most women are able to cut out skins and cloth for boots and parkas with a minimum of measurement. On the other hand, the Temne produce almost no graphics, sculpture or decoration. Clothing, when locally made, is relatively plain and simply designed, although their choice of imported fabrics tends to be colourful. Paintings and carvings are rare, and even religious objects, on which one might expect the highest creative development, are unimaginative and gross. Skill in making maps seems to be lacking among the Temne as well (Littlejohn, 1963), while the Eskimo have been frequently observed making and using them (Bagrow, 1948; Carpenter, 1955). It is apparent, even from these short notes, that the artistic, craft- and map-making skills of the Eskimo are much more highly developed than those of the Temne, and it is not difficult to conceive how practice of these skills could aid in the development of both the observational and spatial abilities required by the land.

SOCIALIZATION PRACTICES The third cultural aid which is considered is the system of socialization practices used by members of a particular society. Barry, Child and Bacon (1959) have investigated the relationship between subsistence economy and socialization practices. They suggested that, to best meet their economic needs, in societies with low food accumulation (hunting or fishing peoples), "adults should tend to be individualistic, assertive and venturesome," while in societies with high food accumulation (pastoral or agricultural peoples), "adults should tend to be conscientious, compliant and conservative." They predicted that the socialization practices of societies would emphasize appropriate training to ensure the development of these traits. By rating a number of societies on the degree of food accumulation and on six aspects of socialization, they were able to demonstrate a significant relationship between the type of subsistence economy of a society and the socialization practices in use. This division of societies into low and high food accumulators provides a useful approach to the study of Temne and Eskimo socialization practices. The Temne and Eskimo economies have already been examined; the Temne with a single crop of rice each year tend to be high food accumulators, while the Eskimo with a hunting and fishing economy tend to be low food accumulators. An examination of their respective socialization practices reveals that the Barry, Child and Bacon findings hold true for both groups.

Temne socialization practices have been examined by Dawson (1963). In general, "the baby is treated with much affection until weaned (2 to 2½ years), after which it is subjected to considerable severity in disciplinary measures, and toilet training is from this stage very strict." Conformity is usually demanded from the child; "a child is generally not allowed to assert individuality," and "witchcraft and swears are used against individuals who have deviated psychologically or socially from accepted forms of behaviour." Eskimo practices, on the other hand, generally avoid the use of punishment. Butt (1950) has summarized much of the material available on Eskimo child training: "Children are treated lovingly and every care and consideration is lavished on them . . . Children are scarcely ever subjected to blows or even to scolding or cross words, and they do practically as they wish, even to the extent of ordering about their parents and getting their own way in everything."

The evidence, then, indicates great differences between Temne and Eskimo methods of child rearing, especially with respect to the severity of discipline and pressures toward conformity. Witkin and his associates (1962) have shown that these opposing modes of socialization have definite consequences for perceptual ability of individuals living in Western culture. They administered a series of orientation and perceptual tests, and found large differences in individual ability. Those people who found it, "difficult to overcome the influence of the surrounding field, or to separate an item from its context," they termed "field-dependent"; those who could carry out these tasks with ease, they termed "field-independent." Several factors were considered to foster field-dependence, including severe disciplining and a stress upon conformity within the home. Field-independence on the other hand, was fostered by home encouragement to assume responsibilities, and by parental stimulation of the child's curiosity and interests. Field-independence was considered to be psychologically more differentiated, and hence they suggested that field-independent persons represented a higher level of perceptual development. Dawson (1963) was the first to apply Witkin's concepts in a cross-cultural setting. Noting that Africans had been found to have considerable difficulties with tests such as Kohs Blocks (Jahoda, 1956; McFie, 1961), Dawson considered that, in addition to a lack of experience with shapes and forms, most African difficulties might be perceptual in nature, and furthermore might be related to Witkin's concept of field-dependence. He suggested that: ". . . in the traditional African family group, although there will be differences between tribal groups, there is a very strong traditional requirement for the development of those characteristics which are field-dependent." To test this assumption, Dawson administered Kohs Blocks to over 500 relatively westernized subjects from a number of tribal groups in Sierra Leone, including some Temne who had taken up employment in an iron mine. Although all scores were well below Western norms, the inter-tribal differences were significantly related to socialization practices.

In the present study, it is considered that, if significant differences in perceptual abilities can be found between members of tribes whose socialization practices tend to foster field-dependence, but to different degrees, then the extreme differences in the practices existing between the Temne and the Eskimo should aid the development of perceptual skills to vastly different extents.

HYPOTHESES

On the basis of the examination of ecological requirements and cultural aids, two sets of specific hypotheses were made concerning Temne and Eskimo perceptual skills:

DISCRIMINATION SKILL   In a test for closure, despite equivalent acuity, the Eskimo will be more aware of small detail than the Temne, and hence less ready to form closure.

SPATIAL SKILL   In four standard tests of spatial ability (Kohs Blocks, Witkin Embedded Figures, Morrisby Shapes, and Raven Matrices): 1. The Eskimo will score significantly higher than the Temne for comparable degrees of westernization. 2. Furthermore, the Eskimo scores will more closely approximate the Scottish scores than the scores of the Temne samples of equivalent westernization. 3. As a result of contact with Western peoples and institutions, the Temne and Eskimo transitional samples will score higher than the respective traditional samples. 4. Within the six samples, these scores will be significantly related to the level of education. 5. Within each sample, those rating themselves as more severely disciplined will score lower than those less severely disciplined. . . .

RESULTS

[The author goes on to test the first hypothesis by presenting to each subject a series of forms (triangles, squares, and rectangles), each with a gap in either the right or left side. In successive exposures, the gap increased in size. After each exposure the subject was asked to draw what he had seen. The Eskimo couples were significantly more aware of small gaps than their Temne counterparts, thus confirming the prediction based on what is required of the Eskimo by their environment.

Tests of spatial ability (Kohs Blocks, Witkin Embedded Figures Test, Morrisby Shapes, Raven Matrices) were also administered. Eskimo scores exceeded Temne scores, and, in fact, closely approximated the Scottish scores. A consistent positive relationship was found between years of education and spatial test scores. (Eds.)]

DISCUSSION

[There were a] large number of significant intercorrelations among the four spatial tests, [which,] especially when they are used cross-culturally, is, in itself, a significant result. In general, they are highest for the Scottish samples, as might be expected, and lowest for the Temne samples. This general high level of intercorrelation suggests that, even in cultures as diverse as those of the Temne and the Eskimo, these tests, designed in Britain and America, are measuring some characteristic fairly consistently; a moderate degree of reliability may therefore be attributed to these tests as used in the present study. . . .

The most striking feature of [the results] is the great gulf between Temne and Eskimo performance, and the minimal difference between the Eskimo and the Scots (*cf.* hypotheses 1 and 2). The second most apparent feature is the fairly consistent difference in all three societies between the rural/traditional samples and the urban/transitional ones (represented by the thick solid and thin broken lines respectively; *cf.* hypotheses 3 and 4).

The age trends are similar for the Scottish and Eskimo samples; low scores in the youngest age groups increase to a maximum at approximately twenty-five years of age, and decrease in later years to scores comparable to those of the 10-15 year old subjects. The Temne samples, on the other hand, have consistently flatter graphs. This peculiarity is considered to reflect the lack of any need to develop these skills; the basic ability to produce a score on the tests apparently exists from the age of ten onwards, and there is little later development through lack of demand by the environment or the society for this particular skill.

In both Pt. Loko and Frobisher Bay, there is a noticeable inflation of scores over the normal pattern in the two age groups 10-15 and 16-20. This trend is particularly strong in the Kohs and Matrices scores for both samples, in EFT scores for the latter sample, and is the strongest in the Shapes scores for the youth of Frobisher Bay. This pattern is considered to be a result of the relatively stronger effects of westernization on the younger, when compared to the older, members of the transitional communities. They are the ones who have gone to the school, have learned the new language, and have directed themselves toward the new way of life.

CONCLUSIONS

Discrimination Skill

It is considered that a strong case has been made for the hypothesis that, despite equivalent acuity, the Eskimo will display a greater awareness of small detail than the Temne. It is apparent that the ecological necessity for detailed discriminations coupled with a long experience in their relatively barren visual environment, have made the Eskimo more aware of minute cues than the Temne.

Spatial Skill

A strong case has also been made for four of the hypotheses concerning the development of spatial skill. Hypotheses 1 and 2 are accepted without reservation; not only have the Eskimo exceeded the Temne performance, but they have come very close to matching the Scottish scores. Hypotheses 3 and 4, that the urban, more westernized samples would perform better, and that this performance would be related to the number of years of education, are also accepted without reservation; contact with Western culture, especially with Western education, produces significantly better spatial scores in both Temne and Eskimo societies. Hypothesis 5, concerning the effects of severity of discipline, tends to be confirmed, but the results are not strong. It is apparent that the self-rating scale suffered from poor discrimination at the extremes in both Mayola and Pond Inlet; no more definite conclusion may therefore be drawn. The analysis of sex differences suggests the conclusion that in societies where women assume a dependent role, they will have more field-dependent perceptual characteristics than the men, but in societies where women are allowed independence, sex differences will disappear. It is possible, of course, that in societies where men assume a dependent role, the usual sex differences might be reversed, but the samples examined in the present study do not allow this possibility to be tested. The age trends suggest that in societies where spatial skills are required, maximum ability is attained between 20 and 30 years of age, but where these skills are not needed, the minimum level of ability already possessed at an early age remains fairly constant and undeveloped throughout life. These trends furthermore demonstrate the relatively greater impact that Western life has on the younger members of transitional communities.

General Conclusions

In general, it may be concluded that ecological demands and cultural practices are significantly related to the development of perceptual skills; it has been shown that perceptual skills vary predictably as the demands of the land and the cultural characteristics vary. It has not been possible, though, to unravel the respective contributions of the ecological demands and the cultural aids, but it is apparent that the cultural characteristics developed by the respective societies *do not inhibit* the development of the skills required by their environments. In some sense, then, cultural and psychological developments are congruent; cultural characteristics allow people to develop and maintain those skills which they have to. We are not arguing for the environmental determination of all perceptual skills; the factors discussed are not considered to be either necessary or sufficient for the production of the observed differences. It is, however, considered that these cultural and ecological factors played a significant role in their determination. But whether the factors considered in this study are the only ones involved in producing perceptual differences, or indeed whether these perceptual differences are the only ones produced by the noted cultural and ecological differences are two questions which cannot be answered from the present data. Race (genetic factors) is frequently held to account

for psychological differences among peoples of the world. But in view of the significant differences between the traditional and transitional Temne and Eskimo samples (and, of course, the minimal differences between the Eskimo and the Scots) on the spatial tests, it is considered that a purely racial explanation is not acceptable. The vast differences between the Temne and the Eskimo, and the minimal differences between the Eskimo and the Scots, in those cultural characteristics held to be, at least partially, responsible for perceptual differences are directly in keeping with both the nature and the extent of the perceptual differences which were observed. In view of this vast Temne-Eskimo difference, it would seem advisable for psychologists engaged in cross-cultural research to distinguish carefully between individual non-Western cultures. It is not the case, as many have supposed, that members of all non-Western societies inevitably perform poorly on Western tests, for it is apparent that some skills may be developed to similar extents by very divergent societies.

The results of the present study support Biesheuvel's view (1952) that "culture-free" tests are unattainable; since peoples with differing cultures and ecologies tend to develop and maintain different sets of skills, then the concept of intelligence, or its equivalent, is bound to be defined somewhat differently in each society. It follows from this that the search for a "culture-free" test is futile insofar as it is hoped to find a *universally* valid test; although some tests might be used with fairness in a limited number of societies, this still leaves us with the problem of comparing the results between these various "test-fair" units.

REFERENCES

Bagrow, L. Eskimo maps. *Imago Mundi,* 1948, 5, 92–95.

Barry, H., Child, I., & Bacon, M. Relation of child training to subsistence economy. *Amer. Anthropologist,* 1959, 61, 51–63.

Biesheuvel, S. The occupational abilities of Africans. *Optima,* 1952, 2.

Biesheuvel, S. *Race, culture and personality.* Johannesburg: South African Institute of Race Relations, 1959.

Biesheuvel, S. The growth of abilities and character. *South African J. Sci.,* 1963, 59, 375–394.

Butt, A. The social organization of the eastern and central Eskimos. Unpublished doctoral dissertation, Institute of Social Anthropology, Oxford University, 1950.

Carpenter, E. S. Space concepts of the Aivilik Eskimo. *Explorations,* 1955, 5, 131–145.

Dawson, J. L. M. Psychological effects of social change in a West African community. Unpublished doctoral dissertation, Keble College, Oxford University, 1963.

Fyfe, C. *History of Sierra Leone.* London: Oxford Univer. Press, 1962.

Gagne, R. Personal communication, 1965.

Jahoda, G. Assessment of abstract behaviour in a non-Western culture. *J. abnorm. soc. Psychol.,* 1965, 53, 237–243.

Littlejohn, J. Temne space. *Anthropol. Quart.,* 1963, 36, 1–17.

McCulloch, M. *People of the Sierra Leone Protectorate.* London: Internat. African Institute, 1950.

McFie, J. The effect of education on African performance on a group of intellectual tests. *Brit. J. educ. Psychol.,* 1961, 31, 232–240.

Michael, D. A cross-cultural investigation of closure. *J. abnorm. soc. Psychol.,* 1953, 48, 225–230.

Postman, L., & Bruner, J. S. Hypothesis and the principle of closure: the effect of frequency and recency, *J. Psychol.,* 1952, 33, 113–125.

Wertheimer, M. Untersuchungen zur Lehre von der Gestalt. II *Psychol. Forsch.,* 1923, 4, 301–350.

Witkin, H. A., Dyk, R. B., Paterson, H. F., Goodenough, D. R., & Karp, S. A. *Psychological differentiation.* London: Wiley, 1962.

THE SOURCES OF STUDENT DISSENT

KENNETH KENISTON

The apparent upsurge of dissent among American college students is one of the more puzzling phenomena in recent American history. Less than a decade ago, commencement orators were decrying the "silence" of college students in the face of urgent national and international issues; but in the past two or three years, the same speakers have warned graduating classes across the country against the dangers of unreflective protest, irresponsible action and unselective dissent. Rarely in history has apparent apathy been replaced so rapidly by publicized activism, silence by strident dissent. . . .

TWO VARIETIES OF DISSENT

Dissent is by no means the dominant mood of American college students. Every responsible study or survey shows apathy and privatism far more dominant than dissent. On most of our twenty two hundred campuses, student protest, student alienation and student unrest are something that happens elsewhere, or that characterizes a mere handful of "kooks" on the local campus. However we define "dissent," overt dissent is relatively infrequent and tends to be concentrated largely at the more selective, "progressive," and "academic" colleges and universities in America. Thus, Peterson's study of student protests finds political demonstrations concentrated in the larger universities and institutions of higher academic calibre, and almost totally absent at teachers colleges, technical institutes and non-academic denominational colleges. And even at the colleges that gather to-

gether the greatest number of dissenters, the vast majority of students—generally well over 95%—remain interested onlookers or opponents rather than active dissenters. Thus, whatever we say about student dissenters is said about a very small minority of America's six million college students. At most colleges, dissent is not visible at all.

Partly because the vast majority of American students remain largely uncritical of the wider society, fundamentally conformist in behavior and outlook, and basically "adjusted" to the prevailing collegiate, national and international order, the small minority of dissenting students is highly visible to the mass media. As I will argue later, such students are often distinctively talented; they "use" the mass media effectively; and they generally succeed in their goal of making themselves and their causes highly visible. Equally important, student dissenters of all types arouse deep and ambivalent feelings in non-dissenting students and adults—envy, resentment, admiration, repulsion, nostalgia and guilt. Such feelings contribute both to the selective over-attention dissenters receive and to the often distorted perceptions and interpretations of them and their activities. Thus, there has developed through the mass media and the imaginings of adults a more or less stereotyped —and generally incorrect—image of the student dissenter.

The Stereotyped Dissenter

The "stereotypical" dissenter as popularly portrayed is both a Bohemian and political activist. Bearded, be-Levi-ed, long-haired, dirty and unkempt, he is seen as profoundly disaffected from his society, often influenced by "radical" (Marxist, Communist, Maoist, or Castroite) ideas, an experimenter in sex and

Reprinted with abridgment by permission of the author and the Society for the Psychological Study of Social Issues from *The Journal of Social Issues*, 1967, **23**, No. 3, 108–37.

drugs, unconventional in his daily behavior. Frustrated and unhappy, often deeply maladjusted as a person, he is a "failure" (or as one U. S. Senator put it, a "reject"). Certain academic communities like Berkeley are said to act as "magnets" for dissenters, who selectively attend colleges with a reputation as protest centers. Furthermore, dropouts or "non-students" who have failed in college cluster in large numbers around the fringes of such colleges, actively seeking pretexts for protest, refusing all compromise and impatient with ordinary democratic processes.

According to such popular analyses, the sources of dissent are to be found in the loss of certain traditional American virtues. The "breakdown" of American family life, high rates of divorce, the "softness" of American living, inadequate parents, and, above all, overindulgence and "spoiling" contribute to the prevalence of dissent. Brought up in undisciplined homes by parents unsure of their own values and standards, dissenters channel their frustration and anger against the older generation, against all authority, and against established institutions.

Similar themes are sometimes found in the interpretations of more scholarly commentators. "Generational conflict" is said to underlie the motivation to dissent, and a profound "alienation" from American society is seen as a factor of major importance in producing protests. Then, too, such factors as the poor quality and impersonality of American college education, the large size and lack of close student-faculty contact in the "multiversity" are sometimes seen as the latent or precipitating factors in student protests, regardless of the manifest issues around which students are organized. And still other scholarly analysts, usually men now disillusioned by the radicalism of the 1930's, have expressed fear of the dogmatism, rigidity and "authoritarianism of the left" of today's student activists.

Activism and Alienation

These stereotyped views are, I believe, incorrect in a variety of ways. They confuse two distinct varieties of student dissent; equally important, they fuse dissent with maladjustment. There are, of course, as many forms of dissent

as there are individual dissenters; and any effort to counter the popular stereotype of the dissenter by pointing to the existence of distinct "types" of dissenters runs the risk of oversimplifying at a lower level of abstraction. Nonetheless, it seems to me useful to suggest that student dissenters generally fall somewhere along a continuum that runs between two ideal types—first, the political activist or protester, and second, the withdrawn, culturally alienated student.

THE ACTIVIST   The defining characteristic of the "new" activist is his participation in a student demonstration or group activity that concerns itself with some matter of general political, social or ethical principle. Characteristically, the activist feels that some injustice has been done, and attempts to "take a stand," "demonstrate" or in some fashion express his convictions. The specific issues in question range from protest against a paternalistic college administration's actions to disagreement with American Vietnam policies, from indignation at the exploitation of the poor to anger at the firing of a devoted teacher, from opposition to the Selective Service laws which exempt him but not the poor to—most important—outrage at the deprivation of the civil rights of other Americans.

The initial concern of the protester is almost always immediate, ad hoc and local. To be sure, the student who protests about one issue is likely to feel inclined or obliged to demonstrate his convictions on other issues as well. But whatever the issue, the protester rarely demonstrates because his *own* interests are jeopardized, but rather because he perceives injustices being done to *others* less fortunate than himself. For example, one of the apparent paradoxes about protests against current draft policies is that the protesting students are selectively drawn from that subgroup *most* likely to receive student deferments for graduate work. The basis of protest is a general sense that the selective service rules and the war in Vietnam are unjust to others with whom the student is identified, but whose fate he does not share. If one runs down the list of "causes" taken up by student activists, in rare cases are demonstrations directed at improving the lot of the protesters themselves; identification with the oppressed is a more important motivating factor than an actual sense of immediate personal oppression.

The anti-ideological stance of today's activists has been noted by many commentators. This distrust of formal ideologies (and at times of articulate thought) makes it difficult to pinpoint the positive social and political values of student protesters. Clearly, many current American political institutions like de facto segregation are opposed; clearly, too, most students of the New Left reject careerism and familism as personal values. In this sense, we might think of the activist as (politically) "alienated." But this label seems to me more misleading than illuminating, for it overlooks the more basic *commitment* of most student activists to other ancient, traditional and credal American values like free speech, citizen's participation in decision-making, equal opportunity and justice. In so far as the activist rejects all or part of "the power structure," it is because current political realities fall so far short of the ideals he sees as central to the American creed. And in so far as he repudiates careerism and familism, it is because of his implicit allegiance to other human goals he sees, once again, as more crucial to American life. Thus, to emphasize the "alienation" of activists is to neglect their more basic allegiance to credal American ideals.

One of these ideals is, of course, a belief in the desirability of political and social action. Sustained in good measure by the successes of the student civil rights movement, the protester is usually convinced that demonstrations are effective in mobilizing public opinion, bringing moral or political pressure to bear, demonstrating the existence of his opinions, or, at times, in "bringing the machine to a halt." In this sense, then, despite his criticisms of existing political practices and social institutions, he is a political optimist. Moreover, the protester must believe in at least minimal organization and group activity; otherwise, he would find it impossible to take part, as he does, in any organized demonstrations or activities. Despite their search for more truly "democratic" forms of organization and action (e.g., participatory democracy), activists agree that group action is more effective than purely individual acts. To

be sure, a belief in the value and efficacy of political action is not equivalent to endorsement of prevalent political institutions or forms of action. Thus, one characteristic of activists is their search for new forms of social action, protest and political organization (community organization, sit-ins, participatory democracy) that will be more effective and less oppressive than traditional political institutions.

THE CULTURALLY ALIENATED   In contrast to the politically optimistic, active, and socially-concerned protester, the culturally alienated student is far too pessimistic and too firmly opposed to "the System" to wish to demonstrate his disapproval in any organized public way. His demonstrations of dissent are private: through nonconformity of behavior, ideology and dress, through personal experimentation and above all through efforts to intensify his own subjective experience, he shows his distaste and disinterest in politics and society. The activist attempts to change the world around him, but the alienated student is convinced that meaningful change of the social and political world is impossible; instead, he considers "dropping out" the only real option.

Alienated students tend to be drawn from the same general social strata and colleges as protesters. But psychologically and ideologically, their backgrounds are often very different. Alienated students are more likely to be disturbed psychologically; and although they are often highly talented and artistically gifted, they are less committed to academic values and intellectual achievement than are protesters. The alienated student's real campus is the school of the absurd, and he has more affinity for pessimistic existentialist ontology than for traditional American activism. Furthermore, such students usually find it psychologically and ideologically impossible to take part in organized group activities for any length of time, particularly when they are expected to assume responsibilities for leadership. Thus, on the rare occasions when they become involved in demonstrations, they usually prefer peripheral roles, avoid responsibilities and are considered a nuisance by serious activists.

Whereas the protesting student is likely to accept the basic political and social values of his parents, the alienated student almost always rejects his parents' values. In particular, he is likely to see his father as a man who has "sold out" to the pressures for success and status in American society: he is determined to avoid the fate that overtook his father. Toward their mothers, however, alienated students usually express a very special sympathy and identification. These mothers, far from encouraging their sons towards independence and achievement, generally seem to have been over-solicitous and limiting. The most common family environment of the alienated-student-to-be consists of a parental schism supplemented by a special mother-son alliance of mutual understanding and maternal control and depreciation of the father.

In many colleges, alienated students often constitute a kind of hidden underground, disorganized and shifting in membership, in which students can temporarily or permanently withdraw from the ordinary pressures of college life. The alienated are especially attracted to the hallucinogenic drugs like marijuana, mescalin and LSD, precisely because these agents combine withdrawal from ordinary social life with the promise of greatly intensified subjectivity and perception. To the confirmed "acid head," what matters is intense, drug-assisted perception; the rest—including politics, social action and student demonstrations—is usually seen as "role-playing."

The recent and much-publicized emergence of "hippie" subcultures in several major cities and increasingly on the campuses of many selective and progressive colleges illustrates the overwhelmingly apolitical stance of alienated youth. For although hippies oppose war and believe in inter-racial living, few have been willing or able to engage in anything beyond occasional peace marches or apolitical "human be-ins." Indeed, the hippie's emphasis on immediacy, "love" and "turning-on," together with his basic rejection of the traditional values of American life, inoculates him against involvement in long-range activist endeavors, like education or community organization, and even against the sustained effort needed to plan and execute demonstrations or marches. For the alienated hippie, American society is beyond redemption (or not worth trying to redeem);

but the activist, no matter how intense his rejection of specific American policies and practices, retains a conviction that his society can and should be changed. Thus, despite occasional agreement in principle between the alienated and the activists, cooperation in practice has been rare, and usually ends with activists accusing the alienated of "irresponsibility," while the alienated are confirmed in their view of activists as moralistic, "up-tight," and "uncool."

Obviously, no description of a type ever fits an individual perfectly. But by this rough typology, I mean to suggest that popular stereotypes which present a unified portrait of student dissent are gravely oversimplified. More specifically, they confuse the politically pessimistic and socially uncommitted alienated student with the politically hopeful and socially committed activist. To be sure, there are many students who fall between these two extremes, and some of them alternate between passionate search for intensified subjectivity and equally passionate efforts to remedy social and political injustices. And as I will later suggest, even within the student movement, one of the central tensions is between political activism and cultural alienation. Nonetheless, even to understand this tension we must first distinguish between the varieties of dissent apparent on American campuses.

Furthermore, the distinction between activist and alienated students as psychological types suggests the incompleteness of scholarly analyses that see social and historical factors as the only forces that "push" a student toward one or the other of these forms of dissent. To be sure, social and cultural factors are of immense importance in providing channels for the expression (or suppression) of dissent, and in determining *which* kinds of dissenters receive publicity, censure, support or ostracism in any historical period. But these factors cannot, in general, change a hippie into a committed activist, nor a SNCC field worker into a full-time "acid-head." Thus, the prototypical activist of 1966 is not the "same" student as the prototypical student bohemian of 1956, but is rather the politically aware but frustrated, academically oriented "privatist" of that era. Similarly, as I will argue below, the most compelling alternative to most activists is not the search for kicks or sentience but the quest for scholarly competence. And if culturally-sanctioned opportunities for the expression of alienation were to disappear, most alienated students would turn to private psychopathology rather than to public activism.

Stated more generally, historical forces do not ordinarily transform radically the character, values and inclinations of an adult in later life. Rather, they thrust certain groups forward in some eras and discourage or suppress other groups. The recent alternation in styles of student dissent in America is therefore not to be explained so much by the malleability of individual character as by the power of society to bring activists into the limelight, providing them with the intellectual and moral instruments for action. Only a minority of potential dissenters fall close enough to the midpoint between alienation and activism so that they can constitute a "swing vote" acutely responsive to social and cultural pressures and styles. The rest, the majority, are characterologically committed to one or another style of dissent.

THE SOURCES OF ACTIVISM

What I have termed "alienated" students are by no means a new phenomenon in American life, or for that matter in industrialized societies. Bohemians, "beatniks" and artistically-inclined undergraduates who rejected middle-class values have long been a part of the American student scene, especially at more selective colleges; they constituted the most visible form of dissent during the relative political "silence" of American students in the 1950's. What is distinctive about student dissent in recent years is the unexpected emergence of a vocal minority of politically and socially active students. Much is now known about the characteristics of such students, and the circumstances under which protests are likely to be mounted. At the same time, many areas of ignorance remain. In the account to follow, I will attempt to formulate a series of general hypotheses concerning the sources of student activism.

It is abundantly clear that no single factor will suffice to explain the increase of politically-motivated activities and protests on American campuses. Even if we define an activist narrowly, as a student who (a) acts together with others in a group, (b) is concerned with some ethical, social, ideological or political issue, and (c) holds liberal or "radical" views, the sources of student activism and protest are complex and inter-related. At least four kinds of factors seem involved in any given protest. First, the individuals involved must be suitably predisposed by their personal backgrounds, values and motivations. Second, the likelihood of protest is far greater in certain kinds of educational and social settings. Third, socially-directed protests require a special cultural climate, that is, certain distinctive values and views about the effectiveness and meaning of demonstrations, and about the wider society. And finally, some historical situations are especially conducive to protests.

THE PROTEST-PRONE PERSONALITY

A large and still-growing number of studies, conducted under different auspices, at different times and about different students, presents a remarkably consistent picture of the protest-prone individual. For one, student protesters are generally outstanding students; the higher the student's grade average, the more outstanding his academic achievements, the more likely it is that he will become involved in any given political demonstration. Similarly, student activists come from families with liberal political values; a disproportionate number report that their parents hold views essentially similar to their own, and accept or support their activities. Thus, among the parents of protesters we find large numbers of liberal Democrats, plus an unusually large scattering of pacifists, socialists, etc. A disproportionate number of protesters come from Jewish families; and if the parents of activists are religious, they tend to be concentrated in the more liberal denominations—Reform Judaism, Unitarianism, the Society of Friends, etc. Such parents are reported to have high ethical and political standards, regardless of their actual religious convictions.

As might be expected of a group of politically liberal and academically talented students, a disproportionate number are drawn from professional and intellectual families of upper middle-class status. For example, compared with active student conservatives, members of protest groups tend to have higher parental incomes, more parental education, and less anxiety about social status. Another study finds that high levels of education distinguish the activist's family even in the grandparental generation. In brief, activists are not drawn from disadvantaged, status-anxious, underprivileged or uneducated groups; on the contrary, they are selectively recruited from among those young Americans who have had the most socially fortunate upbringings.

Basic Value Commitments of Activists

The basic value commitments of the activist tend to be academic and non-vocational. Such students are rarely found among engineers, future teachers at teachers colleges, or students of business administration. Their over-all educational goals are those of a liberal education for its own sake, rather than specifically technical, vocational or professional preparation. Rejecting careerist and familist goals, activists espouse humanitarian, expressive and self-actualizing values. Perhaps because of these values, they delay career choice longer than their classmates (Flacks, 1967). Nor are such students distinctively dogmatic, rigid or authoritarian. Quite the contrary, the substance and style of their beliefs and activities tends to be open, flexible and highly liberal. Their fields of academic specialization are non-vocational—the social sciences and the humanities. Once in college, they not only do well academically, but tend to persist in their academic commitments, dropping out *less* frequently than most of their classmates. As might be expected, a disproportionate number receive a B.A. within four years and continue on to graduate school, preparing themselves for academic careers.

Survey data also suggest that the activist is not distinctively dissatisfied with his college education. As will be noted below, activists generally attend colleges which provide the best, rather than the worst, undergraduate education available today. Objectively then, activists probably have less to complain about in their undergraduate educations than most other students. And subjectively as well, surveys show most activists, like most other American undergraduates, to be relatively well satisfied with their undergraduate educations. Thus, dissatisfaction with educational failings of the "impersonal multiversity," however important as a rallying cry, does not appear to be a distinctive cause of activism.

In contrast to their relative satisfaction with the quality of their educations, however, activists *are* distinctively dissatisfied with what might be termed the "civil-libertarian" defects of their college administrations. While no doubt a great many American undergraduates distrust "University Hall," this distrust is especially pronounced amongst student protesters. Furthermore, activists tend to be more responsive than other students to deprivations of civil rights on campus as well as off campus, particularly when political pressures seem to motivate on-campus policies they consider unjust. The same responsiveness increasingly extends to issues of "student power": i.e., student participation and decisions affecting campus life. Thus, bans on controversial speakers, censorship of student publications, and limitations on off-campus political or social action are likely to incense the activist, as is arbitrary "administration without the consent of the administered." But it is primarily perceived injustice or the denial of student rights by the Administration—rather than poor educational quality, neglect by the faculty, or the impersonality of the multiversity—that agitates the activist.

Most studies of activists have concentrated on variables that are relatively easy to measure: social class, academic achievements, explicit values and satisfaction with college. But these factors alone will not explain activism: more students possess the demographic and attitudinal characteristics of the protest-prone personality than are actually involved in protests and social action programs. Situational, institutional, cultural and historical factors (discussed below), obviously contribute to "catalysing" a protest-prone personality into an actual activist. But it also seems that, within the broad demographic group so far defined, more specific psychodynamic factors contribute to activism.

Activists . . . Not in Rebellion

In speculating about such factors, we leave the ground of established fact and enter the terrain of speculation, for only a few studies have explored the personality dynamics and family constellation of the activist, and most of these studies are impressionistic and clinical. But certain facts are clear. As noted, activists are *not,* on the whole, repudiating or rebelling against explicit parental values and ideologies. On the contrary, there is some evidence that such students are living out their parents' values in practice; and one study suggests that activists may be somewhat *closer* to their parents' values than nonactivists (Flacks, 1967). Thus, any simple concept of "generational conflict" or "rebellion against parental authority" is clearly oversimplified as applied to the motivations of most protesters.

Activists . . . Living Out Parental Values

It does seem probable, however, that many activists are concerned with *living out expressed but unimplemented parental values.* Solomon and Fishman (1963), studying civil rights activists and peace marchers, argue that many demonstrators are "acting out" in their demonstrations the values which their parents explicitly believed, but did not have the courage or opportunity to practice or fight for. Similarly, when protesters criticize their fathers, it is usually over their fathers' failure to practice what they have preached to their children throughout their lives. Thus, in the personal background of the protester there is occasionally a suggestion that his father is less-than-"sincere" (and even at times "hypocritical") in his professions of political liberalism. In particular, both careerism and familism in parents are the objects of activist criticisms, the more so because these implicit goals often conflict with explicit parental values. And it may be that protesters receive both covert and overt support from their parents because the latter are secretly proud of their children's eagerness to implement the ideals they as parents have only

given lip-service to. But whatever the ambivalences that bind parents with their activist children, it would be wrong to overemphasize them: what is most impressive is the solidarity of older and younger generations.

ACTIVISTS . . . FAMILY STRUCTURE

While no empirical study has tested this hypothesis, it seems probable that in many activist-producing families, the mother will have a dominant psychological influence on her son's development. I have already noted that the protester's cause is rarely himself, but rather alleviating the oppression of others. As a group, activists seem to possess an unusual *capacity for nurturant identification*—that is, for empathy and sympathy with the underdog, the oppressed and the needy. Such a capacity can have many origins, but its most likely source in upper-middle-class professional families is identification with an active mother whose own work embodies nurturant concern for others. Flacks' finding that the mothers of activists are likely to be employed, often in professional or service roles like teaching and social work, is consistent with this hypothesis. In general in American society, middle-class women have greater social and financial freedom to work in jobs that are idealistically "fulfilling" as opposed to merely lucrative or prestigious. As a rule, then, in middle-class families, it is the mother who actively embodies in her life and work the humanitarian, social and political ideals that the father may share in principle but does not or cannot implement in his career.

Given what we know about the general characteristics of the families of protest-prone students, it also seems probable that the dominant ethos of their families is unusually equalitarian, permissive, "democratic," and highly individuated. More specifically, we might expect that these will be families where children talk back to their parents at the dinner table, where free dialogue and discussion of feelings is encouraged, and where "rational" solutions are sought to everyday family problems and conflicts. We would also expect that such families would place a high premium on self-expression and intellectual independence, encouraging their children to make up their own minds and to stand firm against group pressures. Once again, the mother seems the most likely carrier and epitome of these values, given her relative freedom from professional and financial pressures.

The contrast between such protest-prompting families and alienating families should be underlined. In both, the son's deepest emotional ties are often to his mother. But in the alienating family, the mother-son relationship is characterized by maternal control and intrusiveness, whereas in the protest-prompting family, the mother is a highly individuating force in her son's life, pushing him to independence and autonomy. Furthermore, the alienated student is determined to avoid the fate that befell his father, whereas the protesting student wants merely to live out the values that his father has not always worked hard enough to practice. Finally, the egalitarian, permissive, democratic and individuating environment of the entire family of the protester contrasts with the over-controlling, over-solicitous attitude of the mother in the alienating family, where the father is usually excluded from major emotional life within the family.

These hypotheses about the family background and psychodynamics of the protester are speculative, and future research may prove their invalidity. But regardless of whether *these* particular speculations are correct, it seems clear that in addition to the general social, demographic and attitudinal factors mentioned in most research, more specific familial and psychodynamic influences contribute to protest-proneness. . . .

[In the last section of this paper, not included here, Keniston examines the characteristics of the colleges or universities attended by the protest-prone student. Colleges with a reputation for academic excellence and freedom, coupled with highly selective admissions policies, tend to attract the potential activist. The existence of advanced students, including large numbers of "exploited, underpaid, disgruntled and frustrated teacher assistants," facilitates dissent by providing leadership. Institutional factors such as largeness, impersonality, and atomization probably do not play as important a role as students claim, says Keniston, but failure to measure up to students' expectations of what a college should be is a factor. (Ed.)]

CRUCIBLE OF IDENTITY:
THE NEGRO LOWER-CLASS FAMILY

LEE RAINWATER

But can a people . . . live and develop for over three hundred years by simply *reacting?* Are American Negroes simply the creation of white men, or have they at least helped create themselves out of what they found around them? Men have made a way of life in caves and upon cliffs, why can not Negroes have made a life upon the horns of the white man's dilemma? . . . American Negro life is, for the Negro who must live it, not only a burden (and not always that) but also a discipline just as any human life which has endured so long is a discipline teaching its own insights into the human conditions, its own strategies of survival. . . .

For even as his life toughens the Negro, even as it brutalizes him, sensitizes him, dulls him, goads him to anger, moves him to irony, sometimes fracturing and sometimes affirming his hopes; even as it shapes his attitude towards family, sex, love, religion; even as it modulates his humor, tempers his joy—it *conditions* him to deal with his life and with himself. Because it is *his* life and no mere abstraction in someone's head. He must live it and try consciously to grasp its complexity until he can change it; must live it *as* he changes it. He is no mere product of his socio-political predicament. He is a product of interaction between his racial predicament, his individual will and the broader American cultural freedom in which he finds his ambiguous existence. Thus he, too, in a limited way, is his own creation.

—*Ralph Ellison*

As long as Negroes have been in America, their marital and family patterns have been subjects of curiosity and amusement, moral indignation and self-congratulation, puzzlement and frustration, concern and guilt, on the part of white Americans. As some Negroes have moved into middle-class status, or acquired standards of American common-man respectability, they too have shared these attitudes toward the private behavior of their fellows, sometimes with a moral punitiveness to rival that of whites, but at other times with a hard-headed interest in causes and remedies rather than moral evaluation. Moralism permeated the

subject of Negro sexual, marital, and family behavior in the polemics of slavery apologists and abolitionists as much as in the Northern and Southern civil rights controversies of today. Yet, as long as the dialectic of good or bad, guilty or innocent, overshadows a concern with who, why, and what can be, it is unlikely that realistic and effective social planning to correct the clearly desperate situation of poor Negro families can begin.

This paper is concerned with a description and analysis of slum Negro family patterns as these reflect and sustain Negroes' adaptations to the economic, social, and personal situation into which they are born and in which they must live. As such it deals with facts of lower-class life that are usually forgotten or ignored in polite discussion. We have chosen not to ignore

Reprinted with abridgment by permission of the author and *Daedalus* from *Daedalus*, Journal of the American Academy of Arts and Sciences, Boston, Massachusetts, **95**, No. 1, 172–216.

these facts in the belief that to do so can lead only to assumptions which would frustrate efforts at social reconstruction, to strategies that are unrealistic in the light of the actual day-to-day reality of slum Negro life. Further, this analysis will deal with family patterns which interfere with the efforts slum Negroes make to attain a stable way of life as working- or middle-class individuals and with the effects such failure in turn has on family life. To be sure, many Negro families live *in* the slum ghetto, but are not *of* its culture (though even they, and particularly their children, can be deeply affected by what happens there). However, it is the individuals who succumb to the distinctive family life style of the slum who experience the greatest weight of deprivation and who have the greatest difficulty responding to the few self-improvement resources that make their way into the ghetto. In short, we propose to explore in depth the family's role in the "tangle of pathology" which characterizes the ghetto.

The social reality in which Negroes have had to make their lives during the 450 years of their existence in the western hemisphere has been one of victimization "in the sense that a system of social relations operates in such a way as to deprive them of a chance to share in the more desirable material and non-material products of a society which is dependent, in part, upon their labor and loyalty." In making this observation, St. Clair Drake goes on to note that Negroes are victimized also because "they do not have the same degree of access which others have to the attributes needed for rising in the general class system—money, education, 'contacts,' and 'know-how.'" The victimization process started with slavery; for 350 years thereafter Negroes worked out as best they could adaptations to the slave status. After emancipation, the cultural mechanisms which Negroes had developed for living the life of victim continued to be serviceable as the victimization process was maintained first under the myths of white supremacy and black inferiority, later by the doctrines of gradualism which covered the fact of no improvement in position, and finally by the modern Northern system of ghettoization and indifference.

When lower-class Negroes use the expression,

"Tell it like it is," they signal their intention to strip away pretense, to describe a situation or its participants as they really are, rather than in a polite or euphemistic way. "Telling it like it is" can be used as a harsh, aggressive device, or it can be a healthy attempt to face reality rather than retreat into fantasy. In any case, as he goes about his field work, the participant observer studying a ghetto community learns to listen carefully to any exchange preceded by such an announcement because he knows the speaker is about to express his understanding of how his world operates, of what motivates its members, of how they actually behave.

The first responsibility of the social scientist can be phrased in much the same way: "Tell it like it is." His second responsibility is to try to understand why "it" is that way, and to explore the implications of what and why for more constructive solutions to human problems. Social research on the situation of the Negro American has been informed by four main goals: (1) to describe the disadvantaged position of Negroes, (2) to disprove the racist ideology which sustains the caste system, (3) to demonstrate that responsibility for the disadvantages Negroes suffer lies squarely upon the white caste which derives economic, prestige, and psychic benefits from the operation of the system, and (4) to suggest that in reality whites would be better rather than worse off if the whole jerry-built caste structure were to be dismantled. The successful accomplishment of these *intellectual* goals has been a towering achievement, in which the social scientists of the 1920's, '30's, and '40's can take great pride; that white society has proved so recalcitrant to utilizing this intellectual accomplishment is one of the great tragedies of our time, and provides the stimulus for further social research on "the white problem."

Yet the implicit paradigm of much of the research on Negro Americans has been an overly simplistic one concentrating on two terms of an argument:

White cupidity ⟶ Negro suffering.

As an intellectual shorthand, and even more as a civil rights slogan, this simple model is both justified and essential. But, as a guide to greater understanding of the Negro situation as human adaptation to human situations, the paradigm is totally inadequate because it fails to specify fully enough the *process* by which Negroes adapt to their situations as they do, and the limitations one kind of adaptation places on possibilities for subsequent adaptations. A reassessment of previous social research, combined with examination of current social research on Negro ghetto communities, suggests a more complex, but hopefully more vertical, model:

White cupidity

creates

Structural Conditions Highly Inimical to Basic Social Adaptation (low-income availability, poor education, poor services, stigmatization)

to which Negroes adapt

by

Social and Personal Responses which serve to sustain the individual in his punishing world but also generate aggressiveness toward the self and others

which results in

Suffering directly inflicted by Negroes on themselves and on others.

In short, whites, by their greater power, create situations in which Negroes do the dirty work of caste victimization for them.

The white caste maintains a cadre of whites whose special responsibility is to enforce the system in brutal or refined ways (the Klan, the rural sheriff, the metropolitan police, the businessman who specializes in a Negro clientele, the Board of Education). Increasingly, whites recruit to this cadre middle-class Negroes who can soften awareness of victimization by their protective coloration. These special cadres, white and/or Negro, serve the very important function of enforcing caste standards by whatever means seem required, while at the same time concealing from an increasingly "unprejudiced" public the unpleasant facts they would prefer to ignore. The system is quite homologous to the Gestapo and concentration camps of Nazi Germany, though less fatal to its victims.

For their part, Negroes creatively adapt to the system in ways that keep them alive and extract what gratification they can find, but in the process of adaptation they are constrained to behave in ways that inflict a great deal of suffering on those with whom they make their lives, and on themselves. The ghetto Negro is constantly confronted by the immediate necessity to suffer in order to get what he wants of those few things he can have, or to make others suffer, or both—for example, he suffers as exploited student and employee, as drug user, as loser in the competitive game of his peer-group society; he inflicts suffering as disloyal spouse, petty thief, knife- or gun-wielder, petty con man.

It is the central thesis of this paper that the caste-facilitated infliction of suffering by Negroes on other Negroes and on themselves appears most poignantly within the confines of the family, and that the victimization process as it operates in families prepares and toughens its members to function in the ghetto world, at the same time that it seriously interferes with their ability to operate in any other world. This, however, is very different from arguing that "the family is to blame" for the deprived situation ghetto Negroes suffer; rather we are looking at the logical outcome of the operation of the widely ramified and interconnecting caste system. In the end we will argue that only palliative results can be expected from attempts to treat directly the disordered family patterns to be described. Only a change in the original "inputs" of the caste system, the structural conditions inimical to basic social adaptation, can change family forms.

Almost thirty years ago, E. Franklin Frazier foresaw that the fate of the Negro family in the city would be a highly destructive one. His readers would have little reason to be surprised at observations of slum ghetto life today:

. . . As long as the bankrupt system of southern agriculture exists, Negro families will continue to seek a living in the towns and cities. . . . They will crowd the slum areas of southern cities or make their way to northern cities where their families will become disrupted and their poverty will force them to depend upon charity.

THE AUTONOMY OF THE SLUM GHETTO

Just as the deprivations and depredations practiced by white society have had their effect on the personalities and social life of Negroes, so also has the separation from the ongoing social life of the white community had its effect. In a curious way, Negroes have had considerable freedom to fashion their own adaptations within their separate world. The larger society provides them with few resources but also with minimal interference in the Negro community on matters which did not seem to affect white interests. Because Negroes learned early that there were a great many things they could not depend upon whites to provide they developed their own solutions to recurrent human issues. These solutions can often be seen to combine, along with the predominance of elements from white culture, elements that are distinctive to the Negro group. Even more distinctive is the *configuration* which emerges from those elements Negroes share with whites and those which are different.

It is in this sense that we may speak of a Negro subculture, a distinctive *patterning* of existential perspectives, techniques for coping with the problems of social life, views about what is desirable and undesirable in particular situations. This subculture, and particularly that of the lower-class, the slum, Negro, can be seen as his own creation out of the elements available to him in response to (1) the conditions of life set by white society and (2) the selective freedom which that society allows (or must put up with given the pattern of separateness on which it insists).

Out of this kind of "freedom" slum Negroes have built a culture which has some elements of intrinsic value and many more elements that are highly destructive to the people who must live in it. The elements that whites can value they constantly borrow. Negro arts and language have proved so popular that such commentators on American culture as Norman Mailer and Leslie Fiedler have noted processes of Negro-ization of white Americans as a minor theme of the past thirty years. A fairly large proportion of Negroes with national reputations are engaged in the occupation of diffusing to the larger culture these elements of intrinsic value.

On the negative side, this freedom has meant, as social scientists who have studied Negro communities have long commented, that many of the protections offered by white institutions

stop at the edge of the Negro ghetto: there are poor police protection and enforcement of civil equities, inadequate schooling and medical service, and more informal indulgences which whites allow Negroes as a small price for feeling superior.

For our purposes, however, the most important thing about the freedom which whites have allowed Negroes within their own world is that it has required them to work out their own ways of making it from day to day, from birth to death. The subculture that Negroes have created may be imperfect but it has been viable for centuries; it behooves both white and Negro leaders and intellectuals to seek to understand it even as they hope to change it.

Negroes have created, again particularly within the lower-class slum group, a range of institutions to structure the tasks of living a victimized life and to minimize the pain it inevitably produces. In the slum ghetto these institutions include prominently those of the social network—the extended kinship system and the "street system" of buddies and broads which tie (although tenuously and unpredictably) the "members" to each other—and the institutions of entertainment (music, dance, folk tales) by which they instruct, explain, and accept themselves. Other institutions function to provide escape from the society of the victimized: the church (Hereafter!) and the civil rights movement (Now!).

THE FUNCTIONAL AUTONOMY OF THE NEGRO FAMILY

At the center of the matrix of Negro institutional life lies the family. It is in the family that individuals are trained for participation in the culture and find personal and group identity and continuity. The "freedom" allowed by white society is greatest here, and this freedom has been used to create an institutional variant more distinctive perhaps to the Negro subculture than any other. (Much of the content of Negro art and entertainment derives exactly from the distinctive characteristics of Negro family life.) At each stage in the Negro's experience of American life—slavery, segregation, *de facto* ghettoization—whites have found it less necessary to interfere in the relations between the sexes and between parents and children than in other areas of the Negro's existence. His adaptations in this area, therefore, have been less constrained by whites than in many other areas.

Now that the larger society is becoming increasingly committed to integrating Negroes into the main stream of American life, however, we can expect increasing constraint (benevolent as it may be) to be placed on the autonomy of the Negro family system. These constraints will be designed to pull Negroes into meaningful integration with the larger society, to give up ways which are inimical to successful performance in the larger society, and to adopt new ways that are functional in that society. The strategic questions of the civil rights movement and of the war on poverty are ones that have to do with how one provides functional equivalents for the existing subculture before the capacity to make a life within its confines is destroyed.

The history of the Negro family has been ably documented by historians and sociologists. In slavery, conjugal and family ties were reluctantly and ambivalently recognized by the slave holders, were often violated by them, but proved necessary to the slave system. This necessity stemmed both from the profitable offspring of slave sexual unions and the necessity for their nurture, and from the fact that the slaves' efforts to sustain patterns of sexual and parental relations mollified the men and women whose labor could not simply be commanded. From nature's promptings, the thinning memories of African heritage, and the example and guilt-ridden permission of the slave holders, slaves constructed a partial family system and sets of relations that generated conjugal and familial sentiments. The slave holder's recognition in advertisements for runaway slaves of marital and family sentiments as motivations for absconding provides one indication that strong family ties were possible, though perhaps not common, in the slave quarter. The mother-centered family with its emphasis on the primacy of the mother-child relation and only tenuous ties to a man, then, is the legacy of adaptations worked out by Negroes during slavery.

After emancipation this family design often also served well to cope with the social disorganization of Negro life in the late nineteenth century. Matrifocal families, ambivalence about the desirability of marriage, ready acceptance of illegitimacy, all sustained some kind of family life in situations which often made it difficult to maintain a full nuclear family. Yet in the hundred years since emancipation, Negroes in rural areas have been able to maintain full nuclear families almost as well as similarly situated whites. As we will see, it is the move to the city that results in the very high proportion of mother-headed households. In the rural system the man continues to have important functions; it is difficult for a woman to make a crop by herself, or even with the help of other women. In the city, however, the woman can earn wages just as a man can, and she can receive welfare payments more easily than he can. In rural areas, although there may be high illegitimacy rates and high rates of marital disruption, men and women have an interest in getting together; families are headed by a husband-wife pair much more often than in the city. That pair may be much less stable than in the more prosperous segments of Negro and white communities but it is more likely to exist among rural Negroes than among urban ones.

The matrifocal character of the Negro lower-class family in the United States has much in common with Caribbean Negro family patterns; research in both areas has done a great deal to increase our understanding of the Negro situation. However, there are important differences in the family forms of the two areas. The impact of white European family models has been much greater in the United States than in the Caribbean both because of the relative population proportions of white and colored peoples and because equalitarian values in the United States have had a great impact on Negroes even when they have not on whites. The typical Caribbean mating pattern is that women go through several visiting and common-law unions but eventually marry; that is, they marry legally only relatively late in their sexual lives. The Caribbean marriage is the crowning of a sexual and procreative career; it is considered a serious and difficult step.

In the United States, in contrast, Negroes marry at only a slightly lower rate and slightly higher age than whites. Most Negro women marry relatively early in their careers; marriage is not regarded as the same kind of crowning choice and achievement that it is in the Caribbean. For lower-class Negroes in the United States marriage ceremonies are rather informal affairs. In the Caribbean, marriage is regarded as quite costly because of the feasting which goes along with it; ideally it is performed in church.

In the United States, unlike the Caribbean, early marriage confers a kind of permanent respectable status upon a woman which she can use to deny any subsequent accusations of immorality or promiscuity once the marriage is broken and she becomes sexually involved in visiting or common-law relations. The relevant effective status for many Negro women is that of "having been married" rather than "being married"; having the right to be called "Mrs." rather than currently being Mrs. Someone-in-Particular.

For Negro lower-class women, then, first marriage has the same kind of importance as having a first child. Both indicate that the girl has become a woman but neither one that this is the last such activity in which she will engage. It seems very likely that only a minority of Negro women in the urban slum go through their child-rearing years with only one man around the house.

Among the Negro urban poor, then, a great many women have the experience of heading a family for part of their mature lives, and a great many children spend some part of their formative years in a household without a father-mother pair. From Table 1 we see that in 1960,

TABLE I

Proportion of Female Heads for Families with Children by Race, Income, and Urban-Rural Categories

	Rural	Urban	Total
Negroes			
under $3000	18%	47%	36%
$3000 and over	5%	8%	7%
Total	14%	23%	21%
Whites			
under $3000	12%	38%	22%
$3000 and over	2%	4%	3%
Total	4%	7%	6%

Source: U. S. Census: 1960, PC (1) D. U. S. Volume, Table 225; State Volume, Table 140.

forty-seven per cent of the Negro poor urban families with children had a female head. Unfortunately cumulative statistics are hard to come by; but, given this very high level for a cross-sectional sample (and taking into account the fact that the median age of the children in these families is about six years), it seems very likely that as many as two-thirds of Negro urban poor children will not live in families headed by a man and a woman throughout the first eighteen years of their lives.

One of the other distinctive characteristics of Negro families, both poor and not so poor, is the fact that Negro households have a much higher proportion of relatives outside the mother-father-children triangle than is the case with whites. For example, in St. Louis Negro families average 0.8 other relatives per household compared to only 0.4 for white families. In the case of the more prosperous Negro families this is likely to mean that an older relative lives in the home providing baby-sitting services while both the husband and wife work and thus further their climb toward stable working- or middle-class status. In the poor Negro families it is much more likely that the household is headed by an older relative who brings under her wings a daughter and that daughter's children. It is important to note that the three-generation household with the grandmother at the head exists only when there is no husband present. Thus, despite the high proportion of female-headed households in this group and despite the high proportion of households that contain other relatives, we find that almost all married couples in the St. Louis Negro slum community have their own household. In other words, when a couple marries it establishes its own household; when that couple breaks up the mother either maintains that household or moves back to her parents or grandparents.

Finally we should note that Negro slum families have more children than do either white slum families or stable working- and middle-class Negro families. Mobile Negro families limit their fertility sharply in the interest of bringing the advantages of mobility more fully to the few children that they do have. Since the Negro slum family is both more likely to have the father absent and more likely to have more children in the family, the mother has a more demanding task with fewer resources at her disposal. When we examine the patterns of life of the stem family we shall see that even the presence of several mothers does not necessarily lighten the work load for the principal mother in charge.

THE FORMATION AND MAINTENANCE OF FAMILIES

We will outline below the several stages and forms of Negro lower-class family life. At many points these family forms and the interpersonal relations that exist within them will be seen to have characteristics in common with the life styles of white lower-class families. At other points there are differences, or the Negro pattern will be seen to be more sharply divergent from the family life of stable working- and middle-class couples.

It is important to recognize that lower-class Negroes know that their particular family forms are different from those of the rest of the society and that, though they often see these forms as representing the only ways of behaving given their circumstances, they also think of the more stable family forms of the working class as more desirable. That is, lower-class Negroes know what the "normal American family" is supposed to be like, and they consider a stable family-centered way of life superior to the conjugal and familial situations in which they often find themselves. Their conceptions of the good American life include the notion of a father-husband who functions as an adequate provider and interested member of the family, a hard working home-bound mother who is concerned about her children's welfare and her husband's needs, and children who look up to their parents and perform well in school and other outside places to reflect credit on their families. This image of what family life can be like is very real from time to time as lower-class men and women grow up and move through adulthood. Many of them make efforts to establish such families but find it impossible to do so either because of the direct impact of economic disabilities or because they are not able to sustain in their day-to-day lives the ideals which they hold. While these ideals do serve as a meaningful guide to lower-class couples who

are mobile out of the group, for a great many others the existence of such ideas about normal family life represents a recurrent source of stress within families as individuals become aware that they are failing to measure up to the ideals, or as others within the family and outside it use the ideals as an aggressive weapon for criticizing each other's performance. It is not at all uncommon for husbands or wives or children to try to hold others in the family to the norms of stable family life while they themselves engage in behaviors which violate these norms. The effect of such criticism in the end is to deepen commitment to the deviant sexual and parental norms of a slum subculture. Unless they are careful, social workers and other professionals exacerbate the tendency to use the norms of "American family life" as weapons by supporting these norms in situations where they are in reality unsupportable, thus aggravating the sense of failing and being failed by others which is chronic for lower-class people.

Going Together

The initial steps toward mating and family formation in the Negro slum take place in a context of highly developed boys' and girls' peer groups. Adolescents tend to become deeply involved in their peer-group societies beginning as early as the age of twelve or thirteen and continue to be involved after first pregnancies and first marriages. Boys and girls are heavily committed both to their same sex peer groups and to the activities that those groups carry out. While classical gang activity does not necessarily characterize Negro slum communities everywhere, loosely-knit peer groups do.

The world of the Negro slum is wide open to exploration by adolescent boys and girls: "Negro communities provide a flow of common experience in which young people and their elders share, and out of which delinquent behavior emerges almost imperceptibly." More than is possible in white slum communities, Negro adolescents have an opportunity to interact with adults in various "high life" activities; their behavior more often represents an identification with the behavior of adults than an attempt to set up group standards and activities that differ from those of adults.

Boys and young men participating in the street system of peer-group activity are much caught up in games of furthering and enhancing their status as significant persons. These games are played out in small and large gatherings through various kinds of verbal contests that go under the names of "sounding," "signifying," and "working game." Very much a part of a boy's or man's status in this group is his ability to win women. The man who has several women "up tight," who is successful in "pimping off" women for sexual favors and material benefits, is much admired. In sharp contrast to white lower-class groups, there is little tendency for males to separate girls into "good" and "bad" categories. Observations of groups of Negro youths suggest that girls and women are much more readily referred to as "that bitch" or "that whore" than they are by their names, and this seems to be a universal tendency carrying no connotation that "that bitch" is morally inferior to or different from other women. Thus, all women are essentially the same, all women are legitimate targets, and no girl or woman is expected to be virginal except for reason of lack of opportunity or immaturity. From their participation in the peer group and according to standards legitimated by the total Negro slum culture, Negro boys and young men are propelled in the direction of girls to test their "strength" as seducers. They are mercilessly rated by both their peers and the opposite sex in their ability to "talk" to girls; a young man will go to great lengths to avoid the reputation of having a "weak" line.

The girls share these definitions of the nature of heterosexual relations; they take for granted that almost any male they deal with will try to seduce them and that given sufficient inducement (social not monetary) they may wish to go along with his line. Although girls have a great deal of ambivalence about participating in sexual relations, this ambivalence is minimally moral and has much more to do with a desire not to be taken advantage of or get in trouble. Girls develop defenses against the exploitative orientations of men by devaluing the significance of sexual relations ("he really didn't do anything bad to me"), and as time goes on by developing their own appreciation of the intrinsic rewards of sexual intercourse.

The informal social relations of slum Negroes begin in adolescence to be highly sexualized. Although parents have many qualms about boys and, particularly, girls entering into this system, they seldom feel there is much they can do to prevent their children's sexual involvement. They usually confine themselves to counseling somewhat hopelessly against girls becoming pregnant or boys being forced into situations where they might have to marry a girl they do not want to marry.

Girls are propelled toward boys and men in order to demonstrate their maturity and attractiveness; in the process they are constantly exposed to pressures for seduction, to boys "rapping" to them. An active girl will "go with" quite a number of boys, but she will generally try to restrict the number with whom she has intercourse to the few to whom she is attracted or (as happens not infrequently) to those whose threats of physical violence she cannot avoid. For their part, the boys move rapidly from girl to girl seeking to have intercourse with as many as they can and thus build up their "reps." The activity of seduction is itself highly cathected; there is gratification in simply "talking to" a girl as long as the boy can feel that he has acquitted himself well.

At sixteen Joan Bemias enjoys spending time with three or four very close girl friends. She tells us they follow this routine when the girls want to go out and none of the boys they have been seeing lately is available: "Every time we get ready to go someplace we look through all the telephone numbers of boys we'd have and we call them and talk so sweet to them that they'd come on around. All of them had cars you see. (I: What do you do to keep all these fellows interested?) Well nothing. We don't have to make love with all of them. Let's see, Joe, J. B., Albert, and Paul, out of all of them I've been going out with I've only had sex with four boys, that's all." She goes on to say that she and her girl friends resist boys by being unresponsive to their lines and by breaking off relations with them on the ground that they're going out with other girls. It is also clear from her comments that the girl friends support each other in resisting the boys when they are out together in groups.

Joan has had a relationship with a boy which has lasted six months, but she has managed to hold the frequency of intercourse down to four times. Initially she managed to hold this particular boy off for a month but eventually gave in.

Becoming Pregnant

It is clear that the contest elements in relationships between men and women continue even in relationships that become quite steady. Despite the girls' ambivalence about sexual relations and their manifold efforts to reduce its frequency, the operation of chance often eventuates in their becoming pregnant. This was the case with Joan. With this we reach the second stage in the formation of families, that of premarital pregnancy. (We are outlining an ideal-typical sequence and not, of course, implying that all girls in the Negro slum culture become pregnant before they marry but only that a great many of them do.)

Joan was caught despite the fact that she was considerably more sophisticated about contraception than most girls or young women in the group (her mother had both instructed her in contraceptive techniques and constantly warned her to take precautions). No one was particularly surprised at her pregnancy although she, her boy friend, her mother, and others regarded it as unfortunate. For girls in the Negro slum, pregnancy before marriage is expected in much the same way that parents expect their children to catch mumps or chicken pox; if they are lucky it will not happen but if it happens people are not too surprised and everyone knows what to do about it. It was quickly decided that Joan and the baby would stay at home. It seems clear from the preparations that Joan's mother is making that she expects to have the main responsibility for caring for the infant. Joan seems quite indifferent to the baby; she shows little interest in mothering the child although she is not particularly adverse to the idea so long as the baby does not interfere too much with her continued participation in her peer group.

Establishing who the father is under these circumstances seems to be important and confers a kind of legitimacy on the birth; not to know who one's father is, on the other hand, seems the ultimate in illegitimacy. Actually Joan had a choice in the imputation of father-

hood; she chose J.B. because he is older than she, and because she may marry him if he can get a divorce from his wife. She could have chosen Paul (with whom she had also had intercourse at about the time she became pregnant), but she would have done this reluctantly since Paul is a year younger than she and somehow this does not seem fitting.

In general, when a girl becomes pregnant while still living at home it seems taken for granted that she will continue to live there and that her parents will take a major responsibility for rearing the children. Since there are usually siblings who can help out and even siblings who will be playmates for the child, the addition of a third generation to the household does not seem to place a great stress on relationships within the family. It seems common for the first pregnancy to have a liberating influence on the mother once the child is born in that she becomes socially and sexually more active than she was before. She no longer has to be concerned with preserving her status as a single girl. Since her mother is usually willing to take care of the child for a few years, the unwed mother has an opportunity to go out with girl friends and with men and thus become more deeply involved in the peer-group society of her culture. As she has more children and perhaps marries she will find it necessary to settle down and spend more time around the house fulfilling the functions of a mother herself.

It would seem that for girls pregnancy is the real measure of maturity, the dividing line between adolescence and womanhood. Perhaps because of this, as well as because of the ready resources for child care, girls in the Negro slum community show much less concern about pregnancy than do girls in the white lower-class community and are less motivated to marry the fathers of their children. When a girl becomes pregnant the question of marriage certainly arises and is considered, but the girl often decides that she would rather not marry the man either because she does not want to settle down yet or because she does not think he would make a good husband.

It is in the easy attitudes toward premarital pregnancy that the matrifocal character of the Negro lower-class family appears most clearly. In order to have and raise a family it is simply not necessary, though it may be desirable, to have a man around the house. While the AFDC program may make it easier to maintain such attitudes in the urban situation, this pattern existed long before the program was initiated and continues in families where support comes from other sources.

Finally it should be noted that fathering a child similarly confers maturity on boys and young men although perhaps it is less salient for them. If the boy has any interest in the girl he will tend to feel that the fact that he has impregnated her gives him an additional claim on her. He will be stricter in seeking to enforce his exclusive rights over her (though not exclusive loyalty to her). This exclusive right does not mean that he expects to marry her but only that there is a new and special bond between them. If the girl is not willing to accept such claims she may find it necessary to break off the relationship rather than tolerate the man's jealousy. Since others in the peer group have a vested interest in not allowing a couple to be too loyal to each other they go out of their way to question and challenge each partner about the loyalty of the other, thus contributing to the deterioration of the relationship. This same kind of questioning and challenging continues if the couple marries and represents one source of the instability of the marital relationship.

Getting Married

As noted earlier, despite the high degree of premarital sexual activity and the rather high proportion of premarital pregnancies, most lower-class Negro men and women eventually do marry and stay together for a shorter or longer period of time. Marriage is an intimidating prospect and is approached ambivalently by both parties. For the girl it means giving up a familiar and comfortable home that, unlike some other lower-class subcultures, places few real restrictions on her behavior. (While marriage can appear to be an escape from interpersonal difficulties at home, these difficulties seldom seem to revolve around effective restrictions placed on her behavior by her parents.) The girl also has good reason to be suspicious of the likelihood that men will be able to perform stably in the role of husband and provider; she is reluctant to be tied down by a man who will not prove to be worth it.

From the man's point of view the fickleness of women makes marriage problematic. It is one thing to have a girl friend step out on you, but it is quite another to have a wife do so. Whereas premarital sexual relations and fatherhood carry almost no connotation of responsibility for the welfare of the partner, marriage is supposed to mean that a man behaves more responsibly, becoming a provider for his wife and children even though he may not be expected to give up all the gratifications of participation in the street system.

For all of these reasons both boys and girls tend to have rather negative views of marriage as well as a low expectation that marriage will prove a stable and gratifying existence. When marriage does take place it tends to represent a tentative commitment on the part of both parties with a strong tendency to seek greater commitment on the part of the partner than on one's own part. Marriage is regarded as a fragile arrangement held together primarily by affectional ties rather than instrumental concerns.

In general, as in white lower-class groups, the decision to marry seems to be taken rather impulsively. Since everyone knows that sooner or later he will get married, in spite of the fact that he may not be sanguine about the prospect, Negro lower-class men and women are alert for clues that the time has arrived. The time may arrive because of a pregnancy in a steady relationship that seems gratifying to both partners, or as a way of getting out of what seems to be an awkward situation, or as a self-indulgence during periods when a boy and a girl are feeling very sorry for themselves. Thus, one girl tells us that when she marries her husband will cook all of her meals for her and she will not have any housework; another girl says that when she marries it will be to a man who has plenty of money and will have to take her out often and really show her a good time.

Boys see in marriage the possibility of regular sexual intercourse without having to fight for it, or a girl safe from venereal disease, or a relationship to a nurturant figure who will fulfill the functions of a mother. For boys, marriage can also be a way of asserting their independence from the peer group if its demands become burdensome. In this case the young man seeks to have the best of both worlds.

. . . In general, then, the movement toward marriage is an uncertain and tentative one. Once the couple does settle down together in a household of their own, they have the problem of working out a mutually acceptable organization of rights and duties, expectations and performances, that will meet their needs.

Husband-Wife Relations

Characteristic of both the Negro and white lower class is a high degree of conjugal role segregation. That is, husbands and wives tend to think of themselves as having very separate kinds of functioning in the instrumental organization of family life, and also as pursuing recreational and outside interests separately. The husband is expected to be a provider; he resists assuming functions around the home so long as he feels he is doing his proper job of bringing home a pay check. He feels he has the right to indulge himself in little ways if he is successful at this task. The wife is expected to care for the home and children and make her husband feel welcome and comfortable. Much that is distinctive to Negro family life stems from the fact that husbands often are not stable providers. Even when a particular man is, his wife's conception of men in general is such that she is pessimistic about the likelihood that he will continue to do well in this area. A great many Negro wives work to supplement the family income. When this is so the separate incomes earned by husband and wife tend to be treated not as "family" income but as the individual property of the two persons involved. If their wives work, husbands are likely to feel that they are entitled to retain a larger share of the income they provide; the wives, in turn, feel that the husbands have no right to benefit from the purchases they make out of their own money. There is, then, "my money" and "your money." In this situation the husband may come to feel that the wife should support the children out of her income and that he can retain all of his income for himself.

While white lower-class wives often are very much intimidated by their husbands, Negro lower-class wives come to feel that they have a right to give as good as they get. If the husband indulges himself, they have the right to indulge themselves. If the husband steps out on his wife, she has the right to step out on him. The commitment of husbands and wives to each other seems often a highly instrumental one after the "honeymoon" period. Many wives feel they owe the husband nothing once he fails to perform his provider role. If the husband is unemployed the wife increasingly refuses to perform her usual duties for him. For example one woman, after mentioning that her husband had cooked four eggs for himself, commented, "I cook for him when he's working but right now he's unemployed; he can cook for himself." It is important, however, to understand that the man's status in the home depends not so much on whether he is working as on whether he brings money into the home. Thus, in several of the families we have studied in which the husband receives disability payments his status is as well-recognized as in families in which the husband is working.

Because of the high degree of conjugal role segregation, both white and Negro lower-class families tend to be matrifocal in comparison to middle-class families. They are matrifocal in the sense that the wife makes most of the decisions that keep the family going and has the greatest sense of responsibility to the family. In white as well as in Negro lower-class families women tend to look to their female relatives for support and counsel, and to treat their husbands as essentially uninterested in the day-to-day problems of family living. In the Negro lower-class family these tendencies are all considerably exaggerated so that the matrifocality is much clearer than in white lower-class families.

The fact that both sexes in the Negro slum culture have equal right to the various satisfactions of life (earning an income, sex, drinking, and peer-group activity which conflicts with family responsibilities) means that there is less pretense to patriarchal authority in the Negro than in the white lower class. Since men find the overt debasement of their status very threatening, the Negro family is much more vulnerable to disruption when men are temporarily unable to perform their provider roles. Also, when men are unemployed the temptations for them to engage in street adventures which repercuss on the marital relationship are much greater. This fact is well-recognized by Negro lower-class wives; they often seem as concerned about what their unemployed husbands will do instead of working as they are about the fact that the husband is no longer bringing money into the home. . . .

Marital Breakup

The precipitating causes of marital disruption seem to fall mainly into economic or sexual categories. As noted, the husband has little credit with his wife to tide him over periods of unemployment. Wives seem very willing to withdraw commitment from husbands who are not bringing money into the house. They take the point of view that he has no right to take up space around the house, to use its facilities, or to demand loyalty from her. Even where the wife is not inclined to press these claims, the husband tends to be touchy because he knows that such definitions are usual in his group, and he may, therefore, prove difficult for even a well-meaning wife to deal with. As noted above, if husbands do not work they tend to play around. Since they continue to maintain some contact with their peer groups, whenever they have time on their hands they move back into the world of the street system and are likely to get involved in activities which pose a threat to their family relationships.

Drink is a great enemy of the lower-class housewife, both white and Negro. Lower-class wives fear their husband's drinking because it costs money, because the husband may become violent and take out his frustrations on his wife, and because drinking may lead to sexual involvements with other women. . . .

Finally, it should be noted that migration plays a part in marital disruption. Sometimes marriages do not break up in the dramatic way described above but rather simply become increasingly unsatisfactory to one or both partners. In such a situation the temptation to move to another city, from South to North, or North to West, is great. Several wives told us that their first marriages were broken when they moved with their children to the North and their husbands stayed behind.

"After we couldn't get along I left the farm and came here and stayed away three or four days. I didn't come here to stay. I came to visit but I liked it and so I said, 'I'm gonna leave!' He said, 'I'll be glad if you do.' Well, maybe he didn't mean it but I thought he did. . . . I miss him sometimes, you know. I think about him I guess. But just in a small way. That's what I can't understand about life sometimes; you know—how people can go on like that and still break up and meet somebody else. Why couldn't—oh, I don't know!"

The gains and losses in marriage and in the post-marital state often seem quite comparable. Once they have had the experience of marriage, many women in the Negro slum culture see little to recommend it in the future, important as the first marriage may have been in establishing their maturity and respectability.

The House of Mothers

As we have seen, perhaps a majority of mothers in the Negro slum community spend at least part of their mature life as mothers heading a family. The Negro mother may be a working mother or she may be an AFDC mother, but in either case she has the problems of maintaining a household, socializing her children, and achieving for herself some sense of membership in relations with other women and with men. As is apparent from the earlier discussion, she often receives her training in how to run such a household by observing her own mother manage without a husband. Similarly she often learns how to run a three-generation household because she herself brought a third generation into her home with her first, premarital, pregnancy.

Because men are not expected to be much help around the house, having to be head of the household is not particularly intimidating to the Negro mother if she can feel some security about income. She knows it is a hard, hopeless, and often thankless task, but she also knows that it is possible. The maternal household in the slum is generally run with a minimum of organization. The children quickly learn to fend for themselves, to go to the store, to make small purchases, to bring change home, to watch after themselves when the mother has to be out of the home, to amuse themselves, to set their own schedules of sleeping, eating, and going to school. Housekeeping practices may be poor, furniture takes a terrific beating from the children, and emergencies constantly arise. The Negro mother in this situation copes by not setting too high standards for herself, by letting things take their course. Life is most difficult when there are babies and preschool children around because then the mother is confined to the home. If she is a grandmother and the children are her daughter's, she is often confined since it is taken as a matter of course that the mother has the right to continue her outside activities and that the grandmother has the duty to be responsible for the child.

In this culture there is little of the sense of the awesome responsibility of caring for children that is characteristic of the working and middle class. There is not the deep psychological involvement with babies which has been observed with the working-class mother. The baby's needs are cared for on a catch-as-catch-can basis. If there are other children around and they happen to like babies, the baby can be over-stimulated; if this is not the case, the baby is left alone a good deal of the time. As quickly as he can move around he learns to fend for himself.

The three-generation maternal household is a busy place. In contrast to working- and middle-class homes it tends to be open to the world, with many non-family members coming in and out at all times as the children are visited by friends, the teenagers by their boy friends and girl friends, the mother by her friends and perhaps an occasional boy friend, and the grandmother by fewer friends but still by an occasional boy friend.

The openness of the household is, among other things, a reflection of the mother's sense of impotence in the face of the street system. Negro lower-class mothers often indicate that they try very hard to keep their young children at home and away from the streets; they often seem to make the children virtual prisoners in the home. As the children grow and go to school they inevitably do become involved in peer-group activities. The mother gradually gives up, feeling that once the child is lost to this pernicious outside world there is little she

can do to continue to control him and direct his development. She will try to limit the types of activities that go on in the home and to restrict the kinds of friends that her children can bring into the home, but even this she must give up as time goes on, as the children become older and less attentive to her direction.

The grandmothers in their late forties, fifties, and sixties tend increasingly to stay at home. The home becomes a kind of court at which other family members gather and to which they bring their friends for sociability, and as a by-product provide amusement and entertainment for the mother. A grandmother may provide a home for her daughters, their children, and sometimes their children's children, and yet receive very little in a material way from them; but one of the things she does receive is a sense of human involvement, a sense that although life may have passed her by she is not completely isolated from it.

The lack of control that mothers have over much that goes on in their households is most dramatically apparent in the fact that their older children seem to have the right to come home at any time once they have moved and to stay in the home without contributing to its maintenance. Though the mother may be resentful about being taken advantage of, she does not feel she can turn her children away. For example, sixty-five-year-old Mrs. Washington plays hostess for weeks or months at a time to her forty-year-old daughter and her small children, and to her twenty-three-year-old granddaughter and her children. When these daughters come home with their families the grandmother is expected to take care of the young children and must argue with her daughter and granddaughter to receive contributions to the daily household ration of food and liquor. Or, a twenty-year-old son comes home from the Air Force and feels he has the right to live at home without working and to run up an eighty-dollar long-distance telephone bill.

Even aged parents living alone in small apartments sometimes acknowledge such obligations to their children or grandchildren. Again, the only clear return they receive for their hospitality is the reduction of isolation that comes from having people around and interesting activity going on. When in the Washington home the daughter and granddaughter and their children move in with the grandmother, or when they come to visit for shorter periods of time, the occasion has a party atmosphere. The women sit around talking and reminiscing. Though boy friends may be present, they take little part; instead they sit passively, enjoying the stories and drinking along with the women. It would seem that in this kind of party activity the women are defined as the stars. Grandmother, daughter, and granddaughter in turn take the center of the stage telling a story from the family's past, talking about a particularly interesting night out on the town or just making some general observation about life. In the course of these events a good deal of liquor is consumed. In such a household as this little attention is paid to the children since the competition by adults for attention is stiff.

Boy Friends, Not Husbands

It is with an understanding of the problems of isolation which older mothers have that we can obtain the best insight into the role and function of boy friends in the maternal household. The older mothers, surrounded by their own children and grandchildren, are not able to move freely in the outside world, to participate in the high life which they enjoyed when younger and more foot-loose. They are disillusioned with marriage as providing any more secure economic base than they can achieve on their own. They see marriage as involving just another responsibility without a concomitant reward—"It's the greatest thing in the world to come home in the afternoon and not have some curly headed twot in the house yellin' at me and askin' me where supper is, where I've been, what I've been doin', and who I've been seein'." In this situation the woman is tempted to form relationships with men that are not so demanding as marriage but still provide companionship and an opportunity for occasional sexual gratification.

There seem to be two kinds of boy friends. Some boy friends "pimp" off mothers; they extract payment in food or money for their companionship. This leads to the custom sometimes called "Mother's Day," the tenth of the month when the AFDC checks come. On this day one

can observe an influx of men into the neighborhood, and much partying. But there is another kind of boy friend, perhaps more numerous than the first, who instead of being paid for his services pays for the right to be a pseudo family member. He may be the father of one of the woman's children and for this reason makes a steady contribution to the family's support, or he may simply be a man whose company the mother enjoys and who makes reasonable gifts to the family for the time he spends with them (and perhaps implicitly for the sexual favors he receives). While the boy friend does not assume fatherly authority within the family, he often is known and liked by the children. The older children appreciate the meaningfulness of their mother's relationship with him—one girl said of her mother's boy friend:

"We don't none of us (the children) want her to marry again. It's all right if she wants to live by herself and have a boy friend. It's not because we're afraid we're going to have some more sisters and brothers, which it wouldn't make us much difference, but I think she be too old."

Even when the boy friend contributes ten or twenty dollars a month to the family he is in a certain sense getting a bargain. If he is a well-accepted boy friend he spends considerable time around the house, has a chance to relax in an atmosphere less competitive than that of his peer group, is fed and cared for by the woman, yet has no responsibilities which he cannot renounce when he wishes. When women have stable relationships of this kind with boy friends they often consider marrying them but are reluctant to take such a step. Even the well-liked boy friend has some shortcomings—one woman said of her boy friend:

"Well he works; I know that. He seems to be a nice person, kind hearted. He believes in survival for me and my family. He don't much mind sharing with my youngsters. If I ask him for a helping hand he don't seem to mind that. The only part I dislike is his drinking."

The woman in this situation has worked out a reasonably stable adaptation to the problems of her life; she is fearful of upsetting this adaptation by marrying again. It seems easier to take the "sweet" part of the relationship with a man without the complexities that marriage might involve.

It is in the light of this pattern of women living in families and men living by themselves in rooming houses, odd rooms, here and there, that we can understand Daniel Patrick Moynihan's observation that during their mature years men simply disappear; that is, that census data show a very high sex ratio of women to men. In St. Louis, starting at the age range twenty to twenty-four there are only seventy-two men for every one hundred women. This ratio does not climb to ninety until the age range fifty to fifty-four. Men often do not have real homes; they move about from one household where they have kinship or sexual ties to another; they live in flop houses and rooming houses; they spend time in institutions. They are not household members in the only "homes" that they have—the homes of their mothers and of their girl friends.

It is in this kind of world that boys and girls in the Negro slum community learn their sex roles. It is not just, or even mainly, that fathers are often absent but that the male role models around boys are ones which emphasize expressive, affectional techniques for making one's way in the world. The female role models available to girls emphasize an exaggerated self-sufficiency (from the point of view of the middle class) and the danger of allowing oneself to be dependent on men for anything that is crucial. By the time she is mature, the woman learns that she is most secure when she herself manages the family affairs and when she dominates her men. The man learns that he exposes himself to the least risk of failure when he does not assume a husband's and father's responsibilities but instead counts on his ability to court women and to ingratiate himself with them.

HEALTH AND THE EDUCATION
OF SOCIALLY DISADVANTAGED CHILDREN

HERBERT G. BIRCH

INTRODUCTION

Recent interest in the effect of social and cultural factors upon educational achievement could lead us to neglect certain biosocial factors which through a direct or indirect influence on the developing child affect his primary characteristics as a learner. Such a danger is exaggerated when health and education are administered separately. The educator and the sociologist may concentrate quite properly on features of curriculum, familial environment, motivation, cultural aspects of language organisation, and the patterning of preschool experiences. Such concentration, while entirely fitting, becomes one-sided and potentially self-defeating when it takes place independently of, and without detailed consideration of, the child as a biological organism. To be concerned with the child's biology is not to ignore the cultural and environmental opportunities which may affect him. Clearly, to regard organic factors as a substitute for environmental opportunity (Hunt 1966) is to ignore the intimate interrelation between the biology of the child and his environment in defining his functional capacities. However, it is equally dangerous to treat cultural influences as though they were acting upon an inert organism. Effective environment (Birch 1954) is the product of the interaction of organic characteristics with the objective opportunities for experience. The child who is apathetic because of malnutrition, whose experiences may have been modified by acute or chronic illness, or whose learning abilities may

Reprinted with abridgment by permission of the author and Spastics International Medical Publications from *Developmental Medicine and Child Neurology*, 1968, **10,** 580–99.

have been affected by some 'insult' to the central nervous system cannot be expected to respond to opportunities for learning in the same way as does a child who has not been exposed to such conditions. Increasing opportunity for learning, though entirely admirable in itself, will not overcome such biologic disadvantages (Birch 1964, Cravioto *et al.* 1960). . . .

PREMATURITY AND OBSTETRIC COMPLICATIONS

Few factors in the health history of the child have been as strongly associated with later intellectual and educational deficiencies as prematurity at birth and complications in the pregnancy from which he derives (McMahon and Sowa 1959). Although a variety of specific infections, explicit biochemical disorders, or trauma may result in more clearly identified and dramatic alterations in brain function, prematurity, together with pre- and perinatal complications, are probably factors which most broadly contribute to disorders of neurologic development (Lilienfeld *et al.* 1955, Pasamanick and Lilienfeld 1955).

A detailed consideration of health factors which may contribute to educational failure must start with an examination of prematurity and the factors associated with it.

Prematurity has been variously defined either by the weight of the child at birth, by the maturity of certain of his physiologic functions, or by gestational age (Coiner 1960). Independently of the nature of the definition in any society in which it has been studied, prematurity has an excessive representation in the lower social strata and among the most significantly so-

TABLE I

Percentage Distribution of 4,254,784 Live-Births by Birth Weight and Ethnic Group, USA 1957

Birth weight (g.)	Total	White	Non-white
1,000 or less	0.5	0.4	0.9
1,001–1,500	0.6	0.5	1.1
1,501–2,000	1.4	1.3	2.4
2,001–2,500	5.1	4.5	8.1
2,501–3,000	18.5	17.5	24.5
3,001–3,500	38.2	38.4	37.2
3,501–4,000	26.8	28.0	19.6
4,001–4,500	7.3	7.8	4.8
4,501–5,000	1.3	1.3	1.3
5,001 or more	0.2	0.2	0.2
Total	100	100	100
Percentage under 2,501 g.	7.6	6.8	12.5
Median weight (g.)	3,310	3,330	3,170
Number of Live Births	4,254,784	3,621,456	633,328

From Baumgartner 1962.

cially disadvantaged. Prematurity in any social group is simultaneously indicative of two separate conditions of risk. In the first place fetuses that are primarily abnormal and characterized by a variety of congenital anomalies are more likely to be born before term than are normal fetuses. Second, infants who are born prematurely, even when no congenital abnormality may be noted, are more likely to develop abnormally than are infants born at term. Thus, Baumgartner (1962) has noted that follow-up studies have 'indicated that malformation and handicapping disorders (neurological, mental and sensory) are more likely to be found among the prematurely born than those born at term. Thus, the premature infant not only has a poorer chance of surviving than the infant born at term, but if he does survive he has a higher risk of having a handicapping condition.' One consequence of this association between prematurity and neurological, mental, sensory and other handicapping conditions is the excessive representation of the prematures among the mentally sub-normal and educationally backward children at school age (Drillien 1964).

Baumgartner (1962) has presented the dis-

tribution of live births by birthweight for white and non-white groups in the United States for 1957 (Table 1). For the country as a whole 7.6 per cent of all live births weighed 2,500 g. or less. In the white segment of the population 6.8 per cent of the babies fell in this category, while 12.5 per cent of the non-white infants weighed 2,500 g. or less. The frequency at all levels of low birthweight was twice as great in non-white infants. Baumgartner attributed the high incidence of prematurity among non-whites to the greater poverty of this group. The studies of Donnelly, *et al.* (1964) in North Carolina, of Thomson (1963) in Aberdeen, Scotland, and of Shapiro *et al.* (1960) in New York suggest that many factors, including nutritional practices, maternal health, the mother's own growth achievements as a child, as well as deficiencies in prenatal care and birth spacing and grand multiparity, interact to produce group differences between the socially disadvantaged and more advantageously situated segments of the population.

It has sometimes been argued that the excess of low birthweight babies among the socially disadvantaged is largely a consequence of ethnic differences (*i.e.,* Negroes 'naturally' give

TABLE 2

Incidence of Obstetric Abnormalities in Aberdeen Primigravidae by Maternal Health and Physique as Assessed at the First Antenatal Examination. (Twin Pregnancies Have Been Excluded.)

	Health and Physique			
	Very good	*Good*	*Fair*	*Poor; very poor*
Prematurity* (%)	5.1	6.4	10.4	12.1
Caesarean section (%)	2.7	3.5	4.2	5.4
Perinatal deaths per 1,000 births	26.9	29.2	44.8	62.8
No. of subjects	707	2,088	1,294	223
Percentage tall (5 ft. 4 in. or more)	42	29	18	13
Percentage short (under 5 ft. 1 in.)	10	20	30	48

* Birthweight of baby 2,500 g. or less (from Thomson 1961).

birth to smaller babies). However, the high association of prematurity with social class in an ethnically homogeneous population such as that in Aberdeen, the finding of Donnelly, *et al.* that within the Negro group higher social status was associated with reduced frequency of prematurity, the findings of Pakter *et al.* (1961) that illegitimacy adds to the risk of prematurity within the non-white ethnic group, and the suggestion made by Shapiro *et al.* that a change for the better in the pattern of medical care reduces the prevalence of prematurity, all make the ethnically based hypothesis of 'natural difference' difficult to retain. . . .

If the low birthweight and survival data are considered distributively rather than categorically, it appears that the non-white infant is subject to an excessive continuum of risk reflected at its extremes by perinatal, neonatal, and infant death, and in the survivors by a reduced functional potential.

THE BACKGROUND OF PERINATAL RISK

Clearly, the risk of having a premature baby or a complicated pregnancy and delivery begins long before the time of the pregnancy itself. A series of studies carried out in Aberdeen, Scotland on the total population of births of that city (Thomson 1963, Walker 1954, Thomson and Billewicz 1963) indicate that prematurity as well as pregnancy complications are significantly correlated with the mother's nutritional status, height, weight, concurrent illnesses, and the social class of her father and husband. Although the relation among these variables is complex, it is clear that the women born in the lowest socio-economic class and who have remained in this class at marriage were themselves more stunted in growth than other women in the population, had less adequate dietary and health habits, were in less good general health, and tended to be at excessive risk of producing premature infants. The mother's stature as well as her habits were determined during her childhood, tended to be associated with contraction of the bony pelvis, and appeared systematically related to her risk condition as a reproducer. In analyzing the relation between maternal health and physique to a number of obstetrical abnormalities such as prematurity, caesarean section and perinatal death, Thomson (1959) (Table 2) has shown each of these to be excessively represented in the mothers of least good physical grade.

The finding of a relation between the mother's physical status and pregnancy outcome is not restricted to Scotland. Donnelly *et al.,* in their study of North Carolina University Hospital births, has shown a clear distribution of height with social class. In Class I (the most advantaged whites) 52 per cent of the women were less than 5 feet 5 inches tall. In contrast in social class IV (the least advantaged non-whites) 75 per cent of the women were under

5 ft. 5 in. in height. The proportion of shorter women increased consistently from Classes I to IV and within each class the incidence of prematurity was higher for women who were less than 5 ft. 3 in. tall. Moreover, within any height range the least advantaged whites had lower prematurity rates than the most advantaged non-whites. Thus in the least advantaged whites less than 5 ft. 3 in. tall the prematurity rate was 12.1 per cent as contrasted with a rate of 19.6 per cent for the non-whites in the same height range. In the tallest of the most disadvantaged whites the rate was 5.6 per cent whereas in non-whites of the same height range who were least disadvantaged the prematurity rate was 10.1 per cent.

DIETARY FACTORS—PRE-WAR AND WAR-TIME EXPERIENCE

The physical characteristics of the mother which affect her efficiency as a reproducer are not restricted to height and physical grade. As early as 1933, Mellanby, while recognizing that 'direct and accurate knowledge of this subject in human beings is meagre,' asserted that nutrition was undoubtedly 'the most important of all environmental factors in childbearing, whether the problem be considered from the point of view of the mother or that of the offspring.' It was his conviction that the reduction of a high perinatal mortality rate as well as of the incidence of maternal ill health accompanying pregnancy could effectively be achieved by improving the quality of the diet. Acting upon these views he attempted to supplement the diets of women attending London antenatal clinics and reported a significant reduction in morbidity rates during the puerperium.

Although Mellanby's own study is difficult to interpret for a number of methodologic reasons, indirect evidence rapidly came into being in support of his views. Perhaps the most important of these was the classical inquiry directed by Sir John Boyd-Orr and reported in *Food, Health and Income* (1936). This study demonstrated conclusively that the long recognised social differential in perinatal death rate was correlated with a dietary differential, and that in all respects the average diet of the lower

income groups in Britain was inadequate for good health. Two years later McCance *et al.* (1938) confirmed the Boyd-Orr findings in a meticulous study of the individual diets of 120 pregnant women representing a range of economic groups ranging from the wives of unemployed miners in South Wales and Tyneside to the wives of professionals. The diet survey technique which they used and which has, unfortunately, been rarely imitated since, was designed to minimize misreport. The results showed that there was wide individual variation in the intake of all foods which related consistently neither to income nor to intake per kilogram of body weight. But when the women were divided into six groups according to the income available for each person per week, the poorer women proved to be shorter and heavier and to have lower hemoglobin counts. Moreover, though economic status had little effect on the total intake of calories, fats and carbohydrates, 'intake of protein, animal protein, phosphorus, iron and Vitamin B_1 rose convincingly with income.' The authors of the study offered no conclusions about the possible outcome of the pregnancies involved, but the poorer reproductive performance of the lower class women was clearly at issue. For as they stated, 'optimum nutrition in an adult implies and postulates optimum nutrition of that person as a child, that child as a fetus, and that fetus of its mother.'

A second body of indirect data supporting Mellanby's hypothesis derived from animal studies on the relation of diet to reproduction. Warkany (1944), for example, demonstrated that pregnant animals maintained on diets deficient in certain dietary ingredients produced offspring suffering from malformation. A diet which was adequate to maintain maternal life and reproductive capacity could be inadequate for normal fetal development. The fetus was not a perfect parasite and at least for some features of growth and differentiation could have requirements different from those of the maternal host.

It would divert us from the main line of our inquiry to consider the many subsequent studies in detail. However, Duncan *et al.* (1952), in surveying these studies, as well as the war-time experiences in Britain, have argued convincingly that the fall in stillbirth and neonatal death rate could only be attributed to a reduction in poverty accompanied by a scientific food rationing policy. Certainly there was no real improvement in prenatal care during the war when so many medical personnel were siphoned off to the armed forces. Furthermore, the improvement took place chiefly among those deaths attributed to 'ill defined or unknown' causes—that is among those cases when low fetal vitality seems to be a major factor in influencing survival—and these types of death 'are among the most difficult to influence by routine antenatal practice.' Of all the possible factors then, nutrition was the only one which improved during the war years (Garry and Wood 1945). Thomson (1959) commented that the result was 'as a nutritional effect' all the more convincing 'because it was achieved in the context of a society where most of the conditions of living other than the nutritional were deteriorating.'

While this National 'feeding experiment' was going on in the British Isles, a more controlled experiment was being carried out on the continent of Europe (Toverud 1950). In 1939 Dr. Toverud set up a health station in the Sagene district of Oslo to serve pregnant and nursing mothers and their babies. Though war broke out shortly after the station was opened, and it became progressively more difficult to get certain protective foods, an attempt was made to insure that every woman being surpervised had the recommended amounts of every essential nutrient, through the utilization of supplementary or synthetic sources when necessary. In spite of food restrictions which became increasingly severe, the prematurity rate among the 728 women who were supervised at the station never went above the 1943 high of 3.4 per cent, averaging 2.2 per cent for the period 1939–1944. Among the unsupervised mothers the 1943 rate was 6.3 per cent and the average for the period 4.6 per cent. In addition, the stillbirth rate of 14.2/1,000 for all women attending the health station was half that of the women in the surrounding districts.

Meanwhile, even as the British and Norwegian feeding experiments were in progress, there were some hopefully never-to-be repeated starvation 'experiments' going on elsewhere.

When they were reported after the war, the childbearing experiences of various populations of women under conditions of severe nutritional restriction were to provide evidence of the ways in which deprivation could negatively affect the product of conception, just as dietary improvement appeared able to affect it positively.

Smith (1947), for example, studying infants born in Rotterdam and the Hague during a delimited period of extreme hunger brought on by a transportation strike, found that the infants were shorter and lighter (by about 240 g.) than those born both before and after the period of deprivation. Significantly enough Smith also found that those babies who were five to six month fetuses when the hunger period began appeared to have been reduced in weight as much as those who had spent a full nine months in the uterus of a malnourished mother. He was led to conclude from this that reduced maternal caloric intake had its major effect on fetal weight beginning around the sixth month of gestation. Antonov's study of babies born during the siege of Leningrad (1947) confirmed the fact of weight reduction as well as Smith's observations that very severe deprivation was likely to prevent conception altogether rather than reduce the birthweight. Antonov found that during a six month period which began four months after the start of the siege, there was an enormous increase in prematurity as judged by birth length—41.2 per cent of all the babies born during this period were less than 47 cm. long and fully 49.1 per cent weighed under 2,500 grams. The babies were also of very low vitality—30.8 per cent of the prematures and 9 per cent of the full-term babies died during the period. Abruptly, during the latter half of the year, the birthrate plummeted—along with the prematurity rate. Thus, while 161 prematures and 230 term babies were born between January and June, 1942, five prematures and 72 term babies were born between July and December. Where information was available it suggested that the women who managed to conceive during the latter part of the year, when amenorrhea was widespread, were better fed than the majority, being employed in food industries or working in professional or manual occupations which had food priorities. Antonov concluded that while the fetus might behave for the most part like a parasite, 'the condition of the host, the mother's body, is of great consequence to the fetus, and that severe quantitative and qualitative hunger of the mother decidedly affects the development of the fetus and the vitality of the newborn child.' . . .

OBSTETRICAL CARE
OF LOWER CLASS WOMEN

Obstetrical care as suggested above is markedly different in socially advantaged and disadvantaged segments of the population. A preliminary view of the obstetrical care received by lower class pregnant women may be obtained from a consideration of Hartman and Sayl's (1965) survey of 1,380 births, at the Minneapolis General Hospital. This hospital which served medically indigent patients living in census tracts having notably high rates of infant mortality delivered 43 per cent of its patients with either no prenatal care or only one third trimester antenatal visit. Of the women who did attend the hospital's prenatal clinic, 3 per cent made their initial visit during the first trimester, 26 per cent in the second trimester and 71 per cent in the last trimester. Infant mortality appeared to vary according to prenatal care. The mothers having no prenatal care experienced fetal deaths at a rate of 4 per cent, a rate considerably higher than the 0.7 per cent fetal death rate for mothers having one or more visits to the prenatal clinic.

Boek and Boek (1956), in upper New York State, collected their sample through an examination of birth certificates. 1,805 mothers were interviewed and grouped according to social class as determined by the child's father's occupation. The amount and type of obstetric care correlated with social class. Mothers in the lowest social classes tended to seek health care later during pregnancy than higher class women. Lower class mothers tended to use a family doctor for both pre- and post-natal care, rather than the obstetric specialists and pediatricians heavily patronized by upper class women. More than twice as many upper class women attended group meetings for expectant parents than did lower class mothers. Lower class women tended to stay in the hospital fewer days than upper

class women, and although the former paid lower doctor's bills, they tended to pay higher hospital bills since more higher than lower class families had hospital insurance. Three months after the birth of the child fewer lower class women had received postnatal checkups than upper class women and fewer mothers in the lowest social class had their babies immunized with a triple vaccine or planned to have this done.

The effects of a good, comprehensive health program on pregnancy losses was studied by Shapiro *et al.* (1960), in a comparison of the infant mortality rates for members of the Health Insurance Plan and the general New York City population. Obstetric-gynecology diplomates delivered 72 per cent of the HIP babies. Only 24 per cent of the general New York population received specialist care, and only 5 per cent of non-white babies were delivered by specialists. Because of these radical differences in type of delivery care, the investigators compared the HIP prematurity and perinatal mortality rates only to those New Yorkers who were patients of private physicians. Socio-economic status was judged by the occupation of the father as recorded on birth and death certificates. The data on prematurity for the three year period are presented in Table 3. The white patients who participated in the Health Insurance Plan had their prematurity rate reduced from the 6 per cent rate characteristic for their group in the city as a whole to 5.5 per cent. This reduction just missed statistical significance at the 5 per cent level. In the non-white group the rate was reduced from 10.8 to 8.8 per cent, a difference significant at the .01 level of confidence. Within each specific category of physician used, Shapiro found that white deliveries had a far lower perinatal mortality than non-white for the general New York City group. General service deliveries had a far greater mortality rate than private physician cases in hospitals for both the white and non-white groups. 'Among white deliveries mortality was considerably higher for general service cases than for those under the care of private doctors in each occupation category . . . This raises the interesting question whether the greater mortality in general service is principally due to factors associated with type of

TABLE 3

*Prematurity Rates by Ethnic Group, New York City, and HIP (Adjusted) 1955–1957**

	Single Live Births Attended by Private Physician in Hospital			
	Prematurity Rate per 100 Live Births[1]			
Ethnic Group	*New York City*[2]	*HIP Adjusted*[2]	*Standard Error of Difference*	*P*[3]
Total (Excluding Puerto Rican)	6.2	5.7	0.23	0.04
White	6.0	5.5	0.24	0.06
Nonwhite	10.8	8.8	0.74	<0.01

[1] Prematurity rate is defined as the number of live births 2,500 gm. or less per 100 live births.
[2] New York City rates are observed rates for deliveries of women of all ages excluding those under 20 and age not stated.
HIP rates are adjusted to age of mother and ethnic distribution of New York City deliveries (excluding deliveries of women under 20 and age not stated).
[3] '*p*' represents the probability that NYC-HIP difference is due to chance factors.
* (From Shapiro 1960).

care or the setting in which it is received, or whether the poorer risk women within each occupation class tend to turn to general service.' . . .

In view of the potential importance of prenatal care on pregnancy course and outcome and the suggestion that such care is deficient in the lowest socio-economic groups it is important to examine the ethnic distribution of antenatal care. The study of Pakter *et al.* (1961) though restricted to New York City is representative of conditions that exist on a national scale. His findings can be replicated in any urban community having a significantly large nonwhite population. In rural areas the situation is equally bad. Approximately 30 per cent of married Negro mothers and 39 per cent of Puerto Rican mothers received no prenatal care during the first six months of the pregnancy. In contrast, only 13 per cent of white married mothers were subjected to a similar lack of care.

POST-NATAL CONDITIONS FOR DEVELOPMENT

Densen and Haynes (1967) have indicated that many types of illness are excessively rep-

resented in the non-white segments of the population at all age levels. I have selected one, nutritional status, as the model variable for consideration. A considerable body of evidence from animal experimentation as well as field studies of populations at nutritional risk (Cravioto *et al.* 1966) have suggested a systematic relation between nutritional inadequacy and both neurologic maturation and competence in learning.

At birth the brain of a full-term infant has achieved about one quarter of its adult weight. The bulk of subsequent weight gain will derive from the laying down of lipids, particularly myelin, and cellular growth. Animal experiments on the rat (Davison and Dobbing 1966), the pig (Dickerson *et al.* 1967, McCance 1960) and the dog (Platt *et al.* 1964) have all demonstrated a significant interference in brain growth and differentiation associated with severe dietary restriction, particularly of protein, during the first months of life. In these animals the behavioral effects have been dramatic with abnormalities in some cases persisting after dietary rehabilitation.

The relation of these data to the human situation is made difficult by the extreme severity of the dietary restrictions. More modest restrictions have been imposed by Widdowson (1965) and Barnes *et al.* (1966) and the latter experiments indicated some tendency for poorer learning in the nutritionally deprived animals. Cowley and Griesel's work (1963) suggests a cumulative effect of malnutrition on adaptive behavior across generations.

The animal findings as a whole can be interpreted either as suggesting a direct influence of malnutrition on brain growth and development, or as resulting in interference with learning at critical points in development. In either case the competence of the organism as a learner appears to be influenced by his history as an eater. These considerations add cogency to an already strongly held belief that good nutrition is important for children and links our general concerns on the relation of nutrition to health to our concerns with education and the child's functioning as a learner.

Incidents of severe malnutrition appear rarely in the United States today, but there is evidence to suggest that the low income segments of the population suffer from subtle, sub-clinical forms of malnutrition which may be partially responsible for the higher rates of morbidity and mortality of children in this group. Brock (1961) suggests that 'dietary sub-nutrition can be defined as any impairment of functional efficiency or body systems which can be corrected by better feeding.' Since 'constitution is determined in part by habitual diet . . . diet must be considered in discussing the aetiology of a large group of diseases of uncertain and multiple aetiology . . .' The relationship between nutrition and constitution is demonstrated by the fact that the populations of developed nations are taller and heavier than those of technically underdeveloped nations and that 'within a given developed nation children from economically favoured areas are taller and heavier than children from economically under-privileged areas.' . . .

[The author goes on at this point to review research on the nutritional status of various economic groups in the United States. The diets of infants and children from low-income families in Boston, North Carolina, South Carolina, New York, and Onondaga County, New York, were found to be significantly less adequate than those of middle class subjects, and the diet of blacks was nutritionally poorer than that of whites. (Eds.)]

CONCLUSIONS

In this review I have examined certain selected conditions of health which may have consequences for education. Other factors such as acute and chronic illness, immunizations, dental care, the utilization of health services and a host of other phenomena, perhaps equally pertinent to those selected for consideration, have been dealt with either in passing or not at all but in fact studies of these factors that do exist reflect the same picture that emerges from those variables which have been discussed. In brief, though much of the information is incomplete, and certain aspects of the data are sparse, a serious consideration of available health information leaves little or no doubt that children who are economically and socially disadvantaged and in an ethnic group exposed to discrimination, are exposed to massively excessive risks for maldevelopment.

Such risks have direct and indirect consequences for the functioning of the child as a learner. Conditions of ill health may directly affect the development of the nervous system and eventuate either in patterns of clinically definable malfunctioning in this system or in sub-clinical conditions. In either case the potentialities of the child as a learner cannot but be impaired. Such impairment, though it may in fact have reduced functional consequences under exceptionally optimal conditions for development and education, in any case represents a primary handicap which efforts at remediation may only partially correct.

The indirect effects of ill health or of conditions of sub-optimal health care on the learning processes may take many forms. . . . Children who are ill nourished are reduced in their responsiveness to the environment, distracted by their visceral state, and reduced in their ability to progress and endure in learning conditions. Consequently, given the same objective conditions for learning, the state of the organism modifies the effective environment and results in a reduction in the profit which a child may derive from exposure to opportunities for experience. Consequently, the provision of equal opportunities for learning in an objective sense is never met when only the school situation is made identical for advantaged and disadvantaged children. Though such a step is indeed necessary, proper and long overdue, a serious concern with the profitability of such improved objective opportunities for socially disadvantaged children demands a concern which goes beyond education and includes an intensive and directed consideration of the broader environment, the health and functional and physical well-being of the child.

Inadequacies in nutritional status as well as excessive amounts in intercurrent illness may interfere in indirect ways with the learning process. As Cravioto, *et al.* (1966) have put it, at least 'three possible indirect effects are readily apparent:

(1) *Loss of learning time.* Since the child was less responsive to his environment when malnourished, at the very least he had less time in which to learn and had lost a certain number of months of experience. On the simplest basis, therefore, he would be expected to show some developmental lags.

(2) *Interference with learning during critical periods of development.* Learning is by no means simply a cumulative process. A considerable body of evidence exists which indicates that interference with the learning process at specific times during its course may result in disturbances in function that are both profound and of long term significance. Such disturbance is not merely a function of the length of time the organism is deprived of the opportunities for learning. Rather, what appears to be important is the correlation of the experiential opportunity with a given stage of development— the so-called critical periods of learning. Critical periods in human learning have not been definitively established, but in looking at the consequences associated with malnutrition at different ages one can derive some potentially useful hypotheses. The earlier report by Cravioto and Robles (1965) may be relevant to the relationship between the age at which malnutrition develops and learning. They have shown that, as contrasted with older patients, infants under six months recovering from kwashiorkor did not recoup their mental age deficit during the recovery period. In older children, ranging from 15 to 41 months of age, too, the rate of recovery from the initial mental deficit varied in direct relation to chronological age at time of admission. Similarly, the findings of Barrera-Moncada 1963 in children, and those of Keys, *et al.* (1950) in adults, indicated a strong association between the persistence of later effects on mental performance and the age at onset of malnutrition and its duration.

(3) *Motivation and personality changes.* It should be recognized that the mother's response to the infant is to a considerable degree a function of the child's own characteristics of reactivity. One of the first effects of malnutrition is a reduction in the child's responsiveness to stimulation and the emergence of various degrees of apathy. Apathetic behavior in its turn can function to reduce the value of the child as a stimulus and to diminish the adults' responsiveness to him. Thus, apathy can provoke apathy and so contribute to a cumulative pattern of reduced adult-child interaction. If this occurs it can have consequences for stimulation, for learning, for maturation, and for interpersonal relations, the end result being significant backwardness in performance on later more complex learning tasks.'

However, independently of the path through which bio-social pathology interferes with educational progress, there is little doubt that ill health is a significant variable for defining differentiation in the learning potential of the child. To intervene effectively with the learning problems of disadvantaged children it would be disastrous if we were either to ignore or to relegate the physical condition and health status of the child with whose welfare we are concerned to a place of unimportance. To do so would be to divorce education from health; a divorce which can only have disorganizing consequences for the child. Unless health and education go hand in hand we shall fail to break the twin curse of ignorance and poverty.

REFERENCES

Antonov, A. N. (1947) 'Children born during the siege of Leningrad in 1942.' *J. Piediat.,* 30, 250.

Barnes, R. H., Cunnold, S. R., Zimmerman, R. R., Simmons, H., MacLeod, R., Krook, L. (1966) 'Influence of nutritional deprivations in early life on learning behaviour of rats as measured by performance in water maze.' *J. Nutr.,* 89, 399.

Barrera-Moncada, G. (1963) Estudios sobre Alleraciones del Crecimiento y del Desarrollo Psicológico de Sindrome Pluricarencial Kwashiorkor. Caracas: Editoria Grafos.

Baumgartner, L. (1962) 'The public health significance of low birth weight in the U.S.A., with special reference to varying practices in providing special care to infants of low birth weights.' *Bull. Wld Hlth Org.,* 26, 175.

———— (1965) 'Health and ethnic minorities in the sixties.' *Amer. J. publ. Hlth,* 55, 495.

Birch, H. G. (1954) 'Comparative psychology.' *In* Marcuse, F. A. (Ed.) Areas of Psychology. New York: Harper.

———— (Ed.) (1964) Brain Damage in Children: Biological and Social Aspects. Baltimore: Williams & Wilkins.

Boek, W. E., Boek, J. K. (1956) Society and Health. New York: Putnam.

———— and co-worker (1957) Social Class, Maternal Health and Child Care. Albany, N.Y.: New York State Department of Health.

Brock, J. (1961) Recent Advances in Human Nutrition. London: Churchill.

Corner, B. (1960) Prematurity. London: Cassell.

Cowley, J. J., Griesel, R. D. (1963) 'The development of second generation low-protein rats.' *J. genet. Psychol.,* 103, 233.

Cravioto, J., De Licardie, E. R., Birch, H. G. (1966) 'Nutrition, growth and neuro-integrative development: an experimental and ecologic study.' *Pediatrics,* 38, 319.

————, Robles, B. (1965) 'Evolution of adaptive and motor behaviour during rehabilitation from kwashiorkor.' *Amer. J. Orthopsychiat.,* 35, 449.

Davison, A. N., Dobbing, J. (1966) 'Myelination as a vulnerable period in brain development.' *Brit. med. Bull.,* 22, 40.

Densen, P. M., Haynes, A. (1967) 'Research and the major health problems of Negro Americans.' Paper presented at the Howard University Centennial Celebration, Washington. (Unpublished.)

Dickerson, J. W., Dobbing, J., McCance, R. A. (1967) 'The effect of under nutrition on the postnatal development of the brain and cord in pigs.' *Proc. roy. Soc. B.,* 166, 396.

Donnelly, J. F., Flowers, C. E., Creadick, R. N., Wells, H. B., Greenberg, B. G., Surles, K. B. (1964) 'Maternal, fetal and environmental factors in prematurity.' *Amer. J. Obstet. Gynec.,* 88, 918.

Drillien, C. M. (1964) The Growth and Development of Prematurely Born Children. Edinburgh: Livingstone; Baltimore: Williams & Wilkins.

Duncan, E. H. L., Baird, D., Thomson, A. M. (1952) 'The causes and prevention of stillbirths and first week deaths. I. The evidence of vital statistics.' *J. Obstet. Gyn. Brit. Emp.,* 59, 183.

Garry, R. C., Wood, H. O. (1945–46) 'Dietary requirements in human pregnancy and lactation: a review of recent work.' *Nutr. Abstr. Rev.,* 15, 591.

Hartman, E. E., Sayles, E. B. (1965) 'Some reflections on births and infant deaths among the low socioeconomic groups.' *Minn. Med.,* 48, 1,711.

Hunt, E. E. (1966) 'Some new evidence on race and intelligence.' Paper read at the meeting of the New York Academy of Sciences—Anthropology Section, Oct. 24, 1966. (Unpublished.)

Keys, A., Brozek, J., Henschel, A., Mikelson, O., Taylor, H. (1950) The Biology of Starvation. Vol. 2. Minneapolis: University of Minnesota Press.

Lilienfeld, A. M., Pasamanik, B., Rogers, M. (1955) 'Relationship between pregnancy experience and the development of certain neuropsychiatric disorders in childhood.' *Amer. J. publ. Hlth,* 45, 637.

McCance, R. A. (1960) 'Severe undernutrition in growing and adult animals. I. Production and general effects.' *Brit. J. Nutr.,* 14, 59.

————, Widdowson, E. M., Verdon-Roe, C. M. (1938) 'A study of English diets by the individual method. III. Pregnant women at different economic levels.' *J. Hyg.* (*Lond.*), 38, 596.

MacMahon, B., Sowa, J. M. (1961) 'Physical damage to the foetus.' *In* Causes of Mental Disorders: A Review of Epidemiological Knowledge, 1959. New York: Milbank Memorial Fund, p. 51.

Mellanby, E. (1933) 'Nutrition and child bearing.' *Lancet,* ii, 1,131.

Orr, J. B. (1936) Food, Health and Income. London: Macmillan.

Pakter, J., Rosner, H. J., Jacobziner, H., Greenstein, F. (1961) 'Out-of-wedlock births in New York City. II. Medical aspects.' *Amer. J. publ. Hlth,* 51, 846.

Pasamanik, B., Lilienfeld, A. M. (1955) 'Association of maternal and fetal factors with development of mental deficiency. I. Abnormalities in the prenatal and perinatal periods.' *J. Amer. med. Ass.,* 159, 155.

Platt, B. S., Heard, R. C., Stewart, R. J. (1964) 'Experimental protein-calorie deficiency.' *In* Munro, H. N., Allison, J. B. (Eds.) Mammalian Protein Metabolism. New York: Academic Press, p. 446.

Shapiro, S., Jacobziner, H., Densen, P. M., Weiner, L. (1960) 'Further observations on prematurity and perinatal mortality in a general population and in the population of a prepaid group practice medical care plan.' *Amer. J. publ. Hlth,* 50, 1,304.

Smith, C. A. (1947) 'Effects of maternal undernutrition upon the new born infant in Holland.' *J. Pediat.,* 30, 229.

Thomson, A. M. (1959) 'Maternal stature and reproductive efficiency.' *Eugen. Rev.,* 51, 157.

———— (1959) 'Diet in pregnancy. III. Diet in relation to the course and outcome of pregnancy.' *Brit. J. Nutr.,* 13, 509.

———— (1963) 'Prematurity: socio-economic and nutritional factors.' *Bibl. paediat. (Basel),* 81, 197.

————, Billewicz, W. Z. (1963) 'Nutritional status, physique and reproductive efficiency.' *Proc. nutr. Soc.,* 22, 55.

Toverud, G. (1950) 'The influence of nutrition on the course of pregnancy.' *Milbank mem. Fd. Quart.,* 28, 7.

Walker, J. (1954) 'Obstetrical complications, congenital malformations and social strata.' *In* Mechanisms of Congenital Malformations. New York: Association for the Aid of Crippled Children, p. 20.

Warkany, J. (1944) 'Congenital malformations induced by maternal nutritional deficiency.' *J. Pediat.,* 25, 476.

Widdowson, E. M. (1966) 'Nutritional deprivation in psychobiological development: studies in animals.' *In* Proceedings of the Special Session, 4th Meeting of the PAHO Advisory Committee on Medical Research, June, 1965. Washington: World Health Organization.

PART THREE

INFANCY

THE NEONATE

In comparison with the newborn of many other species, the human neonate begins life relatively helpless. He can carry on vital functions only if others nurture him and provide for him the environment necessary for life. Furthermore, he is born with a large portion of his central nervous system unprogrammed; most of his adaptations to the environment have to be acquired—a biological factor that insures maximum flexibility of behavior.

But the neonate is not the decorticate organism incapable of discriminatory sensory stimulation he was once described as being. As a result of a tremendous expansion of empirical research under improved laboratory conditions, the picture of a more competent neonate is emerging. For one thing, his reflex behaviors and capabilities include the ability to engage in visual pursuit, to respond to form, to distinguish differences in volume and pitch, and to respond to tactile, thermal, and olfactory stimuli. Some excellent summaries of this research are included in the references at the end of this introduction.

The general procedure for assessing reflex capabilities is to present an appropriate stimulus and to observe the ensuing response. Thus in assessing olfactory sensitivity, the experimenter can present substances classed as pungent, floral, musky, fruity, minty, rancid, and so on and observe such behaviors as facial expression (mimetic), gross motor activity, sucking, and breathing and blood pressure changes. The procedure can become quite sophisticated, as research on vision indicates. The paper by Salapatek included in this volume investigates whether the newborn is capable of responding visually to form. Is the world the fuzzy blur that early investigators described, or are there the beginnings of discrimination in scanning an object? Results show that even within the first eight days of life the newborn fixates differently on a solid black triangle than on a uniform field. How he focuses is revealed by recording reflections of infrared lights from the cornea of the eye.

Such findings on reflex behaviors may strike the reader as trivial and irrelevant. However, such findings have implications for the role of reflexes in adaptation and development. Child development research has been plagued by a "maturational bias" which implies that "the young organism harbors the genetic determinants which will dictate the appearance of certain behaviors at certain stages of development, and that experience plays only a minimal role" (Lipsitt, 1966), a bias which still persists despite evidence *against* genetic determinacy. As knowledge of the organism grows, as we see continuity in development from visual scanning to object constancy to permanence of object to conservation, with all the intervening steps, we can begin to consider seriously the question of what kinds of environmental conditions aid development and what constitutes proper intervention for optimal development.

Both observational and learning studies also have revealed the neonate as competent. Piaget noted in observation of his own children that experience influences the sucking reflex; within a few days after birth, his son Laurent showed a shift from passive response to active search for the nipple, and by the twentieth day, although he might first attempt to suck the skin of the breast, he quickly moved to grope actively with his mouth for the nipple. Experimental studies have subjected the sucking reflex to controlled investigation. Lipsitt and Kaye (1964) report an experiment in which either a nipple only or tubing only was presented to infants in each of two groups, while nipple and tubing were presented alternately, five trials in a session, to a third group. As might be expected, judging by amount of sucking, the nipple proved to be more agreeable than the tubing. More interesting, though, is the fact that within the five-trial blocks for the alternated group, effects from the previously administered stimulus persevered. That is, response to each of the five presentations of the nipple started low and moved higher, while response to the tube started high and moved lower, in comparison to the single-stimulus groups. Sucking appears to be affected by the other oral stimuli that the infant has experienced.

An important variable that must be taken into account in assessing both newborn and older infants is that of *state*. "State" is a concept used to describe a behavioral condition, stable over time, that occurs frequently and in all infants. How alert the infant is, for example, or whether or not he is crying are states that can make for both qualitative and quantitative differences in results. While "state" is difficult to assess, investigators have learned that it is a variable to be considered seriously.

INFANT-MOTHER RELATIONSHIPS

Concern with infant-mother relationships is not a new concern in child development. Freudian theory places a great deal of emphasis on the mother-child dyad, ethologists have given us insights from the behavior of animals, cognitive theorists are interested in cognitive-affective influences, and experimentalists have tested hypotheses generated by various theoretical schools. Two areas in particular will be explored here: object relations and social attachments; and separation, deprivation, and stimulation.

Object Relations and Social Attachments

The helpless nature of the infant and his dependence on others for physical care bring him into close contact with a caretaker, usually the mother. The extremely close tie between mother and child has been of great interest to investigators of different theoretical schools who have attempted to explain the origins and nature of the tie. According to psychoanalytic theory, the biological interaction that takes place in either breast- or bottle-feeding as well as in other caretaking activities becomes invested with psychological content. In the oral experience the infant libido, or psychic energy, is directed toward the mother—she becomes the libidinal object. Out of this relationship develops the first notion of object.

The notion of object is basic to perception and cognition. In fact, we see the world as a world of objects, and we construct relationships among them to build a structure of knowledge. Since the mother appears to be the first object, investigators have done considerable research on infant-mother relationships to find out more about object relations.

The age at which an infant achieves permanence of object provides a mark against which infant cognitive development can be measured. Piaget emphasizes the importance of object permanence in sensorimotor intelligence and traces its slow development. A three-month-old infant may show interest in an object shown to him but lose interest when the object is removed. The object has no permanence; it appears to have left no trace in sensorimotor intelligence. Between four to eight months, there is a dawning awareness of object, shown by such actions as the child removing an obstacle from his face to free perception. In the eight-to-twelve-months period, there is an active search for an object shown to the child and then hidden while he watches where it is hidden. But permanence is still bound to action; if the object is hidden in two successive places, the child searches at the initial place, not at the last-seen place. Between twelve and eighteen months, the object is sought in the place last seen. If the displacement has to be inferred, though, the child searches in the first hiding place.

What connection is there between this development and infant-mother relations? Cobliner (1965), working within the framework of psychoanalytic theory, claims that the quality of these relations determines the motivating factors essential to permanence-of-object attainment. The disappearance of the object causes frustration in the child; unless he can master this momentary frustration, he cannot energize his psychic forces to search for the object. But the frustration can be overcome if the mental image of the object has been invested with a positive cathexis, and objects become positively cathected only after the mother has been established as a permanent object. A close reciprocal relationship with the mother facilitates development of the mother as a permanent object, differentiated from self, which in turn serves as a trailbreaker for formation of the concept of permanence of other objects.

Spitz (1965) has argued that the aspect of mother that first has significance for the infant is the mother's face, particularly the forehead, eyes, and nose. Spitz states that beginning with the second month of life, the human face becomes a "privileged" percept and the infant will respond to its presentation with a smile. Wolff (1963) was able to produce a smiling response (not the "false" smile associated with digestive troubles) as early as three weeks. Even when presentation of the human face is accompanied by other stimuli (auditory, tactile, kinesthetic), in conditioning experiments (Brossard and Décarie, 1968) the visual stimulus alone provides rapid learning. Kagan *et al.* (1966) found that four-month-old babies smile more often at a realistic face stimulus than at a scrambled face or one lacking an eye. Certainly the human face, with its constantly changing features, is a most interesting stimulus, in addition to having reciprocal affective value. When an infant smiles at his mother's face, his mother may be so delighted that "he smiled at me!" that she will respond in kind.

Recognition of an individual face is a later development. Spitz noted the emergence of an anxious response to strangers, which he called "eight-month anxiety." To psychoanalysts, this phenomenon is due to a fear of losing the mother which evidences itself when the mother is absent. It is not that the stranger evokes memories of a disagreeable experience, but that the infant perceives the stranger's face as not identical with the memory traces of the mother's face. Spitz contends that appearance of the eight-month anxiety marks the onset of a new stage in infant development: it is a "critical" period in ego development, marking the time when "the child has found 'the' partner with whom he can form object relations in the true sense of the term." There can be no true libidinal object while the objects remain interchangeable.

Other investigators, such as Bowlby (1969), also a psychoanalyst, conceive of the infant-mother tie as a *social attachment* based on species-characteristic behavioral systems that activate and are activated by stimuli provided by human beings. Such infant behaviors as head-turning, reaching, and crying signal the mother to respond, and her response triggers new responses in the infant; there is a *reciprocal feedback* between mother and baby and baby and mother which is in continual flux, a reciprocal relationship that is increasingly emphasized in the literature. In time the child learns to single out his mother as a particularly satisfying object; he becomes aware of her as an object which is not self and which moves about in a fairly predictable way. In time he seeks also to maintain proximity to her. The onset of specific attachments is generally found in the third quarter of the first year (Schaffer and Emerson, 1964).

Separation, Deprivation, and Stimulation

The closeness of the infant-mother tie raises the question of separation and deprivation. Since the infant must grow into an independent person, separation from the mother is inevitable and indeed begins in infancy, as Rheingold and Eckerman (1970) have shown. Physical separation is possible when the infant is able to move his own body; separation brings with it enormously increased opportunities to interact with the environment. Rheingold emphasizes that the consequences of detachment are as important to study as attachment.

Temporary separation, whether initiated by infant or mother, is endurable and inevitable. Deprivation of the mother for a long period of time, as is the case with institutionalized babies, is a more serious matter; its effects have been noted by Spitz (1945), Bowlby (1952), Goldfarb (1945), and others and summarized by Casler (1961). Most of the studies report the same unfortunate results—that infants abruptly separated from their mothers go into a state of depression, and when raised in institutions, they are retarded in language and concept formation and

develop an apathetic personality, continually seeking affection but unable to establish close, meaningful ties with other people. That such effects of institutionalization and deprivation are neither inevitable nor irreversible has been brought out
in a number of studies. Skeels (1966) found that when mentally retarded girls
performed parenting functions for babies, otherwise deprived of "mothering," in an
orphanage, the babies not only gained spectacularly in IQ and became adoptable
(since, typically, only babies whose IQ's approach the normal range are acceptable
to foster parents), but most of them grew up to be self-sustaining adults. These
results were in sharp contrast to controls receiving no "mothering." Wolins (1970)
found the same thing to be true in a Yugoslav institution. Younger children who
relied on older children in the same institution for their affective ties were not
significantly different at adolescence in intellectual performance and personality
development from family-reared children. (We might note here parenthetically that
kibbutz children in Israel do not fall into the usual category of maternally deprived,
institutionalized children. Children in the kibbutzim see their parents every day
and have a chance to establish affectional ties.)

The cognitive deficit noted in orphanage babies was first attributed to maternal
deprivation, to the lack of a close tie with a single caretaker. Casler (1961), however, proposed that the antecedent condition might be a *perceptual* deficit, that
institutionalized babies spent most of their day in cribs with nothing to see, hear, or
touch and with only minimal contact with human caretakers. Dennis and Najarian
(1957) had shown that institutionalized babies deprived of motor stimulation were
severely retarded in creeping and walking. These studies were confirmed by findings
from animal studies (Zubek, 1969) which also revealed serious deficits in problem-
solving abilities in animals exposed to extreme deprivation of stimulation. These
studies, together with studies of preschool children in socioeconomically disadvantaged families, have raised questions about the appropriate means and time to provide
enrichment to overcome environmental deficit. Must the stimulation come from a
human caretaker in infancy, or can it be administered mechanically?

The Brossard and Décarie study included here investigates the significance of
the caretaker in the development of the young infant. During the first two to four
months, is mechanically administered perceptual stimulation as effective as social
stimulation mediated with a human agent? These and related questions were put to
experimental test with institutionalized infants with the surprising result that while
amount of stimulation is indeed significant, both the perceptual group and the social
group did about equally well, and both did better than the mixed and control groups.
The investigators, however, wisely caution against "monkeying with the mother
myth"; there is still too much to be learned about what is learned in the mother-
child reciprocal relationship to advocate "mechanical mothering" even during the
first few months of life. One is reminded of Harlow's infant monkeys who, reared
with wire "mothers" who furnished food and warmth, turned out to be wretched
mothers. Like Décarie, one wonders about later development—whether, for example,
mechanically stimulated babies will develop the basic trust in other human beings
that Erikson talks about. Will they develop the close attachment to a single human
being revealed by eight-month anxiety? The dogs in Scott's study (Scott *el al.*,
1951), reared in isolation, showed no signs of fear in situations where it would have

been normal to show fear, and it took several months of social living before the isolated dogs caught up.

The question of "critical period" is relevant here, for the notion has been prevalent that the first six months are "critical" for stimulating development. "Critical period," the reader will recall from Part 1, refers to a period in development when the organism is uniquely sensitive to certain environmental stimuli. The "following" response of certain animals (such as ducks and sheep) is an example of *imprinting,* a special kind of learning that occurs during the critical few hours after birth. However, it is now generally believed that though "critical period" is sometimes applied to human learning, the human organism is tremendously flexible: while it is true that the infant is vulnerable from the standpoint of social attachments and need for stimulation, at this point one cannot say that the first six months or any other specified time period in infancy is "critical" in the true sense of that word.

SENSORIMOTOR INTELLIGENCE

We are defining the period of infancy as that period extending from birth to eighteen months. At the start we have an infant whose competencies are real but limited, an organism incapable of intelligent action. At the end of this time, we have a mobile, talking baby with a remarkable repertoire of "schemata" (Piaget's term for Gestalt-like mental structures built out of sensorimotor experiences of the child). For a step-by-step account of the growth of mental structures, we turn to Piaget.

The first stage that Piaget describes in the development of intelligence is the *sensorimotor.* The data on which he bases his analysis come from systematic, detailed observations of his own three children—Jacqueline, Lucienne, and Laurent—each observation labeled with the exact age of the child (e.g., "1:2 (8)" means one year, two months, and eight days). The sensorimotor stage lasts until about eighteen months and is described by Piaget in terms of developments during six periods (also called "stages" by Piaget, which is a bit confusing).

STAGE 1   According to Piaget's theory, development of sensorimotor intelligence begins with the exercise of inborn reflexes such as sucking, grasping, and reflexes controlling vision. The nature of these reflexes is such that they need to be used; they need stimulation, and contact with an object provides the stimulation which is "nourishment" for the reflex, leading to further exercise of it. Sucking, for example, induces more sucking, a "primary circular reaction" in Piaget's terminology.

STAGE 2   Reflexes change as a function of experience, as already noted in Laurent's active search for the nipple; accommodation occurs and the first acquired adaptations make their appearance.

STAGE 3   Piaget made many observations of the coordination of reflexes such as the visual and prehensile, in which the infant becomes capable of looking and grasping, or grasping and looking, which occur during the four- to eight-month period. Piaget emphasizes that this coordination is not a matter of physiological maturation; he finds in his data evidence for his theory that more complex mental structures are based on the simpler ones. Laurent at 0:3 (3) managed to grasp an object in his father's hand, a precocious accomplishment possible only after the visual image of Piaget's hand had been assimilated to the visual image of Laurent's own hands, and this new image had been incorporated into the schema of grasping hands. A whole series of earlier searchings and graspings had to occur before the structure of grasping emerged when he saw the object and the hand simultaneously.

The reader will note a similarity between Piaget's findings on infant behavior and those of learning theorists. However, Piaget does not describe the behaviors we have been discussing here in terms of conditioned reflexes. He does not see "looking at–grasping" emerging as an association established between a visual image and the reflex of prehension; rather, he believes that perceiving an object sets in motion the child's need to grasp, a need that is then gratified by action.

In the third stage also, a stage called "secondary circular reactions," Piaget finds the beginnings of an elaboration of a world independent of self. The infant can now "make interesting sights last"; he has discovered by chance how to produce interesting sensations in his own body and now he tries to conserve those which he himself brings about. Jiggle an eight-month-old infant on your knee, stop, and the infant will bounce up and down, indicating that he knows how to continue the interesting sensations he has enjoyed.

STAGE 4   At about eight to nine months, Piaget notes the first actually intelligent behavior patterns. For Piaget, intelligence is not just reproducing interesting results, but arriving at them as a result of new combinations. Now intention precedes the activity. This is the stage at which the child will actively search for an object shown to him and then hidden. (However, if the object is hidden first in one place and then in another while the infant looks on, the child will search at the initial place and not at the last-seen place.)

STAGE 5   During the twelve- to eighteen-month period, Piaget notes the onset of inventive intelligence. Now the infant is capable of discovering new means to an end by coordinating existing schemata. An object itself out of reach but placed on a pillow within reach can be brought closer by drawing to oneself the pillow on which it is placed.

STAGE 6   From eighteen months on, Piaget sees the infant as capable of inventing new means through mental combinations. The infant tries out a problem solution in his mind and makes a sensorimotor deduction before actually carrying out the action. Lucienne, for example, wanted to remove a watch chain from a matchbox which had a slit too narrow for her finger. She did not explore the slit with her finger, groping until she discovered the procedure. Instead, she opened and closed her mouth while examining the slit, proving, for Piaget, that she was mentally trying out the enlargement of the slit. She was assimilating the slit as perceived to schemata involving other openings, and she then proceeded to a solution.

Excerpts from Piaget's *The Origins of Intelligence in Children* are included in the readings to illustrate each of these stages.

REFERENCES

Bowlby, J., *Attachment and loss*, vol. I: *Attachment* (London: Hogarth Press; New York: Basic Books, 1969).

———, "Maternal care and mental health." *WHO Monograph Series*, 1952, no. 2.

Brossard, L. M., and Décarie, T. G., "Comparative reinforcing effect of eight stimulations on the smiling response of infants." *Journal of Child Psychology and Psychiatry*, 1968, 9, 51–59.

Casler, L., "Maternal deprivation: a critical review of the literature." *Monographs of the Society for Research in Child Development*, 1961, 26.

Cobliner, W., "Appendix: The Geneva school of genetic psychology and psychoanalysis: parallels and counterparts." In R. Spitz, *The First Year of Life* (New York: International Universities Press, 1965), pp. 301–56.

Dennis, W., and Najarian, P., "Infant development under environmental handicap." *Psychological Monographs*, 1957, 71.

Goldfarb, W., "Psychological deprivation in infancy and subsequent adjustment." *American Journal of Orthopsychiatry*, 1945, 15, 247–55.

Kagan, J.; Henker, B.; Hen-Tov, A.; Levine, J.; and Lewis, M., "Infants' differential reactions to familiar and distorted faces." *Child development*, 1966, 37, 519–32.

Lipsitt, L. P., "Learning processes of human newborns." *Merrill-Palmer Quarterly*, 1966, 12, 45–71.

Lipsitt, L. P., and Kaye, H., "Conditioned sucking in the human newborn." *Psychonomic Science*, 1964, 1, 29–30.

Rheingold, H. L., and Eckerman, C. O., "The infant separates himself from his mother." *Science*, 1970, 168, 78–83.

Schaffer, H. R., and Emerson, P. E., "Patterns of response to physical contact in early human development." *Journal of Child Psychology and Psychiatry*, 1964, 5, 1–13.

Scott, J. P., Fredericson, E., and Fuller, J. L., "Experimental exploration of the critical period hypothesis." *Personality*, 1951, 1, 162–83.

Skeels, H., "Adult status of children with contrasting early life experiences." *Monographs of the Society for Research in Child Development*, 1966, 31.

Spitz, R. A., *The first year of life* (New York: International Universities Press, 1965).

———, "Hospitalism: an inquiry into the genesis of psychiatric conditions in early childhood." In *The Psychoanalytic Study of the Child*, vol. I (New York: International Universities Press, 1945), 53–74.

Wolff, P., "Observations on the early development of smiling." In B. M. Foss, ed., *Determinants of Infant Behaviour*, vol. II (London: Methuen; New York: Wiley, 1963), pp. 113–34.

Wolins, M., "Young children in institutions: some additional evidence." *Developmental Psychology*, 1970, 6, 99–109.

Zubek, J. P., ed., *Sensory deprivation* (New York: Appleton-Century-Crofts, 1969).

THE VISUAL INVESTIGATION
OF GEOMETRIC PATTERN BY THE
ONE- AND TWO-MONTH-OLD INFANT

PHILIP SALAPATEK

[Cognitive theorists, following Piaget, place considerable emphasis on the development of object permanence during the first year of life. Along this line, they emphasize the importance of recognition of the human face, and first in importance, in both cognitive and affective development, is the mother's face. These developments, obviously, depend on the infant's ability to focus on an object and to perceive a form. Salapatek and others have been investigating the characteristics of geometric figures that are visually attractive to very young infants. Their findings contradict the previously held notion that the very young infant sees only an undifferentiated blur by revealing that the infant's attention can be captured, and that he will fixate on certain aspects of a stimulus display. (Eds.)]

Seven to eight weeks of life appears to be a rather critical transitional point for many characteristics of infant visual perception. By most accounts sustained binocular fusion is the rule, smiling to specific, simple visual configurations is the rule, variable accommodation to objects at varying distances begins, sustained smooth circular as well as horizontal and vertical tracking is possible, some oculomotor anticipation of visual trajectories occurs, considerable progress in visual acuity has occurred, and certain rather marked reversals in visual preferences occur. There is, for example, a reversal in preference from linear to circular patterns, and from two- to three-dimensional forms.

Reprinted with abridgment by permission of the author from a paper presented at meetings of the American Association for the Advancement of Science, Boston, Massachusetts, December 26–31, 1969.

From the second to the third month of life three developments reported in the literature particularly guided our thinking in the collection of detailed eye-fixation data from infants four to ten weeks of age. In the first place, the rather extensive literature on the responses, particularly smiling, of infants to faces and face-like patterns, summarized by Eleanor Gibson in her book on perceptual development (Gibson, 1969), tends to indicate that certain critical features, particularly the eyes, have become necessary to the infant's definition of a face. The developmental progression from the third month appears to involve expansion of necessary features to include nose, mouth, etc., in their correct arrangement, embedded in an appropriate frame.

The second source of information that influenced our thought is not extensive, but is rather convincing. It has been fairly regularly reported by researchers such as Fantz, and Saayman, Ames, and Moffett, for example (Fantz, 1964; Saayman, Ames, & Moffett, 1964), that the first evidence of memory for specific simple figures, such as circles and crosses, not serving as signals for reinforcing contingencies, emerges during the third month.

Finally, the collected experiments of Thomas Bower (Bower, 1965a, 1965b, 1966a, 1966b, 1966c, 1967) suggest a number of rather surprising properties of the two-month-old infant's visual processing capacities, among which are: (1) the ability to store information regarding specific, simple sizes and shapes, (2) the ability to exhibit size and shape constancy for simple forms, (3) a tendency to store and respond to multiple features in a compound display in a non-configurational fashion, and (4) a tendency to organize elements in the visual field, e.g., good continuation for interposed figures, and common fate for adjacent forms. It is Bower's contention, particularly in the case of size and shape constancy, that mechanisms underlying such abilities are largely *not* developed through experience, and are probably present before the 50–60 days of age of most subjects. Although many theories do not assume directed focal attention for the estimation of size and shape, some theorists, such as Hebb (1949) [and] Piaget (1952), are quite explicit in requiring a period of intensive focal ocular experience (a) with particular shapes and sizes preliminary to the discrimination of specific shapes and sizes, and (b) with real size- and shape-consonant transformations preliminary to the exhibition of size and shape constancy. These theories would require broad scanning of simple geometric figures by six or seven weeks of age—the age at which Bower reports size and shape constancy. However, the theories of Neisser and Eleanor Gibson propose a system that on a gross level of functioning may extract general, structural information from the visual field, with or without central vision, but which for detailed pattern or object identification depends primarily upon focal attention (involving the line of sight). Such a development would not necessarily involve focal attention and a directed line of sight towards rather broad aspects of a visual display prior to the development of general size and shape estimation.

To evaluate these issues we have collected detailed records of sequential eye fixations from 64 infants in two studies. . . .

In Study I, ten infants between four and six weeks of age, and eleven infants between eight and ten weeks of age were presented with five geometric patterns in randomized order (Figure 1). All stimuli were centered directly between the infant's eyes. . . . The stimuli were: (1) a circle, 6 inches in diameter, (2) an upright equilateral triangle, 6 inches to a side, (3) a square, 6 inches to a side, (4) a regular 12-turn shape, and (5) an 11-turn random shape. In addition, all infants were presented six times

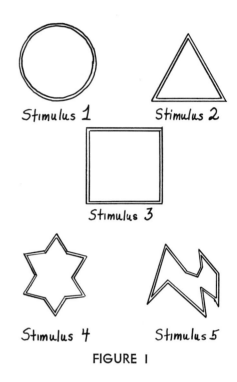

FIGURE I

Geometric patterns presented to infants in Study I.

with a homogeneous, flat-black stimulus panel, once before, once between, and once following figure presentations. . . .

My first task is to demonstrate that the geometric figures introduced during the experimental trials of each infant attracted his attention. . . . An attempt was made to record the eye movements and fixation points of each infant when presented with the five geometric figures and with six homogeneously black stimulus panels interspersed between geometric-figure presentations. In actuality, it was all but impossible to collect such eye fixations during control periods when no geometric figure was centrally placed. During control periods, infants between four and ten weeks of age generally fussed, fell asleep, and/or moved their line of sight to the extreme limits of the visual field, obliterating the corneal reflection of the infrared reference lights. Table 1 summarizes this effect. Only 23 of 126 control

TABLE I

Number of Scorable vs. Unscorable Trials by Age of Infant and Stimulus Condition

			Number of Trials	Fussy	Off to Side or Down	Poor Photography	Asleep or Partially Asleep	?
Exp.	Young N = 50	Scor.	50/50					
		Unsc.	0/50					
	Old N = 55	Scor.	55/55					
		Unsc.	0/55					
Con.	Young N = 60	Scor.	9/60					
		Unsc.	36/60	5	15	1	0	16
		?	15/60	7	0	1	3	5
	Old N = 66	Scor.	14/66					
		Unsc.	46/66	9	26	0	3	11
		?	6/66	1	2	0	1	3

periods of young and older infants were scorable, i.e., consisted of determinable eye fixations directed towards the central portion of the stimulus panel for at least 50 seconds. In contrast, on 105 of 105 experimental trials, when a central geometric figure was present, the infant's line of sight was attracted to the central portion of the visual field. In short, infants between four and ten weeks of age who would direct their line of sight towards the central portion of their visual fields when a geometric pattern was there, would not do so when no geometric pattern was there. . . .

. . . The geometric patterns employed in this study attracted the visual regard of the infants who served as subjects.

Most infants in this study looked with their right eyes towards the right portion of geometric figures centrally placed in their visual fields. This effect was more marked for young infants between four and six weeks of age than for older infants between eight and ten weeks of age. . . . The tendency of younger as compared to older infants to fixate on the right of stimulus figures during more stimulus presentations was significant at the .025 level of confidence. . . .

More younger than older infants exhibited a tight as compared to a loose scan of the central portion of the visual field during more stimulus trials. A tight scan of the central visual field during a stimulus trial was defined as a stimulus trial during which 90 percent of eye fixations fell within a circle of radius 1½ inches ($\sim$ 7 visual degrees) on the stimulus panel during a period of scanning unbroken by eye closure. . . .

. . . Young infants concentrated most of their visual scan on a very limited portion of the stimulus panel in their visual fields on more trials than did old infants. . . .

Most infants, both young and old, fixated the contour rather than the center of geometric patterns. . . . However, more older than younger infants directed some fixations towards the central portion of the stimulus figure in their visual fields. . . .

Young infants fixated mainly a very limited segment of the contour of the geometric figure during most stimulus trials. Older infants tended to examine a more extended segment of the perimeter of the figure than younger [infants] during most stimulus presentations. . . . During 36 to 50 stimulus presentations young infants concentrated their visual attention towards a very limited segment of the contour of the stimulus figure. However, older infants exhibited such focalized visual attention during only 17 of 55 stimulus presentations. . . .

Further, there was no indication that more complex as compared to less complex geometric figures were more effective in eliciting a focalized scan in either young or old infants. However, it must be admitted that the number of trials upon which such a conclusion is based is small.

There was, however, a very significant tendency for focalized scan to be directed towards an angle when an angle was present. Of the 45 trials during which a focalized scan occurred towards a geometric figure containing an angle, 40 focalized scans were directed towards an acute or a right angle. . . . On 19 of the 21 trials during which infants directed a focalized scan towards a triangle or a square, the focalized scan was directed towards an angle of the figure.

The foregoing data suggest the following generalities regarding the visual scan of infants between four and six weeks of age as compared to the visual scan of infants between eight and ten weeks of age towards outline geometric figures in their visual fields:

1. In the presence of a very finely textured, homogeneous visual field, infants between four and six weeks of age do not fixate centrally. Rather they fixate to the extreme portions of their visual fields, become fussy, or fall asleep. Perhaps, this may be regarded as a muscular extension of the tendency of the newborn infant to scan broadly under similar conditions.

2. When a geometric figure is introduced into the central visual field of the infant between four and ten weeks of age, he rapidly fixates and visually scans the figure for an extended period of time. The figure may be either simple, e.g., a circle, triangle, or square, or complex, e.g., a regular 12-turn figure, or an 11-turn random shape.

3. The majority of infants between four and six weeks of age generally exhibit the following visual scan towards a centrally-positioned geometric figure in the visual field:

(a) there is a tendency to fixate mainly on the right as compared to the left half of the figure with the right eyes,

(b) there is a tendency to concentrate the vast majority of fixations within a circular area 13 or 14 degrees in diameter in the visual field,

(c) there is a tendency to direct the vast majority of fixations towards the contour of a geometric figure centrally placed in the visual field,

(d) there is little tendency to direct any fixations towards the central portion of a geometric figure centrally placed in the visual field,

(e) there is a tendency to fixate mainly a very limited portion of the contour of a geometric figure centrally positioned in the visual field,

(f) the limited portion of the contour of a centrally-positioned geometric figure, selected for focal attention, is usually an angle, although a segment of circular contour may be selected when no angle is present,

(g) the foregoing tendencies are present in the four- to six-week-old infant for both simple and complex figures.

4. The majority of infants between eight and ten weeks of age generally exhibit the following visual scan towards a centrally-positioned geometric figure in their visual field:

(a) a tendency to direct fixation towards the right as compared to the left portion of the geometric figure, although less so than infants between four and six weeks of age,

(b) a greater tendency than young infants to direct fixation more loosely in the visual field,

(c) a tendency to direct the vast majority of fixations towards the contour of geometric figures centrally positioned in their visual fields,

(d) a much greater tendency than younger infants to direct some fixations towards the centers of geometric figures centrally positioned in their visual fields,

(e) a tendency, much greater than that of the young infant, to fixate more than a limited segment of the contour of a geometric figure centrally positioned in the visual field,

(f) a tendency to direct most focalized scans towards an angle of a geometric figure centrally positioned in the visual field,

(g) the foregoing tendencies appear to be generally true for both simple figures, e.g., a circle, triangle or square, and for complex, e.g., a regular 12-turn figure, or an 11-turn random shape figure.

REFERENCES

Bower, T. G. R. The determinants of perceptual unity in infancy. *Psychonomic Science,* 1965a, 3, 323–324.

———. Stimulus variables determining space perception in infants. *Science,* 1965b, 149, 88–89.

———. Heterogeneous summation in human infants. *Animal Behavior,* 1966a, 14, 395–398.

———. Slant perception and shape constancy in infants. *Science,* 1966b, 151, 832–834.

———. The visual world of infants. *Scientific American,* 1966c, 2–10.

———. The development of object-permanence: some studies of existence constancy. *Perception and Psychophysics,* 1967, 2, 411–418.

Dayton, G. O., Jr., and Jones, M. H. Analysis of characteristics of fixation reflex in infants by use of direct current electrooculography. *Neurology,* 1964, 14, 1152–1156.

Easterbrook, J. A. The effect of emotion on cue utilization and the organization of behavior. *Psychological Review,* 1959, 66, 183–201.

Fantz, R. L. Visual experience in infants: decreased attention to familiar patterns relative to novel ones. *Science,* 1964, 146, 668–670.

Gibson, E. *Principles of perceptual and learning development.* New York: Appleton-Century-Crofts, 1969.

Hebb, D. O. *The organization of behavior.* New York: Wiley, 1949.

Kessen, W., Salapatek, P., and Haith, M. The visual response of the human newborn to horizontal and vertical linear contour. Paper presented at meetings of American Psychological Association, Chicago, 1965.

Mann, I. *The development of the human eye.* London: British Medical Association, 1964.

Neisser, U. *Cognitive psychology.* New York: Appleton-Century-Crofts, 1967.

Piaget, J. *The origins of intelligence in children.* New York: International Universities Press, 1952.

Saayman, G., Ames, E. W., and Moffett, A. Response to novelty as an indicator of visual discrimination in the human infant. *Journal of Experimental Child Psychology,* 1964, 1, 189–198.

Salapatek, P. Visual scanning of geometric figures by the human newborn. *Journal of Comparative and Physiological Psychology,* 1968, 66, 247–258.

Salapatek, P., and Kessen, W. Prolonged investigation of a plane geometric triangle by the human newborn. Paper presented at meetings of the Society for Research in Child Development, Santa Monica, April, 1969.

———. Visual scanning of triangles by the human newborn. *Journal of Experimental Child Psychology,* 1966, 3, 155–167.

THE DETERMINANTS OF ATTENTION
IN THE INFANT

JEROME KAGAN

A six-month-old infant displays a remarkable ability to focus his attention on interesting events, and he will maintain prolonged orientations to the face of a stranger, the movement of a leaf, or a lively conversation. He seems to be quietly absorbing information and storing it for future use. Since acquiring knowledge about the environment depends so intimately upon how the infant distributes his attention, and for how long, it is important to ask what governs these processes. This question has stimulated fruitful research from which an outline of preliminary principles is emerging.

EARLY DETERMINANTS OF FIXATION TIME: CONTRAST AND MOVEMENT

The most obvious index of attentiveness to visual events is the length of orientation to an object—called fixation time. Like any response it has multiple determinants; the relative power of each seems to change as the infant grows. Ontogenetically, the earliest determinant of length of orientation to a visual event derives from the basic nature of the central nervous system. The infant is predisposed to attend to events that possess a high rate of change in their physical characteristics. Stimuli that move or possess light-dark contrast are most likely to attract and hold a newborn's attention. A two-day-old infant is more attentive to a moving or intermittent light than to a continuous light source; to a design with a high degree of black-white contrast than to one of homogeneous hue

Reprinted by permission of the author and *American Scientist* from *American Scientist*, 1970, **58**, 298–306.

(Haith 1966; Salapatek and Kessen 1966; Fantz 1966; Fantz and Nevis 1967). These facts come from experiments in which stimuli varying, for example, in degree of black-white contrast (e.g., a black triangle on a white background versus a totally gray stimulus) are presented to infants singly or in pairs while observers or cameras record the length of orientation to each of the stimuli. In general, the newborn's visual search behavior seems to be guided by the following rules: (1) If he is alert and the light is not too bright, his eyes open. (2) Seeing no light, he searches. (3) Seeing light but no edges, he keeps searching. (4) Finding contour edges, his eyes focus on and cross them (Haith 1968).

The attraction to loci of maximal contrast and movement is in accord with knowledge about ganglion potentials in the retinas of vertebrates. Some ganglion cells respond to a light going on; others to its going off; still others to both. Since an object moving across a visual field stimulates a set of cells for a short period, it creates onset and offset patterns similar to those of an intermittent light. Figures that contain dark lines on light backgrounds serve better as onset stimuli than do solid patterns because the change in stimulation created by the border of dark on light elicits more frequent firing of nerve cells, and this phenomenon may facilitate sustained attention (Kuffler 1952, 1953).

The preference for attending to objects with high contrast is dependent, however, on the size of the figure; there seems to be an optimal area that maintains fixation at a maximum. Four-month-old infants shown designs of varying areas (Figure 1) were most attentive to the

FIGURE 1

One of a set of random designs shown to four-month infants.

moderately large designs (Figure 2) (McCall and Kagan 1967). Similarly there is a nonlinear relation between the total amount of black-white edge in a figure and attention. Consider

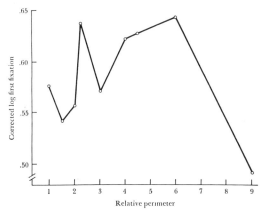

FIGURE 2

Relation between fixation time and approximate area of random design in four-month infants.

a series of black-and-white checkerboards of constant area but varying numbers of squares. The total number of inches at which black borders white increases as the number of

squares increases. Karmel (1966) has suggested, on the basis of studies with young infants, that the longest fixations are devoted to figures with a moderate amount of edge.

Although indices of attention to auditory events are more ambiguous than those to visual ones, intermittent tones, which have a high rate of change, elicit more sustained interest, as evidenced by motor quieting, than continuous tones (Eisenberg 1964; Brackbill 1966). Nature has apparently awarded the newborn an initial bias in his processing of experience. He does not have to learn what he should examine, as the nineteenth-century empiricists argued. The preferential orientation to change is clearly adaptive, for the source of change is likely to contain the most information about the presence of his mother or danger.

THE ROLE OF DISCREPANCY FROM SCHEMA

The initial disposition to attend to events with a high rate of change soon competes with a new determinant based on experience. The child's encounters with events result, inevitably, in some mental representation of the experience, called a schema. A schema is defined as an abstraction of a sensory event that preserves the spatial or temporal pattern of the distinctive elements of the event. A schema is to be regarded as a functional property of mind that permits an organism to recognize and retrieve information. The schema does not necessarily involve a motor response. It is neither a detailed copy of the event nor synonymous with the language label for the event. An example from a recent experiment may be useful here.

A four-year-old looked through a set of 50 magazine pictures illustrating objects, people, or scenes, many of which he had never seen before and could not name when asked. He spent only a few seconds on each picture and flipped through the 50 in less than three minutes. He was then shown 50 pairs of pictures; one of each pair was the picture he saw earlier, the other was new. He was asked to point to the picture he saw before. Although he could recall spontaneously only three or four, the average four-year-old recognized over 45 of the 50 pictures. Some children recognized them all. Since some of the pictures showed objects the child had never seen (say, a lathe or a slide rule), it is unlikely that his performance can be totally explained by assuming that each picture elicited a language label or a fragmentary motor response. What hypothetical entity shall we invoke to explain the child's ability to recognize over 90 percent of the scenes? If we use the concept schema to refer to the processes that permitted recognition, we can say that each picture contained a unique configuration of salient elements, and the schema preserved that configuration, without necessarily preserving an exact spatial analogue of the event. Some psychologists might use the older term memory engram to convey the meaning we attribute to schema. The schema for a visual event is not a photographic copy, for minor changes in the scenes viewed initially do not produce changes in the child's performance. Nor is the schema synonymous with a visual image, for the child is also able to recognize a series of different melodies or sound patterns after brief exposure to each. Early twentieth-century biologists used the concept of the gene to explain demonstrated properties of cells and nuclear material, though no one knew the gene's structure. We use the concept of schema to account for properties of mind, even though we cannot specify its structure.

The notion of schema helps to explain the older infant's distribution of attention. Toward the end of the second month, fixation time is influenced by the degree to which the child's memory for a particular class of events resembles the specific external event encountered originally. Thus the length of orientation to a picture of a strange face is dependent on the child's schema for the faces he has seen in the past. Events which are moderately discrepant from his schema elicit longer fixations than very familiar events or ones that are completely novel and bear no relation to the schema. The relation of fixation time to magnitude of discrepancy between schema and event is assumed to be curvilinear; this assumption is called the discrepancy hypothesis.

The neurophysiologist describes this attentional phenomenon in slightly different language.

The prepotent role of novelty in evoking the orienting reflex suggests that this response is not initiated directly by a stimulus, in the customary sense of the term, but rather by a change in its intensity, pattern or other parameters. A comparison of present with previous stimulation seems of prime significance, with an orienting reflex being evoked by each point of disagreement. The concept of a cortical neuronal model . . . accounts for this induction of the orienting reflex by stimuli whose characteristic feature is their novelty. This model preserves information about earlier stimuli, with which aspects of novel stimulation may be compared. The orienting reflex is evoked whenever the parameters of the novel stimulus do not coincide with those of the model [Magoun 1969, p. 180].

Although an orienting reflex can often be produced by any change in quality or intensity of stimulation, duration of sustained attention seems to be influenced by the degree of discrepancy between event and related schema. Consider some empirical support for the discrepancy hypothesis. One- or two-week-old infants look equally long at a black-and-white outline of a regular face (upper right Figure 3) and a meaningless design, for contrast is still

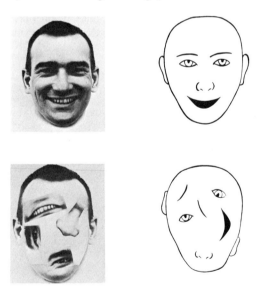

FIGURE 3

Achromatic faces shown to infants.

the major determinant of attention at this early age. Even the eight-week-old attends equally long to a three-dimensional model of a head and an abstract three-dimensional form (Carpenter 1969). But four-month-old infants show markedly longer fixations to the two regular faces in Figure 3 than to the design in Figure 1 (McCall and Kagan 1967). The four-month-old has acquired a schema for a human face, and the achromatic illustrations are moderately discrepant from that schema. However, if the face is highly discrepant from the schema, as occurs when the components are rearranged (the lower faces in Figure 3), fixation time is reduced (Wilcox 1969; Haaf and Bell 1967). The moderately discrepant face elicits more sustained attention than the extremely discrepant form at 16 weeks, but not during the first eight weeks of life (Fantz and Nevis 1967; Wilcox 1969; Lewis 1969). The differences in length of fixation to a normal face and to an equally complex but distorted face is greatest between three and six months of age, when infants normally display long fixations to faces. After six months fixation times to photographs of faces drop by over 50 percent and are equally long for both regular and irregular faces (Lewis 1969).

This developmental pattern confirms the discrepancy hypothesis. Prior to two months, before the infant has a schema for a human face, photographs of either regular or irregular faces are treated as nonsense designs and elicit equal periods of attention. Between two and four months the schema for a human face is established, and a photograph of a strange face is optimally discrepant from that schema. During the latter half of the first year, the schema for a face becomes so firmly established that photographs of regular or irregular faces, though discriminable, elicit short and equal fixations.

A second source of support for the discrepancy hypothesis comes from experiments in which an originally meaningless stimulus is presented repeatedly (usually 5 to 10 times), and afterward a variation of the original stimulus is shown to the infant. Fixation time typically decreases with repetitions of the first stimulus; but when the variation is presented, fixation times increase markedly (McCall and Melson 1969). In one experiment four-month-old infants were shown a stimulus containing three objects (a doll, a bow, and a flower) for five 30-second presentations. On the sixth trial

the infants saw a stimulus in which one, two, or all three objects were replaced with new ones. Most infants showed significantly longer fixations to the changed stimulus than to the last presentation of the original (McCall and Kagan 1970).

The most persuasive support for the curvilinear hypothesis comes from an experiment in which a new schema was established experimentally (Super, Kagan, Morrison, Haith, and Weiffenbach, unpublished). Each of 84 firstborn Caucasian infants, four months old, was shown the same three-dimensional stimulus composed of three geometric forms of different shape and hue for 12 half-minute periods (Figure 4). Each infant was then randomly

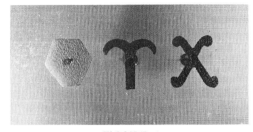

FIGURE 4

One of the two standard mobiles shown to infants in the laboratory.

assigned to one of seven groups. Six of these groups were exposed at home to a stimulus that was of varying discrepancy from the standard viewed in the laboratory. The mother showed the stimulus, in the form of a mobile, to the child 30 minutes a day for 21 days. The seven experimental groups were as follows (Figure 5).

Group 1: Control standard. These infants were exposed to the same stimulus they saw in the laboratory at four months.

Group 2: Subtraction. These infants were shown a four-element stimulus constructed by adding a fourth element to the three-element standard seen in the laboratory. ("Subtraction" referred to the later laboratory session [see below], which used only three elements.)

Group 3: Serial rearrangement. Infants exposed to a stimulus in which the three elements of the original standard were rearranged in the horizontal plane.

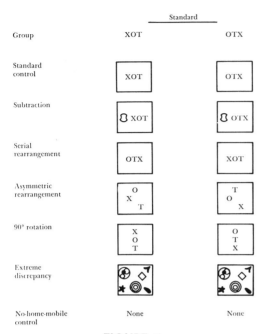

FIGURE 5

Schematic illustration of the mobiles infants saw at home for 21 days.

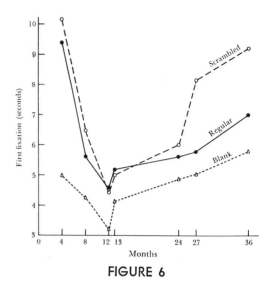

FIGURE 6

Change in fixation time for each of the experimental groups.

Group 4: Asymmetric rearrangement. Infants shown the three-element stimulus rearranged in an asymmetric form.

Group 5: Ninety-degree rotation. Infants shown a stimulus in which the three horizontal elements in the standard were rearranged in a vertical plane.

Group 6: Extreme discrepancy. Infants shown a mobile consisting of many more elements of different shapes and colors than those of the standard.

Group 7: No-mobile control. Infants exposed to no stimulus during the 21-day experimental period.

Three weeks later each subject was brought back to the laboratory and shown the same stimulus viewed initially at four months. The major dependent variable was the change in fixation time between the first and second test sessions. Figure 6 illustrates these changed scores for total fixation time across the first six trials of each session.

The infants who saw no stimulus at home are the referent group to which all the other groups are to be compared. These infants showed no change in fixation time across the three weeks, indicating that the laboratory stimulus was as attractive on the second visit as on the first. The infants who developed a schema for the asymmetric and vertical rotation mobiles (moderate discrepancy) showed the smallest drop in interest across the three weeks. By contrast, the infants who experienced a minimal (groups 2 and 3) or major discrepancy (group 6) showed the greatest drop in interest. (Analysis of variance for total fixation time across the first six trials yielded an F ratio of 5.29 and a probability value of less than .05.) There was a curvilinear relation between attention and stimulus-schema discrepancy. Although the existing data are still not conclusive, they clearly support the discrepancy hypothesis.

The onset of a special reaction to discrepancy between two and three months is paralleled by other physiological and behavioral changes in the infant. . . . The Moro reflex—the spreading and coming together of the arms when the head is suddenly dropped a few inches—begins to disappear, crying decreases, babbling increases, decreased attention to repeated presentations of a visual event becomes a reliable phenomenon (Dreyfus-Brisac 1958; Ellingson 1967), and three-dimensional representations of objects elicit longer fixations than two-dimensional ones (Fantz 1966). Perhaps the infant's capacity to react to discrepancy at this age reflects the fact that the brain has matured enough to permit the establishment of long-term memories and their activation by external events.

THE EFFECT OF THE INFANT'S HYPOTHESES

As the child approaches the end of the first year he acquires a new kind of cognitive structure which we call hypotheses. A hypothesis is an interpretation of some experience accomplished by mentally transforming an unusual event to the form the child is familiar with. The "form he is familiar with" is the schema. The cognitive structure used in the transformation is the hypothesis. Suppose a five-year-old notes a small bandage on his mother's face; he will attempt to find the reason for the bandage and may activate the hypothesis, "She cut her face." A five-month-old will recognize his mother in spite of the bandage but will not try to explain its presence.

To recognize that a particular sequence of sounds is human speech, rather than a telephone, requires a schema for the quality of a human voice. Interpretation of the meaning of the speech, on the other hand, requires the activation of hypotheses, in this case linguistic rules. The critical difference between a schema and a hypothesis resembles the difference between recognition and interpretation. Recognition is the assimilation of an event as belonging to one class rather than another. The performance of the four-year-old in the experiment with 50 pictures illustrates the recognition process. The child requires only a schema for the original event in order to answer correctly. Interpretation involves the additional process of activating hypotheses that change the perception of an event so that it can be understood. It is assumed that the activation of hypotheses to explain discrepant events is accompanied by sustained attention. The more extensive the repertoire of hypotheses—the more knowledge the child has—the longer he can work at interpretation and the more prolonged his attention. The child's distribution of attention at an art museum provides a final analogy. He may be expected to study somewhat unusual pictures longer than extremely realistic ones or surrealistic ones because he is likely to have a richer set of hypotheses for the moderately discrepant scenes. The richer the repertoire of hypotheses, holding discrepancy of event constant, the longer the child will persist at interpretation. There is as yet no body of empirical proof for these ideas, but data that we shall consider agree with these views.

In sum, three factors influence length of fixation time in the infant. High rate of change in physical aspects of the stimulus is primary during the opening weeks, discrepancy becomes a major factor at two months, and activation of hypotheses becomes influential at around 12 months. These three factors supplement each other; and a high-contrast, discrepant event that activates many hypotheses should elicit longer fixation times from an 18-month-old than a stimulus with only one or two of these attributes.

Two parallel investigations attest to the potential usefulness of the complementary principles of discrepancy and activation of hypotheses. In the first, one-, two-, and three-year-old children of middle class families in Cambridge, Massachusetts, and of peasant Indian families from a village in the Yucatan peninsula were shown color prints of male faces—Caucasian for the American children and Indian for the Mexican children (Finley 1967). Fixation time to the faces increased with age. The largest increase between two and three years of age occurred to the discrepant, scrambled face rather than to the nondiscrepant, regular face; the former required the activation of more hypotheses in order to be assimilated.

In the second study 180 white, firstborn boys and girls from the Cambridge area viewed the clay faces in Figure 7 repeatedly at 4, 8, 13, and 27 months of age. There was a U-shaped relation between age and fixation time. Fixation decreased from 4 to 13 months but increased between 13 and 27 months. The longer fixations at 4 months reflect the fact that these stimuli were discrepant from the infant's acquired schema for his parents' faces. Fixations decreased at 8 and 13 months because these masks were less discrepant but did not yet

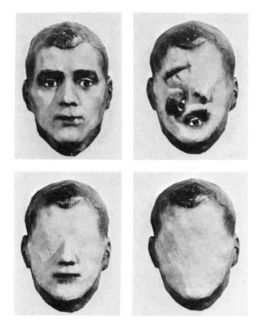

FIGURE 7

Clay masks shown to children at 4, 8, 13, and 27 months.

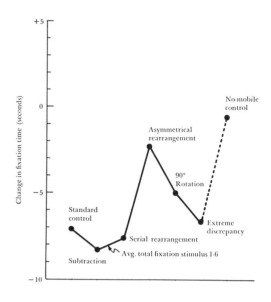

FIGURE 8

Relation between fixation time to faces and age of child.

activate a long train of hypotheses in the service of assimilation. Between one and two years fixations rose because the child was activating hypotheses to resolve the discrepancy.

As with the first study, the largest increase in fixation time, between 13 and 27 months, occurred to the scrambled face. The children's spontaneous comments indicated that they were trying to understand how a face could be so transformed. "What happened to his nose? Who hit him in the nose?" asked a two-year-old. And, "Who that, Mommy? A monster, Mommy?" said another. The function resulting from combining the data of the two studies is illustrated in Figure 8. The U-shaped relation between fixation time and age is concordant with the theoretical argument given earlier.

SOCIAL CLASS AND FIXATION TIME

The number of hypotheses surrounding a class of events should covary, in part, with language competence. Hence any experiences that promote acquisition of language should be associated with longer fixation times toward the end of the first year. The positive correlation between parental educational level and the child's linguistic competence is well known and well documented (see, for example, Cazden 1966). Thus a positive relation between parental education and fixation time should appear toward the end of the first year and grow with time. The data on 180 firstborns indicated that parental education was not highly related to fixation time to faces at 4 and 8 months but was moderately related (correlation coefficient [r] = about 0.4) at 13 and 27 months, and this relation was slightly stronger for girls than for boys. Since the majority of infants either increased in fixation time or showed no essential change between 13 and 27 months, we computed the change in first fixation between 13 and 27 months for each child and correlated that change with parental educational level as well as independent indexes of verbal ability at 27 months. There was a positive relation between increase in fixation time and parents' educational level for the girls (r = .31) but not for boys (r = −.04); 27-month-old girls with the highest vocabulary scores showed the largest increases in fixation time.

It is not clear why the relation between parental education and sustained attention should be stronger for girls than for boys. Other investigators have also reported closer covariation in girls than boys between social class and various indexes of cognitive development including IQ scores and school grades. Moss and Robson (1968) studied the relation between amount of face-to-face interaction mother and infant had in the home and the three-month-old infant's fixation time to photographs of faces in the laboratory. The association was positive for girls (r = .61, *p* < .01) and close to zero for boys. Hess, Shipman, Brophy, and Bear (1968, 1969) and Werner (1969) have reported more substantial correlations for girls than boys between maternal education or verbal ability, on the one hand, and the child's IQ or level of reading achievement on the other. There seems to be a general tendency for indexes of maternal intellectual ability and, by inference, maternal concern with the child's mental development, to be better predictors of cognitive development in daughters than sons.

One interpretation of this puzzling phenomenon rests on the fact that girls are biologically less variable than boys (Acheson 1966). This implies that fewer infant girls would display extreme degrees of irritability, activity, or attentiveness. Let us assume the following principle: the more often the mother attempts to interest her child in an event the stronger the child's tendency to develop a general sensitivity to change and a capacity for sustained attention to discrepancy. This principle is likely to be less valid for infants who temperamentally have a tendency toward apathy or hypervigilance. There are many functional relations in nature that lose their validity when one of the variables assumes an extreme value, and this may be another instance of that phenomenon.

An alternative explanation of the stronger covariation for girls than boys between maternal intelligence and the child's mental development assumes greater differences between well and poorly educated mothers in their treatment of daughters than of sons, especially in maternal actions that promote attention and language acquisition. A mother seems more likely to project her motives, expectations, and self-image on her daughter than on her son, and is more likely to assume that her daughter will come to resemble her. Many poorly educated mothers feel less competent than the college graduate and have greater doubts about their daughters' potential for intellectual accomplishment. Such a mother may set or supply lower standards and less enthusiastic as well as less consistent encouragement to her infant girl to learn new skills. The well educated mother sets higher aspirations and acts as though she held the power to catalyze her child's development.

The situation with sons is somewhat different. Most mothers, regardless of class background, believe their sons will have to learn how to support a family and achieve some degree of independence. Hence mothers of all classes may be more alike in energizing the cognitive development of sons. The restricted range of acceleration of sons, compared with daughters, would result in closer covariation for girls between social class and indexes of cognitive development.

This argument finds support in observations of the mother-child interaction in the home. Well educated mothers are more likely to talk to their four-month-old daughters than mothers with less than a high school education. But this class difference in maternal "talkativeness" does not occur for sons. Observations of an independent sample of 60 mother-daughter pairs at 10 months of age (Tulkin, unpublished) also indicate that middle, in contrast to lower, class mothers spend significantly more time in face-to-face contact with their daughters, vocalize more often to them, and more frequently reward their attempts to crawl and stand. A final source of data is the home observations on some of the 180 children at 27 months. The observer noted each instance in which the mother reproved the child for disobeying a rule. Mothers of all social classes were more likely to reprove sons than daughters. However, reproval for incompetence at a task was most frequently meted out by the well educated mothers of daughters; there was no comparable class difference for mothers of sons.

Thus, independent and complementary evidence supports the idea that differential pressures toward intellectual competence are more likely to covary with social class for mother-daughter than for mother-son pairs. It has usually been assumed that the girl is more concerned with acceptance by parents and teachers than the boy, and that this particular motive for intellectual accomplishment covaries with social class; but intellectual achievement among boys is spurred by more varied motives, including hostility, power, and identification with competent male figures—motives less closely linked to social class. However valid these propositions, they are not operative during the first year of life.

IMPLICATIONS

The influence of contrast, discrepancy, and activation of hypotheses on distribution of attention is probably not limited to the first two years of life. Schools implicitly acknowledge the validity of these principles for older children by using books with contrasting colors and unusual formats and by emphasizing procedures whose aim is to ensure that the child has a relevant hypothesis available when he encounters a new problem. A child who possesses no hypothesis for solution of a problem is likely to withdraw from the task. Many children regard mathematics as more painful than English or social studies because they have fewer strategies to use with a difficult problem in arithmetic than for one in history or composition. The school might well give children more help in learning to generate hypotheses with which to solve problems, and put less pressure on them to accumulate facts.

The principles discussed in this paper are also related to the issue of incentives for acquiring new knowledge. The behaviorist, trying to preserve the theoretical necessity of the concept of reinforcement, has been vexed by the fact that the child acquires new knowledge in the absence of any demonstrable external reward. However, the process of assimilating a discrepant event to a schema has many of the characteristics of a pleasant experience and therefore is in accord with the common understanding of a reward. The central problem in educating children is to attract and maintain focused attention. The central theoretical problem in understanding mental growth is to discern the factors that are continually producing change in schema and hypothesis. Solution of these two problems is not to be found through analyses of the environment alone. We must decipher the relation between the perceiver and the space in which he moves, for that theme, like Ariadne's thread, gives direction to cognitive growth.

REFERENCES

Acheson, R. N. 1966. Maturation of the skeleton. In F. Falkner, ed. *Human development*. Philadelphia: W. B. Saunders, pp. 465–502.

Brackbill, Y., G. Adams, D. H. Crowell, and M. C. Gray. 1966. Arousal level in newborns and preschool children under continuous auditory stimulation. *J. Exp. Child Psychol.* 3:176–88.

Carpenter, G. C. Feb. 1969. Differential visual behavior to human and humanoid faces in early infancy. Presented at Merrill-Palmer Infancy Conference, Detroit, Mich.

Cazden, C. B. 1966. Subcultural differences in child language. *Merrill-Palmer Quart.* 12:185–219.

Dreyfus-Brisac, C., D. Samson, C. Blanc, and N. Monod. 1958. L'électroencéphlograme de l'enfant normal de moins de trois ans. *Études néonatales* 7:143–75.

Eisenberg, R. B., E. J. Griffin, D. B. Coursin, and M. A. Hunter. 1964. Auditory behavior in the neonate. *J. Speech and Hearing Res.* 7:245–69.

Ellingson, R. J. 1967. Study of brain electrical activity in infants. In L. P. Lipsitt and C. C. Spiker, eds. *Advances in child development and behavior*. New York: Academic Press, pp. 53–98.

Fantz, R. L. 1966. Pattern discrimination and selective attention as determinants of perceptual development from birth. In A. H. Kidd and J. J. Rivoire, eds. *Perceptual development in children*. New York: International Universities Press.

Fantz, R. L., and S. Nevis. 1967. Pattern preferences in perceptual cognitive development in early infancy. *Merrill-Palmer Quart.* 13:77–108.

Finley, G. E. 1967. Visual attention, play, and satiation in young children: a cross cultural study. Unpublished doctoral dissertation, Harvard Univ.

Haaf, R. A., and R. Q. Bell. 1967. A facial dimension in visual discrimination by human infants. *Child Devel.* 38:893–99.

Haith, M. M. 1966. Response of the human newborn to visual movement. *J. Exp. Child Psychol.* 3:235–43.

Haith, M. M. March 1968. Visual scanning in infants. Paper presented at regional meeting of Society for Research in Child Development. Clark Univ., Worcester, Mass.

Hess, R. D., V. C. Shipman, J. E. Brophy, and R. M. Bear. 1968 and (follow-up phase) 1969. The cognitive environments of urban preschool children. Report to the Graduate School of Education, Univ. of Chicago.

Karmel, B. Z. 1966. The effect of complexity, amount of contour, element size and element arrangement on visual preference behavior in the hooded rat, domestic chick, and human infant. Unpublished doctoral dissertation, George Washington Univ., Washington, D.C.

Kuffler, S. W. 1952. Neurons in the retina: Organization, inhibition, and excitation problems. *Cold Spring Harbor Symposium in Quantitative Biology* 17:281–92.

Kuffler, S. W. 1953. Discharge patterns and functional organization of mammalian retina. *J. Physiol.* 16:37–68.

Lewis, M. 1969. Infants' responses to facial stimuli during the first year of life. *Devel. Psychol.* no. 2, pp. 75–86.

McCall, R. B., and J. Kagan. 1967. Attention in the infant: effects of complexity, contour, perimeter, and familiarity. *Child Devel.* 38:939–52.

McCall, R. B., and J. Kagan. 1970. Individual differences in the infant's distribution of attention to stimulus discrepancy. *Developmental Psychology* 2:90–98.

McCall, R. B., and W. H. Melson. March 1969. Attention in infants as a function of the magnitude of discrepancy and habituation rate. Paper presented at meeting of the Society for Research in Child Development. Santa Monica, Calif.

Magoun, H. W. 1969. Advances in brain research with implications for learning. In K. H. Pribram, ed., *On the biology of learning*. New York: Harcourt, Brace & World, pp. 171–90.

Moss, H. A. 1967. Sex, age and state as determinants of mother-infant interaction. *Merrill-Palmer Quart.* 13:19–36.

Moss, H. A., and K. S. Robson. 1968. Maternal influences on early social-visual behavior. *Child Devel.* 39:401–8.

Salapatek, P., and W. Kessen. 1966. Visual scanning of triangles by the human newborn. *J. Exp. Child Psychol.* 3:113–22.

Super, C., J. Kagan, F. Morrison, and M. Haith. An experimental test of the discrepancy hypothesis. Unpublished.

Tulkin, S. Social class differences in mother-child interaction. Unpublished.

Werner, E. E. 1969. Sex differences in correlations between children's IQs and measure of parental ability and environment ratings. *Devel. Psychol.* 1:280–85.

Wilcox, B. M. 1969. Visual preferences of human infants for representations of the human face. *J. Exp. Child Psychol.* 7:10–20.

LEARNING PROCESSES OF NEWBORNS

LEWIS P. LIPSITT

The concept of development is generally defined, in the biological tradition, by reference to organismic changes which are essentially time-determined. It is apparent that at least for the study of physical growth characteristics of children, an interest which occupied many of our early child developmentalists, the emphasis on time *is* of paramount importance. The question of whether the passage of time, or increasing age, is as important for *psychological* development is, of course, an empirical one. But before the issue had time for empirical resolution, the field of child development rather wholeheartedly adopted the physical growth model and engaged itself in normative investigations which sought to relate "behavioral growth" to chronological age. We are all familiar with the pictorial representations of Shirley (1933) and the extensive verbal pictures of Gesell and his colleagues (1949)—infants *doing* things, like raising their heads from the bed, or pulling themselves to a standing position, and doing them in a fairly orderly progression and by a fairly predictable age (Bayley, 1955; Cattell, 1940). The norms were so reliable, in fact, that a concept of *developmental* age, homologous with mental age, was devised to provide a numerical representation of the behavioral status of any given infant in relation to the comparably tested performance of similarly aged peers. Child psychologists were reinforced for this increasing concern with the temporal determinants of behavior, moreover, by an indulgent and practical society which soon found age-norms, with their neat means and standard deviations, to be of ostensible psychometric value in assessing progress of individual children. . . .

Reprinted with abridgment by permission of the author and the Merrill-Palmer Institute from the *Merrill-Palmer Quarterly*, 1966, **12**, 45–71.

For the past seven years or so, I have been fortunate to have access to a population of infants who are, with their parents, participants in a longitudinal investigation of child development. The major focus of the project is on neurological aberrations, mental retardation, and the biological and experimental precursors of such disfunctions. Brown University is one of fourteen institutions throughout the country participating in this large study supported by the National Institute of Neurological Diseases and Blindness. It is the intent of the overall project to collect extensive obstetrical, pediatric and psychological data on the prenatal circumstances, the birth events, and developmental progress of about 50,000 children. As part of the so-called core project, which is guided by an extensive protocol that each institution is committed to follow closely, the infants are seen during the first few days of life, then at follow-up centers at 4 months of age, 8 months, and 12 months, and at longer intervals thereafter. . . .

Our newborn laboratory at the Providence Lying-In Hospital is equipped with a stabilimeter crib (Lipsitt and DeLucia, 1960), a six-channel polygraph with an integrator unit, an audio-oscillator and associated speaker, a Physiological Stimulator, and some interval timers for the controlled presentation of stimuli. We can get polygraphic recordings of sucking behavior by means of a pressure-transducer linked with tubing and ordinary bottle-nipples. The stabilimeter provides continuous polygraphic records of the infant's movement and enables the recording of startle or other activity in response to specific stimulation. We record breathing activity by means of an infant pneumograph around the infant's abdomen, linked with an appropriate transducer and to the polygraph.

One of the most easily observed behavioral attributes of the human newborn is that with repetitive stimulation by an initially effective or unconditioned stimulus, response diminution tends to occur. This phenomenon was described in very early literature on child development (Peiper, 1925; Forbes and Forbes, 1927; Disher, 1934), but it has been only relatively recently that this response-decrement or extinction-like process has been systematically studied in newborns (Bridger, 1961; Bartoshuk, 1962). The phenomenon may be documented by recording the startle response as measured by body-movement, respiration, or heart rate, and noting the gradual lessening of reaction to the startle stimulus with repetitive stimulation.

An interesting use of the habituation experiment, as it has come to be called, was reported by Bronshtein et al. in 1958. Bronshtein reported that if a tone or an odor is administered to a sucking infant, that stimulus would at first cause an interruption in the sucking activity, but with successive repetitions of that stimulus, the interruption of sucking activity would gradually diminish, until after a number of trials the previously effective stimulus would lose its eliciting properties. Recovery or dishabituation of the response would occur only if a sufficiently long interval was allowed to elapse, or if the stimulus was discriminably changed. This latter property of the habituation process was, in fact, considered by Bronshtein and his coworkers to provide an important advance in the study of infant behavior. Discriminative abilities of differently aged children could be documented by first habituating to a stimulus, then testing with other stimuli of varying steps removed from the original.

Unfortunately, the promise of this technique, using the sucking response, was not fulfilled in our laboratory attempts, when Kaye and Levin (1963) were unable to replicate the interruptive effects of external stimulation on sucking. We have done several studies of response decrement to olfactory stimuli (Engen, Lipsitt, and Kaye, 1963; Engen and Lipsitt, 1965) using our polygraphically recorded measures of body movement and breathing, and these studies have fared considerably better than our use of the Bronshtein technique. . . .

In one such study of olfactory responsivity

and its decline with successive stimulation, each of 10 subjects was presented two odors, anise oil and asafoetida. Half received 10 trials with anise first and asafoetida second; for the other half the order was reversed. Presentation of stimulus and control trials was alternated. After the 20-trial series with first one odor, then the other, the first-given odor was reintroduced for two additional trials. The time between all trials was one minute, and this interval was the same in going from one odor-stimulus to another. Utilizing the activity and breathing records, judges viewed the records and independently judged a response to have occurred on the odor trial only if the response on that trial exceeded response on the paired control trial. . . . A number of findings are apparent: (1) that response-decrement occurred to repetitive stimulation with both odorants, (2) that there was some cross-odor adaptation, such that stimulation with one odor for ten trials tended to decrease sensitivity to the second-administered stimulus, and (3) most importantly for my present purposes, there was recovery of response to a new stimulus following habituation with another. With respect to the latter point, recovery actually occurred twice, first when the infants were administered the second odor, and then again when they were restimulated with the first odor. This recovery of response to novel stimulation is the sort of phenomenon to which Bronshtein had alluded and which can be used as a test of the newborn's discriminative capacity. . . .

I wish to turn now to some data from neonatal sucking experiments, in which my principal collaborator has been Dr. Herbert Kaye. The first of these studies (Lipsitt and Kaye, 1965) documents a kind of perseverative effect which we think may involve a memorial or learning process. A number of writers (e.g., Gunther, 1961) have suggested that differently shaped nipples, both natural and unnatural, have differential capacity for eliciting sucking responses in newborns, and Piaget (1952) has called attention to the very early influences of experience on this response. We did this study with an "optimizing" and a "non-optimizing" intra-oral stimulus, i.e., a good elicitor of sucking and a poor elicitor. The stimuli used, respectively, were an ordinary bottle nipple and a

piece of straight ¼ in. rubber laboratory tubing. Ten *S*s in this study received stimulation
with just the nipple, ten with just the tube, and
ten with both of these in order to determine
whether sucking on one might be affected by
experience in sucking on the other. All subjects
received 50 trials of intra-oral stimulation, each
of these lasting 10 seconds with an inter-trial
interval of approximately 30 seconds. A Tube-
only and a Nipple-only group received these
50 stimulations with either the tube or the
nipple. A Tube-Nipple alternation group received five trials with the tube, then five with
the nipple, five with tube, and so on. Observational counts of sucks per unit time are highly
reliable. The mechanics of stimulus presentation
were such that the experimenter touched the infant's lips with a stimulus, and when the mouth
opened the stimulus was inserted. The experimenter pushed a button connected with a timer
set at 10 seconds, activating a light signal during which the observers counted. . . .

Regardless of whether just the tube or nipple
is given, or both, the nipple elicits more sucking than the tube [Figure 1]. More pertinent
for our present discussion is the fact that within
5-trial blocks for the alternated group there appears to be a perseverational effect of response
to the previous stimulus administered, such that
response to each block of the nipple starts low
and goes high, while response to the tube starts
high and goes low, relative to comparison trials
in the single-stimulus groups. This effect is seen
best in the next figure (Figure 2), which was

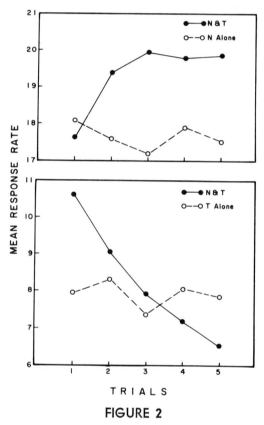

FIGURE 2

Perseverational effect of response to previous stimulus in Groups N and T, compared with response
on comparable trials in Groups N and T, respectively.

drawn by collapsing the blocks of scores, elimi-
nating the first in which no such effect should
be expected. The upward trend within blocks
for nipple-sucking and the downward trend for
tube-sucking in the alternated group are compared with the appropriate data from the nipple-only and the tube-only groups. Statistical
analyses confirmed that both trends for the

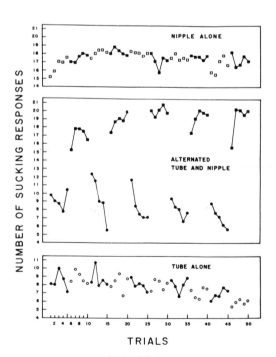

FIGURE 1

Mean numbers of sucking responses on 5-trial
blocks by all three groups of infants.

alternated group are reliable, while in the other two groups responding does not change within blocks. The nature of an intra-oral stimulus, then, determines the frequency with which a newborn sucks, and sucking is affected by other oral stimuli with which the infant has experience.

That study led naturally into the next and further convinces us that newborns do learn. Since the tube proved to be a relatively poor elicitor of sucking, this provided an opportunity to use the tube in the following conditioning study (Lipsitt, Kaye and Bosack, 1965). Twenty infants from 2 to 4 days of age were given one of two treatments. An experimental group received six baseline trials of fifteen-second presentations of tube, followed by a conditioning, then extinction, then reconditioning and extinction periods. During Conditioning and Reconditioning, a 5 per cent dextrose-and-water solution was given through the tube after the first 10 seconds of sucking, 1 cc. being given each trial. A control group was run which received identical treatment with the exception that the dextrose solution was given by syringe between each of the trials comparable to Conditioning and Reconditioning in the experimental group. To control amount of oral stimulation, an empty syringe was used at comparable times for the experimental subjects. Sucking throughout was recorded for the first 10 seconds of each 15-second trial. The figure (Figure 3) shows the difference in response rate for the two groups through the experiment. The difference in Conditioning was reliable, although the difference during Reconditioning fell short of significance. Our conclusion is that a "non-optimizing" sucking stimulus can be transformed into a more effective elicitor of sucking through the pairing with it of a suitable reinforcing agent, a phenomenon previously established in newborn dogs by Stanley et al. (1963).

It may be added that in another study (Lipsitt and Kaye, 1964), classical conditioning of the sucking response was demonstrated utilizing a loud tone as the CS. Sucking in response to the tone was greater, following a basal period, in infants who received paired presentations of the tone than in infants who received unpaired presentations of the same stimuli.

Dr. Kaye (1965) has recently demonstrated

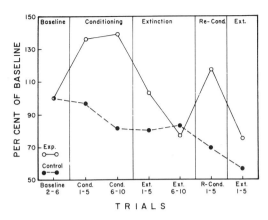

FIGURE 3

Difference in response rate for two groups of infants, age 2–4 days, in conditioning study.

another very striking conditioning effect, utilizing the newly discovered Babkin reflex. The Babkin reflex is elicited by pressing on the neonate's palms, and the response consists of a wide opening of the mouth and a tendency to turn the head toward midline from the tonic-neck-reflex position. In a Pavlovian analogue, Kaye paired this unconditioned stimulation with neutral stimulation consisting of transporting the arms from the infant's sides up over his head just prior to pressing the palms. He gave an experimental group five baseline trials of arm-transport alone prior to 35 conditioning trials, and followed these with 15 extinction trials. A comparable control group received the five baseline trials, followed by 35 trials of palm-press alone with the arms being retained in the upward position, and followed by 15 extinction trials.

. . . All pertinent statistical tests indicate that the experimental group gave reliably more responses to arm-transport in the extinction period than did the control group, although the two groups did not differ in numbers of responses during the pre-conditioning period. It may be added that a second control group was run, involving arm-transport alone on trials comparable to conditioning trials in the experimental group, and no substantial amount of responding was induced in this way. . . . There were no differences in the groups with respect to numbers of responses elicited during this period, and it can be seen also that habituation of the Babkin reflex is apparently a rather slow process.

I have only one other finding to report from a study just recently completed. Based on some suggestions of Papousek (1961), Dr. Einar Siqueland has recently developed a procedure (Siqueland and Lipsitt, 1966) for studying conditioned head-turning behavior utilizing both tactual stimulation and nutritive reinforcement. The procedure, briefly, consists of sounding a buzzer for a 5-second period, during the latter half of which period the experimenter strokes one cheek of the newborn near the mouth. If the infant responds to the tactile stimulation, or in fact to the buzzer preceding it, a bottle is inserted in the mouth for a brief period and the infant is allowed to suck. Under these conditions, we were able to show that although the tactual stimulus is a low-level elicitor of head-turning responses at the outset, the eliciting power of this stimulation can be increased reliably and considerably as an apparent consequence of the reinforcing circumstance. To test the conditioning hypothesis, a control group received the same stimulation and same number of reinforcements as the experimental group, but the reinforcements were administered on a basis not contingent upon the head-turning response of the infant. This procedure seems at this point to have considerable potential for the study of conditioned responding and discriminative behavior in the newborn, and we are looking forward to its further exploration.

Although I do not know whether I have made a forceful case for the proposition that the human newborn is a learning organism, my own conclusion, on the basis of the studies just recited, is that the normal neonate has considerable learning capacity. It will take much research over the coming years, of course, to ferret out the most important parameters controlling such learned changes in infant behavior, to determine the long-term effects of early learning opportunities, and to study learning processes on an individual-difference basis. Already, though, I think that we are beginning to get the picture. And, perhaps not so strangely, the parameters and experimental techniques which seem to have most promise at present are very similar to those known for some time to be effective in manipulating animal behavior and adult behavior—parameters that have received considerable attention over the years in the experimental psychologist's laboratory. Now we can only marvel at the hesitancy with which the child developmentalist has approached their study. This is not to say, incidentally, that any animal researcher knows already all the conditions that are likely to facilitate infant learning. I expect that eventually the researcher of infant learning processes may be able to tell the animal researcher of a few behavioral determinants that have been overlooked typically in studies of infra-human learning. . . .

REFERENCES

Bartoshuk, A. K. Human neonatal cardiac acceleration to sound; habituation and dishabituation. *Percept. mot. Skills*, 1962, 15, 15–27.

Bayley, Nancy. On the growth of intelligence. *Amer. Psychologist*, 1955, 10, 805–818.

Bridger, W. H. Sensory habituation and discrimination in the human neonate. *Amer. J. Psychiat.*, 1961, 117, 991–996.

Bronshtein, A. I., Antonova, T. G., Kamenetskaya, N. H., Luppova, V. A., and Sytova, V. A. On the development of the functions of analyzers in infants and some animals at the early stage of ontogenesis. In *Problems of evolution of physiological functions*. Acad. Sci., U.S.S.R., 1958 (Washington, D.C.: US Dept Hlth., Educ. & Welf., Trans. serv.).

Cattel, Psyche. *The measurement of intelligence of infants and young children*. New York: Psychological Corp., 1940.

Disher, Dorothy R. *The reactions of newborn infants to chemical stimuli administered nasally*. Ohio State Univer. Stud. Inf. Behav., No. 12. Columbus: Ohio State Univer. Press, 1934. Pp. 1–52.

Engen, T. and Lipsitt, L. P. Decrement and recovery of responses to olfactory stimuli in the human neonate. *J. comp. physiol. Psychol.*, 1965, 59, 312–316.

Engen, T., Lipsitt, L. P., and Kaye, H. Olfactory responses and adaptation in the human neonate. *J. comp. physiol. Psychol.*, 1963, 56, 73–77.

Forbes, H. S. and Forbes, H. B. Fetal sense reaction: hearing. *J. comp. Psychol.*, 1927, 7, 353–355.

Gesell, A. and Ilg, Frances L. *Child development: an introduction to the study of human growth.* New York: Harper & Bros., 1949.

Gunther, Mavis. Infant behavior at the breast. In B. Foss (Ed.), *Determinants of infant behavior.* London: Methuen & Co., 1961. Pp. 37–44.

Kaye, H. The conditioned Babkin reflex in human newborns. *Psychonomic Sci.,* 1965, 2, 287–288.

Kaye, H. and Levin, G. R. Two attempts to demonstrate tonal suppression of non-nutritive sucking in neonates. *Percep. mot. Skills,* 1963, 17, 521–522.

Lipsitt, L. P. and DeLucia, C. An apparatus for the measurement of specific response and general activity of the human neonate. *Amer. J. Psychol.,* 1960, 73, 630–632.

Lipsitt, L. P. and Kaye, H. Conditioned sucking in the human newborn. *Psychonomic Sci.,* 1964, 1, 29–30.

Lipsitt, L. P. and Kaye, H. Change in neonatal response to optimizing and nonoptimizing sucking stimulation. *Psychonomic Sci.,* 1965, 2, 221–222.

Lipsitt, L. P., Kaye, H., and Bosack, T. The facilitation of sucking responses in the human neonate through conditioning procedures. 1965 (MS.)

Papousek, H. Conditioned head rotation reflexes in infants in the first months of life. *Acta Pediat.,* 1961, 50, 565–576.

Peiper, A. Sinnesempfindungen des Kindes vor seiner Geburt. *Monatssche. f. Kinderhk.,* 1925, 29, 236–241.

Piaget, J. *Origins of intelligence in Children.* (Trans. by Margaret Cook.) New York: Internat. Univer. Press, 1952.

Shirley, Mary M. *The first two years, a study of twenty-five babies.* Vol. 2. *Intellectual development.* Inst. Child Welf. Mongr., Serial No. 8. Minneapolis: Univer. Minnesota Press, 1933.

Siqueland, E. and Lipsitt, L. P. Conditioned head-turning behavior in newborns. *J. exp. child Psychol.,* 1966, in press.

Stanley, W. C., Cornwell, Anne C., Poggiani, Constance, and Trattner, Alice. Conditioning in the neonatal puppy. *J. comp. physiol. Psychol.,* 1963, 65, 211–214.

SENSORY-MOTOR INTELLIGENCE

JEAN PIAGET

STAGE I:
THE USE OF REFLEXES

[This first excerpt from Piaget's observations of his own three children beginning at birth illustrates the use and early adaptation of the sucking reflex. (Eds.)]

OBSERVATION 1   From birth sucking-like movements may be observed: impulsive movement and protrusion of the lips accompanied by displacements of the tongue, while the arms engage in unruly and more or less rhythmical gestures and the head moves laterally, etc.

As soon as the hands rub the lips the sucking reflex is released. The child sucks his fingers for a moment but of course does not know either how to keep them in his mouth or pursue them with his lips. Lucienne and Laurent, a quarter of an hour and a half hour after birth respectively, had already sucked their hand like this: Lucienne, whose hand had been immobilized due to its position, sucked her fingers for more than ten minutes.

A few hours after birth, first nippleful of colostrum. It is known how greatly children differ from each other with respect to adaptation to this first meal. For some children like Lucienne and Laurent, contact of the lips and probably the tongue with the nipple suffices to produce sucking and swallowing. Other children, such as Jacqueline, have slower coördination: the child lets go of the breast every moment without taking it back again by himself or applying himself to it as vigorously when the nipple is replaced in his mouth. There are some

Reprinted with abridgment from pp. 25, 57, 157–58, 215, 283–84, 337–38 of *The Origins of Intelligence in Children* by Jean Piaget, by permission of International Universities Press, Inc. Copyright 1952 by International Universities Press. Reprinted by permission of the author and Éditions Delachaux & Niestlé.

children, finally, who need real forcing: holding their head, forcibly putting the nipple between the lips and in contact with the tongue, etc. . . .

STAGE II:
THE FIRST ACQUIRED ADAPTATIONS

. . . . .

OBSERVATION 25   I tried to determine with respect to Laurent when there began to be association between the position of the baby and the seeking of the breast. But it seemed to me impossible to affirm the existence of the association before the second month. At 0;0 (6) and the days following, Laurent, it is true, sought to nurse as soon as he was put on the scale, the dressing table, or his mother's bed, whereas previously he sought nothing and cried in his crib. At 0;0 (9) Laurent is half asleep in his crib; he sought nothing as long as he was being carried, but as soon as he was placed on the bed he opened his mouth and turned his head from side to side with more rapid arm movements and tension of the whole body. At 0;0 (10) he no longer seeks while in his crib but as soon as he is in the nurse's arms, etc. This was his behavior until the end of the first month. But is it a matter of pure coincidence or of an actual association between position and sucking? It is impossible for us to decide this question, because the facts can be interpreted quite independently from the existence of an associative transfer. It is sufficient to state, as we have done in Chapter I, how precocious sucking-like movements and the groping characteristic of the reflex are, to understand that the child will try to nurse as soon as he is neither crying, nor asleep, nor distracted by movement. In his crib he does not seek because nothing distracts him from his cries of hunger, and these cries engender others through this sort of reflex repetition of which we have already spoken; so long as he is carried he seeks nothing because the rocking motion absorbs him; but as soon as he is placed on the scale, on the dressing table where his diapers are changed, or in his nurse's or his mother's arms, he tries to suck before recommencing to cry because neither his weeping nor the excitements of motion prevent him any longer from sucking. Does this mean there is a connection between *Trinklage* and sucking? Nothing authorizes us to deny it, or to affirm it either as yet. Besides, when one knows the difficulty of establishing a conditioned reflex in animals and especially the necessity to "strengthen" it all the time in order to preserve it, one can only be prudent in invoking such a mechanism in so far as the behavior patterns of the first weeks are concerned. . . .

STAGE III:
SECONDARY CIRCULAR REACTIONS

. . . Here are some examples of circular reactions relating to the movements the child gives to his bassinet and to the hanging objects:

OBSERVATION 94   At 0;3 (5) Lucienne shakes her bassinet by moving her legs violently (bending and unbending them, etc.), which makes the cloth dolls swing from the hood. Lucienne looks at them, smiling, and recommences at once. These movements are simply the concomitants of joy. When she experiences great pleasure Lucienne externalizes it in a total reaction including leg movements. As she often smiles at her knick-knacks she caused them to swing. But does she keep this up through consciously coördinated circular reaction or is it pleasure constantly springing up again that explains her behavior?

That evening, when Lucienne is quiet, I gently swing her dolls. The morning's reaction starts up again, but both interpretations remain possible.

The next day, at 0;3 (6) I present the dolls: Lucienne immediately moves, shakes her legs, but this time without smiling. Her interest is intense and sustained and there also seems to be an intentional circular reaction.

At 0;3 (8) I again find Lucienne swinging her dolls. An hour later I make them move slightly: Lucienne looks at them, smiles, stirs a little, then resumes looking at her hands as she was doing shortly before. A chance movement disturbs the dolls: Lucienne again looks at them and this time shakes herself with regularity. She stares at the dolls, barely smiles and moves her legs vigorously and thoroughly. At each moment she is distracted by her hands which pass again into the visual field: she examines them for a moment and then returns to the dolls. This time there is definite circular reaction.

At 0;3 (13) Lucienne looks at her hand with more coördination than usually. In her joy at seeing her hand come and go between her face and the pillow, she shakes herself in front of this hand as when faced by the dolls. Now this reaction of shaking reminds her of the dolls which she looks at immediately after as though she foresaw their movement. She also looks at the bassinet hood which also moves. At certain times her glance oscillates between her hand, the hood, and the dolls. Then her attention attaches itself to the dolls which she then shakes with regularity.

At 0;3 (16) as soon as I suspend the dolls she immediately shakes them, without smiling, with precise and rhythmical movements with quite an interval between shakes, as though she were studying the phenomenon. Success gradually causes her to smile. This time the circular reaction is indisputable. Same reaction at 0;3 (24). Same observations during the succeeding months and until 0;6 (10) and 0;7 (27 at sight of a puppet and at 0;6 (13) with a celluloid bird, etc. . . . .

STAGE IV:
COÖRDINATION OF SECONDARY SCHEMATA

. . . . .

OBSERVATION 121   Here is an analogous example, but easier to interpret. At 0;8 (20) Jacqueline tries to grasp a cigarette case which I present to her. I then slide it between the crossed strings which attach her dolls to the hood. She tries to reach it directly. Not succeeding, she immediately looks for the strings which are not in her hands and of which she only saw the part in which the cigarette case is entangled. She looks in front of her, grasps the strings, pulls and shakes them, etc. The cigarette case then falls and she grasps it.

Second experiment: same reactions, but without first trying to grasp the object directly.

At 0;9 (2) Jacqueline tries directly to grasp her celluloid duck when I put its head between the strings I have just described. Not succeeding, she grasps both strings, one in each hand, and pulls. She looks at the duck who shakes when she shakes. Then she grasps both strings in one hand and pulls, then grasps them in the other hand a little higher up and pulls harder until the duck falls.

I begin over again, but attach the duck more firmly. She then at once pulls the strings, systematically, until she can touch the duck with her finger, but does not succeed in making it fall. She then gives up although I shake the duck several times, which shows that she tries to grasp the duck and not to swing it.

It may be seen that these behavior patterns differ from those in [an earlier observation] even though in both cases it is a question of shaking the string to exert influence on a distant object. In the case of [the earlier observation], the child limits himself to utilizing a procedure which he has employed just previously, and to utilizing it in order to prolong a spectacle he has just had before his eyes. On the other hand, in the present case, he tries to grasp an object and to do so he must find the appropriate means. The means to which Jacqueline has recourse is of course borrowed from the schemata of her earlier circular reactions, but the act of intelligence has precisely consisted in finding the right means without limiting herself to repeating that which has already been done.

These behavior patterns must not, however, be overestimated and one must not so soon see in them a utilization of instruments (the behavior pattern of the "stick") or even a utilization of extensions of the object (the behavior pattern of the "string"). There could be no question of instruments for several more months. . . . Jacqueline [at this point] does

not yet consider the strings as extensions of the desired object. . . .

STAGE V:
TERTIARY CIRCULAR REACTIONS

· · · · ·

OBSERVATION 148   At 0;10 (16) . . . Laurent discovers the true relations between the support and the objective and consequently the possibility of utilizing the first to draw the second to him. Here are the child's reactions:

(1) I place my watch on a big red cushion (of a uniform color and without a fringe) and place the cushion directly in front of the child. Laurent tries to reach the watch directly and not succeeding, he grabs the cushion which he draws toward him as before. But then, instead of letting go of the support at once, as he has hitherto done, in order to try again to grasp the objective, he recommences with obvious interest, to move the cushion while looking at the watch. Everything takes place as though he noticed for the first time the relationship for its own sake and studied it as such. He thus easily succeeds in grasping the watch.

(2) I then immediately attempt the following counterproof. I put two colored cushions in front of the child, of identical form and dimensions. The first is placed as before, directly in front of the child. The second is placed behind, at an angle of $45°$, that is to say, so that a corner of the cushion is opposite the child. This corner is placed on the first cushion but I manage to flatten the two cushions at this place, where one is partially superposed on the other, so that the second does not protrude and is not too visible. Finally I place my watch at the other extreme end of the second cushion.

Laurent, as soon as he sees the watch, stretches out his hands, then grasps the first cushion which he pulls toward him by degrees. Then, observing that the watch does not move (he does not stop looking at it), he examines the place where the one cushion is superposed on the other (this is still the case despite the slight displacement of the first one), and he goes straight to the second one. He grasps it by the corner, pulls it toward him over the first cushion, and takes the watch.

The experiment, when repeated, yields the same result the second time.

(3) I now place the two cushions next to each other, the proximal side of the second parallel to the distal side of the first. But I superpose the first on the second on a strip about 20 cm. wide (the watch of course being at the extremity of the second cushion). Laurent immediately pulls the first cushion but, observing that the watch is not displaced, he tries to raise this cushion to reach the second one. At a certain moment he has succeeded in raising up the first cushion, but without removing it, and he holds it against his chest with his left hand while trying to pull the second one with his right hand. He finally succeeds and takes possession of the watch, thus revealing his perfect comprehension of the role of the support.

(4) Finally I place the second cushion as in (2) but sideways, the proximal corner of the second superposed on one of the distal corners of the first. Laurent does not make a mistake and at once tries to reach the second cushion.

These four reactions combined reveal that the relation between the objective and its support has been acquired. . . .

STAGE VI:
INVENTION OF NEW MEANS

. . . . .

OBSERVATION 180   Another mental invention, derived from a mental combination and not only from a sensorimotor apprenticeship was that which permitted Lucienne to rediscover an object inside a matchbox. At 1;4 (0), that is to say, right after the preceding experiment, I play at hiding the chain in the same box used [previously]. I begin by opening the box as wide as possible and putting the chain into its cover (where Lucienne herself put it, but deeper). Lucienne, who has already practiced filling and emptying her pail and various receptacles, then grasps the box and turns it over without hesitation. No invention is involved of course (it is the simple application of a schema, acquired through groping) but

knowledge of this behavior pattern of Lucienne is useful for understanding what follows.

Then I put the chain inside an empty matchbox (where the matches belong), then close the box leaving an opening of 10 mm. Lucienne begins by turning the whole thing over, then tries to grasp the chain through the opening. Not succeeding, she simply puts her index finger into the slit and so succeeds in getting out a small fragment of the chain; she then pulls it until she has completely solved the problem.

Here begins the experiment which we want to emphasize. I put the chain back into the box and reduce the opening to 3 mm. It is understood that Lucienne is not aware of the functioning of the opening and closing of the matchbox and has not seen me prepare the experiment. She only possesses the two preceding schemata: turning the box over in order to empty it of its contents, and sliding her finger into the slit to make the chain come out. It is of course this last procedure that she tries first: she puts her finger inside and gropes to reach the chain, but fails completely. A pause follows during which Lucienne manifests a very curious reaction bearing witness not only to the fact that she tries to think out the situation and to represent to herself through mental combination the operations to be performed, but also to the role played by imitation in the genesis of representations. Lucienne mimics the widening of the slit.

She looks at the slit with great attention; then, several times in succession, she opens and shuts her mouth, at first slightly, then wider and wider! Apparently Lucienne understands the existence of a cavity subjacent to the slit and wishes to enlarge that cavity. The attempt at representation which she thus furnishes is expressed plastically, that is to say, due to inability to think out the situation in words or clear visual images she uses a simple motor indication as "signifier" or symbol. Now, as the motor reaction which presents itself for filling this role is none other than imitation, that is to say, representation by acts, which, doubtless earlier than any mental image, makes it possible not only to divide into parts the spectacles seen but also to evoke and reproduce them at will, Lucienne, by opening her mouth thus expresses, or even reflects her desire to enlarge the opening of the box. This schema of imitation, with which she is familiar, constitutes for her the means of thinking out the situation. There is doubtless added to it an element of magic-phenomenalistic causality or efficacy. Just as she often uses imitation to act upon persons and make them reproduce their interesting movements, so also it is probable that the act of opening her mouth in front of the slit to be enlarged implies some underlying idea of efficacy.

Soon after this phase of plastic reflection, Lucienne unhesitatingly puts her finger in the slit and, instead of trying as before to reach the chain, she pulls so as to enlarge the opening. She succeeds and grasps the chain.

During the following attempts (the slit always being 3 mm. wide), the same procedure is immediately rediscovered. On the other hand, Lucienne is incapable of opening the box when it is completely closed. She gropes, throws the box on the floor, etc., but fails.

THE EFFECTS OF THREE KINDS
OF PERCEPTUAL-SOCIAL STIMULATION
ON THE DEVELOPMENT
OF INSTITUTIONALIZED INFANTS:
PRELIMINARY REPORT
OF A LONGITUDINAL STUDY

MARTINE BROSSARD   THÉRÈSE GOUIN DÉCARIE

Although the association between institutionalization and maternal deprivation has been recognized since the beginning of the twentieth century, it was only around the 1960's that essential distinctions began to appear regularly in the literature. From then on, not only does one see the necessity to describe (and even to name) the institution where the research took place repeatedly stressed but, what is even more important, the complex elements constituting maternal deprivation are slowly becoming disentangled.

In 1962, Ainsworth suggested that if "confusion and controversy is to be avoided, distinctions should be maintained between the following: (a) insufficiency of interaction implicit in deprivation; (b) distortion in the character of the interaction, without respect to this quantity; and (c) the discontinuity of relations brought about through separation" (p. 99).

In his review of the literature, Yarrow (1964) focuses mainly on this last dimension of *discontinuity* of the relationship. Casler (1961), on the other hand, is interested in maternal deprivation considered from the aspect of *insufficiency*. He writes: "Since ill effects may result not from maternal deprivation itself but from the rupture of an already existing emotional bond with the mother, only those separations beginning before the establishment of this bond can furnish data regarding the effects of deprivation *per se*" (p. 3).

This restricted use of the term "maternal deprivation"[1] explains why Casler, in his critical review, concentrates on research studies focusing on institutionalized infants in the first semester of life. His well documented conclusion is far removed from psychoanalytic thinking, his thesis (clearly stated and restated) being that the physical, intellectual and emotional deficits often observed in individuals deprived of "mothering" during early infancy can best be explained in terms of perceptual and/or sensory deprivation. More precisely, in the first months of life, institutionalized infants would suffer, not from a lack of mother love, but from insufficient tactile, visual, auditory, kinesthetic and vestibular stimulation, and from a restriction in exploratory activities.

This conclusion is, of course, in a large

Reprinted by permission of the authors and *Early Child Development and Care* from *Early Child Development and Care*, 1971, **1,** No. 1, 111–30, published by Gordon and Breach, Inc., Science Publishers, New York, London, Paris.

[1] Gewirtz (1968) suggests the use of the terms "privation phenomena" when there is limited availability of stimuli from earliest life onward, and "deprivation phenomena" in the case of the removal of stimuli such as in a shift in the functional environment.

measure, based on animal experimentation. In most of these research studies, the methodology consists essentially of controlled deprivation and the analysis of its ill effects, or of controlled stimulation and the analysis of its beneficial effects (see *Stimulation in early Infancy* [1969]). In contrast to these animal studies, the investigators of early human infancy do not engage, for obvious ethical reasons, in experimental deprivation. They limit their study to the systematic observations of subjects who are "naturally" deprived because of an institutional setting (Spitz, 1945, 1946a, 1946b; Fisher, 1952, 1958; Dennis and Najarian, 1957; Kohen-Raz, 1968; Provence and Lipton, 1962; etc.) or proceed to the controlled enrichment of the environment (Rheingold, 1956; Rheingold, Gewirtz and Ross, 1959; Rheingold and Samuels, 1970; David and Appell, 1961; Gewirtz, 1961, 1965, 1969; White and Castle, 1964; White, Castle and Held, 1964; White and Held, 1966; White, 1967; Casler, 1965a, 1965b; Schaffer and Emerson, 1968; Lezine, 1965, 1970; etc.). In the case of this latter type of research, the enrichment is usually done through the intervention of a human person. It is the nurse or the experimenter who stimulates the subject through handling, talking, smiling, moving about, etc.

This use of the human person as the agent of stimulation raises an important question: Are the positive effects reported in these studies simply due to increased stimulation *per se,* or are the results also influenced by the fact that this increased stimulation is associated with a human person, inevitably involving a human relationship (however precarious and impersonal)? In other words, the amount (in terms of duration) of stimulation being equal, will the kind of stimulation significantly modify the development of deprived infants? Is it possible to hypothesize that the eye-hand coordination of socially stimulated babies, who are not given toys but have a daily interaction with a stable individual, will be just as good as that of babies who are allowed free manipulation of complex inanimate objects? Or is it possible to imagine that—when a focused relationship does not yet exist—social responsiveness of babies stimulated solely by an enrichment of the physical environment will not differ greatly from the social re-

sponsiveness of babies who receive mostly what most authors would call "social or affective" stimulation?

The following experiment was conceived in an effort to shed light on this important issue.

SETTING

Physical environment

The whole experiment took place in an institution which is part of a large hospital, in the heart of Montreal. The main function of the "Crèche de la Miséricorde" is to offer temporary residence to babies born out-of-wedlock. Its usual population varies between 500 to 600 infants whose chronological ages range from birth to twenty-four months. About half of these children have been abandoned for legal adoption by the mother, and the other half are "reserved" by the mother. Each room holds from twelve to twenty-four cots. The walls are of a pale blue color. The lighting is sufficient (there are large bright windows) except in the case of those babies whose beds are nearest to the corridor. In addition to the white colored cots, each room contains three small chairs, three baby-relax and two adult rocking chairs.

Toys are attached to the cot: a pale blue or pink rattle at the head of it, or a rudimentary cradle gym which is fixed to the side railing, often the outer side.

Staff

There are three shifts and the number of persons involved varies from one shift to another. What follows is a description of the typical staff from 8 A.M. to 5 P.M.

Rooms with 24 beds. Permanent staff: two student nurses and a baby-helper. Supplementary staff (at meal time, bath time and change of diapers): two student nurses.

Rooms with 18 beds. Permanent staff: one baby-helper and one untrained person. Supplementary staff: two student nurses.

Rooms with 12 beds. Permanent staff: one baby-helper and one untrained person. Supplementary staff: one student nurse.

Thus the highest adult-infant ratio found at any time of adult-infant interaction was 1:6.

Infants' Daily Schedule

Morning	8:00	Breakfast
	8:30	Bath
	9:30	Feeding
	10:00	Change of diapers
	11:30	Lunch
	12:00	Change of diapers
Afternoon	1:30	Feeding
	2:15	Change of diapers
	3:00	Temperatures
	4:00	Supper
	5:15	Change of diapers
	5:30	Feeding
	6:30	Change of diapers
	9:30	Feeding
	10:30	Change of diapers

THE SUBJECTS

The subjects were forty-eight infants of both sexes who were considered physically normal by medical standards, and whose chronological ages ranged from two to two-and-a-half months. They were divided on the basis of sex, age in weeks, and developmental quotients, into three experimental groups (P, S and M) and one control group (C) (N = 12 in each group). At the end of the experiment proper, twenty-nine of the initial subjects were still available: nineteen were lost because of adoption or episodic sickness.

PROCEDURE

Stimulation

The three experimental groups received systematic stimulation during a period of 15 minutes daily, five days a week, during two consecutive months. Stimulation varied from one group to another in the following manner:

The first group or Group P, which we will refer to as the "perceptually stimulated infants" [for] want of a better term, was offered a bright mobile made of audible toys of varied colors, forms and textures. This mobile was attached to the cot in the field of vision and prehension of the infants who were placed supine in their own beds. Simultaneously, they were exposed to various sounds recorded on a 30-foot magnetic tape. The sounds (ninety of them) were selected by the first author with the permission of the McGill School of Communications. They were more or less usual sounds such as doors opening, rain falling, cars' horns, birds' songs, etc. but excluding the human voice. The tape recorder was moved periodically so that the angle of exposure to sound for each infant was controlled. The second group or Group S, which we will refer to as the "socially stimulated infants" was divided into two sub-groups of six babies each: one sub-group was seen by the first author who is a trained psychologist and the other sub-group by a psychotechnician. The experimenters followed a flexible but standardized routine which is briefly schematized here.

First step. Singing, talking to and smiling at the baby.
2 minutes: 30 seconds talking
            15 seconds singing:
                "Le cerf et le lapin" with gestures
            30 seconds talking
            15 seconds singing:
                "Le cerf et le lapin" with gestures
            30 seconds talking.

Second step. Talking to and caressing the baby.
2 minutes: Caresses head, arms and hands, legs and feet.
This was done playfully, three times, during periods of approximately 30 seconds each.

Third step. Playing with the baby without holding him.
2 minutes: Talking and singing.

twice $\begin{cases} \text{15 seconds arm exercises (singing)} \\ \text{15 seconds pull-to-sitting game} \\ \text{15 seconds leg exercises (singing)} \\ \text{15 seconds pull-to-sitting game} \end{cases}$

Fourth step. Taking the baby in one's arms, talking to him and singing while walking around the room.
2 minutes:

twice $\begin{cases} \text{30 seconds words} \\ \text{30 seconds song "Au clair de la lune"} \\ \quad \text{and "Valse"} \\ \text{30 seconds words} \\ \text{30 seconds song} \end{cases}$

Fifth step. Holding the baby on the experimenter's knees, rocking him, talking to him, smiling at him and singing. Kissing the baby.
4 minutes: Constant rocking.

twice $\begin{cases} \text{30 seconds talking} \\ \text{30 seconds singing} \\ \text{30 seconds talking} \\ \text{30 seconds kissing} \end{cases}$

Sixth step. Putting the baby back in bed.
No sudden or painful separation.
1 minute of playful taking-leave.

The experimenters working with this group never used any toys (or jewelry) but the children were permitted to explore the experimenters' bodies freely. The social stimulation took place in a small room where they and each infant could be. This was an exhausting procedure and the order in which each infant was

TABLE I

*Distribution of Subjects According to Age
(in Weeks), Developmental Quotient and Group
(N = 48)*

	Age in weeks	Developmental Quotient			
		80–100	101–112	113–124	125+
Group P Mean age = 10.5 Mean quotient = 107.5	8				
	9		1	1	
	10	1	3		1
	11	1	1	1	
	12		1		
	13	1			
Group S Mean age = 10.1 Mean quotient = 105.4	8			1	
	9		2		
	10	2	1	2	
	11		2		
	12	2			
	13				
Group M Mean age = 10.1 Mean quotient = 108.0	8		1		
	9		1	1	
	10	1	3	1	
	11		1	1	
	12	1	1		
	13				
Group C Mean age = 9.7 Mean quotient = 106.9	8		1	1	1
	9		2		
	10	2	1	1	
	11	1	1		
	12	1			
	13				

exposed to social stimulation varied to compensate for the factor of fatigue in the handler.

The third group or Group M, which we will refer to as the "mixed group," was exposed to 7 minutes and 30 seconds of stimulation originating from mechanical agents and to 7 minutes and 30 seconds of stimulation given by the experimenter; in other words, they received the same stimulation as the first group but for half the amount of time and the same stimulation as the second group but with each step of the routine reduced by half.

The fourth group or Group C was the control group. This group did not receive any experimental stimulation, but the children in it were nevertheless designated to the staff as "research subjects." This was done in order to equalize the effects of the experimental stimulation *per se* for we knew that, simply because we were interested in them, the three other groups would draw new interest from the staff and therefore receive a certain degree of uncontrolled stimulation.

Evaluation

In order to ascertain the development of the subjects, four techniques (each very different in its conceptualization and aims) were used:

1. The Griffiths Mental Development Scale (Griffiths, 1954) which yields a general global quotient and five sub-quotients for the following specific scales: (a) Locomotor, (b) Personal-Social, (c) Hearing and Speech, (d) Eye and Hand, (e) Performance.

2. An object concept scale based on Piaget's theory (Décarie, 1962). This scale was divided into two sections; one series of tasks to be done with an inanimate object and another with a person (Décarie, 1966; Brossard, 1967; Bell, 1970).

3. A protocol of systematic observations of spontaneous behavior patterns and interaction patterns, lasting for about fifteen minutes.

4. A movement transducer. This small electric apparatus (Electrocraft) was placed in the foam mattress of the cot. It registered only gross motricity.

Besides the initial testing which took place at the beginning of the experimentation before

any stimulation was introduced, an evaluation of the different aspects of development of the subjects was done every fifth week by a third member of the research team. In order to measure the duration of the effects of the different forms of stimulation, a final evaluation also took place in the fifth week after the cessation of stimulation. At that time, however, only nineteen of the initial subjects were still available. We shall not therefore report on this last evaluation.

The third member of the research team who did the lengthy and complex evaluation was a psychologist totally ignorant of the classification of the infants: she did not know which baby belonged to which group.

RESULTS

The results reported here are limited to the quotients (general and specific) obtained on the Griffiths Scale by the twenty-nine subjects still available at the time of the third testing session. Pre-test refers to the initial evaluation which took place during the period when subjects were being selected and their ages ranged from two to two-and-a-half months. Test I refers to the first evaluation which took place during the fifth week after stimulation had been introduced, when the infants were between three and four months. Test II refers to the second evaluation which took place during the tenth week of stimulation when the infants were between four and five months. Group P designates the perceptually stimulated infants, Group S, the socially stimulated ones, Group M refers to the mixed group and Group C to the control group.

All four groups show a significant lowering of quotients between the Pre-test and Test I, but the quotients of the first two experimental groups (i.e. the perceptually and the socially stimulated babies) show a significant rise between Test I and Test II. These results indicate that after ten weeks of stimulation, the quotients were restored to what they were at the beginning of the experiment. Surprisingly, this is not the case for the experimental mixed group, nor (as expected) for the control group: while the change in quotients is not significant

TABLE 2

Mean Scores of the Griffiths General Intelligence Quotients at Each Testing (N = 29)

	Pre-test	Test I	Test II
Group P (n = 7)	103.86	85.86	103.43
Group S (n = 11)	102.27	89.09	102.36
Group M (n = 6)	109.67	91.00	93.83
Group C (n = 5)	102.40	85.80	83.20

when one compares Test I and Test II, it becomes so when one compares the Pre-test and Test II, and it indicates a decrease. The level of significance for all differences reported is $p < .01$.

TABLE 3

Summary of All the Covariance Analyses Between the Three Tests on the Griffiths General Intelligence Scales Quotients

	Pre-test	Test I	Test II
Pre-test	—	—	—
Test I	—	—	*
Test II	*	*	*

— non-significant
* significant, $p < .05$

Table 3 makes it clear that the experimental conditions did not significantly influence the test results between the Pre-test and Test I, but that they did interfere significantly between Pre-test and Test II and also between Test I and Test II.

Considering the General Intelligence Quotients only, it appears that this influence is due mainly to the perceptual and to the affective types of stimulation, the results of these two groups being significantly higher than those of the control group.

TABLE 4

General Intelligence Quotient Group t Values Between Pre-test and Test II and Between Test I and Test II

	t values	
Groups	Pre-test/Test II	Test I/Test II
P/S	.211	.343
P/M	1.942	1.996
S/M	1.928	1.862
P/C	3.703**	3.702**
S/C	3.831**	3.711**
M/C	1.796	1.745

** significant, $p < .01$

The almost identical weight of the perceptual and the social types of stimulation and the lack of influence of the mixed stimulation will require a good deal of interpretation. It is difficult to understand why the mixed stimulation appears to have no influence on the general development of the deprived infants. We had expected that the combination of both perceptual and social stimulation would be extremely effective. In the limited scope of our experiment, this hypothesis proves untenable. However, in the following results obtained on the five different scales of the Griffiths, we find that though the superiority of Group P and Group S, compared to the two other groups, remains strong, the mixed stimulation is not completely without effect.

THE LOCOMOTOR SCALE[2]

Studies similar to ours mention that motricity seems to be the aspect of development least modifiable by an enriched environment (see Rheingold 1956; Casler, 1965a). The counterpart of this statement is that motricity is usually less significantly affected by deprivation than are intelligence, language, or social responsiveness (Bowlby, 1951; Yarrow, 1961; Ainsworth, 1962).

[2] Griffiths' Locomotor Scale includes items referring to posture and prehension as well as to locomotion. (Ex.: item 14: Plays with own toes; item 16: Sits with slight support, etc.).

TABLE 5

Locomotor Sub-Quotient Group t Values Between Pre-test and Test II, and Between Test I and Test II

| | t values | |
Groups	Pre-test/Test II	Test I/Test II
P/S	.409	.574
P/M	2.726*	2.860**
S/M	2.599*	2.588*
P/C	3.543**	3.466**
S/C	3.480**	3.248**
M/C	.921	.724

* significant, p < .05
** significant, p < .01

Though further analysis is needed, our preliminary data are not in accord with these general conclusions: motricity appears as a dimension which responds well to environmental enrichment. The results of both the perceptually and the socially stimulated groups are significantly higher than the results obtained by both the control group and the mixed group. Here again, nevertheless, there is no significant difference between Groups P and S.

THE PERSONAL-SOCIAL SCALE

Surprisingly enough, even on this scale which is supposed to test social responsiveness, the results of the first two groups do not differ significantly, nevertheless Table 6 does show that the rise of quotients on the Personal-Social Scale is due, as could be expected, mainly to the affective type of stimulation.

Group S is superior to the control group throughout and superior to the mixed group at the beginning of the experimentation. The superiority of group P is less marked, for though the perceptually stimulated babies are socially more responsive than the babies of the control group, they do not differ significantly from the babies who received a mixed stimulation. These data could mean, as emphasized by Walters and Parke (1965), that it is "stimulation in general" that develops social responsiveness.

TABLE 6

Personal-Social Sub-Quotient Group t Values Between Pre-test and Test II and Between Test I and Test II

| | t values | |
Groups	Pre-test/Test II	Test I/Test II
P/S	−1.155	−.463
P/M	1.034	.501
S/M	2.234*	.990
P/C	2.646*	2.420*
S/C	3.908**	3.043**
M/C	1.609	1.881

* significant, p < .05
** significant, p < .01

HEARING AND SPEECH SCALE

Here, for the first time, the effects of the mixed stimulation become apparent.

TABLE 7

Hearing and Speech Sub-Quotient Group t Values Between Pre-test and Test II and Between Test I and Test II

| | t values | |
Groups	Pre-test/Test II	Test I/Test II
P/S	.118	.426
P/M	.087	.415
S/M	−.017	.049
P/C	3.437**	3.678**
S/C	3.625**	3.611**
M/C	3.243**	3.176**

** significant, p < .01

The babies of Group M, stimulated both perceptually and socially, fare better in pre-language development than the babies in the control group. Their results do not differ significantly from those of Group P or Group S. The good rating of the mixed group on this particular scale is probably due to the fact that in the 7 minutes 30 seconds of interaction with the experimenter, the verbal stimulation was intense—the six steps of the standardized routine were cut in half, thus retaining a lot of singing and talking throughout.

EYE-HAND SCALE

From the point of view of eye-hand coordination, one might have expected that the babies who were offered a mobile would develop better than those who had only the person of the experimenter to touch and who, in fact (much to the astonishment of the experimenters), did very little body exploration.

TABLE 8

Eye and Hand Sub-Quotient Group t Values Between Pre-test and Test II and Between Test I and Test II

Groups	t values	
	Pre-test/Test II	Test I/Test II
P/S	.415	.485
P/M	2.698*	2.771*
S/M	2.563*	2.575*
P/C	5.157**	4.829**
S/C	5.226**	4.808**
M/C	2.507*	2.124*

* significant, $p < .05$
** significant, $p < .01$

This is not the case. Group P dominates the mixed and control groups, but does not show any significant difference compared with Group S: Group S being also superior to Groups M and C. Here again nevertheless, as on the hearing and speech scales, a superiority of the mixed group over the control group is revealed. This is in agreement with most studies of this type; they usually indicate that even brief periods of perceptual stimulation favor the coordination of sensory-motor schema.

THE PERFORMANCE SCALE

The superiority and almost identical influence of the first two experimental situations are clear once more in this last table.

TABLE 9

Performance Sub-Quotient Group t Values Between Pre-test and Test II and Between Test I and Test II

Groups	t values	
	Pre-test/Test II	Test I/Test II
P/S	.521	.785
P/M	3.537**	3.537**
S/M	3.382**	3.130**
P/C	3.846**	3.785**
S/C	3.708**	3.405**
M/C	.469	.410

** significant, $p < .01$

This scale is supposed to measure the learning capacities of the infants. The babies that were perceptually stimulated and the babies that were socially stimulated have significantly better results throughout than the babies of both the mixed and control groups.

DISCUSSION

It is only when these results will be integrated into the rest of the data that a full discussion will become possible. Nevertheless, though this is only a preliminary report, a few questions might already be asked, if not answered.

This experiment emphasizes the importance of the amount (in terms of duration) of stimulation. In her study on measurement of maternal care, Rheingold (1960) writes:

The difference between care in the home and in the institution appeared to be not in the kinds of caretaking activities . . . but rather in the amount of the different kinds. [p. 570]

Our data show that stimulation of equal duration (15 minutes) though differing considerably in kind (perceptual vs social) can have very similar effects. However, this is true only within certain limits. We have seen that, when we compare infants who have received a combination of perceptual and social stimulation, with infants who received perceptual *or* social stimulation, the latter situation is found to be more effective, stimulation time being constant for all groups.

Our data thus strongly suggest that stimulation *per se* is more important for the overall development of the infant than the *type* of stimulation but they also suggest that there is a minimum duration time for which any stimulation should be applied to have any value. What are the parameters of the time variable? In our experimental schema, they might well be closely related to the amount of time needed by an infant to become active, be it in an interrelationship with an adult or within the circular reaction (Piaget, 1937, 1948) that emerges during the manipulation of inanimate objects.

The psychoanalytic notion of "mothering" and of its influence, *at a time when there is not yet a focused relationship,* needs revision. For at this point in our work, a conclusion seems unavoidable: in an institutional setting, the two-to-three-month-old infant who (during a ten-week period) receives varied perceptual stimulation without the mediation of a human agent presents a developmental profile almost identical to that of an infant who has received the same amount of "affective" stimulation.

Moreover, despite the fact that the two stimulations lasted for only fifteen minutes each day, the general quotients of both these groups of infants are well within the normal range.

Our findings are a partial answer to the important question so clearly formulated by Yarrow (1967):

Can one assume that because focused relationships are not clearly established before three to five months of age that the kind of mothering experienced before this time is not significant for development? The animal research has documented convincingly the importance of early stimulation, and conversely the deleterious effects of early stimulus deprivation. A crucial question is whether it is necessary for the infant to obtain this stimulation from a specially cathected person, or whether appropriate stimulation *per se* during this early period is sufficient. [p. 439]

In the light of our data, appropriate stimulation *per se* does seem sufficient. However,

several warning remarks must be made before accepting this global statement.

First, we do not know whether underlying the normal general quotients of our perceptually (or for that matter, socially) stimulated infants, we will find the usual developmental profiles or deviant ones. This qualitative analysis has not yet been done.

Secondly, one cannot conclude that a varied physical environment can replace a benevolent stable care-taker, a mother or a mother figure, during this period of life, simply because perceptual stimulation appears as effective as social stimulation during this time. A mobile (however fascinating and provocative of activity) cannot lead to a constantly evolving, dynamic, focused relationship, and we know that such a relationship (be it called attachment, dependency or object relations; Ainsworth, 1969) is, normally, an essential element of human socialization. Here, some vital questions need answering. What happens when a five-to-six-month-old infant, who has received a sufficient amount of non-human stimulation to develop "selon toute apparence" as well as a baby who has been mothered, comes into contact for the first time with a mother figure? His previous history has been such that he could not develop a focused relationship, and we have every reason to believe that "a focused individualized relationship with the mother or major caretaker does not appear suddenly, but is rather a gradual development of which there are many stages" (Yarrow, 1967, p. 440). What then will be the evolution of this infant? Will he "telescope" the preceding stages? Will he *fall in love* when offered a stable loving person? Or will he have to "learn the mother" and in so doing take six months before reaching a focused attachment? If there is a décalage, will it leave its mark, or is it easily reversible? And what of the mother? The learning of a baby is a reciprocal process.[3] What happens, then, to a mother who has had little or no contact with a baby before he is six months old?

A certain number of guide lines are offered by animal experimentation, but a great deal of

---

[3] This reciprocal process is beautifully illustrated in Ainsworth's book: *Infancy in Uganda: Infant Care and the Growth of Love* (1967).

research on human infancy must take place before we start "monkeying with the mother myth . . ." (Jensen and Bobbitt, 1968) on the basis of such limited data as ours.

REFERENCES

Ainsworth, Mary (1962). *The effects of maternal deprivation: a review of findings and controversy in the context of research strategy in deprivation of maternal care.* Geneva, W.H.O., 97–165.

——— (1969). Object relations, dependency and attachment: a theoretical review of the infant-mother relationship. *Child Development,* 40, 969–1025.

Bell, Silvia (1970). The development of the concept of object as related to infant-mother attachment. *Child Development,* 41, 291–311.

Bowlby, J. (1951). *Maternal care and mental health.* Geneva, W.H.O.

Brossard, Martine (1967). Notion d'objet appliquée à la personne humaine et réaction à la personne étrangère chez le jeune enfant, *in* T. Gouin Décarie (ed.): *La réaction du jeune enfant à la personne étrangère.* Montréal, Presses de l'Université de Montréal (in press).

Casler, L. (1961). Maternal deprivation: a critical review of the literature. *Monographs of the Society for Research in Child Development,* 26, 1–64.

——— (1965a). The effects of extra tactile stimulation on a group of institutionalized infants. *Genetic Psychology Monographs,* 71, 137–175.

——— (1965b). The effects of supplementary verbal stimulation on a group of institutionalized infants. *Journal of Child Psychology and Psychiatry,* 6, 19–27.

David, Myriam and Appell, Geneviève (1961). A study of nursing care and nurse-infant interaction, *in* B. M. Foss (ed.): *Determinants of infant behavior, I.* New York, Wiley, 121–141.

Décarie Gouin, Thérèse (1962). *Intelligence and affectivity in early childhood.* New York, International Universities Press.

——— (1966). Intelligence sensori-motrice et psychologie du premier âge, *in* Bresson et Montmolin (ed.): *Psychologie et épistémologie génétiques.* Paris, Dunod, 299–307.

Dennis, W. and Najarian, P. (1957). Infant development under environmental handicap. *Psychological monographs,* 71, no. 7 (whole no. 436).

Fischer, Liselotte K. (1952). Hospitalism in six-month-old infants. *American Journal of Orthopsychiatry,* 22, 522–533.

——— (1958). The significance of atypical postural and grasping behavior during the first year of life. *American Journal of Orthopsychiatry,* 45, 368–375.

Gewirtz, J. L. (1961). A learning analysis of the effects of normal stimulation, privation and deprivation on the acquisition of social motivation and attachment, *in* B. M. Foss (ed.): *Determinants of infant behavior, I.* New York, Wiley, 213–301.

——— (1965). The course of infant smiling in four child-rearing environments in Israel, *in* B. M. Foss (ed.): *Determinants of infant behaviour, III.* New York, Wiley, 205–260.

——— (1968). The role of stimulation in models for child development, *in* Laura Dittman (ed.): *New perspectives in early child care.* New York, Atherton Press.

——— (1969). Mechanisms of social learning: some roles of stimulation and behaviour in early development, *in* D. A. Goslin (ed.): *Handbook of socialization theory and research.* Chicago, Rand McNally.

Griffiths, Ruth (1954). *The abilities of babies.* London, University of London Press.

Jensen, J. and Bobbitt, Ruth (1968). Monkeying with the mother myth. *Psychology today,* 1, no. 12, 41–43.

Kohen-Raz, R. (1968). Mental and motor development of kibbutz, institutionalized, and home-reared infants in Israel. *Child Development,* 39, no. 2, 489–504.

Lezine, Irène (1965). Présentation des travaux de l'équipe de recherche sur le premier développement de l'enfant (Gentilly). *Psychologie française,* 10, no. 4, 379–384.

——— (1970). Influence du milieu sur le jeune enfant. Paper presented at the meeting of L'Association de psychologie scientifique de langue française, Lille, 1970 (in press).

Piaget, J. (1937). *The construction of reality in the child.* New York, Basic Books, 1954.

——— (1948). *The origins of intelligence in children.* New York, International Universities Press, 1952.

Poznansky, Ethel (1969). The effects of enrichment on motricity in a group of institutionalized infants. Unpublished thesis presented for the degree of Master of Psychology, Université de Montréal.

Provence, Sally and Lipton, Rose C. (1962). *Infants in institutions.* New York, International Universities Press.

Rheingold, Harriet L. (1956). The modification of social responsiveness in institutional babies. *Monographs of the society for research in child development,* 21, no. 2.

——— (1960). The measurement of maternal care. *Child Development,* 31, 565–575.

Rheingold, Harriet L., Gewirtz, J. L. and Ross, Helen (1959). Social conditioning of vocalizations in the infant. *Journal of Comparative and Physiological Psychology,* 52, 68–73.

Rheingold, Harriet L. and Samuels, Helen (1970). Maintaining the positive behavior of infants by increased stimulations, *in* Stella Chess and A. Thomas (eds.): *Annual progress in child psychiatry and child development*. New York, Brunner-Mazel, 1–13.

Schaffer, H. R. and Emerson, Peggy (1968). The effects of experimentally administered stimulation on developmental quotients of infants. *British Journal of Social and Clinical Psychology*, 7, part 1, 61–67.

Spitz, R. (1945). Hospitalism: an inquiry into the genesis of psychiatric conditions in early childhood. *Psychoanalytic Study of the Child*, 1, 53–74.

———— (1946a). Hospitalism: a follow-up report. *Psychoanalytic Study of the Child*, 2, 113–117.

———— (1946b). Anaclitic depression. *Psychoanalytic Study of the Child*, 2, 313–342.

Stimulation in early infancy (1969). A. Ambrose (ed.), London and New York, Academic Press.

Walters, R. H. and Parke, R. D. (1965). The role of distant receptors in the development of social responsiveness, *in* Lipsitt and Spiker (eds.): *Advances in child development and behavior*, 2, New York, Academic Press, 59–96.

White, B. (1967). An experimental approach to the effects of experience on early human development, *in* J. P. Hill (ed.): *Minnesota Symposia on child psychology*. Toronto, Clark, 201–226.

White, B. and Castle, P. (1964). Visual exploratory behavior following post-natal handling of human infants. *Perceptual Motor Skills*, 18, 497–502.

White, B., Castle, P. and Held, R. (1964). Observations on the development of visually-directed reading. *Child Development*, 35, 349–364.

White, B. and Held, R. (1966). Plasticity of sensorimotor development in the human infant, *in* J. F. Rosenblith and W. Allinsmith (eds.): *Causes of behavior: readings in child development and educational psychology*. Boston, Allyn and Bacon, 60–71.

Yarrow, L. J. (1961). Maternal deprivation: towards an empirical and conceptual re-evaluation. *Psychological Bulletin*, 58, 459–490.

———— (1964). Separation from parents during early childhood, *in* M. L. Hoffman and L. W. Hoffman (eds.): *Review of child development research, I*. New York, Russell Sage Foundation.

———— (1967). The development of focused relationship, *in* J. Hellmuth (ed.): *Exceptional infant, vol. I: The normal infant*. New York, Bruner-Mazel, 429–442.

THE DEVELOPMENT
OF THE CONCEPT OF OBJECT AS RELATED
TO INFANT-MOTHER ATTACHMENT

SILVIA M. BELL

Piaget (1937) suggested that the development of the object concept does not proceed at the same rate with respect to all objects. The purpose of the present study was to explore the relation between the development of person and object permanence and the attachment of an infant to his mother. 3 hypotheses were tested. (a) Babies tend to be more advanced in the concept of persons than in the concept of inanimate objects as permanent, but there are important individual differences. (b) Differences in the rate of development of person permanence are related to the quality of attachment behavior that a baby exhibits toward his mother. (c) Differences in the rate of development of person permanence can affect, in turn, the development of object permanence. The hypotheses were confirmed.

According to Piaget (1937) the child has a concept of "object" when he can conceive of things as substantial, independent of himself, and existing in a context of spatial and causal relations even when they are not present to his perception. The acquisition of this concept is an important facet of development and proceeds gradually throughout the last four of the six main stages which Piaget distinguishes in the sensorimotor period—that is, in the period occupying roughly the first two years of life.

Although Piaget studied the acquisition of the object concept only in reference to inanimate objects, he suggested (1937, 1954) that the concept of persons as permanent objects undergoes a homologous, but more accelerated process of development. The acceleration takes place because a baby finds people the most interesting of objects. The mother, who stimulates simultaneously many of his schemata and

who enters and leaves his perceptual field in rough synchrony with his signals, is *the* most important object in the environment of the young infant, and the one upon which he focuses first. Consequently, Piaget concludes that, while developing in parallel with the concept of object, the concept of person permanence both begins and is completed first. This is an instance of "horizontal décalage"—a term referring to the child's ability, at a given chronological age, to perform with varying degrees of success tasks involving the same basic mental operation, but presented in different contexts. Thus, for example, an 8-month-old baby may be capable of finding his mother in a simple hide-and-seek game, but not of retrieving an interesting toy comparably hidden.

Saint-Pierre (1962) confirmed Piaget's hypothesis, showing that in 23 of 30 infant subjects, person permanence was in advance of object permanence. She found individual differences, however: a few babies showed no décalage, and still others were more adept at finding hidden inanimate objects than the hidden mother.

Reprinted with abridgment by permission of the author and The Society for Research in Child Development, Inc., from *Child Development*, 1970, **41**, 291–311. © 1970 by The Society for Research in Child Development, Inc. All rights reserved.

A hypothesis that these individual differences in the rate of development may be attributable to environmental circumstances is compatible with Piaget's interactionist position. In an early article (1940) on the mental development of the child, published in translation only recently (1967), he ascribes great importance to the degree of "interest" that the environment elicits in the baby. Interest, a term referring to the appropriateness of an object as "aliment" for a particular structure, "is the proper orientation for every act of mental assimilation . . . and plays an essential role in the development of sensorimotor intelligence." Inhelder (1956) stated the relation more explicitly: "the age at which the cognitive structures appear is relative to the environment, which can either provoke or impede their appearance." Since a baby's mother is the key figure in his environment, it is reasonable to suppose that the development of person and object permanence might be especially affected by mother-infant interaction in the first 2 years of life.

The development of "attachment" is also hypothesized to be related to mother-infant interaction. Attachment, according to Ainsworth (Ainsworth & Bell 1970a), is "an on-going condition of an organism and refers to its propensity to behave in ways, characteristic of that organism, which serve to maintain proximity to or interaction with a particular figure—the object of attachment." Proximity seeking, a generic category which subsumes seeking contact, proximity, and/or interaction, is considered as the hallmark of attachment (Ainsworth 1967; Bowlby 1958, 1969; Schaffer 1963). . . .

The purpose of the present research project was to explore the relation between attachment and the development of person and object permanence based on the hypothesis that both processes are influenced by mother-infant interaction in the first year of life. Specifically, the aims were: (*a*) To test further the hypothesis that infants tend to be more advanced in the development of person permanence than in the development of the concept of inanimate objects as permanent, or that there tends to be a "positive décalage"; (*b*) to determine whether the direction of observed discrepancies between the object and person permanence scores for each baby (i.e., whether a baby scored higher or lower on person permanence as compared to object permanence) is related to the quantity and quality of attachment behavior that the infant displays toward his mother; (*c*) to ascertain whether the direction of the discrepancies is associated with the speed with which the development of the object concept is finally completed. . . .

METHOD

Two scales were devised to test for object and person permanence. They were administered to a sample of 33 babies who were tested at home three times between the ages of 8½ and 11 months. Interview information was also obtained from the mother during the course of these home visits. One week after the third testing session, babies were introduced to a strange situation, for the purpose of evaluating attachment behavior. Finally, a restricted portion of the original sample was retested at 13½ months to obtain additional data in regard to the development of the object concept.

Subjects

The sample consisted of 33 subjects, 21 males and 12 females, of middle-class parents whose names were obtained from pediatricians in private practice. All were full-term babies, in good health, who had normal births. Two of the boys had been adopted by their present mothers when they were between 2 and 3 months of age.

Measure of Object and Person Permanence

Since at the time this research was begun Décarie's (1965) scale of object permanence was the only one available, and a more detailed measure of this development seemed preferable, two new scales were devised to assess object and person permanence. They are homologous, consisting of 11 hiding steps which, although based directly on Piaget's account of the stages involved in the acquisition of the object concept, expand his original descriptions to test for behaviors which seemed

TABLE I

The Object Scale

Item No.	Description of Item	Stage Implied Therein	Appropriate Response
1	Object hidden partially in A	3b	S frees object from screen
2	Object hidden completely in A as S is reaching for it	3b → 4	S searches in A and secures the object
3	Object hidden completely in A	4	S searches in A and secures the object
4	Object hidden directly in B, after S found it in A	4 → 5a	S searches in B
5	Object displaced sequentially from A to B	5a incomplete 5a	S searches in A, then in B S searches in B directly
6	Object displaced sequentially from A to B to C	5a → 5b 5b incomplete	S searches in C after checking A and/or B S searches in C directly
7	Object displaced in random alteration: ACB, BAC, CAB	5b	S searches in the last screen directly
8	Single invisible displacement in A. Tried also in B	6a incomplete 6a	S searches in A, but cannot find object when hidden in B S searches in A, or in B appropriately
9	Sequential invisible displacement from A to B	6a → 6b 6b	S searches in B after checking A S searches directly in B
10	Sequential invisible displacement from A to B to C	6b → 6c 6c incomplete	S searches in C after checking A and/or B S searches directly in C
11	Random alternation of invisible displacements: ACB, BAC, CAB	6c complete	S searches directly in the last screen

to represent transitions between the main stages. Although these scales were devised independently of those constructed by Escalona et al. (1967) and Uzgiris and Hunt (1966b), they were subsequently found to be closely comparable to them.

A summarized account of the test will be found in Table 1. The items reflect a progression from hiding a part of the object to hiding the object completely in a complicated series of visible and invisible displacements. A displacement is visible when the infant is allowed to observe the object as it is being hidden. The technique of invisible displacements consists of hiding the object first in a container which

is, in turn, hidden under/behind a screen, and is brought out empty after releasing the object in the hiding place. The subject, who does not watch this transaction, must deduce the object's location after noticing that the container is empty. Three hiding places were used, indicated in the table as *A, B,* and *C*. The test elicited 15 behaviors which were scored following Piaget's stage paradigm.

MATERIALS   The objects used to test for object permanence were small toys interesting to the baby. Generally the same toy was used throughout a sequence of items, but if the baby lost interest the item was administered again with a different object. Piaget uses the term "screen" to refer to anything under or behind which an object is hidden. In the object-permanence test, three 6 × 8-inch felt pads, red, white, and green, were used as screens.

The usual person to hide in the person-permanence test was the mother, but the choice of object was determined on the basis of the baby's responsiveness as well as the mother's ability and willingness to cooperate. On a few occasions the experimenter hid either with the mother, or instead of her. The screens were varied. Doors, couches, and other available places in the house were used, as long as they completely covered the person hiding. An especially constructed screen on wheels, 1½ × 6 feet, was also provided to shield the person from the baby's sight. In addition, three smaller screens, behind which the person could hide if hunched over or kneeling, were utilized when testing a baby who could not crawl, or crawled with difficulty, and thereby failed to become engaged in the testing. These babies were placed on the floor with the screens arranged in a semicircle a short distance from them. They could indicate the person's location by pulling or lifting the correct screen, or by merely reaching toward it. This arrangement proved successful also in the case of a few babies who, although able to crawl with ease, lost interest when the game was tried from a distance.

SCORING AND CLASSIFICATION OF RESULTS
Each subject received two scores in each testing session, one on object permanence and one on person permanence, indicating the most advanced substages he had mastered with inanimate objects and with persons. In order to verify that discrepancies between object- and person-permanence scores were indicative of a true horizontal décalage rather than of mere error, the standard error of measurement was computed for each testing session. Discrepancies between object- and person-permanence scores, monotonically transformed, were considered true indications of a developmental difference when they were larger than the standard error of measurement.

Since there were no reversals in the direction of observed discrepancies in any of the first three testing sessions, the sample could be

unequivocally classified into three distinct groups. Those babies showing a preponderance toward significant discrepancies in favor of person permanence in the first three testing sessions were classified in the positive décalage group; those showing a preponderance toward significant discrepancies in favor of object permanence were designated the negative décalage group. Babies showing either no discrepancy between the two scores, or discrepancies which were smaller than the specified level of significance, were classified in the no décalage group.

Criterion of Attachment: Behavior in a Strange Situation

Since assessment of mother-infant interaction from direct observation can be equivocal unless the mother-infant pair is followed intensively over several months (and this was not feasible for the purposes of the present research project), a means to test attachment was needed which elicited a pattern of response from the infant which was stable, and which adequately reflected the quality of the mother-infant relationship.

The strange situation devised by Ainsworth and Wittig (1969) was designed to elicit exploratory behavior at first, but then to tip the balance toward attachment behavior through a series of increasingly stressful episodes. The evidence indicates that this test situation serves to highlight and intensify attachment behavior differentially in babies who had had different patterns of interaction with their mothers in the first year of life (Ainsworth & Bell 1970b; Ainsworth, Bell, & Stayton, in press; Ainsworth & Wittig 1969). In addition, Ainsworth, Bell, and Stayton (in press) showed that it elicits behavior which is highly correlated with the infant's behavior at home. The babies displayed differences in the quality of the balance between competing tendencies to explore away from the mother and to seek proximity and contact with her which were significantly related to the balance between these two tendencies observed at home. Thus, the strange situation met the desired requirements and was adopted to assess attachment in the present study.

TABLE 2

Strange Situation Episodes

Episode No.	Duration	Participants	Description of Episode
1	30 sec, approximately	Observer, mother, baby	Observer ushers mother and baby in the room. Baby is set down on the floor
2	3 min	Mother, baby	Baby is free to explore. M reads a magazine
3	3 min	Stranger, mother, baby	Stranger enters, sits quietly for a moment, interacts with mother, then with baby
4	3 min*	Stranger, baby	**M leaves.** Stranger remains with baby; responds to his advances or comforts him if necessary
5	Variable	Mother, baby	Stranger leaves as mother enters. Mother comforts the baby if he is distressed, then reinterests him in toys
6	3 min*	Baby	Mother leaves baby alone in room
7	3 min*	Stranger, baby	Stranger enters; attempts to comfort baby if distressed; returns to her chair
8	Variable	Mother, baby	Mother enters as stranger leaves. Observation continued until reunion behavior has been fully recorded

* The duration of episode was curtailed if the baby became very distressed.

The procedure, which has been described in detail elsewhere (Ainsworth & Bell 1970a) consists of eight 3-minute episodes designed to permit observation of a baby's response to two brief separations from the mother, and to subsequent reunion with her (Table 2). . . .

. . . Subgroup distinctions seemed unessential for the purposes of this research project, and thus only their criteria for classifying the subjects into three main groups are reported here. The characteristics of these groups may be summarized as follows:

Group A consisted of infants who showed relatively little proximity-seeking or contact-maintaining behavior, and who manifested striking proximity-avoiding behavior toward the mother in the reunion episodes. The Group A baby ignored the mother's return despite her efforts to attract his attention, or mingled a casual approach or greeting with clear-cut proximity-avoiding responses—moving past the mother, averting the face, and turning away from her. He tended to show little differential responsiveness in his treatment of mother and stranger, except for showing less avoidance of the latter.

Group B babies responded to the mother's return in the reunion episodes with more than a casual greeting. They showed tendencies to approach, and either sought proximity and contact or sought to interact with the mother. These babies were active in seeking contact and/or interaction and were clearly more interested in the mother than in the stranger.

Group C consisted of infants who were very ambivalent upon reunion with the mother and who, in addition, did not explore the strange environment in the preseparation episodes as actively as babies in the other two groups. Some of the babies were very upset by the situation itself, as well as the stranger, even prior to the mother's departure. Others were passive and did not take active initiative either in exploring during the preseparation episodes, or in seeking proximity and contact in the reunion episodes.

Procedures for Interviewing the Mother

A brief interview was conducted with the mother in the hope that her reply to certain questions would elucidate maternal attitudes and practices, as well as aspects of the mother-infant relationship. Several topics were probed, but only those which proved to be directly relevant to the main findings are mentioned here. Specifically, the mother was asked to state how frequently she played peek-a-boo and hide-and-seek games with her baby; whether she tended to take the baby on outings with her regularly or to leave him at home; and what she considered were some salient characteristics of the baby's temperament. The interview was conducted informally during the course of the first three visits.

In addition to recording the interview information, the observer noted instances during the home visits in which the mother punished the baby, physically rejected him (i.e., pushed him away or otherwise impeded him from establishing contact with her), or interfered with his ongoing activity in a way which was unnecessarily abrupt or inappropriate to the circumstances.

The analysis of information obtained from this procedure will be integrated with the main findings in the discussion of this paper. . . .

FINDINGS

The findings will be discussed in three sections corresponding to the specific aims of the study.

Horizontal Décalage*

. . . . .

The positive décalage group includes 23 subjects who showed a preponderance toward discrepancies in favor of person permanence. The negative décalage group includes seven subjects who tended to show discrepancies in the opposite direction. Finally, three babies showing no significant differences by the third

---

* The reader may want to refer back to p. 185, where *décalage* is first discussed. In the context here, it refers to the discrepancy in appearance of two types of permanence of object: person permanence and inanimate or object permanence. Conceivably, one would expect that these two phenomena would emerge at the same time in development. Where person permanence appears first, Dr. Bell reports the décalage as "positive." [Eds.]

testing session were classified in the no décalage group.

Discrepancies in favor of person permanence thus were more prevalent in this sample, as Piaget would have predicted, and seem to be very consistent over time since a sizable décalage of three scale steps on the average tended to persist until subjects had reached the highest substages of both the object- and person-permanence scales. The data indicate that negative discrepancies, in contrast, diminish in size more rapidly and disappear by the third testing session, when the majority of babies in the negative décalage group had reached the middle substages of stage 6. Whereas in the first two testing sessions all of the seven subjects in this group showed differences ranging from two to five steps in favor of object permanence, by the third testing session only two babies still showed a negative décalage, each consisting of two steps. . . .

Relation Between Type of Décalage and Attachment

The babies were also classified into three groups on the basis of their behavior in the strange situation: five infants were placed in Group A, four in Group C, and the remaining 24 in Group B. Table 3 shows the significant relation between décalage and attachment.

TABLE 3

Type of Décalage and Quality of Attachment

Strange Situation Classification	Type of Décalage		
	Positive	None	Negative
Group A	. . .	1	4
Group B	23	1	. . .
Group C	. . .	1	3

Babies classified in Group B were those who actively attempted to gain and maintain contact, proximity, and/or interaction with the mother after the brief separations, and who were able to use the mother as a secure base from which to explore during preseparation episodes. Twenty-three of the 24 infants in this group had a positive décalage—a more advanced concept of the permanence of persons than of inanimate objects. . . .

Five babies were classified in Group A since they displayed little heightening of proximity-seeking attachment behavior after separation, or mingled some degree of responsiveness with tendencies to turn away, go away, look away from the mother, and the like—possibly defensive reactions. In general they turned away from persons in favor of directing attention to the physical objects in the environment. . . .

Finally, three of four babies classified in Group C, since they showed ambivalence to the mother and/or general inability to cope with the strange environment—had a negative décalage. . . .

DISCUSSION

The findings confirm Piaget's (1937) hypothesis that the development of person permanence is homologous with that of object permanence, but proceeds at a different rate and probably begins at a different time. In the present sample, 70 percent of the babies showed a positive décalage—a discrepancy in favor of person permanence—and 27 percent a negative décalage—or discrepancy in favor of object permanence. The positive décalage proved to be more stable than the negative décalage. Differences in favor of person permanence tended to remain until scale ceiling was reached, whereas those in favor of object permanence tended to decrease steadily with age and to disappear in most cases by the time the middle levels of the final stage of this development—stage 6—were reached.

The most significant finding to emerge from this study, however, is that the development of the object concept is intimately associated with the attachment of a baby to his mother. In the present sample there was an almost perfect correspondence between type of décalage and the quality of attachment of a baby to his mother. In the present sample there was an almost perfect correspondence between type of décalage and the quality of attachment ex-

hibited in the strange situation. All of the babies who had a positive décalage displayed active efforts to establish and maintain proximity, contact, and/or interaction with the mother through approaching, reaching, and/or initiating interaction. Babies with a negative or no décalage reacted very differently: some showed little or no interest in interaction, proximity, or contact with the mother, whereas others were highly ambivalent toward her, or seemed passive and generally unable to cope with a strange environment.

Babies with a positive décalage were significantly more advanced in the development of person permanence at all testing sessions than were the babies who tended to have a negative or no décalage. In addition, they had reached the same level of object permanence at 8½ months and 11 months, and even tended to be more advanced with respect to this concept by 13½ months. Since these positive and negative or no décalage groups differed consistently with respect to person permanence, it seems that the type of décalage is an indication of a certain degree of advancement or retardation in the development of the permanence of persons, relative to the development of object permanence which proceeds in a more stable fashion. Thus, in keeping with the interactional emphasis of Piaget's theory, it seems possible to suggest from our findings that the acquisition of person permanence was more sensitive to favorable and unfavorable environmental circumstances.

Given the highly consistent relation between attachment and décalage evident in these findings, it can be hypothesized that the environmental circumstances which affect attachment have affected the development of person permanence, and thus the type of décalage. Ainsworth and Bell (1970b) and Ainsworth, Bell, and Stayton (in press) reported a definitive relationship between the quality of attachment behavior which an infant directs toward his mother in the strange situation, and mother-infant interaction in the first year of life. Babies whose mothers were especially perceptive, responsive, and desirous to gratify them, in the feeding situation as well as in social interaction, tended to manifest clear-cut unambivalent attachment toward the mother.

Generalizing these findings to the behavior of the present sample in the strange situation, it seems likely that the link between attachment and the development of person permanence is to be found in the quality of mother-infant interaction during the formative period of these affective and cognitive structures. A harmonious relationship between mother and infant seems to be the precondition for eliciting the type of "interest" in the baby which, Piaget hypothesized, so pervasively affects the development of sensorimotor intelligence.

In fact, evidence obtained from interviews in the present study strongly corroborates the above assumption. Whereas differences in the direction of décalage were not related to the reported amount of experience infants had with hide-and-seek or peek-a-boo games (which are in some respect comparable to the person-permanence test), maternal attitude as expressed in replies to the interview questions clearly differentiated between the positive and negative–no décalage groups at a statistical level of significance ($p < .05$). Mothers of babies in the positive décalage group tended to go on frequent outings with their babies and to avoid even brief daily separations from them. They tended to comment only on the baby's positive features, and never showed physical rejection or mistreated the infant in front of the observer. Mothers of negative décalage infants instead were significantly more rejecting: they rarely took the baby on outings, and openly found fault with him or commented on negative aspects of his temperament. In addition, they were prone to express disapproval and rejection through inappropriate use of physical punishment, refusal to establish contact with the baby, or abrupt interference with his ongoing activity.

Fortunately, a significantly higher percentage of the babies in the present sample, as well as in an earlier study by Saint-Pierre (1962), had a positive décalage—thus indicating a normative tendency for babies to experience circumstances which are sufficiently favorable to allow for an accelerated development of person permanence. Evidence from the present study suggests that the lack of a positive décalage is indeed atypical, since it indicates a retardation in the development of person permanence which ad-

versely affects the acquisition of the concept of object. Whereas the ability to master the higher substages of object permanence is facilitated by large, consistent, positive discrepancies, a lag in the development of person permanence hinders the growth of these advanced structures and the consolidation of symbolic processes of representation implied therein.

Much of the interest in Piaget's account of sensorimotor development has been aroused by the possibility, inherent in his theory, of accurately evaluating the effects of environmental conditions on specific aspects of cognitive development. In fact, Escalona and Corman (1967) and Uzgiris and Hunt (1966a) suggest that this is one of the primary purposes for which their scales can be utilized. Yet, when their object-permanence scales were used to assess differences in development between "slum" and "middle-class" infants, the results were equivocal. Golden and Birns (1967) could demonstrate no differences at 12, 18, or 24 months in the development of object permanence, among three socioeconomic groups. Wachs, Uzgiris, and Hunt (1967) reported significant differences between a "slum" and a "control" group only at 11 months, which could not be conclusively reconfirmed through testings at 15, 18, and 22 months.

In contrast, the comparison of the negative and positive décalage subgroups within this sample, which was composed only of middle-class subjects, revealed significant differences in their ability for symbolic representation of inanimate objects. These were related, as has been amply discussed above, to consistently observed differences in the development of person permanence which are associated with the quality of a baby's tie to his mother. Thus, it is suggested here that there is an important dimension affecting the development of the object concept which transcends socioeconomic boundaries and often goes unexamined in studies aiming to isolate the essential features of "enrichment" or "deprivation." Specifically, the findings of the present study lead us to the hypothesis that the quality of a baby's interaction with his mother is one of the crucial dimensions of "environmental influence" to affect this type of sensorimotor development.

REFERENCES

Ainsworth, M. D. S. *Infancy in Uganda: infant care and the growth of love.* Baltimore: Johns Hopkins University Press, 1967.

Ainsworth, M. D. S., & Bell, S. M. V. Attachment, exploration, and separation: illustrated by the behavior of one-year-olds in a strange situation. *Child Development,* 1970, 41, 49–67. (a)

Ainsworth, M. D. S. Some contemporary patterns of mother-infant interaction in the feeding situation. In J. A. Ambrose (Ed.), *The functions of stimulation in early post-natal development.* London: Academic, 1970. (b)

Ainsworth, M. D. S.; Bell, S. M. V.; & Stayton, D. J. Individual differences in strange-situation behavior of one-year-olds. In H. R. Schaffer (Ed.), *The origins of human social relations.* London: Academic, in press.

Ainsworth, M. D. S., & Wittig, B. A. Attachment and exploratory behavior of one-year-olds in a strange situation. In B. M. Foss (Ed.), *Determinants of infant behaviour, IV.* London: Methuen, 1969. Pp. 111–136.

Bowlby, J. The nature of the child's tie to his mother. *International Journal of Psychoanalysis,* 1958, 39, 350–373.

Bowlby, J. *Attachment and Loss.* Vol. 1. *Attachment.* London: Hogarth, 1969.

Décarie, T. G. *Intelligence and affectivity in early childhood.* New York: International Universities Press, 1965.

Escalona, S., & Corman, H. H. The validation of Piaget's hypotheses concerning the development of sensori-motor intelligence: methodological issues. Paper presented at the biennial meeting of the Society for Research in Child Development, March 1967.

Escalona, S.; Corman, H.; Galenson, E.; Schecter, D.; Schecter, E.; Golden, M.; Leoi, A.; & Barax, E. Albert Einstein Scales of Sensori-Motor Development. Unpublished, Department of Psychiatry, Albert Einstein School of Medicine, 1967.

Golden, M., & Birns, B. Social class and cognitive development in infancy. Paper presented at the biennial meeting of the Society for Research in Child Development, New York, March 1967.

Piaget, J. *La construction du réel chez l'enfant.* 1937. Neuchâtel: Delachaux et Niestlé, 1963.

Piaget, J. *Six psychological studies.* New York: Random House, 1967.

Saint-Pierre, J. Étude des différences entre la recherche active de la personne humaine et celle de l'objet inanimé. Master's dissertation, University of Montreal, 1962.

Schaffer, H. R. Some issues for research in the study of attachment behavior. In B. M. Foss (Ed.), *Determinants of infant behaviour, II.* New York: Wiley, 1963; London: Methuen, 1963. Pp. 179–199.

Uzgiris, I., & Hunt, J. McV. An instrument for assessing infant psychological development. Unpublished, University of Illinois, February 1966. (a)

Uzgiris, I., & Hunt, J. McV. Ordinal scales of infant development. Paper read at the eighteenth International Congress of Psychology, Moscow, August 1966. (b)

Wachs, T.; Uzgiris, I.; & Hunt, J. McV. Cognitive development in infants of different age levels and from different environmental backgrounds. Paper presented at the biennial meeting of the Society for Research in Child Development, New York, March 1967.

VARIABLES INFLUENCING
THE DEVELOPMENT OF ATTACHMENT

MARY D. SALTER AINSWORTH

The title of this chapter reflects the belief that attachment does not develop willy-nilly according to some inner, genetic, regulating mechanism, but rather is influenced by conditions in the baby's environment. This does not imply that inner, genetic regulators are negligible. On the contrary, the orderly sequence in the emergence of attachment patterns—as well as the fact that there seem to be striking similarities between this sequence among the Ganda and the sequence observable in our society—suggests that the development of attachment is correlated with other processes of development and that all these processes are in part determined by genetic factors characteristic of the human species. Furthermore, as an article of faith, we must concede that there are genetically based individual differences between babies, as well as differences stemming from prenatal development, circumstances surrounding the birth process, and from environmental influences in the neonatal period. In the present study it is quite impossible to differentiate genetic, prenatal, and perinatal influences from environmental influences since only one baby was observed from birth onward, and even in this case observations were too widely spaced to be helpful. Nevertheless, the fact that some environmental variables can be demonstrated to have a significant influence on the development of attachment among the babies of this sample demonstrates that genetic factors are not overwhelmingly important and that infant-care practices can make a difference.

The assertions in the paragraph above may

seem obvious to many readers. Nevertheless, there are some scientific students of infant behavior who attach almost exclusive importance to constitutional determinants of development, who view development as a maturational process of unfolding of genetic potential, who believe that a child can only learn a specific behavior pattern when his maturational level makes him ready, and who do not believe that methods of infant care and child rearing have any significant effect in accelerating or retarding development. There are other psychologists, chiefly concerned with animal learning, who believe that a person's responses can be controlled largely, if not entirely, by environmental contingencies, and who equate development with learning, thereby implying that developmental level is of little significance as long as the environmental contingencies are right. Because these two divergent views are widely held, it seems necessary to assume a stance and to assert that my position rests on a thoroughgoing belief that development is an interactional process—an interaction between the constitutional elements and environmental circumstances.

But here we are concerned with environmental influences. Let us begin with the end result insofar as it is known in the babies of this sample.

CLASSIFICATION OF INFANTS ACCORDING TO STRENGTH AND SECURITY OF ATTACHMENT

The sample may be divided into three groups according to the strength and security of the baby's attachment to his mother: (1) a secure-

Reprinted with abridgment by permission of the author and publisher from pp. 387–400 of *Infancy in Uganda: Infant Care and the Growth of Love*, by Mary D. Salter Ainsworth (Baltimore: The Johns Hopkins Press, 1967).

attached group consisting of sixteen children, subjects #1 to #16; (2) an insecure-attached group of seven children, subjects #17 to #23; and (3) a "non-attached" group of five children, subjects #24 to #28. In all of the tables interspersed throughout the book, the order in which the babies are listed corresponds to these divisions.

The babies in the two attached groups were those who manifested the patterns of attachment behavior found to be typical of their age —at least as judged by the norms of this sample. The third, "non-attached" group did not show any of the patterns of attachment behavior (directed toward the mother) throughout the entire period of observation. Let us consider this third group first, since they have not been dealt with in previous chapters.

The "Non-Attached" Group

First, let it be said that "non-attached" has been placed in quotation marks because the implication is not that these babies are not attached and never will be, but rather that they are not yet attached, and, although they are delayed in the development of attachment, it is entirely likely that they will become attached. Nevertheless, the fact that this small group is behind the rest of the sample in regard to the development of attachment makes it deserving of notice.

The "non-attached" (or "not-yet-attached") group consists of Nora, Kulistina, the younger set of twins—Waswa and Nakato—and Namitala. We shall immediately exclude Namitala from consideration. Although she did not develop any signs of discrimination of her mother from other people during the fifteen weeks she was observed, it could easily be said that she was somewhat delayed in discrimination, and that one cannot expect attachment to have developed by fifteen weeks of age. The other four children were, however, observed long enough to ascertain that they were deviant from their age peers in the development of attachment. In no case do I consider that conditions were such as to prevent the development of any attachment; but, certainly, attachment was delayed in these cases.

Nora, even when one year old, did not show any discrimination between her own mother and Kulistina's mother, who was a familiar caretaker and a member of the household. She did not cry when her mother left the room nor did she attempt to follow. We did not observe any greeting responses, and none were reported to us. Nora liked to explore her world after locomotion developed, but there is no evidence that she used her mother as a secure base for this exploration. Indeed, one might describe her tentatively as precociously independent. The only sign of attachment was to her father. On the weekends when he was at home, Nora was exceptionally active, approaching him, laughing, then retreating, only to approach him again. And at night she called out to him—*taata.* She also showed some preference for one of her half-sisters—one who was home only for occasional visits. Nora was not at all apprehensive of strangers. During our visits she sometimes responded to our advances, sometimes smiled spontaneously, but mostly she wanted to explore without interference from her mother or anyone else.

Kulistina had the unenviable distinction of being the baby in the sample whose start in life had been worst. Her mother did not, or could not, breast feed her, and she did not flourish on artificial feeding, not, at least, until pediatric advice was obtained and put into practice. Kulistina was a friendly baby and smiled a great deal. Her smiling seemed to be quite undiscriminating, even at forty-seven weeks of age. She accepted the attentions of the other wife in the household as readily as she accepted the attentions of her own mother. At thirty-three weeks of age we noted that she was more active and "scrambled" with her mother more than with other people—but aside from this observation, there seemed to be very little differentiation in her mode of responding to different people. At forty weeks Kulistina was said to "know" her mother, and also to "know" her father when he came home—but other babies could make these discriminations in the first quarter of the first year. In short, she seemed to be just beginning to make differential responses in the last quarter of the first year, whereas by this time most of the other babies in the sample were making their attachments clear by active, preferential behavior which showed initiative.

The Younger Twins—Waswa and Nakato. The twins manifested very little attachment behavior during the period of investigation. At twenty-three weeks they were described as lifting their heads up and vocalizing (as though they wanted to sit) in response to the approach of a person, but the response seemed quite non-differential. Nakato at thirty-two weeks was characterized as likely to cry when strangers were present, but Waswa "liked people." Neither baby cried when the mother left the room and both were described as behaving toward the mother no differently than they behaved toward others. The only hint of differential response came from Nakato, who was described as being less likely to cry when with her mother or father than when left with the young girls who were her "nursemaids." Waswa seemed to show no discrimination whatsoever.

One could perhaps argue that these babies were not wholly "non-attached." Nakato showed a few differential responses; Nora seemed especially excited by her father. But, on the whole, there seems little doubt that these four, including Nakato and Nora, were lagging markedly behind their age peers in regard to the development of discrimination and differential response—let alone the development of clear-cut attachment.[1]

The Secure-Attached Group

This is the largest of the three groups, consisting of sixteen children. These children were designated as "attached" according to the criterion of manifesting age-appropriate attachment behavior. Fourteen of the sixteen had reached at least Phase IV in the development of attachment behavior—showing following, approaching, active greeting, and the like. The other two—Alima (twenty-six weeks) and Samwendi (twenty-four weeks)—displayed Phase III behavior, which was appropriate for

[1] If one can judge from brothers and sisters, I could predict that these four babies, and also the fifth—Namitala —would eventually develop attachment to the mother. On the other hand, it seems likely that the attachment developed after the delay might be different in quality from the attachment of other babies who had less of a setback at the beginning.

their age at the end of our period of observations. These sixteen children were judged to be secure in their attachment to their mothers according to the criterion of infrequent crying. . . . To be sure, they might cry if parted from their mothers, or if particularly hungry, or they might be fussy during a period of illness or after weaning, but on the whole they cried very little, and when they were with their mothers they seemed especially content. . . .

Sembajwe was older than any of the other babies at the beginning of our visits to him— over 19 months old—and hence his behavior was not pertinent to an examination of the development of attachment during the first year of life. Nevertheless . . . Sembajwe was clearly attached to his mother before weaning, and, indeed, after weaning as well, but with a difference in behavior.

Senvuma was observed to be very clearly attached to his mother during the period of informal observations I made during my month in the village before the actual beginning of the project, although after weaning and separation . . . he was disturbed.

The Insecure-Attached Group

This group consists of seven babies. All of them had reached at least Phase IV in the development of attachment behavior and thus were classified as attached. They were designated as insecure according to the criterion of frequent crying. They were fussy babies who cried not just when parted from their mothers but even when with their mothers. . . . They cried to be picked up and cried when their mothers put them down and they sought to be in almost continuous physical contact with their mothers. Although seeking for proximity shows attachment, these seven children differed from the secure-attached group both in their relative inability to tolerate a little distance and in the fact that even when in proximity to the mother they continued to be fussy.

This was obviously a mixed group. Although they were all insecure, they were apparently insecure for different reasons. Two were chronically hungry and malnourished:

Waswa and Nakato, the older twins, were

still breast-fed, although the mother obviously had insufficient milk to nourish two babies of their age. They were over thirteen months old when we began to visit and twenty-one months old at the end of the study—and still unweaned. The mother, having been deserted by the father, did not have any money with which to buy milk or any of the protein foods the twins so sorely needed to supplement their diet. . . . The twins characteristically fussed during our visits, competed in their attempts to be picked up by the mother, and when picked up, persistently sought the breast and could not be soothed. Although after we provided dried milk supplement for them they began to gain and were somewhat less fussy, they still cried more frequently than the secure-attached babies.

One was chronically ill and fussy—*Magalita.* Although some of the secure-attached babies had periods of illness during which they were fussy, Magalita was ill and fussy throughout most of the first year of life. *Nakalema,* too, was ill a lot, although perhaps not more than some of the secure-attached babies. The mothers of four of the babies—*Muhamidi, Kasozi,* and the older twins—were themselves highly anxious, having been separated from or deserted by their husbands and finding it difficult to establish a satisfactory mode of life apart from them. *Sulaimani*'s mother must have been preoccupied with marital difficulties and with her conflict with the other wife in the household, and, indeed, Sulaimani seemed more secure after the other wife left the household.

There was some evidence that Nakalema was rejected by her mother, and this was perhaps the chief reason for her insecurity. Nevertheless, there may well have been an element of rejection in the other cases as well. Even Muhamidi's mother, who seemed so devoted and overprotective, was so anxious and depressed that she could not give Muhamidi delighted attention even though she gave him the physical contact that he so constantly demanded. The mother of twins was at her wits' end; she constantly frustrated the babies by withholding the breast that they sought, and their persistent demands obviously contributed to her anxiety. In all of these cases there seemed to be a vicious spiral in which the baby's fussy demands exasperated the mother, who then overtly or covertly rejected the baby, who in turn responded to the rejection by anxiety and by increasing his demands. The mother's and the baby's anxiety seemed to be in spiraling interaction.

Furthermore, the infant-care practices used by the mothers of the insecure-attached babies may have contributed to the babies' insecurity. Kasozi's mother, for example, had to work most of the day in a desperate effort to establish a new garden in order to provide food for her family and she left Kasozi with a neighbor. The father's desertion thus affected Kasozi both through the mother's anxiety and by making it necessary for her to give him less care and attention than most of these Ganda mothers gave their babies. The same was true of the mother of twins, and, moreover, the lack of money for supplementary milk resulted not only in the twins' hunger and malnutrition but also in a frustrating practice of scheduled feedings, for this harassed mother could not possibly accede to the twins' demands for the breast.

MATERNAL-CARE VARIABLES RELATED TO THE STRENGTH AND SECURITY OF ATTACHMENT

On the basis of all that we know about the effects on subsequent development of deprivation of maternal care in infancy and early childhood, it is an essential condition of subsequent satisfactory interpersonal relations for a child to have formed an attachment to someone—his mother or a substitute for her. On the basis of all of our clinical knowledge of the relationship between early parent-child relations and later intimacies, it seems desirable for a baby to have a secure attachment to his mother rather than an insecure one. How then can infant-care practices foster the development of a secure attachment?

This question can be answered only tentatively on the basis of a sample as small as this one and observations as discontinuous and incomplete as ours of necessity were. Nevertheless, a search was made for variables in terms of which the three groups of babies could be differentiated, on the assumption that such variables might help us to understand how it came about that some babies became attached during the first year while others did not, and that the attachment of some was secure while that of others was insecure.

With respect to some of the variables we examined, even this small sample is heterogeneous enough that hypotheses of cause and effect relationships between infant care and "outcome" can be formulated; with respect to other variables the sample is too homogeneous for statistically significant relationships to be found, however significant such relationships may be in another population of cases. Moreover, our search for cause and effect relationships is a retrospective search. Therefore, it has the strength of exploiting to the utmost the relationship between an antecedent condition which appears to be a cause and a consequent outcome which appears to be the effect. It also has the weakness of the *post hoc ergo propter hoc* fallacy in reasoning, because not all antecedent conditions are in a cause and effect relationship to events that follow them.

In full realization of these dangers and limitations let us ask the question: "In terms of what variables can these groups be distinguished from one another?" Both a priori considerations and an examination of the case summaries suggest a number of possibilities. The variables that seem possibly significant may be classified roughly into two groups: those which are related to the feeding situation and those which are not. Let us first consider those which are not directly associated with feeding.

WARMTH OF MOTHER

On a priori grounds it might be assumed that the warmth and affection expressed by the mother in interaction with her baby would have much to do with how secure and attached he became. All but two of these mothers, however, seemed warm and affectionate with their children. The exceptions were the mother of the non-attached twins, Waswa and Nakato, and the mother of the insecure child, Nakalema, who struck me as rejecting. The others all seemed warm with their babies, holding them easily, seeming to enjoy the contact and treating them with apparent affection. In this sample, there-

fore, the warmth of the mother and her observed affectionate contact behavior do not explain the differences between groups, although there is no reason to suppose that warmth would not emerge as a significant variable in another sample with wider range.

MULTIPLE CARETAKERS

The deleterious effects on infants and young children of prolonged periods in institutions and hospitals have been attributed at least in part to the fact that in the typical institutional setting a child is given care by a large number of people, who do different things for him at different times and who come and go with shifts of assignments and changes of job so that the child has no opportunity to establish an attachment with any one of them. Moreover, under these circumstances a caretaker who is responsible for several children is unable to be sensitive to the signals of all and consequently does not time her caretaking interventions in synchrony with the individual child's needs and rhythms. In the context of discussing maternal deprivation, Bowlby said that "what is believed to be essential for mental health is that the infant and young child should experience a warm, intimate, and continuous relationship with his mother (or permanent mother-substitute) in which both find satisfaction and enjoyment."

Margaret Mead, on the other hand, disputed the view that care by a single, continuous mother-figure was a necessary condition for the development of healthy interpersonal relations. On the contrary, her experience in non-literate societies led her to believe that it was not necessary for a child to attach himself to any one person. Indeed, multiple mother-figures serve as catastrophe insurance. The loss of his mother is less disastrous for a child who has been used to other caretakers than for one who has had an exclusive relationship with his mother.

These two points of view are tangential to each other because care by multiple figures in an institutional setting is obviously a different case than care by several figures who spell each other off but who each have the opportunity to give individualized and sensitive attention. Nevertheless, the controversy directs attention to the possible effect of multiple caretakers on the development of attachment.

Although the mothers of the non-attached children in this study all shared their mothering duties with other people, most of the mothers of the other two groups of children did likewise, so that this variable fails to distinguish between the groups at a statistically significant level. Therefore, there is no evidence that care by several people necessarily interferes with the development of healthy attachment. And yet if the sharing of mothering duties unduly reduces the amount of care the mother (or any other one person, presumably) gives the baby, this does seem to have an adverse effect on the development of attachment, as may be seen in the next section.

AMOUNT OF CARE GIVEN BY THE MOTHER

Each mother was rated [on a scale from 1, the lowest rating, to 7, the highest] in regard to the amount of care she gave her baby. . . . Ratings of 1 or 2 occur only in the non-attached group. The mothers of the non-attached infants regularly left their babies for long periods and shared their mothering duties with others even when they themselves were available to give the babies care. Three of the four ratings of 7 occurred in the secure-attached group. These mothers gave their babies much motherly care, and, indeed, took them along wherever they went. This variable does significantly differentiate between the three groups.

TOTAL AMOUNT OF CARE

According to Margaret Mead's position, it might be expected that the total amount of care received from all caretakers combined might be the most crucial variable. A case such as Nabatanzi fits in with this position. Although her mother regularly left her for long periods, she had three other caretakers who gave her much care; she was alone and uncared for only when asleep. And she was clearly secure and attached until the time of weaning; her disturbance at weaning was, however, especially intense and prolonged.

Each child was rated in regard to the total amount of care he received. . . . Nineteen babies received ratings of 7 or 6, implying much total care, and . . . this was true for five of the seven insecure-attached babies as well as for thirteen of the sixteen secure-attached babies. It is probably because of this very skewed distribution that this variable fails to differentiate significantly between the groups. The condition that is not adequately represented in this sample is a high amount of total care and a relatively small amount of care given by the mother, i.e., more infants like Nabatanzi, or with an even greater discrepancy between the ratings. Under these circumstances, and depending on the size of the discrepancy and the extent to which the supplementary care was given by one rather than by several people, one might expect either that the child would become more attached to another caretaker than to his mother or that he might become insecure because he had enough interaction with his mother to become attached to her but not enough to prevent him from from feeling rejected, as, indeed, Nabatanzi seemed to feel after weaning.

In any event, the infants in the non-attached group all received low ratings in both total amount of care and in amount of care given by the mother. Nora and Kulistina were both left in cribs for much of the day, each in her own separate room, quite isolated. The younger twins were together, but spent much of the day by themselves either in a gocart outside the house or in an empty house.

The term "motherly care" is too unspecific. The connotation is one of routine care, of tending to the baby's physical needs. Two more specific variables, which have emerged as highly significant in my subsequent study of American babies during the first year of life, are: (1) the sensitivity of the mother in responding to the baby's signals and (2) the amount and nature of the interaction between mother and baby. Sensitivity of response to signals implies that signals are perceived and correctly interpreted and that the response is prompt and appropriate. The signals may be of need and distress or they may be social signals. Sensitivity to signals tends to ensure that the care the mother gives the baby, including her playful interaction with him, is attuned to the baby's state and mood—at the baby's own timing, not at the mother's timing. Routine care may be undertaken with little interaction. It is interaction that seems to be most important, not mere care, and particularly conspicuous in mother-child pairs who have achieved good interaction is the quality of mutual delight which characterizes their exchanges.

These more subtle and complex variables are subsumed in the present ratings scales of amount of maternal and total care, but they are also obscured by being included together with notions of routine care, amount of time the mother is available, and the like. Unfortunately, a much more intensive and prolonged type of observation is necessary for assessing the subtleties of interaction than was undertaken in this study, and hence more subtle assessments cannot be made even retrospectively. Nevertheless, it is believed that the reason that the amount of care given by the mother emerges as a variable significantly related to the development of attachment is that interaction and sensitivity to signals have as a necessary condition that the mother is available to the child. If the mother is elsewhere, she obviously cannot respond to and interact with the baby, although her mere presence is no guarantee of sensitivity or interaction.

MOTHER'S EXCELLENCE AS AN INFORMANT

This variable first suggested itself as worthy of exploration when it was realized that the information that had been collected about the non-attached babies was more meager than that accumulated about other children to whom we had paid fewer visits. [Dr. Ainsworth includes a rating scale for this variable, as well as for others already discussed, in earlier chapters of her book not reprinted here.] . . .

Of course, more than mere excellence of information is implied by this scale. Implicit in a high rating is that the mother is sufficiently interested in the baby, that she is free enough of preoccupations and anxieties of her own, that she is sensitively perceptive of his idiosyncratic ways of behaving and of the ways in which he expresses his needs, wishes, and preferences,

and that she takes enough interest and pleasure in him to want to talk about him, volunteering information about him rather than talking about other things. Implicit in a low rating is that the mother has not been attentive to her baby, so that she really does not know very much about his special ways of behaving—either because she is with him infrequently or because she is preoccupied with other thoughts or activities when they are together. Also implicit in a low rating is that the mother, when interviewed about her baby, is more interested in other topics of conversation than she is in her baby.

The mothers of the non-attached infants were below the median in excellence as informants, while a higher proportion of the mothers of the secure-attached babies had really high ratings than did the mothers of the insecure-attached babies. This variable significantly differentiates between the three groups and hence seems related to the development of attachment. Of course, in future research it would be better to rate directly the mother's perceptiveness of the baby and her pleasure and interest in him than to infer it from her excellence as an informant. Moreover, it is conceivable that a mother might be uncommunicative in interview for reasons totally unrelated to her attitude toward the baby —although this did not seem to happen in this sample. Next let us consider the variables related to the feeding situation.

SCHEDULED VERSUS SELF-DEMAND FEEDING

It will be recalled that eight babies were fed according to a schedule, and that of those fed "on demand," some were fed when the mothers judged them to be hungry and some also for comfort, even though they were obviously not hungry. . . . The schedule-fed babies are found in each of the three groups, as are those fed on demand. There is a tendency for the mothers of the secure-attached babies to give the breast for comfort whereas none of the mothers of the non-attached babies did so; this tendency, however, was below the level of statistical significance.

Repeated investigations of the effects of scheduled versus demand feedings have yielded similar inconclusive results. If one believes, as

I do, that the mother's sensitivity to the baby's signals significantly influences their interaction and his development, it is difficult to accept these findings. One reason for inconclusive findings is that the mothers interviewed defined self-demand feeding in so many different ways. It is common for women in this country to say that they feed on demand—when the baby is hungry —but to believe that he cannot possibly be hungry until four hours after the previous feeding, and in such cases a distinction between demand and scheduled feedings is negligible. In the Ganda investigation an effort was made to obtain a statement from the mother of how she defined demand feeding, and, moreover, we could observe how hunger signals and feeding were managed during our visits. In this case, it seems likely that the distinctions broke down by reason of the unavailability of the mothers who left their babies behind when gardening. Kasozi's mother fed him for comfort when they were together, for example, but she was absent for at least seven hours a day. It is hoped that future research will overcome difficulties such as these and settle the matter of whether or not demand feeding is better than scheduled feeding.

MOTHER'S MILK SUPPLY

Some of the mothers claimed to have considerable difficulty in maintaining an adequate supply of milk. If the difficulty is a real one, it could make for insecurity as well as hunger in the baby—as indeed it did in the case of the older twins—both directly and indirectly, because it makes the mother anxious. If the difficulty is imagined, it could nevertheless affect the baby through the mother's anxiety. There were eleven mothers who reported no difficulty in milk supply; nine of them were mothers of secure-attached babies. The statistical test shows that the tendency in this sample is below the level of significance, but since the sample is such a small one, the influence of milk supply on the nature of the infant-mother relationship with breast-fed babies cannot be dismissed as negligible.

MOTHER'S ATTITUDE TOWARD BREAST FEEDING

Fourteen mothers stated without qualification that they enjoyed breast feeding—thirteen when Namitala's mother is excluded. Twelve of these were mothers of secure-attached infants, one a mother of an insecure-attached infant; none were mothers of non-attached babies. It is thus obvious that this variable significantly differentiates the groups.

The relationship between a mother and a breast-fed baby is undoubtedly a complex one in which the feelings of the mother and the response of the infant can interact in vicious or virtuous spirals. Suffice it to say that twelve of the sixteen secure-attached babies not only enjoyed their interaction with their mothers but had mothers who enjoyed at least the feeding interaction with them.

SUMMARY

In summary, then, there were three variables which were found to be related significantly to the development of security and attachment: the mother's attitude to breast feeding, the amount of care she gave to the baby, and her excellence as an informant. A fourth variable—mother's milk supply—was only slightly below the level of statistical significance. All of these variables could be described as mere rough approximations of underlying variables which are more crucial in determining the development of infant-mother attachment.

These rough approximations served the useful purpose of directing attention toward a much more elaborate set of refined variables, which can be assessed only in a more intensive study. Some of these, which are believed to be significant in this Ganda sample and which are emerging as significant in my present study of American infants, are: the sensitivity of the mother in responding to the baby's signals of need and distress and to his social signals, and the promptness and appropriateness of her response; the amount of interaction she has with him and the amount of pleasure both derive from it; the extent to which her interventions and responses come at the baby's timing rather than her own; the extent to which she is free from preoccupation with other activities, thoughts, anxieties, and griefs so that she can attend to the baby and respond fully to him; and finally and obviously, the extent to which she can satisfy his needs, including his nutritional needs.

EFFECTS OF VARIOUS MOTHER-INFANT RELATIONSHIPS ON RHESUS MONKEY BEHAVIORS

HARRY F. HARLOW   MARGARET K. HARLOW

During the last eight years we have studied the effects of a wide variety of mother-infant rearing relationships on the social development of rhesus monkeys. At one extreme we have raised monkeys from birth onward without mothers or playmates, and at the other extreme we have raised monkeys with normal mothers and easily available playmates. The intermediate rearing conditions include normal mothering without playmates and a variety of situations in which playmates were available but mothering ranged from total denial of any mother, to inanimate, nonresponsive surrogate mothers, indifferent or brutal mothers, and a rotating series of individual mothers.

EFFECTS OF DENIAL OF BOTH MOTHER AND AGE-MATE RELATIONSHIPS

Our extreme condition of affectionless up-bringing was rearing monkeys in social isolation from birth until various predetermined ages. In isolation there was no opportunity to experience maternal or peer affection or to develop affection for other monkeys. We have employed two conditions of social isolation: Monkeys in *subtotal isolation* were raised in individual wire cages which permitted visual and auditory access to other infants but denied any opportunity for physical interaction. Monkeys in *total isolation* were raised in individual enclosed sheet-metal chambers which prevented viewing of other monkeys or of humans.

Reprinted with abridgment by permission of Harry F. Harlow, B. M. Foss, and the publisher from pp. 15–36 of *Determinants of Infant Behaviour, IV*, edited by B. M. Foss (London: Methuen & Co., 1969).

INDIVIDUAL BEHAVIORS DEVELOPING DURING SOCIAL ISOLATION

Rhesus monkeys raised under either of these isolation conditions for long periods of time develop many aberrant individual and social behavior patterns. Typical individual behavior patterns associated with isolation include: (1) Increased non-nutritional orality directed toward the physical environment or the animal's own body, with almost any body part fixated—thumb, fingers, toes, nipple, or penis. The frequency of this pattern is high during the first two years and then gradually drops to a normal level by the fifth year of life. (2) A second pattern is that of self-clutching in which monkeys, particularly infants, tightly clasp their bodies and/ or heads with their hands and feet. The frequency of this pattern decreases after the first year and reaches a baseline for males by Year 2 and for females by Year 4. (3) A third pattern is that of social indifference with vacant staring; the animal is unresponsive to ordinary stimulation in the environment such as calls or movement of other animals in the room or the activity of caretakers. This pattern of social apathy may take an extremely bizarre form, to which we have given the name 'catatonic contracture.' While a monkey sits in a quiescent state, an arm floats upward with concurrent flexion of the wrist and fingers—a movement made as if the limb were not an integral part of the monkey's own body. (4) A fourth abnormal behavior is that of fixed, stereotyped repetitive movements, such as pacing back and forth or circling over and over from the top to the bottom of the cage. This pattern in one form or another has been observed in many laboratories and for many mammalian species. (5) A fifth pattern is that of aggression. Aggression was measured by having one observer run his hand, covered by a large black laboratory glove (used by handlers when making direct contact with the animals), over the monkey's living cage. The development of two patterns of aggression was traced: aggression directed against the observer, and aggression directed against the animal's own body—biting its own hand, arm, foot, or leg. Both aggressive patterns appeared earlier in the males than in the females, but even for the males externally directed aggression was infrequent until the second year of life and self-directed aggression low until the fourth year. It is the self-directed aggression which differentiates the isolated subjects from normal animals.

EFFECTS OF ISOLATION ON SOCIAL BEHAVIOR

The effects of raising monkeys in total social isolation during the first 3, 6, and 12 months of life on their later capability of adjusting to age-mates in our playroom situation are well established. Two independent studies showed that monkeys socially deprived for the first 3 months were terrified upon release but rapidly adjusted to age-mates. No differences in social threat and no significant differences in play behavior were disclosed, even in the first month of playroom testing. Subsequently an independent, unpublished study by Sackett suggested some depression of exploratory-curiosity behaviors, probably not of a permanent nature.

These data relating to play and sex behavior in 3-month isolates are in strong contrast with the effects of 6 months of total social isolation tested by placing pairs of 6-month isolates in the playroom with pairs of control subjects. Play and social threat during the first two test months were essentially nonexistent for the isolates. Even after 32 test weeks, frequency of play by the isolates was low and limited to contacts with each other, never with the controls.

Twelve months of total social isolation left even more devastating effects. Social behavior on the part of the isolates was almost completely absent. Even individual play, a preliminary to

social play, was negligible, and a similar pattern existed for each of the wide variety of social behaviors measured in the playroom situation. Social testing in the 12-month isolate groups had to be discontinued after 10 weeks because the control animals were mauling and abusing the helpless isolates to the point that they could not have survived continuing interaction.

Long-term deprivation effects have been assessed by testing these isolate animals 2 or 3 years later, after they had been housed in individual wire-mesh cages in a colony room without physical contacts with peers. In social pairings with adults, age-mates, and 1-year-old juveniles, the 6-month isolates, then 2½ to 3½ years of age, showed no normal sexual behavior, and such attempts as they made toward play were inept. Aggression, however, was frequent in these animals, though totally abnormal in objects. They often engaged in near-suicidal acts of threat or assault against the huge adult males. Even though fearful of juveniles, they attacked and bit them, a response we rarely see in socially raised animals, male or female. The 12-month isolates at the same ages exhibited fear of all social contacts, showed essentially no play or sex behavior, and engaged in no acts of physical aggression. However, one year later (at 3½ to 4½ years of age) two 12-month isolates (one male and one female) displayed abnormal aggression toward both adults and age-mates.

It is clear that denial of both maternal and age-mate affection during the first 6 months to 1 year of life produces a syndrome of persisting social and sexual ineptitude and abnormal aggression in monkeys even though in some animals the appearance of aggression is much delayed.

EFFECTS OF PEER DEPRIVATION DURING NORMAL MOTHERING

The consequences of deprivation of peer experience on infants provided normal mothering from birth have been studied by Alexander (1966) in the playpen situation. A control group interacted with their mothers from birth and with each other from the third week onward. Two experimental groups were also raised by normal mothers but were denied sight of, and all association with, other infants and other mothers for the first 4 and the first 8 months of life, respectively, by placement of opaque panels between adjacent cages and play-pens. We refer to the infants in the experi-mental groups as the playmate-deprived or peer-deprived infants. The experimental mothers developed ambiguous relationships toward these offspring; they tended to be oversolicitous and eventually, also, overpunishing as compared with control mothers, the 8-month group be-ing more punitive than the 4-month group, al-though negative behaviors never became a dom-inant feature in treatment of offspring.

The infants that were peer-deprived for 4 months and then allowed to interact with other infants rapidly developed adequate, typical play patterns and appeared to be socially and sex-ually normal except for their wariness of bodily contact, lessened frequency of affectionate in-terchanges with peers, and a tendency toward increased agonistic responses as compared with the control group. The infants in the 8-month playmate-deprived group also made rapid and effective social and heterosexual adjustments when allowed to interact with peers. Compared with the 4-month group, however, the 8-month group showed even less bodily contact, still fewer affectional interchanges, and even more agonistic responses. After separation of the young monkeys from their mothers at 13 months of age, additional tests were made of peer in-teractions and of treatment of stranger 6-month-old infants. The 8-month group was consistently hyperaggressive, the 4-month group intermedi-ate, and the control group low in aggression within groups. In affectionate behavior within groups, the three groups ranked in reverse or-der, the control group scoring high, the 4-month group intermediate, and the 8-month group low. In behavior toward stranger infants, the 8-month group again was most hostile, the 4-month group next, and the control group least hostile. No group showed a tendency to make positive responses toward the infants; rather, absence of aggressive behavior was ac-companied by ignoring the intruders.

We have previously pointed out that six months of combined mother and peer depriva-tion produces serious, long-term social malad-

justment in monkeys. In contrast, eight months of peer deprivation alters social behavior but much less severely although the implications of the social characteristics of the peer-deprived monkeys are not entirely clear. Such animals placed in a heterogeneous social group includ-ing animals of all ages might well become lon-ers or outcasts by virtue of their lower affilia-tive tendencies and higher aggressive tendencies. In a group restricted to age-mates, however, they could conceivably establish themselves as dominant members because of their readiness to aggress. Nevertheless, in a group similarly reared they do show adequate play and normal sex behavior, suggesting that to a large extent mothers may substitute fairly effectively for age-mates in at least the first eight months of the rhesus monkey's life. This occurs in spite of the fact that rhesus mothers engage in little in-teractive play with their infants, unlike chim-panzee mothers and certainly unlike human mothers. The human mother not only plays with her child but continuously debases her play level to that appropriate to the matura-tional age of the infant.

Recently, Joslyn observed the behavior of two young monkeys, a male and a female, nor-mally mothered but peer-deprived for the first 20 months. Both mothers were solicitous and protective but also punished their offspring oc-casionally. When these long-term, peer-deprived juveniles were given the opportunity to associate with each other, they were fearful and neither interacted nor displayed physical contact. Sub-sequently both juveniles were given daily op-portunity to interact or not interact with a nor-mal, unfamiliar peer. The peer-deprived female made no attempt at social interaction through-out 2 months of testing. The male rapidly ad-justed to his playmate with no detectable signs of social abnormality except that his sexual be-havior was poorly developed. The extreme in-dividual differences were striking, since these two peer-deprived animals, raised under identi-cal conditions, would have been at diverse poles of any social adjustment scale. Similar differ-ences developed with sex reversed in an earlier pair of monkeys raised by their mothers and given the opportunity to interact in the playpen at 7 months of age. In this instance the female repeatedly attempted to establish contact but the male never left the living cage in two months of daily exposures to the female; moreover, the male's mother prevented the female from entering the male's living cage. Subsequently in the playroom, after separation from their mothers, this pair developed no interactive play in two months of exposure.

EFFECTS OF PEER DEPRIVATION DURING SURROGATE MOTHERING

Although we have conducted no experiments specifically on the social consequences of raising monkeys from birth on cloth surrogate mothers while denying them any peer interactions during the first half-year or year of life, we do have a considerable body of relevant data. The early mother-surrogate studies showed that infants so raised formed strong attachments to their inanimate mothers and that in a strange situation the cloth surrogates (but not wire surrogates) imparted strong security feelings to the infants, then 3 to 6 months of age. The social contribution of surrogate mothers probably ends with the infant's development of security and trust.

Only one research suggests any long-term effect favoring surrogate-reared animals over those raised in bare wire cages. In this study of mothers raised without real mothers and without peer experience in the first 7 to 12 months, it was found that of the 7 females raised with cloth surrogates, 2 were abusive, 3 were indifferent, and 2 were adequate as compared with 6 abusive, 4 indifferent, and 3 adequate mothers among the 13 wire-cage-raised females. The numbers are too small for conclusiveness but hold out the possibility that surrogate mothering has some long-term effect which reduces the extreme aggression which these 'motherless-mothers' would otherwise exhibit towards their own infants. Nonetheless, the maternal performance of the cloth-surrogate group considered alone is far from exemplary, as is their record of sexual behavior—2 were impregnated involuntarily and none of the remaining 5 fell within normal limits in copulatory behavior. No surrogate-raised male has even achieved a normal mount, and none has achieved intromission. Even in social interactions in the sec-

ond year of life surrogate-raised monkeys, male and female, were as inadequate as wire-cage-raised animals. These shortcomings contrast with those of the mother-reared, peer-deprived infants of the Alexander study [published in 1966], which show social behaviors that are within normal limits or approach normal limits even though they are affectively different from those of animals also provided with early peer experience.

EFFECTS OF TOTAL MATERNAL DEPRIVATION

We have also raised macaque monkeys in situations in which they have had no mothering whatsoever, real or surrogate, but have been given opportunity to interact with other infants, either in pairs, groups of four, or groups of six. We have called these monkeys our 'together-together' infants. These monkeys placed together in the first weeks of life have strong propensities to seek contact comfort, as seen in their quickly developed physical attachments to each other. These attachments resemble those that neonatal and infant monkeys form to real or surrogate mothers, and they largely replace the self-cling patterns typical of infants raised in total or partial social isolation.

Unmothered infants raised in pairs typically enter into [a] tight ventral-ventral clinging pattern. This pattern may persist for many weeks and retard the development of normal play responses. Eventually, however, this pattern is broken and play is established. Unmothered infants raised in unchanging groups of four or six form a dorsoventral clinging pattern, which we have called the 'choo-choo' effect. Such simulated mother-infant attachment patterns in larger groups are more easily broken than are the infant pair patterns, and interactive play is exhibited earlier, although it is delayed by comparison with that obtained under more normal rearing conditions.

Our predictions concerning the eventual social capabilities of these unmothered, 'together-together' infants were gloomy, but the infants' long-term social adjustments have been far better than expected. Interactive play patterns did develop, aggression within groups was low, and normal heterosexual adjustments were the rule, not the exception. One female has thus far become a mother, and her behavior toward her infant has been normal in every respect. Thus, in the special, highly protected environment of the laboratory, infant interactions appear to have compensated reasonably well for lack of mothering. We do not believe, however, that normal mothering is in any sense dispensable under feral conditions, nor could it be put to test, for abandoned or orphaned infants would certainly be adopted very soon or perish. . . .

[The Harlows continue here with data from a study by Chamove, published in 1966, on monkeys living in pairs, either with the same or a changing partner, as compared with monkeys living in a group of six, and monkeys living alone.]

These data strongly suggest that early experience with multiple peers, whether as a group or consecutively, produces ties among group members which maximize play and affiliative behavior and minimize aggression within the group or towards outsiders. Early experience with constant single partners, on the other hand, produces strong partner-ties but little carry-over to peers encountered subsequently, resulting in moderate levels of play and in affiliation within pairs but high aggression between partner-pairs and, sometimes, towards outsiders. Animals raised alone for one year and then placed in a group-living situation show high aggression among themselves and little play or affiliative behaviors. Their aggression carries over to a threatening larger animal although they tend to ignore smaller animals. A second factor is the constancy of association, for there was a tendency for constant-group animals, whether the group of six or the pairs, to show stronger affiliative tendencies to their constant peers than the animals with changing partners or alternate-week partners.

The monkeys raised as a constant group of six in some ways resemble the group of six refugee children studied by Freud & Dann [and published in 1951]. These children who lost their parents at birth or in the early months of life were shifted about as a group for several years with inconstant caretaking and showed social characteristics in common with our unmothered monkey group of six. Most strikingly, the children showed very low hostility and extremely high affiliative tendencies within

their group, as did our monkeys. Their adjustment to other children is not known, nor has this been tested adequately with our monkeys. The child situation demanded an adjustment to adults which the monkey situation did not, and in this respect the comparison of groups cannot be made. Both situations, limited as they are in scope, do certainly point to the important role age-mates may play in the development of affection and socialization, but they both leave untested the potential adjustment of the members to the larger, more heterogeneous social group.

EFFECTS OF SURROGATE MOTHER RAISING WITHOUT PEER DEPRIVATION

As we have already stated, cloth-surrogate mothers are obviously substandard monkey mothers since they are devoid of facial, vocal, and gestural language; cannot protect their infants; cannot punish their infants; and cannot respond reciprocally to their infants' behavior. Even so, macaque monkeys raised on cloth-surrogate mothers but given ample opportunity to interact with other infants show remarkably effective social and sexual development. . . .

. . . Hansen [in a paper published in 1966] compared the social development of a group of four monkeys raised from birth to 21 months with cloth surrogates in the playpen with that of four monkeys raised by their own mothers in the playpen apparatus. Unfortunately, one variable was uncontrolled; the four animals in the surrogate group were balanced for sex but the mother-raised group was all male. Inasmuch as sex differences in activity and play appear by the second and third months and increase subsequently, it is likely that Hansen's differences between groups are enhanced by the sex composition of the groups.

On all social measures the Hansen results showed the mother-raised babies were in advance of the surrogate-raised babies, typified by measures of rough-and-tumble and approach-withdrawal play illustrated in Figure 1, but the group differences lessened with time and by the end of the first year the groups were similar. A third group of two males and two females raised by their mothers from birth in two-unit playpens and transferred at 9 months to four-unit

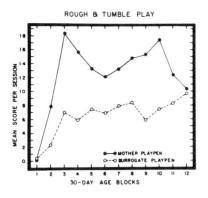
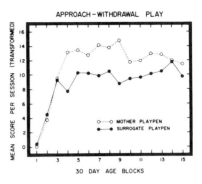

FIGURE I

Development of rough-and-tumble and approach-withdrawal play by mother-raised and by surrogate-raised monkeys.

playpens was closely similar to the surrogate group in the second year. When the 12 animals were separated from their mothers at 18 to 21 months and tested together, the surrogate-raised group was indistinguishable in social behavior, but the sexual behavior of the two surrogate-raised males was not normal in that when testing ended the double foot-clasp pattern had not appeared. One mother-raised male did not display adult-type mounting behavior as of this time.

The results suggest that live mothers impart a social advantage to their offspring in the first half-year, but this is in part negated in the second half-year when the mother-raised infants are subjected to considerable ambivalence from their mothers. It is during this period that disturbance scores rise for the mother-raised group. Surrogate mothers, on the other hand, are constant in their stimulus values. It is likely that the surrogate babies would be disadvantaged if they interacted in the early months with mother-raised infants and that the social consequences could become fixed, but under the experimental condition of interaction with others in the same rearing condition until late in the second year, this problem is avoided.

EFFECTS OF INDIFFERENT AND BRUTAL MOTHERING

Female monkeys raised in subtotal social isolation from birth through adolescence are fre-

quently inadequate mothers to their first infants regardless of the way their impregnation is achieved. These so-called 'motherless mothers', denied both maternal and age-mate affection early in life, are typically indifferent or brutal to their offspring.

Seay, Alexander & Harlow [in a paper published in 1964] traced the course of infant-infant or peer affection in four infants, three males and one female, of near equal ages raised by motherless mothers in the playpen situation. Peer affection, measured by contact play responses, was initially delayed in the motherless-mother infants as compared with infants of normal mothers, but essentially no differences were found from the third month onward. The developmental course of the more complex play pattern of noncontact play was depressed for infants of motherless mothers compared with normal mothers. Although differences persisted throughout the 6-month test period, they were not statistically significant. Early in life these motherless-mother infants exhibited normal, if not precocious, sexual development. There was also a trend of heightened agonistic responses in the group, with the female and one male tending to dominate the other two males. Retested at 3 years of age, these motherless-mother animals showed less adequate play and more aggression than normal-mother-raised monkeys, leaving open the question concerning long-term effects of the early rearing. The social adjustment of the motherless-mother monkeys was, at least, much closer to that of monkeys raised by normal mothers than that of equal-aged monkeys subjected to early subtotal social isolation. . . .

. . . These findings tend to support the trends . . . suggesting that poor mothering retards early peer adjustment and encourages aggressive behavior.

EFFECTS OF MULTIPLE-MOTHER-RAISING ON INFANT SOCIAL ADJUSTMENT

Griffin has recently completed an investigation comparing the social behavior of two groups of four infants raised in playpens by their own mothers with a group of four infants rotated on a biweekly schedule within a group of four mothers. The most notable effect of the multiple-mothering treatment was an abnormally high level of disturbance behavior in these infants as compared with the controls (see Figure 2), and the overall group effect was

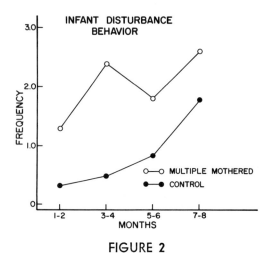

FIGURE 2

Disturbance behavior of multiple-mothered infants and controls.

significant. However, the mothers in the multiple-mother group did not exhibit maternal behaviors significantly different from those of the mothers in the control groups although it is possible that maternal variance was enhanced. When the multiple-mothered infants were allowed to interact with peers, they did not show any deficiencies in play or sexual behavior nor did they show aberrant aggressive responses.

Data collected by Griffin and Sackett on these infants at 8 months of age in a situation where they could choose either a stranger adult or a stranger infant do show differences. The infants from the single-mother groups showed a preference for the infant over the adult, but the multiple-mothered infants showed no preference.

In a series of experiments multiple mothers, normal mothers, motherless mothers, and their infants were given preference tests to see if mothers preferred their own infants and infants their own mothers. The test apparatus allows test monkeys to choose among four compartments to each of which is attached a cage containing a stimulus monkey. The test monkey can be near, see, and hear the stimulus animal by entering the choice compartment but has no physical access to the animal. When the stimuli were mothers, the test animals were infants. When infants were stimuli, test animals were mothers. In all tests one stimulus animal was the test monkey's natural mother or infant. Preference is indicated by the amount of time spent in each choice compartment during the 10-minute trial. The results show that normal mothers and their offspring preferred each other to familiar but unrelated animals. The multiple-mothered infants and mothers did not prefer their own relative. This was expected because these infants spent equal time during rearing with all mothers in the group. Among all the infants, the infants of inadequate motherless mothers had the greatest preference for their own mothers. The motherless mothers, however, did not prefer their own infants. These tests were conducted when the infants were one year old, within one month of final separation from their mothers. Thus, infants reared by indifferent or hostile mothers seem to have developed greater attachment to their mothers than did infants of normal mothers, but motherless mothers appear to lack the attachment to their infants demonstrated by normal mothers.

SUMMARY

This paper has been concerned with assessing the effects of diverse mothering situations for rhesus infants while varying simultaneously the opportunities for peer association. The rearing conditions considered range from total deprivation of mothering and peers to normal mothering and regular peer experience from the first weeks of life.

The isolation conditions have effects that are directly related to duration of the imposed deprivation and degree of isolation. Three months of subtotal or total social isolation followed by extensive opportunity to interact with peers results in rapid adjustment and leaves no obvious deficits. Doubling or quadrupling this period of isolation produces dramatic social debilitation which is far more severe for the total as compared with the subtotal condition. These crippling or devastating effects are not alleviated when social isolates attain adolescence or early adulthood. Prolonged maternal and age-mate deprivation produces affectionless monkeys which exhibit: (*a*) inadequate social and even nonsocial play, (*b*) avoidance of physical contact, (*c*) absence of normal heterosexual behavior, and (*d*) inability to inhibit antisocial aggression when the animal is not too terrified to aggress.

If the deprivation condition is confined to mothering and the monkeys are given regular opportunity to interact socially with multiple age-mates from at least three months of age, they make an adequate social adjustment to their age-mates by all available criteria. Thus far, no negative long-term effects have been uncovered for these animals. Social adjustment is less adequate for monkeys deprived of mothering and provided social experience with only a single peer. They show strong attachments to partners, but otherwise display adjustment inferior to that of multiple-peer groups but in no sense comparable to that of long-term isolates. Similarly, monkeys raised from birth onward with inanimate cloth mothers or with indifferent or brutal natural mothers or passed from one mother to another adjust effectively to age-mates when they are available. Such data as exist indicate either no serious long-term adverse social effects or, at worst, that the infants' social adjustments are within or approach normal limits.

Earlier data led Harlow & Harlow to postulate that the age-mate or peer affectional system, developed through intimate contact play, was the primary socialization mechanism—the basic mechanism through which macaque monkeys developed deep and enduring affection for members of their own species. Whether or not this is the most effective and efficient manner of interpreting the development of intraspecies affection and socialization may be open to question, but the crucial importance of peer affection as a socialization variable is obvious.

Although peer affection is a remarkably efficient substitute for normal mothering, experiments reported in this paper also show that maternal affection may partially substitute for early peer interaction. Infant monkeys raised by normal monkey mothers but denied age-mate contacts for periods of time that would be socially destructive under conditions of subtotal or total social isolation adjust variably to age-mates, some appearing to be essentially normal and others showing extreme difficulties. When they grow to adolescence and early adulthood they may or may not adjust socially to age-mates, older adults, juveniles, and infants—prolonged peer denial, at least in some cases, can be socially destructive. Just as age-mate affection partially compensates for inadequate mothering, so does maternal affection partially compensate for inadequate and delayed peer socialization.

In a broad sense it is inappropriate to pit the importance of one of these affectional systems against the other. The fact that either may compensate in whole or in part for deficiencies in the other provides an enormous social safeguard, since mothers may be deficient or agemates unavailable in the critical early period of social development. In primates—monkeys, apes, and men—socialization is essential to survival, and the hazards of normal socialization are multiple and diverse. The biological utility of compensatory social mechanisms is obvious, and that effective social safeguards should have developed over the course of evolutionary development is in no way surprising.

PART FOUR

PERCEPTUAL AND COGNITIVE DEVELOPMENT

INTELLIGENCE

This section contains among other readings papers on factors associated with and contributing to the development of intelligence. Before we can understand its development, a clear definition of intelligence must be established. For many students, it has come to be equated with whatever intelligence tests measure. However, it should be kept in mind that the intelligence test is basically a measure (and a very good measure) of how much the child has learned about the dominant concepts in his culture; as such, it predicts very well how successful a child will be in schools as we know them today. But no claim is made that it tests intelligence defined as an individual's "in-born, all-around, intellectual ability" (Burt, 1934); or as his "ability to carry on abstract thinking" (Terman, 1925); or as his capacity for equilibration (Piaget, 1947); or as "intellectual capacities based on hierarchically arranged central processes" (Hunt, 1961); or as "an accumulation of learned facts or skills" (Hayes, 1962). The definitions range from those biased in the direction of heredity, like Burt's, to those biased in the direction of environment, like Hayes's.

A summary of some of the major findings with respect to intelligence test scores follows. In each case, only one reference is cited, although countless investigators may have conducted research on the topic. However, the reference cited is a definitive one, and it serves the purpose of directing the reader to other studies.

1. Repeated tests of the same children over time show that, contrary to the notion that it is constant, IQ is quite variable early in life. It becomes relatively stable in children after four to five years (at this age it correlates about .70 with IQ at age seventeen), although there are individual children whose IQ's fluctuate widely (Bloom, 1964).

2. While tests of infant intelligence may be valid measures of cognitive abilities at the time, they have little predictive validity. Tests of infant intelligence are tests of sensorimotor and perceptual abilities before the onset of language. They measure cognitive development during infancy but do not correlate with scores after age six (Bayley, 1970).

3. Children from different ethnic groups differ in patterns of ability on tests of verbal ability, reasoning, number ability, and space (Lesser, Fifer, and Clark, 1965; paper included here). It is presumed that these differences occur because different ethnic groups foster the development of different abilities, not because of hereditary factors.

4. IQ scores differ according to socioeconomic status, with scores decreasing as status decreases. Early studies (Havighurst and Janke, 1945) showed the average IQ of white-collar workers to be 112, compared with 98 for the lowest occupational groups and the down-and-outers. A more recent study by Bayley and Schaefer (1964), included here, also revealed positive correlations of scores with such socioeconomic factors as family income, father's education, mother's education, father's occupation, and composite social rating. Such socioeconomic differences, however, do not affect scores up to sixteen months (Bayley, 1965). A large-scale test by Kennedy *et al.* (1963) of black children in southeastern states showed a mean IQ of 86 for five-year-old blacks as compared with a mean of 101.8 on the Terman-Merrill revision of the Stanford-Binet intelligence test. To what extent data on the blacks have been affected by a compounding of social class and ethnic factors, and by factors in the test situation, is investigated in a paper by Palmer (1970), who found that IQ scores of black children up to the age of three years and eight months did not vary with socioeconomic status when testing was done under specified optimal conditions and a variety of intellective behaviors was assumed.

5. With regard to socioeconomic factors, boys' IQ scores show highest correlations with father's occupation, and girls' with both parents' education (Bayley & Schaefer, 1964; paper included here).

6. Environmental impoverishment during infancy and early childhood can have a depressing effect on IQ scores (Goldfarb, 1945; Skeels *et al.,* 1938). Children in orphanages, for example, where little individual care and stimulation are provided, show a deficit in concept and language development as well as in affective areas. In contrast, stimulation involving social interaction during the early years, even social interaction with mentally retarded adolescent girls, appears to result in higher IQ scores (Skeels, 1966).

7. Severe malnourishment during infancy has a depressing effect on IQ scores (Stoch and Smythe, 1963). Colored children in South Africa, severely malnourished in infancy, tested significantly below an adequately nourished group at seven years of age.

HEREDITY AND THE IQ

The issue of the relative importance of heredity and environment to the development of intelligence has been debated for decades, but the most heated debate so far occurred in 1968–69 over the publication of a paper by Arthur Jensen, "How Much Can We Boost IQ and Scholastic Achievement?" Jensen presents a large body of evidence to substantiate his thesis that genetic factors in intelligence are currently being neglected. He does not attempt to deal with the question of what intelligence "really" is, but points out that "the best we can do is to obtain measurements of certain kinds of behavior and look for new relationships to other phenomena and see if these relationships make any kind of sense and order" (p. 6). This is precisely what makers of intelligence tests do.

Using statistical techniques and evidence from animal breeding experiments and kinship studies on human beings (many of them studies of twins and adopted children), Jensen separates out genetic and environmental components in intelligence test scores. He concludes that genetic factors are more important than environmental factors in producing IQ differences. He then reviews the evidence on social-class and racial differences in intelligence. He cites studies to show that blacks are disproportionately represented in the group identified as educationally disadvantaged, and that blacks test about one standard deviation (15 IQ points) below the average of the white population (Shuey, 1966). He concludes, after reviewing alternate environmental explanations, that various lines of evidence "when viewed all together make it a not unreasonable hypothesis that genetic factors are strongly implicated in the average Negro-White intelligence difference" (p. 82).

Scholars in the fields of genetics, developmental psychology, and measurement, while accepting the data in the studies that Jensen cites, reject the notion that racial differences in intelligence-test scores are attributable in large part to genetic factors. Some of the main points covered in the *Harvard Education Review* (Spring, 1969), where replies to Jensen were printed, are:

1. We have only begun to scratch the surface in ameliorating environmental conditions for blacks. In fact, some black leaders maintain that, because of crowding, growing up in a ghetto like Harlem is worse today than it was in the 1930's and 1940's. We cannot say, as Jensen does, that we have tried remedial education measures like Head Start and that they have failed. We have hardly begun to test the effects on intellectual growth of early, cognitively stimulating experiences for young children. Present compensatory education programs have been neither adequately developed nor satisfactorily evaluated.

2. IQ data collected in standard testing situations may not reflect the actual intelligence of disadvantaged children. Studies like Zigler and Butterfield's (1968) and Palmer's, cited earlier, show that optimizing testing procedures for all children unfamiliar with testing situations and using a variety of tests result in higher IQ scores for lower-class children.

3. It can be argued that being white or black changes one or more aspects of the environment so significantly as to account for differences in scores; the evidence regarding environmental factors is insufficient to say at this point that environment can be discounted and the differences regarded as genetic.

4. Jensen claims a heritability index of 0.80 for intelligence. The heritability index is described by Jensen as the ratio of the genetic variance to the total variance. He arrived at the heritability index by using a formula that included correlations in IQ scores of close relatives, siblings, and twins, as well as environmental correlations in IQ scores of identical twins raised apart. The H index is high, but understandably so, since it describes a population with a specific gene pool and most of whom have developed in similar environments. Such an index, being less than 100 percent, can be affected by changes in the environment. Witness the significant increases in height of children of Japanese ancestry raised in Hawaii, of Mexican children reared in the

American Southwest, and, in a different category, the "stupid" peasantry of Czarist Russia whose children sent Sputnik into space.

Hirsch (1970) quotes Karl Pearson, reflecting a generally accepted attitude toward Jews in England in 1925, to the effect that the Eastern European Jews from Poland and Russia were, "taken on the average, . . . somewhat inferior physically and mentally to the native population." In fact, Pearson explicitly stated that intelligence was a congenital characteristic and that the factors determining the alleged intellectual inferiority of the Jews were "racial and familial." The reader might keep Pearson's statement in mind when reading the Lesser *et al.* paper included here, which shows top performance by Jewish children in most of the mental abilities tested.

The issue of the relation of intelligence to genetic racial differences will undoubtedly keep recurring. It is ironic that it should do so in America, where the descendants of Europe's poor and downtrodden, once given a chance, have been able to build, whatever its faults, a great technological society. Hopefully the blacks and other racial minorities will also, belatedly, have a chance for a decent life and self-development. A truly democratic society will not eliminate individual differences in intelligence, but it will eliminate bias in test scores.

LANGUAGE DEVELOPMENT

A noted authority on the study of language has said, "The ability to learn language is so deeply rooted in man that children learn it even in the face of dramatic handicaps." The grammar that they acquire may not be the "king's English," but even children from impoverished, disorganized homes know and use all parts of speech, with only a few exceptions, by the time they enter kindergarten. Nor is there such a thing as a "primitive" or "emerging" language; linguists and anthropologists have found that people living under the most primitive conditions use languages as rule-bound and complex as our own.

But primitive man, like Western man and like the child, uses language and abides by its rules unconsciously. In fact, it is only as we listen to the young child and hear him violate certain rules that we become aware of them and of the child's gradual mastery of them. When a child says "footses" for "feet," he is revealing a knowledge of one of our rules for forming plurals; he is simply not aware of all the exceptions.

A description of the set of rules governing language is called a *grammar*. Linguists, notably Noam Chomsky, have written generative transformational grammars that describe the cognitive system used in verbal communication. The grammars are, in essence, psychological theories to explain what goes on when we speak and listen. They have stimulated exciting new research in the field of child language. Whereas earlier investigators were concerned with describing and counting (i.e., size of the child's vocabulary; number of verbs used versus number of nouns, etc.), today's researcher, influenced by psycholinguistics, is interested in studying the child's development of a rule-system and in analyzing dialectal differences to discover what the rules are.

A body of utterances presumably representative of a given language and suitable for analysis is called a *corpus*. The most complete corpus to date has been collected by a research group at Harvard, under the direction of Roger Brown. The group, notably Bellugi, Cazden, and Berko, analyzed tape recordings of the language of three children, Adam, Eve, and Sarah, collected on a weekly basis over a three-year period. From their analyses have come many studies that have illuminated our knowledge of how child language develops. Other investigators have also contributed: Labov to dialectal differences; Slobin and the Berkeley group to methodology; Menyuk and McNeill to developmental psycholinguistics. Cazden's *Child Language and Education* (1972) is an excellent reference for the reader without special training in linguistics who wants to build competence in the area.

The following are some of the more important generalizations about language development to date:

1. Man has an innate biological capacity for language learning. Lenneberg (1967) compares the development of language with motor development and finds certain accomplishments in one area paralleled by accomplishments in the other. Table 1 shows the developmental milestones in both areas for the first four years.

2. The child acquires language not so much through imitation as through problem-solving processes. Slobin and Welsh (1967) reported on an investigation in which statements were presented to a two-year-old to imitate. What the child gave back was not a verbatim repetition of what the investigator said, but the product of the processing the child had done; the child reduced what was said to *his* current grammar. The paper by C. Chomsky included here illustrates some of the linguistic subtleties children acquire, without instruction, through a process Piaget calls *self-regulation*.

Studies reveal that a similar processing takes place among speakers of Black English. When children who speak Black English are asked to repeat a sentence uttered in Standard English, they translate what they hear into their dialect. For example, given the sentence, "I asked Alvin if he knew," the child repeats, "I aks Alvin do he know" (Labov *et al.,* 1971). What the children accomplish is simultaneous translation, no small feat, since it involves first decoding the speaker's statement and then recoding it into his own dialect.

3. An important factor in interaction between parent and child that may facilitate language development is the modeling of language by the parents. An earlier hypothesis—that the critical factor might be expansion by the parent of telegraphic speech used by the child—was tested by Cazden. The young child says, "Red truck, Mommy," to which the mother replies, "Yes, that is a red truck," unconsciously expanding the utterance by supplying the words the child has omitted. However, when the hypothesis was tested, Cazden (1965) found that a modeling treatment, while not significantly superior, was favored in the results. That is, a tutor would reply to the child's utterances in a conversational manner, modeling as she did so a rich variety of syntactical forms. She might say, "Yes, it's a furniture truck. Someone on our street is getting new furniture. See, it's stopping at the Browns'." Given a rich variety of syntactical forms, the child can, with his built-in computer for processing language, process what he hears and derive rules which are not explicit but which are revealed in the child's speech (in errors such as "footses" for "feet").

There are social-class differences in the mother's use of language which affect

TABLE I

Developmental Milestones in Motor and Language Development

At the com-pletion of:	Motor Development	Vocalization and Language
12 weeks	Supports head when in prone position; weight is on elbows; hands mostly open; no grasp reflex	Markedly less crying than at 8 weeks; when talked to and nodded at, smiles, followed by squealing-gurgling sounds usually called *cooing*, which is vowel-like in character and pitch-modulated; sustains cooing for 15–20 seconds
16 weeks	Plays with a rattle placed in his hands (by shaking it and staring at it), head self-supported; tonic neck reflex subsiding	Responds to human sounds more definitely; turns head; eyes seem to search for speaker; occasionally some chuckling sounds
20 weeks	Sits with props	The vowel-like cooing sounds begin to be interspersed with more consonantal sounds; labial fricatives, spirants and nasals are common; acoustically, all vocalizations are very different from the sounds of the mature language of the environment
6 months	Sitting: bends forward and uses hands for support; can bear weight when put into standing position, but cannot yet stand with holding on; reaching: unilateral; grasp: no thumb apposition yet; releases cube when given another	Cooing changing into babbling resembling one-syllable utterances; neither vowels nor consonants have very fixed recurrences; most common utterances sound somewhat like ma, mu, da, or di
8 months	Stands holding on; grasps with thumb apposition; picks up pellet with thumb and finger tips	Reduplication (or more continuous repetitions) becomes frequent; intonation patterns become distinct; utterances can signal emphasis and emotions
10 months	Creeps efficiently; takes side-steps, holding on; pulls to standing position	Vocalizations are mixed with sound-play such as gurgling or bubble-blowing; appears to wish to imitate sounds, but the imitations are never quite successful; beginning to differentiate between words heard by making differential adjustment
12 months	Walks when held by one hand; walks on feet and hands—knees in air; mouthing of objects almost stopped; seats self on floor	Identical sound sequences are replicated with higher relative frequency of occurrence and words (mamma or dadda) are emerging; definite signs of understanding some words and simple commands (show me your eyes)
18 months	Grasp, prehension and release fully developed; gait stiff, propulsive and precipitated; sits on child's chair with only fair aim; creeps downstairs backward; has difficulty building tower of 3 cubes	Has a definite repertoire of words—more than three, but less than fifty; still much babbling but now of several syllables with intricate intonation pattern; no attempt at communicating information and no frustration for not being understood; words may include items such as thank you or come here, but there is little ability to join any of the lexical items into spontaneous two-item phrases; understanding is progressing rapidly
24 months	Runs, but falls in sudden turns; can quickly alternate between sitting and stance; walks stairs up or down, one foot forward only	Vocabulary of more than 50 items (some children seem to be able to name everything in environment); begins spontaneously to join vocabulary items into two-word phrases; all phrases appear to be own creations; definite increase in communicative behavior and interest in language

TABLE I (Cont.)

At the completion of:	Motor Development	Vocalization and Language
30 months	Jumps up into air with both feet; stands on one foot for about two seconds; takes few steps on tip-toe; jumps from chair; good hand and finger coordination; can move digits independently; manipulation of objects much improved; builds tower of 6 cubes	Fastest increase in vocabulary with many new additions every day; no babbling at all; utterances have communicative intent; frustrated if not understood by adults; utterances consist of at least two words, many have three or even five words; sentences and phrases have characteristic child grammar, that is, they are rarely verbatim repetitions of an adult utterance; intelligibility is not very good yet, though there is great variation among children; seems to understand everything that is said to him
3 years	Tiptoes three yards; runs smoothly with acceleration and deceleration; negotiates sharp and fast curves without difficulty; walks stairs by alternating feet; jumps 12 inches; can operate tricycle	Vocabulary of some 1000 words; about 80% of utterances are intelligible even to strangers; grammatical complexity of utterances is roughly that of colloquial adult language, although mistakes still occur
4 years	Jumps over rope; hops on right foot; catches ball in arms; walks line	Language is well-established; deviations from the adult norm tend to be more in style than in grammar

From Eric H. Lenneberg, *Biological Foundations of Language* pp. 128–30. Copyright © 1967 by John Wiley & Sons, Inc. Reprinted by permission.

cognitive development. Hess and Shipman (1968) reported that lower-class mothers, in teaching an experimental task to their children, were more likely to use language to give orders and to admonish their children than were middle-class mothers, who generally gave specific directions and help. Maternal teaching styles as reflected in the mother's language were found to be significantly related to school performance as measured by achievement tests.

4. Recent research by Bernstein and Brandis (in Cazden, in press) has identified specific maternal behaviors that correlate higher with language development than the general social-class factor does. Bernstein and Brandis have tried to specify which aspects of social class affect child language and intellectual development. The investigators conclude that a child's cognitive ability, as revealed by standardized tests, is more closely correlated with a maternal index score based on how mothers respond to children's questions than with social class. Scores on the Wechsler Intelligence Scale for Children (WISC), for example, correlate .25 with social class and .38 with a maternal index score. The maternal index included both communication and control (how the mother responded to the child's conversation and questions as well as how she controlled her child, explained her own actions, etc.). Bernstein concludes that the mother's orientation toward the *relevance* of language is related to a child's measured ability on verbal tests.

5. There are social-class differences in children's abilities to use language to meet cognitive demands. These demands, which occur frequently in classrooms, include the ability to give explanations for phenomena and to talk about objects or events not in the immediate present. Krauss and Rotter (1968) asked kindergarten children to describe abstract figures or squiggles and to identify a squiggle from a verbal

description; results indicated that lower-class children were less competent than middle-class children in encoding and decoding.

6. There is a developmental progression in children's acquisition of syntax from the simple to the more complex. Cazden (1965), Bellugi (1967), and C. Chomsky (1969) are among those who have studied certain aspects of the progression: Cazden, the acquisition of noun and verb inflections; Bellugi, the development of negation; and C. Chomsky, acquisition of certain syntactical forms after age six. Excerpts from the Chomsky paper are included here.

Cognitive processes today tend to be identified with Piaget, whose theory we have dealt with in Part 1 and briefly in Parts 2 and 3. The reader will recall that Piaget's is an epigenetic theory, with cognitive development proceeding in age-related stages. This section will deal with attempts to intervene in the developmental process in order to accelerate the onset of a particular stage.

Piaget's postulation of the age-relatedness of stages in cognitive development has served as a potent stimulus to American psychologists. Investigators have been anxious to prove Piaget wrong or to show either that American children are superior to European children or that they can be made into superior thinkers by accelerating logical processes. Tell the typical American investigator that a certain trait is characteristic of an "average" six-year-old, and he will feel challenged to see if the same trait can be developed in a younger child.

As a consequence of Piaget's work, the years since the early 1960's have seen a large number of research studies devoted to the task of acceleration. Most have concentrated on conservation training, attempting to see if children who are non-conservers in pretraining tests can conserve after a training period of a specified length of time. Investigations have attempted to speed up the onset of conservation of number, quantity, length, and weight in subjects in most cases at a preoperational level. Though the phenomenon seems obvious to adults, preoperational children are generally strongly resistant to the notion that a ball of clay continues to have as much "stuff" in it when it is rolled into a long sausage and continues to weigh the same even when broken into little pieces. Early studies by Smedslund (1961) and Wohlwill and Lowe (1962) attempted to test the equilibration model (i.e., that children assimilate information that may upset existing mental structures; then mental structures are changed to accommodate the new data and equilibrium in thought processes is maintained) versus reinforcement. Smedslund tried external reinforcement, which worked only in subjects who were transitional with respect to operational structures. Wohlwill had limited success in inducing number conservation, not through external reinforcement, but through additive operations, lending credence to Piaget's theory that more complex structures are based on the simpler. Other investigators also found conservation resistant to training; children can be taught through reinforcement techniques to make conservation responses, but there is no transfer to new situations.

More recently, investigators have attempted to identify particular strategies children might acquire through training that would be effective in inducing operational structures. These strategies utilize addition-subtraction, perceptual conflict and reversibility procedures, and verbal-rule instruction. The Wallach *et al.* and Smith papers included here will help the reader gauge the value of such techniques. Verbal-rule instruction in particular proved to be effective. Assessment of the success of a training technique, however, is extremely complicated. In one training experiment, for example, Kohnstamm (1967) used verbal instruction to train children on a class inclusion task. His technique was to explain the problem when the child gave a wrong answer, so that the child would learn the thought operation involved. For example, if a child said in response to a question that there were more policemen than men, the experimenter would say, "No, that's not right. You're supposed to say that there are more men, because policemen are also men." Kohnstamm found that even after a change of stimuli and a lapse of several weeks, the technique was effective in producing correct answers, particularly when it was combined with the use of blocks and pictures. Léone and Bovet (1966) of the Geneva staff, however, replicated Kohnstamm's experiment and showed that although nine of eleven subjects did indeed succeed in giving correct answers to the class inclusion questions, only two of eleven succeeded in conservation tasks. Genevan investigators accept as evidence of success not the giving of answers on which children have been drilled, but the giving of responses indicating the use of mental operations such as reversibility. They expect that when a child's judgments are based on these mental operations, there is transfer to other tasks, and the child may be said to be "operational" (see pp. 43–45).

Recent training research conducted in Geneva has concentrated on studying the transition from one stage of logical thinking to another in order to discover the underlying mechanisms that might account for the transition. Language is one such factor. In general, the conclusion of the Geneva school is that acceleration is possible only within the limits imposed by the equilibration model. What is becoming abundantly clear is that short-term, restricted types of training are ultimately ineffective in inducing logical thought structures. Structures so pervasive and powerful take time to develop and require the background of a broad spectrum of experiences before they can be generalized and applied universally.

Investigations of discrimination learning have bearing on cognitive processes, for they deal with specific problems of how the child makes distinctions among stimuli as he acquires knowledge. Typically, however, discrimination studies are done by experimental psychologists, and all too often with little communication between "cognitivists" and experimentalists. Yet discrimination studies such as the Pick paper included here can be helpful to cognitive psychologists in delineating the conditions necessary for superior performance in making simultaneous comparisons. Finally, a paper by Gibson on the development of perception is included here. Gibson discusses perception as an adaptive process akin to the development of locomotion. With interesting cross-species comparisons, the author shows that perception of space develops early, but that the fine-grained discriminations of complex sets of objects are possible only through education.

REFERENCES

Bayley, N., "Comparisons of mental and motor test scores for ages 1–15 months by sex, birth order, race, geographical location, and education of parents." *Child Development,* 1965, 36, 379–411.

———, "Development of mental abilities."

In P. H. Mussen, ed., *Carmichael's Manual of Child Psychology,* 3rd ed., vol. I (New York: Wiley, 1970), pp. 1163–1209.

———, "Mental growth during the first three years. A developmental study of 61 children by repeated tests." *Genetic Psychological Monographs,* 1933, 14, 1–92.

Bellugi, U., "The acquisition of the system of negation in children's speech." Unpublished doctoral dissertation, Harvard University, 1967.

Bernstein, B., and Brandis, W., research reported in C. Cazden, *Child language and education* (New York: Holt, Rinehart and Winston, 1972).

Bloom, B. S., *Stability and change in human characteristics* (New York: Wiley, 1964).

Burt, C.; Jones, E.; Miller, E.; and Moodie, W., *How the mind works* (New York: Appleton-Century-Crofts, 1934).

Cazden, C., "Environmental assistance to the child's acquisition of grammar." Unpublished doctoral dissertation, Graduate School of Education, Harvard University, 1965.

Chomsky, C., *The acquisition of syntax in children from five to ten* (Cambridge, Mass.: M.I.T. Press, 1969).

Goldfarb, W., "Effects of psychological deprivation in infancy and subsequent stimulation." *American Journal of Psychiatry,* 1945, 102, 18–33.

Havighurst, R., and Janke, L., "Relations between ability and social status in a midwestern community." *Journal of Educational Psychology,* 1945, 36, 499–509.

Hayes, K. J., "Genes, drives, and intellect." *Psychological Reports,* 1962, 10, 299–342.

Hess, R. D.; Shipman, V. C.; Brophy, J.; and Baer, R. M., *Cognitive environments of urban preschool Negro children.* Report to the Children's Bureau, Social Security Administration, Department of Health, Education, and Welfare, Washington, D.C., 1968.

Hirsch, J., "Behavior-genetic analysis and its biosocial consequences." *Seminars in Psychiatry,* 1970, 2, 89–105.

Hunt, J. McV., *Intelligence and experience* (New York: Ronald Press, 1961).

Jensen, A. R., "How much can we boost IQ and scholastic achievement?" *Harvard Educational Review,* Winter, 1969, 39, 1–123.

Kennedy, W.; Van de Riet, V.; and White, J., Jr., "A normative sample of intelligence and achievement of Negro elementary school children in the southeastern United States." *Monographs of the Society for Research in Child Development,* 1963, 28.

Kohnstamm, G. A., *An evaluation of part of Piaget's theory. Teaching children to solve a Piagetian problem of class inclusion* (Amsterdam: North-Holland, 1967).

Krauss, R. M., and Rotter, G. C., "Communication abilities of children as a function of status and age." *Merrill-Palmer Quarterly,* 1968, 14, 161–73.

Labov, W., *et al.,* "A study of the non-standard English of Negro and Puerto Rican speakers." In *Cooperative Research Reports,* vol. I (New York City: U.S. Regional Survey, 1971), p. 320.

Lenneberg, E. H., *Biological foundations of language* (New York: Wiley, 1967).

Léone, J. P., and Bovet, M., "L'apprentissage de la quantification de l'inclusion et la théorie opératoire." *Acta Psychologie,* 1966, 25, 334–56.

Palmer, F. H., "Socioeconomic status and intellective performance among Negro preschool boys." *Developmental Psychology,* 1970, 3, 1–9.

Piaget, J., *The psychology of intelligence,* trans. by M. Piercy and D. E. Berlyne (London: Routledge & Kegan Paul, 1947).

Shuey, A. M., *The testing of Negro intelligence,* 2nd ed. (New York: Social Science Press, 1966).

Skeels, H. M., "Adult status of children with contrasting early life experiences." *Monographs of the Society for Research in Child Development,* 1966, 31 (3, Whole No. 105).

Skeels, H. M., *et al.,* "A study of environmental stimulation: an orphanage preschool project." *University of Iowa Studies of Child Welfare,* 1938, 15 (4), 1–191.

Slobin, D. I., and Welsh, C. A., "Elicited imitation as a research tool in developmental psycholinguistics." In C. Lavatelli, ed., *Language Training in Early Childhood Education* (Urbana: University of Illinois Press, 1971).

Smedslund, J., "The acquisition of conservation of substance and weight in children. III. Extinction of conservation of weight acquired 'normally' and by means of empirical controls on a balance scale." *Scandinavian Journal of Psychology,* 1961, 2, 85–87.

Stoch, M. B., and Smythe, P. M., "Does undernutrition during infancy inhibit brain growth and subsequent intellectual development?" *Archives of the Diseases of Childhood,* 1963, 38, 546–52.

Terman, L. M., *Genetic studies of genius.* I.

The mental and physical traits of a thousand gifted children (Stanford, Calif.: Stanford University Press, 1925).

Weir, R. *Language in the crib* (The Hague: Mouton, 1966).

Wohlwill, J. F., and Lowe, R. C., "Experimental analysis of the conservation of number." *Child Development,* 1962, 35, 1113–27.

Zigler, E., and Butterfield, E. C., "Motivational aspects of changes in IQ test performance of culturally deprived nursery school children." *Child Development,* 1968, 39, 1–14.

IMPROVEMENT OF VISUAL
AND TACTUAL FORM DISCRIMINATION

ANNE D. PICK

Gibson, Gibson, Pick, and Osser (1962) demonstrated that children between the ages of 4 yr. and 8 yr. improve in their ability to make visual discriminations among letter-like forms. The present study sought to determine if some kind of learning can produce such improvement in discrimination. The first experiment reported here explored this question with respect to visual discrimination, and the second and third experiments extended the investigation to tactual discrimination.

Two general hypotheses about the nature of learning during improvement of discrimination can be identified. One can be loosely termed a "schema" hypothesis, and is suggested in discussions of Bruner (1957a, 1957b), Vernon (1952, 1955), and in a recent book on perceptual development by Solley and Murphy (1960). Although these investigators deal primarily with identification behavior, i.e., recognition and categorizing behavior, their discussions implicate discrimination behavior as well. According to this point of view, discrimination and identification involve matching sensory data or "cues" about objects to prototypes or models of the objects which have been built up through repeated experience with the objects and "stored" in memory. Improvement in discrimination would involve first constructing schemata or models of the objects to be discriminated, and then matching the sensory data to the models so as to identify them as "same" or "different." Practice with objects to be discriminated, then, would enable S to build up and refine the appropriate schemata.

A second general hypothesis about improvement in discrimination, a "distinctive feature" hypothesis, is suggested by the Gibsons and their colleagues (Gibson & Gibson, 1955; Gibson et al., 1962). It utilizes the concept of distinctive features introduced by Jacobson and Halle (1956) in a discussion of phoneme characteristics. Distinctive features can be thought of as dimensions of difference which distinguish and provide contrasts among objects. The hypothesis developed from the Gibsons' work is that improvement of discrimination consists of learning the distinctive features of the objects to be discriminated. The function of practice, according to this point of view, is to enable S to respond to an increasing number of stimulus variables and to discover which of these variables are "critical" in the sense that they serve to distinguish between one object and another.

The physical conditions resulting in improvement of discrimination do not *necessarily* differ for these two hypotheses. Both would predict that such improvement will occur as a function of practice with the objects to be discriminated. Hence a transfer design can be employed to determine the extent to which prototype learning, distinctive feature learning, or both will occur during training. Specifically, Ss could be presented with initially undifferentiated stimulus forms and trained to discriminate among them. In a transfer task they could then try to discriminate among stimulus forms which *either* differ from each other in the same dimensions as those which they learned to discriminate *or* which have the same prototypes as those which they learned to discriminate. Differential performance in these two transfer conditions should shed light on the function of

Reprinted by permission of the author and the American Psychological Association from *Journal of Experimental Psychology*, 1965, **69**, 331–39.

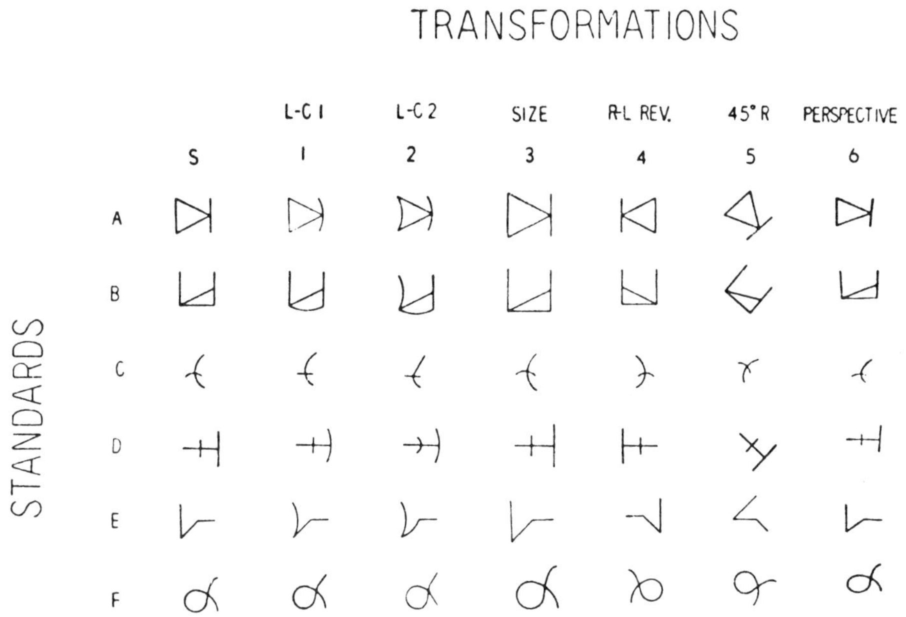

TRANSFORMATIONS

FIGURE I

Standards and transformations used in Experiment I.

prototype learning and distinctive feature learning in improvement of discrimination. Since the two processes are not mutually exclusive, relative transfer in the two conditions described can be determined by comparing them to a control condition in which both the prototypes and dimensions of difference of the forms differ from those used in training.

EXPERIMENT I

Method

SUBJECTS

The *S*s were 60 kindergarteners. Each *S* was randomly assigned to one of three equal transfer groups. There were an approximately equal number of boys and girls among the 20 *S*s in each group.

MATERIALS

The stimulus forms were letter-like forms of the kind used in the developmental study of

Gibson et al. (1962). The forms, approximately 1×1 in., were black and were mounted on rectangular white cardboard cards 3×4 in.

There were six standard forms and six different transformations of each of the standard forms. These transformations were one change of a straight line to a curve, two changes of straight lines to curves, a right-left reversal, a $45°$ rotation, a perspective transformation equivalent to a $45°$ backward tilt, and a 25% increase in size. The standard forms and six transformations for each are shown in Figure 1.

PROCEDURE

Training. The training procedure was the same for all *S*s. The *S* was seated in front of a small table on which a stand similar to a lectern was placed. Three standard forms were placed on this stand and a pack of cards containing two copies of each standard and three transformations of each standard was spread out in front of *S* on the table. The *S* was instructed to look carefully at each of the 15 cards and decide whether it was exactly the same as one of the standards or if it was different. When S found one which was exactly the same as one of the standards, he was instructed to give it to E. When S had made a judgment about every card in the pack (i.e., finished one trial), E shuffled the cards and the procedure was repeated until S reached a criterion of one perfect trial, i.e., gave E only the two copies of each standard. Confusion errors (transformations which S indicated were exact copies of a standard) were recorded. A correction procedure, in which E told S whether each judgment was right or wrong, was used on every trial except the first.

Before the first training trial, a pretraining practice trial with real letters and correction procedure was carried out in order to acquaint Ss with the task and to ensure that they understood that only forms which were "exactly the same" as the standard should be given to E.

Transfer. Following the criterion training trial, the transfer procedure was carried out. The task was the same as in training but only one trial was given and there was no correction given. Confusion errors were recorded as before.

The Ss were divided into three transfer groups in a predetermined arbitrary order. These groups differed in terms of the particular forms used in the transfer trial. Group C provided a base line with which to compare the transfer performance of the other two groups. This group received three standards and three transformations all of which were different from the ones used in training. For example, if in training these Ss had learned to distinguish copies of Standards A, B, and C from line to curve and size transformations of these standards, then their transfer task was to distinguish copies of Standards D, E, and F from rotation, reversal, and perspective transformations.

Group EI reflected the extent to which standard or prototype learning had occurred during training. This group received the same standards as in training, but three new transformations of these standards. For example, if in training these Ss learned to distinguish Standards A, B, and C from line to curve and size

transformations of these standards, then their transfer task was to distinguish these *same* standards from reversal, rotation, and perspective transformations.

Group EII reflected the extent to which distinctive feature learning had occurred during training. This group received three new standards, but the same three types of transformations of these standards as those with which they dealt during training. For example, if in training these Ss learned to distinguish Standards A, B, and C from among reversal, rotation, and perspective transformations of these standards, then, in the transfer trial, their task was to distinguish Standards D, E, and F from reversal, rotation, and perspective transformations of these standards.

In order to balance the design for possible differences in difficulty of discriminating specific combinations of standards and transformations, four subgroups of Ss were used in the training condition. Each was trained with a different combination of standards and transformations. One had Standards A, B, and C with line to curve and size transformations. Another had Standards D, E, and F and these same transformations. A third subgroup was trained with Standards A, B, and C and reversal, rotation, and perspective transformations, and a fourth had Standards D, E, and F and these transformations.

There were also, of course, 4 subgroups within each of the 3 transfer groups since the combination of forms used in transfer for a given S depended on the combination of forms used in training. Thus there were 12 transfer subgroups with five Ss in each.

Results

TRAINING

Differences between the means of the groups in number of confusion errors made on the first trial and in number of trials to criterion were analyzed using t tests. No differences approached the .05 level of significance and hence the null hypothesis that these groups were from the same population could be accepted.

TRANSFER

Confusion errors in the transfer trial constituted the main data of the experiment. Table 1 shows the errors made in the transfer trial

TABLE I

Confusion Errors in Transfer Trial for the 12 Subgroups

	Transformations				
	T 123		T 456		
	Standards				
Group	SABC	SDEF	SABC	SDEF	Total
EI	12	21	17	19	69
EII	11	6	10	12	39
C	23	21	32	25	101

Note: Column headings indicate the particular combination of standards and transformations used in the transfer trial. $n = 5$ in each subgroup.

by each of the 12 subgroups and for the three transfer groups with subgroups combined.

An analysis of variance was performed on the data for the 12 subgroups. Only the effect of transfer groups was significant, F (2, 48) $= 12.69$, $p < .001$. Thus the differences among the three experimental groups obtain regardless of subgroups, i.e., regardless of the particular combination of standards and transformations used.

The differences between the three groups in transfer errors were analyzed with t tests. The three groups were significantly different from each other with a probability level of less than .01 with a two-tailed test.

Discussion

The results of this experiment suggest that learning distinctive features may be a significant component of improvement in visual discrimination of letter-like forms. The Ss who in the transfer trial dealt with forms which they had never seen before but which varied from each

other in familiar ways (the EII group) made the fewest confusion errors. This suggests that during the training trials Ss were learning how the forms varied from each other as they improved in their ability to discriminate among them.

The fact that Group EI, the group having familiar standards and new transformations, was superior to the control group suggests that prototype learning also occurred during training. However, the clear superiority of Group EII implies that such learning may not be essential to improvement in discriminations of this sort.

EXPERIMENT II

The purpose of this second experiment was to investigate the generality of the results of the previous experiment for improvement in tactual discrimination. Adaptations of the procedure and materials of the previous experiment were made in order to provide appropriate conditions for studying improvement in tactual discrimination. These adaptations are noted below. The basic method and design of this experiment were the same as in the previous one.

Method

SUBJECTS

The Ss were 72 first graders. First-grade children were used as Ss because pilot work indicated the task was better suited to this age group than to the kindergarteners used previously.

MATERIALS

The stimulus forms were metal reproductions of some of the letter-like forms used in the previous experiment. The forms (1 × 1 in.) were made by an engraving process and were raised lines on a smooth square metal background about 1¾ × 1¾ in.

There were four standard forms and 10 transformations of each: one, two, and three changes of lines to curves, a 25% increase in

TRANSFORMATIONS

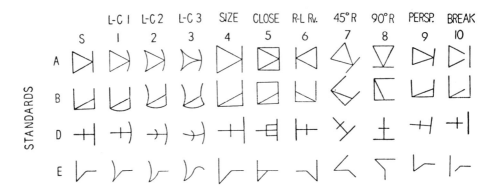

FIGURE 2

Standards and transformations used in Experiment II.

size, two topological transformations: break and close, a right-left reversal, 45° and 90° rotations, and a perspective transformation equivalent to a 45° backward tilt. The standard forms and their transformations are shown in Figure 2.

PROCEDURE

Training. The *S* was seated at a small table on which a form board was placed. This plywood board, 12 × 15 in. with a raised block in the middle, was used to display the forms in front of *S*. The raised block was covered with "velcro" as were the backs of the metal forms and the forms could thus be made to adhere to the block for presentation to *S*. The *S* was blindfolded and a standard form and one of its transformations were placed on the board. The standard was always presented on the left and the transformation on the right.

The *S*'s dominant hand was placed on the board and he was instructed to feel first one form and then the other with that same hand and decide whether the two forms were the same or different. When *S* had made a judgment about the pair of forms, the transformation was removed and replaced by another. After a few presentations, *E* no longer had to guide *S*'s hand to the board. A trial consisted of seven presentations for comparison: one standard form to be compared with each of five

transformations and two copies of the standard in random order. When *S* completed a trial, the procedure was repeated in a different random order until *S* reached the criterion of learning.[1] This criterion consisted of *either* a perfect trial *or* a single confusion error for either the size or perspective transformation (whichever the particular *S* was given). This weaker second condition was accepted as a criterion condition because size and perspective transformations proved in pilot work to be impossible for many *S*s to distinguish from standards long after they were able to distinguish the other transformations from standards.

Preliminary practice prior to training consisted of practice with visual letters followed by both visual and blindfolded practice with letters in the form of tactual stimuli.

Transfer. The same three transfer conditions as before were used. Group C received a different standard and five different transformations of the standard from the ones used in

---

[1] The training task proved too easy for some first graders. Since this was a learning experiment, *S*s who performed the training task successfully on the initial trial were discarded from the experiment. There were also a few *S*s who were never able to learn the training task and who were also discarded. In all, about 100 *S*s were run through the training procedure. The final *n* represents those *S*s who did not perform at criterion level on the first trial and who were eventually able to do so after several training trials.

TABLE 2

Confusion Errors in Transfer Trial for the 24 Subgroups

	Transformations								
	T 12345				T 6789 & 10				
	Standards								
Group	SA	SB	SD	SE	SA	SB	SD	SE	Total
EI	3	8	2	2	4	1	1	3	24
EII	3	2	3	3	3	3	5	3	25
C	9	9	9	2	2	5	5	7	48

Note: Column headings indicate combination of forms used in the transfer trial. $n = 3$ in each subgroup.

training. Group EI received the same standard as in training, but five new transformations of this standard. Group EII received a new standard, but the same five transformations of this standard as those with which they had dealt in training.

Eight subgroups were used in the training condition representing training with each of the four standards and the two groups of transformations. One transformation group consisted of line to curve transformations, the size transformation, and the close. The other group consisted of the reversals, rotations, perspective transformation, and the break.

Results

TRAINING

Differences between the groups in number of confusion errors made on the first trial and in number of trials to criterion were analyzed with *t* tests. None of the differences approached significance.

TRANSFER

Confusion errors made by the subgroups and for the three groups with subgroups combined are shown in Table 2. The analysis of variance indicated a significant effect of transfer groups at less than the .001 probability level, $F (2, 48) = 10.63$. The Transformations × Standards interaction and the triple interaction were also significant at less than the .05 level of probabil-

ity. A comparison of the total errors made by the three groups indicated that Groups EI and EII were not different from each other but both were superior in performance to Group C.

The Transformations × Standards interaction effect seemed to be due to a difference between errors made to Standard E and errors made to the other standards (cf. Figure 2). For Standards A, B, and D more errors occurred with Transformations 1–5 than with Transformations 6–10. This pattern is reversed with Standard E which probably accounted for the fact that the effect of transformations did not reach significance.

The three-way interaction is difficult to interpret meaningfully. Probably its effect was accounted for by the fact that there were only three *S*s in a cell, and one atypical *S* in a given cell could account for the scores in that cell deviating from the overall pattern.

Discussion

Clearly the results of this experiment were different from those of the previous experiment. In that experiment, the group which had opportunity to use in transfer what it had learned about the *distinctive features* of the forms was superior to both the other groups in transfer trial performance. In the present experiment, the comparable group of *S*s was no better in transfer trial performance than the group which had opportunity to use prototypes or memory models of the forms, though both groups were better than the control group.

One interpretation of these results is that the process of improvement in visual discrimination is different from the process of improvement in tactual discrimination and that schema construction and detection of distinctive features may serve equally useful functions in tactual discrimination.

Another interpretation is related to differences in the task required of S. Because S in the tactual experiment explored the forms with only one hand, he made successive comparisons. This task involved memory and perhaps required him to form a memory model of the standard even if his task in learning was to detect distinctive features. In the visual experiment, however, S could look back and forth between the comparison forms without having to remember how they looked in order to discover the differences between them.

If this second interpretation is correct, making the tactual comparison simultaneous should then result in the reappearance of superior performance by Group EII. The third experiment was conducted to test this hypothesis.

EXPERIMENT III

The major difference between this experiment and the previous one is in the nature of S's task. There were minor differences in number of Ss, material, and subgroups as noted below.

Method

Subjects.   The Ss were 60 first graders.

Materials.   The forms were Standards A and D and the 10 transformations of each.

Procedure.   The procedure was the same as in the previous experiment except that throughout this experiment, S explored the two comparison forms simultaneously, one with each hand.[2]

2 Some Ss could not complete the training task successfully and were discarded. Their inability to perform successfully appeared to be a function of an inability to coordinate both hands in exploring the forms. There were also a few Ss who performed the task at criterion level on the first trial, and were discarded. About 80 Ss began the training procedure and the final n, as in the previous experiment, represents those Ss who did not perform at criterion level on the first training trial and who eventually learned the task.

There were four subgroups representing training with each of the two standards and the two groups of five transformations each.

Results

TRAINING

None of the differences between the groups in either number of trials or errors in the first trial approached significance. Hence the groups could be considered equivalent with respect to their ability to handle the forms.

TRANSFER

Transfer trial errors for each subgroup and for subgroups combined are shown in Table 3.

TABLE 3

Confusion Errors in Transfer Trial for the 12 Subgroups

	Transformations				
	T 12345		T 6789 & 10		
	Standards				
Group	SA	SD	SA	SD	Total
EI	10	11	6	4	31
EII	3	3	3	0	9
C	10	10	5	7	32

Note: Column headings indicate combination of forms used in transfer trial. $n = 5$ in each subgroup.

The analysis of variance performed on the data showed the effect of transfer groups to be significant with a probability of less than .001 that the effect was due to chance, $F (2, 48) = 8.62$. The effect of transformations was also significant with a probability of less than .01 that the effect was due to chance. Neither the effect of standards nor any interaction was significant.

A comparison of the total errors made by the three groups showed that Group EII, the group having new forms but familiar transformations in the transfer task, was superior to the other two groups in performance on this task. Group EI, the group having familiar forms but new transformations in the transfer task, was not different from the control group.

The effect of transformations is due to the fact that more errors occurred with Transformations 1–5 than with Transformations 6–10. Except for one standard (E) this was also true in Exp. II. Apparently line to curve transformations are, in general, more difficult to discriminate tactually than rotations and reversals.

Discussion

These results support the hypothesis that under conditions of simultaneous comparison, the group having opportunity to use in transfer what they had learned about the distinctive features of the forms would show superior performance. Not only was this group (EII) superior to the other two groups, but the other experimental group showed no better performance than the control group. In this experiment, the construction of schemata, if such a process occurred at all, showed no effect in the transfer task.

GENERAL DISCUSSION

A consideration of the tasks involved in these experiments may make the three different patterns of results meaningful. The third experiment involved a task of simultaneous comparison. The results suggested that Ss had, in training, learned the distinctive features of the forms since the superior group had no opportunity to construct schemata of the forms used in the transfer task. Those Ss who *could* use schemata in the transfer task performed no better than the control group.

The second experiment involved a task of *successive* comparison. These Ss apparently both constructed schemata of the forms *and* learned distinctive features since groups who could use either distinctive features or prototypes showed similar amounts of transfer relative to the control group.

The first experiment involved a task which might be considered to lie between the tasks of the two tactual experiments in terms of the nature of the comparison. None of the Ss in this experiment had to explore one form thoroughly before exploring the comparison form as did Ss in the second experiment. On the other hand, Ss in this first experiment probably did not receive information from both the standard and comparison forms simultaneously as did Ss in the third experiment. Most likely, Ss in this first experiment quickly looked back and forth several times between the standard and comparison form in order to make a judgment about them. The Ss who could use in transfer what they had learned about distinctive features showed the best transfer task performance. Those Ss who could use schemata also showed transfer but significantly less than the other experimental group.

In terms of the tasks involved in these experiments, one might interpret the results as suggesting that the detection of distinctive features will always facilitate improvement in discrimination but that under conditions of successive comparison, schema construction will *independently* facilitate such improvement.

A more parsimonious interpretation is that the detection of distinctive features may be the *basis* for improvement in discrimination. When such detection is dependent on memory because of the nature of the task (e.g., in Exp. II and to a lesser degree in Exp. I), some schema learning does occur. When no memory requirement is imposed by the task (e.g., Exp. III), schema learning does not occur. In short, detection of distinctive features may be the necessary and sufficient condition for improvement in discrimination. Schema learning may or may not occur depending on the experimental conditions. When it does occur, its function is to make possible the comparison and search for differences, i.e., to make possible the detection of distinctive features.

The data of the present experiments are consistent with this interpretation. In no case did an EI group perform better than an EII group. Furthermore, the EI groups showed better performance than the control group only to the extent that memory was involved in the task of comparison.

Further research is necessary to establish the validity of this interpretation. A direct test might be made by determining whether, under conditions of successive comparison, Ss in fact have learned a prototype or memory model of the standard forms. Can they identify the given standards from a group of unrelated forms, or can they reproduce the standards better than *Ss* who have operated under conditions of simultaneous comparison?

REFERENCES

Bruner, J. S. Neural mechanisms in perception. *Psychol. Rev.,* 1957, 64, 340–358. (a)

Bruner, J. S. On perceptual readiness. *Psychol. Rev.,* 1957, 64, 123–152. (b)

Gibson, E. J., Gibson, J. J., Pick, A. D., & Osser, H. A developmental study of the discrimination of letter-like forms. *J. comp. physiol. Psychol.,* 1962, 55, 897–906.

Gibson, J. J., & Gibson, E. J. Perceptual learning: Differentiation or enrichment? *Psychol. Rev.,* 1955, 62, 32–41.

Jakobson, R., & Halle, M. *Fundamentals of language.* The Hague, Netherlands: Mouton, 1956.

Solley, C. M., & Murphy, G. *Development of the perceptual world.* New York: Basic Books, 1960.

Vernon, M. D. *A further study of visual perception.* Cambridge, England: Cambridge Univer. Press, 1952.

Vernon, M. D. The functions of schemata in perceiving. *Psychol. Rev.,* 1955, 62, 180–192.

THE DEVELOPMENT OF PERCEPTION
AS AN ADAPTIVE PROCESS

ELEANOR J. GIBSON

Since the time of Darwin and the acceptance of the doctrine of evolution of species, psychologists have contemplated the phylogenetic development of behavior as a mark of adaptation to an animal's environment. In the late nineteenth century, the comparative psychologist's eagerness to fit behavior into the evolutionary scheme took some amusing, and by hindsight, naive trends. G. J. Romanes, one of the best of the so-called "anecdotalists," spoke for them when he said, "I hold that if the doctrine of Organic Evolution is accepted, it carries with it, as a necessary corollary, the doctrine of Mental Evolution, at all events as far as the brute creation is concerned" (1895, p. 8). In two volumes called *Mental Evolution in Animals* and *Mental Evolution in Man* he prepared a tree and a chart which served, he thought, to represent the "leading features of psychogenesis throughout the animal kingdom" and also the "principal stages of Mental Evolution in Man."

The chart lists, under "products of intellectual development," a number of faculties which are ranked from lowest to highest—from protoplasmic movements to morality. Then, in a column titled the "psychological scale," there is listed in correlation with the faculties the animal order where each faculty presumably first makes its appearance. "Memory" comes in with the echinoderms, "association by contiguity" with molluscs, "association by similarity" with fish, "recognition of persons" with reptiles and cephalopods, "recognition of pictures, understanding of words, and dreaming" with birds, and "morality" with anthropoid apes and the dog. Along with this, in a third column, is

Reprinted by permission of the author and *American Scientist* from *American Scientist*, 1970, **58,** 98–107.

"psychogenesis in man," and we find the order of appearance of the faculties recapitulated; association by contiguity at 7 weeks, association by similarity at 10 weeks, recognition of persons at 4 months, recognition of pictures and words at 8 months, and so on.

Evidence for this order was based almost entirely on anecdote and informal observation. As comparative psychology developed an experimental method, the work of Romanes and his generation was derided and banished as a shameful page in the history of a new science. Yet the adaptiveness of behavior and evolutionary continuity were never quite forgotten. One no longer looked for faculties but for "laws" of behavior. Hull's theory of learning, which converted half the psychological world, stressed the biological adaptiveness of the conditioned reflex and the principle of reinforcement, which operated by reducing biological drives or need conditions, thereby strengthening behaviors useful to the organism (Hull 1943). The continuity was there too, because it was presumed that one could investigate these mechanisms in the rat and apply the findings to man.

Seeking to understand man's behavior by experimenting with the rat has fallen off in fashion, in its turn, but the ethologists have revived the biological tradition begun by Darwin and furthered by Romanes in a new and more sophisticated spirit of naturalism. Behavior that is specific to the species has become of interest and is studied in relation to the ecology of the species, thus revealing its adaptiveness.

In this abbreviated sketch of the influence of evolutionary concepts on psychology, where does perception come in? Do only executive behaviors like spinning webs, building nests, running through mazes, or pressing bars have adaptive value? Or is there a phylogenesis of perception and a parallel development in the individual? Is there perceptual learning which is adaptive? Or must learning be only on the response side, as behaviorists believed?

Karl Lashley was one of the first to raise these questions and to point out the role of perception in species-specific behavior and in evolution. In the "Experimental Analysis of Instinctive Behavior" (Lashley 1938) he stressed the importance of studying the innate components of "sensory organization," as well as the motor aspects of behavior. The essential first step, he said, was "analysis of the properties of the stimulus situation which are really effective in arousing the behavior." Understanding of the motor activities "hinges on these perceptual problems." Much of his work, from the early naturalistic studies of terns to later studies of stimulus equivalence in the rat, was directed at this problem. He never forgot the importance of evolution for understanding an animal's behavior. In "Persistent Problems in the Evolution of Mind" (1949), he told us that "the limits of capacity of each order of animals are set by the kinds of relations among objects that it can perceive. The development of the individual is a slow maturation of such capacities" (p. 460). "It is not the fact of learning but what is learned that differentiates animals in the evolutionary scale. The learning of higher animals involves a perception of relations which is beyond the capacity of the lower" (p. 458).

The latter statement he illustrated by comparing the behavior of a spider monkey and a chimpanzee in a matching problem. The monkey was required to choose a red or a green square, according as a red or a green square was given as a model. When the squares were placed as in row *a* in Figure 1, the monkey never improved above chance in 1000 trials. But when there was *contact* between the model and the test square, as in rows *b, d, e,* and *g,* he quickly achieved errorless choice. He saw the model, Lashley thought, as a pointer or a signal but did not perceive the relation of similarity. The chimpanzee, on the other hand, grasped it quickly.

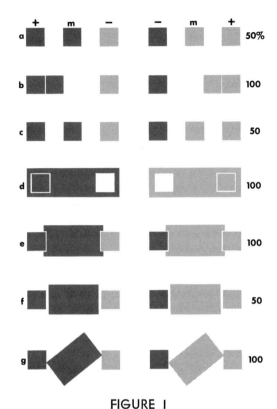

FIGURE I

Arrangements of red and green squares [represented here by gray and black] presented to a spider monkey and a chimpanzee in a matching task. The percentages at the right represent the final level of accuracy attained in each situation (from Lashley 1949; reproduced by permission of the *Quarterly Review of Biology*).

BACKGROUND OF THE THEORY

To tell you how I see perceptual development as a mark of adaptiveness, I must explain first what I think perception is and what perceptual learning is. Then I will distinguish two modes of perceiving and illustrate with experiments what we know about their development in phylogeny and in the individual.

Perception is extracting information from stimulation (Gibson 1966). Stimulation emanates from the objects and surfaces and events in the world around us and it *carries information about* them; though different from them, it *specifies* them. If we were to consider stimulation only as individual rays of light or vibrations in the air, this specification would not be intelligible, because information about objects and layout of the world around us lies in relations, like edges between things; it is not punctuate, but structured over space and time. Not only is there information about things in stimulation; there is rich information, far more, potentially, than we utilize.

Let me give an example. Some animals, especially bats and dolphins, locate food and find their way around by means of echolocation. The dolphin emits clicking sounds at varying rates from one per second to bursts of 500 or more. These clicks are thought to be used for food-finding and navigation. To quote a dolphin expert, "The click trains, or sonar, search the seascape in front of a dolphin in much the same way that the cone of light from a miner's head-lamp shows his way through a mine. In the presence of reflected light, we see where we look. In the presence of reflected sound, or the echoes of their own clicks, dolphins hear where they point their beam of sound. The click-echoes returned from the environment before the moving dolphin are information-bearing. The echoes contain information about the size, shape, location, movement if any, and texture of the living and nonliving things in the water" (McVay 1967, p. 8). It has in fact been demonstrated that dolphins can differentiate in this way objects of different sizes and shape and even different metallic substances, and can swim an obstacle course without collision. Three points emerge from this: one, that potential stimulus information about features of the environment is vast; second, that the information accurately specifies the layout of the world and the objects in it; and third, that perception is an active process, a search for the relevant information that specifies the path an animal needs to travel, the obstacles to be avoided, the mate or the food to be approached.

So perception, functionally speaking, is extracting information about the world from stimulation, a highly adaptive process since the animal must somehow discover where to go, what to seize, and what to avoid. What kind of world is there to perceive? We can describe it in several ways. I choose a classification that refers to properties of the environment. These include properties of the *spatial layout* (sur-

faces, edges, drop-offs); properties of *events* (motion, occlusion, appearance, disappearance, and reappearance); and properties of *objects* that make them distinguishable and identifiable. For man at least we can include another class: man-made symbols—*coded items* that stand for objects and events, such as speech and writing.

Animals perceive the surfaces and objects and events in their surroundings by way of stimulation which specifies them. But they seldom do this perfectly, and the potential information in stimulation is vastly greater than that which becomes effective. To understand how potential information becomes effective we need the concepts of *perceptual development* and *perceptual learning*. As the higher-order invariants and structure that uniquely specify objects and events are progressively extracted from the total stimulus flux, so does perception become more differentiated and more specific to those things. This is a process which goes on in the evolution of species and also, I think, in the development of the individual.

How do animals *learn* to perceive the permanent distinguishable properties of the world in the changing flux of stimulation? Not, I believe, by association, but by a process of extracting the invariant information from the variable flux. I think several processes are involved, all attentional ones. (See Gibson 1969 for a detailed statement of the theory of perceptual learning.) One is perceptual abstraction, akin to what James called "dissociation by varying concomitants" (note the dissociation as opposed to association; something is being pulled *out* from context, instead of being added *on*). Another is filtering of the irrelevant, an attenuation in the perceiving of random, varying, non-informative aspects of stimulation. A third is active, exploratory search. The dolphin beaming his clicking sounds is an example of the latter.

Another example is active touch (Gibson 1962). When a blindfolded subject is handed an unfamiliar object and asked to learn to identify it so as to be able to match it visually to one of a larger set of similar objects, what does he do? He runs his fingers round its contours searching for distinguishing features, and presses it with different finger combinations to determine its proportions. The stimulation to which he exposes himself is constantly varying and, from the point of view of individual receptors, never the same. Yet he picks up from this variable flux of tactual-kinaesthetic stimulation constant structural properties like curves, edges, and indentations which are translatable into visual properties.

With respect to the search process in perceptual learning, a very important question is what terminates the search and thus selects what is learned. For many years no one questioned the proposition that external reinforcement (e.g. food or shock) is the selective principle for learning things like bar-pressing or choosing one arm of a maze rather than another. But is a distinctive feature selected as relevant because it wins a reward or avoids punishment? Is this the way that higher-order structural relations are detected? Although this might happen in a teaching situation, I do not think it is the true principle of perceptual learning. So much of it goes on very early in life and is necessarily self-regulated. No experimenter is on hand to deliver reinforcement; probably not even a parent could provide it deliberately, since he seldom has any way of knowing just what the child is perceiving.

I think the reinforcement is internal—the *reduction of uncertainty.* Stimulation is not only full of potential information; there is too much of it. There is a limit to what can be processed, and variable, random, irrelevant stimulation leads only to perception of confusion—what someone has referred to as cognitive clutter as opposed to cognitive order. But distinctive features, invariants, and higher-order structure serve the function of reducing uncertainty, taking order and continuity out of chaos and flux. The search for invariants, both low-level contrastive features and high-level order, is the task of perception, while detection of them at once reduces uncertainty and is reinforcing.

PERCEPTUAL DEVELOPMENT IN SPECIES AND INDIVIDUALS

With this brief background of theory, I propose to return to my first question. Is there perceptual development, in the animal species and in the individual, and is it adaptive? Are there trends in what is responded to, as Lashley suggested? In order to give some specific answers, I shall compare two modes of perceiving and give evidence, in both cases, of species differences and of development within the life span.

The two modes are perception of *space and events in space* and the perception of *objects and permanent items,* like written letters, that can be approached and examined closely. I have chosen to contrast these because there is reason to think that in their phylogenetic development there is a considerable difference between them. Localizing oneself in the spatial layout or monitoring events going on in the space around one seem to develop earlier and to be neurologically more primitive than fine-grain identification of objects and outline figures such as letters.

This difference is akin to a distinction within visual perception drawn in a recent paper by Trevarthen (1968), who speaks of "two mechanisms of vision." One of these he calls "ambient vision." It has to do with orientations of the head, postural adjustments, and locomotion in relationship to spatial configurations of contours, surfaces, events, and objects. The other he calls "focal vision." It is applied to one space and a specific kind of object; it serves to examine and identify.

"Ambient vision in primates," says Trevarthen, "resembles the vision of primitive active vertebrates. . . . At any instant, an extensive portion of the behavioral space around the body is mapped by this ambient visual mode; in primates, somewhat more than a frontal hemisphere is apprehended. With large rotations of the head or whole body, an animal may quickly scan all of the space close to his body and thus obtain a visual impression of the large features in it. The visual mechanism is strongly stimulated by parallax changes caused by translation of the eye, and the receptor mechanism is particularly sensitive to the velocities of displacement of continuities in the light pattern of the retina" (p. 328).

"In contrast with this vision of ambient space, focal vision, enormously developed in diurnal primates, is applied to obtain detailed vision." Its scope at any given instant is restricted, but it is extended over time by sampling movements of the eyes. An area of interest may thus be brought to full attention and "analyzed as if carried close in by a zoom lens" (p. 329).

Focal vision in primates appears to be primarily a function of the cortex. Even in rodents a comparable, though less pronounced, distinction may exist. Schneider (1967) working with hamsters found that ablation of the visual cortex left the animal with only a minimal ability to tell *what* he was seeing, but left nearly intact his ability to find *where* it was. He was unable to discriminate and identify objects, but could localize them in space. Ablation of the superior colliculus produced the opposite effect; the hamster knew what he was seeing but behaved as if he didn't know where it was.

I shall say no more about this neurological distinction, since I have made no contribution to it, but it supports the point I intend to make; that discrimination of events in space is primitive, both phylogenetically and ontogenetically, while development progresses toward differentiation of form in objects and two-dimensional projections. In other words, fine-grain identification of objects or patterns is the later achievement; its development continues over a long time; learning plays a prominent role in it as compared with perceiving the spatial layout and events; and we can expect to find more striking phylogenetic differences.

PERCEPTION OF SPACE

Consider, first, development of the perception of space and of events in space. Is there phylogenetic continuity here within the vertebrate phylum? Indeed there is. The similarities between species are far greater than their differences in this respect. We can adduce evidence for this in three important cases—perception of imminent collision (called "looming"); perception of depth-downward; and perceived constancy of the sizes of things.

Looming can be defined as accelerated magnification of the form of an approaching object. It is an optical event over time. It specifies a future collision (Schiff, Caviness, and Gibson 1962). If a vehicle or even a small object such

as a baseball is perceived as coming directly toward him by a human adult, he ducks or dodges out of the way. Is the perception of imminent collision together with its avoidance instinctive? If so, in what species, and how early? Schiff (1965) constructed an artificial looming situation in which nothing actually approached the animal observer but there was abstract optical information for something approaching.

In Schiff's experiments, a shadow was projected by a shadow-casting device on a large translucent screen in front of the animal. The screen was large enough to fill a wide visual angle. The projected shadow could be made to undergo continuously accelerated magnification until it filled the screen or, on the other hand, continuously decelerating minification. Magnification resulted in a visual impression of an object approaching at a uniform speed. Minification gave a visual impression of an object receding into the distance. The projected silhouette could be varied in form, so as to compare, for instance, jagged contours with smooth ones, or silhouettes of meaningful objects with meaningless ones. Subjects studied included fiddler crabs, frogs, chicks, kittens, monkeys, and humans.

The crabs responded to magnification (but not to minification) by running backwards, flinching, or flattening out. Frogs jumped away from the ghostly approaching object. Chicks responded more often to magnification than minification by running, crouching, and hopping. Kittens (28 days old) tended to respond to magnification with struggle and head movements, but the kittens were restrained in holders and well-differentiated avoidance behavior did not show up clearly. Rhesus monkeys (including infants five to eight months of age) were observed in the situation under four conditions (magnification, minification, lightening of the screen, and darkening of the screen). Both young and adult animals withdrew rapidly in response to the approach display, leaping to the rear of the cage. Alarm cries frequently accompanied retreat in the younger animals. The receding display brought responses which might be described as curiosity, but never retreat. The lightening and darkening of the screen had no effect, and this served as a control, that is, a change of mere stimulation as compared with change of magnification.

The adaptiveness of the responses to optical magnification is illustrated by the turtle. Hayes and Saiff (1967) investigated what they termed the "visual alarm reaction" in the turtle. A looming shadow on a screen was used, as in Schiff's experiments. The turtles responded to magnification by withdrawing the head into the shell.

What about a human subject? Schiff measured the galvanic skin reflex in adult human subjects in the looming situation. There was decrease of skin resistance in the majority of subjects for magnification but not for minification. Human infants, Burton White found (1969), began to blink at a rapidly approaching object (with air currents controlled) at about three weeks of age. The reliability of the response increased for another 10 or 12 weeks. Perhaps sensitivity to visual approach of a missile takes this long to mature or be learned in the human infant; but perhaps another indicator response would show that it is picked up even earlier. Some observers claim that attempted head withdrawal to visual looming occurs as early as two weeks in human infants.

Does it matter what shape or object characteristics the expanding silhouette has? Schiff tried objects of different shapes as shadow-casters, but he did not find that silhouettes of these objects had a differential influence on avoidance behavior, as long as there was accelerated magnification of the shadow. It was the event of looming as such, not an identifiable object, that controlled the avoidant behavior. The functional usefulness of this lack of specificity is obvious; quick avoidance of a fast approaching object is often necessary for avoidance of collision, while fine-grain identification of the object hardly matters.

Now let me give you some phylogenetic comparisons for avoidance of a falling-off place, that is, a drop-off of the ground. Depth downwards is specified in the light to the animal's eye. Does this information by itself cause the animal to avoid it? Some years ago, Dr. Richard Walk and I constructed an apparatus for answering this question (Gibson and Walk 1960). We called it a "visual cliff." "Cliff," because there was a simulated drop-off downward, and "visual" because we attempted to eliminate all other information for the drop-off. Figure 2 shows an apparatus constructed for testing small animals, such as a rat or a chick. The animal is placed on a center board. A checkerboard floor extends out from the center board on one side, an inch or two below it. A similar floor is 10 inches or more below on the other side. A sheet of glass extends from the center board, above the floor, an inch or two below the board, so that tactual information for the cliff is eliminated, and air currents and echoes are equated.

What is the visual information? Figure 3 shows the difference in the density of optical texture from the two checkered surfaces in the light projected to the animal's eye. For some animals binocular parallax might yield differential information about the two sides. The best information, our experiments suggested, was the motion perspective produced by the animal's own movements—especially head movements—as the cliff edge is observed in comparison to the shallow edge. Differences in texture density were eliminated and a monocular animal was used to make this observation.

Many animal species have been tested on the visual cliff: rodents, birds, turtles, cats (including lions, tigers, and snow leopards), sheep and goats, dogs, and of course primates (Walk and Gibson 1961; Routtenberg and Glickman 1964). All these species, save flying ones or swimming ones, avoided the cliff edge of the apparatus and chose the safe, shallow edge on the basis of visual information alone. Texture must be present on the ground under the animal, however, for a safe surface of support to be perceived. The animal will not walk out upon a homogeneous, untextured surface— he demands "optical support" as well as felt support. This surely has value for survival.

Avoidance of a drop-off and dependence upon optical support must be developmentally primitive. This conclusion is suggested not only by the continuity of the behavior within the vertebrate phylum, but also by ablation experiments and ontogenetic data. When the striate cortex of the cat is removed (Meyer 1963) pattern vision in the sense of identification goes, but a cat will still avoid a cliff, if he can move freely.

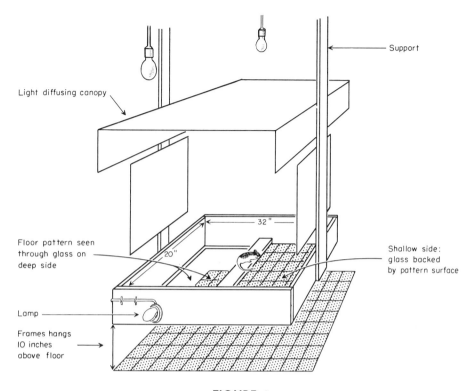

FIGURE 2

Drawing of a visual cliff (from Walk and Gibson 1961; copyright by American Psychological Assoc. and reproduced by permission).

Ontogenetically, Walk and I found that cliff avoidance develops very early and, in some species, without any opportunity for learning. Precocial animals such as chicks and goats avoid a cliff a few hours after birth, as soon as they can be tested. Rats reared in the dark avoid a cliff as soon as they are brought out, with no opportunity for preliminary visual experience. Primates cannot be tested at birth, but human infants avoid a cliff as early as they can crawl. Monkeys, like human infants, are carried by their mothers in early infancy. But monkeys placed on the untextured glass without optical support at three days of age (Rosenblum and Cross 1963) showed indications of emotional disturbance (crouching, vocalization, self-clasping, and rocking), whereas there was no disturbance when they were placed on the glass with a texture just below it.

We may conclude that perception of a safe surface in contrast to a drop-off appears early in evolution and early in life, and that little learning may be required for its appearance. It is modified by biased circumstances, such as prolonged dark rearing, but terrestrial animals do not generally have to be taught this useful adaptation.

Now consider my third case: perceived constancy of the sizes of things. Information for size constancy is given normally by motion; motion of the object toward or away from a stationary observer, or movement of the observer toward the object. Since information for constant size—the rule relating size and distance—is given in motion, it should belong with my "primitive" mode of perceiving. Let us see if it does, if there is continuity over species and early development without any marked dependence on learning with external reinforcement.

As for continuity among animal species, size constancy has been demonstrated in the chimpanzee, by Köhler (1915); in the monkey by

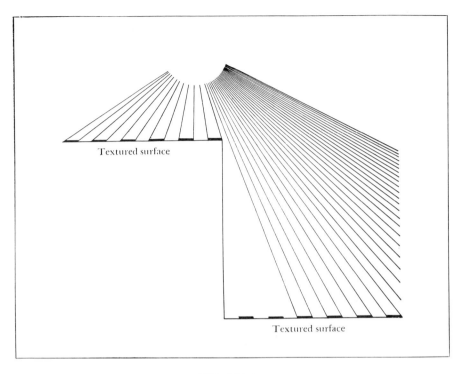

FIGURE 3

Cross section of a visual cliff. The diagram shows the pattern of light projected to the subject's eye from a textured surface at a shallow depth below his station point on a center runway and from an identical surface farther below (from Walk and Gibson 1961; copyright by American Psychological Assoc. and reproduced by permission).

Klüver (1933) and by Locke (1937); in the cat by Gunter (1951) and by Freeman (1968); in the weanling rat (Heller 1968); in the duckling (Pastore 1958); and in fish (Herter 1953). It is no surprise to the thoughtful biologist that animals other than man exhibit size constancy. How indeed could they locomote or seize things accurately if the apparent sizes of things around them were constantly shrinking or expanding as distance changed with the target's movement or the observer's position?

Is learning involved in perceiving things as constant in size? It might well be, since the conditions for extracting the invariant depend on motion of an object or of the observer in relation to it. The mother's face approaches the baby as she bends to pick it up; the baby moves his hand toward and away from his eyes and moves them together and apart, for hours at a time. These are guaranteed opportunities for presenting him with appropriately structured stimulation. But such learning would have to take place very early, for Bower (1966) has found evidence of size constancy as young as two months in the human infant. He used the method of operant conditioning, the response being a leftward turning of the head. The infant was trained to respond thus to a 30-cm. white cube placed one meter from his eyes. The reinforcement for the head-turning response was an experimenter popping up and "peek-a-booing" at the infant and then disappearing again (an ingenious and, it turns out, remarkably effective reinforcement. The infant learns to do something to *get a perception*). After training, three new stimuli were introduced for generalization tests. These were the 30-cm. cube placed 3 meters away; a 90-cm. cube placed 1 meter away; and the 90-cm. cube placed 3 meters away (see Figure 4). These and the original training situation were presented in a counterbalanced order.

The conditioned stimulus situation would be

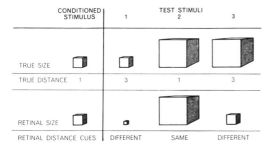

CONDITIONED STIMULUS		TEST STIMULI	
	1	2	3

FIGURE 4

Schematic representation of cubes of different sizes placed at different distances in Bower's investigation of size constancy in infants (from Bower 1966; copyright by Scientific American, Inc., and reproduced by permission).

expected to elicit the most head-turnings, and the one appearing to the infant most like it, the next most. If the infant has size constancy, one would expect the cube identical with the training one to evoke the next most responses, even when it is farther away (test stimulus 1). If size constancy hasn't been attained, one might expect the cube projecting the same-sized retinal image (test stimulus 3) to elicit most response. The infants, in practice, responded to test stimulus 1 next most often after the training situation, evidence that they perceived the cube in its true, objective size. Next most often came the larger cube placed at the same distance as the training cube; and last of all, the large cube placed at 3 meters where it projected the identical-sized retinal image.

Does this result mean that *no* learning is involved in the development of size constancy? Definitely not, since even eight weeks gives a lot of opportunity for visual experience. But it means that any learning could not have involved association with specific motor acts, such as reaching a certain distance or walking so many paces. But perceived motion of an object could provide an opportunity for discovery of the rule relating projective size of object to nearness of the object. Dark-reared rats (Heller

1968) did not exhibit size constancy when first brought into the light, despite normal performance on the visual cliff. Some visual experiences with objects moving in space may be necessary, therefore, for size constancy to develop, but it does so very early. Later changes, appearing when judgmental methods are used (Piaget 1961), probably indicate development of a more analytical attitude toward perceiving objects rather than the mere localizing of things in their true sizes.

PERCEPTION OF OBJECTS

Now, let me turn to my other class of perceptions—the fine-grain identification of objects, and the use of coded stimuli to substitute for them. Is there continuity over species and early appearance as there is with the spatial perceptions?

There is continuity, yes, but in this instance there is a good case for a striking evolutionary change, and also for a long course of perceptual learning in the individual. The human child must learn the distinctive features of the objects, representations, and symbolic items that human life requires him to differentiate.

What about the *phylogeny* of object identification? Certainly animals identify some objects at quite an early age. The herring gull chick identifies by a spot of red the beak of its parent hovering over it. This information is referred to by the ethologists as an "innate releaser." Releasers seem in many cases to be very simple unlearned signals for the discharging of a fixed unlearned pattern of responses, like the chemical signal that releases attack behavior in some species of snake. A mere trace of the chemical in a box will bring the attack. Sometimes the effective stimulus pattern is more complex, as is the visual pattern that constitutes "owlness" and releases mobbing behavior in the chaffinch, or the quite complex and informative song patterns of many birds, but the role of learning is still minimal in these cases.

Do we have studies of learned object identification in any animals but primates? Of course, the studies of imprinting in precocial animals come to mind. Certain properties of an object like high brightness contrast and motion release in the newborn animal a following response, and following the moving object serves, presumably, to "impress" its features on the "mind" of the subject so that he will later discriminate it from other objects and approach it rather than others. Here, in a manner insuring that the precocial animal will take to his parent or at least to his species, is a very immediate kind of learning that seems to contain the rudiments of perceptual learning. It is not a matter of association of stimulus and response; the response is ready to go at once and, besides, recognition can be measured by other responses than following. There is no external reinforcement; the mother can butt an infant goat away and he will follow her just the same. What is learned is typical of perceptual learning: an increased specificity of response to visual and auditory stimulation characteristic of the releasing object. To what extent there is increased differentiation we really don't know, for early imprinting is quickly followed by opportunities for learning to discriminate feature-contrasts that insure more precise differentiation.

We can study this latter process most easily in the young human animal, so I shall trace some of the steps in his learning to differentiate complex objects in his environment. Does he begin, like the precocial animal, with innate attention to high-contrast visual stimulation and to motion? Some people think so and like to compare the turning of the eyes or head toward a voice or a shiny moving thing to imprinting. One of the first and most prominent objects in an infant's world is the face of his caretaker. Studies of development of recognition of a human face tell us much (Gibson 1969, Ch. 16). At first, it appears to be motion of the head (like a nod) that is compelling, but very shortly the eyes emerge as a prominent feature—the dominant feature for a discriminative response. They are bright, and they move. After a time, the facial contour, the contours of brow and nose around the eyes, and later the mouth (especially in motion) differentiate as critical features. But not until nearly four months must these features be present in an invariant and "face-like" relation for the recognition response to occur. At four months, a "realistic" face is smiled at more. Not until six months are individual faces differentiated, and not until much later still are facial expressions. We know little

as yet about how this learning goes on, but it is perceptual learning; there is increasing differentiation of more and more specific stimulus information. Motor responses play little or no role, nor does reinforcement.

"Learning-to-learn" about objects was demonstrated in a long-term experiment with infants 6 to 12 months old by Ling (1941). She presented infants with a pair of solid wooden objects, differently shaped. Both were colored bright yellow and were of a graspable size. They were presented to the infant on a board within reaching distance. One was fastened tightly to the board. The other was removable and was furthermore sweet to taste, having been dipped in a saccharine solution. The infant learned over a period of days to reach at once for the shape that was sweetened. Then five series of problems were presented to him. The first series had four problems: circle vs. cross, circle vs. triangle, circle vs. square, and circle vs. oval. After successive mastery of these, the child progressed to a series in which one of the forms was rotated; then a series in which sizes were transformed; a fourth, in which the number of "wrong" blocks was increased; and a fifth, in which the positive and negative shapes were reversed. There was evidence of more and more rapid learning as the series continued, as well as transfer of discriminations with rotation and change of size. What were the babies learning that transferred? Distinctive features of the shapes they were comparing, to be sure, but something more general too, Ling thought. They learned search strategies of systematic observation and comparison, "attention to form differences, rather than improvement in form discrimination *per se*." Compared with control babies of the same age, they made a more immediate and minute examination of the stimulus patterns and inhibited extraneous bodily movement.

Now I want to finish with the top-level achievement of fine-grain identification—the identification of written symbols. Only man does this and only a well-grown, well-tutored man at that. Monkeys can indeed learn to discriminate a pair of fairly small line drawings from one another, but they are much slower at this task and make many more errors than human children of four or five (Hicks and Hunton 1964; Hunton and Hicks 1965). Both phylogenetically and ontogenetically, this is the peak of perceptual achievement. Here we find that education is most essential. How is one letter discriminated from another? I think by learning the distinctive features for the set of letters. There is evidence to show that this is the way letters really are discriminated, that there is a set of distinctive features, not idiosyncratic to an individual perceiver or to a given graphic character but characterizing the set and permitting each letter to be distinguished by its unique pattern of features within the set.

The set of letters, in this case, must be differentiated as a set from other outline drawings or similar things. Linda Lavine, at Cornell, found that this is done quite early. Children from three to five were shown a systematically chosen sample of graphic items: hand-written Roman letters, numerals, lower-case letters, cursive handwriting, artificial letters, scribbles, and simple line drawings of objects—a flower, a stick man, a child's attempt at drawing a house or a face, and so on. The children were asked to "tell me which of these are writing." Most children of three and four could separate the drawings of objects from the rest, but not the scribbling. Most children of five could differentiate the numbers and letters, whatever type or case, from both scribbling and pictures although they could seldom identify individual numbers or letters. Habits of observing differences between

small objects, like those shown by Ling's babies, probably carry over from object perception to the perception of line drawings, and the set of graphic symbols is somehow differentiated from other marks on paper before individual items can be identified.

To discover what features are actually noted in comparing letters and identifying them, we performed a number of discrimination experiments using both children and adults (Gibson, Schapiro, and Yonas 1968). These experiments, which simply required the subject to decide whether a pair of letters was the same or different, allowed us to construct a "confusion matrix" for a set of letters. The time taken to judge same or different and the errors were entered in matrices to show which pairs were most often confused and which least. Then the matrices were analyzed to find what proximities or clusters underlie the structure of the matrix. This tells us what features are being used by the observer when he must decide whether a given pair is the same or different.

The method of analysis was a hierarchical cluster analysis (Johnson 1967). It looks progressively (in steps) for the most compact and isolable clusters, then for the next most compact, and so on till one winds up with loose clusters and finally the whole set. The results can be turned upside down and diagrammed in a tree structure. Figure 5 shows on the left the

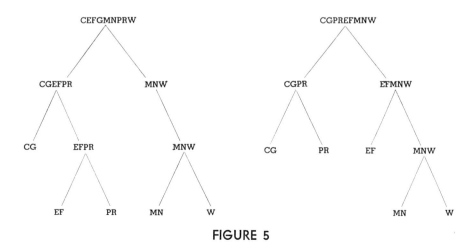

FIGURE 5

Tree structure yielded by confusions in making same-different judgments. The structure on the left was obtained with adult subjects; that on the right with seven-year-old children.

tree resulting from an analysis of 48 adult subjects' latency data for 9 letters. The first split separates the "sharp" letters with diagonality from all the others. On the left branch, the "round" letters, C and G, next split off from the others. At the next branch, the square right-angular letters E and F split off from letters differentiated from them by curvature. The error data for these letters with the same subjects reveal an identical structure.

On the right of Figure 5 is the hierarchical structure for 60 seven-year-old children, with the same letters. It is similar to the adults' but not quite the same. The first split is a simple curve-straight one. On the second branch, the round letters are split off from the P and R. The square letters are now split off from those with diagonality. This is very neat, and it suggests to me that children at this stage are doing straightforward sequential processing of features, while adults have progressed to a more Gestalt-like processing, picking up higher orders

of structure given by redundancy and tied relations. This is speculative, but it would be a highly adaptive kind of development, achieving the highest level of differentiation with the greatest economy of processing.

CONCLUSION

Is the development of perception an adaptive process? It is as much so as the development of locomotion. Nature seems to have insured first the means of detecting the information needed for getting around and avoiding such dangers as obstacles, pitfalls, and missiles. Discrimination of objects by simple signs based on single physical characteristics of high vividness is primitive too. But fine-grain differentiation of multidimensional complex sets of objects is high in the evolutionary scheme and in development, a process where adaptation is achieved only through education.

REFERENCES

Bower, T. G. R. 1966. The visual world of infants. *Scient. Amer.* 215:80–92.

Freeman, R. B. 1968. Perspective determinants of visual size-constancy in binocular and monocular cats. *Amer. J. Psychol.* 81:67–73.

Gibson, E. J., and R. D. Walk. 1960. The "visual cliff." *Scient. Amer.* 202:64–71.

Gibson, E. J., F. Schapiro, and A. Yonas. 1968. Confusion matrices for graphic patterns obtained with a latency measure. Pp. 76–96 in Final report, Project No. 5-1213, Contract No. OE6-10-156, Cornell University and the U. S. Office of Education.

Gibson, J. J. 1962. Observations on active touch. *Psychol. Rev.* 69:477–91.

Gibson, J. J. 1966. *The senses considered as perceptual systems.* Boston: Houghton-Mifflin.

Gunter, R. 1951. Visual size constancy in the cat. *Brit. J. Psychol.* 42:288–93.

Hayes, W. N., and E. I. Saiff. 1967. Visual alarm reactions in turtles. *Anim. Behav.* 15:102–06.

Heller, D. P. 1968. Absence of size constancy in visually deprived rats. *J. Comp. Physiol. Psychol.* 65:336–39.

Herter, K. 1953. *Die Fischdressuere und ihre sinnes physiologischen Grundlagen.* Berlin: Akademie-Verlag.

Hicks, L. H., and V. D. Hunton. 1964. The relative dominance of form and orientation in discrimination learning by monkeys and children. *Psychon. Sci.* 1:411–12.

Hull, C. L. 1943. *Principles of behavior.* New York: Appleton.

Hunton, V. D., and L. H. Hicks. 1965. Discrimination of figural orientation by monkeys and children. *Percept. Mot. Skills* 21:55–59.

Johnson, S. C. 1967. Hierarchical clustering schemes. *Psychometrika* 32:241–54.

Klüver, H. 1933. *Behavior mechanisms in monkeys.* Chicago: Univ. Chicago Press.

Köhler, W. 1915. Untersuchungen am Schimpansen und am Haushuhn. *Abh. preuss. Akad. Wiss.* (phys.-math.) No. 3, 1–70.

Lashley, K. S. 1938. Experimental analysis of instinctive behavior. *Psychol. Rev.* 45:445–71.

Lashley, K. S. 1949. Persistent problems in the evolution of mind. *Quart. Rev. Biol.* 24:28–42.

Ling, B. C. 1941. Form discrimination as a learning cue in infants. *Comp. Psychol. Monogr.* 17, Whole No. 86.

McVay, S. 1967. How hears the dolphin? *Princeton Alumni Weekly,* October, pp. 6–9.

Meyer, P. M. 1963. Analysis of visual behavior in cats with extensive neocortical ablations. *J. Comp. Physiol. Psychol.* 56:397–401.

Pastore, N. 1958. Form perception and size constancy in the duckling. *J. Psychol.* 45:259–61.

Piaget, J. 1961. *Les mécanismes perceptifs.* Paris: Presses Universitaires de France.

Romanes, G. J. 1893. *Mental evolution in man.* New York: D. Appleton.

Romanes, G. J. 1895. *Mental evolution in animals.* New York: D. Appleton.

Rosenblum, L. A., and H. A. Cross. 1963. Performance of neonatal monkeys on the visual cliff situation. *Amer. J Psychol.* 76:318–20.

Routtenberg, A., and S. E. Glickman. 1964. Visual cliff behavior in undomesticated rodents, land and aquatic turtles, and cats (panthera). *J. comp. physiol. Psychol.* 58:143–46.

Schiff, W. 1965. The perception of impending collision: A study of visually directed avoidant behavior. *Psychol. Monogr. 79,* Whole No. 604.

Schiff, W., J. A. Caviness, and J. J. Gibson. 1962. Persistent fear responses in rhesus monkeys to the optical stimulus of "looming." *Science* 136: 982–83.

Schneider, G. E. 1967. Contrasting visuo-motor functions of tectum and cortex in the Golden Hamster. *Psychol. Forsch.* 31:52–62.

Trevarthen, C. B. 1968. Two mechanisms of vision in primates. *Psychol. Forsch.* 31:299–337.

Walk, R. D., and E. J. Gibson. 1961. A comparative and analytical study of visual depth perception. *Psychol. Monogr. 75,* No. 15.

White, B. L. 1969. Child development research: An edifice without a foundation. *Merrill-Palmer Quarterly* 15:49–80.

CORRELATIONS OF MATERNAL AND CHILD BEHAVIORS WITH THE DEVELOPMENT OF MENTAL ABILITIES: DATA FROM THE BERKELEY GROWTH STUDY

NANCY BAYLEY   EARL S. SCHAEFER

INTRODUCTION

In the course of the past fifty years, since Binet gave us a practical method for assessing intelligence, research in the field has carried us through increasingly sophisticated theories about the composition of intellectual processes, their rates of growth and change over time, and the adequacy of their measurement by various kinds of tests. The etiology of intellectual functions is another aspect of intelligence which has been the subject of much theoretical controversy. In general the trend in the past fifty years in theories of intelligence has been from the assumption of an inherited, stable, general capacity, toward an increasing complexity of multiple factors, whose development and manifestations are determined by inheritance alone, environment alone, or, more realistically, by some combination or interaction of the two. It is our concern here to investigate some of the correlates of intelligence that may throw light on its etiology. This systematic study of a small but relatively constant sample that has been studied for the first 18 years of life will afford a view of both stable and changing correlations of other variables with the processes of intellectual development. . . .

Reprinted with abridgment by permission of the authors and The Society for Research in Child Development, Inc., from *Monographs of the Society for Research in Child Development*, 1964, **29,** Ser. no. 6, Whole no. 97, 5, 7–8, 17–34, 67–71. © 1964 by The Society for Research in Child Development, Inc. All rights reserved.

SUBJECTS AND GENERAL CHARACTERISTICS OF THE STUDY

The children of the Berkeley Growth Study were selected in 1928 and 1929 as healthy newborns (28). The original sample of 61 children was reduced somewhat over time; and ten younger children, added during the first three years of the study, were retained for part or all of their growth. At least 47 of the children were tested at most of the 39 mental-test ages, and in the first eight years 53 of them were tested at almost every age.

The study was oriented from the start toward investigating several primarily developmental aspects of growth in the child. These aspects may be broadly classified as mental and motor development, and physical growth and maturing. In the past thirty years, data from the study have furnished the materials for a series of reports on the growth of intelligence by Bayley (3, 5, 7, 8, 9, 10, 11) and by Bayley and Jones (12). These reports have been concerned with the lack of consistency of mental scores in infancy, with the individuality in patterns of intellectual growth, with the general relevance of genetic and socioeconomic factors to scores on the tests, with evidences for the changing character of mental processes as they become increasingly complex with growth, and with evidences that some intellectual functions continue growing at least into young adulthood. So far, however, because the problems of emotional aspects of development were not the main objectives of the study, only two reports (1, 6) have dealt with the relation of the children's emotions and attitudes to the functioning and the measurement of their intelligence.

The necessity for recording emotional and related behavioral data became evident in the early months of the study. The babies often grew tense, cried and sometimes struggled when weighed and measured, or they cried from colic or because they were hungry or sleepy and for a variety of other reasons. Their individual modes of response to the tests and to persons raised questions of reliability and validity of scores. Also, the mothers reacted in many different ways to their babies' happy or stressed behavior. These variables altered, in unpredictable and not clearly understood ways, the standard testing situations and procedures. In order to record these behaviors for possible use in interpreting measures and test scores, rating scales were devised, including estimates on a 4-point scale of wakefulness at beginning and end of the test, and 7-point ratings on strangeness, responsiveness to toys and to persons, activity, speed of movement, irritability, positive vs. negative behavior, and happiness. The babies' crying was coded and timed with a stop watch. Immediately after each visit the children were rated, and notes were written, describing the mothers and their behaviors toward their children. As the children grew, the rating scales were changed several times to more age-appropriate forms. Starting at 13 years the ratings were replaced by descriptive notes of the child's behavior and appearance. After the children were three years of age, the mothers were rarely present in the testing situation and were seen only briefly. However, information-gathering home visits were made from time to time, and at some time between the children's ages of 9 and 14 years, 34 of the mothers were interviewed intensively about their children, and comprehensive notes on these visits were recorded.

The early efforts to relate emotional behaviors to intelligence did not yield much of significance. In a study of crying, mental test scores in the first year were correlated with the amount the babies cried during the examination and found to be essentially zero (1). In a later study (6) an "optimal score" utilized ratings of the infant's behavior between 10 and 36 months and "facility" and "attitude" scores based on 3- to 7-year ratings. The optimal score was the sum of the ratings on eight of the variables ("irritability" was omitted). The ratings were arranged so a high score indicated conditions favorable for the child to make his best possible performance. The optimal scores were found to correlate about .30 with the concurrent intelligence scores. But rank difference *rhos*, computed for twenty individual children between their optimal and mental scores over time on repeated observations for samples of 11 to 13 tests per child, ranged from +.77 to −.33. Similarly, for the same cases, *rhos* between attitude scores and mental scores ranged between +.68 and −.46. It seemed evident, from these correlations, and from inspection of the children's age trends in optimal, attitude, and mental scores, that for some children the mental scores they earned did not fluctuate with their state of emotional well-being or their attitudes toward the tests. Periods of consistently slow or rapid development seemed to override the fluctuations in behavioral scores.

These studies, however, made use of only a small portion of the available material. This material had potentials for extensive studies of the interrelations of healthy children's emotional, social, and task-oriented behaviors over time, with their own development, with their mothers' behaviors, and with other documented aspects of their environment. But many of the data were not in appropriate form for statistical analysis. Furthermore, they were not organized into a useful conceptual framework. It was necessary first to convert some descriptive notes into ratings or numerical scores, and then to organize the entire array of ratings into meaningful patterns of behavioral relations. In 1955 Earl S. Schaefer and Richard Q. Bell undertook to develop rating scales for maternal behavior, utilizing both the 0- to 3-year observational notes and the reports of the 9- to 14-year interviews (36). The scales were found to be reliable, and to characterize the mothers very well. Schaefer's continued work on the data, organizing both the maternal scales and the child behavior ratings, gave us a rational order of behavior variables, and facilitated the study of their patterns of intercorrelation and their consistencies over time. These studies have been reported in a series of publications (13, 14, 32, 33, 34, 35). The most recent of these publications is a monograph which summarizes and extends the entire series of behavioral studies, and discusses the complex patterns of relations between the behaviors of mother and child, from birth to 18 years, as observed in the subjects of the Berkeley Growth Study. That monograph is an exploration into observed mother-child relations as they bear on the children's social and emotional behaviors over time. The present monograph is written as a companion to this preceding one, "Maternal Behavior, Child Behavior, and Their Intercorrelations from Infancy through Adolescence" (35). The earlier monograph should be consulted for a more detailed treatment of the behaviors which are used here but described only briefly. . . .

MATRIX OF INTERCORRELATED MATERNAL-CHILD VARIABLES

In the present study each of the 13 age-level mental scores (covering ages 1 month through 18 years) has been correlated, for the sexes separately, with similarly averaged age-level child behavior ratings. The behaviors include three sets of ratings that cover the age range 10 months through 12½ years plus a set of adolescent behavior scores. Each of these scores (e.g., activity at 10, 11, and 12 months) is correlated with each of the 13 mental scores. The mental scores are also correlated with five parental socioeconomic variables, and with two sets of scores for maternal behaviors, one toward their infants and one toward their preadolescents.

Thus, for most of the 18 years for which we have records of the children's intelligence, we have a series of concurrent estimates (ratings) of their social, emotional, and task-oriented behaviors (these behavior ratings cover the ages 10 months through 18 years). We have an indirect indicator of parental ability (socioeconomic status), and we have two separate estimates of maternal behaviors based on observations made about ten years apart by different people and under different circumstances.

The 18-year runs of intelligence test scores show inconstant rates of growth in the first two or three years, but by five or six years they have settled into fairly predictable IQs, or stable rates of growth in mental ability. There are, however, distinctive individual patterns of growth, and in all parts of the 18-year span children were found with rather marked changes in IQ (or standard scores) (7, 10). Similar individual patterns have been reported by others (e.g., 17, 22, 26, 38). In trying to understand the relations of these patterns in IQ to the children's own characteristic attitudes and behaviors and to those of their mothers, we must compare the mental scores with a considerable variety of rated behavior variables which appear in most instances to be much less stable than the intelligence scores.

It will not, of course, be possible to indicate causal sequences. However, patterns of relations found for this one sample should serve at least to raise questions and to suggest hypotheses for further testing. Already to some extent we have cross-validation of the findings from similar data in other longitudinally-studied samples. A thorough study of published reports should yield many more tests of the validity of our results. If it should happen that many of the relations found here are unique to the Berkeley Growth Study, there remains the impressive fact that, within the universe of data recorded for these children, the findings are repeatedly supported and reinforced as they are viewed in varying combinations and organizations of the available data. Therefore, to the extent that these patterns of correlation show internal consistency, it would appear that we have some fairly accurate descriptions of one sample of children, as seen in relatively standard testing situations.

Correlations of Parent Socioeconomic Status with Children's Intelligence

For many years the conventional measures used in studying parental relationships to child's intelligence have been socioeconomic variables which are indicative of parental status and ability: education, occupation of father, income, and some form of social rating.

In several of the earlier reports on the Berkeley Growth Study (5, 8, 12), the children's intelligence was correlated with these measures of parental status, but only in the 1954 study were the correlations presented by the sex of the child. In that paper *r*s were given for individual tests at ten ages comparing boys' and girls' mental scores separately with attained education of mother and of father. It was noted then that the girls' scores correlated more highly with education of both parents than did the boys' with either parent.

The more complete set of *r*s between socioeconomic status and mental score, for the 13 age levels, is shown here in bar diagram form in Figure 1. The parent-son *r*s are on the left, the parent-daughter *r*s are on the right.

The boys' mental scores tend to be negatively correlated in the first year, most strongly so around 4 to 6 months, while the girls' *r*s at this age are essentially zero with parents' education, occupation, and social rating. Starting about

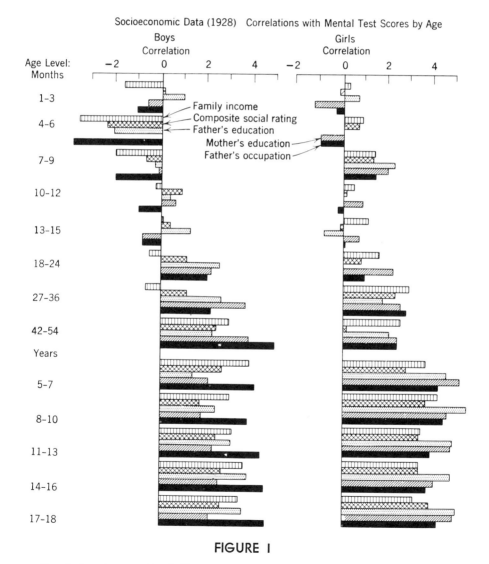

FIGURE I

Correlations between five indicators of socioeconomic level and mental test scores, sexes separated, for all age levels.

two years in both sexes the *r*s become positive, in this case more strongly for the girls. We cannot assume, however, that this growing correlation with age is a simple function of the effects of parental environment (9). Contrary evidence includes, for example, similar shifts in correlation of adopted children with their natural mothers but not with their foster parents (24). The evidence repeatedly points to a change after infancy in the nature of the developing intellectual processes (3, 9, 23). The change in correlation between children's mental scores and parental status also coincides with the change in stability over time of the children's test scores.

The interpretation of these *r*s with socioeconomic status is further complicated by the finding reported earlier (14) that the mothers' behaviors are correlated with their socioeconomic status. Higher status mothers are rated as more cooperative, equalitarian, and affectionate toward their children, while lower status mothers are more irritable, punitive, and ignoring. The relations are more clear for the mothers of boys. The one marked sex difference was that higher status mothers maintained closer contact with their daughters, lower status mothers with their sons.

It would appear from a survey of the correlations thus far that the better-circumstanced mothers (who more often treated their infant sons with relative freedom and affection) had sons who as infants were slow in developing but who later earned high IQs. The different pattern of correlations for the girls might be related to the greater stimulation to development in infancy of girls whose high-status mothers were closely interacting with them as well as being affectionate and equalitarian. These tentative suggestions may be tested by the direct comparison between the maternal behaviors and the children's intelligence.

Correlations of Early Maternal Behavior with Children's Intelligence

Keeping in mind these socioeconomic variables and the correlations for consistency of intelligence scores, as well as the different consistencies in the behavior ratings, we may now turn to the relation of intelligence to the behavioral or attitudinal-emotional variables, considering first those of the mother (Tables 1 and 2). The bar diagram in Figure 2 shows the correlations of the 0- to 3-year maternal behavior ratings with the children's mental scores during the first year. The mother-son *r*s are on the left, the mother-daughter *r*s on the right. The maternal traits are arranged in Schaefer's circumplex order of neighboring of maternal behaviors (36). Starting at granting autonomy, these behaviors move down the chart through loving acceptance to controlling, hostile, rejecting, and ignoring behaviors. Opposite each of these maternal variables the *r*s are given for four age levels of the children's mental scores (1 to 3, 4 to 6, 7 to 9, and 10 to 12 months).

For all four age levels of these first 12 months, the patterns within a sex are consistent. The boys' scores are correlated negatively with the maternal ratings of *equalitarianism, expressing affection,* and related behaviors, but are correlated positively with such variables as *punishing, use of fear to control,* and *strictness.* It is as though the hostile controlling (often lower socioeconomic status) mothers stirred their sons into activity (the sons of hostile mothers were more active at this age) and this increased activity facilitated test performance at this early age level. It can, however, be argued equally well that these energetic babies forced their mothers to punishments and to active controlling behavior. It is also true that active boy babies tend to score higher on the motor tests, and the *r*s between the mental and motor tests are of the order of .50 (4, p. 25).

The relations for the girls are different. Throughout the first year the girls' mental scores are positively correlated with the accepting-loving half of the maternal circumplex, from *positive evaluation* through *intrusiveness.* The *r*s then become negative in the hostile-rejecting segment—just that part in which the *r*s with the boys' mental scores are positive and highest. The only segment in which the *r*s are positive for both sexes covers the span of controlling behaviors, from *achievement-demand* through *anxiety.*

The girls' correlations with maternal behavior are in agreement with the pattern of correlations between maternal behavior and socioeconomic status. Thus it would appear that intelligent well-circumstanced mothers have a

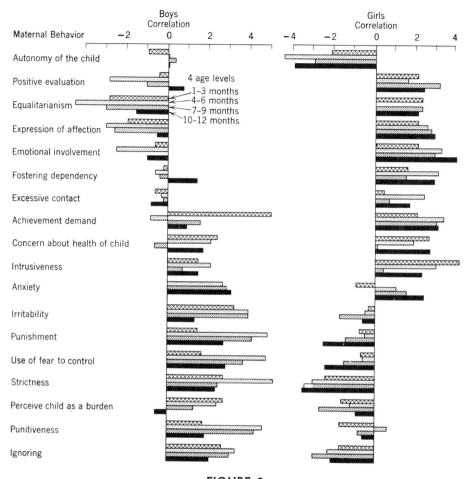

FIGURE 2

Correlations between ratings of maternal behavior in the first three years and intelligence scores of boys and of girls at four age levels, 1 to 12 months. The *r*s for all four sets of mental scores are opposite each maternal behavior item.

close relation to their girl babies, treat them well, and their babies thrive and develop rapidly, earning high scores on the tests. This, together with the positive *r*s with controlling behavior, raises the question whether control, and specifically for the girls closeness of contact, may be of very general, though by no means predominant, importance in determining the mother-child correlates with intelligence in infancy.

As we move along into the preschool ages (13 to 54 months) we see in Figure 4 a tendency for the patterns to shift. The boys develop positive *r*s where they had been negative

earlier and vice versa. By four years of age the boys with equalitarian, positively evaluating mothers tend to make higher scores; there is no correlation with achievement-demand and other forms of control; and the four-year-olds with irritable, rejecting, punitive mothers tend to make low scores. As for the girls, their pattern of correlations in infancy seems to be maintained or even strengthened through three years, though here, too, in the segment of control the *r*s break down.

At the school-age years a new pattern of correlation emerges. This pattern is congruent with the fact that by four years of age the children's

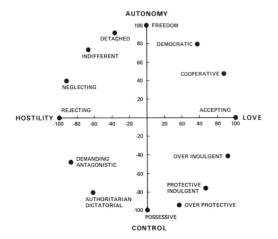

FIGURE 3

A circumplex model for maternal behavior. From E. S. Schaefer, "A Circumplex Model for Maternal Behavior," *Journal of Abnormal and Social Psychology,* 1959, 59, 226–35.

levels of intellectual function are fairly well set, and except for a few individual cases their IQs remain relatively stable thereafter, at least through the next 17 years of our records. The *r* for the total sample between intelligence tests at age levels 4 and 17 years is .62. This is similar to the *r* of .68 for maternal consistency, in love–hostility ratings, a consistency which, as we have noted, is found for mothers of both boys and girls. It is not surprising, therefore, that we find here a stable relation between maternal behaviors and intelligence scores.

The correlations of the behavior of the mothers toward their infants with the children's school-age intelligence are shown in Figure 5. For the boys the pattern of *r*s is an almost exact reversal from the pattern of infancy, and is in line with that established at four years. The only unchanged segment is in the area of maternal control. *Fostering dependency* and *excessive contact* remain unrelated to intelli-

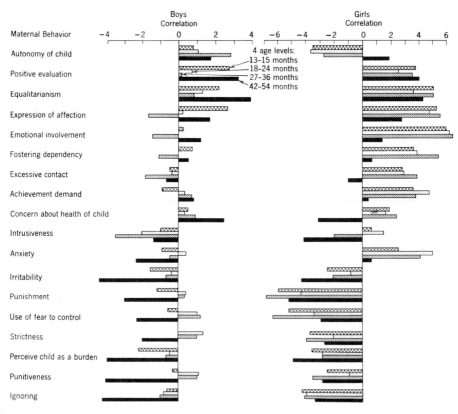

FIGURE 4

Correlations between ratings of maternal behavior in the first three years and intelligence scores of boys and of girls at four age levels, 13 to 54 months.

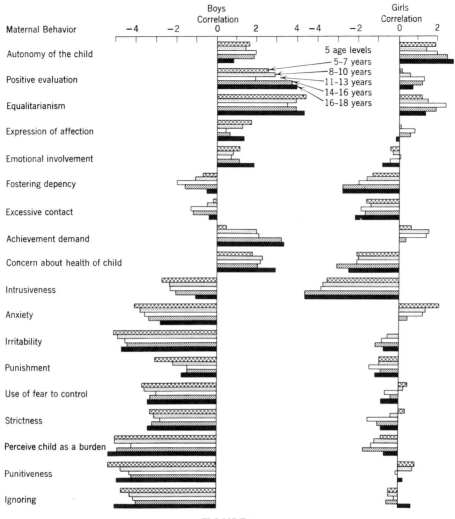

FIGURE 5

Correlations between ratings of maternal behavior in the first three years and intelligence scores of boys and of girls at five age levels, 5 to 18 years.

gence scores; *achievement demand* and *concern about health* maintain low positive *r*s. The boys' patterns of correlation now suggest that for *them* high tested intelligence throughout the school years goes with loving, accepting mothers of high socioeconomic status. The converse of this is seen more compellingly in the consistently large negative *r*s between early maternal hostility and intelligence. Mothers who with their infant sons are seen as *anxious. irritable, using fear to control, strict, perceiving the child as a burden, punitive,* and *ignoring,* have school-age sons whose IQs are in general below

the group averages. Over half of the *r*s for the eight maternal variables in this segment of the circumplex range between −.40 and −.52. As we have already noted, this type of maternal behavior is also more characteristic of the low socioeconomic woman. It remains, therefore, to test whether these relations result from the maternal behavior (which may be culturally influenced), or from other, possibly genetic, factors. However, it may very well be that maternal hostility toward boy babies serves to interfere with their subsequent optimal intellectual development.

As for the girls, the correlations at school ages with early maternal behavior appear to break down completely, with one exception. The girls whose mothers were *concerned about health* and *intrusive* now tend to make lower scores; the *r*s between girls' intelligence and mothers' *intrusiveness* are −.36, −.38, −.39, −.47, and −.47. It is interesting to note that Moss and Kagan (31), who have been making similar studies of the Fels data, find somewhat similar sex differences on a similar variable. They report that mothers' restrictiveness correlated −.41 with daughters' IQ, but only −.16 with sons' IQ. However, at three years they found a significant *r* of .42 between maternal acceleration and boys' IQ, with no mother-daughter relationship for this variable. These last two correlations are not in complete agreement with ours for three-year-olds, but are very much like those for five-year-olds and older in the Berkeley data. A very recent study by these authors (Moss and Kagan, unpublished) for subjects tested from birth to adulthood is in close agreement with ours for correlations of intelligence with socioeconomic status, and with maternal restriction (intrusiveness) and acceleration (achievement-demand). Where there are minor differences these may easily be accounted for by differences in the variables used and the situations in which the behaviors were observed.

In reviewing the arrays of correlations, it is important to keep in mind that we are comparing maternal behavior toward the infant and child under three years of age with *that* child's mental test scores from 1 month through 18 years. The early test scores, therefore, were made at the same ages for which the maternal ratings were made. Thus we should expect some correlations to be heightened by the concurrent mother-child interactions. Consequently, the patterns of correlation for the girls are most in line with expectations of change through time. Girl babies with loving mothers tend to do well, but with the lengthening intervals between the times of the maternal observations and the daughters' test scores (and in spite of some consistency in maternal ratings), the relations become attenuated.

What is most remarkable is the systematic pattern of mother-son correlations. This pattern has two aspects. First, there is the clear reversal over time in correlations between the love-hostility dimensions of maternal behavior and sons' scores. Second, there is the remarkably stable set of correlations between early maternal behaviors and sons' later scores.

These and other groups of correlational comparisons point toward an hypothesis that there are some basic differences in the determiners of the boys' and girls' intellectual growth patterns. For one thing, the correlation between the boys' mental scores and ratings of the mothers' intelligence remains about .3 after 15 months (Table 1). That is, there are much stronger correlations between the boys' IQs and some of the expressed maternal behaviors than between their IQs and what might be considered to be more basic or inherent, the assessed level of maternal intelligence.

The girls' mental scores on the other hand, after the first two years, are consistently correlated around .5 with their mothers' estimated intelligence (Table 2). These sex differences in mother-child *r*s of intelligence hold most clearly for the first of two independently made sets of ratings on the mother; one set from the infancy protocols and one set from the 9- to 14-year interviews.

Another, more objective, indicator of parental ability is their achieved educational level. . . . The girls in this sample showed a higher correlation between their intelligence scores and the education of both their mothers and fathers than did the boys. Although the differences are small, they recur in other reports in which parent-child correlations are given for boys and girls separately. For example, Honzik (24, 25) for the Berkeley Guidance Study, and Kagan and Moss (29), for the Fels Growth Study, report sex differences, with the girls' IQs correlating more highly than the boys' with the education of their parents. The Fels Study also shows a tendency toward the same sex differences in *r*s with mother's IQ.

In looking further for tests of the generality of this sex difference, we have utilized the material from a study by Skodak and Skeels (37), who published all of the individual data on 100 children who were placed in adoptive homes as infants. These data include, in addition to the children's IQs at five testings, the education of

TABLE I

Relationship of Mental Test Scores to Maternal Behavior Ratings from Zero to Three Years

Data on boys. N varies from 22 to 26.

	1-3 Mos.	4-6 Mos.	7-9 Mos.	10-12 Mos.	13-15 Mos.	18-24 Mos.	27-36 Mos.	42-54 Mos.	5-7 Yrs.	8-10 Yrs.	11-13 Yrs.	14-16 Yrs.	16-18 Yrs.
						Mental Test Scores							
Autonomy	−09	01	04	01	08	11	29	18	16	14	19	18	08
Ignoring	26	33	30	20	−08	−14	−11	−44*	−46	−42	−40	−39	−49
Punitiveness	17	46	42	18	−03	11	10	−42	−52	−46	−42	−41	−48
Perceives Child as Burden	27	24	13	−06	−23	−05	−07	−41	−49	−49	−46	−48	−52
Strictness	27	51	24	23	00	14	10	−21	−33	−31	−28	−32	−32
Use of Fear to Control	16	48	37	28	−06	10	12	−24	−37	−36	−30	−33	−34
Punishment	14	48	41	27	−12	04	03	−21	−31	−22	−15	−15	−18
Irritability	32	39	39	13	−16	−04	−07	−45	−51	−49	−45	−44	−47
Anxiety	17	19	21	00	−09	04	−05	−24	−41	−38	−36	−34	−28
Intrusiveness	15	21	07	15	−10	−21	−36	−14	−28	−24	−24	−21	−11
Concern about Health	24	21	−06	17	05	03	09	25	17	22	21	19	28
Achievement-Demand	50	−08	16	09	−09	03	07	08	04	19	20	31	32
Excessive Contact	−06	−03	−02	−08	−05	−04	−19	−07	−02	−05	−13	−12	−04
Fostering Dependency	−02	−06	−04	14	07	00	−11	05	−07	−11	−20	−16	−05
Emotional Involvement	−06	−25	−07	−10	02	00	−15	12	11	08	07	11	18
Expression of Affection	−19	−30	−26	−05	27	02	−17	17	17	12	04	06	13
Equalitarianism	−27	−45	−30	−15	22	13	08	40	44	38	35	39	43
Positive Evaluation	−04	−28	−10	08	28	07	01	33	25	29	24	37	39
Rejection of Home-making	31	28	27	11	00	−04	−15	−50	−62	−75	−69	−70	−74
Negative Emotional States	09	21	03	−04	−11	−11	−16	−43	−44	−38	−49	−52	−51
Mood Swings	33	39	28	15	−02	06	−02	−33	−40	−44	−47	−46	−44
Financial Stress	29	20	−08	−26	−31	−46	−47	−41	−48	−30	−32	−33	−33
Poor Physical Health	−03	−14	−26	−25	−27	−24	−32	−20	−32	−31	−35	−34	−29
Suppression of Aggression	21	27	13	21	−19	−07	00	02	−08	07	07	12	14
Dominance	38	10	06	04	−19	−15	−17	−15	−40	−33	−25	−16	−14
Self-Abasement	11	08	−14	−22	−09	−11	−14	−14	−03	−02	−09	−12	−05
Dependency	32	04	01	15	−12	−18	−12	−18	−12	−15	−14	−12	−08
Over-Conscientiousness	03	−07	−35	−16	02	06	04	18	19	22	12	13	24
Sociability	07	00	−07	00	−14	−13	−29	−03	−04	−18	−17	−14	−15
Cooperativeness	−20	−26	−33	−23	17	21	25	42	38	36	38	36	39
Estimated Intelligence	−03	−26	−11	−14	19	28	31	34	26	15	29	26	27
Narcissism	42	24	34	46	04	−16	−13	−26	−44	−32	−26	−14	−18

* Underlined entries significant beyond the .05 level.

TABLE 2

Relationship of Mental Test Scores to Maternal Behavior Ratings from Zero to Three Years

Data on girls. N varies from 24 to 27.

	1-3 Mos.	4-6 Mos.	7-9 Mos.	10-12 Mos.	13-15 Mos.	18-24 Mos.	27-36 Mos.	42-54 Mos.	5-7 Yrs.	8-10 Yrs.	11-13 Yrs.	14-16 Yrs.	16-18 Yrs.
							Mental Test Scores						
Autonomy	−20	−43*	−28	−38	−28	−29	−22	14	19	14	20	25	28
Ignoring	−16	−22	−29	−20	−34	−31	−32	−26	−05	−05	−02	−06	06
Punitiveness	−16	07	−07	−05	−20	−09	−28	−22	08	07	−01	00	02
Perceives Child as Burden	−15	−11	−26	−08	−28	−22	−22	−39	−09	−12	−14	−18	−07
Strictness	−23	−29	−33	−34	−29	−16	−31	−21	03	−04	−16	−11	−09
Use of Fear to Control	−06	−05	−14	−23	−41	−27	−50	−23	04	02	−07	−04	−09
Punishment	−06	−04	−13	−24	−47	−34	−54	−41	−10	−10	−15	−09	−12
Irritability	−02	−03	−16	−05	−20	−06	−16	−34	00	−06	−09	−12	−08
Anxiety	−08	11	16	25	20	39	32	05	20	13	12	04	00
Intrusiveness	42	31	05	24	05	12	−16	−33	−36	−38	−39	−47	−47
Concern about Health	27	20	02	28	15	13	19	−25	−21	−20	−21	−31	−25
Achievement-Demand	22	35	31	32	28	37	30	03	06	15	14	03	00
Excessive Contact	05	25	08	18	22	23	30	−08	−16	−14	−19	−17	−22
Fostering Dependency	17	32	16	30	28	30	42	05	−13	−16	−20	−28	−28
Emotional Involvement	22	34	30	41	46	48	50	11	−04	−03	01	−04	−08
Expression of Affection	22	27	29	30	41	37	43	21	00	01	08	06	−01
Equalitarianism	24	20	24	22	39	28	39	33	12	15	24	19	14
Positive Evaluation	22	17	33	25	29	20	27	31	02	06	13	12	07
Rejection of Home-making	04	20	−03	09	−20	−18	−13	−33	−09	−05	00	−13	00
Negative Emotional States	−43	−22	−25	−10	−14	−22	−18	−32	−16	−17	−22	−16	−13
Mood Swings	−07	10	−08	02	−15	07	−14	−30	03	04	01	−04	−06
Financial Stress	−14	−20	−24	−17	−18	−34	−27	−29	−34	−28	−20	−09	−21
Poor Physical Health	−17	06	−11	09	−04	00	−20	−41	−36	−33	−29	−25	−16
Suppression of Aggression	−22	07	−06	−13	−25	04	−07	−15	02	−04	−14	−16	−12
Dominance	28	34	34	42	18	24	16	−04	18	21	20	10	11
Self-Abasement	06	−12	−11	01	04	02	14	−20	−32	−41	−31	−40	−36
Dependency	30	26	−10	17	00	01	18	−42	−22	−29	−21	−35	−22
Over-Conscientiousness	10	13	01	20	15	24	27	−24	−16	−19	−14	−21	−15
Sociability	37	31	25	38	31	23	14	−09	−14	−14	−02	−15	−12
Cooperativeness	−05	−31	02	−16	18	11	33	53	18	16	22	24	16
Estimated Intelligence	−11	−21	14	00	20	20	31	55	51	46	55	50	50
Narcissism	54	34	28	33	13	18	00	−07	21	17	24	13	21

* Underlined entries significant beyond the .05 level.

TABLE 3

Correlations of Child's IQ with Indicators of True Parents' and Adoptive Parents' Mental Ability

Data from Skodak and Skeels (1949)

	Test:	1	2	3	4	4L
Mean Age at Test of Total Group*		2 years, 3 months	4 years, 3 months	6 years, 7 months	13 years, 6 months	13 years, 6 months
Child's IQ by	N	r	r	r	r	r
True M's IQ						
Boys	23	−.34	.23	.33	.07	.29
Girls	40	.20	.30	.36	.52	.47
True M's Ed						
Boys	35	−.30	.05	.11	.24	.25
Girls	56	.33	.42	.46	.48	.44
True F's Ed						
Boys	23	−.13	.18	−.02	.35	.13
Girls	37	.20	.48	.41	.49	.56
Foster M's Ed						
Boys	40	−.06	−.31	−.04	−.29	−.28
Girls	60	.02	−.41	.10	.21	.19
Foster F's Ed						
Boys	40	.16	.12	.03	−.03	−.09
Girls	60	−.02	.35	.01	.13	.06

* Mean ages for the various subgroups are within six months of the ages for the total group.

most of the true fathers and mothers and all of the foster parents, and the Stanford-Binet (1916) IQs of 63 of the true mothers. The children's average ages at the five testings were approximately 2 years, 4, 7, and twice at 13½ years. These rs are given in Table 3. Whether the parent-child comparisons utilize education (the only measure available except for the true mothers) or IQ as indicators of parental ability, there is a clear picture of higher correlation between girls and their true parents than between boys and their true parents. For example, at the 13½-year testing, on the 1916 Stanford-Binet, the girls' IQs correlate with their mothers' IQs .52, while the mother-son r is only .07. Also at 13½ years on the children's 1937 Form L test, the mother-child r for the girls is .47, for the boys .29. These same 13½-year tests correlated with their true fathers' education: for the girls .49 and .56 and for the boys .35 and .13.

In this instance, not only do these sex differ-

ences corroborate our findings from the Berkeley Growth Study, they occur in a population of children for whom there has been no opportunity for environmental influence by the true parents. What is more, the correlations with the foster parents' education remain essentially zero except perhaps for the 4-year tests. For these 4-year tests we have the problem of explaining, if true, the negative rs with foster mothers' education, and the girls' positive r with foster fathers' education.

Another study for which we have available parent-child correlations by sex of the child is the Conrad and Jones (16) study of familial resemblance in intelligence of a Vermont population in which the number of cases for any one comparison ranges between 216 and 263. When the Army Alpha test was used for both parents and offspring, the parent-daughter r is .57, the parent-son r is .40. However, we do have in this same study an instance of a slight reversal in size of correlation: for children tested on a different scale, the Stanford-Binet, the parent-daughter *r* is .48, the parent-son *r* is .51. In a study by Goodenough (18) the IQs of boys and girls tested twice at each of three ages (at 2, 3, and 4 years) were correlated with mothers' and fathers' education. For the 12 resulting pairs of *r*s (for *N*s of 31 to 41) eight *r*s were higher for girls with parents, one was equal, and three were higher for boys with parents.

We find thus not overwhelming but considerable evidence for a sex difference in parent-child correlations in intelligence. The fact that in the Kagan and Moss study (29) the differences are more consistent with parents' education than with their IQs may point to a greater conformity, among girls, with parental values toward intellectual goals. An attractive alternative interpretation fits in with our other mother-child correlations. When the higher parent-daughter correlations in mental abilities are compared with the higher mother-son relations between maternal behaviors and child's mental abilities, we may hypothesize a genetic sex difference in resistance to or resilience in recovery from environmental influences. This sex difference *may* be selective, and the effects of the environment may be either enhancing or depressing in their effect on a given structure or function. But our data show a great preponderance of maternal behavior variables that correlate higher with boys' than with girls' IQ.

Such a sex difference would be in accord with a number of observed physical sex differences. It is common knowledge that the infant mortality rate is greater for boys than for girls. One example of greater male vulnerability is to be found in the effect of the atomic bombings on children who survived the Hiroshima and Nagasaki attacks. When several hundred first-graders were examined two years after the bombings, boys were found to be significantly more retarded than girls in skeletal age (21). Similarly for children in the Marshall Islands who were accidentally exposed to radioactive fall-out, Conrad *et al.* (15) found that two years later growth in height of boys was two inches less than expected, but the girls' heights were not affected. The studies of socioeconomic effects on sex differences in growth in height and weight are conflicting, evidently because of

complex factors that are often not controlled (20). In the discussion of Graffar's paper, Van der Werff Ten Bosch summarizes the conflict. Pointing out J. B. Hamilton's findings that males of a large number of species are more vulnerable than females and the suggestion that the sex difference is related to gonadal activity, he says: "Could it be that the relatively short-term response of girls to adverse environmental conditions, as expressed in altered height and weight development, constitutes a homeostatic mechanism which serves long-term purposes and that this is somehow related to the sex differences surveyed by Hamilton? The male hormone would be responsible for higher vulnerability because it fails to make the body respond to changes in the environment through alterations in body growth" (20, pp. 159–190).

Whether or not the male hormone is the effective agent, some such pervasive physical differences in adaptability might also be reflected in behavioral flexibility and capacity for a given organism to return to its own homeostatic norm. Obviously we need more carefully controlled studies of these variables. At present they are suggestive rather than definitive. Also, the relations are probably very complex and their behavioral manifestations are often indirect as well as varying in degree. . . .

[The authors go on at this point to present data on later maternal behavior and children's intelligence, as well as relations between other characteristics of the mother and intelligence of children. The findings are summarized in the discussion that follows. (Eds.)]

DISCUSSION

In reviewing these patterns of relations between behaviors, both maternal and child, and the child's intelligence over an 18-year span, clear trends emerge. In the first place, there are marked and consistent sex differences in the patterns of correlation for these Berkeley children. The boys appear to establish early a pattern of relations with their mothers' behavior toward them in regard to their own behaviors and to their intelligence scores. There is evidence, in the boys, of a strong persistence in the effects of these early interaction patterns. In the girls, by contrast, the relations often show up clearly on a concurrent basis, but then drop out. For girls, there is little relation between either their mother's behavior or their own in the first two or three years and their later intelligence.

Again, when we consider various kinds of early behavior as they relate to the child's mental development, our findings indicate that it makes an important difference whether the child is a girl or a boy. The persistently recurring hypotheses concerning the lasting effects of early maternal influence on subsequent development are only partially substantiated, and even then in no simple clear-cut way.

For the boys there is a group of mother-son correlations that are systematically related to the patterns of mental growth. Mothers who evaluate their boy babies positively, behave toward them in an equalitarian way, and to some degree both grant them autonomy and express affection for them—such mothers more often have sons who as infants are happy, positive in their responses, and calm. These boys tend to make below-average mental scores in the first year but to make rapid gains in the next two or three years, so that by five and thereafter they are more likely to have high IQs.

The converse of this is the cluster of hostile, punitive maternal behaviors, related to active, unhappy, negative, excitable, responsive-to-persons boy babies, who tend to make high developmental scores in the first year, and to have low IQs after four years. It looks as though we could make our best predictions of the boys' later intelligence from a combination of non-intellective variables. That is, we might predict a high IQ after five years for a boy who at six months made a rather low mental score but was happy, inactive, and placid, with a loving, accepting mother, and a father in a professional occupation. It might also help for him to have parents with a high education or to be rated or scored as high in intelligence. A little later on, at 27 to 36 months, the boy who also responds positively to the tests is a good candidate for a high IQ.

High mental test scores of the girls during infancy tend to be positively correlated with involved, close, and loving behaviors of their mothers. The girl babies who are happy, posi-

tively responding, not shy, and responsive to persons, usually have affectionate, controlling mothers who are more likely to have high socioeconomic status and to be rated high in intelligence. Although their daughters' mental scores in infancy are not related to parental socioeconomic variables, the daughters of mothers with loving and controlling behavior ratings do tend to make above average mental scores through the first three years. The well-adjusted, happy girl babies also tend to make above average mental scores over these same ages (through three years). But so also do girl babies who are rapid and active (variables for which there is no clear mother-daughter relation). This correlation of mother-daughter behavior with early mental development is just the reverse of the mother-son correlation. After three years, however, these relations with daughters' intelligence drop out almost entirely. The only correlations that even give a hint of a positive relation between the early ratings and girls' later (5 to 18 years) intelligence are the girls' 2- and 3-year ratings of *activity, freedom from shyness,* and *happiness.* There is also evidence from the correlations that the mothers who are *intrusive* with their girl babies have daughters who earn low IQs after four years. An inspection of cases shows a trend for low school-age IQs to be related to hostile maternal behavior toward daughters who are responsive to persons.

In going over the data on the girls, then, we find fewer and usually different predictive criteria available than for the boys. In any effort to predict the girls' later IQs from records collected in the first three years we must rely primarily on parents' education, fathers' occupational level, and a rating (or measure) of the mothers' intelligence. We might possibly add the negative relation of maternal intrusiveness. Only when the girls have reached the age of three years can we include (in a very limited degree) the girls' own ratings on the variables: *not shy, active,* and *happy.*

Where we might say of the boys that early mothering pays off in the long run, for girls we would have to say that so far as intelligence is concerned these early "good" mother-daughter interactions are of little avail, and that genetic inheritance appears to be the important determiner for later intellectual growth. But, where they occur, we must be cautious about assuming that these age changes in correlation are the result of maternal behaviors in themselves. The rs with maternal behaviors must be interpreted in the light of such facts as (a) that parental behaviors and parental intelligence (or education) are correlated, and (b) that the children's early mental behavior and their intelligence measured in school-age mental tests are very different in kind, and therefore we may expect them to be related differently to the behavior variables.

However, over and above these relations there is evident need for further explanation of the complex of intercorrelations reported here. Perhaps one of the most challenging of the findings is the sex difference in the relations of intelligence to social, emotional, and goal-oriented behaviors of both mother and child. The findings lend themselves to an hypothesis that in infancy males are more permanently affected than females, not only physically, but also psychologically, in both emotional and intellectual aspects of adjustment and growth. There is some evidence that the effective environmental factors appear to be both enhancing and inhibiting, in both short-range and long-range effects. What seems to be the case (if we venture to generalize from the data we have presented here) is that the male infant's response to the emotional climate of his life situation is more readily fixed and stabilized than is the case for the female infant. If this is true, his response tendencies may tend to become fixed and to color all of his later development, not only in such behavioral dimensions as introversion–extraversion and love–hostility, but also in intellectual attitudes, values, and preoccupations of the kind which enhance or depress growth in intelligence.

The girls, on the other hand, although responsive to emotional climates, are less permanently conditioned. Their mental development appears to be more closely determined by genetic factors. Good mother-daughter relations tend to go with enhanced mental scores in the first three years, but after this age the girls' intelligence appears to develop with little regard to the maternal behavior variables we have observed. It is interesting to note that the general lack of sex difference in intelligence when total scores are compared not only smooths out sex differences in certain types of intellectual function but apparently also obscures sex differences in responsiveness to environmental pressures.

Obviously, there are many determiners of intellectual growth besides the ones considered here. It is in the very nature of these behavior variables that their correlations with IQ should be moderate. It is also true that the sex differences represent averages, with considerable spread of scores and ratings within the sex. Consequently, with our small samples, the relations we find are only tentative. However, it is evident that emotional and other behavioral variables do play important roles, though in complex ways that repeatedly limit us in any tendencies we may have to make broad generalizations about specific relations. It should be possible to test these findings further by comparisons with other longitudinal studies, such as those of Kagan and Moss (29, 30, 31) with the Fels material. But also new studies should be designed and carried out for the express purpose of investigating these hypothesized interrelations: to clarify and to confirm, or to negate them.

On the basis of the findings to date, however, one should at least be warned against making across-the-board general statements about the effects of "mothering" in infancy on later development. This caution is relevant whether the generalizations refer to the kind or the adequacy of interpersonal relations or of intellectual functioning. The nature of the maternal behaviors, the nature of the child's own behaviors, the sex of the child, as well as a multitude of other genetic and environmental conditions all play some part in the complex patterns of interaction. Nevertheless, if our findings are substantiated they can be of considerable importance for theories of the nature of etiological determiners in the development of intelligence.

SUMMARY

In the subjects of the Berkeley Growth Study the intercorrelations of maternal and child behaviors with children's intelligence over the 18-year span of their growth reveal a number of congruent but complex patterns of relation. The correlations exhibit systematic shifts in pattern with changing age of the children, and these age changes in pattern differ according to sex. In general, the boys' intelligence is strongly related to the love–hostility dimension of maternal behavior. Hostile mothers have sons who score high in intelligence in the first year or so, but have low IQs from 4 through 18 years. The highly intelligent boys, in addition to having loving mothers, were characteristically happy, inactive, and slow babies, who grew into friendly, intellectually alert boys and well-adjusted extraverted adolescents. The girls who had loving, controlling mothers were happy, responsive babies who earned high mental scores. However, after three years the girls' intelligence scores show little relation to either maternal or child behavior variables, with the

exception of negative *r*s with maternal intrusiveness. The girls' childhood IQs are correlated primarily with education of the parents and estimates of the mothers' IQ. These differences, together with other findings on sex differences, have led to an hypothesis of genetic sex differences. The impact of the environment (maternal behaviors) on infant boys is persistent: both their behaviors and their intellectual functioning tend to become fixed by the third year and to persist, at least through 18 years. The girls' intellectual functioning, on the other hand, appears to be more genetically determined. It is as though the girls continually readjust their behavior to the concurrent environmental conditions. However, their intelligence is relatively independent of those maternal and child behaviors which are evidently important for the boys. . . .

REFERENCES

1. Bayley, N. A study of the crying of infants during mental and physical tests. *J. genet. Psychol.*, 1932, 40, 306–329.
2. Bayley, N. *The California First-Year Mental Scale*. Univer. of California Press, 1933.
3. Bayley, N. Mental growth during the first three years: a developmental study of 61 children by repeated tests. *Genet. Psychol. Monogr.*, 1933, 14, 1–92.
4. Bayley, N. The development of motor abilities during the first three years. *Monogr. Soc. Res. Child Develpm.*, 1935, 1, No. 1 (Serial No. 1).
5. Bayley, N. Mental growth in young children. Chapter II. In G. M. Whipple (Ed.), Intelligence: its nature and nurture. *Yearb. Nat. Soc. Stud. Educ.*, 1940, 39 (II), 11–47.
6. Bayley, N. Factors influencing the growth of intelligence in young children. Chapter III. In G. M. Whipple (Ed.), Intelligence: its nature and nurture. *Yearb. Nat. Soc. Stud. Educ.*, 1940, 39 (II), 49–79.
7. Bayley, N. Consistency and variability in the growth of intelligence from birth to eighteen years. *J. genet. Psychol.*, 1949, 75, 165–196.
8. Bayley, N. Some increasing parent-child similarities during the growth of children. *J. educ. Psychol.*, 1954, 45, 1–21.
9. Bayley, N. On the growth of intelligence. *Amer. Psychologist*, 1955, 10, 805–818.
10. Bayley, N. Individual patterns of development. *Child Develpm.*, 1956, 27, 45–74.
11. Bayley, N. Data on the growth of intelligence between 16 and 21 years as measured by the

Wechsler-Bellevue Scale. *J. genet. Psychol.*, 1957, 90, 3–15.
12. Bayley, N., & Jones, H. E. Environmental correlates of mental and motor development: A cumulative study from infancy to six years. *Child Develpm.*, 1937, 8, 329–341.
13. Bayley, N., & Schaefer, E. S. Maternal behavior and personality development: data from the Berkeley Growth Study. In C. Shagass & B. Pasamanick (Eds.), *Psychiatric research reports 13*. Amer. Psychiat. Ass., 1960. Pp. 155–173.
14. Bayley, N., & Schaefer, E. S. Relationships between socioeconomic variables and the behavior of mothers toward young children. *J. genet. Psychol.*, 1960, 96, 61–77.
15. Conrad, R. A., Huggins, C. E., Cannon, B., Lowrey, A., & Richards, J. B. Medical survey of Marshallese two years after exposure to fall-out radiation. *J. Amer. med. Ass.*, 1957, 164, 1192.
16. Conrad, H. S., & Jones, H. E. A second study of familial resemblance in intelligence: environmental and genetic implications of parent-child and sibling correlations in the total sample. In G. M. Whipple (Ed.), Intelligence: its nature and nurture. *Yearb. Nat. Soc. Stud. Educ.*, 1940, 39 (II), 99–141.
17. Dearborn, W. F., & Rothney, J. W. M. *Predicting the child's intelligence*. Sci-Art, 1941.
18. Goodenough, F. L. The relation of the intelligence of preschool children to the education of their parents. *Sch. & Soc.*, 1927, 26, 1–3.
19. Goodenough, F. L., & Maurer, K. M. *The*

mental growth of children from two to fourteen years. Univer. of Minnesota Press, 1942.

20. Graffar, M. Influence du milieu social sur la croissance. *Mod. Probl. Paediat.*, 1962, 7, 159–170. (Karger, Basel/New York)

21. Greulich, W. W., Crismon, C. S., & Turner, M. L. The physical growth and development of children who survived the atomic bombing of Hiroshima or Nagasaki. *J. Pediat.*, 1953, 43, 121–145.

22. Hilden, A. H. A longitudinal study of mental development. *J. Psychol.*, 1949, 28, 187–214.

23. Hofstaetter, P. R. The changing composition of "intelligence": a study of *t*-technique. *J. genet. Psychol.*, 1954, 85, 159–164.

24. Honzik, M. P. Developmental studies of parent-child resemblance in intelligence. *Child Develpm.*, 1957, 28, 215–228.

25. Honzik, M. P. Fluctuations in mental test scores. In J. P. Ambuel (Ed.), *Physical behavior and growth: report of the twenty-sixth Ross Pediatric Research Conference.* Ross Laboratories, 1958. Pp. 54–57.

26. Honzik, M. P., Macfarlane, J. W., & Allen, L. The stability of mental test performance between two and eighteen years. *J. exp. Educ.*, 1948, 17, 309–324.

27. Jaffa, A. S. *The California Pre-School Mental Scale.* Univer. of California Press, 1934.

28. Jones, H. E., & Bayley, N. The Berkeley Growth Study. *Child Develpm.*, 1941, 12, 167–173.

29. Kagan, J., & Moss, H. A. Parental correlates of child's IQ and height: a cross-validation of the Berkeley Growth Study results. *Child Develpm.*, 1959, 30, 325–332.

30. Kagan, J., & Moss, H. A. *Birth to maturity: a study in psychological development.* Wiley, 1962.

31. Moss, H. A., & Kagan, J. Maternal influences on early IQ scores. *Psychol. Rep.*, 1958, 4, 655–661.

32. Schaefer, E. S. A circumplex model for maternal behavior. *J. abnorm. soc. Psychol.*, 1959, 59, 226–235.

33. Schaefer, E. S. Converging conceptual models for maternal behavior and for child behavior. In J. C. Glidewell (Ed.), *Parental attitudes and child behavior.* Charles C Thomas, 1961. Pp. 124–146.

34. Schaefer, E. S., & Bayley, N. Consistency of maternal behavior from infancy to preadolescence. *J. abnorm. soc. Psychol.*, 1960, 61, 1–6.

35. Schaefer, E. S., & Bayley, N. Maternal behavior, child behavior and their intercorrelations from infancy through adolescence. *Monogr. Soc. Res. Child Develpm.*, 1963, 28, No. 3 (Serial No. 87).

36. Schaefer, E. S., Bell, R. Q., & Bayley, N. Development of a maternal behavior research instrument. *J. genet. Psychol.*, 1959, 95, 83–104.

37. Skodak, M., & Skeels, H. M. A final follow-up study of one hundred adopted children. *J. genet. Psychol.*, 1949, 75, 85–125.

38. Sontag, L. W., Baker, C. T., & Nelson, V. L. Mental growth and personality development: a longitudinal study. *Monogr. Soc. Res. Child Develpm.*, 1958, 23, No. 2 (Serial No. 68).

39. Terman, L. M. *The measurement of intelligence.* Houghton Mifflin, 1916.

MENTAL ABILITIES OF CHILDREN FROM DIFFERENT SOCIAL-CLASS AND CULTURAL GROUPS

GERALD S. LESSER   GORDON FIFER   DONALD H. CLARK

INTRODUCTION

The purpose of this study was to examine the patterns among various mental abilities in young children from different social-class and cultural backgrounds. The patterns among four mental abilities (verbal ability, reasoning, number facility, and space conceptualization) were studied in first-grade children from four cultural groups in New York City (Chinese, Jewish, Negro, and Puerto Rican), with each cultural group divided into middle-class and lower-class groups.

Until recent years, there has been little empirical study of differential mental abilities in young children. In contrast, much theoretical and methodological progress (e.g., Balinsky, 1941; Burt, 1939, 1941, 1944, 1949, 1954; Carroll, 1941; Clark, 1944; Garrett, 1946; Guilford, 1956, 1958, 1959; Kelley, 1928; Meyer & Bendig, 1961; Swineford, 1948, 1949; Thurstone, 1948; Vernon, 1950) has been made in defining the organization of differentiated mental operations in adults and in children old enough to respond to group tests. Within the past decade, however, sufficient knowledge has accumulated (e.g., Davis, Lesser, & French, 1960; Meyers & Dingman, 1960; Meyers, Orpet, Attwell, & Dingman, 1962) to indicate that differentiated mental abilities can be identified in children who are too young to read and write.

Reprinted with abridgment by permission of Gerald S. Lesser, Gordon Fifer, and The Society for Research in Child Development, Inc., from *Monographs of the Society for Research in Child Development*, 1965, **30,** Ser. no. 102, Whole no. 4, 1–4, 11–12, 80–84. © 1965 by The Society for Research in Child Development, Inc. All rights reserved.

Our purpose was to extend the general demonstration that differential mental abilities exist in young children by examining the variations in the *patterns* of these diverse abilities that are associated with variations in social-class and cultural conditions. While it has been established that group factors beyond a general-ability factor exist in young children, little has yet been discovered about the differences in *patterns* of intellectual expression related to the influences of different social classes and cultures.

General Implications of the Research

This research problem has several theoretical and practical implications. Certain of these implications are part of the growing discussion (e.g., Passow, 1963; Riessman, 1962) of the problems of the "disadvantaged" or "culturally deprived" children from "depressed" areas. However, in the absence of clear, consensual definitions of these concepts and of substantial empirical evidence relevant to the opinions presented, it is difficult to formulate rigorous and testable propositions about the problems of disadvantaged children. When these problems are viewed within the context of evolving theories of intelligence and analyses of the sociological forces associated with social-class and cultural influences, testable questions can be asked with greater scientific meaning and precision.

The attempt to establish similarities and differences between the structures of mental abilities of young children in different social-class and cultural groups is linked to several scientific issues. One such issue is the long history of investigation of trait organization and intra-individual variations in test performance (see Anastasi, 1958a, Chs. 10, 11). Social class and cultural-group determinants of the structure of mental abilities are also related to the development of mathematical procedures for identifying the dimensions of human behavior (e.g., Guttman, 1954; Hotelling, 1933; Kelley, 1935; Thurstone, 1947) and to a psychological issue with a most venerable background, the heredity *versus* environment controversy (e.g., Anastasi, 1958b; Carmichael, 1954; Gesell & Thompson, 1929; Loevinger, 1943). Evidence concerning the environmental antecedents and correlates of diverse mental abilities is also central to theory construction in developmental psychology (e.g., Hunt, 1961). Such evidence provides a clarification of the basic nature, function, and organization of the mental abilities themselves and of the characteristics of the environmental conditions that influence their development.

Implications for Psychological Assessment and Educational Procedures

Perhaps the most important implications of this research on patterns of mental ability in young children relate to the practical efforts to determine the optimum educational conditions and the most valid assessment instruments for children from diverse backgrounds. The loss of outstanding intellectual talent in groups labeled "culturally deprived" has been a source of increasing concern (e.g., McClelland, 1958; Wolfle, 1954, 1960). American society is dedicated to the development of intellectual ability wherever it is found. However, before talent can be developed, it must be located and identified. In the last few decades, intellectual ability has been located primarily with the aid of a few popular tests of intelligence (e.g., the Revised Stanford-Binet Intelligence Scale). For better or worse, we have, in practice, defined "intelligence" in terms of the most popular tests that presume to measure it.

These intelligence tests have been frequently criticized (e.g., Anastasi, 1958a; Freeman, 1962) for being too heavily loaded with verbal items that are both unfair to certain groups

within our population and too narrow as assessments of intellectual functioning. A score based on a test that is heavily loaded with one factor can tell little about the quality and quantity of the various talents that an individual has. Perhaps because of such intelligence measures, or for reasons as yet undiscovered, we are failing conspicuously to discover outstanding talent in certain strata of our society. It is clear from the research literature (e.g., Anastasi, 1960a; Strodtbeck, 1958; Wolfle, 1960) that lower socioeconomic groups and certain cultural groups do not contribute their proportion of intellectually productive individuals.

Teachers must make both immediate and continuing educational decisions about children from different social-class and cultural backgrounds in order to provide effective classroom instruction. There is, however, a serious lack of valid information available regarding the abilities of these children. When a child is classified on the basis of a single, global score, such as a general-intelligence quotient (even if the test is appropriate and valid for his social class and cultural group), much remains to be known about the range and operation of his abilities. However, if that single global score is not only too narrow but is also inappropriate and invalid for his group, the information available to the teacher becomes even more obscure and less useful.

The study of cultural differences in mental abilities attacks a fundamental, persistent problem for education and psychology: How do we provide valid psychological evaluation of children from widely dissimilar cultural groups? There is no doubt that one of the most pressing needs expressed by teachers and school administrators is for testing instruments that will provide fair, accurate, and broad assessment of the abilities of young children from cultural backgrounds other than those typical of our total school population.

School personnel in "underprivileged areas" contend that their children cannot possibly perform well on the available psychological tests because the tasks required of them are either unimportant or alien. The claim has often been made (e.g., Davis, 1948, 1951) that intelligence tests (such as the Stanford-Binet Intelligence

Scale) were originally designed to measure those aspects of mental ability in which middle-class children excelled, ignoring those other aspects of mental ability in which the lower class, through its culture, encourages its children to perform favorably. This is understandable since intelligence tests were developed to answer the need for prediction of performance in school. As long as schools function to train children who are best able to understand and work within standards that are based on middle-class, white, urban values, such tests should do a reasonably good job of predicting those children of superior academic "ability."

We are no longer satisfied with such limited educational goals, however. We must educate children who can contribute to our changing society in ways that we may well not be able to anticipate today. This means we must broaden our definition of "ability" or "talent" to include behaviors based on values that, thus far, have not been prominent in middle-class culture. We must be able to identify relative intellectual strengths *within* an individual, and we must be able to identify his individual intellectual strengths, no matter what his social-class or cultural identity may be. Having done this psychological assessment job, we must develop educational techniques that will help the most talented children develop their talents fully, although radical departure from traditional educational procedures may be necessitated thereby.

Before the psychological assessment job can be begun, however, information is needed on the possible variations in the *patterns* of diverse mental abilities as they relate to variations in social class and culture. In order to understand the relative strengths of an individual child's mental abilities, we must have information on how children of a particular background (e.g., middle-class Puerto Rican or lower-class Chinese) tend to express their intellectual abilities, in contrast to how the majority of the school population tends to express its intellectual abilities. Perhaps intelligence tests can then be developed that will yield intra-individual profiles of scores for the various mental abilities of children, with contrasting normative profiles for children of similar social-class and cultural identity and for children in the entire nation.

The Social-Status Variables Studied

This study examines the effect of three independent variables—social class, cultural background, and sex (and the interactions among these variables)—upon various mental abilities of young children. . . .

Hypotheses

Anastasi (1958a) concluded that one reason for the slow progress of studies of cultural variations in intellectual development is that our concept of intelligence is itself culturally conditioned and restricted. "It is not so much that tests are unfair to lower-status groups, as that lower-class environment is not conducive to the effective development of 'intelligence' as defined in our culture" (p. 534).

Our culture, however, has gradually begun to supply several definitions of intelligence. The most popular definition to date has been, of course, the concept of general intelligence, and for this concept, Anastasi's conclusion appears inescapable. For many reasons, however, the *differential* approach to the definition and measurement of ability is becoming one of the chief distinguishing characteristics of contemporary psychology and education (see Anastasi, 1961, Ch. 13). Adopting the differential definition that intelligent behavior can be manifested in a wide variety of forms, we can then examine in detail the relative degrees to which different social environments are conducive to the effective development of various mental skills. This position provides the premise for the hypotheses tested in the current study: Cultural influences differ not only in degree but in kind, with the consequence that different kinds of intellectual skills are fostered in different environments.

The hypotheses to be tested are as follows:

1. Significant differences exist among groups of children from different social classes and cultures in each of four mental ability areas, i.e., verbal ability, reasoning, number facility, and space conceptualization.

2. Significant differences exist among groups of children from different social classes and cultures in the *pattern* or configuration of scores

on measures of these diverse areas of mental ability.

3. Significant interactions exist between the variables of social class and cultural group in determining the level of each mental ability and the nature of the patterns among them.

To test these hypotheses, the Hunter Aptitude Scales (Davis et al., 1960) were revised and adapted. These scales were constructed originally to provide a broad assessment of diverse mental abilities in young children; they are reliable measures of verbal ability, reasoning, number facility, and space conceptualization in a middle-class sample of four- to five-year old children. Through the earlier application of these tests, certain psychometric properties of the scales (e.g., reliability coefficients; intercorrelations; amount of unique, nonchance variance contributed by each test, etc.) were established (Davis et al., 1960). The present research extended the application of these instruments to the study of young children from different social classes and cultures. The original scales and the present adaptations are described in detail in a later chapter.

In the present study, first-grade children were studied from both middle- and lower-class families among the following cultural groups in New York City: Chinese, Jewish, Negro, and Puerto Rican. . . .

This study of social-class and cultural variations in diverse mental abilities departs in general strategy from earlier test-making approaches (e.g., Davis & Eells, 1953; Eells et al., 1951) that were designed to reduce cultural bias in test results; the procedure of selecting test items principally on the grounds that they do *not* discriminate between cultural groups is an extremely restrictive, if not reversed, approach to the study of intellectual functioning (Charters, 1963). . . .

THE MENTAL-ABILITY SCALES   The descriptions of the four mental abilities studied are as follows:

Verbal. The skill is defined as memory for verbal labels in which reasoning elements, such as those required by verbal analogies, are reduced to a minimum. Verbal ability has long been regarded as the best single predictor of success in academic courses, especially in the language and social-science fields. It is involved to a marked degree in the work of all professions and in most of the semiprofessional areas.

Reasoning. Reasoning involves the ability to formulate concepts, to weave together ideas and concepts, and to draw conclusions and inferences from them. It is, almost by definition, the central element of aptitude for intellectual activities and, therefore, is of primary importance in all academic fields and in most vocations.

Number. The ability is defined as skill in enumeration and in memory and use of the fundamental combinations in addition, subtraction, multiplication, and division. It is of great importance in arithmetic in elementary schools and in mathematics in secondary schools.

Space Conceptualization. The ability refers to a cluster of skills related to judging spatial relations and sizes of objects and to visualizing their movements in space. It is involved in geometry, trigonometry, mechanics, and drafting; in elementary-school activities, such as practical arts and drawing; and in occupations such as mechanics, engineering, and architecture.

THE VERBAL SCALE   The Verbal Scale consists of 30 Picture Vocabulary items and 30 Word Vocabulary items.

Picture Vocabulary. As indicated earlier, the Picture Vocabulary subtest was extended considerably from the form it took in the earlier scale, since it was thought that the measurement of verbal concepts in terms of a child's observation of his environment would be less contaminated by the sort of naming behavior that allegedly takes place in a middle-class environment. The items selected, then, were those that would necessarily be represented in the environments of all urban children in the sampled population. Naturally, the urban areas of New York City were primarily drawn upon, although it seemed that the materials ultimately utilized in the subtest would be equally appropriate for any metropolitan area in the United States. The items selected were chosen on the basis of visibility to any child regardless of where he lived in an urban culture. A definite attempt was made to avoid the sort of rural emphasis that is prevalent in many of the group intelligence tests now in use in the United States. In picturing the items, the artists were instructed to make drawings of people neutral in tone and to include a minimum of the frills often appearing in the pictures in popular children's books. The Picture Vocabulary items . . . consisted of 18 pictures of people and objects, which the subject was asked to name, and 12 pictures of activities, which the subject was asked to identify. In the weighted scoring key that was developed for this subtest, the possible range of scores was from 0 to 60.

Word Vocabulary. The Word Vocabulary items were administered at separate testing sessions in two parallel forms of 15 words each. This technique was employed because of the length of time required to administer the items. . . . The development of the Word Vocabulary tests entailed the greatest difficulty in test construction. Extended tryouts of words were necessary to meet the following criteria:

1. No word unknown by a large percentage of either middle- or lower-class children during tryout was used.

2. No word unknown by a large percentage of one or more of the ethnic groups during tryout was used.

3. No word known only by a large percentage of either middle- or lower-class children was used.

4. No word known only by a large percentage of three or fewer ethnic groups was used.

5. Only words were used for which there were suitable equivalents in Spanish, Chinese, and Yiddish that indicated the same verbal concepts at approximately the same difficulty level for children aged six to seven and one-half years.

Numerous words were selected and grouped into categories of nouns, verbs, adjectives, and a limited number of adverbs of very frequent usage as judged by word counts (Thorndike & Lorge, 1944). The list was then analyzed to determine if each word had a counterpart in the native language of each of the ethnic groups and if each translated word would be of a difficulty approximately equivalent to its difficulty

level in the American usage of the English word.

During a tryout period, English words were translated into Spanish and then given to other persons to translate from Spanish back to English to see whether the resulting English words were the original ones. This procedure was successful in producing an extensive list of words that was suitable for testing the Puerto Rican children. The success of this procedure for the Puerto Rican children was crucial to this study because 75 of the 80 Puerto Rican children were tested either in Spanish, exclusively, or in some combination of Spanish and English.

For the Chinese group, it was difficult to follow the same procedure since there are several different Chinese dialects used in New York City. In the group we sampled, we found primarily the Cantonese dialect, but other dialects of southern China were also found. Among the middle-class Chinese, we found either the Mandarin or Shanghai dialect, if Chinese was spoken at all. The resolution of this situation was the most difficult problem in developing the Word Vocabulary subtest. The attempted solution was to locate consultants who spoke both English and Chinese and who were familiar with the local urban conditions in New York City. They proposed the verbal concept in Chinese that most closely represented each English word and that could be expected to be known by a Chinese child of normal ability at about the same age as an American child. Extensive tryouts of these Chinese words were then conducted.

A second obstacle arose in building an equivalent list of Chinese vocabulary words because the only possible translations of certain words into Chinese demanded contextual references. For example, the word "shade" in Chinese has no meaning by itself and is accompanied by a modifier such as "tree shade," "lampshade," etc. The only possible way of scoring responses to these items would be on the basis of the child's ability to use the word in a context, and this was not the verbal skill we were attempting to assess through the Word Vocabulary test. Thus, many additional words had to be discarded.

A final criterion for retention of a Chinese word in the vocabulary list was whether the word could be assigned an equivalent translation in Mandarin and Shanghai dialects as well as in the Cantonese.

As a result of these efforts, the Word Vocabulary list seemed fair for comparing Chinese children with English-speaking children. It is not known precisely if this development of the subtest had any detrimental effect upon its efficacy for measuring verbal ability in general. However, as vocabulary tests tend to be quite highly correlated with each other regardless of the words they contain when used for measuring English-speaking subjects, the test was probably quite suitable for the age range for which it was designed.

During the tryout of the words, it was discovered that it was not necessary to be too concerned about a careful Yiddish translation of the test. It was found that lower-class Jewish children were less likely to speak Yiddish than were the middle-class, and the middle-class Jewish children tended to be more fluent in English even if they knew some Yiddish or Hebrew. Ultimately, with . . . four exceptions . . . the entire sample of Jewish children was tested in English.

Following these procedures, it was possible to obtain a list of 40 words that met all the original criteria, passed the standards set for Spanish and Yiddish as determined by the testers and the language consultants representing the two groups, and also met the approval of the Chinese testers and consultants. The final 30 vocabulary words included in the test were those displaying the best difficulty levels in the tryouts with the four ethnic groups. The instability of the word lists during the tryouts precluded obtaining reliable discrimination indices. The 30 words were then divided into two matched lists based upon the composite rankings of the words made by the psychologists serving as test administrators and by the test constructors.

THE REASONING SCALE   The Reasoning scale subtests used in this study are more similar in content and format to those of the earlier study than any of the other subtests. (The only early subtest not included in the current battery was Verbal Analogies.) The

major changes in items within the subtests consisted of revisions of the drawings for the Picture Analogies and Picture Arrangement subtests. Drawings were made with a view to minimizing the picture-book quality previously present. A further modification was the addition of more abstract drawings; that is, a number of geometrical line drawings were added to measure the ability to recognize various relations outside the usual context of the picture book or story book. All items included in the Reasoning scale subtests were such that no naming of objects was required. If the subject could perceive the relations involved, the correct answer could be indicated without naming any object or, indeed, without knowing the names of any of the objects in the drawings. Verbal skills were thus minimized.

Picture Analogies.   Each picture analogy item consisted of two large cards. The first contained three drawings, two of which were paired. The paired objects were similar and were related to each other in some way, e.g., small-large, young-old, narrow-wide, upright-turned. The second card consisted of drawings of four objects similar to the single object on the first card. One of the four objects on the second card bore the same relation to the single object on the first card as did the paired objects to each other. *S* was required to select the analogous pair.

Picture Arrangement.   The subtest consisted of a series of picture stories and abstract object sequences. The series consisted of from three to five drawings, each on a separate card. Each item was presented in a predetermined mixed order and the subject was asked to arrange the cards so the pictures made a good story or were in a good order.

Jump Peg.   The subtest consisted of a specially designed board with large holes in it (similar to a Chinese Checkers board) and several large wooden pegs. The subject was presented with a set of increasingly more difficult arrangements in the board and instructed to jump and eliminate pegs until only one peg remained, and that one in the center hole of the board.

The Jump Peg subtest was retained in almost precisely the same form as that used in the earlier research. Although the use of a certain amount of spatial visualization seemed to contaminate this reasoning subtest, it was retained in the Reasoning scale with the intention of presenting a sufficient number of sample items so that individual differences in spatial ability would be neutralized before the scored items were presented. It was expected that the obtained variance in Jump Peg scores would thus primarily reflect differences in the subjects' abilities to reason.

All Reasoning items were tried out on both lower- and middle-class children of all four ethnic groups. The results of the trial suggested a weakness of the Jump Peg subtest for the current study—that it was similar to certain children's games. It is possible that children whose families purchased this type of game had an advantage that was difficult to counteract completely and that applied mainly to the middle-class children. Consequently, the directions for the subtest were designed to acquaint each subject so thoroughly with the procedure required before scoring began that the advantage could be minimized as much as possible. The opposite possibility of associative interference also existed; since the Jump Peg subtest resembled but was not identical to other children's games, familiarity with such games may have acted to confuse the child and depress his Jump Peg score. Again, the thorough directions and the use of sample items operated against such interference.

The detailed directions for the administration and scoring of these subtests indicate the steps that were taken in each case to be certain that the subjects understood the procedure before scored items were presented.

THE NUMERICAL SCALE   The Number scale used in the earlier study of gifted children, in spite of its uniqueness and high reliability, was obviously unsuitable for use in the present study. Successful performance on the scale required not only familiarity with the basic arithmetic operations generally taught in the first two grades in school but also knowledge of the symbols $+$, $-$, $\times$, $\div$. In the current study, an attempt was made to measure numerical concepts prior to formal training in the mechanics of computation or the operational symbols.

The resulting numerical test consisted simply of two pictures: one for the Enumeration, Addition, and Subtraction subtests, and one for the Multiplication and Division subtests. The first picture was a street scene showing houses, trees, autos, children, and other objects in quantity. The second was of a fruit and vegetable stand with some children in the scene. The test items required the subject to enumerate, add, subtract, multiply, and divide the persons or objects in the scene. On the Enumeration subtest, the subject was permitted to count by actually touching the picture with his finger, if necessary, as the test was introduced into the scale in order to determine the subject's ability to count. On all other subtests the subjects were required to compute without touching the pictures.

The risk of introducing unwanted verbal variance in presenting the numerical tests in this manner was recognized. However, the names of objects to be manipulated, the phrasing of the questions, and the directions given were all put in the simplest possible language. Various versions of the specific methods applicable to each of the subtests were tested during item tryouts, and the wording producing the least confusion was adopted. Furthermore, the examiner was prepared to give the entire test in the native language of the child, if necessary. . . .

THE SPACE SCALE   The original Spatial-Conceptualization battery consisted of eight subtests but was shortened in this version to only four. The Cubes subtest was dropped because it was the most difficult for the gifted children and it was considered unlikely that enough easy items could be constructed to measure the abilities of children in this study. The Hidden Pictures, Roll-Up, and Judging Sizes subtests employed in the earlier study were also discarded because they could not be extended to an easier level and because earlier reliability estimates were too low to retain the subtests without increasing their lengths.

Object Completion. The subtest consisted of 16 incomplete pictures of familiar objects that S was requested to identify. . . .

The Object Completion subtest was, perhaps, less suitable for measuring spatial conceptualization than was desirable because it required verbal identification as well as visual perception. The attempt was made to minimize the verbal component by selecting extremely simple and familiar objects (e.g., dog, spoon, car). In addition, the subtest was scored so that if a child could not name the object precisely, but indicated a suitable identification of it, his response was marked correct.

Estimating Path. This subtest consisted of 12 drawings of airplanes. Five drawings showed a single plane entering a cloud, and 7 showed two planes on intersecting routes. The drawings indicated the planes' directions of flight. In the first set, the subject was asked to select from four choices the point at which the plane would come out of the cloud if it continued on the same flight path. In the second set, the subject selected from four options the point at which the flight paths of the two planes would cross.

The Estimating Path subtest from the earlier battery was retained although it tended to have a somewhat limited three-dimensional quality. As it was reasonably easy for the gifted children, it seemed suitable for measuring spatial conceptualization in normal children. Furthermore, being a completely novel test, it was unlikely that knowledge of any current children's game could bias the results.

Jigsaw Puzzles. Each item in this subtest consisted of two identical squares, triangles, or circles, made of a colorful, heavy plastic. One figure of each shape was cut into two or more pieces. The subject was required to fit the pieces together to match the uncut shape that was left in view but out of the subject's reach.

The Jigsaw Puzzles subtest was retained because it was the most successful subtest in the Space battery given to gifted children. For the purposes of this study, the only change made was to use the easier items. It was likely that this test yielded a valid and reliable spatial-visualization factor. Such a finding was made in the study of gifted children, and the estimates

of difficulty levels suggested that an appropriate set of items had been included in the current battery.

Perspective. This subtest consisted of three large drawings, two of street scenes and one of a children's playground. Each scene contained three or four persons. The subject was asked to identify from four to six options the part of the scene a particular person would be able to see from his position in the scene.

The Perspective subtest provided a good spatial measure, if one can assume a minimum reasoning ability. To reduce the contribution of individual differences in reasoning ability, the items were designed to present perspective in its simplest form, directions were simplified as much as possible, and sample items were used. . . .

SUMMARY

This study examined the patterns among various mental abilities in six- and seven-year-old children from different social-class and cultural backgrounds. The main intent was to extend the empirical analyses of the development of differential mental abilities in children, but the findings of this research also bear directly upon the problems of building valid and precise assessment instruments for children from different cultural groups.

Despite the considerable amount of work in the field of mental abilities in an attempt to create "culture-free" or "culture-fair" tests, little has been shown to yield consistent and valid results. The problem still remains of how to evaluate the intellectual potential of children whose backgrounds necessarily handicap them seriously on the usual tests of mental ability. This study focused on two major aspects of the problem: first, to devise tests that would be as free as possible of any direct class or cultural bias but still would be acceptable measures of intellectual traits and, second, to structure a testing situation that would enable each child to be evaluated under optimal conditions.

Hypotheses were tested regarding the effects of social-class and ethnic-group affiliation (and their interactions) upon both the level of each mental ability considered singly and the pattern among mental abilities considered in combination. Four mental abilities (Verbal ability, Reasoning, Number facility, and Space Conceptualization) were studied in first-grade children from four ethnic groups (Chinese, Jewish, Negro, and Puerto Rican), with each ethnic group divided into middle- and lower-class groups.

The following specific predictions were made:

1. Significant differences will exist between the two *social-class* groups in the *level* of scores for each mental ability.

2. Significant differences will exist among the four *ethnic* groups in the *level* of scores for each mental ability.

3. *Social class* and *ethnicity* will interact significantly in determining the *level* of scores for each mental ability.

4. Significant differences will exist between the two *social-class* groups in the *pattern* of scores from the four mental-ability scales.

5. Significant differences will exist among the four *ethnic* groups in the *pattern* of scores from the four mental-ability scales.

6. *Social class* and *ethnicity* will interact significantly in determining the *pattern* of scores from the four mental-ability scales.

To test these hypotheses, a $4 \times 2 \times 2$ analysis-of-covariance design (completely balanced randomized blocks) was used. The four ethnic groups (Chinese, Jewish, Negro, and Puerto Rican) were each divided into two social-class groups (middle and lower), each in turn divided into equal numbers of boys and girls. A total of 16 subgroups, each composed of 20 children, was represented. The total sample was thus composed of 320 first-grade children. Three test influences were controlled statistically in the analysis-of-covariance design: effort and persistence, persuasibility or responsiveness to the tester, and age of the subject.

The major findings were as follows:

1. Differences in *social-class* placement *do* produce significant differences in the absolute *level* of each mental ability but *do not* produce significant differences in the *patterns* among these abilities.

2. Differences in *ethnic-group* membership *do* produce significant differences in *both* the absolute *level* of each mental ability and the *patterns* among these abilities.

3. *Social class* and *ethnicity do* interact to affect the absolute *level* of each mental ability but *do not* interact to affect the *patterns* among these abilities.

Thus, predictions 1, 2, 3, and 5 were strongly confirmed. No statistically significant support was found for predictions 4 and 6. The following other specific results were found:

1. Regarding social-class effects upon mental abilities, middle-class children are significantly superior to lower-class children on all scales and subtests.

2. Regarding ethnic-group effects upon mental abilities: (*a*) On Verbal ability, Jewish children ranked first (being significantly better than all other ethnic groups), Negroes ranked second and Chinese third (both being significantly better than Puerto Ricans), and Puerto Ricans fourth. (*b*) On Reasoning, the Chinese ranked first and Jews second (both being significantly better than Negroes and Puerto Ricans), Negroes third, and Puerto Ricans, fourth. (*c*) On Numerical ability, Jews ranked first and Chinese second (both being significantly better than Puerto Ricans and Negroes), Puerto Ricans third, and Negroes, fourth. (*d*) On Space, Chinese ranked first (being significantly better than Puerto Ricans and Negroes), Jews second, Puerto Ricans third, and Negroes, fourth.

3. Regarding sex differences, boys were significantly better than girls on the total Space scale, on the Picture Vocabulary subtest (but not on the total Verbal scale), and on the Jump Peg subtest (but not on the total Reasoning scale).

4. Regarding the interactions of social class and ethnicity, two effects combined to produce the statistically significant interaction effects upon each scale of mental ability: (*a*) On each mental-ability scale, social-class position produced more of a difference in the mental abilities of the Negro children than in the other groups. That is, the middle-class Negro children were more different in level of mental abilities from the lower-class Negroes than, for example, the middle-class Chinese were from the lower-class Chinese. (*b*) On each mental-ability scale, the scores of the middle-class children from the

various ethnic groups resembled each other to a greater extent than did the scores of the lower-class children from the various ethnic groups. That is, the middle-class Chinese, Jewish, Negro, and Puerto Rican children were more alike in their mental-ability scores than were the lower-class Chinese, Jewish, Negro, and Puerto Rican children.

5. Regarding the interactions of sex and ethnicity, the significant interactions for both Verbal and Space reflected the higher scores for boys than for girls in all ethnic groups, except for the Jewish children; Jewish girls were superior to Jewish boys for both Verbal and Space scales.

It was concluded that social-class and ethnic-group membership (and their interaction) have strong effects upon the level of each of four mental abilities (verbal ability, reasoning, numerical facility, and space conceptualization).

Ethnic-group affiliation also affects strongly the pattern or organization of mental abilities, but once the pattern specific to the ethnic group emerges, social-class variations within the ethnic group do not alter this basic organization. Apparently, different mediators are associated with social-class and ethnic-group conditions. The mediating variables associated with ethnic-group conditions do affect strongly the organization of abilities, while social-class status does not appear to modify further the basic pattern associated with ethnicity.

These findings allow a reassessment of the various proposed explanations of cultural influences upon intellectual performance. The importance of the mediators associated with ethnicity is to provide differential impacts upon the development of mental abilities, while the importance of the mediators associated with social class is to provide pervasive (and not differential) effects upon the various mental abilities. This conclusion allows selection among the several explanations offered to interpret cultural influences upon intellectual activity; the explanations based upon natural selection, differential reinforcement, motivation, problem-solving tactics, work habits, and so forth, were re-examined in the light of the present results.

In summary, the findings lend selective support to Anastasi's premise (1958a, p. 563) that "Groups differ in their relative standing on different functions. Each . . . fosters the development of a different *pattern* of abilities." It seems true that social-class and ethnic groups do "differ in their relative standing on different functions." However, ethnic groups do "foster the development of a different pattern of abilities," while social-class differences do not modify these basic organizations associated with ethnic-group conditions.

The present effort to construct suitable testing procedures for studying children from culturally diverse groups must now incorporate the broader educational considerations of curriculum development, teacher training, and school organization. We have shown that several mental abilities are related to each other in ways that are culturally determined. We propose that the identification of relative intellectual strengths and weaknesses of members of different cultural groups must now become a basic and vital prerequisite to making enlightened decisions about education in urban areas.

LANGUAGE DEVELOPMENT AFTER AGE SIX

CAROL CHOMSKY

INTRODUCTION

This study deals with several aspects of the acquisition of syntactic structures in children between the ages of 5 and 10. It is concerned with the general question of the extent to which children in this age group have achieved mastery of their native language, and explores areas of disparity between adult grammar and child grammar. We find that the grammar of a child of 5 differs in a number of significant respects from adult grammar, and that the gradual disappearance of these discrepancies can be traced as children exhibit increased knowledge over the next four or five years of their development. The method of inquiry is designed to ascertain the child's competence with respect to the grammatical structures under investigation, and undertakes an active exploration of his comprehension by means of questioning and discussion. A number of grammatical structures are investigated which are present in adult grammar and are part of ordinary language usage, but which are found to be absent in the grammar of 5-year-olds. These structures are studied in the grammar of children up to the age of 10, when the children's command of the structures is found to approach that of adults. The stages found in the intervening years reveal an interesting and orderly picture of gradual acquisition.

A common assumption among students of child language has been that the child has mastered the syntax of his native language by about age 5. Accordingly most of the research carried out in the area of acquisition of syntax has

concentrated on children under 5 years of age, dealing with the period of rapid progress and more readily observable changes in the child's degree of knowledge. Summaries and discussion of the literature dealing with this early period are presented in several comprehensive works, among them Slobin (1967) and McNeill (in press).

Our study deals with the later period, after age 5. Clearly, by this age the rate of acquisition of syntactic structures has decreased markedly, and differences between the child's grammar and adult grammar are no longer so readily discernible in the child's spontaneous speech. Such differences are brought to light, however, when we begin to explore the child's comprehension of particular syntactic structures. Under direct examination, the child's lack of knowledge of a number of constructions which are commonplace to the adult becomes apparent. The process may be viewed as analogous to a study of an individual's vocabulary range. Differences in command of vocabulary between children and adults are revealed more readily by tests based on words of increasing difficulty than by observations of spontaneous conversation. Similarly, differences in command of syntactic structures can be revealed most readily by comprehension tests involving selected constructions of a relatively complex nature. The children's observed failure to correctly interpret a number of such constructions is indicative of several areas in which their underlying syntactic knowledge falls short of the adult's. Furthermore, the nature of the children's mistakes in interpreting these constructions is important in bringing out various aspects of the implicit linguistic knowledge which they do possess. For we find that the children do in fact assign an interpretation to the structures that we present to them. They do not, as they see it, fail to understand our sentences. They understand them, but they understand them wrongly. The information thus revealed about discrepancies between child grammar and adult grammar affords considerable insight into the processes of acquisition, and in addition, into the nature of the structures themselves.

Our procedure is to elicit information from the child about several test constructions by direct interviewing. By age 5, most children have become amenable to questioning. It is possible to work with them in an interview situation, to enlist their cooperation in carrying out tasks, playing games and answering questions, all geared to revealing various aspects of their knowledge of the syntactic structures in question. We find them quite willing, even eager, to participate in such activities, and the interview acquires the spirit of interesting play. We are thus able to observe a variety of responses indicative of the children's interpretations of the structures under study. We select four constructions which are part of ordinary language usage but which we consider, on the basis of notions of linguistic complexity, to be candidates for late acquisition. We test the comprehension of these constructions in a group of children starting with age 5, at which age most children give evidence of not yet knowing the constructions. We continue to test children of increasing ages up to the point at which we find that most children exhibit a command of the structures comparable to that of adults, about age 10. Of particular interest in our observations is that variation in age of acquisition does not seem to affect order of acquisition for particular constructions. A number of related structures, for example, are observed to be acquired by all children tested in the same order, illustrating areas in which linguistic development, whether it occurs earlier or later, nevertheless proceeds along similar paths. Our sample consists of forty children, in kindergarten through grade 4, interviewed at elementary schools in the Boston area. In the report which follows, the theoretical considerations of complexity which underlie the choice of structures are discussed in detail, the experimental method is described fully, and results are presented together with transcriptions of representative interviews with the children.

Recent work in the field of generative transformational grammar has provided the motivation for a study of this sort, as well as the grammatical insights and material necessary for its development. Briefly we may say that the mature speaker who knows his language has internalized an intricate and highly complex set of rules which constitute the grammar of his language. A child who is acquiring language has the task of constructing for himself a similar set of rules which will characterize the language that surrounds him and enable him to use it for both speaking and understanding. When the child speaks, he gives us evidence of various aspects of his internalized grammar, but there are certainly many aspects of grammar that are not at all evident from spontaneous speech. Just as the vocabulary that we comprehend exceeds that which we may ever produce in speaking, the grammatical constructions that we understand are of a greater variety and perhaps a greater complexity than we may ever produce. Work in generative grammar over the last decade has considerably extended our knowledge of the depth and nature of the complexities of grammatical structures, and has given rise to the suspicion that the child of 5 or 6 may still not have mastered certain—perhaps surprisingly many—aspects of the structure of his language that the mature speaker takes for granted and commands quite naturally. Very little syntactic questioning has been done with children of this age, perhaps because until recently the notions of the complexities of language were not sufficiently developed to permit the selection of grammatical constructions which might be candidates for late acquisition. Examples of this nature may now be found in the literature of the field of generative grammar, if one undertakes to examine the literature with an eye to questions of language acquisition. Structures which have potential for late acquisition would be those, for example, which deviate from a widely established pattern in the language, or whose surface structure is relatively inexplicit with respect to grammatical relationships, or even simply those which the linguist finds particularly difficult to incorporate into a thorough description, whatever the reason. All of these might be con-

sidered as candidates for late acquisition. Fortunately, a few of these constructions do lend
themselves to exploration in young children.

As we have stressed, it is the children's interpretations of the constructions under investigation that we undertake to study. As an example,
every speaker of English knows, for sentences
(a) and (b),

(a) John promised Mary to shovel the driveway.
(b) John told Mary to shovel the driveway.

that in (a) it is John who intends to do the
shoveling, and that in (b) it is Mary who is
supposed to do it. Many children of 5 or 6,
however, have not yet learned to make this
distinction, and interpret that it is Mary who
is to do the shoveling in (a) as well as in (b).
They make this interpretation on good authority, for in fact almost all verbs in English which
can replace *told* in sentence (b) require the
interpretation as in (b), namely, that Mary
is to shovel the driveway: cf. *ordered, persuaded, wanted, advised, allowed, expected*, etc.
The fact is that *promise* in this construction
appears to be an exception to the general pattern of the language, and most 6-year-olds have
just not yet learned this fact about their language, although they do know what a promise
is, and are able to use and correctly interpret
sentences containing *promise* in other syntactic
environments.

By age 8, most children have learned this
special grammatical fact about *promise,* and
are able to interpret sentences such as (a) correctly. This observation brings us to a clearer
understanding of what it means to have learned
a word in one's language, i.e., the nature of
the information about a word which the speaker
of a language has available when he knows the
word. There are two aspects to this knowledge,
which are distinct from one another. On the
one hand, the speaker knows the concept attached to the word, and secondly he knows the
constructions into which the word can enter.
The child who has acquired the concept of the
word but does not yet control some of the
constructions into which it can enter gives us
clear evidence of the distinctness of these
two aspects of his knowledge. A complete

knowledge of the word includes both this semantic knowledge and all the syntactic knowledge relating to the word. For a word like
promise, where there is a particular difficulty
attached to the syntactic aspect of the word,
we see that the child first acquires semantic
knowledge, and later progresses to full syntactic knowledge. It is syntactic knowledge of
this sort, which all adults share as part of their
knowledge of their language, but which is in a
grammatical sense fairly complex or subtle,
that we deal with in this investigation.

It is of interest that a study of this kind may
be revealing not only with respect to language
acquisition, but also with respect to the notions
of linguistic complexity on which it is based.
We are studying the stage of language learning
in which children are at the border of adult
competence. The sorts of things that they do
know at this late stage bear a close relation to
the characteristics and complexities of the ultimate linguistic system that they will one day
command. An increased understanding of these
complexities is currently developing among
linguists and psychologists concerned with general questions of the nature of language and
human cognitive capacities. Investigation of
the child's knowledge as he approaches linguistic maturity contributes to this understanding
and provides additional insights into degrees of
linguistic complexity that are otherwise difficult
or perhaps even impossible to detect.

THEORETICAL CONSIDERATIONS OF LINGUISTIC COMPLEXITY

The initial task involved in approaching a
study of the child's acquisition of syntactic
structures after age 5 is to characterize notions
of linguistic complexity. The natural assumption is that children acquire later those structures which are more complex. Accordingly,
our procedure is first to take up notions of
complexity, next to hypothesize on the basis
of these notions which structures will tend to
be acquired late, and finally to proceed to investigate these structures in children's grammar.

We have found that the results bear out our
original hypotheses in many respects, and furthermore that the results contribute to a clarifi-

cation and a sharpening of our original notions of complexity.

Our approach to the question of syntactic complexity is from the point of view of a listener performing the operation of understanding a sentence. He is essentially acting as a recognition device faced with the task of assigning a structural interpretation to a string of words which he receives as input. It is the specific operation of determining the syntactic structure of the S(entence) which is our concern here. In order to understand a S, the listener must be able to determine the grammatical relations which hold among the words and phrases that make it up. We postulate that the difficulty of this interpretive task is increased by the presence of the following four conditions:

(A) The true grammatical relations which hold among the words in a S are not expressed directly in its surface structure.

(B) The syntactic structure associated with a particular word is at variance with a general pattern in the language.

(C) A conflict exists between two of the potential syntactic structures associated with a particular verb.

(D) Restrictions on a grammatical operation apply under certain limited conditions only.

We will discuss each of these conditions, and indicate what structures and test Ss were selected in accordance with them.

(A) The true grammatical relations which hold among the words in a S are not expressed directly in its surface structure.

In order to understand a S, a listener must be able to determine the actual grammatical relations that hold among the words that make it up. When these relations are explicit in the surface structure of the S, as in (1), the task of the listener is facilitated.

(1) John saw Mary.

In (1), the listener has no difficulty in deter-

mining that John is the subject of the S, and that Mary is the object of the verb. These relations are expressed directly in the surface structure of the S by the order of the words, according to the standard subject-verb-object pattern of English, and are readily observable. In some Ss, however, these grammatical relations are not represented in the surface structure and cannot be directly observed by the listener. Nevertheless, he must, in order to understand the S, determine what these relations are. The less clearly these relations are expressed in the surface structure, the more analysis he must perform in order to recover them, and the more knowledge he must bring to bear on the situation.

In the simple case of (1), the subject-verb-object order appears intact in the surface structure of the S. Consider now the familiar examples (2) and (3).[1]

(2) John is eager to see.
(3) John is easy to see.

In (2) standard grammatical order is maintained. To understand this S, the listener interprets that *John* is the subject of the S, *eager* is an adjective predicated of John, and that *John* is also the subject of the infinitival complement verb *see,* i.e., that it is John who will be doing the seeing in this S. In (3), however, this order is not maintained. Although *John* appears to be the subject in both cases, closer inspection reveals that in (3) it is the superficial subject only. In (2) it is John who is eager, but in (3) it is not John who is easy. The adjective *easy* is not predicated of John in (3) as *eager* is in (2). In (3) what is easy is for someone to see John. Thus (4) is a paraphrase of (3),

(4) To see John is easy.

whereas (5) is not a paraphrase of (2).

(5) * To see John is eager.

The deep subject of (3) is actually *to see John.* Further, in (3) *John* is not the subject of the

[1] Discussion of these examples is to be found in Lees (1960) p. 216, and Chomsky (1964) pp. 34–35.

complement verb *see* as it is in (2), but is instead its object. In (2) John is performing the action, but in (3) John is acted upon. In (3) it is someone else who is seeing John.

Thus we see that in (2) the true grammatical relations in the S are far more readily ascertained by an inspection of the surface structure than in (3). To interpret (3) correctly, then, is a more complex task, and ought to require more extensive syntactic knowledge. We hypothesize that the child will learn to assign the correct interpretation to (2) earlier than to (3). We assume that interpretation (2) is the simpler of the two, in the sense of more accessible, or more readily applied, and also earliest learned. For the child who is in the process of learning the rules for interpreting these two types of Ss, we assume that the tendency to assign interpretation (2) will predominate. What this would mean in practice is that given a S of type (3), the child whose rule system is still in a state of flux would tend to assign to it a (2) interpretation. Once the rule system has become firmly established, we would expect this tendency to disappear, and to find that the child assigns the (3) interpretation where required.

The fact that children have more difficulty with constructions in which word order differs from the standard has been noted by other researchers. Luria and Yudovich (1959) describe a case of 5-year-old twins with retarded speech development who interpret passive Ss in Russian as active, understanding *Petia was struck by Vasia* to mean that Petia struck Vasia. The tendency is to interpret the S as if standard order of words is exhibited. This primacy of the active S form over the passive has been noted also in English for very young children by Fraser, Bellugi, and Brown (1963), Turner and Rommetveit (1967), and Slobin (1966).

(B) The syntactic structure associated with a particular word is at variance with a general pattern in the language.

We will now take up a set of constructions in which elements crucial to the understanding of the S are omitted from its surface structure, and must be supplied by the listener. Consider Ss such as

(6) John told Bill to leave.
(7) John persuaded Bill to leave.
(8) John ordered Bill to leave.

In each of these Ss, the subject of the infinitival complement verb *leave* is not expressed, but must be filled in by the listener. In order to understand these Ss, he must be aware that the implicit subject of *leave* is *Bill* in each case. Although two candidate noun phrases (*NP*s) are present in the main clause, *John* and *Bill,* the listener must know to select *Bill* as complement subject. He must have learned a rule for interpreting Ss of this type in which the complement has an infinitival verb lacking a subject. The rule must say, in essence, that

(9) For Ss of the form
NP_1 V NP_2 to inf vb
assign NP_2 as subject of the infinitive verb.

Rule (9) applies very generally in English, holding for almost all verbs which take complement constructions similar to (6–8) above. A partial list of examples is:

(10) a. John told Bill to leave.
   b. John persuaded Bill to leave.
   c. John encouraged Bill to leave.
   d. John ordered Bill to leave.
   e. John permitted Bill to leave.
   f. John allowed Bill to leave.
   g. John urged Bill to leave.
   h. John caused Bill to leave.
   i. John advised Bill to leave.
   j. John enticed Bill to leave.
   k. John forced Bill to leave.
   l. John selected Bill to leave.
   m. John compelled Bill to leave.
   n. John required Bill to leave.
   o. John believed Bill to be a sociable fellow.
   p. John understood Bill to be a sociable fellow.
      . . . . .
[At this point, Mrs. Chomsky considers other sentences where the subject of the infinitive is a pronoun referring to the proper noun nearest the infinitive: John told Bill that *he* (Bill) must leave. The verbs in such sentences are of the command type: *tell, order, force, require,* and

so on. The author then contrasts sentences containing command-type verbs with sentences containing the verb *promise,* which carries a very different meaning. (Eds.)]

. . . *Promise* is in a distinct semantic category from these command verbs. We may say that each semantic class—command verbs on the one hand, and *promise* on the other—has associated with it a separate syntactic process. For the command verbs, the infinitival complement verb relates to the main clause object; for *promise,* it relates to the main clause subject.

Semantic class	Syntactic process
1. command verbs	1. complement vb relates to main clause object
2. *promise*	2. complement vb relates to main clause subject

Thus we have two semantic classes, and an unambiguous syntactic process associated with each. Now notice that there is in addition a third class of verbs which lies semantically somewhere between a command and a promise. These are verbs like *ask* and *beg* which are in the nature of a request. Interestingly enough, the semantics of *ask* and *beg* permit both syntactic processes to be associated with them. The complement verb may relate either to the main clause object, as in (17), or to the main clause subject, as in (18).

(17) a. The teacher asked the child to leave the room.
     b. John begged Bill to change the tire.
(18) a. The child asked the teacher (for permission) to leave the room.
     b. John begged Bill (to be allowed) to change the tire.

Thus we may insert a third semantic class into our above representation, with which both syntactic processes may be associated:

Semantic class	Syntactic process
1. command verbs	1. complement vb relates to main clause object
2. request verbs	2. complement vb relates to main clause subject or object
3. *promise*	3. complement vb relates to main clause subject

To approach the difference between *promise* and our other verbs in another way, we may consider the different categories of verbs which introduce indirect speech or quoted speech in the complement clause. If we look at the characteristics of this indirect speech when it is transposed into direct speech, we will notice that for our command verbs, the result is an imperative:

John ordered Mary to move the car. →
"Move the car!"

Promise, however, does not have this characteristic. *Promise* is not in the nature of a command, and the indirect speech cannot be transposed into an imperative. Obviously when the direct speech is in the first person it cannot be an imperative:

John promised Mary that he would pay his debts. →
"I will pay my debts."

But even when the direct speech is in the second person, it is not an imperative:

John promised Mary that she would get a bicycle for her birthday. →
"You will get a bicycle for your birthday."

Notice that a verb like *told* exhibits two possibilities for the transposition of the indirect speech into direct speech in the second person. Depending on the structure of the complement, the direct speech may be either in the imperative or not:

Imperative: John told Mary to get a bicycle. →
"Get a bicycle!"
Nonimperative: John told Mary that she would get a bicycle. →
"You will get a bicycle."

Promise differs in that it permits only the latter possibility, the nonimperative.

There is another aspect of the verb *promise* which is discussed by Austin (1962), and which may have a bearing on its unusual syntactic characteristics. Austin distinguishes between 'statements' and 'performative utterances,' pointing out that whereas many Ss that a speaker utters state a fact or report something, in other Ss the speaker is actually doing an action by uttering the S. That is, the speaker is not just saying something about an action, but is actually performing the action by uttering the S. Examples of such Ss from Austin (1962) are:

I bet you it will rain tomorrow.
I apologize for the error.
I deny having been there.
I promise you to try harder.

The act of betting, apologizing, denying, and promising is performed by the very utterances of the Ss. Perhaps this aspect of the verb *promise* may provide additional insight into its syntactic nonconformity.

Promise, then, constitutes an exception to the MDP,* which applies very generally in English. Since the MDP applies so extensively throughout the language, it would seem likely that the child learns this principle, and applies it across the board, so to speak, for a period of time. We hypothesize that this is the case, and will investigate the child's interpretation of Ss in which a correct interpretation requires a violation of the MDP. We expect to find a stage of development in which children have learned the MDP and have not yet learned rule (16). These children should select NP_2 as subject of the infinitival complement verb in (19) as well as (20), and report that it is Bill who is supposed to do the work in both cases.

(19) John promised Bill to shovel the driveway.
(20) John told Bill to shovel the driveway.

Once rule (16) is learned, the child should distinguish these two cases, and correctly report that in (19) it is John who intends to do the work.

A second verb which signals violation of the MDP is *ask* in constructions of the form

(21) I	asked	him	what	to	do.
NP^1	ask	NP_2	wh-	to	inf vb

Consider the contrast between (22) and (23):

(22) I asked him what to do.
(23) I told him what to do.

The paraphrase of (22) is *I asked him what I should do,* whereas the paraphrase of (23) is *I told him what he should do.* When the subject is omitted from the wh-clause as in (22) and (23), the resulting surface structures are identical, and the task of distinguishing them falls to the listener. He must know to employ the MDP in one case, and to violate it in the other. To do this, the listener must know a special fact about *ask:* that in constructions such as (22), *ask* signals violation of the MDP. He must acquire a rule for *ask* similar to rule (16) for *promise:*

(24) For a S of the form
NP_1 ask NP_2 wh- to inf vb
violate the MDP and assign NP_1 as subject of the inf vb.

We hypothesize that the child will learn the correct interpretation for (22) later than the correct interpretation for (23). Before he acquires rule (24), we expect that the child will assign to (22) the interpretation

I asked him what he should do.

Once rule (24) is learned, he should correctly assign the interpretation

I asked him what I should do.

(C) A conflict exists between two of the potential syntactic structures associated with a particular verb.

We would like to draw a distinction here between examples (19) and (22) in the preceding section.

(19) John promised Bill to shovel the driveway.

* The MDP, or Minimal Distance Principle, states that when the subject of a complement verb is not given (as in *John wanted to leave,* with *to leave* being the complement verb), the implicit subject is the noun phrase most closely preceding the complement verb (*John,* in this case). [Eds.]

(22) I asked him what to do.

In both of these Ss the Minimal Distance Principle is violated and we have postulated that as a result they will be correctly interpreted by the child later than Ss (20) and (23).

(20) John told Bill to shovel the driveway.
(23) I told him what to do.

We would like now to discuss a difference in the degree of complexity evidenced by Ss (19) and (22), and to show that (22) is considerably more complex than (19).

The difference between these two constructions lies in the nature of the verbs *ask* and *promise*. If we consider the information that a speaker has available when he knows a verb in his language, we see that part of this information concerns the types of structures that may be associated with the verb. That is, a verb may permit, for example, a direct object:

(25) John ate dinner.

Or it may permit complements of various sorts:

(26) John believed Bill to be a thief.
(27) John knew that Bill was hungry.

and so on. The total set of constructions permitted by a verb is part of the information that a speaker has learned and has available in using his language. Fodor, Garrett, and Bever (1968) have advanced the view that this information about the 'lexical character' of the verb is an important factor in sentential complexity. They consider that in interpreting a S, a listener must consider the lexical character of its main verb, and that 'in general, the greater the variety of deep structure configurations the lexicon associates with the main verb of a sentence, the more complicated the sentence should be.'[2] They present experimental evidence to show that increased complexity is evidenced by Ss whose main verbs have a higher number of potential syntactic structures associated with them lexically.

2 Fodor, Garrett, and Bever, "Some Syntactic Determinants of Sentential Complexity, II: Verb Structure," *Perception and Psychophysics*, 3 (1968), p. 454.

We would like to add to this view, and consider that it is not just the *number* of potential syntactic structures associated with a verb lexically that contributes to complexity, but also the nature of these structures with respect to one another. If two different structures associated with the same verb happen to require conflicting rules for their analyses, then the degree of complexity will be considerably increased. The verb *ask* is a case in point, with respect to the MDP described above.

Consider the example dealt with above:

(28) John asked Bill what to do.

We said that in order to learn to interpret this S, the child must acquire a special rule which says, 'In the case of *ask* + *wh-* + *to* + *inf vb*, violate the MDP.' But notice that *ask* also permits the structure

(29) John asked Bill to leave.

which follows the MDP, i.e., it is Bill who is to leave. To interpret this S, the child must follow the rule: 'In the case of *ask* + *to* + *inf vb*, follow the MDP.' Thus the final system which the child must acquire must contain two opposing rules for *ask:*

(30) For *ask* + *to* + *inf vb*, follow the MDP.
(31) For *ask* + *wh-* + *to* + *inf vb*, violate the MDP.

The task of acquiring two contradictory rules for the same verb certainly poses a problem of considerable difficulty.

The notion of 'same verb' must be analyzed further. Notice that *ask* is used in two different senses in (30) and (31). Ss exemplifying these two constructions are (32) and (33).

(32) John asked Bill to leave.
(33) John asked Bill what to do.

In (32) ask is used in the sense of *request* (ask_r), and in (33) it is used in the sense of *question* (ask_q). In other languages, these two verbs are distinguished lexically. In German, ask_r is *bitten*, and ask_q is *fragen*. In Russian, ask_r is *poprosit'*, and ask_q is *sprosit'*. Since Eng-

TABLE I

Three Levels of Complexity with Regard to MDP Application

Complement construction	Rule for MDP application

1. *Normal pattern*
   a. John told Bill to leave.
   b. John asked$_1$ Bill to leave.
	APPLY MDP, SUBJ = NP$_2$

2. *Consistent exception* c. John promised Bill to leave.	VIOLATE MDP, SUBJ = NP$_1$

3. *Inconsistent exception*
   d. John asked$_2$ Bill what to do.
   e. John asked$_3$ Bill (for permission) to leave.
	VIOLATE MDP, SUBJ = NP$_1$

lish has only one lexical item for these two senses of *ask,* the syntactic complexity of the word and its associated structures is increased.

The analysis of *ask* is further complicated by the fact that (32) has a second less likely interpretation, namely

(34) John asked Bill (for permission) to leave.

in which *John* is the subject of *leave*. This ambiguity was pointed out . . . in our discussion of the three semantic classes of verbs with which we are dealing:

Semantic class	Syntactic process
1. command verbs	1. complement vb relates to main clause object
2. request verbs	2. complement vb relates to main clause subject *or* object
3. *promise,* *ask*$_q$	3. complement vb relates to main clause subject

Ask$_r$ as in (32) belongs in class 2, and has both syntactic processes associated with it. *Ask*$_r$ is therefore inconsistent both within itself and with respect to *ask*$_q$, which belongs in class 3 along with *promise.*

Considering these various complications pertaining to *ask,* we propose three levels of complexity with regard to the application of the MDP.

The important constructions to note here are Ss (b), (d), and (e), with *ask* labeled ask$_1$, ask$_2$, and ask$_3$. We expect that the inconsistency between ask$_1$ on the one hand, and ask$_2$ and ask$_3$ on the other, will cause children difficulty in learning ask$_2$ and ask$_3$. We hypothesize that Ss (a) and (b), which exhibit the normal pattern, will be learned first; that (c) will be learned second; and that (d) and (e) will be learned last. For *promise* the child must learn to violate the MDP, but at least *promise* is consistent within itself.[3] For *ask* he must learn the rather curious property: Keep the MDP, but violate it some of the time. We expect this difficulty to result in relatively late acquisition of the conditions of violation.

(D) *Restrictions on a grammatical operation apply under certain limited conditions only.*

Under this heading we would like to deal with an aspect of the general question of pronominalization, and the information used by the listener who must make decisions about the reference of pronouns in the Ss that he hears. In many ways the problem is an extremely complicated one, as shown by Ross (1967) in his detailed treatment of pronominalization. If we

---

[3] *Promise* also has the characteristic that it can be followed by a direct object plus complement clause, in which case the complement verb refers to the direct object. In the S *They promised him a secretary to type his letters.* it is the secretary who will do the typing. If the indirect object *him* is omitted from this S, the resulting S is ambiguous. In *They promised a secretary to type his letters.* the subject of *type* is either *they* or *secretary,* depending on whether *secretary* is considered to be the indirect object or the direct object of *promise.* We are indebted to Karl V. Teeter for pointing out this feature of the verb *promise.*

consider some Ss which contain both a pronoun and an NP, we see that in many cases the pronoun may refer to the NP which is present elsewhere in the S:

(35) a. John knew that he was going to win the race.
    b. When he was tired, John usually took a nap.
    c. After John took a drink, he felt better.
    d. Knowing that he was going to be late bothered John.
    e. John expected Mary to like him.
    f. John's mother was disappointed in him.

In all of these Ss, the pronoun *he* or *him* may refer to *John,* i.e., identity of the pronoun with the occurring NP is possible. However, this identity is not required in the Ss of (35). The pronouns in (35) may also refer to someone else not mentioned in the S. The structure of the S does not impose a restriction on the pronoun's reference, but permits the pronoun either an identity or a nonidentity relationship with the occurring NP. Factors other than structure may be present which influence the pronoun's interpretation in a given S, such as semantic effect, or stress placement. For example, in (35b),

When he was tired, John usually took a nap.

the most likely interpretation is that *he* refers to *John,* but it can also refer to someone else, in the spirit of

(36) When the mother feels cold, the child puts on a sweater.

In (35c) and (35d),

After John took a drink, he felt better.
Knowing that he was going to be late bothered John.

the most likely interpretation again is that *he* refers to *John,* but if the pronoun is contrastively stressed, the nonidentity interpretation becomes the more likely one. The Ss of (35), then, do not restrict pronominal reference by

their structure, but exhibit both possibilities of reference.

There are cases, however, in which the structure of the S does restrict the pronoun's reference. In (37) the pronoun cannot refer to *John,* but must refer to someone else outside the S:

(37) a. He knew that John was going to win the race.
    b. He expected Mary to like John.
    c. Knowing that John was going to win the race bothered him.

Nonidentity is required in these constructions, as opposed to the constructions of (35). Restriction of pronominal reference to nonidentity is apparently the only type of structural restriction which occurs in English. We do not find Ss in which the pronoun's reference is restricted on the basis of structure to an identity relationship.

It is difficult to characterize the conditions under which this restriction applies, i.e., under which nonidentity of pronoun with NP is required. Ross (1967) treats this question in detail, and indicates that a satisfactory account covering all occurrences still remains to be worked out. For our purposes here, we do not wish to enter into a discussion of these complexities, but merely to point out that they have been discussed in the literature, and have served as our motivation for exploring the question of pronominal reference in children's grammar. Since the eventual system of rules for nonidentity that a speaker must acquire is fairly complex, we might expect that the child accomplishes the task relatively late. We wish to confine ourselves in this study to a much simpler question than that of the whole system of restrictive rules for nonidentity that the mature speaker commands. We wish to investigate only a very elementary question concerning the onset of this acquisition, namely, at what stage of development the child becomes aware that a nonidentity restriction on pronominal reference exists in his language at all. A common and simple construction exhibiting this restriction is the one illustrated in (37a):

He knew that John was going to win the race.

We will attempt to determine, for children of different ages, whether they recognize that in (37a) the pronoun cannot refer to *John,* whereas in Ss like (38), the pronoun may refer to *John.*

(38) a. If he wins the race, John will be happy.
b. John knew that he was going to win the race.

To do this they must be aware, first, of the notion of nonidentity restriction on pronominal reference, and second, they must know to apply this restriction selectively, to (37a) and not to (38). The underlying principles governing this selectivity are not completely understood, but roughly we can say that a pronoun which precedes the NP in a S, (37a) and (38a), is restricted to nonidentity when in a main clause (37a), but not when in a subordinate clause (38a). For a more specific statement, and an account of exceptions, see Ross (1967).

We hypothesize that children who have not yet learned to apply the nonidentity requirement to constructions such as (37a) will interpret Ss of this form as if the pronoun has unrestricted reference, and report for some such Ss the interpretation

(39) John knew that John was going to win the race.

Once a child has learned that a nonidentity requirement applies to Ss of this construction, he should report only the interpretation

(40) Somebody else knew that John was going to win the race.

At both stages we expect the child to interpret Ss of the form of (38) with unrestricted pronominal reference. . . .

SUMMARY

We have studied children's acquisition of four syntactic structures that are considered candidates for late acquisition according to criteria of syntactic complexity:

Structure	Difficulty
1. John is easy to see.	1. subject of sentence subject of *see*
2. John promised Bill to go.	2. subject of *go*
3. John asked Bill what to do.	3. subject of *do*
4. He knew that John was going to win the race.	4. reference of *he*

We tested the comprehension of these structures by forty children between the ages of 5 and 10. Considerable variation was found in the ages of children who knew the structures and those who did not, and we were able to draw the following conclusions about acquisition for the children in our sample. Structures 1, 2, and 3 are strongly subject to individual rate of development. Structures 1 and 2 are acquired between the ages of 5.6 and 9, and are known by all children 9 and over. Structure 3 is still imperfectly learned by some children even at age 10, and structure 4 is acquired fairly uniformly at about age 5.6.

The significance of these results lies in the surprisingly late acquisition of syntactic structures that they reveal, and in the differences that they bring to light concerning the nature of the linguistic processes studied. Contrary to the commonly held view that a child has mastered the structures of his native language by the time he reaches the age of 6, we find that active syntactic acquisition is taking place up to the age of 9 and perhaps even beyond. Second, our observations regarding *order* and *rate* of acquisition for related structures in different children are in agreement with the findings of investigators who have worked with younger children. By tracing the child's orderly progress in the acquisition of a segment of his language, we are able to observe, for a set of related structures, considerable variation in rate of acquisition in different children together with a common, shared order of acquisition. Quite simply, although we cannot say just when a child will acquire the structures in question, we can offer a reliable judgment about the relative order in which he will acquire them. Third, we find several distinct patterns of acquisition in our study, each characteristic of one or more of the test constructions. These observed differences in the way the structures are acquired point up interesting distinctions in the nature of the structures themselves. Last, the methods and general approach of this study are shown to be fruitful for investigating questions of linguistic complexity. Children at the stage of language learning which borders on adult competence can offer valuable material for studying degrees of complexity that may be otherwise difficult to detect. The differences between their grammar and adult grammar can be described in terms of the adult linguistic system, and reflect the intricacies of that system. Our understanding of linguistic complexity in general can be enhanced by inquiring into the children's underlying competence and studying these differences.

SYSTEMATIC RELATIONS OF STANDARD AND NON-STANDARD RULES IN THE GRAMMARS OF NEGRO SPEAKERS

WILLIAM LABOV   PAUL COHEN

In this paper, we will discuss the intersection of the non-standard vernacular of the urban ghettos and standard English, drawing on some preliminary data from our investigation. Although Negro speech patterns have been explained as the product of dialect mixture of two originally uniform grammars, our data do not support such a construct. We will describe some rules embodying continuous variation at all age levels, and others which represent adjustments in conditions on standard rules which have proved unstable in the history of English. The general indication of our work so far is that the differences between this dialect and standard English are greater on the surface than in the underlying grammatical structure.

Since the last Project Literacy Conference, we have continued our studies into the structural and functional conflicts between standard English and the non-standard vernacular of the urban ghettos. Perhaps one of the most difficult tasks, technically, was the completion of interviews with a random sample of 100 adults in three areas of South Central Harlem. The resistance to interviewing on the part of the most critical age groups (working class Negro men 20 to 30 years old) has reached a peak for many reasons, social and political, but by various devices we did succeed in completing the cells of our stratified sample: we are now able to compare subjects along the axes Northern vs. Southern, older vs. younger, middle class vs. working class, and male vs. female.

Reprinted with abridgment by permission of the authors from *Project Literacy Reports*, (mimeo), Cornell University, July, 1967, No. 8, 66–84.

In these face-to-face interviews we utilized our knowledge of the culture and of the factors which control language behavior to stimulate a range of language behavior from most casual to most formal styles. Many of the questions were focused upon the intersections of two or more of the "focal concerns" of lower class culture in general and also the particular concerns of the Negro people. We are analyzing these materials with particular attention to the functions for which verbal skills are positively evaluated. More immediately, we have been able to draw from these interviews a complex set of quantitative phonological and morphological variables which display the general sociolinguistic structure of the speech community. Table 1 shows some preliminary figures derived from the phonological analysis of every fourth speaker in the sample. These three variables show similar systematic patterns in the white community, but at different levels and without the North-South complication. The (r) index is essentially the percentage of final and pre-consonantal (r); the (dh) index is constructed from the frequency of fricative, affricate and stop for morphophonemic *th* initially in *this, then, that,* etc. The higher the index number, the more non-standard forms are recorded. The (ing) variable is the percentage of *-in'* forms in all occurrences of unstressed -ing. Note that these three variables illustrate certain general principles:

1. In careful speech, the middle class speakers are much closer to the prestige norm than working class speakers.

2. Both working class and middle

TABLE I

Three Phonological Variables of Non-Standard Negro Adults in South Central Harlem

	Style	*Raised in the North*	*Raised in the South*	*Middle Class*	*Working and Lower Class*
(r)	Casual	00	07	13	03
	Careful	25	08	40	09
(dh)	Casual	151	79	45	123
	Careful	59	79	26	83
(ing)	Casual	28	04	00	14
	Careful	48	13	59	22

speakers shift away from the prestige norm when they move from careful to casual speech.

3. The shift of the middle class speakers is more extreme: in casual speech they approach or surpass the working class in distance from the standard.

4. Speakers raised in the South do not participate in this set of sociolinguistic variables (*-ing* is an exception to this; here Southerners follow the same pattern at a lower level).

It is important to obtain a clear understanding of this sociolinguistic structure in approaching the more complex variables which are located at the intersection of phonological and grammatical rules, such as the simplification of consonant clusters. These are the elements which are probably most relevant to locating structural interference in reading problems. For linguists who have been raised in the tradition of categorical rules without exceptions, there is a great temptation to regularize these variables by some bold abstraction from the data. It is simple to assume that such variation as shown in Table 1 is due to mechanical dialect mixture, external to linguistic structure, and that behind all this are two pure dialects: one with stops for all *th-'s,* for example. Such an assumption is even more convenient in disposing of the frequent *-ed* forms which occur with apparent irregularity in this speech community. The process of inferring the rules for competence from the facts of performance is then simplified to the act of discarding inconvenient data. But close study of adults, adolescents and preadolescents shows that such systematic variation occurs at

all age levels; it is an inherent part of the structure of the language, and rules must be written to reflect this fact. . . .

. . . We have frequently encountered cases where sentences differ strikingly from standard English in their surface structure, yet in the final analysis appear to be the result of minor modifications of conditions upon transformational rules, or late stylistic options.

One of the most well-known characteristics of this dialect of English is the absence of the copula in the present before predicate nouns and adjectives, locatives, and comitative phrases, and the parallel absence of the forms of *to be* in the auxiliary unit *be . . . ing:*

He a friend.	He with us.
He tired.	He working with us.
He over there.	

This pattern is paralleled and reinforced by the frequent absence of *is* and *are* in questions: *Why he here? He with you?*

. . . . .

[The authors go on at this point to discuss such sentences as those above, considering regularities in usage that appear with respect to the copula:

1. *ain't* appears in the negative:
    He ain't here.
2. *was* appears in the past:
    He was here.
3. *'m* remains in the first person:
    I'm here.

(Eds.)]

We could follow similar arguments on a more complex phenomenon, the non-standard *Ain't nobody see it; ain't nobody hear it*. This differs strikingly from standard English in that the order associated with questions (tense marker and first element of the auxiliary-noun phrase-balance of the verb phrase) is here used in a declarative statement, equivalent to standard *Nobody saw it; nobody heard it*. We cannot discuss this problem in detail here, but the general outline of the argument can be presented. We first note that this form occurs only with indefinite subjects. This suggests that it is associated with the negative concord rules which produce the well-known double negative pattern. For standard English, there is a rule which moves a negative element to combine with the first indefinite; for white non-standard English, a rule which distributes the negative to all the indefinite elements of the sentence. In the case of *Ain't nobody see it,* we have a typical pleonastic form characteristic of negative concord: one negative element in the deep structure (one meaningful negative in this case) corresponding to two negatives in the surface structure.

In this case, the negative moves to the beginning of the sentence with the tense marker, and assumes the regular form *ain't;* it also distributes to *anybody* to produce *nobody*. Such a transposition of the negative might appear strange at first, until we consider the wide range of such phenomena in standard English. Adverbs which contain negative elements move with the tense marker to the beginning of the sentence as a regular stylistic device, with roughly the same emphatic (focus) significance as the non-standard form. Thus we get *Never did he come here; Scarcely did I think so; Rarely would he do that*. Finally, we can even find a standard parallel to the movement of the negative element plus tense marker without the adverb, in the more or less archaic *Nor did anybody see him*. Thus the considerations outlined here lead us to relate the non-standard *Ain't nobody see him* to the standard rules of negative attraction: first, as the absence of the limiting condition that negatives are distributed to the *first* negative only; second, as an extension of the rule that brings negative adverbs to the beginning of the sentence with reversal of

auxiliary and subject (or more simply as a continuation of the archaic standard rule with different surface formatives).

Similar arguments bring us to the conclusion that sentences such as *It ain't no cat can't get in no coop* (= There isn't any cat which *can* get in any coop) are simple modifications and extensions of standard transformational rules.

We do not mean to imply that there are no differences in the underlying structure of the language of the Negro speech community. There are two elements which appear immediately as candidates for independent phrase structure rules. One is the use of *be* to indicate generality, repeated action, or existential state in sentences such as *He be with us; They be fooling around*. We do not believe that there is any simple translation of standard rules which will produce these grammatical forms. Another such element is *done* to indicate an intensive or perfective meaning as in *The bullet done penetrate my body; I done got me a bat*. Both of these are part of an aspectual system which is plainly distinct from tense; there still remains the problem of specifying their use and limitations precisely, and then relating them to the tense system. Since there is considerable disagreement on the relative roles of tense and aspect in the standard English verbal system, it is easy to understand why there is disagreement in this area.

In approaching these grammatical rules, it is not enough to determine their relative order and relation to standard English rules. We must also say something about their relative constancy within casual and spontaneous speech, the ease with which they alternate with other rules in formal speech, and their resistance to change or correction within the schoolroom situation. Of course these characteristics of the grammatical rules of non-standard English also bear upon their position in the grammar as a whole, as well as their importance in relation to reading problems.

One approach to this question is through the techniques that were used in the study of phonological variables cited above. A first step in studying syntactic patterns is to note the existence of particular forms of interest; a second step is to place them in the total population of forms which represent the same meaning and with which they alternate. The definition of this class of complementary forms or rules is not simple in many cases; but we should certainly know how frequently pre-adolescents say *He's here* as opposed to *He here* and *He be here,* together with the frequency of the relevant adverbs and other contexts which help define this alternation. In this case, and many others, there is an inherent pattern of variation in the non-standard dialect, not reducible to any constant or fixed rule.

Recently, we have begun a series of investigations which lead more directly into the problem of estimating the firmness or depth of embedding of grammatical rules in the language of children. We have utilized the device of asking for instant repetitions of standard and non-standard sentences of varying length, which has been used effectively in studying much younger children. In this case, we have been working with a group of Negro boys, ages 11 to 14, whom we know quite well. We provide strong motivation for this task by various means, and obtain all the signs of strong effort to repeat the sentences back as heard. In general, we find that standard sentences of moderate length will be repeated without delay in the non-standard form if they contravene certain deeply embedded grammatical rules:

"I asked Alvin if he knows how to play basketball."
→"I aks Alvin do he know how to play basketball."

Even if the standard sentence is said very slowly, and repeated many times, we may obtain the non-standard form repeatedly from many of the speakers. However, this is not the result with cases where the non-standard rule seems to be relatively late in the grammar. For example, we regularly obtain such repetitions as:

"Honey, who is eleven, can't spit as far as Boo can."
→"Honey, who is eleven, can't spit as far as Boo can."
"Larry is a stupid fool."
→"Larry is a stupid fool."

In fact, in our first series of tests, 21 out of 22

cases of *is* were repeated back without omission. In contrast, half of the sentences with negatives and indefinites were repeated back with the non-standard forms.

In a later series, we found that sentences beginning with *Nobody ever* . . . were persistently produced as *Nobody never* . . . , even after many repeated attempts. No difficulties whatever were found with the simple *is* of the copula. When we add this information to our findings on the inherent variability of copula deletion in actual speech, and the structural arguments given above, we are forced to the conclusion that the presence or absence of *is* and *are* is governed by the operation of a low-level rule controlled by variable stylistic factors.

The behavior produced in response to the memory test leads us to a more far-reaching conclusion about the linguistic structure available to our subjects. We can ask, what linguistic competence is required to explain the rapid repetition:

A "I asked Alvin if he knows how to play basketball."
B →"I aks Alvin do he know how to play basketball."

In the most obvious view, we can observe that the subject failed to perform the task required. But we cannot overlook the fact that B is the correct equivalent of A; it has the same meaning and is produced by the non-standard rule which is the nearest equivalent to the standard rule. In the standard form, the order of the yes-no question is re-reversed when it is embedded with the complementizer *if* = 'whether or not.'

(A1) I asked Alvin - # - Q - he knows how to play basketball #
(A2) I asked Alvin - # - Q - does he know how to play basketball #
(A3) I asked Alvin if he knows how to play basketball.

In the non-standard form, the order of the yes-no question is preserved when it is embedded without a complementizer.

(B1) I aks Alvin - # - Q - he knows how to play basketball #

(B2) I aks Alvin - # - Q - do he know how to play basketball #

(B3) I aks Alvin do he know how to play basketball.

Thus the original *Q* of the deep structure is represented in the standard sentence as *if,* and in the non-standard sentence as reversal of auxiliary and subject noun phrase. The non-standard rules differ from the standard only in the absence of the *if*-complementizer placement A3.

Since the listener does perform the translation, it is clear that he does understand the standard sentence. He then rapidly produces the correct non-standard equivalent B3. Understanding here must mean perception, analysis and storage of the sentence in some relatively abstract form. If the non-standard were converted to standard, it would mean the *addition* of the *if*-complementizer rule. But as standard is converted to non-standard, we can only infer that the perceived sentence is decoded at least to the depth of A2-B2 from the point of view of production, but at least to A1-B1 from the point of view of perception and understanding. . . .

In the first part of this paper, we showed that there are general principles which govern the phonological shifting of middle class and working class speakers as they move towards and away from standard English. It may be argued that in Harlem both standard and non-standard rules are part of a larger linguistic structure which governs the shift between them. The data on syntactic behavior are not yet rich enough for us to show such systematic alternation, and we do not argue that it necessarily follows the same pattern. We do argue, however, that standard and non-standard syntactic rules can be shown to be variants of slightly more general rules. Furthermore, the competence of native speakers of the non-standard vernacular clearly includes the ability to perceive, abstract and re-produce the meaning of many standard forms which they do not produce. It is reasonable to assume that a single grammar can be constructed which accounts systematically for the syntactic variation inherent in all styles of the speech of this community.

THE EFFECTS OF TRAINING PROCEDURES
UPON THE ACQUISITION OF
CONSERVATION OF WEIGHT

IAN D. SMITH

One aspect of Piaget's developmental theory of thinking which has provoked considerable research effort is the nature of the transition from preoperational to operational thinking. The distinctive feature of the transition, occurring at about the age of 7 years, is said to be the child's newly acquired ability to perform mental operations. The application of the principles characteristic of logic and mathematics to concrete problems now becomes possible for the child. Also, as a consequence of being able to reverse mental operations, the child can understand the concept of conservation—the fact that an object's weight, for instance, remains constant despite changes in its physical shape.

Since the concept of conservation has been closely associated by Piaget (1952) with the onset of operational thinking, it has become the dependent variable in a considerable number of experimental studies during the past decade. During a period of research at Piaget's Geneva laboratory, Jan Smedslund (1959) conducted a study designed to determine the influence of two treatment conditions upon the acquisition of conservation of weight. The two treatments were reinforced practice—achieved by demonstrating on a pair of scales that objects do not change their weight despite changes in shape—and a combination of the reinforced practice technique and the addition or subtraction of a small piece to or from one of two objects. A control group took no part in either of the two

Reprinted by permission of The Society for Research in Child Development, Inc., from *Child Development*, 1968, **39**, 515–26. © 1968 by The Society for Research in Child Development, Inc. All rights reserved.

practice sessions. Smedslund found that a considerable, but unspecified, amount of learning took place in both of the experimental groups and that there was no significant difference between them, although the group which received only reinforced practice trials performed slightly better.

This finding differs from that of Wohlwill (1959), who reported an insignificant, but suggestive, superiority of a group receiving addition/subtraction training when compared with the performance of a group trained directly with deformed objects. However, this discrepancy may have been caused by either of two factors: first, the difference in the dimension studied, Wohlwill being concerned with conservation of number while Smedslund studied the dimension of weight; second, the lack of two clearly differentiated conditions in Smedslund's experiment.

In the accounts of subsequent experiments, Smedslund (1961a, 1961b, 1961d, 1961e, 1961f, 1962) has proposed and tested the hypothesis that the transition to operational thinking takes place after "cognitive conflict" has been experienced by the child. He conceives of cognitive conflict as being similar to Festinger's (1957) "cognitive dissonance." The conflict is said to occur when the addition/subtraction and the deformation conceptual frameworks or schemata come into contact. If a child believes that the lengthening of a piece of plasticine makes it heavier (because it is now longer) and yet knows that subtracting a piece from the object makes it lighter, then in those cases where both of these schemata are activated with precisely the same strength, cognitive conflict will occur. This conflict is sometimes accompanied by such overt signs as hesitation, looking back and forth, tension, and uneasiness. Smedslund has successfully employed the addition/subtraction method to accelerate the concepts of conservation of weight and substance.

The second experimental procedure which has been successful in accelerating the concept of conservation has involved verbal instruction of the principle of conservation, together with a demonstration of reversibility. In a well-controlled study of conservation of number, Beilin (1965) found that the "verbal rule instruction" method was the only one of four experimental treatments which facilitated the learning process. Furthermore, Kohnstamm (1963) claims to have accelerated the concept of class inclusion by applying an intensive learning program involving explanation of the rule. Also relevant is the finding of Gruen (1965) that a group which undertook addition/subtraction trials plus verbal pretraining performed significantly better on a conservation-of-number posttest than did a control group which was given no verbal pretraining. Finally, in another experiment concerned with number conservation, Wallach, Wall, and Anderson (1967) argued that recognizing reversibility is necessary for conservation to develop.

The main purpose of the present study was to determine the relative efficiency of Smedslund's addition/subtraction method and Beilin's verbal rule instruction method in accelerating the development of the concept of conservation of weight. The stimulus materials, as well as other aspects of the experimental design, were standardized so as to render the training procedures directly comparable. A second concern of this study was to examine the influence of these experimental treatments on children at different stages of cognitive development. Those subjects who undertook the training procedures were classified on the basis of a conservation pretest as being either consistent nonconservers or transitional conservers who had reached an intermediate stage between nonconserver and consistent conserver.

The purpose of including these Ss was to ascertain the effects of training on the development of a concept which is at a formative stage.

It was predicted that the various training methods would have more influence on these Ss than on consistent nonconservers, particularly upon the group trained with the addition/subtraction procedure, since "cognitive conflict" should be aroused more readily in these Ss.

A further objective was to investigate Smedslund's claim that the concept of conservation is resistant to the countersuggestion involved in apparent nonconservation. Briefly, Smedslund (1961c) asserts, and presents evidence which suggests, that once a child is genuinely conserving he will resist the suggestion that a change in the shape of an object alters its weight. This claim gains support from Inhelder's (1962) view that a conserving child does not revert to an explanation of conservation based on the object's perceptual features, such as length and height, which were previously used to arrive at an incorrect judgment of nonconservation.

METHOD

Subjects

Tests were performed on 139 subjects, comprising three first-grade classes and one second-grade class at Greenacre Public School, which is situated in the western area of Sydney. Of the total number of subjects tested, nine were omitted from the experimental procedure, seven of them because they failed to demonstrate understanding of the concepts of "heavier," "lighter," and "the same weight." The remaining two Ss were omitted toward the end of the main testing session because their criterion category of transitional conservers had been filled and only nonconservers were required for the training procedures. The other 130 Ss consisted of 10 children who were consistent conservers in the pretest and posttest, and who undertook the countersuggestion stage only as informal conservers, as well as 120 Ss divided equally into 60 each of nonconservers and transitional conservers. These were randomly divided into four groups of 15 Ss, each group undertaking one of the four treatment conditions. The mean ages for the nonconservers, transitional conservers, and conservers were 6 years and 6 months, 6 years and 8 months, and 6 years and 7 months, respectively, with corresponding standard deviations of 6.6, 5.9, and 6.3 months. The number of boys and girls in each treatment group was not controlled, since there is no evidence of a sex difference in the age at which the concept of conservation is acquired.

Apparatus

The main piece of apparatus consisted of a primitive balance constructed from a children's model-building set. The dimensions of the balance were as follows: base, $5\frac{1}{2} \times 2\frac{1}{2} \times 1\frac{1}{2}$ inches; overall height, 10 inches; length of supporting arm, $12\frac{1}{2}$ inches; two pans, $2\frac{1}{2} \times 2\frac{1}{2}$ inches each; length of each of eight pieces of nylon, $5\frac{1}{2}$ inches; distance from supporting arm to center of each pan, 5 inches. The objects weighed on the pans were pieces of plasticine. Two pieces each of red, yellow, green, blue, brown, and white plasticine were employed, each piece weighing approximately $\frac{1}{2}$ ounce. The plasticine was rolled into a variety of shapes on a masonite board, of dimensions $13 \times 6\frac{1}{4}$ inches, with a cream face.

Procedure

Each child was tested individually. After introducing the child to the experimental situation, E completed a preliminary inquiry to insure that each S understood the meaning of the concepts of "heavier," "lighter," and "the same weight." Each child was asked the standard question, "Do you think this one [pointing to one of the plasticine objects] weighs heavier than, or the same as, or lighter than this one?" This inquiry proved to be generally easy for the children, only seven of the Ss failing at this stage.

The conservation-of-weight pretest consisted of five nonreinforced trials:

1. Two equal balls of the same color, one rolled into a sausage.
2. The sausage rolled into a snake.
3. The snake made into a ring.
4. Another two equal balls of the same color, one ball flattened into a cake.
5. The cake flattened into a pancake.

On the basis of his results on the pretest, each child was classified as being a nonconserver, transitional conserver, or conserver according to the following criteria:

Nonconserver: No correct responses, together with no correct explanations of conservation following Smedslund's (1961b) definitions.

Transitional conserver: At least one correct response.

Conserver: All five correct responses, as well as five correct explanations.

STAGE 1: TRAINING

Four treatment conditions were employed in the present experiment. There were three training procedures: (*a*) addition/subtraction (A.S.), (*b*) reinforced practice (R.P.), and (*c*) verbal rule instruction (V.R.I.). All training was administered in one session, lasting in all from about 15 to 20 minutes.

In addition, a control group for each of the two criterion groups of nonconservers and transitional conservers undertook no training whatsoever. Instead, each S was requested to draw a picture, using colored pencils, of himself and his family in a picnic scene. The training procedures were as follows:

Addition/Subtraction. This method was a replication of the first of three sessions employed by Smedslund (1961e). Only one session was used because of Smedslund's claim that very little change occurred from Session I to Session III. As was the case during the pretest, E remained as neutral as possible to all of the S's responses. The child was always presented with the information that the two identical objects weighed the same. Each of the 12 items consisted of one deformation and either the addition or subtraction of a small piece of plasticine, followed by the standard question; then of the reverse transformation of either the addition/subtraction or the opposite deformation, also followed by the standard question. For instance, the first item involved a transformation of one sausage into a much thicker sausage, together with the addition of a small piece of plasticine to this deformed object, followed by the subtraction of that piece of plasticine. Each of the 12 items is presented in Table 1. The

TABLE I

Items in the A.S. Training Procedure

Item No.	Objects	1st Transformation	2nd Transformation
1	Yellow sausages	Much thicker sausage $+ V$	$- V$
2	Red logs	$+ V$ a little thinner log	Equal logs
3	White snakes	Much thinner snake $- V$	Equal snakes
4	Green cakes	$- K$ ball	$+ K$
5	Blue blocks	Ball $+ K$	Equal blocks
6	Brown balls	$+ K$ slightly squeezed ball	$- K$
7	Green snakes	A little thicker snake $- V$	Equal snakes
8	Red sausages	$- V$ snake	$+ V$
9	White logs	A little thinner log $+ V$	$- V$
10	Brown blocks	$+ K$ a little higher block	Equal blocks
11	Yellow cakes	Much thicker cake $- K$	Equal cakes
12	Blue balls	$- K$ slightly squeezed ball	$+ K$

Note. $+$ = addition; $-$ = subtraction; V = deformed object; K = undeformed object.

deformations were either very small (e.g., a log squeezed into a little thinner log), medium sized, or large. If a piece was removed from the object, it was placed nearby on the board; if a piece was to be added, it was stuck on top of the object. The additions and subtractions in the same item refer to the same piece of plasticine.

Reinforced practice. In this method, the same objects were employed as in the A.S. procedure outlined above. After S was told that both objects weighed the same, one object was deformed. When S had answered the standard question, the two objects were weighed in order to demonstrate their equality. The S's answers were not commented upon, nor was he asked to explain them. The order of presentation of the 12 items was the same as that for the A.S. procedure.

Verbal rule instruction. This treatment condition was a modification of Beilin's V.R.I. procedure (1965). As in the previous two training methods, the standard order of presentation of the objects was maintained. After deforming one of the two objects, E posed the standard question. An incorrect response prompted the following statement of the principle of conservation of weight, together with a demonstration of reversibility: "If we start with a . . . [e.g., sausage, log] like this one [pointing to undeformed object] and we don't put any pieces of plasticine on it or take any pieces away from it, then it still weighs the same even though it looks different. See, I can make it back into a . . . , so it hasn't really changed." In this procedure there were also 12 trials.

A conservation posttest, identical to the pretest, followed each treatment condition.

STAGE 2: COUNTERSUGGESTION

The second or countersuggestion stage of the experiment was administered only to those Ss who reached the criterion of five correct responses ("same") in the posttest. The countersuggestion was achieved by manipulating one of the pans of the primitive balance as one of the objects was placed upon it, with the result that this pan was forced to the table and, conversely, the other pan was raised further from the table. Thus the deformed object could be made to appear as though it weighed more or less than the undeformed object merely by applying an extra amount of force to one of the pans when the object was placed on it. Resistance to countersuggestion was defined (after Smedslund, 1961c) as the omission of any reference to the perceptual "change" in the weight of an object after a change in its shape had taken place.

Before each of the five trials, the child was informed again that both objects weighed the

TABLE 2

Posttest Means and t Statistics for the Three Training Groups Compared with the Control Group of Nonconservers

Item	Treatment Condition			
	A.S.	*R.P.*	*V.R.I.*	*Control*
$\overline{X}$ post	0.07	0.47	2.45	0.20
t	−0.32	0.63	5.37*	. . .

* Significant beyond the .01 level.

same. The deformation of one object was followed by the standard question which was succeeded by the demonstration of apparent nonconservation. After each of the five demonstrations, the child was asked: "Why do you think the . . . [deformed object] weighs heavier [or lighter]?" The five trials were made up of the three employed by Smedslund (1961c) with two additional trials, as follows:

1. Two brown balls, one rolled into an apparently lighter sausage.
2. Two red blocks, one squashed into an apparently heavier cake.
3. Two green sausages, one rolled into an apparently lighter ball.
4. Two yellow snakes, one squashed into an apparently lighter sausage.
5. Two white cakes, one squashed into an apparently heavier pancake.

The order of the direction of the "change" in weight (i.e., from "same" to "heavier" or "lighter") was determined so that no consistent sequence of responses could be correctly given by the subject.

Finally, at least 1 week after the main testing session, a delayed posttest was administered to all those who had participated in the countersuggestion trials. In order to avoid the possibility of direct retention of the individual items of the posttest and countersuggestion trials influencing performance on the delayed posttest, five different trials were employed as follows:

1. Two snakes, one rolled into a sausage.
2. One snake and a sausage, the sausage rolled into a ball.
3. One snake and a ball, the ball rolled into a ring.

4. Two pancakes, one squeezed into a cake.
5. One pancake and a cake, the cake rolled into a ball.

Other than the modified stimulus objects, the procedure was identical with that of the pre- and posttests. This final session lasted no longer than 5 minutes per subject.

RESULTS

The hypotheses for the first or training phase of the experiment were tested separately for the nonconservers and for the transitional conservers. A type I error rate of .05 was adopted in testing all null hypotheses.

STAGE 1: TRAINING

Nonconservers. The posttest means of the four groups are presented in Table 2. Since the overall differences between the means were significant,[1] the three training group means were compared individually with the control group mean by using a technique outlined by Winer (1962, pp. 88–89).

There was found to be no difference between the posttest performance of the group of nonconservers trained by the A.S. method and the control group of nonconservers. Furthermore, contrary to Smedslund's observation, no *S*s manifested even the slightest improvement in

[1] The original *F* value was significant at the .01 level. However, the assumption of homogeneity of variance was violated. Nevertheless, an analysis of variance which corrects for heterogeneity of variance (Winer, 1962, pp. 240–241) produced an *F* value of 14.13, which is greater than the critical value of 8.86 at the .01 level of significance.

TABLE 3

Pre- and Posttest Means, Gain Scores, and t Statistics for the Transitional Conservers

Item	A.S.	R.P.	V.R.I.	Control
$\overline{X}$ pre	2.07	1.47	2.20	1.67
$\overline{X}$ post	2.47	3.33	4.27	1.33
G	0.40	1.87	2.07	−0.33
t	1.36	4.46*	4.09*	. . .

* Significant beyond the .01 level.

their understanding of the concept as a result of A.S. training.

Similarly, no difference was observed between the posttest performance of the R.P. group and the control group. This finding was unexpected, since the R.P. method was considered to be a simple rote-learning task. However, the result may have been caused by the primitive nature of the balance. The pieces of nylon to which the two pans were tied tended to slip unevenly with the weights being placed on the pans. Consequently, one pan may have appeared to be lower than another when, in fact, both pieces of plasticine weighed the same. In other words the correct response ("same") may not have been consistently reinforced.

The group which received V.R.I. training, however, did perform significantly better than the control group. The obtained t statistic of 5.37 was larger than the value of 2.79 required to reject the null hypothesis at the .01 level of significance. This finding lends support to the result that was reported by Beilin.

Transitional conservers. The pre- and posttest means of the four groups of transitional conservers are presented in Table 3. The gain scores are also included in the table. Since the assumption of homogeneity of within-class regression was violated, an analysis of covariance was replaced by an analysis of variance of the gain scores. It was found that there were no significant differences among the pretest means, indicating that no single group was placed at a disadvantage prior to training. The obtained F value of 9.27 was significant at the .01 level, showing that there were differences in the

amount of improvement of the four groups. The gain scores of the three training groups were then compared individually with that of the control group.

As was the case with the corresponding groups of nonconservers, there was no significant difference between the improvement of the A.S. trained group and the control group of transitional conservers. Since the observed t value of 1.36 is less than the critical value of 2.11 at the .05 level of significance, the null hypothesis must be retained. This finding proved to be contrary to the prediction based on Smedslund's experience.

On the other hand, the R.P. group did improve to a significantly greater degree than the control group, the obtained t value of 4.09 exceeding 2.79, the critical value at the .01 level of significance. Four Ss satisfied the posttest criterion of five correct responses and qualified for the second or countersuggestion stage. In addition, the group trained with V.R.I. showed significantly greater improvement than the control group, with a t value of 4.46 being significant at the .01 level, further confirming Beilin's results. Furthermore, a majority of both R.P. and V.R.I. Ss who qualified for the countersuggestion phase gave fewer than three correct responses in the conservation pretest.

STAGE 2: COUNTERSUGGESTION

The second phase of the experiment was concerned with the relative effects of the countersuggestion trials. The effects were gauged by two variables. The first was a measure of resistance to countersuggestion, while the second

TABLE 4

Mean Scores and Size of Groups in the Countersuggestion Phase

Criterion Group	Countersuggestion Trials	Delayed Posttest	No. in Group
A.S.	2.80	2.00	5
R.P.	2.00	2.75	4
V.R.I.	1.23	2.77	13
I.C.	2.20	0.90	10

was the number of correct responses on the delayed posttest of conservation of weight. The mean scores, together with the number of Ss in each of the four criterion groups, are contained in Table 4.

An analysis of variance of the countersuggestion means indicated that there were no significant differences among the four groups. Similarly, another analysis of variance found no significant differences among the delayed posttest performances of the four groups.

Of particular interest is the finding that the informal conservers were no more resistant to countersuggestion than were those Ss who had been trained on R.P. items. Contrary to Smedslund's experience, neither group proved to be generally resistant to the countersuggestion. The typical correct explanation found by Smedslund (i.e., "you must have taken a little away from that one") was almost nonexistent in the present experiment. Instead, the most common explanations referred incorrectly to perceptual features of the objects (e.g., "that one is heavier because it is longer") or correctly, to the fact that one pan was lower or higher than the other.

Finally, the finding of a regression to nonconservation by a majority of Ss as measured by the delayed posttest responses and explanations was most unexpected. That the influence of the countersuggestion procedure has been maintained despite the lapse of a considerable period of time emphasizes the general lack of resistance to countersuggestion.

DISCUSSION

Two major conclusions may be drawn from stage 1 of this experiment. In the first place,

Smedslund's success with the A.S. method of accelerating the concept of conservation was not repeated. Second, a procedure involving V.R.I. in the principle of conservation and demonstration of reversibility, which was employed with some success by Beilin, proved to be an effective training method.

The A.S. method failed to accelerate conservation not only for the nonconservers but also, more surprisingly, for the transitional conservers. If, as Smedslund claims, the A.S. method arouses cognitive conflict, then it would be expected that a child who has reached a transitional stage in his cognitive development would readily have this conflict aroused. Furthermore, the readiness of a transitional conserver might be predicted to be superior to that of a consistent nonconserver. There is no evidence in the present findings, however, to support either of these predictions. Future research in this area might profitably be directed toward the issues of the particular developmental stage and stimulus conditions which most readily arouse cognitive conflict.

For both nonconservers and transitional conservers, the V.R.I. method resulted in improvement in conservation performance that was significantly greater than that of the respective control groups. Furthermore, seven of the nine transitional Ss who scored five correct posttest responses also gave five correct explanations of conservation. One of the four nonconserving Ss to satisfy the posttest criterion also achieved this standard. Thus, the findings of Kohnstamm and, more directly, of Beilin have been substantiated in that a procedure involving the repeated statement of a guiding principle has accelerated the formation of a concept in a relatively brief period of training.

Unlike Smedslund's interpretation of the process of cognitive development, Beilin does not attribute any complex theoretical significance to the efficiency of this method. He merely asserts that the most salient feature of the procedure is that it supplies the child with a "model" for the solution of the problem. Further, the model is expressed in verbal terms. One problem with this interpretation is the common finding of a lack of transfer to other conservation dimensions by children who have manifested conservation in one dimension. This finding suggests that the model is restricted initially to one or possibly two dimensions of conservation. That conservation extends gradually to stimuli of increasing complexity implies also that the model is restricted to certain stimuli, at least in the early stages of operational thinking.

In the second or countersuggestion phase, no difference was observed between the performance on the countersuggestion trials of the informal conservers and the *S*s trained by the R.P. method. Thus, support has not been obtained for the view that resistance to countersuggestion is a feature of a "genuine" concept of conservation. On the contrary, the informal conservers were no more resistant to countersuggestion than were those *S*s who had performed well in a simple rote-learning task.

Perhaps resistance to countersuggestion might be demonstrated in another way. After manipulating the balance so that one deformed object appears to weigh more or less than the other object, *E* might ask the question, "Does this object weigh more than, the same as, or less than that one?" Resistance to countersuggestion could then be defined as resistance to the misleading perceptual cues of the relative positions of the two pans, and demonstrated by *S*'s maintaining that the two objects still weigh the same. The suggested measure of resistance to countersuggestion may support Smedslund's claim that resistance is characteristic of genuine conservers.

The delayed posttest yielded no significant differences among the four criterion groups. The time lapse of at least 1 week between the countersuggestion trials and the delayed posttest had no differential influence on restoring the conservation responses of the four groups. This finding is especially surprising in the case of the informal conserving group. It had been expected that the effect of the week-long lapse would have been to reinstate the conservation response as dominant in the response hierarchy. That this did not occur indicates that the countersuggestion procedure had successfully trained a response contradictory to conservation of weight, one which was still manifest a week later.

REFERENCES

Beilin, H. Learning and operational convergence in logical thought development. *Journal of Experimental Child Psychology,* 1965, 2, 317–339.

Festinger, L. A. *A theory of cognitive dissonance.* New York: Row, Peterson, 1957.

Gruen, G. E. Experiences affecting the development of number conservation in children. *Child Development,* 1965, 36, 963–979.

Inhelder, B. Some aspects of Piaget's genetic approach to cognition. In W. Kessen & C. Kuhlman (Eds.), Thought in the young child. *Monograph of Society for Research in Child Development,* 1962, 27 (No. 2), 19–34.

Kohnstamm, G. A. An evaluation of part of Piaget's theory. *Acta Psychologica,* 1963, 21, 313–356.

Piaget, J. *The child's conception of number.* Translated by C. Gattegno & F. M. Hodgson. London: Routledge & Kegan Paul, 1952.

Smedslund, J. Apprentissage des notions de la conservation et de la transitivité du poids. *Etudes d'Epistémologie génétique,* 1959, 9, 85–124. Cited by J. Smedslund (1961 a).

Smedslund, J. The acquisition of conservation of substance and weight in children, I: Introduction. *Scandinavian Journal of Psychology,* 1961, 2, 11–20. (a)

Smedslund, J. The acquisition of conservation of substance and weight in children, II: External reinforcement of conservation of weight and of the operations of addition and subtraction. *Scandinavian Journal of Psychology,* 1961, 2, 71–84. (b)

Smedslund, J. The acquisition of conservation of substance and weight in children, III: Extinction of conservation of weight acquired "normally" and by means of empirical controls on a balance. *Scandinavian Journal of Psychology,* 1961, 2, 85–87. (c)

Smedslund, J. The acquisition of conservation of substance and weight in children, IV: Attempt at extinction of the visual components of the weight concept. *Scandinavian Journal of Psychology,* 1961, 2, 153–155. (d)

Smedslund, J. The acquisition of conservation of substance and weight in children, V: Practice in conflict situations without external reinforcement. *Scandinavian Journal of Psychology,* 1961, 2, 156–160. (e)

Smedslund, J. The acquisition of conservation of substance and weight in children, VI: Practice on continuous vs. discontinuous material in problem situations without external reinforce-ment. *Scandinavian Journal of Psychology,* 1961, 2, 203–210. (f)

Smedslund, J. The acquisition of conservation of substance and weight in children, VII: Conservation of discontinuous quantity and the operations of adding and taking away. *Scandinavian Journal of Psychology,* 1962, 3, 69–77.

Wallach, L., Wall, A. J., & Anderson, L. Number conservation: the roles of reversibility, addition/subtraction, and misleading perceptual cues. *Child Development,* 1967, 38, 425–442.

Winer, B. J. *Statistical principles in experimental design.* New York: McGraw-Hill, 1962.

Wohlwill, J. F. Un essai d'apprentissage dans le domaine de la conservation du nombre. *Etudes d'Epistémologie génétique,* 1959, 9, 125–135. Reported in J. Smedslund (1961a).

NUMBER CONSERVATION: THE ROLES
OF REVERSIBILITY, ADDITION-SUBTRACTION,
AND MISLEADING PERCEPTUAL CUES

LISE WALLACH   A. JACK WALL   LORNA ANDERSON

The present experiment was designed to answer several questions arising from a previous study (Wallach & Sprott, 1964) in which number conservation was induced in children. The *S*s in that experiment had been 6- and 7-year-olds who recognized that the number of a set of dolls and the number of a set of beds were equal when there was one doll in each bed, but who said the number was different when subsequently, before their eyes, the dolls were taken out of the beds and placed closer together. The procedure which led them to recognize that the number remained equal was to show them repeatedly that the dolls could be fitted back into the beds again when they had been placed closer together or further apart, though not when a doll or a bed was added or taken away.

The results of this previous experiment were interpreted as indicating that conservation under operations that remove defining attributes could be induced through experience with reversibility of these operations. However, it has been proposed (Wohlwill & Lowe, 1962; Smedslund, 1962) that experience with addition and subtraction may be critical for conservation, and such experience, as well as experience with reversibility, was involved in the training procedure. Our first question, therefore, was whether conservation could be induced by training in reversibility alone—that is, whether the procedure would still be effective if it showed only

Reprinted by permission of Lise Wallach, A. Jack Wall, and The Society for Research in Child Development, Inc., from *Child Development*, 1967, **38,** 425–42. © 1967 by The Society for Research in Child Development, Inc. All rights reserved.

that the dolls could be fit back into the beds again when they had been put closer together or further apart and did not show what happened when a doll or bed was added or removed.

Secondly, we wished to see whether conservation could be induced by training in addition and subtraction alone without training in reversibility. We thought that the answer might throw some light not only on the question of the effectiveness of experience in addition and subtraction itself, but also on the suggestion made by Zimiles (1963) that a brief experimental procedure which appeared to induce number conservation might do so only because a number set was aroused by the procedure. Addition and subtraction should certainly be at least as capable of arousing such a set as reversibility.

The earlier study had found that the induced number conservation transferred readily to new sets of objects. We now wished to see whether a wider kind of transfer might also occur; specifically, whether number conservation induced by experience with the dolls and beds would transfer to conservation of the amount of a liquid. Much direct transfer of this kind seemed unlikely, so we included a transitional series of tasks less and less like the dolls and beds and more and more like the liquids, for use when the children did not transfer directly.

A final question that we hoped to answer, if possible, was whether conservation of the quantity of a liquid could itself be induced by training in reversibility. The procedures were thus arranged so that children who did not acquire conservation of the quantity of a liquid through transfer were given an opportunity to acquire it through reversibility training.

METHOD

Subjects

The *S*s were 56 children whose ages ranged from 6 years and 1 month to 7 years and 8 months with a mean of 6 years and 11 months. They were all in the first grade of a predominantly middle-class public school in a small university town.

Pretests

The child was seated at a table with *E,* and another adult sat nearby recording.

DOLL PRETEST   Six dolls and six beds were on the table, the beds lined up and the dolls in a pile in front of them. The *S* was asked to put one doll in each bed. The *E* then asked, "Are there more dolls than beds?" If *S* said there were not, *E* went on, "Are there more beds than dolls?" If *S* again said there were not, *E* continued, "Are there the same number of dolls as beds?"

If all three questions were answered appropriately, *E* said, "Now watch what I do." One by one, he took each doll out of its bed and placed it in a row in front of the beds but closer together, so that the last bed had no doll in front of it. Then *E* asked, "Now are there the same number of dolls as beds?" If *S* said there were, *E* asked, "How do you tell?" If *S* said there were not, *E* asked, "Which are more?"

LIQUID PRETEST   The *E* filled two identical, narrow glasses to the very top from a pitcher of green-colored water. The child was asked whether both glasses were filled exactly to the top, and adjustments were made if necessary. The *E* then asked, "Is there the same amount to drink in each glass?"

If *S* said there was, *E* again said, "Now watch what I do." Explaining what he was doing as he did it, he poured the water from one of the two identical, narrow glasses into a low,

wide glass. Then, indicating the two glasses with water in them, *E* asked, "Now is there the same amount to drink in this glass and in this glass?" If *S* said there was, *E* asked, "How do you tell?" If *S* said there was not, *E* asked, "Which has more?"

Classification of Subjects

On the basis of their performance on the pretest, the *S*s were classified into five categories, as follows:

1. Not meeting criteria: The *S*s who did not assert equality between the dolls and beds when the dolls were in the beds, or between the amount of water in the two identical, filled glasses (three *S*s), or who failed to follow instructions (one *S*). Placement in this category precluded placement in any other.

2. Conservation: The *S*s who asserted both that the number of dolls was the same as the number of beds when the dolls were closer together, and that the amount of liquid in the wide glass was the same as that in the narrow one.

3. Nonconservation. The *S*s who asserted neither that the number of dolls was the same as the number of beds when the dolls were closer together, nor that the amount of liquid in the wide glass was the same as that in the narrow one.

4. Partial conservation—dolls: The *S*s who asserted that the number of dolls was the same as the number of beds when the dolls were closer together, but who did not assert that the amount of liquid in the wide glass was the same as that in the narrow one.

5. Partial conservation—liquid: The *S*s who did not assert that the number of dolls was the same as the number of beds when the dolls were closer together, but who did assert that the amount of liquid in the wide glass was the same as that in the narrow one.

Participation in the experiment ended with the pretest for *S*s in the not meeting criteria and conservation categories. The *S*s in the other categories received additional training and testing as follows (details of the procedures will be described below): The nonconservation *S*s and the partial conservation—liquid *S*s were divided

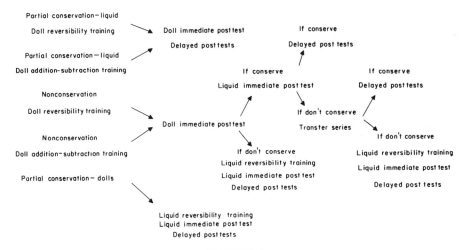

FIGURE I

Sequence of procedures for different groups.

within each category by alternate assignment (the order of *S*s was at the convenience of the teacher) into groups receiving doll reversibility training and doll addition-subtraction training. Immediately following the training, both groups were given a doll posttest which, except for the delayed posttest, was the end of the experiment for the partial conservation—liquid *S*s. Nonconservation *S*s who did not show conservation in the doll posttest were then given liquid reversibility training and subsequently a liquid posttest. Nonconservation *S*s who did show conservation in the doll posttest were immediately given the liquid posttest to test for direct transfer. If direct transfer did not occur, they were then given training on the transfer series, and, if this also did not lead to liquid conservation, they were given liquid reversibility training, and the liquid posttest was repeated. The *S*s in the partial conservation—dolls category were given liquid reversibility training and then the liquid posttest immediately following the pretest. Nonconservation and both partial conservation groups of *S*s were given both doll and liquid delayed posttests 2–6 weeks after the training. See Figure 1.

Doll Training Procedures

DOLL REVERSIBILITY TRAINING   As in the pretest, *S* was again asked to put one of the six

dolls in each of the six beds. Then *E* took the dolls out of the beds and put them closer together. This time, however, *E* asked, "Do you think a doll can be put back in every bed now? Or will there be a bed without a doll? Or a doll without a bed?" Regardless of *S*'s answer, he was then asked to try to put a doll back in each bed.

When the dolls were back in the beds, *E* once more took them out and now placed them further apart, so that the last doll had no bed behind it. The *S* was asked the same questions concerning the possibility of putting the dolls back in the beds and then again asked to try to put them back.

This procedure was repeated, with the dolls being placed closer than the beds one time and further the next, until *S* had correctly predicted four times in succession that the dolls could be put back in the beds.

DOLL ADDITION-SUBTRACTION TRAINING   The *S* was again asked to put one of the six dolls in each of the six beds. Then, however, a low screen was placed between *S* and the beds in such a way that the beds were effectively hidden. (The screen was used so that *S* could not simply rely on perception to tell whether there was a doll in each bed, but he would have to make use of his knowledge of dolls or beds being taken away or added.) The *E* said, "I'm going to take one doll away," and he reached behind the screen and took a doll out of its bed. Indicating a box with one doll in it at S's side, E gave the doll to S, saying, "Would you put it in this box?" when S had complied, E asked, "Do you think there is a doll in every bed now? Or is there a bed without a doll? Or a doll without a bed?" Regardless of S's answer, the screen was then removed, and he was allowed to see that there was one bed without a doll.

The screen was replaced, and E said, "Now would you give me one doll from the box and I'll see if I can put it in a bed." The E took the doll which S gave him and placed it, behind the screen, into the empty bed. Then E asked, "Do you think every doll is in a bed now? Or is there a doll without a bed? Or a bed without a doll?" After S answered, the screen was again removed, and he was allowed to see that every doll was in a bed, with no beds left over.

After this, the screen was again put back, and E said, "Would you please give me one doll from the box again, and I'll see if I can put it in a bed again." The doll which S handed E was laid down, behind the screen, next to the row of beds. Then E asked again, "Do you think every doll is in a bed now? Or is there a doll without a bed? Or a bed without a doll?" After S answered, the screen was again taken away.

The screen was replaced, and E said, "Now I'm going to take one doll away again." He took the doll that was lying on the table without a bed from behind the screen and gave it to S, saying, "Would you put it in the box?" Then E asked, "Do you think there is a doll for every bed now? Or is there a bed without a doll? Or a doll without a bed?" After S answered, the screen was taken away again.

This sequence was repeated until S had correctly described the situation behind the screen four times in succession.

Immediate Posttests

DOLL IMMEDIATE POSTTEST   The six dolls were again in the six beds standing in a row. (This was automatically the case at the end of the reversibility training; E added or took away where necessary to make it the case at the end

of addition-subtraction training.) As in the pretest, E took the dolls out of the beds and put them closer together so that the last bed had no doll in front of it. Then E said, "Now I'll ask you something else again. Are there the same number of dolls as beds?" If S said there were, E asked, "How do you tell?"

LIQUID IMMEDIATE POSTTEST   The first part of the liquid posttest was the same as the liquid pretest, with the same glasses being used. Now, however, if S said there was not the same amount to drink in the one narrow glass and in the wide glass into which the water from the other narrow glass had been poured, E stopped without asking which had more. If, on the other hand, S said there was the same amount to drink in these two glasses, E asked how he knew this and then repeated the procedure with several variations.

The first variation was to have the two identical, narrow glasses filled only part way, with S serving to judge when the second had "just the same amount" as the first. If S showed conservation again when the water from one of the narrow glasses was poured into the wide one, this procedure was repeated with two identical vases and a square pitcher in place of the original glasses. Finally, regardless of whether the new containers were used and of whether conservation occurred with them, the original glasses were filled to the top once more. The original procedure was followed again except that now, instead of all the water, only about two-thirds was poured from the narrow glass into the wide one.

Liquid Training Procedures

TRANSFER-SERIES TRAINING   The transfer series consisted of a series of successive tasks, all of which were presented only if S answered each question correctly. If at any point an incorrect answer occurred, transfer-series training was discontinued, and liquid reversibility training was instituted. The tasks were as follows:

1. Again, the six dolls were put in the six beds. Then E took them out and put them closer together so that the last bed had no doll

in front of it. The *E* asked, "Are there the same number of dolls as beds?"

2. Five 3 × 5-inch cards were laid out in a row, and *S* was given five checkers and asked to put one on each card. The *E* asked, "Are there the same number of checkers as cards?" Then *E* took the checkers off and put them closer together in a row in front of the cards so that there was one card without a checker in front of it, and asked, "Now are there the same number of checkers as cards?"

3. Five black checkers were placed in a row parallel to and aligned with five red ones. The *E* asked, "Are there the same number of red and black checkers?" Then *E* put the black checkers much closer together and asked, "Now are there the same number of red and black checkers?" After *S* answered, *E* spread the red checkers far apart and out of line and repeated the question.

4. The *S* was given one large bead at a time and asked to put them in a row. The *E* took one bead for himself every time he gave *S* a bead and made a row parallel to and aligned with *S*'s. When each row had six beads, *E* asked, "Are there the same number of beads in your row as in my row?" Then *E* put his beads much closer together and asked, "Do we still have the same number of beads?" After *S* answered, *E* spread *S*'s beads further apart and out of line and asked the same question again.

5. The *E* again gave *S* one large bead at a time and gave himself a bead each time he gave one to *S*, but this time *S* was asked to put the beads in a pile, and *E* did likewise. When there were seven beads in each pile, *E* asked, "Do we have the same number of beads?" Then *E* spread his beads out and asked, "Do we still have the same number of beads?" When *S* had answered, *E* put his beads into a glass and repeated the question.

6. The *E* gave *S* and himself each eight small beads, one at a time, and each of them put his beads into a little glass. (The two glasses were identical and different from those used previously.) The *E* asked, "Do we have the same number of little beads?" Then *E* took his beads out of the glass and spread them out on the table, asking, "Now do we have the same number of beads?" Then he said, "Now let me put them back in the glass," and he did so. When

they were back in, *E* said, "Now I'll pour them into another glass," and he poured them into a larger, wider one (different from that used previously). Then *E* asked, "Do we still have the same number of beads?"

7. The little glasses, first empty, were dipped into a basket containing small beads so that they were filled with beads. The *E* asked, "Are both glasses filled to the top?" and he made adjustments when necessary. Then *E* asked, "Are there about the same number of beads in each glass?" After *S* answered, *E* poured the beads from one of the little glasses into the larger, wider glass and, indicating the two glasses with beads in them, asked, "Now are there about the same number of beads in this glass and in this glass?"

8. Little stones (of the kind used for mosaics) were poured from a pitcher into the two little glasses, filling them, and *E* asked, "Are they both filled to the top?" and made adjustments if necessary. Then *E* asked, "Are there about the same amount of little stones in each glass?" Then *E* poured the little stones from one of the little glasses into the larger, wider one and, indicating the two glasses with stones in them, asked, "Now are there about the same amount of little stones in this glass and in this glass?"

9. The green water was poured into the two little glasses, filling them, and *E* asked, "Are they both filled exactly to the top?" and made adjustments when necessary. Then *E* asked, "Is there the same amount to drink in each glass?" After *S* answered, *E* poured the water from one glass into the larger, wider one and, indicating the two glasses with water in them, asked, "Now is there the same amount to drink in this glass and in this glass?"

10. The liquid posttest was repeated.

LIQUID REVERSIBILITY TRAINING   Depending on whether water had just been used or not, *E* said, "Now we're going to do something more with water," or "Now we're going to do something with water again." He placed two identical glasses different from any used previously next to each other and filled each glass, saying, "I'm going to pour it into this glass to the very top just like we did before, and now I'm going to pour it into the other glass to the very top." Then E asked, "Are they both filled exactly to the top?" and made adjustments if necessary.

Then E said, "Watch me," and poured the water from one of the two identical glasses into a new, wide glass, which stood next to the glass which still had water in it. The E said, "Now I'm going to ask you something different. If I pour this water back in the empty glass, will it be filled just like this one?" After S had made a prediction, E poured the water back and asked, "Is it . . . ?" (full, or like the other, etc., whatever S has predicted) or "Did it . . . ?" (run over, etc.).

With the appropriate modifications in wording, this procedure was repeated until S had made three correct predictions in succession. Three different sets of glasses were used in order.

Delayed Posttests

DOLL DELAYED POSTTEST   Three tasks were given in succession:

1. The E gave S six toy soldiers and asked him to line them up. The E then aligned another row of six to S's row and asked, "Are there the same number of soldiers in your row and in my row?" Then E put his soldiers closer together so that one of S's stood alone and asked, "Now are there the same number of soldiers in your row and in my row?"

2. The E asked S to put one of five spoons in each of a row of five bowls, and asked, "Are there the same number of spoons as bowls?" Then E took the spoons out and put them in a row closer together so that there was one bowl without a spoon in front of it and asked, "Now are there the same number of spoons as bowls?"

3. The E asked S to put the six dolls in the six beds, asked if they were the same number, and then took out the dolls and put them closer together so there was a bed without a doll in front of it, as previously. The E asked, "Now are there the same number of dolls as beds?" If S said there were, E pointed to the bed without a doll in front of it and said, "But look, here is a bed without a doll in front of it. Aren't there more beds?"

LIQUID DELAYED POSTTEST   Four tasks were given in succession:

1. The E filled one of two identical opaque cups (not used previously) part way, then said he wanted to put "just the same amount" into the other cup and adjusted until S said he had done so. The E then asked, "Is there the same amount to drink in each cup?" Then, saying, "Now watch what I do" and explaining as he went along, E poured the water from one of the cups into a transparent jar. Indicating the two containers with water in them, E asked, "Now is there the same amount to drink in the jar and this cup?"

2. The second task was the same as the first except that both cups were filled exactly to the top (as judged by S) instead of only part way.

3. The third task was again like the first except that now the previous test glasses were used instead of the two cups and the jar.

4. The fourth task was like the second, but still using the previous test glasses. At the end, if S said there was the same amount in the two different glasses, E said, "But look, in this glass the water goes all the way up to the top, but in this glass it doesn't go nearly so high. Isn't there more water in this glass?"

RESULTS

Pretests

NUMBER AND AGE OF CHILDREN IN EACH CATEGORY   As may be seen in Table 1, approximately the same number of children fell into the conservation and the nonconservation categories. Liquid conservation was present without doll conservation for a sizable number of children, while doll conservation was present without liquid conservation for fewer. The ages of the children were quite comparable in all the categories.

NONCONSERVATION ANSWERS   As was found previously, most children who did not show number conservation said there was a greater number of the items which were more spread out. Of the 28 giving nonconservation answers in the doll pretest, 26 said there were more beds than dolls, while only 2 said there were more dolls.

Most, if not all, of the children giving nonconservation answers in the liquid pretest said there was more liquid in the narrow glass, in

TABLE I

Number and Age of Children in Each Category

Category	N	Mean Age[a]	Age Range[a]
Nonconservation	16	6–10	6–1 to 7–4
Doll reversibility training	8	6–10	6–7 to 7–4
Doll addition-subtraction training	8	6–10	6–1 to 7–4
Partial conservation—liquid	12	6–11	6–6 to 7–5
Doll reversibility training	6	6–11	6–8 to 7–5
Doll addition-subtraction training	6	6–11	6–6 to 7–3
Partial conservation—dolls	5	7–1	6–5 to 7–8
Conservation	19	7–0	6–7 to 7–5
Not meeting criteria	4	6–11	6–7 to 7–4
Grand total	56	6–11	6–1 to 7–8

[a] In years and months.

which it reached a greater height. This was true for 19 subjects; the data are not clear for the other 2.

Doll Reversibility versus Addition-Subtraction Training

CONSERVATION ON DOLL IMMEDIATE POST-TEST   Doll reversibility training had a strong effect on conservation, while addition-subtraction training did not. When the dolls were closer together than the beds in the first posttest, only 2 of the 14 Ss given doll reversibility training still said the number of dolls and the number of beds were not the same; the other 12 all changed to conservation answers. On the other hand, 12 of the 14 Ss given doll addition-subtraction training continued with nonconservation, while only 2 changed to conservation. (χ^2 for the difference is 11.57, $p < .001$ with 1 *df*.)

DOLL DELAYED POSTTEST   All Ss who after training changed to conservation in the doll immediate posttest also gave conservation answers throughout the entire doll delayed posttest, except that 2 of the 12 Ss who had received reversibility training succumbed at the end to E's suggestion against conservation.

NUMBER OF TRAINING TRIALS TO CRITE-RION   Doll reversibility training, with a median of 4, took somewhat fewer trials to criterion than doll addition-subtraction training, with a median of 6, but the difference is

not significant. (χ^2 for the median test is 2.30, $.10 < p < .20$ with 1 *df*.)

Transfer to Liquid

DIRECT TRANSFER   Only nonconservation Ss, who had shown neither doll nor liquid conservation in the pretest, could be used to test for direct transfer to liquid when they had acquired doll conservation through training. This meant that there were only eight Ss available, as doll conservation was developed by only one of the eight nonconservation Ss given addition-subtraction training, and seven of the eight given reversibility training. Of these eight, only one S showed conservation on the liquid posttest after training with the dolls, thus providing essentially no indication of direct transfer at all.

TRANSFER SERIES   With this one S removed, only seven Ss remained for the transfer series. Four of these seven gave liquid conservation answers in the liquid posttest at the end of the series, although one of the four answered incorrectly on the last question. All four continued to maintain liquid conservation in the delayed posttest. The other three Ss gave incorrect answers in the third task of the transfer series.

Liquid Reversibility Training

Sixteen Ss were available for liquid reversibility training. These included the three Ss above who failed to transfer either on the direct test or on the transfer series, the seven addition-subtraction-trained *S*s and the one reversibility trained nonconservation *S* who did not acquire doll conservation with training, and the five partial conservation—dolls *S*s.

CONSERVATION ON LIQUID POSTTESTS   Only 4 of these 16 *S*s gave clear conservation answers in the liquid posttest following liquid reversibility training; 1 more gave a nonconservation answer first but immediately corrected himself; and 11 gave clear nonconservation answers. The 5 *S*s who did give conservation answers at this point, immediately or not, continued to give them throughout the delayed posttest, except that one succumbed to the nonconservation suggestion at the end. These data do not, however, provide much support for the effectiveness of reversibility training for liquid conservation, a point to be further discussed below.

ABILITY TO PREDICT   The predictions called for in liquid reversibility training were clearly very easy. Of the 16 *S*s, 14 made correct predictions on every trial—that is, predicted from the start that the initial glass would be full again when the water was poured back. The remaining 2 *S*s predicted incorrectly only on the first trial.

How Ss Said They Could Tell Number or Amount Were the Same

It will be recalled that *S*s who said number or amount were the same in the pretest or in the immediate posttest were thereupon asked, "How do you tell?" The answers to this question were independently coded by two of the investigators into the following nine categories:

1. Equality Before. Referred to the fact that every bed had a doll in it before the dolls were taken out, or that the two identical glasses had been equally full before the water from one was poured into the different glass.

2. Reversibility. Referred to the fact that a doll could be put back in every bed, or that the water could be poured back into the original glass and the two identical glasses would both be full again.

3. Addition-Subtraction. Referred to the fact that nothing had been added or taken away.

4. Closer or Wider. Noted that the dolls were closer together than the beds, or that the glass into which the water had been poured was wider than the original one.

5. Number. Referred to specific numbers (possible only with dolls, not with liquid).

6. Matching. Showed how the dolls could be matched with the beds, pointing to successive doll-bed pairs saying something like, "this goes with this, this goes with this," etc. (again possible only with dolls).

7. Extra Doll. Showed that there was one doll between two beds, or without a bed, or that two dolls were "sharing" a bed (again possible only with dolls).

8. Don't Know. Indicated lack of knowledge by saying, "Don't know," by not answering, or by restating the equality without a reason (e.g., "because this has as much as this").

9. Miscellaneous. Any other answers.

If a child gave two different reasons for saying the number or amount were the same, his answer was scored as half in one category and half in the other. The investigators agreed on the coding of all but five of the 79 answers; these five were coded again by one of the investigators. The frequency with which answers in the different categories were given by *S*s who first said the number or amount were the same after various experiences may be seen in Table 2. (It should be noted that these answers are not all independent; a given *S* may appear both under dolls and under liquid.)

Table 2 supports the effectiveness of training in that the reasons which *S*s gave after training for saying the number or amount were the same were not appreciably different from the reasons which *S*s gave who did not require training to say they were the same. The main difference seems to be that the latter *S*s somewhat more often gave answers in the "Don't know" or "Miscellaneous" categories. This would suggest that the trained *S*s were, if anything, clearer about the reasons for conservation than the untrained ones.

However, contrary to expectation, neither reversibility nor the lack of anything having been added or removed was very often given as the reason for number or amount being the same. The most frequent reason, by far, with the dolls was that there was an extra doll in the line. With the liquid, two reasons were much more

TABLE 2

Frequency of Different Reasons for Saying Number or Amount Were the Same

Point at Which S Said Number and Amount Were the Same	Equality Before	Reversibility	Addition-Subtraction	Closer or Wider	Number	Matching	Extra Doll	Don't Know	Miscellaneous
Dolls									
Pretest (conservers)	2	0	1	0	2½	1	9½	5	3
After reversibility training	3	2	0	1	1	1	4	0	0
After addition-subtraction training	0	0	0	0	0	0	2	0	0
Total for dolls	5	2	1	1	3½	2	15½	5	3
Liquid									
Pretest (conservers)	17	0	0	12	...	...	...	2	0
After doll training (direct transfer)	0	0	0	0	...	...	...	0	1
After transfer series	2	½	0	1½	...	...	...	0	0
After liquid reversibility training	2	0	0	1	...	...	...	2	0
Total for liquid	21	½	0	14½				4	1

frequent than any others: that the amount had been the same before, and that the glass into which the water had been poured was wider than the glass from which it came. These points will be further considered in the Discussion.

DISCUSSION

Several of the questions which gave rise to this experiment are clearly answered by the results. Our first question was whether, in order to induce number conservation, it was necessary for the reversibility-training procedure which had been found effective in a prior experiment to include, as it had, experience with addition and subtraction. The answer is no; the procedure was as effective here without addition-subtraction experience as it was previously with such experience.

This suggests—but does not necessarily imply —that number conservation is not affected by training in addition and subtraction. In the absence of reversibility training, training with addition and subtraction might still lead to conservation. Our second question was whether this was the case. The answer again is no, at least for the particular addition-subtraction training procedure that we used.

Further, the lack of effectiveness of this procedure indicates that the basis for the success of the reversibility training is not that it arouses a number set, as implied by Zimiles' (1963) suggestion. Such training in addition and subtraction ought to be at least as likely, if not much more likely, to arouse a number set as the training in reversibility.

Another question which seems clearly answered is whether the number conservation induced by our reversibility-training procedure transfers directly to such different conservations as that of the amount of a liquid: it does not. Such transfer is not expected from the point of view that what is critical for conservation of a property is recognition of the reversibility of operations that remove the defining attributes of this property, as suggested by Wallach and Sprott (1964). Our number-conservation training procedure was designed to lead to the realization that when objects had been paired together—a defining attribute of equality—they could be paired again despite intervening changes in arrangement. The procedure would not be expected to indicate that when a liquid which had originally filled one of two identical containers had been poured into a different container, it would exactly fill the first again if it was poured back.

On the other hand, it was found that conservation of the amount of liquid did follow upon the number-conservation training procedure for some children, when the differences between conserving amount of liquid and number were minimized by a series of intervening steps. What this was due to cannot be clearly answered at present. It is possible that the series led the children to realize that the pouring of a liquid is reversible as well as the rearrangement of the dolls, but it is also possible that other processes, particularly that of direct suggestion, were responsible.

The results so far discussed were all essentially in line with expectation and as such appear to support the view that conservation was induced as the result of recognition of reversibility. However, some doubt is thrown upon this interpretation by two other results: (*a*) the reasons which Ss gave for conservation answers, and (*b*) the failure of liquid reversibility training to have a strong effect.

It will be recalled that one reason was given more frequently than reversibility or any other for saying the number of dolls was the same as the number of beds when the dolls were closer together, whether or not training had been necessary for number conservation to be shown. This reason was that there was an extra doll in the line not aligned with a bed—that is, that there was a doll between two beds, or that two dolls were "sharing" a bed, etc. This suggests that the effectiveness of the doll reversibility-training procedure may have been due, not to

the experience with reversibility per se, but to the opportunity which this experience gave for the removal of a distorted perception. That is, initial nonconservation answers may have resulted from seeing the dolls and beds as paired with one bed left over; the training procedure may then have led to the realization that this was not correct—that the dolls and beds were not paired with one another, and that therefore the bed apparently left over at the end did not imply inequality in the number of dolls and beds.

The main effect of the reversibility-training procedure with the dolls, then, may have been to lead the Ss to stop using a misleading perceptual cue. Conservation probably never occurs when a situation provides what the subject takes to be a clear perceptual cue for nonconservation. Removing such cues has been shown to be effective in an experiment by Frank (Bruner, Olver, & Greenfield, et al., 1966), and making the Ss stop using such a cue although it is still present may have been—with or without the experience of reversibility per se as well—a crucial factor in the success of our doll reversibility-training procedure.

If this was the case, it would not be hard to understand why reversibility training was relatively ineffective with the liquid although it was so effective with the dolls. While reversibility training in the doll situation may have indicated that the bed left over at the end of the line was misleading by showing that the other dolls and beds were not paired, there was nothing in the reversibility training in the liquid situation to discourage the use of misleading cues (such as the height of the liquid).

The doll reversibility-training procedure, then, may well have been successful, not because it led the Ss to recognize reversibility, but because it led them to stop relying on a misleading cue. It is, in fact, not clear to what extent the recognition of reversibility—which did, of course, exist—resulted from the experience with reversibility provided by this training procedure and to what extent it was due to prior experience. Both in the present study and in our earlier one (Wallach & Sprott, 1964), sizable proportions of the Ss predicted correctly the first time they were asked that the dolls could be put back into the beds; others did not. It is clear that the Ss who did predict correctly the first time already knew about reversibility from prior experience, though they may not have thought about it until the question was asked. The *S*s who did not predict correctly the first time may also already have known about reversibility and been misled by misperceiving the dolls and beds as paired with a bed left over— that is, they might have been able to predict correctly in a situation which was less misleading perceptually. It is possible, then, that the experience with reversibility provided by the training procedure actually contributed very little to the recognition of reversibility.

In view of the new interpretations suggested by this study, the success of the doll reversibility-training procedure can no longer be regarded as providing evidence for the role of the recognition of reversibility in conservation. This procedure, which previously appeared to induce conservation by leading the *S*s to recognize reversibility, probably did so, at least in large part, by leading them to stop using misleading cues.

We still believe, nonetheless, that the recognition of reversibility is necessary for conservation. The *S*s would not have conserved, we submit, if they had not realized (whether on the basis of the training procedure or prior experience) that the dolls could be fit back into the beds again. The lack of use of misleading cues is not in itself sufficient to account for their believing at the end of the experiment that the number of dolls was equal to the number of beds despite the rearrangement. If a *S* stopped seeing the dolls and beds as paired with a bed left over, this would just mean that a previous reason for believing in inequality no longer obtained; it would not yet provide a basis for believing in equality. Why should the number of dolls and beds be regarded as remaining the same? It seems clear that the use of appropriate perceptual cues does not provide the answer either; seeing the dolls first in the beds and then being taken out is a crucial part of the procedure. When *S*s who had attained conservation were shown the dolls and beds as arranged in the conservation test situation without first seeing the dolls in the beds, they typically took a much longer time to say whether the number of dolls and beds was the same and often answered incorrectly.

An explanation is still needed, then, given that the *S*s stopped using misleading cues, of the fact that—at the end of the experiment— number was thought to remain the same after the dolls had been taken out of the beds and placed closer together. We believe that recognition of the fact that the dolls could be fit back into the beds again—that the rearrangement was reversible—can explain this; no factor suggested by other interpretations of conservation seems capable of doing so (cf. Wallach & Sprott, 1964). In order for conservation answers to be given, a *S* must, we think, realize that the dolls and beds could be exactly paired again, as well as not use misleading perceptual cues.

Quite generally, recognizing reversibility as well as not using misleading perceptual cues would seem to be necessary for conservation. Conservation cannot be attained when a cue for nonconservation is relied on. But that misleading cues are not used is insufficient per se to account for a property being regarded as the same after certain transformations. The only factor that does seem able to account for this is recognition of the reversibility of the transformations. We believe, therefore, that in order for a child to conserve, he must both recognize reversibility and not rely on inappropriate cues.

REFERENCES

Bruner, J. S., Olver, Rose R., & Greenfield, Patricia M., et al., *Studies in cognitive growth.* New York: Wiley, 1966.

Smedslund, J. The acquisition of conservation of substance and weight in children: VII. Conservation of discontinuous quantity and the operations of adding and taking away. *Scandinavian Journal of Psychology*, 1962, 3, 69–77.

Wallach, Lise, & Sprott, R. L. Inducing number conservation in children. *Child Development*, 1964, 35, 1057–1071.

Wohlwill, J. F., & Lowe, R. C. Experimental analysis of the development of the conservation of number. *Child Development*, 1962, 33, 153–167.

Zimiles, H. A note on Piaget's concept of conservation. *Child Development*, 1963, 34, 691–695.

PART FIVE

SOCIALIZATION PROCESSES

The word *socialization* is used here to refer to the process by which the child learns the ways of society and thus becomes acculturated. In the process, he or she develops a conscience, becomes psychologically male or female, and acquires the character traits valued in his or her society. According to the psychoanalytic school of psychology, socialization involves developing a superego, learning to postpone immediate gratification, and learning to channel one's energy into socially constructive activities. For the learning theorists, it involves development and control of certain drive systems: dependence, independence, achievement, aggression, and sexuality. For still a third school, the interactionists, there is emphasis on interaction between the nature of the child and his environment, and on reciprocal relations between the child and "significant others."

This section emphasizes *process,* the mechanisms involved in socialization. Some of the mechanisms have already been described in earlier sections. One in particular, *attachment* (the term is increasingly being used in the literature in preference to dependency), was introduced in Part 3; factors associated with its development in the Uganda infant were discussed in the Ainsworth paper, and the relationship between object constancy and attachment was examined in the Bell paper. In this section, Bowlby discusses attachment (which he regards as *behavior,* not as a *drive*) and sees it occurring as a result of interaction between infant and mother. He postulates that the infant is born with a behavioral system ready to be activated by certain stimuli and that there is an innate bias to respond to stimuli arising from the human voice, face, arms, and body. The infant responses produce a *reciprocal action* in the mother; infant and mother behave so as to maintain closeness to one another.

A different analysis of attachment behavior is presented in a paper by Cairns (1967). The Cairns model is derived from learning theory and views the development of attachments as a "by-product of a continuous conditioning process." He examines research findings on mammals with respect to social attachments, and discusses the effects of such factors as extended exposure to another animal, the stimulus properties of the cohabitant, and continual separation from the attachment-object. While Cairns considers the model to be incomplete, it is useful in identifying variables that need to be considered in understanding and studying attachment, and it is interesting to compare with the Bowlby model.

SOCIAL LEARNING THEORY

In this section we also return to a consideration of the concept of *identification,* first introduced in Part 1. The reader will recall that psychoanalytic theory places great emphasis on the role of identification in the socialization process. It is through identification with the like-sexed parent and incorporation of that parent's attributes that the child learns to take on the appropriate sex role. The boy strives to become like the father in order to deal with his competitive fantasies toward his father and his libidinal attachment to his mother. (Note the power of such a theory in the development of masculinity.) And, since the identification results in part from fear of castration by the father, the boy makes the moral standards of the father his own and develops a conscience that will keep his aggressive drives and libidinal impulses in control even when there is no possibility of being discovered in a transgression.

Although it would be very elegant to explain acquisition of sex-typing, conscience, and other aspects of character and personality by the single process of identification, it is exceedingly difficult to do so. Attempts have been made in the literature, but by and large the results have been inconclusive or negative (see Mischel, 1970).

While theoreticians may not accept the whole Freudian package of erotic attachment, Oedipal conflict, and castration fears, nevertheless it is true that most girls do grow up to be more feminine than masculine, just as most boys grow up to be more masculine than feminine. In addition, many children incorporate or acquire traits of the like-sexed parent, even when they profess to dislike in their parents the very characteristics they themselves develop. It is also true that the child develops a conscience; he internalizes the values of his parents and through them the values of society. If these acquisitions to personality are not made through the single process of identification, how are they acquired?

The Gewirtz and Stingle paper included here explores one possible answer: the identification phenomenon can be explained by a process of "generalized imitation," derived from learning theory. By applying conditioning principles, they show how a child can learn to want to be like another. Their work is in the tradition of Sears and his students, who elaborated on and extended classic learning theory to explain many social behaviors.

Bandura and his followers have also elaborated on a social learning approach, but theirs is one that emphasizes imitation and modeling rather than reinforcement. That is, they believe that a child may form behavior patterns by imitating a model's behavior without reinforcement. Not only superficial behavior may be so acquired but also highly abstracted, generalized attitudes and beliefs. A parent, a teacher, or even television characters may serve as models for imitation.

Imitation may even occur when a particular behavior is negatively reinforced. For example, a child whose parents utilize physical punishment to curb aggressive behavior may actually exhibit more of such behavior outside the home than do children who are not so punished. Despite the punishment, they imitate the aggressive behavior of their parents. The model furnished by the parent is more potent in shaping behavior than is the negative reinforcement. This phenomenon is similar to the psychoanalytic concept of identification with the aggressor (see pp. 55–60).

Social learning theorists maintain that a major weakness of classic learning theory is its failure to account for the acquisition of novel responses not already in the subject's repertoire, which occur in the absence of any eliciting stimulus (apart from cues provided by others) and without reinforcement. Again imitation and modeling are useful to explain how such novel responses are acquired. In one study, O'Connor (1969) demonstrated how patterns of social withdrawal can be changed. In his study, children who displayed extreme social withdrawal were shown films of children who progressively engaged in more social interaction and then were reinforced for their behavior. A second group of withdrawn children was shown films that contained no human characters. The children given the modeling treatment showed a significant increase in their social interaction, provided their social behavior met with peer approval; the children who did not receive treatment, however, showed no change in social responsiveness. Thus new patterns of behavior were acquired on the basis of observation of a model, despite the fact that they received no reinforcement while the behavior was being observed. O'Connor points out that it is difficult to effect such changes in socially withdrawn children through reinforcement, since these responses occur either very infrequently or not at all.

Modeling can also effect changes in the frequency or intensity of previously acquired responses. Lövaas (1961), for example, found that children exposed to aggressive cartoons chose more aggressive play subsequently than children who had watched a nonaggressive movie. Recently CBS did a telecast entitled "The Selling of the Pentagon" in which Marines, as part of a Fourth of July exhibition, fought savagely in hand-to-hand combat, throwing one another on the ground and stomping on one another's stomachs. When the "show" was over, TV cameras picked up the behavior of children who had been spectators and were now swarming onto the field and engaging in wild acts of violence and sadism—a most telling and chilling example of modeling. We are left with the question of how the endless violence and sadism children are exposed to, ranging from that depicted in TV crime shows and Westerns to scenes of the Vietnam war, affects young children's tastes, sensibilities, and regard for human life. The concept of generalized imitation should give pause to those who accept the catharsis theory, which holds that passively viewing acts of aggression enables one to work out aggressive feelings vicariously and safely.

Personality traits of the subjects exposed to the modeling treatment influence the amount of imitative behavior that occurs. Individuals, for example, with low self-esteem, high dependency needs, or those previously rewarded for imitative behavior are more likely to imitate the behavior of a model. An individual also is more prone to imitation if he sees resemblances between the model and himself. For example, students exposed to a bigoted model became more prejudiced if the model was presented as being similar to themselves, but they showed no change in their prejudicial attitudes if the model was presented as being dissimilar to themselves (Bandura and Walters, 1963).

In the process of growing up, children are exposed to many different models. Whether they choose a particular one depends in part on the characteristics of the model. Some observers believe that imitative behavior is more likely to occur as a response to a highly nurturant model. Bandura and Huston (1961) exposed one group of nursery-school children to a female model who interacted in a highly nurturant fashion and a second group to the same model who then acted in a distant, non-nurturant manner. Aggressive responses were imitated regardless of how nurturant the model was, but all other social responses were imitated to a significantly greater extent by the children exposed to the nurturant, rewarding model.

The sex of the model may also be significant. Bandura, Ross, and Ross (1961) showed that exposure to an aggressive male model had more effect on boys than girls. A second study by the same investigators (1963) showed that exposure to an aggressive male model resulted in more imitative aggressive behavior in boys than exposure to an aggressive female model.

Finally, the extent of imitation may depend on response consequences for the model as perceived by the child. Children who observed an aggressive model being rewarded imitated his behavior more readily than did children who saw his behavior punished, despite the fact that those who saw the behavior rewarded were simultaneously extremely critical and disapproving of his behavior. Thus observation of a model rewarded for his behavior may lead to imitation even when the behavior is deviant and contrary to social norms.

In summary, the Bandura *et al.* school of social learning theory attempts to account for the acquisition of social behaviors by emphasizing imitation and modeling. We include in this section Bandura's own paper on the role of imitation, as well as that of Grusec, who shares Bandura's theoretical orientation. Baer, Peterson, and Sherman, whose paper is included here, also deal with modification of behavior through imitation, but they work within the framework of behavioral modification with emphasis on shaping responses through reinforcement.

BEHAVIOR MODIFICATION

Behavior modification is a particularly active field of research at the present time. Investigators working in the field attempt to modify a child's deviant or antisocial behavior by providing certain reinforcers, like praise or a material reward, when the child produces the desired response. The method is called *operant conditioning;* it is a systematic use of consequences to follow operant behavior, that is, behavior that operates on the environment. For example, if a child has been continually disrupting a classroom, the teacher may reward him when she "catches him being good" by giving him praise and attention (Becker, 1969).

A key procedure in behavior modification is *shaping* behavior. There are many cases where the desired behavior does *not* appear and so cannot be strengthened by reinforcing. Then the teacher or experimenter selects a behavior for reinforcement that approximates the desired one. For example, a child who has been flitting from task to task and getting no work done might be praised or receive a token reward for staying with a task for a specified amount of time. The amount of time necessary to spend with a task in order to receive a reward is gradually lengthened, and eventually, when conditioning is successful, the new behavior will maintain itself without reward.

Behavior modification has been criticized by many as smacking of Aldous Huxley's *Brave New World*. However, behavioral psychologists in the Skinner tradition point out that adults are already using operant techniques with children, but they are using them poorly. They more often admonish children for bad behavior (and thus unwittingly provide positive reinforcement by giving attention) than they reward for the good. Actually, the techniques in and of themselves are neutral. Depending on the values of the adult using them, operant techniques can be used to shape child behavior in the direction of overconformity and lack of creativity, or they can be used to encourage the development of a free, creative individual who can learn more freely and creatively because behaviors that interfere with learning have been eliminated. The techniques, however, though they may be considered an adjunct to psychotherapy, are no substitute for therapy in cases of severe emotional disturbance.

MORAL DEVELOPMENT

How moral development, another important area of socialization, proceeds is a matter of concern to many investigators. We have already pointed out that psychoanalysts use the concept of identification as the principal explanatory mechanism. Other writers, working within the framework of social learning theory, emphasize the cognitive aspects of conscience acquisition. Piaget's early work on stages of moral development traced the child's progress toward a concept of justice, beginning with an early stage at which the child believes implicitly in the sacredness of rules and judges acts in terms of the consequences; breaking fifteen cups accidentally is worse than breaking one cup while sneaking jam. At a more advanced stage, the child's judgment of right and wrong causes him to place more emphasis on a person's *intent* to do good or evil. Kohlberg (1963), who has done the most extensive follow-up of Piaget's stage theory, identified six developmental stages on the basis of ideas used by children in working moral judgments: stage 1, where the child obeys out of deference to the power and prestige of the parent and to avoid the pain of punishment; stage 2, where right and wrong are defined in relation to what is satisfying to self; stage 3, where the child is oriented toward pleasing and helping others; stage 4, where the child is oriented toward "doing his duty" and maintaining the social order; stage 5, where the child accepts institutionalized rules on a rational basis; and stage 6, where the child is guided by individual principles of conscience. In the Kohlberg model, *cognitive* factors predominate. The child moves away from the cognitive naiveté of early childhood as he participates more and more in social groups, and as a result he changes his views about authority and authority relations.

The influence of parental methods of control on internalization of standards has also been studied. How should parents discipline their children to be reasonably self-critical and to feel twinges of guilt over transgressions? Hoffman (1970) reviews various factors that parents use: love withdrawal ("I won't love you any more if you do those bad things"); induction (pointing out the effect the child's behavior has on others); affection (supplying nurturance so that the child is positively oriented toward the parent and thus more receptive to his influence). In general, the threat of withdrawing love is likely to produce anxiety in the child; he may restrain his hostile impulses but it will be because of his anxiety rather than because he has internalized the parent's standards. Induction serves the cognitive function of helping the child to take the viewpoint of another. This type of discipline is very effective, especially when it is combined with affection so that the child is predisposed to its reception.

After an extensive review of the literature, Hoffman concludes that moral development is a "complex, multifaceted phenomenon," possibly proceeding along four tracks toward behavioral conformity, perception of authority as rational, impulse inhibition, and consideration for others. Two types of experiences are important here: the taking of reciprocal roles with peers and exposure to adults who express empathy for the feelings of others. Through these experiences the child comes to understand the motives of others as well as the consequences of his own behavior.

SEX-TYPING

To be a man, a boy must be able to distinguish between masculine and feminine behaviors so that he will know which ones are appropriate to his male status. According to Kohlberg (1966), the child has acquired a concept of his sexual identity by the age of five, an acquisition accounted for, says Kohlberg, by the same cognitive processes as any other concept.

The child's display of sex-appropriate behaviors receives constant reinforcement by parents and peers. Our culture, like all others, has certain stereotypes of what is sex-appropriate and what is not. The nursery rhyme that contrasts what little boys are made of (snips and snails and puppy-dog tails) with what little girls are made of (sugar and spice and all that is nice) epitomizes the stereotype, and, as Kagan (1964) put it, the stereotypes serve as standards to guide an individual's behavior. The boy is told early in life that "Little men don't cry" and the girl that "Little girls don't fight," as well as scores of other stereotypes; and the child's behavior is reinforced according to how well it conforms with the sex-appropriate behavior. Sex-role *identity* is achieved with the matching of one's self-assessment against sex-role standards (Kagan, 1964). Kohlberg (1966) emphasizes the underlying cognitive processes in these self-categorizations, though whether cognition (*knowing* what is masculine or feminine) is causal or not is debatable.

There are certain tentative conclusions drawn by investigators regarding the correlates of sex-typing, if not the causes. Sears, Rau, and Alpert (1965) found that a "closed, anxious, nonpermissive attitude on the part of either or both parents was conducive to femininity in both sexes of children, as were the use of physical punishment and severe control of aggression" (p. 198). Permissiveness or nonpermissiveness has been found in other studies to be related to masculine traits; Sears (1961) found that boys of permissive parents tended to be more aggressive than boys from restrictive homes. It would appear that the effect of restrictiveness is to make the child more dependent and compliant, behaviors usually typed as feminine.

It should be noted that serious attempts are being made to transcend the stereotypes. In one community, for example, members of the Women's Liberation Movement have set up a nursery school where aggression on the part of female children is not only tolerated, but even encouraged. And on a different level, new laws are being enacted to insure equal job opportunities and equal pay for women. We are a long way from the millennium, but we are making progress.

The two remaining papers in this section deal with the elementary-school child and take a new point of view regarding the psychological tasks of the latency period. We have seen in Part 1 how the Oedipus complex is resolved through the process of identification: the child internalizes the moral codes and ethics of the parents, and the superego is established in a more final form. The child now has an internalized set of standards on which to model his behavior. The child's ego is also growing during this time, and must become more adept at taking into account and negotiating the demands of the id, the superego, and reality. The ego fears the consequences from both the superego and society of unchecked instinctual gratification. Anxiety develops, and this sets in motion a set of defensive operations to aid in control of the aggressive and libidinal drives. In most healthy children these drives are repressed and then channeled into socially constructive activities. For the post-Oedipal child, these activities usually involve the school and peer group. The relationship with mother and father becomes somewhat less intense as more of the instinctual energies are invested in schoolwork and playmates. The ego grows during this time and develops skill in controlling the immediate expression of instinctual wishes and in conforming to the requirements of the supergo and reality. The instinctual energies previously tied up in the Oedipal situation are now channeled into socially useful activities. For example, the feelings of rivalry the boy has for his father may now be expressed through his participation in competitive games or his desire to excel in the classroom; the girl's wish to have a baby by her father may now find expression in creative activities in art or literature. Psychoanalytic theory refers to the period in which ego controls are developed and sublimations established as *latency*. The Bornstein paper included in this section enlarges on the psychological tasks of this period.

Development of achievement motivation is seen in a very different light in the Rosen and D'Andrade paper. These investigators analyzed the interactions between parents and sons in performance of certain tasks from the standpoint of relations between achievement training, independence training, and parental sanctions. The investigators, writing in 1959, were prophetic in their recognition of the reciprocal influences between parent and child and child and parent, a reciprocity which, as we have previously pointed out, is receiving increasing attention in socialization research.

REFERENCES

Bandura, A., and Huston, A., "Identification as a process of incidental learning." *Journal of Abnormal and Social Psychology,* 1961, 63, 311–18.

Bandura, A.; Ross, D.; and Ross, S. A., "Transmission of aggression through imitation of aggressive models." *Journal of Abnormal and Social Psychology,* 1961, 63, 575–82.

————, "Imitation of film-mediated models." *Journal of Abnormal and Social Psychology,* 1963, 66, 3–11.

Bandura, A., and Walters, R., *Social learning and personality development* (New York: Holt, Rinehart and Winston, 1963).

Baumrind, D., and Black, A. E., "Socialization practices associated with dimensions of competence in preschool boys and girls." *Child Development,* 1967, 38, 291–328.

Becker, W.; Thomas, D.; and Carmine, D., *Reducing behavior problems: an operant conditioning guide for teachers* (Urbana: ERIC Clearinghouse on Early Childhood Education, University of Illinois, 1969).

Bowlby, J., *Attachment and loss,* vol. I (New York: Basic Books, 1970).

Cairns, R., "Attachment behavior of mammals." *Psychological Review,* 1967, **73**, 409–26.

Feshbach, S., "Effects of exposure to aggressive content in television upon aggression in boys." Submitted to the Joint Committee for Research on Television and Children, 1967.

Hoffman, M., "Moral development." In P. H. Mussen, ed., *Carmichael's Manual of Child Psychology* (New York: Wiley, 1970).

Kagan, J., "Acquisition and significance of sex typing and sex role identity." In M. Hoffman and L. Hoffman, eds., *Review of Child Development Research,* vol. I (New York: Russell Sage, 1964), pp. 137–67.

Kohlberg, L., "The development of children's orientations toward a moral order: I. Sequence in the development of moral thought." *Vita Humana,* 1963, 6, 11–33.

————, "A cognitive-developmental analysis of children's sex-role concepts and attitudes." In E. E. Maccoby, ed., *The Development of Sex Differences* (Stanford, Calif.: Stanford University Press, 1966), pp. 82–173.

Lövaas, O., "Effect of exposure to symbolic aggression on aggressive behavior." *Child Development,* 1961, 32, 37–44.

Mischel, W., "Sex-typing and socialization." In P. H. Mussen, ed., *Carmichael's Manual of Child Psychology,* vol. II (New York: Wiley, 1970).

O'Connor, R., "Modification of social withdrawal through symbolic modeling." *Journal of Applied Behavior Analysis,* 1969, 2, 15–22.

Sears, R. R.; Maccoby, E. E.; and Levin, H., *Patterns of child rearing* (Evanston, Ill.: Row, Peterson, 1957).

Sears, R. R., "Relation of early socialization experiences to aggression in middle childhood." *Journal of Abnormal and Social Psychology,* 1961, 63, 466–492.

Sears, R. R.; Rau, L.; and Alpert, R., *Identification and child rearing* (Stanford, Calif.: Stanford University Press, 1965).

Walter, R. H., and Thomas, E., "Enhancement of punitiveness by visual and audiovisual displays." *Canadian Journal of Psychology,* 1963, **17**, 244–55.

THE CHILD'S TIE TO HIS MOTHER: ATTACHMENT BEHAVIOUR

JOHN BOWLBY

I began by stating the two facts which have struck me as new: that a woman's strong dependence on her father merely takes over the heritage of an equally strong attachment to her mother, and that this earlier phase has lasted for an unexpectedly long period of time.

Everything in the sphere of this first attachment to the mother seemed to me so difficult to grasp in analysis . . .

SIGMUND FREUD (1931)

ALTERNATIVE THEORIES

Understanding of the response of a child to separation or loss of his mother-figure turns on an understanding of the bond that ties him to that figure. In psychoanalytic writings discussion of this theme has been conducted in terms of object relations.[1] Thus in any description of traditional theory the terminology of object relations must often be used; in the presentation of a new theory, however, terms such as 'attachment' and 'attachment-figure' are preferred.

For long, psychoanalysts have been at one in recognising a child's first human relationship as the foundation stone of his personality; but there is as yet no agreement on the nature and origin of that relationship. No doubt because of its very importance differences are sharp and feelings often run high. Although it can now be taken for granted that all are agreed on the empirical fact that within twelve months almost

[1] This terminology derives from Freud's theory of instinct in which the object of an instinct is defined as 'the thing in regard to which or through which the instinct is able to achieve its aim' (Freud, 1915a, *S.E.*, **14,** p. 122).

all infants have developed a strong tie to a mother-figure, there is no consensus on how quickly this comes about, by what processes it is maintained, for how long it persists, or what function it fulfils.

Until 1958, which saw the publication of Harlow's first papers and of an early version of the views expressed here (Bowlby, 1958), four principal theories regarding the nature and origin of the child's tie were to be found in the psychoanalytical and other psychological literature. They are:

i. The child has a number of physiological needs which must be met, particularly for food and warmth. In so far as a baby becomes interested in and attached to a human figure, especially mother, this is the result of the mother's meeting the baby's physiological needs and the baby's learning in due course that she is the source of his gratification. I shall call this the theory of Secondary Drive, a term which is derived from Learning Theory. It has also been called the cupboard-love theory of object relations.

ii. There is in infants an in-built propensity

to relate themselves to a human breast, to suck it and to possess it orally. In due course the infant learns that, attached to the breast, there is a mother and so relates to her also. I propose to term this the theory of Primary Object Sucking.[2]

iii. There is in infants an in-built propensity to be in touch with and to cling to a human being. In this sense there is a 'need' for an object independent of food which is as primary as the 'need' for food and warmth. It is proposed to term this the theory of Primary Object Clinging.

iv. Infants resent their extrusion from the womb and seek to return there. This is termed the theory of Primary Return-to-Womb Craving.

Of these four theories by far the most widely and strongly held has been the theory of secondary drive. From Freud onwards it has underlain much, though by no means all, psychoanalytic writing, and it has also been a common assumption of learning theorists. Representative statements are as follows:

> love has its origin in attachment to the satisfied need for nourishment (Freud, 1940, *S.E.,* 23, p. 188).

> probably the feeding experience can be the occasion for the child to learn to like to be with others (Dollard and Miller, 1950). . . .

The hypothesis to be advanced here is different from any of those listed above and is built on the theory of instinctive behaviour already outlined. It postulates that the child's tie to his mother is a product of the activity of a number of behavioural systems that have proximity to mother as a predictable outcome. Since in the human child ontogeny of these systems is slow and complex, and their rate of development varies greatly from child to child, no simple statement about progress during the

first year of life can be made. Once a child has entered his second year, however, and is mobile, fairly typical attachment behaviour is almost always seen. By that age in most children the integrate of behavioural systems concerned is readily activated, especially by mother's departure or by anything frightening, and the stimuli that most effectively terminate the systems are sound, sight, or touch of mother. Until about the time a child reaches his third birthday the systems continue to be very readily activated. Thenceforward in most children they become less easily activated and they also undergo other changes that make proximity to mother less urgent. During adolescent and adult life yet further changes occur, including change of the figures towards whom the behaviour is directed.

Attachment behaviour is regarded as a class of social behaviour of an importance equivalent to that of mating behaviour and parental behaviour. It is held to have a biological function specific to itself and one that has hitherto been little considered.

In this formulation, it will be noticed, there is no reference to 'needs' or 'drives'. Instead, attachment behaviour is regarded as what occurs when certain behavioural systems are activated. The behavioural systems themselves are believed to develop within the infant as a result of his interaction with his environment of evolutionary adaptedness, and especially of his interaction with the principal figure in that environment, namely his mother. Food and eating are held to play no more than a minor part in their development.

Of the four principal theories found in the literature those of primary object sucking and primary object clinging come closest to the hypothesis now proposed: each postulates an autonomous propensity to behave in a certain kind of way towards objects with certain properties. Theories with which the present hypothesis has nothing in common are those of secondary drive and primary return-to-womb craving: the former is discussed; the latter is dismissed as both redundant and biologically implausible.

The hypothesis proposed represents a development of that advanced by me in 1958. The principal change is due to better understanding of control theory and to recognition

---

[2] In this nomenclature, the terms 'primary' and 'secondary' refer to whether the response is regarded as developing autonomously or as being wholly derived, through a process of learning, from some more primitive system; throughout they will be used in this sense. The terms have no reference either to the period of life when the response appears or to the primary and secondary processes postulated by Freud.

of the very sophisticated forms that behavioural systems controlling instinctive behaviour may take. In the present version of the hypothesis it is postulated that, at some stage in the development of the behavioural systems responsible for attachment, proximity to mother becomes a set-goal. In the earlier version of the theory five patterns of behaviour—sucking, clinging, following, crying, and smiling—were described as contributing to attachment. In the new version these same five patterns are still held to be of great importance, but it is postulated that between the ages of about nine and eighteen months they usually become incorporated into far more sophisticated goal-corrected systems. These systems are so organised and activated that a child tends to be maintained in proximity to his mother.

The earlier version of the theory was described as a theory of component instinctual responses. The new version can be described as a control theory of attachment behaviour.

Before this theory is described in greater detail . . . it is useful to compare the attachment behaviour seen in human children with that seen in young animals of other species and to consider what is known of the natural history of such behaviour.

ATTACHMENT BEHAVIOUR AND ITS PLACE IN NATURE

In the countryside in springtime there is no more familiar sight than mother animals with young. In the fields, cows and calves, mares and foals, ewes and lambs; in the ponds and rivers, ducks and ducklings, swans and cygnets. So familiar are these sights and so much do we take it for granted that lamb and ewe will remain together and that a flotilla of ducklings will remain with mother duck that the questions are rarely asked: What causes these animals to remain in each other's company? What function is fulfilled by their doing so?

In the species referred to, young are born in a state of development sufficiently advanced for them to be able to move freely within a few hours; and in each case it is observed that when mother moves off in some direction her young commonly follow her. In other species,

including carnivores and rodents and including also man himself, development of the neonate is much less advanced. In these species weeks or even months may pass before the young acquire mobility; but once they have done so the same tendency to keep in the vicinity of the mother animal is evident. Admittedly there are times when the young animal strays and the mother may then herself behave in such a way that proximity is restored; but just as frequently the young animal, on finding itself alone, is itself the principal agent for restoring proximity.

The kind of behaviour described is characterised by two main features. The first is maintaining proximity to another animal, and restoring it when it has been impaired; the second is the specificity of the other animal. Often within hours of hatching eggs or giving birth to young, a parent can distinguish its own young from any others and then will behave parentally only to them; the young in their turn come soon to distinguish their own parents from all other adults and thenceforward behave in a special way towards them. Thus both parent and young usually behave towards each other in ways very different from the ways in which they behave towards all other animals. Individual recognition and highly differentiated behaviour are, then, the rule in the parent–young relations of birds and mammals.

Naturally, as with other forms of instinctive behaviour, the usual pattern of development may miscarry. In particular, a young animal may seek proximity to an animal other than its mother, or even to some inanimate object. But in natural conditions such anomalies of development are rare, and they need not detain us further at this point.

In most species there is more than one kind of behaviour shown by young that results in young and mother staying close to one another. For example, a young's vocal calls attract mother to it, and its locomotory movements take it to her. Since both kinds of behaviour, and others as well, have the same consequence, namely proximity, it is useful to have a general term to cover them all; and for this purpose 'attachment behaviour' is used. Any one form of juvenile behaviour that results in proximity can then be regarded as a component of attachment behaviour. This type of terminology follows established ethological tradition. Whenever several different sorts of behaviour commonly have the same consequence (or at least contribute to the same consequence) they are usually gathered into a category and labelled by reference to that consequence. Nest-building behaviour and mating behaviour are two well-known examples.

The behaviour of parents that is reciprocal to the attachment behaviour of juveniles is termed 'caretaking behaviour'. . . .

Attachment behaviour, and also caretaking behaviour, are common in ground-nesting birds which leave the nest soon after hatching, and both forms of behaviour are present in all species of mammal. Unless there is some mishap of development, attachment behaviour is initially always directed towards the mother. In species where the father plays a major role in upbringing it may come to be directed towards him as well. In humans it may be directed also towards a few other persons.

The proportion of the life-cycle during which attachment behaviour is manifested varies greatly from species to species. As a rule it continues until puberty though not necessarily until full sexual maturity is reached. For many species of bird the phase when attachment behaviour ceases is the same for both sexes, namely when the young are ready to pair, which may be at the end of their first winter or, as in geese and swans, at the end of their second or third winter. For many species of mammal, on the other hand, there is a marked difference between the sexes. In the female of ungulate species (sheep, deer, oxen, etc.), attachment to mother may continue until old age. As a result a flock of sheep, or a herd of deer, is built up of young following mother following grandmother following great grandmother and so on. Young males of these species, by contrast, break away from mother when they reach adolescence. Thenceforward they become attached to older males and remain with them all their lives except during the few weeks each year of the rutting season.

Attachment behaviour in monkeys and apes is exhibited strongly during infancy and childhood, but during adolescence the bond to mother wears thin. Although in the past it has been tacitly assumed that it then ceases, recent evidence shows that, at least in some species, the bond persists into adult life; by so doing it produces sub-groups of animals all of which have the same mother. Reviewing the reports of Sade (1965) for rhesus monkeys and of Goodall (1965) for chimpanzees, Washburn, Jay, and Lancaster (1965) remark that these kinship sub-groups are 'determined by the necessarily close association of mother with newborn infant, which is extended through time and generations and allowed to ramify into close associations between siblings'; and they express their belief 'that this pattern of enduring social relations between a mother and her offspring will be found in other species of primates'.

Because the human infant is born so very immature and is so slow to develop, there is no species in which attachment behaviour takes so long to appear. This is probably one reason why until recent years the behaviour of the human child towards his mother seems not to have been recognised as belonging to the same general category of behaviour that is seen in so many animal species. Another probable reason is that it is only in the past two decades that attachment behaviour in animals has become the subject of systematic study. Whatever the reasons, that the child's tie to his mother is the human version of behaviour seen commonly in many other species of animal seems now indisputable; and it is in this perspective that the nature of the tie is examined.

Nevertheless caution is necessary. The two lines of animal evolution that led ultimately to birds and to mammals have been distinct since the days of the early reptiles, and it is therefore nearly certain that attachment behaviour has evolved independently in the two groups. That, and the fact that brain structure in birds is very different from what it is in mammals, make it more than probable that the behavioural mechanisms mediating attachment behaviour are also very different for the two groups. Any argument used here that is derived from what is known about bird behaviour must, therefore, be recognised as no more than argument from analogy. Argument from what is known about the attachment behaviour of young mammals, on the other hand, has a much better status. And whatever behaviour is found in sub-human primates we can be confident is likely to be truly homologous with what obtains in man.

The growth of attachment behaviour in the human child and the course of its change over time are in fact still very poorly documented. Partly because of this but chiefly in order to provide a broader perspective in which to view the human case, the discussion starts with what is known about attachment behaviour in monkey, baboon, and great ape.

ATTACHMENT BEHAVIOUR IN SUB-HUMAN PRIMATES

At birth or soon after, all primate infants, bar the human, cling to their mothers. Throughout early childhood they are either in direct physical contact with mother or only a few feet or yards from her. Mother reciprocates and keeps the infant close to her. As the young grow older the proportion of the day when they are in direct contact with mother diminishes and the distance of their excursions increases; but they continue to sleep with her at night and to rush to her side at the least alarm. In higher species, it is probable that some attachment to mother is present until adolescence, and in some species the tie continues in weakened form into adult life.

Female young are less active and adventurous than males. During adolescence females are likely to be found in the centre of a group, often in proximity to adult males, whereas adolescent males are likely to be found at the periphery or even on their own.

Descriptions follow of the course of attachment behaviour in the young of four primate species—two Old World monkeys, the rhesus macaque and the baboon, and two great apes, the chimpanzee and the gorilla. Reasons for this selection are:
a. All four species, and especially baboon and gorilla, are adapted to a terrestrial existence;
b. good field studies are now available for all four;
c. for two species, rhesus and chimpanzee, experimental data are also available.

Although for the sake of brevity much of the description that follows is in the form of un-

qualified statements, it must be remembered not only that there is considerable variation of behaviour between different animals of the same species but that the behaviour typical in one social group of a species may differ in some respects from that typical in another group of the same species. Whilst some of these differences between groups can be accounted for by differences in the habitat that each is living in, some of them appear to be due to innovation started by an animal in one group and passed on to others in its group by social tradition.

Attachment Behaviour in Rhesus Monkeys

Rhesus monkeys have been observed in fairly natural conditions and have been the subjects of much laboratory observation and experiment. They are common throughout Northern India where some still live in forest though many more live in villages and cultivated land. Although rather more of an arboreal than a terrestrial species, much of their day is spent on the ground; at night they resort to the tree tops or a roof. Bands, comprising adults of both sexes, juveniles, and young, are stable over long periods and spend their days and nights in a particular and quite limited locality. In size the bands vary from about fifteen to over a hundred members.

The rhesus monkey reaches puberty at about four years, is full-grown at about six years and may then live another twenty years. Until it is about three years of age a young rhesus monkey in the wild remains close to its mother. At that age 'most males leave their mothers and associate with other adolescents at the edge of the band or shift to other bands' (Koford, 1963a). Females, it is thought, probably remain with their mothers for longer. Sons of high-ranking females also sometimes remain with their mothers; as soon as they become adult these favoured sons are likely to assume a dominant position in the band.

Hinde and his associates have given a very detailed account of infant–mother interaction during the first two and a half years of life in small captive groups of animals (Hinde, Rowell, and Spencer-Booth, 1964; Hinde and Spencer-Booth, 1967).

As soon as they are born some infants immediately cling to their mother's fur, and they tend also to climb up her body. Other infants, however, at first hold arms and legs flexed and are then supported solely by their mother. By no infant was the nipple taken until several hours had elapsed, the longest interval being over nine hours. Once found, the nipple is gripped for long periods, though only a small proportion of that time is spent sucking.

During the first week or two of its life the infant is in continuous ventro-ventral contact with its mother, spending almost all the daytime hours gripping its mother with hands, feet, and mouth, and at night-time being held by her. Thereafter the infant begins to make short daytime excursions from mother and she from it; but until it is six weeks old virtually none of these excursions extends beyond a two-foot radius—close enough, in fact, for mother to gather the infant to her whenever she wishes. Thenceforward its excursions extend further and last longer. Not until it is about ten weeks old, however, is it spending half the daytime off its mother, and not until after its first birthday does the proportion rise above 70 per cent.

Although during their second year infants spent most of their daytime hours in sight of but out of physical contact with mother, most of them nonetheless are in actual contact with her for a substantial fraction of their day—usually from 10 to 20 per cent of it—and for the whole night. Only after their second birthday does amount of time in physical contact during the day become negligible.

Initiative for breaking and resuming contact lies partly with mother and partly with infant, and the balance changes in a complex way as the infant gets older. During the first few weeks the infants sometimes set out to explore 'in an apparently intrepid manner', and the mothers often restrain them. After the first two months the balance begins to shift. Mother restrains less and starts occasionally to hit or reject: 'From this time the infant comes to play an increasing role in the maintenance of proximity with its mother'. Nevertheless mother continues to take an important part—perhaps discouraging the infant from too close proximity when she is sitting quietly and no danger threatens but initiating quick contact when she is about to move or becomes alarmed.

When the mother moves any distance the infant usually travels under her belly, grasping mother's fur with hands and feet and a nipple with its mouth. During the first week or two some mothers give a little additional support with a hand. Babies quickly learn to adopt this carrying position and also to respond appropriately to a light touch of mother's hand on back of neck or shoulders, which seems to act as a signal that she is moving off. After they have reached three or four weeks of age babies may occasionally ride on mother's back.

During the weeks after the baby first leaves its mother, if it is on the ground and she moves away, it usually follows; and even though it can barely crawl it will still attempt to follow.

These early following attempts are often actively encouraged by the mother, who moves away only slowly and hesitantly, repeatedly looking back at the baby, or even pulling at it to encourage it to come.

Should mother move too fast or depart suddenly the baby 'geckers' and the mother responds by hugging it to her. On other occasions when it is away from its mother it may give a short, high squeaking call, and this too brings mother instantly to pick it up. A baby that loses its mother makes very long calls through protruded lips; and this may lead another female to pick it up. In the event of any sudden disturbance occurring when the baby is off its mother, each at once runs to the other; the baby clings to her in the ventro-ventral position and takes the nipple. Such behaviour continues for some years.

Though after the age of two and a half or three years juveniles usually move away from their mothers, evidence is accumulating that the bond may nevertheless persist and play a large part in determining adult social relationships. In a semi-wild colony that has been observed systematically over the course of many years and where the family history of individuals is known, it has become evident not only that in each band there are stable sub-groups, composed of several adult animals of both sexes and a number of juveniles and infants all of which remain in proximity to one another, but that all the members of such a sub-group may be the children and grandchildren of a single elderly female (Sade, 1965).[3]

Attachment Behaviour in Baboons

The chacma baboon, which is roughly twice the size of a rhesus monkey, has been observed in its natural habitat in several localities in Africa, where it is very common south of the Equator. Some troops live in forested ground but many occupy open savanna. In either case they spend most of their day on the ground, taking to trees or cliffs for sleeping and for refuge from predators. Like rhesus monkeys they live in stable bands, comprising adults of both sexes, juveniles, and young. Bands vary in size from about a dozen individuals to over a hundred. Each band keeps to a limited area of ground, though areas of adjacent bands overlap. Relations between bands are friendly.

The maturation rate of young baboons is a little slower than that of rhesus monkeys. Puberty is reached at about four years and the female becomes adult at about six years. The male, however, who grows to be far larger than the female, is not fully grown until about eight years.

A baby baboon remains in close contact and association with its mother throughout its first year of life and for part of the second, but seems to break the tie nearly a year earlier than does the rhesus infant.

Almost the whole of its first month of life a baby baboon spends clinging to its mother in a ventro-ventral position, exactly like the rhesus monkey. After about five weeks of age the infant departs from its mother occasionally, and it is at this age too that it begins to ride on mother's back. By about four months of age its excursions from mother are more frequent and it may move as far as twenty yards from her. This is also the age when riding mother jockey-style becomes popular (except when she runs

[3] There seems to be a marked tendency for sons (half-brothers) to stay close to one another and for daughters (half-sisters) also to stay close together. Since in adolescent and adult life sons tend to leave their mother whereas daughters tend not to, a sub-group of relatives of several generations tends always to contain a higher proportion of females than males.

or climbs, when the infant resumes ventral clinging), and social play with peers begins. From six months onwards play with peers increases and absorbs a large part of the young baboon's time and energy. Nevertheless, until about twelve months it remains fairly close to mother and always sleeps with her. It rides her less and follows more often on foot.

The second year of a young baboon's life is spent mostly with peers and is full of conflict with its mother. As long as she is lactating a female baboon does not go through her normal sexual cycles; but when the infant is aged about ten months and lactation is ceasing, cycles and mating are resumed. At these times the mother rebuffs her infant's attempts either to take the nipple or to ride on her back, and is rejecting even at night-time. Such rebuffs, DeVore reports, 'seem to make the infant more anxious than ever to be in her arms, to hold her nipple in its mouth, and to ride her back to the sleeping trees'. When the sexual swelling has subsided a mother 'often accepts the infant again'. Despite these rebuffs, when either mother or infant is alarmed, they seek each other out; and, when her infant is in trouble with peers or with adult males, mother tries to protect it.

By the end of its second year an infant's mother is likely to have a new baby and thenceforward relations between two-year-old and mother come almost to an end. When alarmed, the two-year-old runs to one of the adult males who, until an infant is nearly three years old, are most protective.

By the age of four years females tend to join adult females and to behave as adults. Males take another four years to reach maturity and during their prolonged adolescence tend to live on the periphery of the group. Once adult they become central figures in the life of the band. Since no band has been observed long enough for individual kinships to be traced, it is unknown whether a legacy of the mother–infant bond plays any part in determining the adult social relationships of baboons.

Attachment Behaviour in Chimpanzees

Chimpanzees have been observed in the forested regions and wooded uplands of Central

Africa, which is their natural habitat; and they have for long been the subjects of laboratory experiment. Though they are skilled in arboreal locomotion and sleep in trees, when they travel distances of more than fifty yards they usually keep to the ground; and they always run from an intruder on the ground. Unlike any other primate studied, chimpanzees do not keep close together in stable social groups. Instead, the individuals belonging to what is believed to be a single social group of from sixty to eighty animals break into an ever-changing variety of temporary sub-groups. Each sub-group can comprise animals of any age, sex, or number; but two kinds of sub-group are specially common, one a party of several males together and the other a party of several females with infants.

Chimpanzees are much slower to mature than are rhesus monkeys or baboons. Adolescence is not reached until about seven years and the animal is not fully mature until ten or eleven years. Although chimpanzees are usually found in company with others, companions are constantly changing with the result that the only stable social unit is that of a mother with her infant and older offspring. Goodall (1965) believes that 'mother–infant ties may persist well into adult life and may [then] form the main link in a group comprising a female with infant and older child, adolescent, and a young mature animal'.

As in all other primate infants, the baby chimpanzee spends the whole of its infancy in close proximity to its mother. During its first four months it clings to her in the ventral position and only very occasionally is seen apart from her, and usually then is sitting beside her. Should it venture more than a couple of feet from her, she pulls it back; and should she observe a predator approach she hugs it more closely.

Between the ages of about six and eighteen months the infant more often travels jockey-fashion on mother's back than on her belly, and the time it spends not actually clinging to mother increases. By the end of the period it is out of physical contact with her for as much as 25 per cent of the day, usually playing with age-mates; but it is never out of its mother's

sight. Not infrequently it breaks off play to run back to her to sit on her lap or beside her. When mother is about to move off she signals her intention by reaching out to touch the infant, gesturing to it, or, when it is up a tree, tapping softly on the trunk. The infant at once obeys and assumes the carrying position.

The next eighteen months, until the age of three years, see increasing activity away from mother and play with companions, and the young chimpanzee is out of physical contact with mother for as much as 75 to 90 per cent of the day. Nevertheless it continues to be transported by her, jockey-fashion unless she is moving fast, and it still sleeps with her.

During the next four years, until puberty is reached at the age of about seven, the small chimpanzee becomes independent of its mother for feeding, transport, and sleeping. It spends much time playing with age-mates, and sometimes also with infants or with adolescents. As it gets older it may leave its mother and join a nursery group of up to a dozen juveniles and adolescents which are moving about in company with one or two mature females; nevertheless, there are times when it is still likely to return to its mother to move about with her.

Adolescence extends from about seven years to eleven years, and during this phase animals of both sexes often associate with mature males. Even so, some of them at least spend days back with their mothers and siblings. It was Goodall's impression that, throughout the years of increasing independence, the initiative for departures and return lay with the young animal. There was no sign of a mother discouraging or rejecting one of her offspring.

Attachment Behaviour in Gorillas

Gorillas, like chimpanzees, inhabit the tropical rain forests and wooded uplands of Central Africa and have also been the subjects of systematic field observation in recent years. Though animals often sleep in trees and the young play in them, for the rest of the time gorillas are almost entirely terrestrial. Apart from a few adult males, they live in social groups made up of both sexes and all ages, the numbers in a group ranging from half a dozen to nearly thirty. Membership of groups is fairly stable but more so in some groups than in others. As in the case of chimpanzees, it seems probable that all the animals in a neighborhood know each other, and meetings between groups and also departures are peaceful.

Biological evidence suggests that gorilla is man's nearest relative.

The rate of maturation of gorillas is roughly the same as that of chimpanzees though, if anything, gorillas mature a little earlier. The course of the young's relation to mother is very similar to that seen in the chimpanzee.

During the first two or three months of life the young gorilla lacks the strength to clasp its mother's hair securely and receives support from its mother's arms. By the age of three months, however, it can cling efficiently and may begin to ride on mother's back. During the period from three to six months a young animal is occasionally on the ground beside mother and then she might, by walking slowly away, encourage it to follow her. An infant is rarely permitted to stray beyond a ten-foot radius, however, before its mother pulls it back. Until it is about eight months of age it is not aware when mother is about to move off and so has to be gathered by her. After that age it is clearly alive to her location and behaviour, and at the first sign of movement rushes back and climbs aboard.

By the age of a year infants may wander amongst the other animals whilst the group is resting and may be out of mother's sight for short periods. They also begin spending time sitting beside mother instead of on her lap. After they have reached eighteen months mothers are often reluctant to carry them.

A frequent sight was a female walking slowly with an infant toddling at her heels [sometimes with one or both hands grasping her rump hairs]. However, at the first sight of danger or the onset of rapid movement all infants up to the age of nearly three years rushed to their mothers and climbed aboard (Schaller, 1965).

Schaller's observations were not extended over sufficient time for him to be confident about the interaction of juveniles aged from three to seven years with their mothers, but it appears to be not unlike that seen in chim-panzees. The juvenile is no longer transported, and it feeds and sleeps on its own. Much of its day it spends with other juveniles. But some juveniles seemed still to be associating with their mothers, and Schaller concludes that ties persist in some cases at least until the juvenile is four and a half years old.

Though most of the initiative to move away from mother seems to come from the juveniles themselves, there are times when gorilla mothers discourage their offspring from remaining too close. For example, a one-year-old infant that was holding on to its mother's rump hairs as she walked along was brushed off with a hand, and one of nearly two years that ran up to its sitting mother was pushed away and rolled playfully on to its back. 'Rebuffs were always gentle'.

Relations of Young Monkeys and Apes to Other Animals in Their Groups

During the period of infancy (up to one year in rhesus and baboon, and up to three years in the great apes) the infant spends little time with adults other than its mother. When away from her it is most likely to be playing with other infants or juveniles. Not infrequently, however, adult females without young of their own seek to mother a baby and sometimes they succeed in obtaining possession of it. In most species this is much disliked by the mother, who soon gets her infant back. The Indian langur monkey, however, permits other adult females to cradle her infant; and Schaller (1965) describes how two infant gorillas were observed to have strong ties with females other than their mothers: one of six months would spend periods of up to an hour or more with the 'aunt', and another over a period of six months during its second year 'spent most of its time . . . with a female and small infant, returning to its mother only intermittently during the day and apparently at night'.

In most species adult males take considerable interest in mothers with babies and not only willingly permit mothers carrying young to remain close to them but may stay behind specially to escort them. As a rule, however, adult males never or only rarely carry young themselves. An exception to this is the Japanese macaque (a relative of the rhesus). In a few troops of that species adult males of high rank commonly 'adopt' a one-year-old infant after the mother has produced a new baby. For a period of limited duration their behaviour 'is quite similar to the behaviour of a mother toward her infant, except for the lack of suckling' (Itani, 1963). Sometimes a second period of 'adoption' occurs a year later when the older child is two, but is then confined to female infants or weakly males. This paternal type of behaviour is not shown by the Indian rhesus male, who is either uninterested in young or hostile to them.

In many species, as the young grow older, association with adult males increases, but the age at which this occurs seems to vary greatly. As early as their second year juvenile baboons when alarmed begin to run to an adult male rather than to mother. Baby gorillas are attracted by the dominant male and when the group rests often sit by or play near him. On occasion they climb on to him or even hitch a lift. Provided the play is not too boisterous the male is remarkably tolerant. Juvenile gorillas also sometimes seek the company of an adult male and will leave the group to tag behind him. These amiable relationships are not reported for chimpanzees; when they become adolescent, however, chimpanzees of both sexes often associate with mature males.

Since in all these species mating within a group is promiscuous, there is no way of telling which male has fathered which infant. In so far as fatherly behaviour occurs, therefore, it is directed towards any of the young in the group, or in the case of the Japanese macaque to one special infant.

Roles of Infant and of Mother in the Relationship

From what has been said it is clear that during the earliest months of infancy mothers of all these species of sub-human primate play a large part in ensuring that their infants remain close to them. If the infant is unable to grip efficiently the mother gives it support. If it strays too far she pulls it back. When a hawk flies overhead or a human approaches too closely she hugs it to her. Thus even if the infant were disposed to go far it is never allowed to do so.

But all the evidence is that the infant is not disposed to stray far. This is shown whenever an infant is brought up away from its mother, as infants of many different species of monkey and ape have been. In several cases in which an infant has been raised in a human home a biographical account is available. Good examples are those by Rowell (1965) of a young baboon, by Bolwig (1963) of a young patas monkey (also a terrestrial species, and with a maturation rate similar to that of a baboon), by Kellogg and Kellogg (1933) and by Hayes (1951) of young chimpanzees, and by Martini (1955) of a young gorilla. Of the cases in which an infant has been brought up on an experimental dummy the best-known reports are those of Harlow and his colleagues (Harlow, 1961; Harlow and Harlow, 1965).

All those brave scientists who have acted as a foster-parent to a young primate testify to the intensity and persistence with which it clings. Rowell writes of the little baboon she looked after (from the fifth to the eleventh week of age): 'when alarmed by a loud noise or a sudden movement he ran to me and clung desperately hard to my leg'. After she had had the infant ten days: 'he no longer allowed me out of his sight, and refused to accept dummy or apron, but clung the more fiercely'. Of the little patas monkey that Bolwig cared for from a few days old he writes that from the first 'he firmly gripped any object placed in his hand and protested by screaming if it was removed' and that 'his attachment quickly grew closer and closer until in the end it became almost unbreakable'. Hayes, describing Viki, the female chimpanzee she reared from three days of age, reports how, at four months old when Viki was walking well, 'from the moment she left her crib until she was tucked up at night, with time out for only an hour's nap, she clung to me like a papoose'. All the accounts contain similar passages.

Discrimination of Mother by Infant

Attachment behaviour has been defined as seeking and maintaining proximity to another individual. Whilst these reports leave no possible doubt that young primates of all species cling to objects with the utmost tenacity, it still remains to be considered how soon they come to discriminate, and to attach themselves to, a particular individual.

Harlow believes that a rhesus infant 'learns attachments to a specific mother (*the* mother)' during the first week or two of life (Harlow and Harlow, 1965). Hinde (personal communication) endorses that view: he points out that, within a few days of birth, a rhesus baby orients towards its mother in preference to other monkeys. For example, at the end of its first week it may leave mother briefly and crawl towards another female; but it soon about-turns and moves towards mother. A capacity so soon to recognize a particular individual is less surprising now that evidence suggests that subhuman primates have some degree of pattern vision at birth (Fantz, 1965).

The reports of human foster-parents are also of interest in this connection.

Bolwig's little patas monkey began discriminating individual members of the household very soon after it arrived, then aged between five and fourteen days. This was shown only three days after its arrival when the monkey, which had been looked after mainly by Miss Bolwig, ran after her to the door, screaming, on being left with Dr. Bolwig, and stopped crying when she returned and picked it up.

During the following days the attachment shifted from my daughter to me, and it became so strong that I had to carry him on my shoulder wherever I went . . . right up to the age of 3½ months he could be very troublesome if left in the care of some other member of the family.

Although at the end of five months the monkey was spending much time in the company of other humans and of other monkeys of its own species, its preference for Dr. Bolwig continued, especially when it was in distress; and this same preference was again in evidence no less than four months later (when it was aged nine months) although Dr. Bolwig had been absent throughout the intervening period.

Rowell's baboon was about five weeks old when she became its foster-mother. Already during its first week the little baboon could dis-

tinguish familiar people from strangers and could recognise its primary caretaker. At first, provided it was not hungry, it was content to stay alone with its dummy and its caretaker's apron. After ten days, however, 'he no longer allowed me out of his sight. . . . If he saw me move or even caught my eye he would drop the dummy and run to me'.

These reports leave no doubt, therefore, that in some species of Old World monkey attachment behaviour comes, within a week or so, to be directed especially towards a certain preferred individual, and that once it is so directed the preference is extremely strong and persistent.

In keeping with their slower rate of maturation, chimpanzee infants appear to be slower to show a clear preference for their caretaker. Once it has developed, however, the preference is no less strong than it is in monkey species. A reading of Hayes's account suggests that Viki was about three months old before she was greatly concerned about whom she was with. Around that age, however, her preference became unmistakable. For example, Hayes describes how Viki, when a little under four months, attended a party and how she alternately explored guests and retreated to be beside her foster-mother. When the guests moved to an adjacent room Viki inadvertently caught hold of another lady's dress; but when she happened to glance up and see her mistake she gave a short cry and transferred at once to climb up her foster-mother.[4]

Changes in Intensity of Attachment Behaviour

In every description of primate infants in the wild it is reported that at the least alarm an infant away from its mother will rush to her and that one already near her will cling more tightly. That attachment behaviour is exhibited without fail on such occasions is of much importance for our understanding of both cause and function.

Some other conditions that lead attachment

---

[4] Accounts by Yerkes also suggest that young chimps are some months old before they are very discriminating. A pair of twins brought up by their mother did not appear to 'recognise one another as social objects' until nearly five months old (Tomilin and Yerkes, 1935).

behaviour to be shown, or shown more intensely, are reported in the accounts of infants raised by human foster-parents. Rowell reports that when her young baboon was hungry 'he was insistent in maintaining contact and screamed continually if left'. Both Rowell and Bolwig describe how, when the infant was a little older and was disposed to explore, the slightest sign that the caretaker was moving off was noticed at once and brought the little animal quickly to cling. A short separation had the same effect. Bolwig records that when his little patas monkey was released from a cage in which it had been left for a few hours with other monkeys of its own kind,

he would cling to me and refuse to leave me out of sight for the rest of the day. In the evening when asleep he would wake up with small shrieks and cling to me, showing all signs of terror when I tried to release his grip.

The Waning of Attachment Behaviour

In the accounts of the attachment behaviour of young primates in the wild it has been described how, as they get older, they spend a decreasing amount of time with mother and an increasing amount of time with peers and, later, with other adults, and how the change is mainly a result of their own initiative. The extent to which the mother herself promotes the change seems to vary much from species to species. A baboon mother does a good deal of rebuffing of her infant after it has reached ten months of age, especially if she is about to have another baby. The rhesus mother also does some rebuffing. Neither chimpanzee nor gorilla appears to do very much.

From such evidence as is available, however, it seems clear that, even with few or no maternal rebuffs, after a certain age attachment behaviour diminishes both in its intensity and in the frequency with which it is elicited. In all likelihood several different processes are at work. One probably is a change in form taken by the behavioural systems mediating attachment behaviour itself. Another is an increase of curiosity and of exploratory behaviour, on the effects of which Harlow (1961) and other workers lay much emphasis.

Bolwig's account of the waning of attachment behaviour as it occurred in his patas monkey is illuminating. He describes vividly how, from the first days, the monkey was inquisitive and liked to stare at hands and faces. Its interest in exploring inanimate objects, present from the start, increased steadily, and by the end of its second month in the household it spent much time climbing over the furniture. At the age of nearly four months it enjoyed itself so much with a crowd of students that it refused to come when called; subsequently such refusals became more numerous. Bolwig concludes that the young monkey's interest in play and exploration 'acted as an antagonist to the phase of attachment and gradually became dominant over it during his hour to hour activity'.

The rate at which attachment behaviour wanes is no doubt affected by many variables. One is the frequency of alarming events: all accounts agree that when alarmed even older juveniles instantly resume proximity to mother. Another is the frequency of enforced separation at too early an age. Bolwig describes the intense clinging shown by his little patas monkey after its caretaker had been persuaded (against his better judgment) to discipline it, for example by locking it out of the house or putting it in a cage. 'Every time I tried . . . it resulted in a setback in the monkey's development. He became more clinging, more mischievous and more difficult'.

Although in the natural course of events attachment behaviour directed towards the mother gradually wanes in sub-human primates, it does not disappear altogether. There is, however, too little evidence from field studies for firm conclusions to be drawn regarding its role in adult life, and the same is true in respect of animals brought up in captivity.

All the human-raised monkeys and apes referred to in these reports have been placed in zoos or in laboratory colonies whilst still juvenile. The general experience with such animals is that, though they usually become reasonably sociable with members of their own species, they continue to show a much stronger interest in humans than do naturally raised animals. Some of them, moreover, become sexually aroused by, and direct sexual behaviour towards, humans. The nature of the figure towards whom attachment behaviour is directed during infancy has, therefore, a number of long-term effects.

ATTACHMENT BEHAVIOUR IN MAN

*Differences from and Similarities with
That Seen in Sub-Human Primates*

At first sight it might appear that there is a sharp break between attachment behaviour in man and that seen in sub-human primates. In the latter, it might be emphasised, clinging by infant to mother is found from birth or very soon afterwards whereas in man the infant only very slowly becomes aware of his mother and only after he has become mobile does he seek her company. Though the difference is real, I believe it is easy to exaggerate its importance.

First, we have seen that in one at least of the great apes, gorilla, the infant at birth has not strength enough to support its own weight and that for two or three months its mother supports it. Secondly, it must be remembered that in the simpler human societies, especially those of hunters and gatherers, the infant is not placed in cot or pram but is carried by his mother on her back. Thus the difference in infant–mother relations in gorilla and in man is not so great. In fact, from lowest primates to Western man a continuum can be discerned. In the least advanced members of the primate order, for example lemur and marmoset, the infant must from birth forward do all the clinging; it receives no support whatever from its mother. In the more advanced Old World monkeys, such as baboon and rhesus, it must do most of the clinging but in the early days of its life its mother gives some assistance. In the most advanced, gorilla and man, the infant continues to cling but has not strength to support himself for long; in consequence, for some months the infant is kept in proximity to mother only by the mother's own actions; but keep in proximity mother and infant do. Only in more economically developed human societies, and especially in Western ones, are infants commonly out of contact with mother for

many hours a day and often during the night as well.

This evolutionary shift in the balance from infant taking all the initiative in keeping contact to mother taking all the initiative has an important consequence. This is that, whereas a rhesus monkey is already clinging strongly before it learns to discriminate its mother from other monkeys (and inanimate objects), the human infant is able to distinguish his mother from other persons (or objects) before he can either cling to her or move actively towards her. This fact leads to a minor difficulty in deciding by what criteria to judge the beginning of attachment behaviour in man.

*Growth of Attachment Behaviour
During the First Year*

There is good evidence that in a family setting most infants of about four months are already responding differently to mother as compared with other people. When he sees his mother an infant of this age will smile and vocalise more readily and follow her with his eyes for longer than he does when he sees anyone else. Perceptual discrimination, therefore, is present. Yet we can hardly say that there is attachment behaviour until there is evidence that the infant not only recognises his mother but tends also to behave in a way that maintains his proximity to her.

Proximity-maintaining behaviour is seen at its most obvious when mother leaves the room and the infant cries, or cries and also attempts to follow her. Ainsworth (1963, 1967) reports that, in one group of African infants, crying and attempts to follow occurred in one infant as early as fifteen and seventeen weeks respectively and that both sorts of behaviour were common at six months of age. All but four of these infants attempted to follow a departing mother as soon as they could crawl. . . . [Bowlby continues here with a further discussion of the Ainsworth study, a section of which is included in Part 3.]

The age at which attachment behaviour develops in the Ganda [by six months], as observed by Ainsworth, does not differ greatly from the age at which Schaffer and Emerson

(1964a) found it to develop in Scottish children. Their study covered sixty infants from birth until twelve months of age. Information was obtained from parents at intervals of four weeks. Criteria of attachment were restricted to responses to being left by mother; seven possible situations, e.g. left alone in room, left in cot at night, were defined, and intensity of protest was scored. First-hand observations were limited, and greeting responses were not taken into account.

In the Scottish investigation one-third of the infants were showing attachment behaviour by six months of age and three-quarters by nine months. As in the case of the Ganda, a few infants were slow to show it: in two it was still not reported when the children were twelve months old.

Taken at their face value Schaffer and Emerson's findings suggest that Scottish children are a little slower to develop attachment behaviour than are Ganda children. This may well be so and would be in keeping with the notably advanced motor development of the Ganda. An alternative explanation is that such differences as are reported are a result of the different criteria of attachment and methods of observation that were employed in the two studies. By being present and making the observations herself Ainsworth may be expected to have recorded the earliest signs of attachment, whereas Schaffer and Emerson in relying on mother's reports may not have done so.[5] However that may be, the two reports agree well on many findings. These include the great range of age at which attachment behaviour is first shown by different children—from before four months to after twelve months. This wide individual variation must never be forgotten. . . .

There is also agreement regarding the frequency with which attachment behaviour is directed towards figures other than mother. Schaffer and Emerson found that, during the month after the children first showed attachment behaviour, one-quarter of them were directing it to other members of the family, and by the time they had reached eighteen months of age

all but a handful of children were attached to at least one other figure and often to several others. Father was the most frequent of other figures to elicit attachment behaviour. Next in frequency were older children, 'not only very much older children, who might occasionally take over the mother's routine care activities, but also preschool children'. Schaffer and Emerson found no evidence that attachment to mother was less intense when attachment behaviour was directed to other figures also; on the contrary, in the early months of attachment the greater the number of figures to whom a child was attached the more intense was his attachment to mother as his principal figure likely to be.

Not only do both studies record great variation in speed of development between children, but both report also that in any one child the intensity and consistency with which attachment behaviour is shown can vary greatly from day to day or hour to hour. Variables responsible for short-term changes are of two kinds, organismic and environmental. Amongst the organismic Ainsworth lists hunger, fatigue, illness, and unhappiness as all leading to increased crying and following; Schaffer and Emerson likewise list fatigue, illness, and pain. As regards environmental factors both studies note that attachment behaviour is more intense when a child is alarmed. Ainsworth was particularly well placed to make such observations because, as a white-skinned stranger, she was especially apt to arouse alarm. No Ganda child showed alarm before forty weeks of age but in the subsequent weeks practically all those observed did so: 'Children whom we met for the first time in this [the fourth] quarter seemed to be terrified of me. . . . Clinging in fright was noticed in this context'. A further point noted by Schaffer and Emerson was that intensity of attachment was increased for a period after mother had been absent.[6]

It will be noticed that all the variables reported as influencing the intensity of attachment in human infants in the short term are the same

5 The possibility that the earliest and less consistent instances of attachment behaviour were not reported to Schaffer and Emerson is suggested by their finding that, when first reported, protests at being left by mother were already at or near their maximum intensity.

6 Schaffer and Emerson report that they were unable to identify the factors responsible for some fluctuations of intensity and that 'some appeared spontaneous in nature'. It is not unlikely, however, that more frequent and first-hand observation might have revealed events not reported by mothers at monthly interviews.

as those reported as influencing its intensity in the short term in monkey and ape infants.

Although there is abundant evidence to show that the kind of care an infant receives from his mother plays a major part in determining the way in which his attachment behaviour develops, the extent to which an infant himself initiates interaction and influences the form it takes must never be forgotten. Both Ainsworth and Schaffer are among several observers who call attention to the very active role of the human infant.

Reviewing her observations of the Ganda, Ainsworth (1963) writes:

One feature of attachment behaviour that struck me especially was the extent to which the infant himself takes the initiative in seeking an interaction. At least from two months of age onwards, and increasingly through the first year of life, these infants were not so much passive and recipient as active in seeking interaction.

Schaffer (1963) writes in the same vein about his Scottish infants:

Children often seem to dictate their parents' behaviour by the insistence of their demands, for quite a number of the mothers we interviewed reported that they were forced to respond far more than they considered desirable . . .

Apart from crying, which is never easily ignored, an infant often calls persistently and, when attended to, orients to and smiles at his mother or other companion. Later, he greets and approaches her and seeks her attention in a thousand attractive ways. Not only does he by these means evoke responses from his companions but 'he maintains and shapes their responses by reinforcing some and not others' (Rheingold, 1966). The pattern of interaction that gradually develops between an infant and his mother can be understood only as a resultant of the contributions of each, and especially of the way in which each in turn influences the behaviour of the other. . . .

Subsequent Course of Attachment Behaviour in Man

Although the growth of attachment behaviour during the first year of life is reasonably well

chronicled, the course it takes during subsequent years is not. Such information as there is strongly suggests that during the second and most of the third year attachment behaviour is shown neither at less intensity nor with less frequency than it is at the end of the first year. An increase in an infant's perceptual range and in his ability to understand events in the world around him leads, however, to changes in the circumstances that elicit attachment behaviour.

One change is that a child becomes increasingly aware of an *impending* departure. During his first year an infant protests especially when put down in his cot and, a little later, on seeing his mother disappear from sight. Subsequently a child who, when his mother leaves him, is otherwise engrossed, begins to notice that she is gone and then protests. Thenceforward he is keenly alert to his mother's whereabouts: he spends much time watching her or, if she is out of sight, listening for sound of her movements. During his eleventh or twelfth month he becomes able, by noting her behaviour, to anticipate her imminent departure, and starts to protest before she goes. Knowing this will happen, many a parent of a two-year-old hides preparations until the last minute in order to avoid a clamour.

By most children attachment behaviour is exhibited strongly and regularly until almost the end of the third year. Then a change occurs. This is well illustrated by the common experience of nursery school teachers. Until children have reached about two years and nine months most of them, when attending a nursery school, are upset when mother leaves. Though their crying may last only a short time, they are nonetheless apt to remain quiet and inactive and constantly to demand the attention of the teacher—in marked contrast to how they behave in the same setting should mother remain with them. After children have reached their third birthday, however, they are usually much better able to accept mother's temporary absence and to engage in play with other children. In many children the change seems to take place almost abruptly, suggesting that at this age some maturational threshold is passed.

A main change is that after their third birthday most children become increasingly able in a strange place to feel secure with subordinate attachment-figures, for example a relative or a school teacher. Even so, such feeling of security is conditional. First, the subordinate figures must be familiar people, preferably those whom the child has got to know whilst in the company of his mother. Secondly, the child must be healthy and not alarmed. Thirdly, he must be aware of where his mother is and confident that he can resume contact with her at short notice. In the absence of these conditions he is likely to become or to remain very 'mummyish', or to show other disturbances of behaviour.

The increase in confidence that comes with age is well illustrated in the account given by Murphy and her associates (1962) of the different ways in which children aged between two and a half and five and a half years respond to an invitation to come for a play session. During a preliminary visit to a child's family a plan was made for the researchers to call again a few days later to take the child by car to the session. Though the children were encouraged to go on their own, no obstacle was put in the way of mother coming too should child protest or mother prefer to do so. Though the mothers were familiar with the researchers, to the children they were strangers, except for a meeting during the researchers' preliminary visit.

Not unexpectedly, when the researchers called at the children's homes to take them to the centre, most of the young ones refused to go unless mother came too. Refusal was highly correlated with age: whereas all but two of seventeen four- and five-year-olds accepted mother's assurances and encouragement and were willing to go alone with the researchers, only a small minority of the fifteen two- and three-year-olds would do so. Not only did most of the younger children insist that mother came too, but during the first session they made sure also of remaining in physical contact with her by sitting beside her, clinging to her skirts, holding her hand, or pulling her along. Given this support they became during later sessions steadily more confident. A majority of the older children, by contrast, went happily on their own to the first session and began soon or at once to enjoy the toys and tests provided. None of those older than four and a half years showed the clinging behaviour so typical of the younger children. To illustrate these differences Murphy gives a number of vivid sketches of the behaviour of individual children.

The children Murphy describes in this study were all from skilled artisan and professional white families and came mostly of old American stock. Their upbringing had tended to be conservative and strict. They had not, therefore, been mollycoddled, and there is no reason to suppose that they were in any way atypical.

English children are no different. The occurrence and incidence of attachment behaviour in a sample of 700 four-year-olds in the English Midlands are well chronicled by Newson and Newson (1966, 1968). To a question whether their four-year-old 'ever comes clinging round your skirts wanting to be babied a bit', the mothers of 16 per cent answered 'often' and of 47 per cent 'sometimes'. Though the mothers of the remaining third answered 'never', in some cases it seemed likely that that was wishful thinking. Common reasons for a child who was not usually given to clinging behaviour to show it were his being unwell and his being jealous of a younger sibling. Although almost all the mothers described themselves as responsive to their child's demands, a quarter of them claimed that they responded only reluctantly. In this connection the Newsons remark on what proved to be a recurrent theme in their conversations with mothers, namely the power that a child exerts, and exerts successfully, to attain his own ends. This is a truth, the Newsons remark, 'which most parents come to realise, but of which they are too seldom warned by manuals of child care'.

Thus, although most children after their third birthday show attachment behaviour less urgently and frequently than before, it nonetheless still constitutes a major part of behaviour. Furthermore, though becoming attenuated, attachment behaviour of a kind not very different from that seen in four-year-olds persists throughout early school years. When out walking, children of five and six, and even older, like at times to hold, even grasp, a parent's hand, and resent it if the parent refuses. When playing with others, if anything goes badly wrong, they at once return to parent, or parent-substitute. If more than a little frightened, they seek immediate contact. Thus, throughout the latency of an ordinary child, attachment behaviour continues as a dominant strand in his life.

During adolescence a child's attachment to

his parents grows weaker. Other adults may come to assume an importance equal to or greater than that of the parents, and sexual attraction to age-mates begins to extend the picture. As a result individual variation, already great, becomes even greater. At one extreme are adolescents who cut themselves off from parents; at the other are those who remain intensely attached and are unable or unwilling to direct their attachment behaviour to others; between the extremes lie the great majority of adolescents whose attachment to parents remains strong but whose ties to others are of much importance also. For most individuals the bond to parents continues into adult life and affects behaviour in countless ways. In many societies the attachment of daughter to mother continues more strongly than that of son to mother. As Young and Willmott (1957) have shown, even in a Western urbanised society the bond between adult daughter and mother plays a great part in social life.

Finally, in old age, when attachment behaviour can no longer be directed towards members of an older generation, or even the same generation, it may come instead to be directed towards members of a younger one.

During adolescence and adult life a measure of attachment behaviour is commonly directed not only towards persons outside the family but also towards groups and institutions other than the family. A school or college, a work group, a religious group or a political group can come to constitute for many people a sub-ordinate attachment-'figure', and for some people a principal attachment-'figure'. In such cases, it seems probable, the development of attachment to a group is mediated, at least initially, by attachment to a person holding a prominent position within that group. Thus, for many a citizen attachment to his state is a derivative of and initially dependent on his attachment to its sovereign or president.

That attachment behaviour in adult life is a straightforward continuation of attachment behaviour in childhood is shown by the circumstances that lead an adult's attachment behaviour to become more readily elicited. In sickness and calamity, adults often become demanding of others; in conditions of sudden danger or disaster a person will almost certainly seek proximity to another known and trusted person. In such circumstances an increase of attachment behaviour is recognised by all as natural. It is therefore extremely misleading for the epithet 'regressive' to be applied to every manifestation of attachment behaviour in adult life, as is so often done in psychoanalytic writing where the term carries the connotation pathological or, at least, undesirable (e.g., Benedek, 1956). To dub attachment behaviour in adult life regressive is indeed to overlook the vital role that it plays in the life of man from the cradle to the grave.

Note: Dr. Bowlby's references are not included here. The reader will find some of them listed in the references for Parts 2 and 3. [Eds.]

THE ROLE OF MODELING PROCESSES
IN PERSONALITY DEVELOPMENT

ALBERT BANDURA

I remember reading a story reported by Professor Mowrer about a lonesome farmer who decided to get a parrot for company. After acquiring the bird, the farmer spent many long evenings teaching the parrot the phrase, "Say Uncle." Despite the devoted tutorial attention, the parrot proved totally unresponsive and finally, the frustrated farmer got a stick and struck the parrot on the head after each refusal to produce the desired phrase.

But the visceral method proved no more effective than the cerebral one, so the farmer grabbed his feathered friend and tossed him in the chicken house. A short time later the farmer heard a loud commotion in the chicken house and upon investigation found that the parrot was pummeling the startled chickens on the head with a stick and shouting, "Say Uncle! Say Uncle!" While this story is not intended as an introduction to a treatise on parrot-training practices, it provides a graphic illustration of the process of social learning that I shall discuss in this paper.

One can distinguish two kinds of processes by which children acquire attitudes, values, and patterns of social behavior. First, there is learning that occurs on the basis of direct tuition or instrumental training. In this form of learning, parents and other socializing agents are relatively explicit about what they wish the child to learn and attempt to shape his behavior through rewarding and punishing consequences.

Although a certain amount of socialization of a child takes place through such direct train-

ing, personality patterns are primarily acquired through the child's active imitation of parental attitudes and behavior, most of which the parents have never directly attempted to teach. Indeed, parental modeling behavior may often counteract the effects of their direct training. When a parent punishes his child physically for having aggressed toward peers, for example, the intended outcome of this training is that the child should refrain from hitting others. The child, however, is also learning from parental demonstration how to aggress physically and this imitative learning may provide the direction for the child's behavior when he is similarly frustrated in subsequent social interactions.

Research bearing on modeling processes demonstrates that, unlike the relatively slow process of instrumental training, when a model is provided, patterns of behavior are rapidly acquired in large segments or in their entirety (Bandura, 1962). The pervasiveness of this form of learning is also clearly evident in naturalistic observations of children's play in which they frequently reproduce the entire parental role, including the appropriate mannerisms, voice inflections, and attitudes, much to the parents' surprise and embarrassment. Although the process whereby a person reproduces the behavior exhibited by real-life or symbolized models is generally labelled "identification" in theories of personality, I shall employ the term imitation or modeling because it encompasses the same behavioral phenomenon and it avoids the elusiveness and surplus meanings that have come to be associated with the former concept.

Let us now consider a series of experiments that both illustrates the process of learning through imitation and identifies some of the factors which serve to enhance or to reduce the occurrence of imitative behavior.

TRANSMISSION OF AGGRESSION

One set of experiments was designed primarily to determine the extent to which aggression can be transmitted to children through exposure to aggressive adult models (Bandura, Ross, & Ross, 1961). One group of children observed an aggressive model who exhibited relatively novel forms of physical and verbal aggression toward a large inflated plastic doll; a second group viewed the same model behave in a very subdued and inhibited manner, while children in a control group had no exposure to any models. Half the children in each of the experimental conditions observed models of the same sex as themselves, and the remaining children in each group witnessed opposite-sex models.

This investigation was later extended (Bandura, Ross, & Ross, 1963a) in order to compare the effects of real-life and film-mediated or televised aggressive models on children's behavior. Children in the human film-aggression group viewed a movie showing the same adults who had served as models in the earlier experiment portraying the novel aggressive acts toward the inflated doll. Children in the cartoon-aggression groups saw a film projected on a glass lenscreen in a television console. In this film a female model was costumed as a cat and exhibited aggressive behavior toward a plastic doll. After exposure to their respective models all children, including those in the control group, were mildly frustrated and tested for the amount of imitative and nonimitative aggression.

The results of these experiments leave little doubt that exposure to aggressive models heightens children's aggressive responses to subsequent frustration. As shown in Figure 1, children who observed the aggressive models exhibited approximately twice as much aggression than did subjects in the nonaggressive model group or the control group. In addition, children who witnessed the subdued nonaggressive model displayed the inhibited behavior characteristic

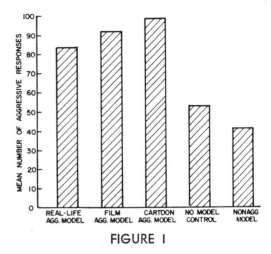

FIGURE I

Mean number of aggressive responses performed by children in each of five groups.

of their model and expressed significantly less aggression than the control children.

Some evidence that the influence of models is partly determined by the sex appropriateness of their behavior is provided by the finding that the aggressive male model was a more powerful stimulus for aggression than the aggressive female model. Some of the children, particularly the boys, commented spontaneously on the fact that the female model's behavior was out of character (e.g., "That's no way for a lady to behave. Ladies are supposed to act like ladies" . . .).

In contrast, aggression by the male model was generally viewed as appropriate and approved by both the boys ("Al's a good socker, he beat up Bobo. I want to sock like Al.") and the girls ("That man is a strong fighter. He punched and punched, and he could hit Bobo right down to the floor and if Bobo got up he said, 'Punch your nose.' He's a good fighter like Daddy.").

Furthermore, the data reveal that aggressive models are highly influential not only in reducing children's inhibitions over aggression, but also in shaping the form of their behavior. Children who observed the aggressive models displayed a great number of precisely imitative aggressive acts, whereas such responses rarely occurred in either the nonaggressive model group or the control group. Illustrations of the way many of the children became virtual

FIGURE 2

Photographs of two children exhibiting precise imitation of the female model whom they had previously observed on film.

carbon copies of their models are presented in Figure 2. The top frames show the female model performing four novel aggressive responses; the lower frames depict a boy and a girl reproducing the behavior of the female model whom they had observed in the film presentation.

Although the children were somewhat less inclined to imitate precisely the cartoon character than the real-life aggressive model, all three experimental conditions—real-life, film-mediated, and cartoon-aggressive models—produced equivalent increases in overall aggressive behavior based on a variety of measures of both imitative and nonimitative aggression.

The finding that film-mediated models are as effective as real-life models in eliciting and transmitting aggressive responses indicates that televised models may serve as important sources of behavior and can no longer be ignored in conceptualizations of personality development. Indeed, most youngsters probably have more

exposure to prestigeful televised male models than to their own fathers. With further advances in mass media and audiovisual technology, models presented pictorially, mainly through television, are likely to play an increasingly influential role in shaping personality patterns and in modifying attitudes and social norms.

It has been widely assumed on the basis of psychoanalytic theory and other hydraulic energy models of personality that children's vicarious participation in film-mediated aggression or the direct expression of aggressive behavior will serve to discharge "pent-up energies" and affects. Guided by this catharsis hypothesis, many parents, educators, and mental health workers encourage hyperaggressive children to participate in aggressive recreational activities, to view highly aggressive televised programs, and to aggress in psychotherapeutic playrooms and other permissive settings.

In contrast to this "drainage" view, social

learning theory (Bandura & Walters, 1963) would predict that the provision of aggressive models and the inadvertent positive reinforcement of aggression, which inevitably occurs during the encouragement of cathartic expressions, are exceedingly effective procedures for enhancing aggressive response tendencies. It is not surprising, therefore, that studies in which children or adolescents have been exposed to film-mediated aggressive models (Bandura, Ross, & Ross, 1961, 1963a, b; Hartmann, 1965; Lovaas, 1961; Mussen & Rutherford, 1961; Siegel, 1956; Walters, Llewellyn-Thomas, & Acker, 1962) have uniformly demonstrated that vicarious participation in aggressive activity increases, rather than decreases, aggressive behavior.

On the other hand, providing aggressive children with examples of alternative, constructive ways of coping with interpersonal frustration has been found to be highly successful in modifying aggressive-domineering personality patterns (Chittenden, 1942). Additional comparisons of social-learning theory and the traditional approaches to personality development will be presented later.

MODIFICATION OF FEARS THROUGH MODELING

Results of a recent study (Bandura, Grusec, & Menlove, 1967a) disclose that well-established fears and inhibitions can be effectively eliminated by having fearful children observe a graduated sequence of modeling activities beginning with presentations that are easily tolerated. Nursery school children who were fearful of dogs, as revealed by parental ratings and an actual test of dog-avoidance behavior, participated in eight brief sessions in which they observed a fearless peer model exhibit progressively longer, closer, and more intimate interactions with a dog. In order to assess both the generality and the stability of treatment effects, the children were readministered tests for avoidance behavior toward two dogs following completion of the treatment series and approximately one month later. In the initial tasks, the dog was enclosed in a playpen and the children were asked to walk up and look

down at the dog, to touch her fur, and to pet her. Following assessment of avoidance of the dog in the playpen, the children were instructed to remove her from the pen, to walk her on a leash, and to pet her. In subsequent tasks the children were asked to remain alone in the room with the animal and to feed her dog biscuits. The final and most difficult set of tasks required the children to climb into the playpen with the dog, to pet her, and to remain alone in the room with her under the confining conditions.

The modeling treatment proved surprisingly effective in reducing the children's fears. Indeed, two-thirds of the children overcame their fear of dogs completely, as shown in the fact that they were willing to remain alone in the room confined with the dog in the playpen. These favorable outcomes are largely corroborated by a second experiment (Bandura & Menlove, 1967b) in which fearful children observed similar modeled performances in filmed presentations, while others, assigned to a control group, watched some entertaining movies. In addition, at the completion of the experiment, the control children, whose fear of dogs remained unchanged, were shown the therapeutic films. Their inhibitions were substantially reduced. The increased boldness of one of the control children who had been subsequently treated is portrayed in Figure 3. The top frames show the model's dauntless behavior; the lower frames depict the girl's fearless interaction with the two canine research assistants.

The influential role of modeling processes in personality development is further revealed by studies demonstrating that children adopt, through observation of behavior exemplified by adults and peers, relatively complex attributes including standards of achievement and self-evaluation (Bandura & Kupers, 1964; Bandura, Grusec, & Menlove, 1967b; Bandura & Whalen, 1966; Mischel & Liebert, 1966), patterns of emotional responsivity (Bandura & Rosenthal, 1966), syntactic styles (Bandura & Harris, 1966), moral judgmental orientations (Bandura & McDonald, 1963), and patterns of self-gratification (Bandura & Mischel, 1965).

It is apparent that children do not reproduce

FIGURE 3

Photographs of two children exhibiting reduced fear of dogs following observation of a fearless peer model.

the personality characteristics of every model with whom they come into contact, nor do they imitate every element of behavior exhibited even by models whom they may have selected as their primary sources of social behavior. The experiments discussed in the remaining sections of this paper are mainly concerned with some of the psychological variables determining the selection of models and the degree to which their behavior will be imitated.

RESPONSE CONSEQUENCES TO THE MODEL

The manner in which rewarding or punishing consequences to the model's behavior influences imitation is demonstrated in an experiment in which nursery school children observed either an aggressive model rewarded, an aggressive model punished, or had no exposure to the models (Bandura, Ross, & Ross, 1963b). The models were two adults and the film presented to the children was projected into a television console. In the aggression-rewarded condition, Rocky, the aggressive model, appropriates all of Johnny's attractive play possessions and tasty foodstuffs through aggressive-domineering means. The film shown to the children in the aggression-punished condition was identical with that shown to the aggression-rewarded group except for a slight rearrangement of the film sequence so that the aggression exhibited by Rocky resulted in his being severely punished by Johnny. Following exposure to the models the children were tested for the incidence of post-exposure aggressive behavior. Children who observed Rocky's aggressive behavior rewarded readily imitated his physical and verbal aggression, whereas children who saw him punished exhibited relatively little imitative behavior and did not differ from a group of control children who had no exposure to the models.

At the conclusion of the experiment each child was asked to evaluate the behavior of Rocky and Johnny and to select the character he preferred to emulate. These data yielded some interesting and surprising findings. As might be expected, children who observed Rocky's aggressive behavior punished both failed to reproduce his behavior and rejected him as a model for emulation. On the other hand, when Rocky's aggression was highly successful in amassing rewarding resources, he was chosen by most of the children as the preferred model for imitation. The surprising finding, however, is that without exception these children were highly critical of his behavior (e.g., "Rocky is harsh" . . . "Rough and bossy" . . . "Mean" . . . "Wicked" . . . "He whack people" . . .).

It was evident from the children's comments that the successful payoff of aggression rather than its intrinsic desirability served as the primary basis for emulation (e.g., "Rocky beat Johnny and chase him and get all the good toys" . . . "He came and snatched Johnny's toys. Get a lot of toys . . ."). The children resolved the conflict by derogating the unfortunate victim, apparently as justification for Rocky's exploitive-assaultive behavior. They criticized Johnny for his inability to control Rocky ("He's a cry baby. Didn't know how to make Rocky mind"), for his miserliness ("If he'd shared right in the beginning, Rocky might have played nice"), and generally described him as "Sulky," "Mean," and "Sort of dumb."

This study clearly demonstrates the way in which rewarding consequences to the model may outweigh the value systems of the observers—children readily adopted successful modeling behavior even though they had labelled it objectionable, morally reprehensible, and publicly had criticized the model for engaging in such behavior.

In many televised and other mass media presentations antisocial models amass considerable rewarding resources through devious means but are punished following the last commercial on the assumption that the punishment ending will erase or counteract the learning of the model's antisocial behavior. The findings of an experiment by Bandura in 1965 reveal that although punishment administered to a model tends to inhibit children's performance of the modeled behavior, it has virtually no influence on the occurrence of imitative learning. In this experiment children observed a film-mediated aggressive model who was severely punished in one condition, generously rewarded in a second condition, and received no response-consequences to the model in the third condition.

Consistent with the findings cited earlier, a post-exposure test of imitative behavior showed that children who observed the punished model performed significantly fewer imitative responses than children in the model-rewarded and the no-consequences groups. Children in all three groups were then offered attractive incentives contingent on their reproducing the model's behavior. The introduction of the rewards completely wiped out the previously observed performance differences, revealing an equivalent amount of learning among the children in the model-rewarded, model-punished and the no-consequences groups. Moreover, girls had acquired approximately as much imitative aggression as did the boys.

It might be concluded from these findings that exposure of children to punished antisocial or other types of models is likely to result in little overt imitative behavior. Nevertheless, the observed behavior is learned and may be exhibited on future occasions given the appropriate instigation, the instruments necessary for performing the imitative acts, and the prospect of sufficiently attractive positive rewards contingent on the successful execution of the behavior.

NURTURANCE

The role of nurturance in facilitating imitative learning has been emphasized in most theories of identification. Through the repeated association of the parent's behavior and attributes with warm, rewarding, and affectionately demonstrative caretaking activities, it is assumed that the parent's behavioral characteristics gradually take on positive value for the child. Consequently, the child is motivated to reproduce these positively valenced attributes in his own behavior.

Some empirical support for the nurturance hypothesis is provided in an experiment in which the quality of the rewarding interaction between a female model and nursery school children was systematically varied (Bandura & Huston, 1961). With one group of children the model behaved in a warm and rewarding manner, while a second group of children experienced a distant and nonnurturant relationship with the model. Following the experimental social interactions the model and the children played a game in which the model exhibited a relatively novel pattern of verbal and motor behavior and the number of imitative responses performed by the children was recorded.

Children who had experienced the rewarding interaction with the model displayed substantially more imitative behavior than did children with whom the same adult had interacted in a nonrewarding way. Exposure to a model possessing rewarding qualities not only elicited precisely imitative verbal responses but also increased the level of nonimitative verbalization. These results are essentially in agreement with those of Milner (1951), who found that children receiving high reading readiness scores had more verbal and affectionately demonstrative maternal models than children in the low reading ability group.

The importance of attaching positive valence to the activities and behavior which the parent or teacher wishes the child to reproduce is dramatically illustrated in a case report by Mowrer (1960). A 2-year-old girl, who suffered from an auditory defect, was seriously retarded in language development, a condition that resulted primarily from her refusal to wear a hearing aid. In analyzing the mother-child verbal interaction, it became readily apparent that the girl was hearing only language responses of high amplitude which the mother uttered in a raised voice during disciplinary interventions. Considering the repeated association of the mother's verbal behavior with negative emotional experiences, it was not surprising that the child refused to wear a hearing aid, and exhibited little interest in, or desire for, vocalization.

The mother was instructed to follow a remedial program in which she deliberately and frequently associated her vocalizations with highly positive experiences, and refrained from using language punitively. Within a brief period of time the child began to show an active interest in the mother's verbalizations, was quite willing to wear the hearing aid, and made rapid progress in her language development.

In discussions of the process of education and socialization, considerable emphasis is generally placed on direct training procedures. As the above case illustrates, however, the attachment of positive valence to modeling behavior may be an important precondition for the occurrence of social learning. Indeed, once the behavior in question has acquired positive properties, the child is likely to perform in the absence of socializing agents and externally administered rewards.

SOCIAL POWER

In the studies to which reference has been made, children were exposed to only a single model. During the course of social development, however, children have extensive contact with multiple models, particularly family members, who may differ widely in their behavior and in their relative influence. Therefore, a further study, designed to test several different theories of identificatory learning, utilized three-person groups representing prototypes of the nuclear family (Bandura, Ross, & Ross, 1963c).

In one condition of the experiment an adult assumed the role of controller of highly rewarding resources including attractive play material, appetizing foods, and high-status objects. Another adult was the recipient of these resources, while the child, a participant observer in the triad, was essentially ignored. In a second condition, one adult controlled the resources; the child, however, was the recipient of the positive resources, while the other adult was assigned a subordinate and powerless role.

An adult male and female served as models in each of the triads. For half the boys and girls in each condition the male model controlled and dispensed the rewarding resources, simulating the husband-dominant home; for the remaining children, the female model mediated the positive resources as in the wife-dominant home. Following the experimental social interactions the adult models exhibited divergent patterns of behavior in the presence of the child, and measures were obtained of the degree to which the child subsequently patterned his behavior after that of the models.

According to the status-envy theory of identification proposed by Whiting (1959, 1960), where a child competes unsuccessfully with an adult for affection, attention, food, and care, the child will envy the consumer adult and consequently identify with him. This theory represents an extension of the psychoanalytic defensive identification hypothesis that identification is the outcome of rivalrous interaction between the child and the parent who occupies an envied consumer status. In contrast to the status-envy hypothesis, the social power theory of identification (Maccoby, 1959; Mussen & Distler, 1960) predicts that children will reproduce more of the behavior of the adult who controls positive resources than that of the powerless adult model.

The results of this experiment reveal that children tend to identify with the source of rewarding power rather than with the competitor for the rewards. In both experimental triads, regardless of whether the rival adult or the children themselves were the recipients of the rewarding resources, the model who possessed rewarding power was imitated to a considerably greater extent than was the competitor or the ignored model. Moreover, power inversions on the part of the male and female models produced cross-sex imitation, particularly in girls. These findings suggest that the distribution of rewarding power within the family may play an important role in the development of both appropriate and deviant sex-role behavior.

Although the children adopted many of the characteristics of the model who possessed rewarding power they also reproduced some of the response patterns exhibited by the model who occupied a subordinate role. The children's behavior represented a synthesis of behavioral elements selected from both models, and since the specific admixture of elements varied from child to child, they displayed quite different patterns of imitative behavior. Thus, within one family even same-sex siblings may exhibit different personality characteristics, owing to their having selected for imitation different elements of their parents' attitudes and behavior. Paradoxical as it may seem, it is possible to achieve considerable innovation through selective imitation.

SOCIAL LEARNING, PSYCHOANALYTIC, AND STAGE THEORIES OF PERSONALITY

It was pointed out in preceding sections of this paper that laboratory data have failed to support predictions derived from several widely accepted psychoanalytic principles of personality development. Research generated by social learning theory also raises some questions about the validity of stage theories that typically depict the developmental process as involving a relatively spontaneous emergence of age-specific modes of behavior as the child passes from one stage to another. According to Piaget's theory of moral development (1948), for example, one can distinguish two clearcut stages of moral orientations demarcated from each other at approximately seven years of age.

In the first stage, defined as objective morality, children judge the gravity of a deviant act in terms of the amount of material damages and disregard the intention of the action. By contrast, during the second or subjective morality stage, children judge conduct in terms of its intent rather than its material consequences. The sequence and timing of these stages are presumably predetermined and, consequently, young children are incapable of adopting a subjective orientation, while objective moral judgments are rarely encountered in older children.

However, in an experiment designed to study the influence of models in transmitting and modifying children's moral judgments (Bandura & McDonald, 1963), objective and subjective moral judgments were found to exist together rather than as successive developmental stages. The vast majority of young children were capable of exercising subjective judgments and most of the older children displayed varying degrees of objective morality.

Children who exhibited predominantly objective and subjective moral orientations were then selected and exposed to adult models who consistently expressed moral judgments that were counter to the children's orientations. The provision of models was highly effective in altering the children's moral judgments. Objective children modified their moral orientations toward subjectivity and, similarly, subjective children became considerably more objective in their judgmental behavior. Furthermore, the children maintained their altered orientations in a new test situation in the absence of the models.

A second study (Bandura & Mischel, 1965), utilizing a similar design, demonstrates that other personality characteristics generally viewed as predetermined age-specific phenomena can also be altered through the application of appropriate social learning principles. Children who showed decided preferences for either immediate or delayed gratification observed adult models who displayed a self-gratification pattern opposite to the children's dominant tendencies. It was found that high-delay children increased their preference for immediate but less valued rewards after having witnessed models favoring immediate gratification; conversely, children who had exhibited a marked disposition toward immediate gratification increased their willingness to wait for more highly valued rewards following exposure to models exemplifying high-delay behavior.

Despite the voluminous clinical and theoretical literature pertaining to child development, the available body of empirically verified knowledge is comparatively meager. The recent years, however, have witnessed a new direction in theorizing about the developmental process which has generated considerable laboratory research within the framework of social learning theory. These studies are beginning to yield relatively unambiguous statements about the influence of particular antecedent events on the behavior and attitudes of children. This approach evidently holds promise of providing both more reliable guidelines for educational practice and the type of evidence necessary for discarding procedures that prove to be ineffective in, or even a hindrance to, the successful realization of desired developmental, educational, and psychotherapeutic objectives.

REFERENCES

Bandura, A. Social learning through imitation. In M. R. Jones (Ed.), *Nebraska Symposium on Motivation*. Lincoln: Univ. of Nebraska Press, 1962, 211–269.

———. Influence of model's reinforcement contingencies on the acquisition of imitative responses. *J. pers. soc. Psychol.*, 1965, 1, 589–595.

Bandura, A., Grusec, Joan E., & Menlove, Frances L. Vicarious extinction of avoidance behavior. *J. pers. soc. Psychol.*, 1967, 5, 16–23. (a)

———. Some social determinants of self-monitoring reinforcement systems. *J. pers. soc. Psychol.*, 1967, 5, 449–455. (b)

Bandura, A. & Harris, Mary B. Modification of syntactic style. *J. exper. child Psychol.*, 1966, 341–352.

Bandura, A. & Huston, Aletha C. Identification as a process of incidental learning. *J. abnorm. soc. Psychol.*, 1961, 63, 311–318.

Bandura, A. & Kupers, Carol J. The transmission of patterns of self-reinforcement through modeling. *J. abnorm, soc. Psychol.*, 1964, 69, 1–9.

Bandura, A. & McDonald, F. J. The influence of social reinforcement and the behavior of models in shaping children's moral judgments. *J. abnorm. soc. Psychol.*, 1963, 67, 274–281.

Bandura, A. & Menlove, Frances L. Psychotherapeutic application of symbolic modeling. Unpublished manuscript. Stanford Univ., 1967.

Bandura, A. & Mischel, W. Modification of self-imposed delay of reward through exposure to live and symbolic models. *J. pers. soc. Psychol.*, 1965, 2, 698–705.

Bandura, A. & Rosenthal, T. L. Vicarious classical conditioning as a function of arousal level. *J. pers. soc. Psychol.*, 1966, 3, 54–62.

Bandura, A., Ross, Dorothea, & Ross, Sheila A. Transmission of aggression through imitation of aggressive models. *J. abnorm. soc. Psychol.*, 1961, 63, 575–582.

———. Imitation of film-mediated aggressive models. *J. abnorm. soc. Psychol.*, 1963, 66, 3–11. (a)

———. Vicarious reinforcement and imitative learning. *J. abnorm. soc. Psychol.*, 1963, 67, 601–607. (b)

———. A comparative test of the status envy, social power, and secondary reinforcement theories of identificatory learning. *J. abnorm. soc. Psychol.,* 1963, **67**, 527–534. (c).

Bandura, A. & Walters, R. H. *Social Learning and Personality Development.* New York: Holt, Rinehart & Winston, 1963.

Bandura, A. & Whalen, Carol K. The influence of antecedent reinforcement and divergent modeling cues on patterns of self-reward. *J. pers. soc. Psychol.,* 1966, **3**, 54–62.

Chittenden, Gertrude E. An experimental study in measuring and modifying assertive behavior in young children. *Monogr. Soc. Res. child Develpm.,* 1942, **7** (Serial No. 31).

Hartmann, D. The influence of symbolically modeled instrumental aggression and pain cues on the disinhibition of aggressive behavior. Unpublished doctoral dissertation, Stanford Univ., 1965.

Lovaas, O. I. Effect of exposure to symbolic aggression on aggressive behavior. *Child Develpm.,* 1961, **32**, 37–44.

Maccoby, Eleanor E. Role-taking in childhood and its consequences for social learning. *Child Develpm.,* 1959, **30**, 239–252.

Milner, Esther. A study of the relationship between reading readiness and patterns of parent-child interaction. *Child Develpm.,* 1951, **22**, 95–112.

Mischel, W. & Liebert, R. M. Effects of discrepancies between observed and imposed reward criteria on their acquisition and transmission. *J. pers. soc. Psychol.,* 1966, **3**, 45–53.

Mowrer, O. H. *Learning Theory and the Symbolic Processes.* New York: John Wiley, 1960.

Mussen, P. & Distler, L. M. Child-rearing antecedents of masculine identification in kindergarten boys. *Child Develpm.,* 1960, **31**, 89–100.

Mussen, P. & Rutherford, E. Effects of aggressive cartoons on children's aggressive play. *J. abnorm. soc. Psychol.,* 1961, **62**, 461–464.

Piaget, J. *The Moral Judgment of the Child.* Glencoe, Ill.: Free Press, 1948.

Siegel, Alberta E. Film-mediated fantasy aggression and strength of aggressive drive. *Child Develpm.,* 1956, **27**, 365–378.

Walters, R. H., Llewellyn-Thomas, E., & Acker, C. W. Enhancement of punitive behavior by audio-visual displays. *Science,* 1962, **136**, 872–873.

Whiting, J. W. M. Sorcery, sin, and the superego. In M. R. Jones (Ed.), *Nebraska Symposium on Motivation.* Lincoln: Univ. of Nebraska Press, 1959, 174–195.

———. Resource mediation and learning by identification. In I. Iscoe & H. W. Stevenson (Eds.), *Personality Development in Children.* Austin: Univ. of Texas Press, 1960, 112–126.

THE DEVELOPMENT OF IMITATION
BY REINFORCING BEHAVIORAL
SIMILARITY TO A MODEL

DONALD M. BAER   ROBERT F. PETERSON   JAMES A. SHERMAN

. . . . .

The development of a class of behaviors which may fairly be called "imitation" is an interesting task, partly because of its relevance to the process of socialization in general and language development in particular, and partly because of its potential value as a training technique for children who require special methods of instruction. Imitation is not a specific set of behaviors that can be exhaustively listed. Any behavior may be considered imitative if it temporally follows behavior demonstrated by someone else, called a model, and if its topography is functionally controlled by the topography of the model's behavior. Specifically, this control is such that an observer will note a close similarity between the topography of the model's behavior and that of the imitator. Furthermore, this similarity to the model's behavior will be characteristic of the imitator in responding to a wide variety of the model's behaviors. Such control could result, for example, if topographical similarity to a model's behavior were a reinforcing stimulus dimension for the imitator.

There are, of course, other conditions which can produce similar behaviors from two organisms on the same occasion, or on similar occasions at different times. One possibility is that both organisms independently have been taught the same responses to the same cues; thus, all children recite the multiplication tables in very

Reprinted with abridgment by permission of the authors and the Society for the Experimental Analysis of Behavior, Inc. from *Journal of the Experimental Analysis of Behavior*, 1967, **10**, 405–16. Copyright 1967 by the Society for the Experimental Analysis of Behavior, Inc.

similar ways. This similarity does not deserve the label imitation, and hardly ever receives it; one child's recitation is not usually a cue to another's, and the similarity of their behavior is not usually a reinforcer for the children. Nevertheless, the children of this example have similar behaviors.

The fact that the world teaches many children similar lessons can lead to an arrangement of their behaviors which comes closer to a useful meaning of imitation. Two children may both have learned similar responses; one child, however, may respond at appropriate times whereas the other does not. In that case, the undiscriminating child may learn to use this response when the discriminating one does. The term imitation still need not be applied, since the similarity between the two children's responses is not functional for either of them; in particular, the second child is not affected by the fact that his behavior is similar to that of the first. This arrangement approaches one which Miller and Dollard (1941) call "matched-dependent" behavior. One organism responds to the behavior of another merely as a discriminative stimulus with respect to the timing of his own behavior; many times, these behaviors will happen to be alike, because both organisms will typically use the most efficient response, given enough experience.

It should be possible, however, to arrange the behavior of two organisms so that one of them will, in a variety of ways, produce precise topographical similarity to the other, but nothing else. A study by Baer and Sherman (1964) seemingly showed the result of such prior learning in several young children. In that study, reinforcements were arranged for children's imitations of three activities of an animated, talking puppet, which served both as a model and a source of social reinforcement for imitating. As a result of this reinforcement, a fourth response of the puppet was spontaneously imitated by the children, although that imitation had never before been reinforced. When reinforcement of the other three imitations was discontinued, the fourth, never-reinforced imitation also decreased in strength; when reinforcement of the original imitations was resumed, imitation of the fourth response again rose in rate, although it still was never reinforced. In short, these children apparently generalized along a stimulus dimension of similarity between their behaviors and the behaviors of a model: when similarity to the model in three different ways was reinforced, they thereupon displayed a fourth way of achieving similarity to the model. Thus, similarity between their behavior and the model's was a functional stimulus in their behavior.

Metz (1965) demonstrated the development of some imitative behavior in two autistic children who initially showed little or no imitative response. In this study, responses similar in topography to demonstrations by the experimenter were reinforced with "Good" and food. Metz found that, after intensive training, several imitative responses could be maintained in strength even when not reinforced with food, and that the subjects had a higher probability of imitating new responses after training than before. However, in one of the conditions used to evaluate the subjects' imitative repertoire before and after imitative training, "Good" was still said contingent upon correct new imitations. Thus, for one subject who initially showed a non-zero rate of imitation, it could be argued that the increased imitation in the test after training was due to an experimentally developed reinforcing property of "Good," rather than to the imitation training as such. Further, in the Metz study, due to a lack of extinction or other manipulation of the behavior, it is difficult to specify that the higher probability of imitating new responses, and the maintenance of unreinforced imitative responses, were in fact due to the reinforcement

of the initial imitative responses during training.

Lovaas, Berberich, Perloff, and Schaeffer (1966) used shaping and fading procedures to establish imitative speech in two autistic children. They reported that as training progressed and more vocal behavior came under the control of a model's prior vocalization, it became progressively easier to obtain new imitative vocalizations. When reinforcement was shifted from an imitative-contingent schedule to a basically non-contingent schedule, imitative behavior deteriorated. In an additional manipulation, the model presented Norwegian words interspersed with English words for the children to imitate. Initially, the children did not reproduce the Norwegian words perfectly. However, the authors judged that the subjects gradually improved their imitations of the Norwegian words even though these imitations were not reinforced.

The studies by Baer and Sherman (1964), Metz (1965), Lovaas *et al.* (1966), and other reports (Bandura, 1962) suggest that for children with truly imitative repertoires, induction has occurred, such that (1) relatively novel behaviors can be developed before direct shaping, merely by providing an appropriate demonstration by a model, and (2) some imitative responses can be maintained, although unreinforced, as long as other imitative responses are reinforced.

The purpose of the present study was to extend the generality of the above findings and to demonstrate a method of producing a truly imitative repertoire in children initially lacking one.

METHOD

Subjects

Three children, 9 to 12 years of age, were selected from several groups of severely and profoundly retarded children in a state school. They were chosen not because they were retarded, but because they seemed to be the only children available of a practical age who apparently showed no imitation whatsoever. (The success of the method to be described suggests that it may have considerable practical value for the training of such children.) The subjects were without language, but made occasional grunting vocalizations, and responded to a few simple verbal commands ("Come here," "Sit down," *etc.*). They were ambulatory (but typically had developed walking behavior relatively late in their development, in the sixth or seventh year), could dress themselves, were reasonably well toilet trained, and could feed themselves. Fair eye-hand coordination was evident, and simple manipulatory skills were present.

The subjects were chosen from groups of children initially observed in their wards from a distance over a period of several days. No instances of possible imitation were noted in the subjects finally selected. (That is, on no occasion did any subject display behavior similar to that of another person, except in instances where a common stimulus appeared to be controlling the behaviors of both persons, *e.g.,* both going to the dining area when food was displayed on the table.) Subsequently, an experimenter approached and engaged the subjects in extended play. In the course of this play, he would repeatedly ask them to imitate some simple response that he demonstrated, such as clapping his hands, or waving. The children failed to imitate any of these responses, although they clearly were capable of at least some of them. Finally, during the training itself, every sample of behavior was initially presented to the child as a demonstration accompanied by the command, "Do this"; at first, none of these samples was imitated, despite extensive repetition.

First Training Procedures

Each subject was seen at mealtimes, once or twice a day, three to five times a week. The subject's food was used as a reinforcer. It was delivered a spoonful at a time by the experimenter, who always said "Good" just before putting the spoon into the subject's mouth. The subject and experimenter faced each other across the corner of a small table, on which were placed the food tray and the experimenter's records. Elsewhere in the room was another small table on which were placed some materials used later in the study, a desk with a telephone on it, a coat rack holding one or

more coats, a wastebasket, and a few other chairs.

The basic procedure was to teach each subject a series of discriminated operants. Each discriminated operant consisted of three elements: a discriminative stimulus (S^D) presented by the experimenter, a correct response by the subject, and reinforcement after a correct response. The S^D was the experimenter's command, "Do this," followed by his demonstration of some behavior. The response required was one similar to the experimenter's. Thus, what the operant learned was always topographically imitative of the experimenter's demonstration. The reinforcement was food, preceded by the word "Good."

Since none of the subjects was imitative, none of the initial S^D's was followed by any behavior which resembled that demonstrated by the experimenter. This was true even for those behaviors which the subjects were clearly capable of performing. Subject 1, for example, would sit down when told to, but did not imitate the experimenter when he said "Do this," sat down, and then offered her the chair. Hence, the initial imitative training for all subjects was accomplished with a combination of shaping (Skinner, 1953) and fading (Terrace, 1963a, 1963b) or "putting through" procedures (Konorski and Miller, 1937).

The first response of the program for Subject 1 was to raise an arm after the experimenter had raised his. The subject was presented with a series of arm-raising demonstrations by the experimenter, each accompanied by "Do this," to which she made no response. The experimenter then repeated the demonstration, reached out, took the subject's hand and raised it for her, and then immediately reinforced her response. After several trials of this sort, the experimenter began gradually to fade out his assistance by raising the subject's arm only part way and shaping the completion of the response. Gradually, the experimenter's assistance was faded until the subject made an unassisted arm-raising response whenever the experimenter raised his arm. The initial responses for all subjects were taught in this manner whenever necessary.

Occasionally during the very early training periods a subject would resist being guided through a response. For example, with a response involving arm raising, Subject 3 at first pulled his arm downward whenever the experimenter attempted to raise it. In this case, the experimenter merely waited and tried again until the arm could be at least partially raised without great resistance; then the response was reinforced. After subjects had received a few reinforcements following the experimenter's assistance in performing a response, they no longer resisted. As the number of responses in the subjects' repertoire increased, the experimenter discontinued the guiding procedure and relied only on shaping procedures when a response did not match the demonstration.

A number of responses, each topographically similar to a demonstration by the experimenter, was taught to each subject. Training of most responses was continued until its demonstration was reliably matched by the subject. The purpose of these initial training procedures was to program reinforcement, in as many and diverse ways as practical, whenever a subject's behavior was topographically similar to that demonstrated by the experimenter.

Further Training Procedures

PROBES FOR IMITATION   As the initial training procedures progressed, and the subjects began to come under the control of the experimenter's demonstrations, certain responses were demonstrated which, if imitated perfectly on their first presentation, were deliberately not reinforced on the first or any future occasion. These responses served as probes for the developing imitative nature of the subject's repertoire. A list of the responses demonstrated, including the reinforced ones for the initial training procedure and the unreinforced probe demonstrations, is given in Table 1 for Subject 1. These responses are listed in the order of first demonstration. Subject 1 had 95 reinforced and 35 unreinforced responses. Similar responses were used with Subjects 2 and 3. Subject 2 had 125 reinforced and five unreinforced probes; Subject 3 had eight reinforced responses and one unreinforced probe.

During the probes, the experimenter continued to present S^D's for imitation. If the re-

sponse demonstrated belonged to the group of reinforced responses and the subject imitated within 10 sec, reinforcement ("Good" and food) was delivered and the next response was demonstrated. If the subject did not imitate within 10 sec, no reinforcement was delivered and the experimenter demonstrated the next response. If it belonged to the unreinforced group of responses (probes), and if the subject imitated it, there were no programmed consequences and the experimenter demonstrated the next response no sooner than 10 sec after the subject's imitation. If it was not imitated, the experimenter performed the next demonstration 10 sec later. The purpose of the 10-sec delay was to minimize the possibility that the subjects' unreinforced imitations were being maintained by the possible reinforcing effects of the presentation of an S^D for a to-be-reinforced imitative response. Demonstrations for reinforced and unreinforced responses were presented to subjects in any unsystematic order.

NON-REINFORCEMENT OF ALL IMITATION
After the probe phase, and after stable performances of reinforced and unreinforced imitative responses were established, non-reinforcement of all imitative behavior was programmed. The purpose of this procedure was to show the dependence of the imitative repertoire on the food reinforcement which was apparently responsible for its development.

Non-reinforcement of imitation was instituted in the form of reinforcement for any behavior other than imitation. Differential reinforcement of other behavior is abbreviated DRO (Reynolds, 1961). The experimenter continued saying "Good" and feeding the subject, but not contingent on imitations. Instead, the experimenter delivered reinforcement at least 20 sec after the subject's last imitation had taken place. Thus, for the group of previously reinforced responses, the only change between reinforcement and non-reinforcement periods was a shift in the contingency. For the group of unreinforced or probe responses there was no change; food reinforcement still did not follow either the occurrence or non-occurrence of an imitative response. This procedure involved simultaneously the extinction of imitation and also the reinforcement of whatever other responses may

TABLE I

The Sequence of Responses Demonstrated to Subject 1

(Asterisks indicate unreinforced responses.)

1. Raise left arm
2. Tap table with left hand
3. Tap chest with left hand
4. Tap head with left hand
5. Tap left knee with left hand
6. Tap right knee with left hand
7. Tap nose
*8. Tap arm of chair
9. Tap leg of table
10. Tap leg with left hand
11. Extend left arm
*12. Make circular motion with arm
13. Stand up
14. Both hands on ears
15. Flex arm
16. Nod yes
17. Tap chair seat
18. Extend both arms
19. Put feet on chair
20. Walk around
21. Make vocal response
22. Extend right arm sideways
23. Tap shoulder
24. Tap head with right hand
25. Tap right knee with right hand
26. Tap leg with right hand
27. Tap left knee with right hand
28. Raise right arm overhead
29. Tap chest with right hand
30. Tap table with right hand
31. Move chair
32. Sit in chair
33. Throw paper in basket
34. Pull up socks
35. Tap desk
36. Climb on chair
37. Open door
38. Move ash tray
39. Put paper in chair
40. Sit in two chairs (chained)
41. Tap chair with right hand
42. Move paper from basket to desk
43. Move box from shelf to desk
44. Put on hat
45. Move hat from table to desk
46. Move box from shelf to desk
47. Nest three boxes
48. Put hat in chair
49. Tap wall
50. Move wastebasket
51. Move paper from desk to table
52. Stand in corner
53. Pull window shade
54. Place box in chair
55. Walk around desk
56. Smile
57. Protrude tongue
58. Put head on desk
*59. Ring bell
60. Nest two boxes
61. Crawl on floor
*62. Walk with arms above head
63. Sit on floor
64. Put arm behind back (standing)
65. Walk with right arm held up
66. Throw box
*67. Walk to telephone
*68. Extend both arms (sitting)
69. Walk and tap head with left hand
70. Walk and tap head with right hand
*71. Walk and clap hands
*72. Open mouth
73. Jump
74. Pat radiator
*75. Nod no
76. Pick up phone
77. Pull drawer
78. Pet coat
79. Tear kleenex
80. Nest four boxes
81. Point gun and say "Bang"
*82. Put towel over face
*83. Put hands over eyes
*84. Tap floor
*85. Scribble
*86. Move toy car on table
87. Place circle in form board
88. Place circle, square, and triangle in form board
*89. Crawl under table
*90. Walk and clap sides
*91. Lie on floor
*92. Kick box
*93. Put foot over table rung
*94. Fly airplane
*95. Rock doll
*96. Burp doll
*97. Tap chair with bat
*98. Open and close book
99. Work egg beater
100. Put arm through hoop
101. Build three block tower
*102. Stab self with rubber knife
103. Put blocks in ring
104. Walk and hold book on head
105. Ride kiddie car
106. Sweep with broom
107. Place beads around neck
108. Ride hobby horse
*109. Put on glove
110. Use whisk broom on table
111. Work rolling pin
*112. Push large car
113. Put beads on doorknob
*114. Put hat on hobby horse
115. Sweep block with broom
116. Place box inside ring of beads
117. Put glove in pocket of lab coat
118. Push button on tape recorder
*119. Bang spoon on desk
120. Lift cup
121. Use whisk broom on a wall
*122. Put a cube in a cup
123. Rattle a spoon in a cup
*124. Throw paper on the floor
*125. Hug a pillow
126. Tap pegs into pegboard with hammer
*127. Wave a piece of paper
*128. Shake a rattle
*129. Hit two spoons together
130. Shake a tambourine

have been taking place at the moment of reinforcement.

For Subject 1, the DRO period was 30 sec. For Subject 2, DRO periods were 30, 60, and 0 sec. (DRO 0-sec meant reinforcement was delivered immediately after the S^D, before an imitative response could occur.) This sequence of DRO intervals was used because, as displayed in the Results section, Subject 2 maintained stable imitation under the initial DRO procedures, unlike the other subjects. For Subject 3, the DRO period was 20 sec. After the DRO procedure for each subject, contingent reinforcement of imitation was resumed and the procedures described below were instituted.

IMITATIVE CHAINS   After reinforcement for imitative behavior was resumed with Subjects 1 and 2, the procedure of chaining together old and new imitations was begun. At first only two-response chains were demonstrated; then three-response chains, after two-response chains were successfully achieved; and so on. During chaining, the experimenter demonstrated the responses the subject was to imitate as an unbroken series. In all cases, the demonstrated chain contained both responses previously learned by the subject and relatively new ones. Walking from one locale to another in the process of performing these behaviors was not considered part of the imitative chain and was not judged for imitative accuracy.

VERBAL IMITATIONS   Late in the training program for Subjects 1 and 3, when virtually any new motor performance by the experimenter was almost certain to be imitated, vocal performances were begun with simple sounds. The experimenter, as usual, said "Do this," but instead of making some motor response made a vocal one, for example, "Ah." Subjects 1 and 3 repeatedly failed to imitate such demonstrations. Different procedures were then employed to obtain vocal imitations. For Subject 1, the vocal response to be imitated was set into a chain of non-vocal responses. For example, the experimenter would say, "Do this," rise from his chair and walk to the center of the room, turn towards the subject, say "Ah," and return to his seat. To such a demonstration Subject 1 responded by leaving her seat, walking toward the center of the room, turning toward the experimenter, and then beginning a series of facial and vocal responses out of which eventually emerged an "Ah" sufficiently similar to the experimenter's to merit reinforcement. This coupling of motor and vocal performances was maintained for several more demonstrations, during which the motor performance was made successively shorter and more economical of motion; finally, the experimenter was able to remain seated, say "Do this," say "Ah," and immediately evoke an imitation from the subject. Proceeding in this manner, simple sounds were shaped and then combined into longer or more complex sounds and finally into usable words.

Subject 3, like Subject 1, initially failed to imitate vocalizations. In his case, the experimenter proceeded to demonstrate a set of motor performances which moved successively closer to vocalizations. At first the experimenter obtained imitative blowing out of a lighted match, then blowing without the match, then more vigorous blowing which included an initial plosive "p," then added a voiced component to the blowing which was shaped into a "Pah" sound. Proceeding in this manner, a number of vocalizations were produced, all as reliable imitations.

GENERALIZATION TO OTHER EXPERIMENTERS   When the imitative repertoire of Subject 1 had developed to a high level, new experimenters were presented to her, of the opposite or the same sex as the original male experimenter. These novel experimenters gave the same demonstrations as the original experimenter in the immediately preceding session. The purpose of this procedure was to investigate whether the subject's imitative repertoire was limited to demonstrations by the original male experimenter. During this procedure, the new experimenters delivered reinforcement in the same manner as the original experimenter; *i.e.*, previously reinforced imitations were reinforced and probes were not.

RESULTS

Reliability of Scoring Imitative Responses

Checks on the reliability of the experimenter's scoring of any response as imitative were made at scattered points throughout the study for Subjects 1 and 2. The percentage of agreement between the experimenter's scoring and the independent records of a second observer exceeded 98%.

First Training Procedures

The initial training procedure contained occasions when the extent of the developing imitative repertoire of each subject could be seen. These were occasions when behavior was demonstrated by the experimenter to the subject for the first time. Any attempt by the subject to imitate such new behavior before direct training or shaping could be attributed to the history of reinforcement for matching other behavior of the experimenter. Thus, it was possible to examine the sequence of initial presentations to each subject to discover any increasing probability that new behavior would be imitated on its first presentation.

The sequence of 130 responses in Subject 1's program was sufficient to increase her probability of imitating new responses from zero at the beginning of the program to 100% at the end. This was demonstrated by grouping the 130 responses into 13 successive blocks of 10 each. As shown in Figure 1, the proportion imi-

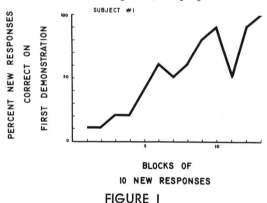

FIGURE I

The development of imitation in Subject 1.

tated on the first presentation within each block rose, not too steadily, but nonetheless clearly, to 100% by the 13th block.

The proportion of new responses successfully imitated by Subject 2 upon their first presenta-

tion rose from 0% to 80%, through a sequence of 130 new responses, as shown in Figure 2.

Subject 2 displayed both more variable and less thorough imitation of new responses on their first presentation than did Subject 1, al-

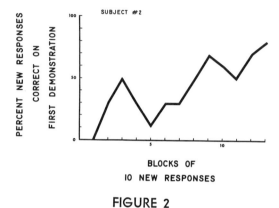

FIGURE 2

The development of imitation in Subject 2.

though the general form of the data is similar.

Subject 3 was taught only eight discriminated operants of imitative topography, which he acquired much more rapidly than did either Subject 1 or 2. He imitated the ninth spontaneously on its first presentation, although he had not imitated it before training.

The progressive development of imitation was apparent in other aspects of the data as well. The number of training sessions required to establish new imitations was displayed by plotting this number of sessions for each successive block of 10 new responses. The criterion for establishment of a new imitative response was that, for one trial, a subject displayed the response demonstrated by the experimenter with no shaping or fading procedures required for that trial. This is shown in Figure 3 for Subject 1 and in Figure 4 for Subject 2, as solid lines. Both graphs show a systematically decreasing number of sessions required to establish successive new imitations. The dotted portions of each graph represent deviations from the usual type of training procedure and thus are plotted differently. For Subject 1 the dotted portion represents a period in which verbal responses were introduced (not plotted as part of Figure 3, but discussed later in this report). For Sub-

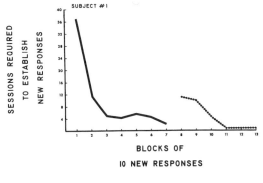

FIGURE 3

The rate of development of imitation in Subject 1.

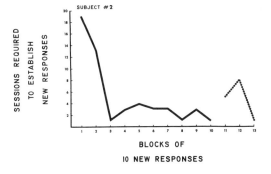

FIGURE 4

The rate of development of imitation in Subject 2.

ject 2 the dotted portion represents a sequence of sessions in which few new imitative responses were introduced. Rather, two previously established imitative responses of similar topography, which the subject no longer clearly displayed, were worked on intensively.

DRO Procedures

For all subjects, both reinforced and unreinforced imitative behavior was maintained over continuing experimental sessions as long as food reinforcement was contingent upon at least some imitative behavior. When reinforcement was no longer contingent upon imitative behavior during the DRO periods, both the previously reinforced imitations and the never-reinforced probe imitations decreased markedly in strength.

Figure 5 is a plot of the percentages of each type of imitative response by Subject 1. It shows that her probability of imitating the 35 probes varied between 80 and 100%, as long as the other 95 imitations, within which the

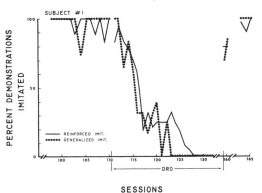

FIGURE 5

The maintenance and extinction of reinforced and unreinforced imitation in Subject 1. (The breaks in the data before and after session 160 represent periods of experimentation aimed at other problems.)

probes were interspersed, were reinforced. The application of the DRO 30-sec procedure extinguished virtually all imitative behavior within about 20 hr. The previously reinforced imitations and the probe imitations extinguished alike in rate and degree. All imitative behavior recovered when, with a small amount of shaping, reinforcement was again made contingent upon imitative behavior.

Figure 6 is a similar plot of the imitative be-

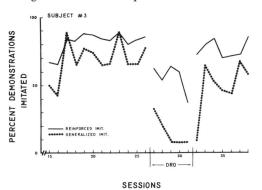

FIGURE 6

The maintenance and extinction of reinforced and unreinforced imitation in Subject 3.

havior of Subject 3. It shows the maintenance of the one probe imitation and eight reinforced imitations during reinforcement of imitation, a marked decrease in both types of imitative behavior during the DRO 20-sec period, and a recovery when contingent reinforcement of imitations was resumed.

Figure 7 is a plot of the imitative behavior

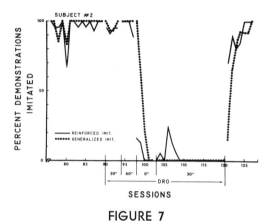

FIGURE 7

The maintenance and extinction of reinforced and unreinforced imitation in Subject 2.

of Subject 2. Her results were similar to those obtained for Subjects 1 and 3, in terms of the maintenance of 125 reinforced and five probe imitations, under conditions of reinforcement of imitations. However, her data depart from the others' during the DRO period. Initially, this subject showed no reliable signs of extinction after four sessions of DRO with a 30-sec delay. Next, DRO 60-sec was instituted for four sessions, still without any reliable effect. At that point, a procedure of DRO 0-sec was begun, meaning that the experimenter demonstrated some behavior, and instantly, before the subject could respond, said "Good" and delivered the food to her mouth. Thus, reinforcement served to forestall the durable imitative responses this subject was displaying. Figure 7 demonstrates the immediacy of effect of this procedure. After four sessions of DRO 0-sec, it was possible to resume the procedures of DRO 30-sec and produce only a brief and partial recovery of the rate of imitation, which then declined to zero. A return to contingent reinforcement, with a small amount of shaping, quickly

reinstated the high rate of imitation previously displayed.

In all cases, then, it is clear that the imitative repertoire depended on reinforcement of at least some of its members. It is noteworthy that those responses which had developed and been maintained previously without direct reinforcement could not survive extinction applied to the entire class of behaviors.

Imitative Chains

Subjects 1 and 2 were exposed to the procedure of chaining together old and new imitative responses. At the end of 10 hr of the procedure for Subject 1, lengthy chains containing already established and new imitative responses became practical. It was possible to obtain perfect imitation on 90% of the chains, some of which involved as many as five responses. Subject 2 received only 2 hr of training on chains. At the end of this time, she would imitate 50% of the three-response chains demonstrated to her, and 80% of the two-response chains.

Verbal Behavior

Subjects 1 and 3 were used in the procedures for the development of verbal imitation. Verbal imitations were established for Subject 1 by chaining together motor and vocal behaviors and then fading out the motor components. Twenty hours of training resulted in 10 words which were reliably imitated such as, "Hi," "Okay," the subject's name, and the names of some objects. Subject 3's training in vocal imitations was accomplished by evoking a set of motor imitations which moved successively closer to vocalizations. Approximately 10 hr of training produced the reliable imitative vocalizations of seven vowel and consonant sounds.

Generalization to Other Experimenters

When Subject 1 was presented with new experimenters, of both the opposite and same sex as the original male experimenter, she showed approximately the same degree of imitation displayed to the original experimenter. That is, she imitated all of the three probe demonstrations given by one new male experimenter and imitated 12 or 15 reinforced demonstrations by a second new male experimenter on the first demonstration and the remaining three by the third demonstration. On another occasion, the second new male experimenter re-presented the 15 demonstrations; all were imitated on their first demonstration. The subject also imitated all of a series of demonstrations by a female experimenter.

DISCUSSION

The procedures of this study were sufficient to produce highly developed imitation in the experimental subjects. However, a noteworthy point is the relative difficulty experienced in obtaining initial matching responses from a subject even when the response required (*e.g.*, arm raising) clearly was in the subject's current repertoire. This suggests that the subjects were not so much learning specific responses as learning the instruction, "Do as the experimenter does." Initially, then, the procedures of this study seem to have involved bringing a number of the subjects' responses under the instructional control of the experimenter's demonstration.[1] To establish this type of instructional control by demonstration requires that the subjects either have or develop responses of observing their own behavior as well as the experimenter's behavior.

As an increasing number of the subjects' behaviors came under the instructional control of demonstration, additional behavior, not previously observed in the subjects' repertoires, became increasingly probable, merely as a result of presenting an appropriate demonstration by a model. In the terminology suggested by Miller and Dollard (1941), a sufficiently extensive arrangement of one child's behavior into matched-dependent response with a model's behavior was sufficient to induce a tendency to achieve similarity in more ways than were originally taught.

[1] The authors are indebted to Israel Goldiamond for his suggestions in clarifying this point.

The development of imitative repertoires, including the unreinforced imitation of probe demonstrations, could be accounted for by the effects of conditioned reinforcement. Conditioned reinforcement may have operated in the present study in the following way: the basic procedure was that of teaching the subject a series of responses, each of which was topographically similar to a demonstration just given by a model. Initially, each response had to be established separately. When established, such responses were imitative only topographically and would better be called matched-dependent behavior; the fact that a subject's response was similar to the experimenter's behavior at that point had no functional significance for any of the subject's other responses. Nevertheless, topographical similarity between child and experimenter was there to be attended to by the child, and this similarity was potentially discriminative with respect to the only reinforcement delivered in the experimental situation. One of the most effective ways of giving a stimulus a reinforcing function is to make it discriminative with respect to reinforcement. In these applications, the stimulus class of behavioral similarity was, in numerous examples, made discriminative with respect to positive reinforcement. Hence, similarity could be expected to take on a positive reinforcing function as well as a discriminative function. As a positive reinforcer, it should strengthen any new behavior that produced or achieved it. Behaviors that achieve similarity between one's self and a model are, of course, imitative behaviors; furthermore, they are imitative by function and not by coincidence.

This analysis is simple only at first inspection. In particular, it should be noted that "similarity" is not a simple stimulus dimension, like the frequency of sound or the intensity of light. Similarity must mean a correspondence of some sort between the stimulus output of the child's behavior and the stimulus output of the model's. A correspondence between two stimuli is not too esoteric a stimulus to consider as functional in controlling behavior. However, for an imitative repertoire to develop, a class of correspondences must become functional as stimuli. The child must learn to discriminate a correspondence between the appearance of his hand and the model's hand, his arm and the model's arm, his leg and the model's leg, his voice and the model's voice, *etc*. It would seem reasonable that each of these kinds of difference must require some prior experience on the child's part to appreciate. A scantiness of such experience may well be characteristic of retarded children, and makes them intriguing subjects for such studies. The ability to generalize similarities among a considerable variety of stimuli, which the children of these studies evidenced, suggests that the training they were subjected to was adequate to the problem. An immediate next problem, it would seem, is the detailed analysis of those procedures to find out which of them accomplished what part of this generalization. That analysis might yield a fair understanding of imitative behavior.

REFERENCES

Baer, D. M. and Sherman, J. A. Reinforcement control of generalized imitation in young children. *J. exp. Child Psychol.*, 1964, 1, 37–49.

Bandura, A. Social learning through imitation. In M. R. Jones (Ed.) *Nebraska symposium on motivation*. Lincoln: University of Nebraska Press, 1962, pp. 211–269.

Konorski, J. and Miller, S. On two types of conditioned reflex. *J. gen. Psychol.*, 1937, 16, 264–272.

Lovaas, O. I., Berberich, J. P., Perloff, B. F., and Schaeffer, B. Acquisition of imitative speech by schizophrenic children. *Science,* 1966, 151, 705–707.

Metz, J. R. Conditioning generalized imitation in autistic children. *J. exp. Child Psychol.*, 1965, 2, 389–399.

Miller, N. E. and Dollard, J. *Social learning and imitation.* New Haven: Yale University Press, 1941.

Reynolds, G. S. Behavioral contrast. *J. exp. Anal. Behav.*, 1961, 4, 57–71.

Skinner, B. F. *Science and human behavior.* New York: Macmillan, 1953.

Terrace, H. S. Discrimination learning with and without "errors." *J. exp. Anal. Behav.*, 1963, 6, 1–27 (*a*)

Terrace, H. S. Errorless transfer of a discrimination across two continua. *J. exp. Anal. Behav.*, 1963, 6, 223–232. (*b*)

LEARNING OF GENERALIZED IMITATION
AS THE BASIS FOR IDENTIFICATION

JACOB L. GEWIRTZ   KAREN G. STINGLE

After the response of another (a "model") has been witnessed, the observer will often exhibit a response resembling that of the model. This response class, termed *imitation,* does not consist of a specific set of responses classifiable by content or by similarity alone. Rather, a behavior is termed imitative if it is matched to the cues provided by the model's response and is similar to his behavior, but is not emitted because of common stimulus antecedents or environmental constraints. The term *generalized imitation* can be used when many different responses of a model are copied in diverse situations, often in the absence of extrinsic reinforcement. In contrast, the term *identification* has usually referred to a person's taking on abstract psychological characteristics of a model like those termed motives, attitudes, values, roles, or affective states, rather than specific behavior patterns. . . .

IMITATION

Miller and Dollard (1941) did much to bring imitation into a behavior-theory framework by suggesting that it is based on both the individual's capacity to learn to imitate and environmental conditions that have positively reinforced him for such learning. Copying, which by their definition involves the copier's knowing when his response is the same as the model's, is learned in a trial-and-error fashion when an external "critic" (reinforcing agent) rewards randomly occurring similarity and punishes dissimilarity, or when copying is followed by the

Reprinted with abridgment by permission of the authors and the American Psychological Association from *Psychological Review*, 1968, **75,** 374–97.

same reinforcer that followed the model's response. Eventually, as the copier's discrimination improves, he emits anticipatory discrimination responses that produce anxiety if his copying response is different from the model's response or reduce anxiety if his copying response is the same. Thus, the copier in time becomes his own critic.

Also in a learning-theory framework, Mowrer (1950, 1960) advanced a theory of imitative learning in which he postulated that imitation (particularly of vocal behaviors) of a model occurs because cues from that model's behaviors have acquired reinforcing value through their pairing with primary reinforcers, and through generalization their imitation acquires secondary reinforcement value for the copier and is thereby maintained. Thus, imitation is learned through a process of self-contained instrumental learning, without direct (extrinsic) reinforcement for imitation. In a preliminary analysis, Skinner (1953) briefly sketched how the cues from models' responses can become discriminative for the extrinsic reinforcement of matching responses, but he did not develop the case for a functional matching-response class maintained by intermittent reinforcement.

The mechanism for the acquisition of imitative (-identificatory) behaviors stressed by Bandura (1962, 1965, 1968) is that of *observational learning,* in which matching behaviors are acquired by an observer through simple exposure to a model's response, independent of the observer's overt response or of its reinforcement. Specifically, Bandura assumes that stimuli from the model's behavior elicit perceptual responses in the observer that become associated on the basis of the temporal contiguity of the stimuli provided by the environment (e.g., the model's behavior). After repeated contiguous stimulation, these perceptual responses come to form verbal or imaginal representations of the stimuli involved. These representational systems mediate response retrieval and reproduction, in that they provide cues which elicit or are discriminative for overt responses corresponding to those of the model. Thus, according to Bandura, it is primarily on the basis of stimulus contiguity and symbolic mediation that imitative behaviors are acquired. The rate and level of observational learning are conceived to be determined by a variety of what Bandura terms perceptual, motoric, cognitive, and incentive variables. Included under such categories are setting conditions (e.g., the saliency and complexity of modeling cues), the availability of necessary component responses in the observer's behavior repertoire, and overt and covert rehearsal of the matching response. However, Bandura assumes that performance of imitative responses, once they are learned, is primarily governed by extrinsic, self-administered, or vicariously experienced reinforcing events. Bandura's conceptualization of observational learning is considered further in a subsequent section.

Varying cognitive approaches to imitation (and identification) have also been put forth by Piaget (1951), and more recently in different ways by Kohlberg (1966) and Aronfreed (1967, 1968). Kohlberg rejects an S-R instrumental learning conception apparently on the basis of a narrow conception in which reinforcement is equated with organismic drive reduction. And although Aronfreed does not deny the role of instrumental learning for certain behaviors, he does qualify the learning mechanism with unindexed "representational" processes. Both theorists, however, minimize the importance of extrinsic reinforcement of the child subject's (*S*'s) responses for imitative learning. Instead, they stress *observational learning* (as does Bandura) and *intrinsic reinforcement* of responses. Kohlberg assumes intrinsic reinforcement to result somehow from "motives" for "competence-mastery" and "interesting" consequences, while Aronfreed assumes that it derives from the child's observation of the model's behavior and the "affective" value that becomes attached (conditioned) to the model and his

behavior as well as to the child's "cognitive representation" or "template" of the model's behavior. This last-mentioned implicit response concept appears to be not dissimilar to the earlier-surveyed concepts of Bandura. . . .

A Simple Mechanism for the Acquisition and Maintenance of Generalized Imitation

In this context, a simple mechanism for the acquisition and maintenance of generalized imitation will be detailed. The first imitative responses must occur by chance, through direct physical assistance, or through direct training (with shaping or fading procedures applied by a reinforcing agent to occurring responses). When such responses occur, they are strengthened and maintained by direct extrinsic reinforcement from environmental agents. After several imitative responses become established in this manner, a class of diverse but *functionally equivalent* behaviors is acquired and is maintained by extrinsic reinforcement on an intermittent schedule. Differences in response content of the imitative behaviors are thought to play a minimal role as long as the responses are members of the imitative response class as defined functionally *by reinforcing agents*. This process is thought to be the same as the way in which, for example, variations in the content of successively emitted plural nouns or first-person pronouns or even in the seemingly homogeneous free-operant bar-pressing output are irrelevant as long as most of the response variants are members of the response class reinforced.

Much past work on imitation (and even more on identification, as we shall see) has emphasized imitative responses as such, with only an implicit consideration of the relevant environmental stimuli that give that response class its functional meaning. The important difference between those approaches and the one presented here is that, in addition to an emphasis on the environmental stimuli (from the model's responses and discriminative settings) that cue the occurrence of imitative responses, we emphasize also those stimuli that maintain (reinforce) them as essential in the process. Thus, the term imitation implies for us just one type of stimulus control over responses. As with any functional response class under some kind of stimulus control, the response class has no special intrinsic value independent of the stimulus conditions controlling it. In a given context, an otherwise trivial response class like bar pressing can gain a functional status comparable to that of imitative responses in natural settings. . . .

Life Conditions for Learning Generalized Imitation

Conditions in life settings make our analysis particularly appropriate in accounting for the rapid acquisition of topographically accurate imitative behavior sequences that typically occur. Theorists like Mowrer (1960) and Bandura (1962) have argued that a trial-and-error process would be too slow to account for this rapid acquisition. However, that point does not seem cogent when one considers the abundance of extrinsic reinforcement occasions and efficient shaping processes during all stages of the child's development, particularly for response classes like imitation. Because these reinforcers come from a variety of sources, on an intermittent schedule overall, and for diverse imitative behaviors, generalized imitation will be acquired relatively early in the child's socialization, maintained at high strength, and relatively resistant to change. This is in keeping with the observation that gross imitative behaviors appear to occur early in life (Walters & Parke, 1965). Although, as a learned social behavior, imitation should be reversible, its extinction would rarely occur, since strict elimination of reinforcement for such pervasive response classes is unlikely to be implemented in complex life settings.

Parents often deliberately set out to teach the child to imitate, using direct tuition, shaping, and fading of the sort employed by Baer et al. (1965, 1967) or Lovaas et al. (1966). The child's imitation can be highly reinforcing *to* parents or models (when contingent on their behaviors). Sometimes a parent may himself imitate the child, either as a spontaneous response or as a step in the process of teaching him to imitate. Among other effects, this may facilitate the child's discrimination of the degree of similarity between his and the model's responses, and can constitute steps in a shap-

ing procedure wherein the child's response is matched to the model's with increasing closeness through successive approximations. This procedure very likely plays an important role in the child's language learning.

Indeed, it is thought that generalized imitation constitutes a most important basis for the initial occurrence and acquisition of many language responses by the child, and for the subsequent expansion of his language repertoire, and may play an even more important role in this acquisition than does simple direct instrumental training without matching. Once such verbal responses are acquired, they will be maintained by responses made to them in conversational interchanges, according to the same principles that account for the maintenance of any other responses (Gewirtz, 1968).

Behaviors of the child that are in the direction of increasing competence and are thus reinforced by socializing agents are almost invariably behaviors the child has observed older models perform (e.g., walking, talking, writing), and his performance of those behaviors is frequently reinforced in the presence of models who are exhibiting them. In a sense, these behaviors are also imitative. Thus, reinforcement for progress toward increasing competence can at the same time be reinforcement for generalized imitation. As the child is subjected increasingly to the socialization process with age, the behaviors for which he is reinforced will change with his growing capacities. The agents reinforcing him will also vary and increase in number, each reinforcing on a different schedule and for different behaviors. In the face of this continual change, one thing remains constant for the child: The imitative response class continues to be reinforced at a high rate throughout his development.

Like other social behaviors, the appropriateness of imitative responses varies from one situation to another. Thus, the imitative behavioral unit usually includes a *discriminative occasion* indicating that an imitative response is likely to be reinforced. Reinforceable occasions may be preceded by an explicit verbal cue, like Baer, Peterson, and Sherman's "Susy, do this," or by a less explicit cue indicating that imitation is appropriate. The imitator learns to discriminate those cue stimuli from cues indicating that noncopying, complementary interactive responses—for instance, dependence—are appropriate. For example, based on differential reinforcement of the child's behaviors in the past, the model's *being oriented toward* the child (physically or otherwise), or his *not being occupied* in some ongoing activity, may acquire discriminative stimulus value for the child's emitting *complementary* interaction responses and for suppressing copying responses, which would be clearly inappropriate. Imitative behaviors are more likely to be reinforced when the model is busily engaged in a *solitary* activity and can more readily reinforce the child's parallel behaviors (like imitation) than his approach or interactive behaviors, as the model can then continue his activity without long interruption. If the child is frequently reinforced for making disruptive dependency initiations in this situation, he may not learn to discriminate that such behaviors are inappropriate and may interrupt the model at will, thus in extreme cases becoming what could be termed "spoiled." It is possible that such children do not learn to imitate to as great an extent as children whose models discourage interruptions of the model's task. It is also likely that at the same time they do not acquire autonomous task-oriented behavior patterns independent of frequent reinforcement from their socializing agents.

There remains a considerable need for a detailed analysis of the discriminative cues that indicate to the child, in specific and more general cases, when it is appropriate to imitate (i.e., when imitation is likely to be reinforced) and which model it is most appropriate to imitate when alternative models are available. An analysis from our intentionally simple approach would attend only in passing to developmental changes in imitative behaviors and learning that occur in typical life settings. Our conception of generalized-imitation learning in principle is not incompatible with cognitive-developmental analyses based on observation in life settings, like Piaget's (1951) conception of "stages" of imitation and other naturalistic approaches that stress change in the child's capacities during the early years as well as developmental differences in the organization of imitative behaviors. However, we assume that the basic mode of acquisition and maintenance of imitation is not altered by such developmental changes.

Focused versus Nonfocused Generalized Imitation

The generalized-imitation paradigm as we have used it up to now has been relatively *nonfocused* with regard to the model imitated, summarizing imitation of diverse responses of *many* models. Yet an important case where such imitation appears to be *focused* more on one particular model than on others often occurs. This model is usually a parent, and the focused imitation involved is thought to provide an important basis for identification, as will be detailed later in this article. Such a selective imitation pattern can result from a combination of relatively frequent contact with one model and frequent reinforcement by the model and by others for imitating a variety of the behaviors of that model. That model's behaviors will therefore acquire discriminative value for the child, indicating that his imitation of them has an even higher probability of being reinforced than does imitation in general.

Much of the child's early socialization takes place in the family setting, where he interacts with parents and siblings. Although a differential distribution of the child's interaction with the members of his family is bound to result, it should be less important for his generalized-imitation learning than should differential reinforcement for imitation of those members. Children of both sexes typically interact more with their mothers than with their fathers, but the boy comes to imitate his father and the girl her mother because of differential reinforcement for copying each of them. As noted earlier, the child will be reinforced for imitating different models in diverse contexts. In the family setting, however, he will discriminate which single model it is usually most appropriate to imitate, on the basis of being differentially reinforced for such imitation; and because of frequent chances to observe that model, the child will imitate an extensive range of his behaviors. More will be said on this issue when we consider sex typing. . . .

Generalized Imitation Extended

Thus far, we have shown that generalized-imitation learning based on extrinsic reinforcement can plausibly account for the acquisition and maintenance of imitative responses in the apparent absence of extrinsic reinforcement, can be facilitated by the heavy extrinsic reinforcement of developmental behavioral advances by the child in the presence of models performing those responses, can be focused on a single model under the proper circumstances, and can come under the discriminative control of gross behavioral settings in which the model is engaged. We will now see how the generalized-imitation concept can account for related behavioral phenomena that will be relevant to our analysis of identification. These include imitation of the model's behavior in his absence, imitation of a large portion of a model's behavior role in play settings, and wide-ranging similarities in abstract values or attitudes.

IMITATION IN THE MODEL'S ABSENCE   Delayed imitation, including imitation of the model's behavior in his absence, can be regarded as a simple variant of the generalized-imitation paradigm. This point, which is also pertinent to observational learning, becomes clearer when one considers that all imitative behaviors occur *after* the model's performance providing the relevant cue has terminated and often while the child is not even looking at the model, and in that sense they are always performed in the *absence* of the model. The delay between the model's performance and the imitative behavior may be further lengthened through shaping techniques, implemented either deliberately or in an unplanned way by reinforcing agents. Immediate direct reinforcement for delayed imitation in the model's absence may frequently be provided by agents other than the model, and sometimes in the form of statements like "you are acting just like your father" or "like a big boy." In addition, the agent may indicate explicitly that what is being reinforced is not only performance of the response, but its performance in the model's absence.

IMITATION OF THE MODEL IN PLAY   Imi-tation of large segments of a model's behavior role in play situations where the model is not present may also be facilitated by ecological factors. Props given to the child can be appropriate to the model's role, as in the case of toy kitchen utensils being made available to a young girl. Reinforcement can be provided through the reciprocal role play of other children, or through occasional direct reinforcement from the model or other adult witnesses. These toys may serve a dual purpose, in that they can also provide a sanctioned discriminable context for the child's imitation of a model's behaviors in his absence when these behaviors might be hazardous or inappropriate in their usual context.

GENERALIZED IMITATION OF VALUES   The generalized-imitation concept can also be extended readily to account for wide-ranging similarities in abstract values (attitudes, life styles, or motives). For example, often a child will act as the model might in a situation even if he has not actually witnessed the model in that situation, or he will strive for the same goals as the model. (As we shall see in the next section, these behaviors are often termed identification.)

An example of a model's value is "tidy housekeeping." A mother's behavior may exemplify that value, and her daughter either may be extrinsically reinforced for nonimitative tidying responses or may exhibit these responses through simple generalized imitation (with or without extrinsic reinforcement), as we have been emphasizing. An important assumption for extending our analysis is that a daughter generally reinforced for acting like her mother may come to discriminate the common elements of responses exhibited by the model in a class of related stimulus contexts (such as housekeeping), which she might also inductively characterize with a statement like, "Mom keeps a tidy house." The child's value is based on her discrimination of such a functional class of the model's responses (some would term it a "concept"), which would then apply to situations in which the child, as generalized imitator, may not actually have seen the model perform. The daughter may also exhibit verbal responses that reflect the value, for instance, "It's good to keep the house tidy," which have been acquired together with tidy-housekeeping responses via generalized-imitation learning. Although some of the daughter's responses may be quite different in topography from those of her mother (because of changed climatic conditions, technological and socioeconomic levels, etc.), they will produce the same outcome: a tidy house. Once the value has been acquired in this manner, the mother is likely to reinforce the resulting responses, and the value will be maintained. As is true of all learned behaviors, however, the permanence of a value will depend on the continuation of the same reinforcement matrix for the class of responses implying that value, and thus it is potentially subject to change.

The analysis thus far has stressed primarily those situations in which cues from the model and extrinsic reinforcement to the child provide the context for the child's imitative behaviors. The above examples show the potential utility of the generalized-imitation paradigm in situations where some of the relevant discriminative and reinforcing stimuli for imitation are absent. In the next section we will argue that a substantial proportion of the phenomena grouped under the concept of identification may be ordered by the concept of generalized imitation and these extensions.

IDENTIFICATION

The child's acquisition of the motives, values, ideals, roles, and conscience of an important other person (the model), particularly of his parents and especially the same-sex parent, has been termed identification. The term has been used variously to refer to the process by which these characteristics are acquired, to the person's desire to possess the characteristics of the model and his belief that he does, and to the resulting similarity of behavior patterns of child and model. Several of these usages are often found in the same analysis. The identification term has also been used often as if it were a unitary concept that involves a single, incompletely specified complex paradigm with demographically defined independent variables (e.g., gender of S in an intact nuclear family) and no consensually valid dependent variable.

Psychoanalytic theory provided the earliest framework for the approach to the phenomena of identification, and much of identification theory still relies on those early attempts. While Freud dealt with identification in a scattered way through half a century of his writing, and there were apparent variations in his approach, he seems to have employed the term in at least two ways: as a *process* and as the behavior-similarity *outcome* of that process. Thus, Freud (1933) regarded identification as the process by which "one ego becomes like another one, which results in the first ego behaving . . . in certain respects in the same way as the second; it imitates it, and as it were takes it into itself [p. 90]." And, in one of his writings, Freud's (1920) index of the outcome of identification was imitation of the model's behaviors. When assumed to result from complete instrumental dependence upon and an emotional tie to the model (typically the parent), identification has been termed "anaclitic" in Freud's approach and by Sears (1957; Sears et al., 1965) and "developmental" by Mowrer (1950); while "aggressive" or "defensive" identification (Freud, 1937; Mowrer, 1950) is assumed to result from fear of punishment from the model, with the child avoiding punishment by becoming like the model. The child's superego, the locus of self-observation, conscience, and ideals, has been assumed to be based largely on this latter type of identification and to be built upon the model of the parents' superego rather than on their actual behavior.

Although many would agree that the child can learn to imitate a range of behaviors on the basis of simple trial-and-error learning (as involved in generalized imitation), imitation has typically been treated in the literature as somehow distinct from identification. Thus, despite an early instance where Freud (1920) used imitation to index identification, the typical psychoanalytic view appears to be that the relatively precise matching to the model's overt behavior in imitation is a transient, surface, even symptomatic process, whereas the wider-ranging, less precise behavioral matching in identification results from a more fundamental or dynamic underlying process.

Kohlberg (1963) has proposed that identification differs from imitation on three counts: (*a*) Identification is a "motivated disposition" because of the intrinsic reinforcing properties of perceived similarity to the model; (*b*) similarity between the behavior of *S* and the model often occurs in the absence of the model; and (*c*) many aspects of the model's behavior are reproduced. These factors appear to have been the bases for many theorists' considering identification as a "higher-order" process than generalized imitation. (More recently, Kohlberg, 1966, has proposed that attachment follows [generalized] imitation, and that the combination of those two factors leads to identification, but it is not clear what are the roles of the above three criteria in his recent approach.)

Within the learning-theory tradition, Miller and Dollard (1941) in a brief comment suggested that imitation mechanisms are also involved in identification, while Seward (1954) suggested that identification is a high-level abstraction from numerous imitative habits. Bandura (1962) and Bandura and Walters (1963) have noted that observational learning is often termed imitation in behavior-theory approaches to personality development and identification in more traditional personality theories, with no substantial differences between the two usages. In our similar view, often the only reason that generalized-imitation learning is assumed inadequate to account for identification phenomena is that factors like a motivation to be like, an emotional attachment to, or envy of the model that are assumed relevant for identification are just not considered at all relevant to generalized imitation, and, indeed, some even appear to think of them as outside the sphere of simple learning.

Generalized Imitation as the Basis for Identification

Such distinctions may have made the analysis of identification needlessly complex. They also point up the necessity for a more systematic approach to identification phenomena and their underlying mechanism(s). We have shown earlier that: (*a*) The seeming intrinsic reinforcing property of certain behavior classes, in particular imitation, depends entirely upon oc-casional extrinsic reinforcement of members of that class; and that (*b*) the performance of diverse imitative behaviors in the absence of the model is also accountable by straightforward application of the generalized-imitation paradigm, as is (*c*) the tendency to focus generalized imitation on one model and to imitate not only a range of his overt behaviors, but also behaviors implied in such general dispositions as are often termed motives, values, or attitudes. In this way, it has been automatically proposed under our functional approach that most if not all the phenomena usually grouped under identification may reasonably be assumed to be the direct consequences of generalized-imitation training, and thus can be reduced to that more parsimonious instrumental training conception.

It appears that another distinction implicit in most definitions of imitation and identification is that while both terms refer to behaviors matched to those of a model, the latter behaviors are maintained exclusively by social stimuli while the former may be maintained by both social and nonsocial ones. Thus, all identificatory acts may be imitative, but not all imitative acts are identificatory. Because the specification of which stimulus contexts and reinforcers are social is often arbitrary, we contend that in a similar manner the distinction between identification and imitation is to a large degree an arbitrary semantic one, with no fundamental differences in the way in which they are learned. Under a learning analysis, the major reason we would prefer to use a single term like social imitation rather than both imitation and identification is that the use of both terms implies that such differences exist and are meaningful, an implication that can only cloud the issue. The use of more learning-oriented terms precludes such interpretations and facilitates the fitting of existing and future data on identification processes into a framework that allows us more easily to tie in other important aspects of the learning process.

Thus, it often appears that the only real distinction in use between identification and imitation may be that the identification process is typically defined in a less precise, more complex, and more inclusive way than is imitation. Further, a large number of loosely related and often overlapping terms at varying levels of conceptual analysis, like introjection, incorporation, internalization, modeling, role copying, and sex typing, all of which lead to similarities between the model's and the identifier's behavior patterns, are included under identification. This situation has further complicated the concept of identification and appears to have implied, as an artifact, a larger number of seemingly distinct processes than is warranted. The level from which such concepts typically are approached makes it difficult to make clear-cut differentiations between identification and overlapping concepts like introjection or sex typing. Reduction of these terms to the same level of analysis in basic paradigms open to a learning analysis is necessary and may show that apparent differences among them can be attributed to the methods of measurement, the segments of the stream of behavior emphasized, the particular stimuli evoking the responses, and the functional reinforcers available, factors that do not ordinarily justify separate paradigms. Such a reduction can be implemented by regarding identification concepts as based on the simpler generalized-imitation paradigm, with behavioral similarity as the outcome.

For example, *introjection* is often defined as the act of incorporating a value system in its entirety, with identification as its result (Fuchs, 1937). Thus, while introjection appears to refer to the acquisition process and identification to its result, those terms may only reflect emphasis on different stages in the behavior process by which generalized imitation is learned and maintained, with introjection pointing to a somewhat earlier phase of the learning than does identification. The use of two different terms therefore seems to emphasize arbitrarily what may for most purposes be a trivial distinction. Similarly, *sex typing* usually denotes identification with models of the same sex as the child, and has itself been broken down further into sex-role identification, sex-role preference, and sex-role adoption (Lynne, 1959). Thus, it refers to the shaping of the child's behaviors to match behaviors specifically appropriate to his sex category. These behaviors are usually assumed to be acquired through observation of a model or a class of models. So defined, they can be regarded as the result of generalized imitation, with the gender of the

model serving as a discriminate stimulus for a higher frequency of extrinsic (immediate or delayed) reinforcement for imitation. Kohlberg (1966) has reported that a shift from generalized imitation of the mother to imitation of the father typically occurs in boys between ages 4 and 7, which he interpreted as reflecting changes in boys' conceptualization of age and sex roles. The approach being advanced in this paper is open to such possibilities, but we would conceive them as resulting from a systematic shift in the discriminative conditions under which imitative behaviors are reinforced. Mischel (1966) has reviewed a number of other results of sex-typing studies done to date and interpreted them from a learning approach very much like ours.

At this point in its evolution, the research area of identification can benefit from a deliberate approach, both theoretical and operational. In the context of a profusion of overlapping concepts and the need to reduce the frequently used demographic independent variables to component functional stimuli, the salient issues for our analysis must be operational, such as whether or not discriminative stimuli for imitation are present and whether or not functional extrinsic reinforcers follow imitative responses. In addition to reducing demographic variables to a more useful level of analysis, such factors can provide the basis for distinguishing among possibly diverse paradigms. By attending to the actual stimuli, responses, and the sequential details of their interaction, this level of analysis makes possible a flexible, individual-oriented approach to identification phenomena. Although in representative life settings some general outcomes do occur, for example, children typically do imitate behaviors appropriate to their sex category, this approach provides greater precision and flexibility in detailing the history of the individual child in question in terms of what similarity behaviors have been acquired and how they are evoked and maintained. But equally important, it can also highlight the conditions responsible for a failure to acquire particular identification behaviors and the conditions that may facilitate, extinguish, or otherwise modify such behaviors. Reversibility or change in identification-behavior patterns is almost never assumed or tested, yet is a perfectly reasonable corollary of the conception of learning, in representative life settings as in the laboratory. A functional analysis such as we propose would also make it possible to determine which antecedent process determines a particular behavior-similarity outcome and whether or not there are different combinations of antecedents that could lead to an identical outcome. The continuous-differentiation process involved would lead routinely to new concept groupings and labels, with previously unidentified but relevant phenomena brought under the identification concept and ordered by novel or derived paradigms.

Empirical research studies of identification, quite reasonably, have typically employed behavioral similarity between the child and his parents as a measure of identification (though often, when verbal reports have provided these indexes, the variables generated were at too removed a level to allow precise leverage on the process). At the level of analysis emphasized here, direct measures of similarity between the child's and the adult's responses (including those summarized as traits) in structured stimulus settings would be useful operational indexes of identification, with variations in discriminative and reinforcement parameters as independent variables. It will be necessary to show in such settings that the behaviors of the child that are termed identification are acquired under the control of the discriminative cues provided by the model's behaviors rather than being determined by environmental constraints or independent but parallel acquisition processes, and that they are, in the absence of the model, under the control of the same discriminative stimuli as were the model's behaviors.

The present approach, then, regards the development of identification behaviors as due to extrinsic reinforcement of the child's imitation of his parent's (or model's) behaviors. The degree to which a child is identified with a particular model is thus grossly determined by the value to the child of the reinforcers contingent upon his imitation of that person's behavior. His identification will also be a function of the amount of exposure to other potential models and reinforcement for imitating them, the frequency of reinforcement for original, nonimitative behaviors, and the value of the reinforcers provided for each of these behavior classes. Identification with the model at the level of abstract values may require finer discriminations by the child but, as we have already shown, should follow the same principles as simpler imitation.

The advantages of this functional approach are evident when one looks at such work as that by Lovaas (1967) with schizophrenic children. Besides teaching the children to imitate vocalizations and to converse, as was described earlier, Lovaas reinforced nonverbal imitation in order to teach behaviors in the areas of personal hygiene, games, drawing, and affectionate behavior, with the intention of eventually shifting the control of these behaviors (by fading procedures) away from the model to control by more appropriate or general stimuli. Noting that the behaviors learned by these children were neither as representative nor did they occur in as wide a range of settings as those covered by such terms as identification, Lovaas nevertheless implied that bringing about this more extensive imitation is not incompatible with the procedures he had been using and may primarily involve increasing the reinforcing value of stimuli from the model and others. Thus, besides permitting a more precise evaluation of the factors involved in the children's failure to identify, this approach suggests specific areas of attack to remedy the deficiencies.

REFERENCES

Aronfreed, J. Imitation and identification: An analysis of some affective and cognitive mechanisms. Paper presented at the biennial meeting of the Society for Research in Child Development, New York, March 1967.

Baer, D. M., Peterson, R. F., & Sherman, J. A.

Building an imitative repertoire by programming similarity between child and model as discriminative for reinforcement. Paper presented at the biennial meeting of the Society for Research in Child Development, Minneapolis, March 1965.

Baer, D. M., Peterson, R. F., & Sherman, J. A.

The development of imitation by reinforcing behavioral similarity to a model. *Journal of the Experimental Analysis of Behavior,* 1967, 10, 405–416.

Bandura, A. Vicarious processes: A case of no-trial learning. In L. Berkowitz (Ed.), *Advances in experimental social psychology.* Vol. 2. New York: Academic Press, 1965. Pp. 1–55.

Bandura, A. Social-learning theory of identificatory processes. In D. A. Goslin (Ed.), *Handbook of socialization theory and research.* Chicago: Rand-McNally, 1968. Ch. 3.

Bandura, A., & Walters, R. H. *Social learning and personality development.* New York: Holt, Rinehart & Winston, 1963.

Freud, A. *The ego and the mechanisms of defense.* London: Hogarth, 1937.

Freud, S. *A general introduction to psychoanalysis.* Garden City, N.Y.: Garden City Publishing Co., 1920.

Freud, S. *New introductory lectures on psychoanalysis.* London: Hogarth, 1933.

Fuchs, S. H. On introjection. *International Journal of Psychoanalysis,* 1937, 18, 269–293.

Gewirtz, J. L. Mechanisms of social learning. In D. A. Goslin (Ed.), *Handbook of socialization theory and research.* Chicago: Rand-McNally, 1968. Ch. 2.

Kohlberg, L. Moral development and identification. In H. W. Stevenson (Ed.), *Child psychology: The sixty-second yearbook of the National Society for the Study of Education.* Chicago: University of Chicago Press, 1963. Pp. 277–332.

Kohlberg, L. A cognitive-developmental analysis of children's sex-role concepts and attitudes. In E. E. Maccoby (Ed.), *The development of sex differences.* Stanford: Stanford University Press, 1966. Pp. 82–173.

Lovaas, O. I. A behavior therapy approach to the treatment of childhood schizophrenia. In J. P. Hill (Ed.), *Minnesota symposia on child psychology.* Vol. 1. Minneapolis: University of Minnesota Press, 1967. Pp. 108–159.

Lovaas, O. I., Berberich, J. P., Perloff, B. F., & Schaeffer, B. Acquisition of imitative speech by schizophrenic children. *Science,* 1966, 151, 705–707.

Lynn, D. B. A note on sex differences in the development of masculine and feminine identification. *Psychological Review,* 1959, 66, 126–135.

Miller, N. E., & Dollard, J. *Social learning and imitation.* New Haven: Yale University Press, 1941.

Mischel, W. A. A social-learning view of sex differences in behavior. In E. E. Maccoby (Ed.), *The development of sex differences.* Stanford: Stanford University Press, 1966. Pp. 56–81.

Mowrer, O. H. *Learning theory and personality dynamics.* New York: Ronald Press, 1950.

Mowrer, O. H. *Learning theory and the symbolic processes.* New York: Wiley, 1960.

Piaget, J. *Play, dreams and imitation in childhood.* New York: Norton, 1951.

Sears, R. R. Identification as a form of behavioral development. In D. B. Harris (Ed.), *The concept of development.* Minneapolis: University of Minnesota Press, 1957. Pp. 149–161.

Sears, R. R., Rau, L., & Alpert, R. *Identification and child rearing.* Stanford: Stanford University Press, 1965.

Seward, J. P. Learning theory and identification: II. Role of punishment. *Journal of Genetic Psychology,* 1954, 84, 201–210.

Skinner, B. F. *Science and human behavior.* New York: Macmillan, 1953.

Walters, R. H., & Parke, R. D. The role of the distance receptors in the development of social responsiveness. In L. P. Lipsitt & C. C. Spiker (Eds.), *Advances in child development and behavior.* Vol. 2. New York: Academic Press, 1965. Pp. 59–96.

Walters, R. H., Parke, R. D., & Cane, V. A. Timing of punishment and the observation of consequences to others as determinants of response inhibition. *Journal of Experimental Child Psychology,* 1965, 2, 10–30.

THE ANTECEDENTS OF SELF-CRITICISM

JOAN GRUSEC

The development of guilt and, therefore, of one of its behavioral manifestations—self-criticism—has typically been conceptualized within theories of identification (e.g., Freud, 1924; Maccoby, 1959; Mowrer, 1950; Sears, 1957). These theories suggest that certain child-rearing practices will be more effective than others for this development. The study reported here was an attempt to assess, in an experimental setting, the importance of two of these child-rearing variables in the development of self-criticism— the technique of punishment employed by the socializing agent and the rewarding characteristics of that agent.

In his theory of identification Sears (1957) suggests that the attributes of the caretaker take on secondary-reward value for the child because of their association with primary-drive reduction (e.g., feeding). In the caretaker's absence the child can provide secondary reinforcement for himself by matching the caretaker's behavior, including his criticism. On the basis of this theory Sears predicts that a punishment technique involving withdrawal of love (WOL) should be more effective for the development of conscience and hence, self-criticism, than one involving withdrawal of rewards or physical punishment. For only under conditions of WOL would a child have to engage in role practice of parental behavior, including parental value statements, in order to provide for himself the reinforcement that had been withdrawn. It seems improbable, however, that a child practices parental behavior which is aversive, such as criticism, in order to provide himself with reinforcement. Recent extensions of identification theory (e.g., Kagan, 1958; Maccoby, 1959; Mussen & Distler, 1959) have

Reprinted by permission of the author and the American Psychological Association from *Journal of Personality and Social Psychology*, 1966, **4,** 244–52.

avoided this difficulty by suggesting that the control exercised by a parent over resources important for the needs of the child—including positive reinforcement *and* power to determine and deliver punishment—will determine the amount of role practice in which the child engages. According to Maccoby (1959), since all aspects of parental behavior are important to the child in guiding his plans about future actions, he will attend to, and covertly practice, all parental behavior. A child whose parents characteristically react to his deviation by WOL will respond to later deviations by withdrawing love from himself because that is the behavior he has rehearsed most frequently in that particular stimulus situation. Thus he will be exhibiting behavior indicative of high conscience development.

Sears, Maccoby, and Levin (1957) found that mothers who used WOL as punishment, provided they were warm, had children who exhibited higher conscience development than those whose mothers used other techniques of punishment. Thus the formulations of both Sears and Maccoby were supported. Hill (1960), however, has suggested that this result may be an artifact of the way WOL is typically used by parents. Specifically, it, as opposed to physical punishment or withdrawal of material reward (WOMR), probably much more often lasts until the child has made some symbolic renunciation of his wrongdoing, and the return of parental love which accompanies this renunciation serves to reinforce it. Hill predicted that if physical chastisement or loss of privileges were also used so that cessation of punishment were contingent upon renunciation, high conscience development would result. On the basis of this reasoning it was predicted that in the experimental situation described in this report WOL would be no more effective for the development of self-criticism than WOMR, provided contingencies for the termination of both were the same. Thus, children reinforced for self-criticism by the cessation of punishment (return of love *or* material reward) should increase in their use of it, while those not reinforced for self-criticism should eventually extinguish in its use.

The initial use of a self-critical response, before the opportunity for reinforcement has occurred, seems adequately accounted for by a theory such as Maccoby's which stresses the model's power as a determinant of attention to and covert rehearsal of that model's criticism. Aronfreed (1964), however, has rejected identification theory as an explanatory device for the origin of self-criticism, stressing, instead, the *timing* of punishment as an important determinant. He showed that a critical response paired by the experimenter with the offset of punishment, and hence with the reduction of anxiety, was used more often by subjects than one paired with the onset of punishment and thereby with the onset of anxiety. Aronfreed (1964) also concluded, on the basis of his experimental evidence, that ". . . the reproduction of social punishment can be subsumed under the consequences of a model's rewarding characteristics [pp. 212–213]."

This latter conclusion, however, may be premature, for Aronfreed's manipulations of the model's rewarding characteristics could well have been ineffective. They were brief and consisted solely of expressions of verbal and physical affection made during the experimental procedure. Other studies which have provided evidence that the social characteristics of a model affect the extent to which an observer imitates his behavior (e.g., Bandura & Huston, 1961; Bandura, Ross, & Ross, 1963; Mischel & Grusec, 1966) have employed relatively long (approximately 20 minutes) nurturance periods prior to the modeling phase during which the model has dispensed many social and material rewards to the subject. Accordingly, it was predicted that, in the present situation, children who interacted with a model who was nurturant and controlled resources important to them—in short, a highly rewarding (HR) model—would be more likely to apply that model's criticism to themselves than would

those exposed to a model who was low in rewardingness (LR), even though the model's criticism preceded punishment and should, according to Aronfreed, not be reproduced because it was paired with the onset of anxiety. A rationale for this prediction comes from Maccoby's (1959) theory, described above. Because an HR model's criticism is the response which has been acquired through attention and covert practice, it is the one which will be evoked when the stimulus conditions under which it was learned arise again.

In this study eight groups of kindergarten children were exposed either to a model who was highly rewarding or to one who was not rewarding. After this exposure, the model and the child played a game devised so that the child could plausibly be criticized for his play on certain arbitrarily preselected trials. The model accompanied this criticism with either WOMR or WOL, making reinstatement of the reward either contingent or noncontingent on the child's applying the critical response to himself. Generalization of the self-critical response and its resistance to extinction were also measured.

METHOD

Subjects

Eighty kindergarten children from a Mountain View, California, school, ranging in age from 5 years, 5 months to 6 years, 11 months, served as subjects. The sample was of middle-class background and heterogeneous with respect to racial origin. Five boys and five girls were assigned randomly to each of eight experimental groups. The same female experimenter was used for each subject.

Experimental Design

A $2 \times 2 \times 2$ factorial design was employed. In the first phase of the experiment half the subjects were exposed to an HR model, while the other half were exposed to an LR model. In the second phase all children participated individually in a game which was designed so that the model could punish them for the way they played and pair the onset of this punishment with a distinctive critical response. For half the subjects in each of the HR and LR conditions the punishment consisted of WOMR, while for the other half it consisted of WOL. Each of these four groups (HR-WOMR, LR-WOMR, HR-WOL, and LR-WOL) was divided into two new groups. For one of these new groups reinforcement (considered in this study as the termination of punishment, i.e., the return of withdrawn material reward or withdrawn love) was contingent on their application of the model's criticism to themselves (C). For the other group it was not contingent on this self-criticism (NC). After a series of punishment trials, generalization of the self-critical response to a new situation was tested. Finally, a number of extinction trials were run in which punishment was no longer administered.

Manipulation of the Model's Rewardingness

HIGH-REWARD CONDITIONS   In the HR conditions the model brought the child from his classroom to a trailer parked near the kindergarten room. They entered an attractive room in the trailer which contained a number of pleasing toys, for example, battery-run cars and airplanes, a bowling set, puppets, dolls, and attractive blocks. The subject and the model played with these toys. The model was warm and friendly, asked the child questions about himself, and was generally highly noncontingently rewarding. During the play session, the model also dispensed cookies and stickers.

LOW-REWARD CONDITIONS   In the LR conditions the model did not take the subject into the trailer, but brought him to the back of it. She remarked that they could not go into the trailer since it did not belong to her, but that the people who owned it had allowed her to set up her belongings behind it. The model informed the child that she had some work to do and that he would have to play by himself for a while. She directed him to a few unattractive toys arranged on the ground, for example, a broken horn, a broken toy accordion, a much-used coloring book, and worn crayons. The model commented that she did not have too many

toys, but suggested that he might color. She then sat down at a table and worked busily at some papers. If the child approached her at any time, she reminded him, in a neutral manner, that she had to get her work finished and that he was to play by himself.

These sessions each lasted for 15 minutes. At the end of this time the model told the subject that they were now going to play a special game. He was seated at a table in front of apparatus for the game while the model sat at the other side of the table.

Apparatus

GAME   The game was similar to one used by Aronfreed (1963). The subject sat in front of a black, triangular-shaped box that was 7 inches high and 15 inches at its base. The base, which faced the model, had no side, and the whole box had no bottom. The box could be removed to reveal 20 plastic soldiers thickly clustered in triangular formation. At the apex of this formation there was a wooden block. Pasted on this block was a colorful and attractive picture of a donkey. Just beyond the base of the formation, beside the model, was a large cardboard box which rested on the floor and could not be seen by the subject. There was a hole at the apex of the box through which the handle of a pushing device could be placed.

DISPENSER   Beside the game there was a small black box which, in the WOMR conditions, was used to dispense chips which subjects could trade for toys at the end of the experimental session. In the WOL conditions the chips were removed. The dispenser could be activated by a switch located on top of it so that, if it was filled, chips automatically emerged from it every 15 seconds. A small red light beside the switch came on when the dispenser was in operation.

TIMER   Beside the dispenser was a timer. Subjects were informed that there was a time limit on the availability of chips and that when the dispenser was off rewards were not only delayed but lost.

The dispenser and the timer were also present

for the WOL groups in order to keep stimulus conditions as similar as possible for all groups.

Procedure

WITHDRAWAL OF MATERIAL REWARD CONDITIONS   Sometime during the week before their interaction with the model children who had been assigned to the WOMR groups were brought to the trailer in groups of 10 by a male experimental confederate. The model was not present. The confederate's task was to explain the operation of the dispenser. This confederate, who described himself as the owner of the dispenser and the toys which could be gotten for chips, was used so that the model's control of resources remained equivalent for WOMR and WOL groups. For if the model had owned the material reward employed in the WOMR conditions she would have controlled more material resources than in the WOL conditions. The confederate demonstrated to subjects that when the dispenser was on, as indicated by the red light, chips emerged from it. These chips, he told them, could be saved and traded for toys which were kept in another room. It was emphasized that the more chips subjects could collect the more toys they would get, and the nicer they would be. Subjects were told that they would all have a chance to return to the trailer where the dispenser would be turned on for them, and they would have a chance to collect chips and trade them for toys.

Any reference to the kind and number of toys for which the chips could be traded was deliberately kept ambiguous. Since it was impossible to equate the amount of the two kinds of punishment, the amount of material reward was left unspecified so that comparison of the effects of WOMR and WOL would be a more reasonable undertaking.

In the experimental session proper, when the model brought subjects in the WOMR conditions to the trailer, no mention was made of the previous visit with the male confederate. After Phase I of the experiment, as the subject was sitting in front of the table which held the game, dispenser, and timer, the model reminded him of how the dispenser worked. She said that she had been asked by the male confederate to turn it on for the subject and give him toys in exchange for the chips he collected. Referring to the timer, the model demonstrated how it worked and said that they would play a game as long as the timer was going. The dispenser would also be in operation until the timer reached the top and rang. At that point, the model explained, the subject would no longer be able to collect chips.

WITHDRAWAL OF LOVE CONDITIONS   No child in these conditions had been to the trailer before his interaction with the model. After Phase I of the experiment, as he was sitting in front of the table which held the game, dispenser, and timer, the model referred to the dispenser which now was empty of chips. She said the dispenser belonged to someone else, but that she was going to use it to tell the subject whether or not she was happy with the way he was playing the game. The dispenser's operation was explained, and the model said that when it was on she was "very pleased and happy" with the way he was playing, but when it was off she was "unhappy and disappointed" in the way he was playing. The operation of the timer was also described, and the subject was told that the game would be played until the timer reached the top and rang. He was urged to try and keep the dispenser on while the game was being played.

Game Instructions

After they had been instructed about the dispenser and timer, subjects in all groups were given the same instructions about how the game was to be played. Removing the cover from the soldiers, the model said:

This is an army game and all the soldiers here are fighting in a war. This is a donkey that was left with the soldiers and they have to look after him. Whenever there's any fighting the donkey has to go into this box so he'll be safe. It's your job to push him off with this pusher so he won't get hurt in the fighting. It's very important that you knock down as few soldiers as possible when you're pushing off the donkey—in fact, the idea of the game is to see how few soldiers you can knock down. If you knock down a few that's good, but if you knock down a lot that's not so good.

We have to put a cover on the soldiers and the donkey so enemy planes can't see them and shoot at them. [The pusher's handle was placed through the hole in the box, and the box was placed over the donkey and soldiers.] That makes your job a bit harder because you won't be able to see them either. But you do as well as you can, and remember to be very, very gentle, both with the donkey and with the soldiers and try to knock down just as few soldiers as you can.

If you hurt the soldiers you'll hear this. [A buzzer was sounded.] That means you were a "hurter" and that's the worst thing you can be in this game. So try not to be a "hurter." Remember that this [the buzzer was sounded] means you were a "hurter" and that's a bad thing to be.

Now I'll turn the box on and set this. [The dispenser was turned on, and the timer set to 20 minutes.] Remember that we'll be using the box until this [referring to the timer] gets to the top and it rings.

Punishment Procedure

Each time the subject pushed the donkey into the cardboard box was counted as a trial. Of the first 15 trials 8 were punished. These, chosen randomly, were trials 2, 4, 5, 7, 8, 9, 12, and 14. On every trial, as soon as the donkey fell into the cardboard box, the model looked into the box as though to count how many soldiers had fallen with it. At the same time she made one or two statements of the following kind: "Let's see how the war is going," and "Let's see what fell." On unpunished trials she replaced the soldiers and donkey and told the subject to push the donkey off again. On punishment trials the buzzer sounded immediately after the neutral statements, thereby indicating to the subject that he had been a "hurter." On Trial 2 (the first punishment trial), immediately after the buzzer, the model said, "You're a 'hurter.' Remember in this game that's the worst thing you can be." From Trial 4 on the model used WOMR or WOL as punishment. Her manner of punishing and the probes she used in an attempt to elicit the self-critical response of "hurter" from the child were as follows.

Punishment in Withdrawal of Material Reward Conditions

On Trial 4, immediately after the buzzer sounded, the model said, "You're a 'hurter.' Because you were a 'hurter' the chips will have to stop coming." She then turned off the dispenser and busied herself with straightening the soldiers, all the while assuming a neutral manner toward the subject. If, within 15 seconds, he said nothing about being a hurter, he was asked, "What happened?" If this question failed to elicit the self-critical label, he was asked, "Can you tell me why the chips aren't coming?" If this question was still not successful, two more attempts were made with, "Was it because of the way you pushed?" and "What did we say you were?" Finally, if the child failed to emit the label, he was reminded once again that he had been a hurter.

On Trial 5 the model said, "The chips will have to stop coming," and turned off the dispenser. If the subject did not respond appropriately within 15 seconds, she said, 'What happened?" If the self-criticism was not verbalized, the model made two more attempts to elicit it with, "Can you tell me why the chips aren't coming?" and "What did we say you were?" If the subject still did not respond, he was reminded, for the last time, that he had been a hurter.

On trials 7, 8, 9, 12, and 14 the model said, "The chips will have to stop coming," and turned off the dispenser. After 15 seconds, two attempts were made to elicit the self-criticism with, "What happened?" and "Can you tell me why the chips aren't coming any more?"

Punishment in Withdrawal of Love Conditions

The model's behavior was identical to her behavior in the WOMR conditions except that, on punishment trials, she substituted, "I'm not happy with the way you're playing" for "The chips will have to stop coming," and "Can you tell me why I'm unhappy with you?" for "Can you tell me why the chips aren't coming?" Also, as soon as she had turned off the dispenser the model bowed her head and looked very unhappy, rather than maintaining her neutral manner of the WOMR conditions. She did nothing in the punishment period but ask eliciting questions and glance occasionally at the subject with a distressed look on her face.

Contingent Reinforcement Conditions

In the C conditions, as soon as the child called himself a hurter, the model said, "When you say that it makes the chips come again" (WOMR conditions) or "When you say that it makes me happy with you again" (WOL conditions). In the WOL conditions she accompanied her verbal reinforcement with a happy smile. The model then turned the dispenser back on and proceeded to the next trial, setting up the donkey and the soldiers in their original positions and saying, "Push the donkey off again." If the subject did not use the self-critical label, the model waited for 10 seconds after her last question and then turned the dispenser on and proceeded to the next trial.

Noncontingent Reinforcement Conditions

In the NC conditions the model waited for 15 seconds after the child made the self-critical response, or for 10 seconds after her last question if he did not call himself a hurter, and then said, "I guess we've waited long enough." She turned on the dispenser and began the next trial.

Generalization Test

Trial 16 was used to test generalization of the self-critical response to a new situation. After the subject had pushed off the donkey, the model looked into the box and exclaimed, "Oh my, you've torn the picture. And I don't have another one here to put in its place." She then showed him a picture which had been hidden in the box and which was identical to the original picture of the donkey except for a large gash across it. The model asked, "Why do you think it got torn?" If the child did not reply to the effect that he was a hurter, the model inquired, "In this game, when you do something like this, what do you call yourself?" If the child used the self-critical response, he was not reinforced for it. The model then "found" another untorn picture, and the game continued.

Extinction Test

Trials 17–25 were an extinction series. On trials 17, 19, 20, 22, and 24 the buzzer sounded, but the model ignored it and did not turn off the dispenser. If the subject did not call himself a hurter within 15 seconds, she asked in an off-hand manner, "What happened?"

Terminal Procedure

At the end of the experiment each child was warmly praised for his performance on the game and told that he had done better than most of the other boys and girls who had played. Children in the WOMR conditions traded in their chips for small toys, while those in the WOL conditions were given toys "because they had done so well." The toys were placed in brown paper bags, and children were asked to keep all information about the game and the toys they had received secret from their classmates so as not to spoil the surprise for them.

Scoring

Only the responses "hurter" or "I hurt[ed] the donkey" were scored as self-critical. The score assigned to indicate the strength of the self-critical response was determined by the speed with which subjects verbalized it. The highest score was assigned for verbalization at the first possible moment, that is, immediately after the buzzer and prior to punishment onset, and the second highest score for verbalization after punishment onset and before the model began to ask eliciting questions. The next highest score was assigned for self-criticism which occurred in response to the model's first question, and so on. Thus the highest possible score for Trial 4 was 6, while it was 4 for Trials 7–14. Although three eliciting questions were asked on trial 5, the last one was ignored in the scoring procedure so that the possible assigned scores would be the same for all punishment trials but Trial 4 (which was treated separately in the analysis of variance).

On Trial 16 no subject called himself a hurter in response to the model's first question. Thus, if the self-critical response was made in reply to the model's second question, a score of 1 was assigned.

For Trials 17–24 (extinction) a score of 2 was assigned if the self-critical response was verbalized within 15 seconds of the buzzer, and a score of 1 was assigned if it occurred in response to the model's first, and only, question. . . .

DISCUSSION

The hypothesis that interaction with an HR model is more likely to induce a child to adopt the critical label she applies to him than is interaction with an LR model was clearly supported in this study, at least with respect to the initial occurrence of self-criticism. Children who had been exposed to an HR model, moreover, reproduced the model's criticism even though it was always paired with the onset of punishment and should therefore have been negatively reinforcing. Aronfreed's (1964) contention that "the internalization of punishment does not rest on a broader predisposition to reproduce the behavior of an otherwise nurturant model [p. 212]" was not supported. Although Aronfreed has clearly shown that the timing of punishment can be of great importance for the acquisition of self-critical labels, the present data reveal that the characteristics of the critical model are of more than tangential importance for this acquisition.

The difference between groups which interacted with an HR model and those which interacted with an LR model in initial use of the self-critical response may have been, as predicted, a result of differences in acquisition of the response. This, in turn, could have been mediated by a difference in the degree to which these groups attended to the model. Children who perceived the model as highly rewarding may have been more likely to attend to and covertly practice her behavior, and hence more able to reproduce her criticism, than children who perceived her as low in rewardingness. This is consistent with Maccoby's (1959) formulation which was discussed earlier. In fact, Grusec and Mischel (1966) have shown that one of the variables determining the amount of modeled behavior which an observer learns is the social characteristics possessed by the model. The hypothesis of acquisition differences in the present study is subject to experimental test by the introduction of external incentives for all groups to reproduce the model's criticism immediately after punishment on Trial 4. If groups exposed to an LR model did not attend

to her initially, and hence never learned the response, they would be unable to reproduce it no matter how great their motivation for doing so had now become.

The technique of punishment used by the model did not differentially affect the initial occurrence of the self-critical response. This was as predicted. However, the prediction that WOL and WOMR would be equally effective for the development of self-criticism if the contingencies for their termination were the same was not supported. The subsequent development of the self-critical response was differentially affected by the technique of punishment which the model employed. In the WOL conditions a combination of high model rewardingness and C for verbalization of the self-critical response produced the strongest self-critical response, while low model rewardingness and NC produced the weakest response. These same combinations in the WOMR conditions produced a self-critical response of intermediate strength. The data thus provide some experimental support for the correlational findings (Sears at al., 1957) that WOL employed by a warm mother (an HR model) is more effective as a punishment technique for the development of conscience than is WOMR. This holds, however, only when C is also employed. It is plausible that in the socialization process some warm mothers who use WOL also use C—hence the correlational findings.

It was hypothesized that subjects who were not reinforced for the verbalization of self-criticism would extinguish in their use of it. This did not happen, however, at least within the course of seven punishment trials. What, then, prevented extinction? It is possible that subjects expected certain positive consequences from their use of the self-critical label, even in the absence of reinforcement from the model, and that these expectancies were sufficiently persistent to maintain their behavior. One subject in an HR-NC group, for example, remarked after she called herself a hurter, "I'm smart. I learn. I do what the teacher tells me." As a result of past experience with teachers and parents, this subject may have expected the model to be pleased that she understood why she was being punished. The model's pleasure, even if merely inferred, might have been sufficiently reinforcing to maintain her behavior as long as these inferences or expectancies were not directly disconfirmed. Moreover, one would expect this reinforcement to be greater if it derived from the inferred pleasure of an HR model. (It is possible, too, that this same incentive—the model's expected pleasure—was responsible in part or completely for the initial verbalization of self-criticism on Trial 4. Explanation of the obtained difference in terms of acquisition differences may therefore be unnecessary.)

There were, then, two possible incentives for subjects to increase their use of the self-critical response. One was the cessation of punishment in groups where the model was contingently reinforcing and the other was the model's inferred pleasure which would be especially great where the model was perceived as highly rewarding. Looking first at the performance of the WOL groups, it is clear that both incentives could have influenced the behavior of the group exposed to high model rewardingness and C—hence its superior performance. On the other hand, neither incentive existed for the group exposed to low model rewardingness and NC, and so it performed poorly. Where only one of these incentives was present—in the LR-C and HR-NC groups—intermediate performance was the result.

These possible incentives did not, however, appear to differentially influence the performance of the WOMR groups. Contrary to prediction, the performance level of the group in which high model rewardingness and C were combined never reached that of the comparable WOL group. A possible explanation of this poor performance is that the material reward was distracting. Subjects spent much time in the punishment interval counting their chips, piling them up, commenting on the number they had, etc. Subjects in the WOL group, on the other hand, had little to do during the punishment interval and therefore may have focused their attention on the model to a greater degree. They could thus have had more time for both covert and overt rehearsal of the model's criticism.

Again, contrary to prediction, the performance of the WOMR group in which low model rewardingness and NC were combined was superior to that of the comparable WOL group. Note, however, that in the NC groups the model's expected approval was the incentive postulated for the verbalization of self-criticism. In the WOL group the model was continually withdrawing her approval in the course of punishment trials, while the model in the comparable WOMR group never withdrew her approval, but always maintained a neutral manner. Subjects in the WOL group who had never experienced the model's approval, and who experienced much of her disapproval, may soon have had any expectancy that she could ever be pleased extinguished. Subjects in the WOMR group, on the other hand, had less reason to believe that the model was impossible to please.

It is suggested that the difference obtained between punishment involving WOL and that involving WOMR may be limited to the experimental paradigm used here and may not be a basic one. Punishment for the WOMR groups may have been less severe than that for at least the WOL groups who interacted with an HR model. The cessation of material reward may have had reduced impact because it occurred in the context of visible material rewards that had already been gained. Although the chip dispenser was turned off, subjects were still being rewarded by the sight of chips, lying on the table in front of them, which they had already won. If the experimental situation had been arranged so that all distracting evidence of previously gained material rewards had been eliminated, the performance of at least the HR-C group might well have improved. This is a possibility which requires further investigation.

REFERENCES

Aronfreed, J. The effects of experimental socialization paradigms upon two moral responses to transgression. *Journal of Abnormal and Social Psychology,* 1963, 66, 437–448.

Aronfreed, J. The origin of self-criticism. *Psychological Review,* 1964, 71, 193–218.

Bandura, A., & Huston, A. C. Identification as a process of incidental learning. *Journal of Abnormal and Social Psychology,* 1961, 63, 311–318.

Bandura, A., Ross, D., & Ross, S. A. A comparative test of the status envy, social power, and secondary reinforcement theories of identificatory learning. *Journal of Abnormal and Social Psychology,* 1963, 67, 527–534.

Freud, S. The passing of the Oedipus-complex. In E. Jones (Ed.), *Collected papers.* Vol. 2. London: Hogarth, 1924. Pp. 269–282.

Grusec, J., & Mischel, W. Model's characteristics as determinants of social learning. *Journal of Personality and Social Psychology,* 1966, 4, 211–215.

Hill, W. F. Learning theory and the acquisition of values. *Psychological Review,* 1960, 67, 317–331.

Kagan, J. The concept of identification. *Psychological Review,* 1958, 65, 296–305.

Maccoby, E. E. Role-taking in childhood and its consequences for social learning. *Child Development,* 1959, 30, 239–252.

Mischel, W., & Grusec, J. Determinants of the rehearsal and transmission of neutral and aversive behaviors. *Journal of Personality and Social Psychology,* 1966, 3, 197–205.

Mowrer, O. H. *Learning theory and personality dynamics.* New York: Ronald Press, 1950.

Mussen, P. H., & Distler, L. Masculinity, identification, and father-son relationships. *Journal of Abnormal and Social Psychology,* 1959, 59, 350–356.

Sears, R. R. Identification as a form of behavioral development. In D. B. Harris (Ed.), *The concept of development.* Minneapolis: University of Minnesota Press, 1957. Pp. 149–161.

Sears, R. R., Maccoby, E. E., & Levin, H. *Patterns of child rearing.* New York: Harper, 1957.

RESISTANCE TO TEMPTATION IN RELATION TO SEX OF CHILD, SEX OF EXPERIMENTER, AND WITHDRAWAL OF ATTENTION

ROGER V. BURTON   WESLEY ALLINSMITH   ELEANOR E. MACCOBY

This experiment is part of a larger study designed to investigate the factors influencing resistance to temptation. A paper has already reported the relationships between child-rearing practices and temptation behavior and indicated the complex nature of this area of study (Burton, Maccoby, & Allinsmith, 1961).

The theoretical bases for this experiment came mainly from modifications of Freudian identification theory as delineated by Allinsmith (1954), Maccoby (1959), Sears, Maccoby, and Levin (1957), and Whiting (1954, 1959), and the work on nurturance-withdrawal of Hartup (1958). Sears et al. proposed a theory of identification which predicts that girls will be more strongly identified with their mothers than boys will be with their fathers. The rationale for this theory is that the mother is the main agent for important resources, especially for nurturance and discipline, during infancy and early childhood regardless of the sex of the child, and is therefore the first object of identification for both boys and girls. She continues in this role for her growing daughter; but the father becomes more and more the boy's model for identification as he takes a more active disciplinary role in his son's life, and as he possesses more of the skills his maturing son wants to have. From this theory the prediction was that girls would conform to standards established by an adult experimenter more than would boys and that this would be especially so when the experimenter was a woman. Furthermore, a female

Reprinted by permission of the authors and the American Psychological Association from *Journal of Personality and Social Psychology*, 1966, **3,** 253–58.

experimenter should produce more conformity than a male experimenter in both boys and girls who are only 4 years old.

Using the work of Hartup (1958) as a basis, we also hypothesized that withdrawal of attention by a formerly nurturant experimenter would arouse dependency anxiety which would mediate the motive to reestablish a nurturant relationship with the experimenter. We would expect, from this reasoning, that interrupting the attention the experimenter paid to the subject would produce greater identification with the experimenter's rules and thus greater conformity to such rules than would continuous attention.

These predictions assume that: acceptance of adult standards will be mediated by the identification process; at this early age there has not been enough time for the boy to shift his main object of identification to his father; there will be generalization from the child's mother and father to the female and male experimenters, respectively.

The standards established in the experimental situation were rules of a very simple game. The adult experimenter taught the child subject these rules and the child was then tempted to deviate from these rules in order to get a "good score." This experiment was designed to answer the following questions concerning the sex of the child subject, the sex of the experimenter, and withdrawal of attention:

1. Is there an overall difference between 4-year-old boys and girls in conforming to the rules of a game?

2. Does the sex of the experimenter affect the behavior of the child in a resistance to temptation setting?

3. Does the sudden withdrawal of attention just prior to the temptation test affect the child's behavioral tendencies to resist temptation or to deviate from the rules?

4. Are there any interaction effects from sex of the subject, sex of the experimenter, and withdrawal of attention on resistance to temptation?

METHOD

Subjects

The 112 children in this study were all 4 years old and enrolled in private nursery schools. They came from well-established, middle-class homes, with well-educated parents. The fathers were professional men, executives in business, or graduate students. None of the children showed any noticeably "abnormal" characteristic.

Procedure

The experimenter brought the subject, individually, from the classroom to the room used for the experiment, telling him, "We have a game for you children to play, and it is your turn." The experimenter talked with the subject while walking to the experimental room and tried to be warm and friendly during this time. In a few cases, the teacher had to accompany the child to the testing room, but she remained only a minute or two until the subject became fascinated with operating the game.

The game consisted of a 1 x 4 foot board with five lights which came on, accompanied by a chime, whenever a string behind the board was hit. One light came on at a time and remained lit until the experimenter reset the game. The rules of the game were to stand on a foot marker, placed about 5 feet from the game, and to try to hit the string with bean bags which were to be thrown only once over the front board. The game was placed against a backstop so that all bags which went over the 1 foot high board would land somewhere near

the string. Since the string was behind this front board, the subject could not see whether or not his bag actually hit the string when he was standing on the marker. In fact, a hidden experimenter (E_2) completely controlled these lights and chimes. He was behind a one-way mirror in a portable observation booth which could be installed in whatever room the school let us use for testing.

A standardized script was followed in showing the subject how the game "worked" and in teaching him the rules of standing on the marker when throwing and of throwing each bag only once over the board. All subjects received the same schedule of three "hits," out of the possible five, for two practice games. After the subject clearly demonstrated he understood the rules, E_1 took the subject to a nearby table and said, "We'll play with this again later. Now I have another game to show you." This new activity, with which the child was to be engaged for a 3-minute period, consisted of little plastic pieces which could be fitted together by their ball-and-socket connections to make Walt Disney animals.

After 1 minute of play during which E_1 was very nurturant and attentive to the subject, E_2 signaled E_1 in the event that this subject was to receive interrupted instead of continuous attention. The treatment for the subject was kept from E_1 to avoid any influence such knowledge might have had on his behavior during the first part of the procedure. E_2 tapped his pencil once against the wall to signal interrupted attention. E_1 would then go to another table, without any explanation to the subject, and start to fill out a rating form on the subject's behavior. In response to the subject's questions or requests, E_1 said, "You go ahead and play. I'm busy," or "I have some work to do now." The attempt was to make as much contrast as possible between the "warm" and "cold" relationships during this interrupted play treatment. At the end of 2 minutes, E_1 said, "Well, that's done," and returned to the subject. For the continuous attention treatment, no signal was given to E_1 so that he continued to play very nurturantly with the subject for the 3 minutes.

At the end of this period, for both interrupted and continuous attention treatments, E_1 put the construction toys in a box and out of sight and reach of the subject while saying, "Now we'll play the bean bag game again." A tray of toys, pretested for attractiveness, and including items of appeal to both sexes as well as sex-neutral toys, was uncovered and the subject was told that he could win the toy of his choice if he "got enough lights on." The subject was then asked which one he would choose if he should get enough lights to win the prize. This was done to insure that all subjects focused on a toy they would really like. This was our method of maximizing temptation in order to control for differential arousal to deviate from the rules. E_1 tested the subject on whether he knew the rules for the game, and, if necessary, reviewed them with him. Just as the subject was about to play the game, E_1 looked at his watch and said, "I have to go out to make a telephone call, but you go ahead and play the game according to the rules while I'm gone." To eliminate fear of being caught, E_1 took the subject to the door and showed him how he was to hook the door so that no one could come in and "bother" him while he was playing the game. E_1 said he would knock when he returned. All children understood the instructions and locked E_1 out as we intended.

Only one light, after the second throw, was given to the subject during the 3-minute test period if he followed the rules. Additional lights were given for each act of breaking the rules: stepping forward, moving the foot marker, retrieving bags that had already been thrown and rethrowing them, and hitting the string with the hand. During this test period, E_2 recorded the subject's behavior and controlled the lights.

After the 3 minutes, E_1 returned, knocked on the door for admittance, and said to the subject "Let's play the game again and this time will be for the prize." E_1 ignored the lights the subject obtained during the test period. If the subject indicated he wanted E_1 to consider that score for the prize or for some sign of approval, E_1 said, "You certainly know how to play the game now, and this time will be for the prize." This last game was played to have a check on whether the subject really understood and would follow the rules with E_1 present, to eliminate any guilt or feelings of failure which might have resulted from the subject's behavior

during the test period, and to avoid reinforcing any cheating.

Resistance to Temptation Measure

The resistance measure was a 7-point scale based on a count of the number of bags the subject threw correctly before deviating from the rules. If the subject deviated immediately, he received a score of 1. His score was 2 if he threw one bag correctly and then deviated. If he threw all five bags correctly and then cheated, he had a score of 6. If he never deviated during the test period, his score was 7. The scoring reliability of this measure was almost perfect.

RESULTS

Table 1 gives the means and n's for each group in the experimental design. Bartlett's (1937) test indicated there was nonhomogeneity

TABLE I

Mean Number of Bags Correctly Thrown Before Deviation (Total Sample)

	Sex of subjects			
	Boys		Girls	
	Sex of experimenter			
Treatment	Male	Female	Male	Female
Continuous attention	5.3 ($n = 11$)	6.1 ($n = 24$)	5.8 ($n = 10$)	4.4 ($n = 26$)
Interrupted attention	3.7 ($n = 11$)	4.9 ($n = 10$)	5.6 ($n = 10$)	4.5 ($n = 11$)

of variance among the cells, which, with unequal n's, precluded a straight analysis of variance with appropriate weightings for each cell. Table 2 shows the means of a reduced sample with each group having 10 subjects.

Table 3 presents the results of an analysis of variance of the reduced sample.

It can be seen that none of the main effects were significant by themselves. The only signif-

TABLE 2

Mean Number of Bags Correctly Thrown Before Deviation (Reduced Sample)

	Sex of subjects			
	Boys		Girls	
	Sex of experimenter			
Treatment	Male	Female	Male	Female
Continuous attention	5.6	5.9	5.8	4.3
Interrupted attention	3.7	4.9	5.6	4.4

TABLE 3

Analysis of Variance of Number of Bags Correctly Thrown Before Deviation (Reduced Sample)

Source	df	SS	MS	F
Sex of subject (A)	1	.00	.00	.000
Sex of experimenter (B)	1	1.80	1.80	.392
Treatment (C)	1	11.25	11.25	2.449
A × B	1	22.05	22.05	4.799*
A × C	1	9.80	9.80	2.133
B × C	1	1.80	1.80	.392
A × B × C	1	.45	.45	.098
Error	72	330.80	4.5944	
Total	79	337.95		

$* p < .05.$

icant F ratio is the interaction between sex of subject and sex of experimenter. An inspection of the means shows that this result is due to greater resistance in the cross-sex groups.

The means of the different groups in Tables 1 and 2, however, indicated that boys and girls should be analyzed separately, especially in regard to any treatment effects. As there is no indication from these means of any interaction between sex of experimenter and type of treatment, we have returned to the full sample to make two-way comparisons of the groups controlling on sex of subjects. Table 4 summarizes

TABLE 4

Differences Between Means of Groups in Total Sample

Contrast (Means)	t	df
Boys		
Male experimenter (4.524) versus female experimenter (5.735)	2.289*	53
Continuous (5.829) versus interrupted (4.300)	2.745**	53
Girls		
Male experimenter (5.700) versus female experimenter (4.459)	2.07*	55
Continuous (4.806) versus interrupted (5.048)	0.405	55

$* p < .05.$
$** p < .01.$

these contrasts. These contrasts indicate there is a cross-sex effect for both boys and girls—such that there is more cheating with a same-sex experimenter and more conformity to the rules with an opposite-sexed adult. Furthermore, the treatment effect remains significant for boys and, though in the opposite direction, is clearly not significant for girls. Continuous attention for boys produced a greater abiding by the rules and interrupted attention produced deviation from the rules.

In order to assess the effect of individual experimenters, comparisons were made for the three male experimenters and the seven female experimenters. There were no significant differences among any of these within-sex experimenter comparisons.

DISCUSSION

Referring to our original predictions, it is clear that 4-year-old girls did not abide by rules more than boys, and that the sex of experimenter was significant only in interaction with the sex of subject. Further, withdrawal of attention had an effect only on boys and this effect was opposite to what would be expected were dependency arousal to increase identification with—and consequently, conformity to—the experimenter's standards.

Sex Interaction

A reexamination of the assumptions underlying the derivations of our hypotheses indicates that conformity with the rules would be related to the degree to which the subject identified with the experimenter. It is clear, post hoc, that this assumption may not have been correct, and that the data are more in line with predictions reasoned from a theoretical scheme of the stages in the identification process as originally depicted by Freud (1933). According to this picture, the child of 4 would not yet have identified with the parent of the same sex but would be experiencing increasing libidinal attachment toward the parent of the opposite sex. Identification with the same-sex parent should occur with the Oedipal resolution around 6 years of age. From such a theoretical position, one could derive the hypothesis that resistance to temptation in 4-year-olds would be greater with opposite-sex adults in order to please them. Our results are certainly more in line with such considerations. However, if we are dealing with pre-Oedipal-resolution children who have a greater cathexis for the opposite-sex parent, the predictions regarding conformity to the rules of our game would not be based on "internalization" of parental strictures. The issue of pleasing the no-longer-present experimenter in our test situation becomes ambiguous in that obtaining a good score to please the experimenter is as likely as conforming to his rules. Thus, to make precise differential predictions from either the pre-Oedipal-resolution or post-resolution psychoanalytic conception is difficult. Data on 7-year-olds are now necessary for a more complete test of this theory since after the Oedipal resolution the significant interaction should be for greater compliance with the rules established by a same-sex experimenter.

Other experiments investigating sex of experimenter and of child as independent variables demonstrated their effect on performance and are relevant for our post hoc considerations. Stevenson (1961) found that a female experimenter was more effective than a male experimenter as a dispenser of social reinforcements to increase performance in 3–4 year olds. But for ages older than 4, the results often indicate that reinforcements dispensed by an opposite-sex experimenter are more effective than those by an experimenter of the same sex as the subject (Gewirtz & Baer, 1958a, 1958b; Gewirtz, Baer, & Roth, 1958; Stevenson, 1961). The results of these studies and of our experiment all conform to the hypothesis that young children are motivated to please an opposite-sex adult more than an adult of the same sex.

This interpretation of our results is based on the assumption that, in order to please an adult of the opposite sex, the child will conform to the rules, rather than cheat to obtain a high score in order to please an adult of the same sex. In fact, however, each of these motives may be contributing to our findings if conforming behaviors are more associated with gaining love from the opposite-sex parent and achievement behaviors are more often instigated by the relationship with the same-sex parent. It is also possible that the wish to please, though operating in our results, is different for boys and girls. In the case of boys, it is the desire to please a father figure by achieving; hence, by contrast, conformity would be associated with an opposite-sex experimenter. For girls, it is the wish to please a father figure by conforming compared with less conformity with a same-sex adult. Though less parsimonious than a single factor model in positing a different basis in boys from that in girls, this interpretation—that both conformity to restrictions of opposite-sex adults and achievement arousal by same-sex adults produce an association of conformity with having an opposite-sex experimenter—does seem reasonable for our results and would be consonant with the results of other research cited above and below.

Withdrawal of Attention

Manipulating the relationship of the child to the experimenter has also produced differential performance in other studies. Withdrawal of attention (Hartup, 1958; Rosenblith, 1959, 1961) and complete isolation from social contacts (Gewirtz & Baer, 1958a, 1958b; Gewirtz et al., 1958; Stevenson & Odom, 1962; Walters & Ray, 1960) have tended to increase performance, although these results are inconsistent in regard to whether withdrawal is more effective when the experimenter is the same or opposite sex as the subject. These results were interpreted as supporting dependency arousal (Hartup, 1958; Rosenblith, 1959, 1961), social deprivation and drive (Gewirtz, 1958a, 1958b; Gewirtz et al., 1958; Stevenson & Odom, 1962), and anxiety arousal (Walters & Ray, 1960).

If performance in these experiments is increased in order to please the experimenter, then the results just reviewed might suggest that withdrawal or isolation would increase this motive. Our data conform to this interpretation if one assumes that for boys a motive to please the experimenter by getting a high score is operating (Table 4). For the effect found is that in boys withdrawal increases cheating. If conformity to the rules of the game is increased in boys by wanting to please a female (opposite-sex) adult, then withdrawal seems to decrease this motive. Perhaps there is some feeling of being rejected which reduced any motive to need to conform to the rules to please the experimenter. Were this the case, the motive to resist temptation would be decreased in the subject by withdrawal of attention, leaving as a greater influence on his behavior the motive to cheat in order to win a prize for himself. In the case of girls, there is a very slight difference in favor of withdrawal to increase conformity, but this is mainly due to the larger number of girls in the continuous attention cell to have had a female experimenter.

Arousal of Achievement

In our post hoc discussion we have repeatedly felt the need to consider the arousal of achievement in accounting for our findings. The temptation test used appears to be strongly loaded with components relevant for achievement motivation. This consideration was given support in the somewhat parallel study by Grinder (1960) which produced its clearest results when he analyzed the resistance to temptation data in such a way as to control for achievement motivation. If the degree of achievement motive aroused in the subject were increased by withdrawal of attention, and the amount of cheating were correlated with this increase in motivation to obtain a high score, then the increase in cheating in boys under the withdrawal of attention is understandable. The lack of this effect on girls would be consistent with other failures to obtain increased achievement motivation in girls (McClelland, Clark, Roby, & Atkinson, 1958).

With such different interpretations possible, it seems that no single explanation presently available can account for the results of studies such as this. Clearly, additional studies investigating the motives involved in temptation tests are required to assess the extent to which these and possibly other motivational components determine whether a person will cheat or not.

REFERENCES

Allinsmith, W. The learning of moral standards. Unpublished doctoral dissertation, University of Michigan, 1954.

Bartlett, M. S. Some examples of statistical methods of research in agriculture and applied biology. *Journal of the Royal Statistical Society Supplement,* 1937, 4, 137–170.

Burton, R. V., Maccoby, Eleanor E., & Allinsmith, W. Antecedents of resistance to temptation in four-year-old children. *Child Development,* 1961, 32, 689–710.

Freud, S. The passing of the Oedipus-complex. In *Collected papers.* Vol. 2. London: Hogarth Press, 1933. Pp. 269–282.

Gewirtz, J. L., & Baer, D. M. Deprivation and satiation of social reinforcers as drive conditions. *Journal of Abnormal and Social Psychology,* 1958, 57, 165–172. (a)

Gewirtz, J. L., & Baer, D. M. The effect of brief social deprivation on behaviors for a social reinforcer. *Journal of Abnormal and Social Psychology,* 1958, 56, 49–56. (b)

Gewirtz, J. L., Baer, D. M., & Roth, C. H. A note on the similar effects of low social availability of an adult and brief social deprivation on young children's behavior. *Child Development,* 1958, 29, 149–152.

Grinder, R. E. Behavior in a temptation situation and its relation to certain aspects of socialization. Unpublished doctoral dissertation, Harvard University, 1960.

Hartup, W. W. Nurturance and nurturance-withdrawal in relation to the dependency behavior of preschool children. *Child Development,* 1958, 29, 191–201.

Maccoby, Eleanor E. The generality of moral behavior. *American Psychologist,* 1959, 14, 358.

McClelland, D. C., Clark, R. A., Roby, T. B., & Atkinson, J. W. The effect of the need for achievement on thematic apperception. In J. W. Atkinson (Ed.), *Motives in fantasy, action, and society.* Princeton, N.J.: Van Nostrand, 1958. Pp. 64–82.

Rosenblith, Judy F. Learning by imitation in kindergarten children. *Child Development,* 1959, 30, 69–80.

Rosenblith, Judy F. Imitative color choices in kindergarten children. *Child Development,* 1961, 32, 211–223.

Sears, R. R., Maccoby, Eleanor E., & Levin, H. *Patterns of child rearing.* Evanston, Ill.: Row, Peterson, 1957.

Stevenson, H. W. Social reinforcement with children as a function of CA, sex of *E,* and sex of *S. Journal of Abnormal and Social Psychology,* 1961, 63, 147–154.

Stevenson, H. W., & Odom, R. D. The effectiveness of social reinforcement following two conditions of social deprivation. *Journal of Abnormal and Social Psychology,* 1962, 65, 429–431.

Walters, R., & Ray, E. Anxiety, social isolation and reinforcer effectiveness. *Journal of Personality,* 1960, 28, 358–367.

Whiting, J. W. M. Fourth presentation. In J. M. Tanner & B. Inhelder, *Discussions on child development.* Vol. 2. London: Tavistock, 1954. Pp. 185–212.

Whiting, J. W. M. Sorcery, sin, and superego: A cross-cultural study of some mechanisms of social control. In M. R. Jones (Ed.), *Nebraska symposium on motivation: 1959.* Lincoln: Univer. Nebraska Press, 1959. Pp. 174–195.

THE IMPACT OF COGNITIVE MATURITY ON THE DEVELOPMENT OF SEX-ROLE ATTITUDES IN THE YEARS FOUR TO EIGHT

LAWRENCE KOHLBERG   EDWARD ZIGLER

INTRODUCTION

This monograph reports a set of studies designed to clarify the role of intelligence in personality organization. These studies examine the relationship of intellectual maturity to social development in the area of sex-role attitudes.

An impressive accumulation of research findings has indicated the empirical importance of intelligence (IQ) as a correlate of social behavior and attitudes. With the exception of such nonbehavioral variables as age, sex, and social class, intelligence appears to be the most powerful single general predictor of personality traits and social behavior, both in terms of cross-sectional [see Cattell (12)] and of longitudinal predictive correlations [see Anderson (3), and Havighurst *et al.* (32)].

How are we to account for this powerful role of intelligence in general personality functioning? It is the writers' opinion that these empirical findings on intelligence have not yet attained their proper significance for the theoretical understanding of personality. The major current theories of personality including those of Freud, Murray, Allport, Erikson, and Sullivan do not provide a well articulated role for intelligence in personality development. While developmental theories of intelligence [see Piaget (54), Vygotsky (65), and Werner (67)] also fail to provide a detailed guide to the understanding of the role of intelligence in personality, they do suggest two considerations which are basic for such understanding. First, these theories suggest that the importance of

Reprinted with abridgment by permission of the authors and The Journal Press from *Genetic Psychology Monographs*, 1967, **75,** 91–123, 159–61, 162–65.

intelligence rests on its being a definer of rate or level of development. Second, these theories suggest that all aspects of personality development have a basic cognitive-structural component, and that both intellectual and social-emotional functioning represent parallel manifestations of these underlying structural features of development.

While these two basic interpretive assumptions are central to developmental theorizing, they have not formed a systematic focus for research studies of the relationship between personality and intelligence. The monumental studies of Terman (61, 62, 63), of Hollingworth (34, 35), and of others which have compared children of high and of average IQ, have rather been guided by Terman's (62) descriptive question, "In what respects does the typical gifted child differ from the child of normal mentality?"

The general answer of these studies is that gifted children are superior to average children in traits deemed socially desirable—e.g., in moral and social conformity, stability, and leadership—and do not differ systematically from the average children with regard to other personality traits (49). The fact that the traits that differentiate the gifted children are all in a socially desirable direction may indicate that a unitary factor of more rapid general development, reflected in both the intellectual and the social-emotional spheres, is involved.

Two major qualifications must be made to such a conclusion, however. In the first place, comparisons of bright and average children do not in themselves allow us to distinguish personality differences due to the advanced developmental rate of bright children from differences due to their history of greater success and interpersonal status or from differences due to hereditary correlates of intelligence like greater physical health. In the second place, the classical studies of personality correlates of intelligence have tended to deal with a wide variety of areas of personality, rather than selecting an area of clear significance to personality theories and studying this area in depth.

The present study was designed to cope with these qualifications by comparing bright and average children both cross-sectionally and longitudinally on a variety of measures of development of sex-role attitudes. This area was selected because it has been considered in detail by a number of theories of personality development. These theories have focused upon age-linked biological and cultural forces rather than upon cognitive factors in sex-role development. If cognitive maturity were found to play an important part in sex-role development, it would have considerable importance for personality theory. The study concentrated on the age period 4 to 8, since this period is considered crucial in both theories of psychosexual development, such as Freud's, and theories of cognition, like Piaget's. Data relating sex-role attitudes to intelligence in this age range are extremely scanty.

The purpose of the study, then, was to assess a cognitive-developmental interpretation of *IQ*-personality correlations. This purpose requires a brief consideration of certain general issues and findings concerning the nature of intelligence and its relationship to personality development.

Theoretical Interpretations of the Relationship Between Intelligence and Personality Variables

Factor-analytic studies indicate that intelligence has a great number of personality correlates and that it is a major definer of personality factor(s) outweighing such emotional factors as neuroticism or extroversion-introversion (12). Of more importance, however, are recurrent findings of the predictive power of intelligence with regard to later traits of social adjustment and social maturity. Documentation of the long-range predictive power of intelligence comes from longitudinal studies, such as

that of Terman (61), of Anderson *et al.* (4), and of Havighurst *et al.* (32). Anderson (3) concludes,

We were surprised at the emergence of the intelligence factor in a variety of our instruments (family attitudes, responsibility and maturity, adjustment) in spite of our attempts to minimize intelligence in selecting our personality measures. Next we were surprised that for prediction over a long time, the intelligence quotient seems to carry a heavy predictive load in most of our measures of outcomes. It should be noted that in a number of studies, adjustment at both the child and the adult level, whenever intelligence is included, emerges as a more significant factor than personality measures (3, p. 91).

An understanding of the power of intelligence in predicting personality variation requires the assumption that intelligence is a relatively stable trait. The stability of intelligence involves two implications. The first is that intelligent behavior in young children that is phenotypically similar to intelligent behavior in older children reflects an underlying or genotypical commonality. The second is that individuals maintain their position relative to one another in respect to intelligence over time.

In regard to the first implication, factor analytic studies indicate that "intelligence" has a relatively stable and unitary functional meaning throughout the school years. While increased age seems to lead to an increased differentiation of intellectual abilities, a gross general factor in intellectual performance may be found throughout postinfant development. In regard to the second implication, longitudinal studies indicate a high degree of stability of relative position of children on *IQ* tests throughout the school years.

The stability and predictive power of intelligence stands in considerable contrast to that of noncognitive personality traits. Recent longitudinal findings suggest that a variety of personality traits are markedly less stable than is intelligence (17, 39, 47, 70). In part this lower stability of noncognitive traits undoubtedly represents difficulties in obtaining and scoring reliable and representative samples of social-emotional behaviors. In part it may also be due to the fact that most of these traits represent differential outcomes or balancings of conflicting motivational forces. Since these balancings differ at various points in the life cycle, the traits they determine would not be expected to be stable over time. Because of this fact it is not surprising that temperamental aspects of personality appear to be more stable than the more dynamic personality or motivational traits (17).

There is some reason to think, however, that the greater longitudinal stability of intelligence than of social-emotional traits is less the result of its being a "conflict-free" trait than of its being defined in a developmental manner. Because intelligence is defined as a developmentally cumulative trait, transformations in cognitive structure and functioning during the life cycle are still consistent with overall predictability of development. In contrast, need and attitude traits have typically been defined in a fashion that does not allow for regular developmental transformations. Accordingly, it may be questioned whether most noncognitive personality traits studied are "really" the same traits at various ages in the sense of reflecting the same underlying genotypical commonalities in behavior. As an example a trait like aggression, which seems to have little predictive stability from age 5 to adolescence (39, 47, 58), also seems to have different functional meanings at different ages in the sense of having different factor analytic structures and having different childrearing antecedents (17, 58).

A definition of personality characteristics that allows for age-developmental transformations in the structure of social attitudes may lead to a picture of greater continuity of personality. Emmerich (17) has found that a personality factor or cluster of behaviors at one age may be quite different from a personality factor at a later age, but that the individual child's location with regard to the earlier personality factor allows good longitudinal prediction with regard to his location on a second later factor.

Such findings are consistent with developmental theories of personality that conceptualize the continuity of personality development in terms of an orderliness of sequence, rather than a fixity of personality traits. Such a conceptualization is suggested by John Dewey's statement, "Psychology is concerned with life-careers, with behavior as it is characterized by changes taking place in an activity that is serial and continuous, in reference to changes in an environment which is continuous while changing in detail" (16, p. 131).

While continuity in personality development may be defined in terms of a number of alternative sequences available to different individuals in different social settings, most developmental theories of personality-sequence have employed some notion of a single, universal sequence of personality stages (Freud, Gesell and Ilg, Erikson, Piaget). Such stage theories view the child's social behavior as reflections of age-typical world-views and coping mechanisms rather than as reflections of fixed character traits. As the child moves from stage to stage, developmental theorists expect his behavior to change radically, but to be predictable in terms of knowledge of his prior location in the stage sequence and of the intervening experiences stimulating or retarding movement to the next stage.

An example of such continuity is provided by a longitudinal study of moral judgment (40). At one stage an individual child judges in terms of punishment and obedience, still later in terms of maintenance of a social system of role-expectations and authority, still later in terms of moral principles. The moral ideology of the child, then, looks very different at various ages. Nevertheless, his position relative to other children who are also changing remains quite constant. The child's moral ideology is relatively predictable from one period to another three or six years later if prediction is based on a notion of "moral quotient" or relative level of development of ideology rather than stability of its content.

This same model is applicable to stability in intellectual development. The stability of *IQ* does not necessarily imply an innate, fixed capacity, but may be the result of continuity in cognitive transformations which are sequential and cumulative in character. The constancy of the *IQ,* just like the constancy of the "moral quotient," need not derive from a lack of change in underlying behavior structures but may derive from a constancy of the child's position relative to other children of the same age who are also changing in cognitive structures. From a point of view like Piaget's, considerable longitudinal stability of *IQ* follows from the existence of invariant sequences in cognitive restructuring (36, 42). Whether due to genetic or experiential factors, precocious attainment of a particular cognitive level leads to the expectation of precocious attainment of subsequent cognitive levels in the sequence.

While "continuity in transformation" interpretations of the stability of intelligence are most applicable to Piaget developmental measures, they are also applicable to psychometric or capacity measures of intelligence. While psychometric mental age tests are not built in terms of theoretical sequences and are not developmentally scalable as are Piaget tests, there is an obvious component of developmental cumulativity in these tests which would lead to the expectation of longitudinal stability without postulation of an innate rate factor (7). Furthermore, while Piaget measures of cognitive maturity may be factor analytically distinguished from psychometric measures, the two types of measures may be roughly equated: i.e., mental age may be grossly interpreted as cognitive level or *vice versa* (43). Evidence for this is that factor-analytic distinctions between psychometric and Piaget stage tasks are not massive or clear-cut, since both sets of tasks correlate well with one another and yield a gross first general mental age factor. The correlation between children's Stanford-Binet mental ages and their summed scores on Piaget tests are of the order of the correlations between the Stanford-Binet and other individual psychometric tests.

Within a cognitive developmental viewpoint, such as Piaget's, then, the predictive power of intelligence for personality traits lies in the fact that both cognitive and social behaviors develop through regular structural stages and that developments in both domains are closely interrelated. In Piaget's view, both forms of thought and forms of valuing and feeling are schemata whose organization develops in accordance with certain structural characteristics of psychological equilibrium. To some extent, Piaget's (56) view is that the social-emotional and the intellectual represent different perspectives upon, or aspects of, the same phenomena of structural development. To some extent, Piaget's (54, 55) view is also one in which social and intellectual development may be distinguished, but in which

social-developmental forces and cognitive-developmental forces interact in development.

The "double-aspect" implication of Piaget's concept of structural parallelism implies that there are basic structural dimensions of social development and social concepts which are also structural dimensions of "pure" cognitive development and of physical concepts. As an example, the capacity to use structures involving reciprocity is believed by Piaget (54) to be basic both to the development of logic and to the development of social sentiments of justice in the child.

The "interactional" implication of Piaget's concept of structural parallelism is a double implication with regard to the correlations of intelligence with personality. The first implication is that of a more profound causal role for intellectual growth in social development than that implied by views of intelligence as an increased capacity to learn relevant skills and adjust to a given environment. It suggests that intellectual growth involves transformed perceptions of the child's environment. While views of intellectual maturity as capacity suggest its role is one of facilitating adjustment to developmental tasks initiated by environmental socialization pressures, views of intellectual maturity as structural transformation suggest that intellectual growth involves redefinitions of the child's world raising new problems and requiring new modes of adaptation. Accordingly, the structural transformation view suggests that intellectual growth represents a basic initiating force in social development as well as a facilitating factor in it.

The second implication of the structural parallelism view is that social experiential factors play a more profound role in cognitive growth than that ordinarily entertained. As an example Piaget holds that the development of logical structures represents a socialization of thought through the social experiences of role-taking and cooperation, especially in the peer group. Not only is intellectual growth held to play a profound initiating role in social development, but intellectual growth is held to result itself largely from past social developmental forces and achievements rather than representing a purely innate trait or resulting from purely intellectual types of stimulation.

The area of social development that Piaget has attempted to explore in most detail from the structural parallelism point of view is that of moral judgment (55). In this area, Piaget attempts to show how the development of moral judgment parallels the age development of the child's modes of thought and conceptions of the physical world. While the details of Piaget's theory of moral stages have not stood up well before systematic research, the findings do support Piaget's general assumption as to important parallelisms between cognitive and moral judgment development (41). This is true both in the "double-aspect" sense that the basic dimensions of moral development are largely cognitive-structural and in the "interactional" sense that "nonmoral" cognitive development variables, such as *IQ*, and moral-social variables, are correlated with one another.

Werner (67) and his followers (69) adopt a rather similar "structural parallelism" view as to the relations between intellectual and social-emotional development. A structural dimension of development, such as "differentiation," is considered to characterize all aspects of the personality—the social-emotional, the perceptual, and the intellective. As measured by age-developmental perceptual tasks, "differentiation" is quite highly correlated with standard psychometric intelligence measures as well as with a variety of social attitudes and traits. Harvey, Hunt, and Shroeder (31) also elaborate a "structural parallelism" view of personality development in terms of increased structural differentiation and integration of conceptions of self and others, implying both cognitive and attitudinal correlates.

While the most radical view of the relations of intelligence to social development comes from the structural parallelism theories just outlined, virtually all coherent views of intelligence would lead us to expect important relations between it and other aspects of personality. One of the most influential alternative views is the "capacity" view already mentioned, the view of intelligence as a fixed general ability influencing rate of complex learning. In this view, the stability of the *IQ* is not the result of its representing continuity of sequence in development but rather the result of fixed heredity.

This view leads us to expect *IQ* to relate to learning of social concepts and skills as well as to more clearly "intellectual" forms of learning and problem solving. The inability to distinguish performance on tests of "social intelligence" from tests of "general intelligence" supports this view [see Thorndike and Stein (64)]. Insofar, then, as social development may be characterized as complex social learning, bright children would be expected to be advanced in such development. The general predictions as to gross correlations between intellectual and social development derived from the stage and capacity or psychometric views of intelligence are not too dissimilar then. Both lead us to expect correlations between *IQ* and personality traits when those traits reflect differential social learning or development. In general, the findings have been consistent with such expectations. Intelligence appears to be related in a positive direction to "ego" or character traits but not to traits of temperament and mood (12, 49, 62). These ego or character traits include stability, achievement motivation, honesty, and leadership. These traits are closely tied to age-maturity as well as social desirability.

In contrast to the capacity view of intelligence, however, the stage view leads us to expect that the general advance of bright children in social development should also lead to differences of social behavior in areas outside the socially desirable. In these other areas, however, what is developmentally mature may vary from age to age. As stage theories, such as Gesell's (25) or Erikson's (20) suggest, developmental tendencies in one direction at one age may be replaced by opposing tendencies at another age. Thus traits reflecting "inwardness" at one age might be replaced by traits reflecting "outwardness" at another age. If this were the case, differences between bright and average children would be expected to cancel out across varying age groups and subject populations. Accordingly, it is not surprising that most of the *IQ*-personality correlations have been found for aspects of development definable in terms of unidirectional social desirability.

While the general findings on personality correlates of intelligence are consistent with both cognitive-developmental and capacity-psychometric interpretations, they also are consistent with a "social status" view of intelligence. In this view the relationship between intelligence and other aspects of personality is mediated by social status and success. The view here is that intellectual achievement is partly the product of various forms of favored status associated with optimal sociocultural stimulation and teaching. Furthermore, intellectual achievement leads to experiences of status and success in the peer group, the school, and the family. Higher status and a history of success should not only yield higher character ratings, but genuinely higher self-esteem and feelings of competence, reflected in the various socially desirable traits mentioned.

A fourth interpretation of personality-*IQ* correlations which is roughly similar to the social status interpretation may be labelled the "socialization" view. Important here are the socialization antecedents of variations in intellectual abilities. As an example, socialization pressures and techniques associated with high achievement and independence motivation appear to influence general *IQ* scores, as well as special "analytic" abilities (46). From this point of view, personality-*IQ* correlations would be expected insofar as both the relevant personality traits and high *IQ* scores reflect similar socialization factors.

A fifth possible interpretation of the personality correlates of intelligence combines certain aspects of the social status and the structural parallelism views. Recent research and theory has made it plausible to conceive of general effectance tendencies or motives as present from birth [see White (68)]. If hereditary or environmental factors should cooperate to produce general and stable individual differences in such effectance motivation by the end of the preschool years, it would be plausible to attribute a considerable amount of the stable and general element of individual differences in *IQ* to such a source [see Hayes (33)]. Differences in effectance motivation should lead not only to differential rate of exploration and learning of the novel, but to differential rate of cognitive development in the sense of the restructuring of the child's basic stage of mental organization (36, 56). Whether attributed to the impact of effectance motivation on cognitive ability, or to the impact of ability-produced success upon self-esteem, the empirical correlation between

IQ and effectance motivation are clear-cut. Kagan and Moss (39) report high correlations (.53 for boys, .80 for girls) between blind ratings of mastery motivation and *IQ*.

It is apparent that, like the social status view, the view of *IQ* as effectance motivation differs from "the capacity" and the "structural parallelism" views in suggesting important social differences between bright and average children which are not a product of level of cognitive learning or development. Whether the greater curiosity, effectance motivation, and self-esteem of bright children are seen as byproducts of their history of success and status, or whether they are seen as a primary cause of their greater relative mental maturity, this motivation presumably differentiates the bright child from the older average *IQ* child of the same mental age. The effectance view, however, like the structural parallelism view, might lead us to expect differences in social attitudes and behavior that may be characterized as aspects of developmental advance going beyond socially desirable traits associated with favored status. Higher effectance motivation should lead to the earlier formation of new modes of social attachment and of social relationships, as has been argued elsewhere (42).

In summary, then, while the empirical findings on personality correlates of intelligence are consistent with the developmental or structural parallelism view, they are also consistent with major alternative views of intelligence. It was hoped that the present study would clarify these alternatives in the area of sex-role development.

Physiological Development, Cognitive Development, and Socialization Antecedents of Children's Sex-Role Attitudes

While almost all views of intelligence suggest important social correlates of intelligence, it is not clear that these correlates of *IQ* should include basic sex-role attitudes. The most influential theory of sex-role development, psychoanalytic libido theory, would predict that general growth trends in children's sex-role behavior would be tied to the maturational sequence of instinctual drives. The most important age-developmental trend postulated by Freudian theory is the maturation of phallic sexuality at about age 3 to 5, its expression in a sexualized or Oedipal attachment to the opposite-sex parent, and the decline of sexuality and this attachment during the latency period (ages 7 to 11). Freud expected the timing of these developmental trends to be "lawful" or "periodic" and to parallel chronological age and physical maturation: "It seems certain that the newborn child brings with it the germs of sexual feeling which continue to develop for some time and then succumb to a progressive suppression. . . . Nothing is known concerning the laws and periodicity of the oscillating course of development. It seems, however, that the sexual life of the child mostly manifests itself in the third or fourth year in some form accessible to observation" (24, p. 583).

Freud viewed both the onset and inhibition of sexuality as largely the product of such maturational forces: "It is during the period of total or at least partial latency that the psychic forces develop which later act as inhibitions on the sexual life. . . . We may gain the impression that the erection of these dams in the civilized child is the work of education, and surely education contributes much to it. In reality, however, this development is organically determined and can occasionally be produced without the help of education" (24, p. 583).

The Freudian view then suggests that psychosexual developmental trends are a function of chronological age and the physiological development associated with age. Various additional maturational factors besides sheer age might be expected to lead to general advance or retardation in "anatomical preparation" and consequent psychosexual attitudes. There is relatively clear evidence that the early onset of puberty is associated with the early arousal of genital sexual fantasies and behaviors (15). Onset of puberty is in turn predictable from knowledge of the child's earlier level or rate of physiological maturity (60). It might be plausible to expect physiologically advanced children to be advanced in psychosexual attitudes, if such attitudes reflected instinctual maturation.

The psychoanalytic view of libidinal maturation does not, however, lead to the expectation of psychosexual advance in intellectually advanced children. While it might be plausible to attribute advance in instinctual sexual maturation to children who are generally advanced in physiological development, there is no reason to expect such advance in children generally advanced in intellectual development. Physiological and mental maturity measures do not correlate with one another to any appreciable degree. When social class and chronological age are controlled, very small or zero correlations have been found between measures of physiological and mental maturity (1, 5, 6, 52). In light of the absence of a relationship between intellectual and physiological advance, there is little reason to expect purely maturational sexual development to be advanced in bright children.

Freud later added a footnote to the paragraph previously quoted saying, "The *complete* synchronization of anatomical preparation and psychical development is naturally not necessary." Psychoanalytic theory, however, does not suggest that the discrepancies between anatomical preparation and psychical development should be due to cognitive development. These discrepancies would rather be interpreted as the result of differences in "education": i.e., of the socialization pressures of the family and culture and of differential opportunities for, and restrictions upon, identification with parents. It seems unlikely that the timing or severity of sexually repressive training by the adult culture would be systematically determined by the child's relative intellectual maturity. Insofar as there were age-regularities in sex-role socialization, they would be more likely to be related to chronological age grading, to the child's bodily maturity, and to the physiological maturation of his sexual instincts.

These considerations of the timing of cultural training suggest that intellectual maturity would also not be an important factor in social learning theories of psychosexual development (38, 45, 50, 59). While these theorists have not given clear-cut considerations to intellectual factors in sex-role development, their research use of age-related sex-role measures without making use of controls for *IQ* suggests that they do not consider it a major factor in such development. In these theories psychosexual development is defined as appropriate sex-role identification: i.e., as increased learning of the attitudes and behaviors typed by the adult culture as sex-appropriate. Such development is seen as the product of adult and peer labeling and reinforcement of role-appropriate behavior and of identification with sex-appropriate parental behavior. From this point of view, bright children might be expected to show advance in acquisition of verbal sex-role labels and norms. Since discrimination of adult sex-role labeling and reinforcement and of adult sex-role behavior would appear to be relatively simple, these effects of intelligence would probably not be expected to be major, however. The reinforcement learning and identification mechanisms postulated by these theories do not involve much cognitive complexity, so that the timing of this learning should be determined more by environmental timing than by the child's cognitive capacities. As mentioned earlier, it seems likely that such environmental timing of sex-role socialization should be determined primarily by chronological age-grading, with cultural adjustment of timing to the individual child being influenced more by his physical than by his intellectual maturity.

In contrast to maturational and social learning theories of psychosexual development, a theory based on Piaget's notions of the structural development of intelligence and of social-cognitive parallelism clearly leads to the expectation of developmental advance in the psychosexual attitudes of bright children. As elaborated and empirically documented elsewhere (41, 43), such a cognitive-developmental theory implies the following considerations.

1. The concrete, physicalistic, and symbolic nature of the child's thought and interests leads him to conceive of interpersonal relationships in terms of body actions and to define social roles in terms of physical characteristics and differences. The elaboration of the physical bases of sex-role concepts in the concrete thought of the child leads to a core of common meaning to these concepts, regardless of cultural and family variations in sex-role definition.

2. Accordingly, there are "natural" developmental trends or sequences in sex-role attitudes, trends not directly structured by cultural teaching, which are the products of cognitive development. Because of the universal physical dimensions of sex-role concepts and because of culturally universal developmental transformations in modes of conceptualizing, it is plausible to expect some relatively invariant developmental trends in sex-role concepts and attitudes.

3. The fact that sex-role concepts have physical dimensions suggests that the formation of a sex-role identity is in large part the comprehension and acceptance of a physical reality rather than a process primarily determined by sexual fantasies, social reinforcement, or identification with models. The child's basic sex-role identity is largely the result of a self-categorization as a male or female made early in development. While dependent on social labeling, this categorization is basically a cognitive reality judgment rather than a product of social rewards, parental identifications, or sexual fantasies. The reality judgment, "I really am and will always be a boy" or "I really am and will always be a girl" are judgments with a regular course of age development relatively independent of the vicissitudes of social labeling and reinforcement.

4. The motivational forces implied in such reality judgments are general "drive-neutral" motives of effectance, or competence, which orient the child both toward cognitive adaptation toward a structured reality and toward the maintenance of self-esteem. Accordingly sex-typed preferences in activities and social relationships (masculinity-femininity) are largely the product of such reality judgments of sex-identity. The boy, having labeled himself as male, goes on to value masculine modes because of the general tendency to value positively objects and acts consistent with one's conceived identity.

5. To a large extent, the value of social reinforcers to the child is determined by his sex-identity rather than the reverse. As opposed to a social learning sequence, "The boy wants rewards, the boy is rewarded by boy things, therefore he wants to be a boy," a cognitive theory assumes a sequence, "The boy asserts he is a boy. He then wants to do boy things; therefore the opportunity to do boy things and the presence of masculine models is rewarding."

6. The tendency to value positively and imitate self-like objects tends to radiate out in the child's development in the form of imitation

and liking for the same-sex parent. The boy's preferential attachment to the father as against the mother proceeds from, rather than causes, basic sex-role identity and basic tendencies to imitate the father preferentially.

7. The formation of a stable sex-role identity, and its channelization into patterns of parent identification, are dependent upon complex modes of cognitive organization and development. As an example the stabilization of sex-role identity implied in the judgment, "I really am and will always be a boy" or "I really am and will always be a girl," is apparently dependent upon the types of cognitive reorganization discussed by Piaget. Stabilization of these judgments apparently is not completed until age 6 to 7, at a time when other forms of physical constancy or physical conservation become fully stabilized. The stabilization of judgments of sex-role constancy and of physical constancy closely parallel one another in terms of individual development as well as age group norms. The radiation of sex-role identity into identification with the same-sex parent also seems dependent upon complex cognitive reorganizations (at least in boys). As an example, the boy's increased identification with the father doll in doll play appears to be associated (both in terms of age groups and of individual differences) with the development of abstract cognitive categories of likeness involved in the boy's inclusion of himself and his father in a category of "we males."

8. Because of such cognitive mediators, then, regular developmental trends in sex-role attitudes are to a considerable extent linked to rate of cognitive growth, rather than to physiological or chronological development.

While a cognitive-developmental theory of psychosexuality suggests that cognitive advance should have an important impact on sexual attitudes in the early school years, it also suggests that this impact should be greater for boys than for girls. For both boys and girls, the mother is the earliest and most available and meaningful adult model. In the normal course of development, the boy shifts to preferring the father as a model. This shift occurs as a result of a variety of cognitive conceptual mechanisms consolidating the boy's sex-role identity, leading to common categorization of the self and the fa-

ther and giving meaning and prestige to the father's work role. In contrast, the girl's psychosexual development does not appear to require a radical shift in parental model mediated by complex cognitive mechanisms.

In addition to demanding radical shifts in model based on various conceptual equations, the urban boy's father-identification must be based largely on rather abstract forms of behavioral equivalence. A large part of the male adult role is a work role which is distant and vague in meaning. The boy is given little opportunity to observe this role and less opportunity to imitate it overtly. Furthermore, the boy has little reason to expect that he will play an adult work role that will be concretely like his father's, so that the elements of the father's role relevant to his own identity must be quite general and abstract. In contrast, the girl's mother-identification involves very concrete forms of domestic behavior which the girl has an opportunity to observe and practice, and which she expects to perform when she grows up. A cognitive-developmental interpretation of *IQ*-personality correlates, then, suggests that *IQ* should be more determining of the development of sex-role attitudes of boys than of girls because the girl's parental identification can be based on more concrete imitative learning processes under conditions of greater exposure to the model, and because such identification does not require a radical developmental shift in model.

Previous Findings on Relationships Between Intelligence and Sex-Role Attitudes

The research literature reports a number of incidental findings of correlations between *IQ* and tests of sex-typing that have suggestive, though not clear-cut, implications for the issues raised. Epstein and Leverant (19) report no correlation between intelligence and masculinity (on the It Scale) in boys aged 5 to 6. Lefkowitz (44) reports a low positive correlation between a game-preference masculinity measure and *IQ* among 10-year-old boys. Gough (28) reports a low positive correlation between his femininity scale and *IQ* in both boys and girls. Some of the inconsistencies among these find-

TABLE I

Findings of Clark (13) on It Scale Scores of Mentally Retarded Children

Measure	Boys	Girls
Mean C.A.	11, 7	12, 4
Mean *IQ*	49	48
Mean M.A.	5, 9	5, 11
Mean It scores	61	48
Mean It scores of normals of same M.A. (10)	66	52
Correlation of *IQ* with It Scale for Children	.56	.42
Correlation of C.A. with It Scale for Children	.47	.43
Correlation of M.A. with It Scale for Children	.69	.64

ings may be due to the different measures of masculinity-femininity employed. It appears, however, that these varying relationships are due to the fact that the relationships between intelligence and sex-role attitudes are age-specific: i.e., that intelligence affects sex-role attitudes in different ways at different ages rather than in an absolute manner. At younger chronological or mental ages *IQ*s appear to be positively correlated with masculinity of interest in boys, because masculinity scores at younger ages reflect earlier learning of basic sex-typing. As masculinity tests like the It Scale reach a ceiling in which almost all children in a chronological age group can get perfect scores, individual variation is no longer related to intelligence and is only determined by strong forces for deviance in the child's personality or family culture. By adolescence, intelligence may be related to femininity in boys because of developmental advances toward greater heterosexual interests or generally greater breadth of interests. . . .

While Terman found his gifted children of 8 to 10 more same-sex oriented in game preferences than are average children, he found them to be less so in choice of playmates. If same-sex orientation were to be viewed as a single personality trait differentiating gifted children from average children, these results would be confusing. If a developmental view is taken, however, these results merely suggest that the bright children attain earlier the adolescent attitude of heterosexual social interests, while retaining same-sex activity interests. Consistent with this

interpretation, Campbell (11) reports age findings on ratings of children's behavior toward the opposite sex. She found a U-shaped age trend in items reflecting positive attitudes toward the opposite sex, which she used to define a measure of "social sex development." A moderate positive correlation was found between this measure and *IQ*. This positive correlation between *IQ* and this U-shaped developmental scale, then, indicates that the direction of relationship of *IQ* to same-sex *versus* opposite-sex interest in this area is contingent on the developmental status (age or mental age) of the children being considered.

Studies of sex-typing among retardates indicate some more striking relationships to intelligence and also underline the fact that the direction of these relationships is not always in the conforming direction but is contingent on developmental trends in the mental or chronological age range studied. The most clear-cut findings of relationships to intelligence were found in Clark's (13) study of retardates' responses to the It Scale for Children. These findings are summarized in Table 1.

As Table 1 indicates, Clark found the It Scale scores of the retardates to be close to those of younger normal subjects of the same mental age. Correlations between It Scale scores and both *IQ* and mental age among the retarded population are high. For both the boys and the girls, *IQ*, mental age, and chronological age are all correlated with increased preference for masculine objects. For retarded girls, both *IQ* and chronological age operate in a culturally "deviant" direction in the mental age range involved (mental age 4 to 9). Similar chronological age trends toward increased masculinity appear among normal girls in this same mental age range (10, 30). They are the combined result of an artifact in the It Scale and of genuine attitude trends, as is discussed later.

In another study, Fisher (22, 23) analyzed the sex of the figure drawn first by retardates when asked to draw a person. Normal children and adults tend to draw a same-sex figure first, suggesting that this may indicate the child's "sex-role identification." Fisher found that retarded males, both adults and children, draw a same-sex figure first less often than did normals of the same chronological age, but only the differences between retarded and normal adults were statistically significant. Among mentally retarded boys there was no significant relationship between drawing the same-sex figure and either chronological age or *IQ*. These rather ambiguous results correspond to ambiguous or conflicting results as to age developmental trends on this measure in a normal population (37, 66). Fisher also found that retarded girls drew a same-sex figure first significantly less often than did normal girls, and that the duller retarded girls drew a same-sex figure first significantly less often than did the brighter retarded girls.

Fisher found, however, that there was an age trend among his brighter retarded girls toward less same-sex orientation on the figure drawing after the age of 12 (an age trend found also in the normal population). Corresponding to this trend, Fisher found that normal women were not more same-sex oriented on the figure drawing than were retarded women, nor were the brighter retarded women more same-sex oriented than the duller retarded women.

Consideration of the findings of the studies of retardates by Clark and by Fisher suggests, then, the following conclusions. First, *IQ* is an important determinant of measures of sex-typing, but only when these measures reflect age-developmental trends. Second, the direction of differences between retardates and normals on a measure depends on the developmental trends on the measures for the mental age range in-

volved. Differences between male normals and retarded males on the It Scale are clear-cut because there is a monotonic age increase in masculinity on this measure. Differences between male retardates and normals on the figure drawing are not clear-cut as age developmental trends are not clear-cut on this measure, some studies reporting age trends among normals and some not. Among younger girls, retardates are *more* same-sex oriented on the It Scale than are normals, but *less* same-sex oriented on the figure drawing. This was probably due to the fact that the developmental trend on the It Scale for the mental age range considered was toward less same-sex orientation, while this was not true for the figure drawings. Among older girls and adults, however, retardates are slightly *more* same-sex oriented on the figure drawing than are normals. This is probably due to the fact that there is a developmental trend in this older mental age range toward less same-sex orientation on the figure drawing.

The research findings, then, suggest that intelligence does have a fairly important influence upon sex-role attitudes, and that it influences these attitudes in a developmental fashion. It appears that bright children differ from average children (or average children differ from retarded children) in opposed fashion at different ages as successive developmental tasks concern them. At some ages bright children appear higher in "sex-role identification" than do average children, at some ages they appear lower, but in all cases these differences appear to be in line with age-developmental advance by the bright children.

This developmental interpretation of the findings, however, is subject to numerous qualifications, since the studies reporting them were not directed at the theoretical issues raised here and did not incorporate the features of design elaborated in the next section of this monograph. Thus the Terman results on sex-role attitudes are based on a single paper-and-pencil measure that is theoretically ambiguous; differences between bright and average children are confounded with social class differences; and the data on sex-role attitudes were not gathered longitudinally. Studies of retardates have not employed matched average *IQ* controls and have grouped mental age ranges in which *IQ* influences responses in conflicting directions.

General Hypotheses and Design Rationale of the Present Studies

The first general hypothesis of the studies here reported, then, was that intelligence (as indicated by Stanford-Binet *IQ*) was an important[1] correlate of sex-role attitudes in children of 4 to 8. The more theoretical hypothesis tested was that these *IQ*-personality correlations were primarily the result of the impact of general cognitive development upon the development of sex-role attitudes. A subsidiary hypothesis was that intelligence would be a more influential correlate of sex-role attitudes in boys than in girls.

In regard to the theoretical hypothesis, the authors reviewed earlier a number of views of intelligence that offer explanations of *IQ*-personality correlations in terms other than those of cognitive advance. As opposed to the cognitive-developmental view, all of these alternative views suggest that the differences between bright and average children are fixed differences in socially desirable characteristics rather than differences due to the developmental advance of the bright children. In addition all involve questioning the cognitive mediation of the *IQ*-personality relations, suggesting noncognitive correlates of *IQ* as mediating the relationships in question.

In order to discriminate the developmental interpretation from other interpretations of *IQ* differences, it seemed important to incorporate the following features of study design:

1. The study should examine the performance of children differing in intelligence at different ages, preferably in a longitudinal manner. As originally planned, these aims were to be met by comparing groups of bright and average children at each of four ages (4, 5, 6, 7). The results of this first study suggested the desirability of further observations to determine whether the developmental trends for the bright and average groups were really the

same in nature and varied only in rate or acceleration. Accordingly, the available original subjects were retested after an interval of one year, so that cross-sectional trends could be compared with longitudinal trends. In addition, an older group (age 10) was tested on one of the measures to clarify the developmental trends involved.

2. The study must include measures that detected developmental reversals. As long as age development in a measure consisted simply of increased movement to the adult definition of the socially desirable, it would be very difficult to differentiate developmental advance in bright children from their location on nondevelopmental attributes of social desirability. Accordingly, measures were required in which age development would involve movement in one direction at one age period and movement in an opposite direction during a later age period. If bright children differ from average children in one direction at one age and in an opposite direction at another age, but both directions represent advance in age development, then these differences in social behavior may be taken as due to rate of development rather than to differences in social status and desirability.

In line with this consideration, the measurement focus of the present study was upon assessments of preferential attachment and imitation of parent-figures. As is discussed in the next section, psychoanalytic, cognitive-developmental, and social learning theories all postulate developmental reversals in parent-orientations in the age period studied, and prior research findings and methods offered some promise for detecting such developmental reversals in this period. Accordingly, it was decided to employ an experimental measure of orientation of dependency to a male as opposed to a female experimenter, a similar measure of sex-typed imitation of these experimenters, and a doll play measure of orientation of dependency and imitation to the father as opposed to the mother doll.

Because of their wide use in previous theory and research, it was also decided to include measures of sex-typed interests or "sex-role identification" and of sex-typing of peer preferences. While it was not theoretically clear that developmental reversals would occur in such

---

[1] "Important" is a vague term whose meaning in this study will range from conventional assessment as to whether differences are beyond those expected by chance (statistical significance at the .05 level) to assessments as to whether important chronological age differences are primarily accounted for by mental age or intelligence.

measures, prior research suggested such a possibility.

As is discussed in the next section, expectations as to age-developmental trends and reversals could be set up on the basis of prior theory and research. The basic strategy of the present studies, however, was to establish empirical age trends in various sex-role behaviors and to test the hypothesis that these trends occurred earlier in groups of bright children than in groups of average children.

3. In addition to focusing upon measures indicating developmental reversals, the study should include a variety of methods of measurement that would minimize or at least vary the effects of verbal skills and sophistication. The central hypothesis of the study is that the bright children should be developmentally advanced in the *possession* of basic sex-role concepts and attitudes, and not merely advanced in their *expression* of these concepts and attitudes. The distinction between developmental advance in possession of a concept or attitude and sophistication in its expression is, of course, a difficult one. In general, however, if the same differences appear between bright and average children using test forms varying in verbal complexity or indirectness, we may conclude that the differences are not merely matters of verbal sophistication.

For the present study, then, it was decided to include both verbal tests, "projective" doll play tests, and direct behavioral assessments in an experimental situation. Behavioral measures of orientation to strange adults presumably represent a vehicle whereby development of sex-linked attitudes may be expressed without much intervening test awareness or verbal sophistication. They are ambiguous, however, in their reference to the child's attitudes to mother and father roles. In contrast, doll play responses to questions about father and mother are relatively direct in reference but can be checked against the less test-like experimental situation.

Specific Measures Employed and the Rationale for Their Use

A detailed review of theories and findings as to age-developmental trends and sequences in sex-role attitudes is presented elsewhere (40).

For this paper, the authors will merely sketch the considerations that led them to select certain measures and to anticipate certain developmental reversals upon them.

The central developmental reversals considered in the present research design were those suggested by the psychoanalytic theory of the Oedipus complex. Psychoanalytic theory views children of both sexes as originally attached to the mother, then postulates an increase in attachment to cross-sex adult figures from about 3 to 5 (Oedipal period) followed by a decrease in such attachment and an increasing identification with the same-sex adults in the early school years (latency period).

While the cognitive-developmental and social-learning theories of psychosexual development do not postulate an Oedipal (cross-sex) trend, they agree with psychoanalytic theory in the origin and terminus of the age trends in this period (41). They assume that children of both sexes are originally (age 0 to 3) preferentially oriented to the mother and that they then (4 to 8) become oriented to the same-sex parent. All theories lead to an expectation of a developmental shift by the boy from the mother to the father. The psychoanalytic theory, however, postulates a double reversal for the girl (mother at age 0 to 3, father at age 4 to 5, mother at age 6 to 8), while the alternative theories imply a continuing mother orientation for the girl.

Previous experimental findings suggested that the developmental trends postulated by psychoanalytic theory might be reflected in overt behavior in a standardized situation. These findings were based on studies in which children's social dependency was assessed in two parallel experimental situations, one involving a male and one involving a female. Accordingly, it was decided to make use of such an assessment for the present study, based on procedure used in a study by Emmerich and Kohlberg (18). In previous work with this method, Gewirtz (26), Gewirtz and Baer (27), Emmerich and Kohlberg (18), and McCarthy (48) have found that 3-, 4-, and 5-year-old children display significantly more verbal dependency and more responsiveness to social reinforcers with cross-sex than with same-sex adults (mainly under conditions of limited access to the experimenter or after brief social isolation). The opposite-sex preference was clearer for boys than for girls, so that the trends might be consistent with cognitive-developmental theory rather than with the Oedipal theory. In either case, however, the authors were led to expect a more rapid developmental shift to the male by bright than by average boys in the period 4 to 8, with the possibility of a more rapid shift by bright than average girls first toward, and then away from, the male.

Discussion of developmental trends in parent-orientation sometimes refers to these trends as "identifications," implying both preferential affiliation and preferential modeling of one parent. In the psychoanalytic theory of psychosexual development, preferential imitation and preferential affiliation converge at some age points and diverge at others. First, both tendencies converge on the mother (0 to 3), then they tend to diverge in the "Oedipal" period (attachment is to the opposite-sex parent but the child desires to imitate or play the role of the same-sex parent, 4 to 6) and then to converge again on the same-sex parent (6 to 10). In cognitive-developmental and most social learning theories, the two tendencies are viewed as converging on the same object, though cognitive-developmental theory views shift in modeling as preceding shifts in affiliation, while social learning theories tend to assume that preferential dependency precedes preferential imitation (41).

Experimental studies of imitation in preschool and kindergarten children employing the same general design as the social dependency studies suggested tendencies grossly consistent with either the psychoanalytic or the cognitive-developmental theories. Rosenblith (57) and Hartup (29) found that children of both sexes imitatively learned more from a male than a female at an age (kindergarten) at which they appeared to be more affiliative or responsive to the opposite sex. These findings for boys are consistent with either the psychoanalytic or cognitive-developmental theories which postulate that boys shift to modeling the father at an age where they are still preferentially attached to the mother. Accordingly, it was decided to include the Emmerich and Kohlberg (18) measures of imitation in the experimental situation involving the male and female adults. The expectation was that there would be an age

increase in male imitation by boys and that bright boys would be advanced on this tendency. Expectations for girls were not clear.

Interpretations of interactions between sex of child and sex of experimenter in amount of dependency or imitation have been based largely on viewing dependency or imitation responses to strange male or female adults as representing a generalization of responses toward the child's own mother or father. It could be argued, however, that responses to strange adults differ completely from those to parents, either because they represent displacements or compensations of relations with the parents, or because they develop in independence of parent attitudes. As an example, the boy who is absorbed in a close attachment to the mother at home might have no need of adult female figures on the outside and might take the opportunity of exploring relations with male figures. In addition it could be argued that the direction of overt expressions of dependency (or imitation) would not be directly related to the direction of "covert" or "fantasy" expressions of dependency as in doll play techniques. In fact, previous findings on children's orientation of dependency and imitation toward parent dolls in semistructured interviews appeared to be at variance with the findings on orientation toward adult experimenters. Findings on a measure of imitation of the father *versus* the mother doll in children aged 3 to 5 suggest that both sexes preferentially imitate the same-sex parent and that this tendency increases with age (29). Findings with a similar technique measuring preferential attachment or dependency upon the mother *versus* the father in children aged 3 to 5 indicated that girls were mother-oriented, while boys were neutral in orientation of dependency (2). These doll play findings seem most consistent with the cognitive-developmental theory which expects both sexes to be first mother-oriented and expects boys to move then to a father orientation; first in imitation, then in dependency. In contrast, the experimental findings involving orientation of dependency toward adult experimenters suggested trends consistent with Oedipal theory. In any case, it was decided to include the Ammons and Ammons and Hartup measures. It was expected that boys would move to greater father-orientation with age on both measures, and that young bright boys would be advanced in father orientation relative to average boys. Expectations for girls were less clear-cut.

The findings of Campbell (11), based on ratings of attitudes toward opposite-sex peers in a club situation in the years 6 to 16, suggested that this was an area of developmental reversal in which a U-shaped curve defining a "latency period" was to be found. In line with this reversal, Terman found that preadolescent (8 to 11) bright children were slightly less same-sex oriented in friendship choices than were average children. These findings suggested that, in the earlier age period of the present study, bright children would be first (age 4 to 5) more same-sex oriented in friendship choices than average children and would later (age 6 to 7) be less, or no more, same-sex oriented than the average children.

While developmental reversals in measures of sex-typed interests or "sex-role identification" also appeared in the adolescent years in Terman's studies, it appeared unlikely that they would appear in the years 4 to 8. Age trends on one measure of sex-role identification, the It Scale, did suggest such a shift for girls, however. While boys become increasingly masculine in choice with age on this measure, girls' choices become increasingly feminine from age 2 through 4 (30), increasingly masculine from 4 to 9 (9), and then increasingly feminine again. Accordingly, the It Scale was included in the present study. The developmental hypothesis implies that bright boys would be more masculine than average boys and that bright girls would be more "advanced" in masculine choice than average girls at some point in the age period studied. Several results of the initial cross-sectional study showed that the age decline in girls' femininity on the It Scale was largely due to an artifact in the test. Therefore, a second test of sex-typed preference, Sears, Rau, and Alpert's (59) Pictures Test, was added on longitudinal retesting.

METHOD

Subjects and Research Design of Cross-Sectional Studies

A group of 64 middle-class children between the ages of 4 and 8 constituted the core group of subjects for the studies of sex-typed interests, sex-typed peer preferences, and orientation to parent dolls. The core group of children were drawn from two private nursery schools and two suburban elementary schools in southern Connecticut. The children were chosen to fill a 4 × 2 × 2 factorial design, involving chronological age (4, 5, 6, and 7), intelligence, and the sex of the child. Intelligence was measured by the Stanford-Binet for all children, with the exception of the 4-year-olds whose scores were based on the Intellectual Adaptive parts of the Gesell Developmental Examination. The mean *IQ*s of the bright and average groups were 132 and 104, respectively. The *IQ* ranges were from 120 to 149 for the bright group and from 92 to 114 for the average group. . . .

PROCEDURE AND MEASURES   The original study required four separate individual sessions with each child, sessions separated in time by two to three weeks. Data on dependency and imitation directed toward the experimenters were gathered first to avoid the sensitizing to sex-typing represented by the later tasks. Collection of these data (two sessions) was followed by the verbal measures of sex-typing and peer preferences (one session) and finally by the doll play measures (one session).

As mentioned, two male and two female experimenters were used in the experimental dependency-imitation assessment in both cross-sectional and follow-up studies. The remaining tests were conducted by one of two male *E*s in the cross-sectional study and by one of two female *E*s in the follow-up study.

EXPERIMENTAL DEPENDENCY AND IMITATION MEASURES   Procedure for the dependency-imitation assessment was adapted from that used by Emmerich and Kohlberg (18). Each child spent 10 minutes in a situation "making designs," while an adult experimenter sat near him also making designs. After a one-week interval, the child had a similar session with an experimenter of the opposite sex from the first.

The experimenter initiated conversation to gain rapport with the child on the way to the experimental room. When he reached the room, the experimenter pointed out four representations of animals or objects made by attaching adhesive colored geometrical shapes to a piece of paper. The child was told that these designs had been made by other children. He was told that he was also to make sticker designs and that the experimenter would make some too, and that he (the child) could make anything he liked. The use of sticker designs and the presentation of models "made by other children" was dictated by a desire to reduce the role of ability variables in tendency to imitate the experimenter. A minimum of four designs were made by the child during each experimental session.

After the initial instructions, the experimenter did not initiate any verbalization to the child except to name his own design and later to ask the child to name his design if he had not done so spontaneously. The experimenter made minimal but friendly "Uh-huh" responses to verbalizations initiated by the child. The aim of this procedure was to minimize and standardize the experimenter's role in eliciting or reinforcing the verbal output of the child.

Verbal dependency was recorded by the experimenter. A four-point scale of dependency was used, based on Gewirtz's (26) classification. A score of 3 was assigned to a verbal request of the child, which called for something more than information in reply. Asking for help, for praise, for permission, or for direct attention were responses which fell in this category. A score of 2 was assigned to a simple question or request for verbal information. A score of 1 was assigned to any declarative statement by the child which did not call for an actual reply or response by the experimenter, but which the child seemed to expect would be attended to by the experimenter. In support of this weighting, Gewirtz has found Guttman scale-like relations between these three classes of response: i.e., all children asking help also asked questions of information and made declarative comments, but many children only made declarative comments or only made comments and asked questions of information.

A fourth scale point was added to Gewirtz's scale by scoring egocentric comments as one-half a point. The "parallel-play" nature of the experimental situation seemed to elicit a considerable amount of this type of response. Included in this category were utterances classified as "talking to oneself" because they were mut-

tered *sotto voce* so as to be inaudible to the experimenter. Also included were statements more truly egocentric, in Piaget's (53) sense, such as the following comments of one of the subjects:

Where's a nose, a funny, funny nose? Here's a nose, a funny, funny nose. Get back there nose.

A child's dependency score for each experimental session was the sum of his verbal remarks for the 10 minutes, with each verbal remark weighted as just described.

The similarity of the child's drawings to those of the experimenter was used as the basis for an imitation score. If the child gave his design the same name as the experimenter had, a score of 2 was given. If there was some degree of similarity to the designs, but the name was different, a score of 1 was assigned to the design.

DOLL PLAY MEASURES OF RELATIVE ATTACHMENT AND IMITATION OF MOTHER AND FATHER The doll play test consisted of two parts. Half the items, adapted from Hartup (29), involved choices between imitation of the father and of the mother. The other half of the items, adapted from Ammons and Ammons (2), were meant to measure relative attachment or dependency.

Father, mother, and same-sex child Renwall dolls were used together with a miniature table, chairs, bed, and kitchen equipment. The child was told he would play a game and help the experimenter make up stories about a family. Nineteen situations were then presented to the child, consisting of the 10 imitation situations adapted from Hartup (29) and the nine attachment situations adapted from Ammons and Ammons (2). The imitation and attachment situations were alternated in an arrangement forming a sequence carrying the child doll from the beginning to the end of the day. An example of the imitation situations is:

The mommy takes a cookie from the bowl on this table. The daddy takes a cookie from a bowl on this (other) table. Show me the boy (girl) taking a cookie.

If the subject had the child doll take a cookie

from the father's bowl, he received a score of 2 on the item. If the subject had the child doll take a cookie from the mother's bowl, he received a score of zero on the item. If the subject managed to evade the choice, or compromised by having the child doll take a cookie from each bowl, he received a score of 1 on the item.

An example of the attachment items is:

Now the boy (girl) has to go to bed. Whom does he want to put him to bed and say good night?

A choice of the father was scored 2, of the mother 0, and of both or of some other person, 1.

MEASURES OF SEX-TYPED INTERESTS   Our first measure of sex-typed preferences was the It Scale for Children (9). The It Scale involves asking the child to choose between pictures of various objects or persons having sex-typed characteristics. The preferences are to be made, not for the child himself, but for a drawing of a sexless figure called "It," which makes the test more or less "projective."

In scoring the test, the authors deviated from Brown's convention and scored a same-sex choice as positive for both boys and girls, retaining Brown's differential weighting of scores for choices on various items. The authors eliminated the eight least sex-differentiating pictures from the 16 pictures in the first section of the test and doubled the weights of the remaining eight pictures. This left a total of 14 choices in the scaling, allowing scores ranging from zero to 88 according to Brown's weightings.

On follow-up, the authors also included the Sears (59) Pictures test measure of sex-typed preference. In this test, adapted from Fauls and Smith (21), the child indicated his preferred choice of two activities that were presented to him in the form of pictures placed side by side in front of him. For example, one pair showed a child (of the same sex as the subject) washing a car, while another showed the child setting a table for tea. The original Sears, Rau, and Alpert procedure required 12 paired comparison choices. In the present use, only eight comparisons were required to reduce the reduplication of the paired comparison procedure. These choices led to scores for sex-appropriate choice ranging from zero to 8.

MEASURES OF SEX-TYPED PEER PREFERENCES
The sex-typing of playmate preferences measure was based on the child's response to the question:

Tell me the names of three children in school whom you like, who are nice.

This was followed by the question: "Do you like girls (boys)?"

Responses were scored on the following seven point scale:

1. All three friends named are of the opposite sex.
2. Two of the children mentioned are of the opposite sex.
3. One of the children mentioned is of the opposite sex.
4. No children mentioned are of the opposite sex, but subject says he (or she) likes opposite-sex children on probe.
5. Subject says he (or she) likes opposite-sex children sometimes or a little on probe.
6. Subject says he (or she) doesn't like opposite-sex children on probe.
7. Subject vocalizes antipathy or avoidance of opposite-sex children.

Reliability of Measures

EXPERIMENTAL DEPENDENCY AND IMITATION
In order to ascertain the interjudge agreement of the scoring of dependency by the experimenter, the experimental sessions were tape-recorded. A research assistant scored dependency from the tapes to compare with the experimenter's scoring during the session. The product-moment correlation of the research assistant's scoring of each child's total weighted verbal dependency with that of the experimenter's was .98.

The fact that each child had two experimental sessions a week apart, one with a male and one with a female experimenter, provides a gross measure of the test-retest reliability of the authors' dependency measure. Analysis of the within-groups covariance of the two sessions results in a test-retest correlation coefficient of .80 for the dependency measure. This correlation, of course, represents a measure of stability of dependency in the experimental situation rather than a measure of stability of sex-typing of dependency.

Emmerich and Kohlberg (18) found there was 90 per cent agreement between two judges on the three-category measure of imitation.

The within-groups correlation coefficient on the imitation measures in the two sessions was only .53.

DOLL PLAY DEPENDENCY AND IMITATION   In order to obtain a measure of test-retest reliability, a second form of the doll play test was constructed and administered to 27 of the children about equally selected from the 4-, 5-, and 6-year-old age levels. The second form was administered from two to five weeks after the first form of the test. The product-moment correlation between total scores on the two forms of the test was .74, between the imitation scales was .92, and between the attachment scales was .58.

An item analysis was conducted on the first form of the test. Thirteen of the 19 items were significantly ($p < .05$) associated with total score of the combined imitation and attachment scales.

MEASURES OF SEX-TYPED INTERESTS   Brown (9) reports product-moment test-retest reliability coefficients of .71 for boys and .84 for girls for the It Scale, administered to kindergarten children. Borstelmann (8) reports similar coefficients for preschool children. Borstelmann reports test-retest reliability coefficients after a one-month interval of .37 for boys and .38 for girls for the Pictures Test of sex-typing.

SEX-TYPED PEER PREFERENCES   A measure of retest reliability of sex-typed peer preference was not carried out. Sociometric studies indicate quite high test-retest stability in the names of children chosen as first, second, and third choice as companions. Northway (51) asked nursery school children for three choices and asked them to choose again four months later. She found that 83 per cent of first choices were unchanged, 78 per cent of second choices were unchanged, and 74 per cent of third choices were changed. Somewhat similar, though slightly lower, retest stability was found

among elementary school children by Criswell (14).

SUMMARY AND CONCLUSIONS

The major hypothesis of the series of studies reported here was that mental age, as an index of conceptual growth, is an important determinant of the development of sex-role attitudes in the young child, holding chronological age constant. The hypothesis derives from cognitive-developmental theories, such as Piaget's, which see intellectual growth as transforming the perceived world of the child, and hence his social attitudes.

In contrast, the most influential theories of sex-role development have linked it to the maturation of instincts (Freudian theory) or to the pressures and reinforcements of socializing agents (social-learning theory). For either of these two latter types of theory, developmental trends would be related more closely to chronological age (representing physiological maturity and sociological age-status) than to mental age.

The basic design of the investigation involved establishing trends on a variety of sex-role attitude measures for matched bright and average groups of middle-class children at each year of age from 4 to 8. Retesting on the measures, after an interval of a year, was carried out in order to validate the developmental character of the cross-sectional trends. The hypothesis of the study led to the expectation of parallel age trends in the bright and average groups, with these trends occurring earlier for the bright than for the average group.

The measures on which the children were compared were the following:

1. Sex-typing of verbal dependency in an experimental situation with a male and a female *E*.

2. Sex-typing of imitation of the adult *E*s.

3. Doll play choices designed to express relative attachment to mother and father, adapted from Ammons and Ammons (2).

4. Doll play choices designed to express relative tendencies to imitate father *versus* mother, adapted from Hartup (29).

5. The It Scale for Children—a projective

TABLE 2

Summary of Age Trends from 4 to 8 Found on Measures of Sex-Role Attitudes

Measures	Boys	Girls
It Scale, Pictures Test, and Peer Preferences	All boys become more same-sex oriented until 6 (then less so for peer preferences)	All girls become less same-sex oriented with age on It Scale and Peer Preferences, slight increase on Pictures Test
Verbal Dependency to Experimenter	Average boys change from opposite-sex orientation at 4 to same-sex orientation at 7	Average girls remain slightly same-sex oriented
	Bright boys change from same-sex orientation at 4 to opposite-sex orientation at 7	Bright girls remain slightly opposite-sex oriented
Parent Attachment and Imitation	Average boys become more father-oriented with age	Average girls, initially mother-oriented, become more father-oriented with age
	Bright boys do not change their initial father orientation	Bright girls do not change their initial neutrality of choice

picture test of sex-typing developed by Brown (9).

6. The Pictures Test—another picture test of sex-typed preference (8, 59).

7. A measure of sex-typing of preference for other children.

Significant differences between the bright and average children were found for all of the above measures except Measure 2. Although statistically significant simple age trends were not found for all the measures, in every case (except in the case of girls' responses to Measure 5 in which a test artifact was found), the *IQ* differences could be plausibly interpreted as indicating that the bright children were more advanced in terms of age trends found among the average subjects. The actual trends for the major measures are summarized in Table 2.

The developmental trends for the various groups do not fit any simple theory, such as the psychoanalytic theory of the Oedipus complex. The findings indicate that the preschool children preferentially orient to feminine figures. A clear general developmental trend displayed by both boys and girls in most of the studies is toward an increased orientation to the father. This trend is complicated by evidence that sex-typing of verbal dependency becomes differentiated on a "same *versus* cross-sex" dimension, rather than a "father *versus* mother" dimension.

The results of most interest—i.e., those *IQ* differences that would be least likely to be expected from points of view other than cognitive-developmental theory—were obtained with the sex-typing of dependency toward a strange adult in an experimental situation. The bright children higher on male-preference at 4, moved toward greater female-preference at age 7, whereas the average children moved toward a greater male-preference during this period. It was found that the average children of 10 showed a pattern roughly similar to that of their bright 7-year-old mental age counterparts, just as the average children of 6 to 7 showed a pattern roughly similar to that of their bright 4-year-old counterparts. These trends for the behavioral measures with strange adults were broadly consistent with trends with doll-figure representations of the parents.

Thus actual developmental reversals occurred on measures for both bright and average children and the timing of these reversals appeared to be determined by mental rather than chronological age. These findings suggested that at least some of the personality correlates of intelligence represent the role of cognitive transformations of the perceived social environment in initiating new developmental trends rather than simply representing a more facile learning of, or adjustment to, a given social environment.

The results then indicate an important developmental role for intelligence in the sex-role attitudes of both boys and girls as late as age 7. This suggests the incompleteness of cultural-transmission theories which account for sex-role development as the result of adult labeling and reinforcement or as the result of identification with simple parental behaviors. Such theories would have little difficulty in explaining differences in sex-typed preferences between *IQ* groups at a young age, differences explainable as the result of differential rate of learning of parental labels and expectations. The *IQ* differences found at later ages in less stereotyped measures of sex-role attitudes involving reversals in choice of object of dependency and imitation cannot, however, be readily explained as reflections of varied rates of learning of the sex-role norms of socializing agents.

If the *IQ* differences seem incompatible with cultural transmission theory, they seem even less compatible with theories of biological maturation of sexual instincts or attitudes, such as psychoanalytic libido theory. The findings were taken as most compatible with a cognitive-developmental theory of the formation of sex-role attitudes, which has been elaborated elsewhere (40).

REFERENCES

1. Abernathy, E. H. Relationships between mental and physical growth. *Monog. Soc. Res. Child Devel.,* 1936, 1, No. 7.
2. Ammons, R., & Ammons, H. Parent preference in young children's doll play interviews. *J. Abn. & Soc. Psychol.,* 1949, 44, 490–505.
3. Anderson, J. The prediction of adjustment over time. In I. Iscoe & H. Stevenson (Eds.), *Personality Development in Children.* Austin: Univ. Texas Press, 1960.
4. Anderson, J., *et al.* The Prediction of Adjustment over Time. Minneapolis, Minn.: Univ. Minnesota Press, 1961.
5. Bayley, N. Factors influencing growth of intelligence in young children. *Yearbook Nat. Soc. Stud. Educ.,* 1940, 39, 49–79.
6. Blommers, P., Kneif, L., & Stroud, J. B. The organismic age concept. *J. Educ. Psychol.,* 1955, 46, 142–150.
7. Bloom, B. Stability and Change in Human Characteristics. New York: Wiley, 1964.
8. Borstelmann, L. Sex of experimenter and sex-typed behavior of young children. *Child Devel.,* 1961, 32, 519–525.
9. Brown, D. B. Sex-role preference in young children. *Psychol. Monog.,* 1956, 70, No. 14 (Serial No. 287).
10. ———. Masculinity-femininity development in children. *J. Consult. Psychol.,* 1957, 27, 197–205.
11. Campbell, E. H. The social-sex development of children. *Genet. Psychol. Monog.,* 1939, 21, No. 4.
12. Cattell, R. B. Personality and Motivation; Structure and Measurement. Yonkers: World Book, 1957.
13. Clark, E. Sex-role preference in mentally retarded children. *Amer. J. Ment. Defic.,* 1963, 67, 606–610.
14. Criswell, J. H. Social structure revealed in a sociometric test. *Sociometry,* 1939, 2, 69–75.
15. Dennis, W. Adolescence. In L. Carmichael (Ed.), *Manual of Child Psychology.* New York: Wiley, 1946.
16. Dewey, J. Conduct and experience. In C. Murchison (Ed.), *Psychologies of 1930.* Worcester, Mass.: Clark Univ. Press, 1930.
17. Emmerich, W. Continuity and stability in early social development. *Child Devel.,* 1964, 35, 311–333.
18. Emmerich, W., & Kohlberg, L. Imitation and attention-seeking in young children under conditions of nurturance, frustration and conflict. Mimeograph, Chicago, Illinois, 1952.

19. Epstein, R., & Leverant, S. Verbal conditioning and sex-role identification in children. *Child Devel.*, 1963, 34, 99–106.
20. Erikson, E. Childhood and Society. New York: Norton, 1950.
21. Fauls, L. B., & Smith, W. D. Sex-role learning of five-year-olds. *J. Genet. Psychol.*, 1956, 89, 105–119.
22. Fisher, G. M. Sexual identification in retarded male children and adults. *Amer. J. Ment. Defic.*, 1960, 65, 42–45.
23. ———. Sexual identification in mentally subnormal females. *Amer. J. Ment. Defic.*, 1961, 66, 266–269.
24. Freud, S. Three contributions to the theory of sex. In *The Basic Writings of Sigmund Freud*. New York: Modern Library, 1938 (originally published in 1905).
25. Gesell, A., & Ilg, F. Infant and Child in the Culture of Today. New York: Harpers, 1943.
26. Gewirtz, J. Three determinants of attention-seeking in young children. *Monog. Soc. Res. Child Devel.*, 1954, 19, No. 2 (Serial No. 59).
27. Gewirtz, J., & Baer, D. The effect of brief social deprivation on behaviors for a social reinforcer. *J. Abn. & Soc. Psychol.*, 1958, 56, 49–57.
28. Gough, H. G. Factor relations to the academic achievement of high school students. *J. Educ. Psychol.*, 1949, 40, 65–78.
29. Hartup, W. W. Nurturance and nurturance withdrawal in relation to dependency behavior in young children. *Child Devel.*, 1958, 39, 191–201.
30. Hartup, W. W., & Zook, E. Sex-role preferences in three- and four-year-old children. *J. Consult. Psychol.*, 1960, 24, 420–426.
31. Harvey, O. J., Hunt, D., & Shroeder, A. Conceptual Systems and Personality Organization. New York: Wiley, 1961.
32. Havighurst, R. J., *et al.* Growing Up in River City. New York: Wiley, 1962.
33. Hayes, K. Genes, drives, and intellect. *Psychol. Rep.*, 1962, 10, 299–342.
34. Hollingworth, L. S. Gifted Children, Their Nature and Nurture. New York: Macmillan, 1926.
35. ———. Children Above 180 I.Q., Stanford-Binet. New York: World Book, 1942.
36. Hunt, J. McV. Intelligence and Experience. New York: Ronald Press, 1961.
37. Jolles, J. A. A study of the validity of some hypotheses for the qualitative interpretation of the H-T-P for children of elementary school age: I. Sexual identification. *J. Clin. Psychol.*, 1952, 8, 113–118.
38. Kagan, J. The acquisition and significance of sex-typing and sex-role identity. In M. & L. Hoffman (Eds.), *Review of Child Develop-*

ment Research *(Vol. 1)*. New York: Russell Sage Foundation, 1964.
39. Kagan, J., & Moss, H. Birth to Maturity. New York: Wiley, 1962.
40. Kohlberg, L. A cognitive-developmental analysis of children's sex-role concepts and attitudes. In E. Maccoby (Ed.), *Development of Sex Differences*. Stanford, Calif.: Stanford Univ. Press, 1966.
41. ———. Stage and sequence: The developmental approach to moralization. In M. Hoffman (Ed.), *Moral Processes*. Chicago, Ill.: Aldine Press, in press.
42. ———. Psychosexual Development in Children: A Cognitive Interpretation. New York: Holt, Rinehart and Winston, in press.
43. ———. Stages in the development of physical and social concepts in the years four to eight. Unpublished paper, Chicago, Illinois, 1967.
44. Lefkowitz, M. M. Some relationships between sex-role preference of children and other parent and child variables. *Psychol. Rep.*, 1962, 10, 43–53.
45. Lynn, D. A note on sex differences in the development of masculine and feminine identification. *Psychol. Rev.*, 1959, 66, 126–136.
46. Maccoby, E. Sex differences in intellectual functioning. In E. Maccoby (Ed.), *Development of Sex Differences*. Stanford, Calif.: Stanford Univ. Press, 1966.
47. MacFarlane, J., Allen, L., & Honzik, N. A Developmental Study of Behavior Problems of Children Between Twenty-one Months and Four Years. Berkeley: Univ. Calif. Press, 1954.
48. McCarthy, D. Language development of the preschool child. *Inst. Child Welfare Monog., No. 4*. Minneapolis, Minn.: Univ. Minn. Press, 1930.
49. Miles, C. C. Gifted children. In L. Carmichael (Ed.), *Manual of Child Psychology (2nd ed.)*. New York: Wiley, 1954.
50. Mussen, P., & Distler, L. Child-rearing antecedents of masculine identification in kindergarten boys. *Child Devel.*, 1960, 31, 89–100.
51. Northway, M. L. Social relationships among preschool children: Abstracts and interpretations of three studies. *Sociometry*, 1943, 6, 429–433.
52. Paterson, D. G. Physique and Intellect. New York: Century, 1930.
53. Piaget, J. Language and Thought of the Child. London: Routledge & Kegan Paul, 1926.
54. ———. The Psychology of Intelligence. London: Routledge & Kegan Paul, 1947.
55. ———. The Moral Judgment of the Child. Glencoe, Ill.: Free Press, 1948 (originally published in 1932).
56. ———. Les relations entre l'intelligence et l'affectivité dans le développement de l'en-

fant. *Bull. Psychol.,* Paris, 1953–1954, 7, 143–701.

57. Rosenblith, J. Learning by imitation in kindergarten children. *Child Devel.,* 1959, 30, 69–81.

58. Sears, R. R. Relations of early socialization experience to aggression in middle childhood. *J. Abn. & Soc. Psychol.,* 1961, 63, 466–493.

59. Sears, R. R., Rau, L., & Alpert, R. Identification and child-rearing. Stanford, Calif.: Stanford Univ. Press, 1965.

60. Tanner, J. Education and Physical Growth. London: Univ. London Press, 1961.

61. Terman, L. M., & Oden, M. The Gifted Child Grows Up. Stanford, Calif.: Stanford Univ. Press, 1947.

62. Terman, L. M., *et al.* Genetic Studies of Genius. Vol. I. Mental and Physical Traits of a Thousand Gifted Children. Stanford, Calif.: Stanford Univ. Press, 1925.

63. ———. Genetic Studies of Genius. Vol. III.

The Promise of Youth. Stanford, Calif.: Stanford Univ. Press, 1930.

64. Thorndike, R. L., & Stein, S. An evaluation of the attempts to measure social intelligence. *Psychol. Bull.,* 1937, 34, 275–285.

65. Vygotsky, L. M. Thought and Language. New York: Wiley, 1962.

66. Weider, R., & Noller, P. A. Objective studies of children's drawings of human figures. II. Sex, age, intelligence. *J. Clin. Psychol.,* 1953, 9, 20–23.

67. Werner, H. The Comparative Psychology of Mental Development. Chicago, Ill.: Wilcox & Follett, 1948.

68. White, R. Motivation reconsidered: The concept of competence. *Psychol. Rev.,* 1959, 66, 297–333.

69. Witkin, H., *et al.* Psychological Differentiation. New York: Wiley, 1962.

70. Yarrow, L. (Ed.). Symposium on personality, consistency, and change: Perspectives from longitudinal research. *Vita Humana,* 1964, 7, 65–146.

ON LATENCY

BERTA BORNSTEIN

. . . . .

Before we speak about latency and the [psychoanalytic] technique applied during that period, let me review briefly the main factors which precede latency. The ego as a mediator between the inner and outer world adopts at an early point defensive measures against painful stimuli from within and without. Under the influence of reality, the ego is enabled gradually to tolerate greater amounts of tension. The open pursuit of the child's gratifications is hindered by the parents' opposition. The growing functions of intellect and judgment assist the child further to postpone gratifications and to block impulses from direct discharge. A partial resolution of the oedipus complex leads, via the identification with the objects of the oedipus complex, to the establishment of the sugerego. From now on the ego has to observe not only the demands of instinctual drives and of the outside world, but also the demands coming from the superego. This means that certain demands which originally were only complied with under the pressure of the parents or their substitutes, are now complied with even if there is no threat of external danger.

With the resolution of the oedipus complex and with the establishment of the superego, the latency period is introduced. Although it is common practice to refer to the latency period as if it were uniform, at least two major divisions within it can be discerned; the first from five and one half to eight years, and the second from eight until about ten years. There are, of course, more than chronological differences between them. The element common to both is

Reprinted with abridgment from pp. 279–85 of *The Psychoanalytic Study of the Child*, Vol. VI, edited by Ruth S. Eissler *et al.*, by permission of the Estate of Berta Bornstein and International Universities Press, Inc. Copyright 1951 by International Universities Press.

the strictness of the superego in its evaluation of incestuous wishes—a strictness which finds expression in the child's struggle against masturbation.

Let me now describe the characteristics of the first period of latency. The ego, still buffeted by the surging impulses, is threatened by the new superego which is not only harsh and rigid but still a foreign body. This first phase of latency is complicated because of the intermingling of two different sets of defenses: the defense against genital and the defense against pregenital impulses. As a defense against genital impulses a temporary regression to pregenitality is adopted by the ego. First these pregenital drives appear as less dangerous than the genital ones. Still they are threatening enough for the child to have to evolve new defenses against the pregenital impulses. Reaction formations, developed as defense against the pregenital impulses, mark the first character changes in early latency.

The result of the conflicts between the superego and the drives can be observed in a heightened ambivalence. This increased ambivalence is a regular feature of early latency, even if the child is not in the process of developing an obsessive neurosis. The ambivalence is expressed in the child's behavior by an alternation between obedience and rebellion: and rebellion is usually followed by self-reproach. However, at this time of life, the child can tolerate his own feelings of guilt as little as he can tolerate criticism from the outside, nor is his behavior modified right away by either. Anna Freud has described what happens at "this intermediate stage of superego development": The attempt to internalize the criticism from the outside sometimes does not lead further than to an identification with the aggressor, "often supplemented by another defensive measure, namely the projection of guilt." Both defenses in turn thrust the child into greater inner and outer conflicts.

It appears to me that the statement frequently made that infantile neurosis decreases during latency requires some modification. It is correct as far as the second period is concerned, but it does not correspond to my own experience as far as the first period is concerned. When the ego is faced by conflicts it cannot overcome during the first period behavior difficulties arise and neurotic symptoms manifest themselves in new ways. To give a few examples: Early animal phobias are replaced by a new wave of separation anxiety and open castration fear is substituted by fear of death. The symptom of insomnia occurs more frequently during that period than is generally known.

Some children in early latency give the appearance of being in an emergency situation; they are conscious of their emotional distress and under such conditions they are ready to accept the analyst as a potential helper. Though they usually expect instantaneous relief and become disappointed and distrustful if this does not occur, they can be very co-operative during treatment. Due to the facts that the child is aware of his suffering, that the ego is in rebellion against both id and superego, that the libido is still in a fluid state and the superego still open to modification, and thus that the ego is not yet completely crippled by neurotic defenses, therapeutic chances seem to be better in early latency than at any other time.

In the second period of latency the situation is different: The ego is exposed to less severe conflicts by virtue of the facts that, on the one hand, the sexual demands have become less exerting and, on the other, the superego has become less rigid. The ego now can devote itself to a greater extent to coping with reality. The average eight-year-old is ready to be influenced by the children around him and by adults other than his parents. As he is able to compare them with other adults, his belief in the omnipotence of his parents subsides. Coinciding with a partial degradation of parents, there is a parallel change in the attitude of the ego toward the superego.

Even if this period is not quite as smooth as described, even if children manifest character disturbances, ego restrictions or slight obsessive symptoms, these symptoms are ego-syntonic.

During the second period, the temptation to masturbate is not completely overcome but the child is so sincerely opposed to the temptation as well as to the occasional breakthroughs, that he must deny or repress both. His concern to forego the masturbatory temptations is accompanied by the desire that defenses should not be upset by any interference. Since he is further along in the process of consolidation of ego defenses than the younger latency child, and is more oriented to coping with problems of the outside world, and since he has more gratifications in reality, the older latency child is less aware of his suffering.

He fears nothing more than the upsetting of his precarious equilibrium. The fear of upsetting this equilibrium becomes the decisive force in his resistance toward analysis. The child's distrust of the enmity toward the analyst is thus often a displacement of his enmity and distrust of his instinctual impulses.

We repeat: during both periods of latency, neurotic children see as a principal task the warding off of incestuous fantasies and masturbatory temptations. They accomplish this task by means of partial regression. The ego during this period is engaged in deflecting the sexual energy from its pregenital aims and is utilizing it for sublimation and reaction formation. But in neither periods do they fully succeed and a close-up of this period shows the ego in a ceaseless, though quickly repressed, battle against the temptation to masturbate. It appears to us that adult patients give a distorted picture of their latency. They are inclined to remember this period as one in which they had in reality attained what Freud described as the *ideal of latency:* the successful warding off of instinctual demands. The impression retained of latency period is understandable when one takes into account with what amazing rapidity (even in analysis) children repress or deny the occasional breakthroughs of their masturbatory activities. The child's behavior during the latency period might be described as one of persistent denial of the struggle against the breakthrough of instinctual impulses, a denial which extends into adulthood as a partial amnesia for this period. This may be one of the reasons why one learns relatively little about latency from the analysis of adults.

The form of analytic technique with latency children must be in accordance with the specific characteristics of the psychic structure we have just described. Because the child battles against his impulses and needs to keep up his defenses, we must be particularly careful to respect his resistance, and to work through his defenses before we approach the material which is warded off. We know how difficult it is for a child in latency to tell us anything about his inner life.

We have learned to utilize substitutes for free associations, such as play, drawings and stories, which enable us to draw conclusions about id contents, but unlike the adult's free association, these substitute media do not, to the same extent, furnish material on defenses or their genesis. Whatever these media represent, we do not use them for the interpretation of id contents, but as a source of knowledge of the child, and as a stepping stone toward the analysis of defense and of affects.

Since free association is not applicable in latency, defense analysis is more complicated in the analysis of children than in that of an adult. We are forced to search for defenses by microscopic observation of the total behavior of the child.

So far my remarks were theoretical. Let me now turn to an example, illustrating the technique of defense analysis as it was employed in the handling of a daydream a ten-year-old boy told during his treatment. The patient's character disturbance found expression in his complicated relationship with his father and his brothers with whom he competed and toward whom he harbored strong passive desires. Like most children he was apt to forget painful experiences in reality.

His daydreams were important for us not only because they represented a superstructure of a masturbatory fantasy, but because their appearance in the analytic situation signaled a current humiliating experience and permitted the reconstruction of his reaction to such experiences.

After a period of analysis in which we had worked on his desire to compete with his father

and his older brothers which at times had not led further than to an identification with their gestures, he made a *conscious* effort to combat his display of competition. At the beginning of his analysis, he openly played at being important men like generals and admirals; now, in his daydreams, he revealed a modification of these wishes. Motivated by the desire to please the analyst, he made a strong point of telling me that in his daydream he himself was a ten-year-old boy and that in reality he no longer sought to compete with his father but wanted to remain a boy of his own age.

In his daydreams, however, young as he was, he was a famous brain surgeon, and had also discovered a cure for cancer. He attended school during the day, of course, but nevertheless General Eisenhower had heard that our patient was a famous brain surgeon and ordered the boy night after night to the battle field to perform his famous operations on outstanding generals. The brains of those generals were shattered by bullets or their lives were endangered by brain tumors. It was through his restoring the generals' mental capacity that the United States won the war.

Up to this point his daydream emphasized that nobody at school knew about his fame as a brain surgeon. One day a variation of the daydream occurred. A policeman entered the class room and asked about a car that was not parked correctly. It turned out to be our patient's car; in this way everyone at school suddenly learned that he not only had, as he said, a "doctor's certificate," but in recognition of his outstanding services, he had also been granted a driver's license. Our knowledge of his tendencies to react to slight narcissistic injuries with ideas of greatness made us inquire about a defeat at school. We asked whether anything had happened at school, whether anyone had offended him, etc. He told us, though not immediately, that a man teacher had commented on his continuous yawning during class and that it was at this moment that his exhibitionism broke through in his daydream.

As we said before, our interest in a daydream is not aimed at immediately reaching the masturbatory fantasy which it elaborates. What we take out of it, is a knowledge of the typical defenses and the reaction to affects. Although this would be true of almost any production of the child, I have selected the daydream precisely because it is so close to the unconscious; yet it should be used to deal with defense and affect rather than with the instinctual impulses. Since defense and affect are closer to the ego than the impulse, we are able, through them, to make interpretations which the child can recognize and accept without undue resistance. Once a defense appears, we can assume that it is typical for particular situations, and that the identical affect or impulse is present whenever the defense reappears. This being so, whenever a defense is noticed, one can bring to the child's attention the event and the affect to which he had reacted. What has been said about defenses applies in a general way to affects. Wherever we observe an inappropriate expression of affect, we can assume that the ego has intervened. As Anna Freud said: from the transformations which the affect has undergone, we can deduce the specific defenses used against them and we can also assume that the same defenses are used against the instinctual impulses which originally gave rise to these affects.

Let us return to the daydream and scrutinize it from the standpoint of defense and affect. Our young daydreamer, we have seen, reacted to a painful reality situation by *denial in fantasy*. He was not the little boy whom a teacher could scold, but an important surgeon who wielded the power of life and death over the commanders of many men.

Another element in his reaction to the reprimand was a feeling of shame. The shame could not be consciously admitted, because of its associative connection with his passivity. In his daydream, he reverses the shame into glory. The shame was secret, the glory was public. Whenever our patient used the mechanism of reversal, we were sure that behind it was an instinctual impulse which clamored for discharge, and against which the boy rebelled. For instance, the daydream in which our patient performs nocturnal brain surgery on generals becomes meaningful if understood as representing its opposite. You will not be surprised to hear that the daydream took form in a period in which the boy fought against his identification with women. His surgical activity, and his removal of foreign bodies from the head, was the opposite of his *unconscious wish* to be a woman who gives birth to a child.

There were other affects involved which had to be examined. In a school situation, in which a teacher reprimanded a pupil, we would expect the child to experience some anger. This the child did not. No anger had appeared. It was obvious that he consciously could not tolerate any aggression against men. In order to prevent the impulse from appearing, the appropriate affect had to be repressed. Asked about how he had really felt, the child answered good-humoredly: "I really was not angry, I had fun with my daydream. I would really like to become a brain surgeon."

Some time after the boy spoke scornfully about his daydream: "Gee, I'm really a fool, here I am talking about curing the generals from brain tumors, and I don't even know anything about the brain, how the nerves are working and the blood cells, and what makes the heart beat, and what makes a man's muscles hard as bones."

His thirst for knowledge, the desire to learn about physiology and anatomy, remained untouched by our analytic interpretation, although they were rooted in the same conflicts that showed up in the daydream.

In concluding I should like to emphasize that I have discussed primarily the neurotic child and his latency. All children in latency, however, not only the neurotic ones, use their free energies for character development. Therefore it is particularly important during latency not to interfere with healthy character formation. The utmost care has to be exercised in the analysis of latency to strengthen weak structures and to modify those which interfere with normal development. The selection of material for interpretation and the form of interpretation itself must be geared to these ends.

THE PSYCHOSOCIAL ORIGINS
OF ACHIEVEMENT MOTIVATION

BERNARD C. ROSEN   ROY D'ANDRADE

The purpose of this study is to examine the origins of achievement motivation (*n* Achievement) within the context of the individual's membership in two important groups: family and social class. Specifically, this paper explores, through the observation of family interaction, the relationship between achievement motivation and certain child-training practices, and the relationship between these practices and the parents' social class membership.

The importance of group membership for personality development has been demonstrated many times. Perhaps the most important of these groups is the family, whose strategic role in the socialization process has led investigators to study the nexus between child-rearing practices and motivation formation. Thus, Winterbottom (1958) examined the relationship between independence-mastery training and achievement motivation and found that achievement motivation is strongest among boys whose mothers (all of whom were middle class) expected relatively early indications of self-reliance and mastery from them.

Since many socialization practices are known to be dissimilar between social groups (Ericson, 1947; Havighurst & Davis, 1955), it might be expected that independence training practices would also differ. A study by McClelland, Rindlisbacher, and de Charms (1955), later replicated by Rosen (1959), demonstrated this to be the case: middle-class parents place greater stress upon independence training than lower class parents. The deduction from this finding that classes differ in their level of *n*

Reprinted by permission of the authors and the American Sociological Association from *Sociometry*, 1959, **22,** 185–95, 215–18.

Achievement was shown to be correct by Rosen (1956) who found that, on the average, *n* Achievement scores for middle-class adolescents were significantly higher than those for their lower class counterparts.

Significantly, although these studies flow logically from one another, in none of them were all three variables—group membership, child training practices, and *n* Achievement—studied simultaneously. Furthermore, there were certain gaps in these studies which called for theoretical and methodological modifications and additions. The nature of these gaps, and the contributions which it was the research objective of this study to make, are as follows:

THEORETICAL   The keystone around which studies of the origins of achievement motivation have been built is the notion that training in independent mastery is an antecedent condition of *n* Achievement (McClelland & Friedman, 1952; Winterbottom, 1958). This approach grew out of McClelland's and his associates' theory of the nature and origins of motivation. They argue that all motives are learned, that "they develop out of repeated affective experiences connected with certain types of situations and types of behavior. In the case of achievement motivation, the situation should involve 'standards of excellence,' presumably imposed on the child by the culture, or more particularly by the parents as representatives of the culture, and the behavior should involve either 'competition' with those standards of excellence or attempts to meet them which, if successful, produce positive affect or, if unsuccessful, negative affect. It follows that those cultures or families which stress competition with standards of excellence or which insist *that the child be able to perform certain tasks well by himself* . . . should produce children with high achievement motivation" (McClelland, Atkinson, Clark, & Lowell, 1953).

Two distinctly different kinds of child-training practices are implicit in this theory. The first is the idea that the child is trained to do things "well"; the second, the notion that he is trained to perform tasks "by himself." The former has been called *achievement training* (Child, Storm, & Veroff, 1958) in that it stresses competition in situations involving standards of excellence; the latter has been called *independence training* in that it involves putting the child on his own. The failure to disentangle these two concepts has resulted in a focus of attention upon independence training largely to the exclusion of achievement training, although the former is primarily concerned with developing self-reliance, often in areas involving self-caretaking (e.g., cleaning, dressing, amusing, or defending oneself). Although both kinds of training practices frequently occur together, they are different in content and consequences and needed to be examined separately. We believe that of the two training practices, achievement training is the more effective in generating *n* Achievement.

There is another component of independence training—one which is explicit in the idea of independence—that needed further exploration: *autonomy*. By autonomy, we mean training and permitting the child to exercise a certain amount of freedom of action in decision making. Although a related aspect of autonomy—*power*—was studied by Strodtbeck (1958), who examined the relationship between power distribution in the family, *n* Achievement, and academic achievement among a group of Jewish and Italian adolescents, no study had examined simultaneously the self-reliance and autonomy components of independence training. The operation of both components, we believed, tends to increase the power of independence training to generate *n* Achievement, since in itself high parental expectations for self-reliance may cause rebellion, feelings of rejection, or of apathy on the part of the child, while autonomy without parental expectations for self-reliance

and achievement may be perceived as mere permissiveness or indifference.

In association with parental demands that the child be self-reliant, autonomous, and show evidence of high achievement, there must be sanctions to see that these demands are fulfilled. Winterbottom found that mothers of children with high *n* Achievement gave somewhat more intense rewards than mothers of children with low *n* Achievement. Little was known about the role of negative sanctions, or of the relative impact of sanctions from either parent. Further study was required of the degree and kind of sanctions employed by both parents to see that their demands are met.

METHODOLOGICAL   This study departed from two practices common in studies of the origins of *n* Achievement. The first practice is to derive data exclusively from ethnographic materials; the second, to obtain information through questionnaire-type interviews with mothers. Interviews and ethnographies can be valuable sources of information, but they are often contaminated by interviewer and respondent biases, particularly those of perceptual distortion, inadequate recall, and deliberate inaccuracies. There was a need for data derived from systematic observation of parent-child relations. It is not enough to know what parents *say* their child-rearing practices are; these statements should be checked against more objective data, preferably acquired under controlled experimental conditions, that would permit us to *see* what they do. In this study, experiments were employed which enabled a team of investigators to observe parent-child interaction in problem-solving situations that were standardized for all groups and required no special competence associated with age or sex.

An equally strong objection can be raised against the tendency to ignore the father's role in the development of the child's need to achieve. Apart from an earlier study of father-son power relations, no efforts had been made to determine the father's contribution to achievement and independence training—a surprising omission even granted the mother's importance in socializing the child in American society. Although we were not prepared to take a position on the nature of the role relationships between father, mother, and son with respect to this motive, we deliberately created experimental conditions which would enable us to observe the way in which the three members of the family interacted in a problem-solving situation. Finally, this study incorporated in one design the variables of group membership, child-training practices, and motivation, variables that heretofore had not been studied simultaneously. In so doing we hoped to establish the nexus among class membership, socialization practices, and achievement motivation.

HYPOTHESES

This study was designed to provide data that would permit testing two basic hypotheses.

1. Achievement motivation is a result of the following socialization practices: (a) *achievement training,* in which the parents set high goals for their son to attain, indicate that they have a high evaluation of his competence to do a task well, and impose standards of excellence upon tasks against which he is to compete, even in situations where such standards are not explicit; (b) *independence training,* in which the parents indicate to the child that they expect him to be *self-reliant,* while at the same time permit him relative *autonomy* in situations involving decision making where he is given both freedom of action and responsibility for success or failure; (c) *sanctions,* rewards and punishments employed by parents to ensure that their expectations are met and proper behavior is reinforced. Although each contributes to the development of achievement motivation, achievement training is more important than independence training. Neither [is] effective without supporting sanctions.

2. Differences in the mean level of achievement motivation between social classes is in part a function of the differential class emphases upon independence and achievement training: middle-class parents are more likely than lower class parents to stress self-reliance, autonomy, and achievement in problem-solving situations, particularly those involving standards of excellence. They are more likely to recognize and reward evidences of achievement, as well

as to be more sensitive of and punitive toward indications of failure.

EXPERIMENTAL PROCEDURE

The subjects selected to provide data needed for the testing of these hypotheses about the origins of achievement motivation were 120 persons who made up 40 family groups composed of a father, mother, and their son, aged nine, ten, or eleven. The selection of the family groups began with testing the boy. Seven schools in three northeastern Connecticut towns were visited by the same field worker who administered a Thematic Apperception Test individually and privately to 140 boys, aged nine, ten, or eleven. As is customary in the TAT procedure, the subject was presented with a set of four ambiguous pictures and asked to tell a story about each. His imaginative responses were then scored according to a method developed by McClelland and his associates which involves identifying and counting the frequency with which imagery about evaluated performance in competition with a standard of excellence appears in the thoughts of a person when he tells a brief story under time pressure. Experience has shown that this imagery can be identified objectively and reliably. It is the assumption of this test that the more the individual shows indications of evaluated performance connected with affect in his fantasy, the greater the degree to which achievement motivation is part of his personality (McClelland et al., 1953). The stories were scored by two judges; the Pearsonian coefficient of correlation between scorers was .87, a level of reliability similar to those reported in earlier studies with this measure.

Subjects with scores of plus 2 to minus 4 (approximately the bottom quartile) were labeled as having low *n* Achievement, those with scores of plus 9 to plus 22 (approximately the top quartile) as having high *n* Achievement. Any boy with an I.Q. score below 98, with physical defects, whose parents were separated, or who had been raised during part of his life by persons or relatives other than his parents (e.g., grandparents) was eliminated from the sample.

Forty boys, matched by age, race, I.Q., and social class were chosen for further study. All were white, native born, and between nine and eleven years of age; the average was ten years. Half of the boys had high *n* Achievement scores, half had low scores. In each achievement motivation category, half of the boys were middle class, half were lower class. Their social class position was determined according to a modified version of the Hollingshead Index of Social Position (1953) which uses the occupation and education of the chief wage-earner—usually the father—as the principal criteria of status. The middle-class father (class II or III) held either a professional, managerial, white-collar position or was self-employed as an owner of a small- to medium-size business. Often one or both parents in middle-class families were college graduates; all were high-school graduates. The parents of lower class (IV or V) boys were quasi-skilled or skilled workers in local factories, or owners of very small farms—often the farmers held factory jobs as well. Relatively few of these parents had completed high school, none had gone beyond high school.

It can be seen that the study was designed in such a way that the subjects fell into one of four cells, with the achievement motivation level of the boys and the class position of the parents as the classificatory variables. Within each cell there were ten families. This four-cell factorial design was constructed so as to facilitate the use of the analysis of variance technique in the statistical analysis of the data.

. . . A pair of observers visited each family group, usually at night. There were two teams of observers, each composed of a man and woman. Both teams had been trained together to ensure adequate intra- and interteam reliability.

Once in the home, the observers explained that they were interested in studying the factors related to success in school and eventually to a career, and that the son was one of many boys selected from a cross-section of the community. When rapport had been established, the parents and their son were placed at a table—usually in the kitchen—and it was explained that the boy was going to perform certain tasks.

Experimental Tasks

. . . Tasks were devised which the boy could do and which would involve the parents in their son's task performance. The tasks were constructed so that the subjects were often faced with a choice of giving or refusing help. . . . A category system, similar to the Bales system (1951), was devised to permit scoring interaction between parents and son so that the amount and form of each subject's participation could be examined. The investigators were able to learn from . . . interaction data how self-reliant the parents expected their son to be, how much autonomy they permitted him in decision-making situations, and what kind and amount of affect was generated in a problem-solving situation. . . .

The five tasks used in this study are as follows:

1. *Block Stacking.* The boys were asked to build towers out of very irregularly shaped blocks. They were blindfolded and told to use only one hand in order to create a situation in which the boy was relatively dependent upon his parents for help. His parents were told that this was a test of their son's ability to build things, and that they could *say* anything to their son but could not touch the blocks. A performance norm was set for the experiment by telling the parents that the average boy could build a tower of eight blocks; they were asked to write down privately their estimate of how high they thought their son could build his tower. The purposes of this experiment were (a) to see how high were the parents' aspirations for and evaluations of their son, e.g., if they set their estimates at, above, or below the norm; (b) to see how self-reliant they expected or permitted their son to be, e.g., how much help they would give him.

There were three trials for this task. The first provided measures of parental evaluations and aspirations not affected by the boy's performance; the second and third trial estimates provided measures affected by the boy's performance. The procedure for the third trial differed from the first two in that the boy was told that he would be given a nickel for each block he stacked. Each member of the family was asked to estimate privately how high the boy should build his tower. No money would be given for blocks stacked higher than the estimate nor would the subject receive anything if the stack tumbled before he reached the estimate. Conservative estimates, hence, provided security but little opportunity for gain; high estimates involved more opportunity for gain but greater risk. The private estimates were then revealed to all and the family was asked to reach a group decision. In addition to securing objective measures of parental aspiration-evaluation levels, the observers scored the interaction between subjects, thus obtaining data as to the kind and amount of instructions the parents gave their son, the amount of help the son asked for or rejected, and the amount and kind of affect generated during the experiment.

2. *Anagrams.* In this task the boys were asked to make words of three letters or more out of six prescribed letters: G, H, K, N, O, R. The letters, which could be reused after each word was made, were printed on wooden blocks so that they could be manipulated. The parents were given three additional lettered blocks, T, U, and B, and a list of words that could be built with each new letter. They were informed that they could give the boy a new letter (in the sequence T, U, B) whenever they wished and could say anything to him, short of telling him what word to build. There was a ten-minute time limit for this experiment. Since this is a familiar game, no efforts were made to explain the functions of the task.

The purposes of this experiment were: (a) to see how self-reliant the parents expected their son to be, e.g., how soon they would give him a new letter, how much and what kind of direction they would give him, if they would keep him working until he got all or most of the words on the list or "take him off the hook" when he got stuck. And (b) to obtain, by scoring interaction between the subjects, measures of the affect generated by the problem-solving process, e.g., the amount of tension shown by the subjects, the positive and negative remarks directed toward one another.

3. *Patterns.* In this experiment the parents were shown eight patterns, graduated in difficulty, that could be made with Kohs blocks.

The subjects were informed that pattern 1 was easier to make than pattern 2, pattern 3 was more difficult than 2 but easier than 4, and so forth. The subjects were told that this was a test of the boy's ability to remember and reproduce patterns quickly and accurately. Each parent and boy was asked to select privately three patterns which the boy would be asked to make from memory after having seen the pattern for five seconds. All three patterns were chosen *before* the boy began the problem solving so that his performance in this task would not affect the choice of the patterns. Where there were differences of choice, as inevitably there were, the subjects were asked to discuss their differences and make a group decision. Insofar as possible the observers took a verbatim account of the decision-making process, scoring for three kinds of variables: (a) the number of acts each subject contributed to the decision-making process, (b) the number of times each individual initiated a decision, and (c) the number of times each subject was successful in having the group accept his decision or in seeing to it that a decision was made.

The purposes of this experiment were: (a) to obtain another measure of the parents' evaluations of and aspirations for the boy, e.g., whether they would pick easy or difficult tasks for him to do; (b) to get a measure of the autonomy permitted the boy, e.g., whether they would let him choose his own patterns or impose their choices upon him; and (c) to see how much help they would give him and what affect would be generated by the experiment.

4. *Ring Toss.* In this experiment each member of the group was asked to choose privately ten positions, from each of which the boy was to throw three rings at a peg. The distance from the peg was delineated by a tape with 1-foot graduations laid on the floor. The subjects were told that this was a test of discrimination and judgment and that after each set of three tosses they would be asked to make a judgment as to the best distance from which to make the next set of tosses. Group decisions were made as to where the boy should stand. The purposes of this experiment were: (a) to see whether the parents imposed standards of excellence upon a task for which no explicit

TABLE I

The System of Categories Used in Scoring Parent-Child Interaction

+X	Expresses approval, gives love, comfort, affection
+T	Shows positive tension release, jokes, laughs
+E	Gives explicit positive evaluation of performance, indicates job well done
+P	Attempts to push up performance through expression of enthusiasm, urges, cheers on
N	Gives nonspecific directions, gives hints, clues, general suggestions
S	Gives specific directions, gives detailed information about how to do a task
aa	Asks aid, information, or advice
ra	Rejects aid, information, or advice
−P	Attempts to push up performance through expressions of displeasure; urges on, indicating disappointment at speed and level of performance
−E	Gives explicit negative evaluation of performance, indicates job poorly done
−T	Shows negative tension release, shows irritation, coughs
−X	Expresses hostility, denigrates, makes sarcastic remarks

standard had been set, e.g., whether the parents would treat this as a childish game or see it as a task which could and should be done well. Would they choose easy or difficult positions? (b) To determine how much autonomy they permitted their son, e.g., would they let him choose his own position?

5. *Hatrack.* The Maier Hatrack Problem was used in this experiment. The boy was given two sticks and a C-clamp and instructed to build a rack strong enough to hold a coat and hat. His parents were told that this was a test of the boy's ability to build things. In this task no one was given the solution at the beginning of the experiment. For the first time the parents had no advantage over the boy—a most uncomfortable position for many parents, particularly the fathers. This stress situation was created deliberately to maximize the possibility of the problem generating affect, as was often the case, with some hostility being directed at the observers. After seven minutes the parents were given the solution to the problem. The purposes of this experiment were: (a) to see how self-reliant the parents expected their son to be. After receiving the solution what kind of clues would the parents give the boy? How hard would they expect him to work on his own? (b) to obtain measures of the affect

created in an unusually frustrating situation. How would the parents handle their frustration? Would they turn it against the boy?

Category System

References have been made to the use of a category system for scoring interaction between subjects. A brief description of this system, shown in Table 1, is in order. Most of the subjects' verbal and some of their motor behavior (e.g., laughing, handclapping, scowling) was scored in one of twelve categories. In eight of these categories were placed acts involving relatively strong affect. Four additional categories were used to distinguish between various kinds of statements—either giving, requesting, or rejecting directions—which contained very little or no affect. A distinction was made between negative and positive affective acts. Affective acts associated with explicit or implicit evaluations of the boy's performance which aimed at motivating or changing his behavior were scored differently from affective acts which involved reactions to the boy and only indirectly to his performance.

Directional acts by the parents were remarks designed to help the boy perform his task. A distinction was made between *specific* directions (S) which were acts instructing the subject to do particular things which would facilitate task completion, and *nonspecific* (N) which were acts aimed at giving the subject some information but not specific enough to enable him to rely entirely upon it. It was believed that nonspecific statements were more likely than specific statements to create self-reliance in the child.

The affective acts were schematized in two sets—one positive, the other negative. The first set was comprised of acts involving direct expressions of emotions toward another person, not necessarily in the context of task performance, either of a positive character (+X), such as expressions of love or approval, or of a negative character (−X), such as indications of hostility and rejection. Another set was of acts involving release of tension, either associated with positive affect (+T) such as grins, laughter, jokes, or negative affect (−T) such as scowls, coughs, or irritated gestures. Tension-release acts differ from acts of direct emotion (X) in that the former were not focused toward any person but were diffused, undirected reactions to the general situation. The next set of acts involved parental evaluation of the boy's performance. Those acts in which the parents stated that the boy was doing the task well were scored as positive evaluations (+E), while statements that the boy was doing poorly were scored as negative evaluations (−E). The last two categories involved acts aimed at urging or pushing the boy to perform more effectively. These "pushing up the performance level acts" were scored in one of two categories. Those acts in which the parents "cheered" the boy on while at the same time indicating that they expected him to do better were scored as positive pushing acts (+P); negative pushing acts (−P) were statements in which the parents sought to improve the boy's performance by indicating in a threatening way that they thought he could do better.

Only four kinds of acts were scored for the boy: whether he asked for aid (aa), rejected aid (ra), showed positive tension (+T) or negative tension (−T). An act was defined as the smallest segment of verbal or motor behavior which could be recognized as belonging to one of the twelve categories in the system.

The actor rather than the target of the acts was used as the observer's frame of reference. . . .

DISCUSSION AND SUMMARY

The question of how achievement training, independence training, and sanctions are related to achievement motivation may be rephrased by asking, How does the behavior of parents of boys with high *n* Achievement differ from the behavior of parents whose sons have low *n* Achievement?

To begin with, the observers' subjective impressions are that the parents of high *n* Achievement boys tend to be more competitive, show more involvement, and seem to take more pleasure in the problem-solving experiments. They appear to be more interested [in] and concerned with their son's performance; they tend to give him more things to manipulate rather than fewer; on the average they put out more affective acts. More objective data show that the parents of a boy with high *n* Achievement tend to have higher aspirations for him to do well at any given task and they seem to have a higher regard for his competence at problem solving. They set up standards of excellence for the boy even when none is given, or if a standard is given will expect him to do "better than average." As he progresses they tend to react to his performance with warmth and approval, or, in the case of the mothers especially, with disapproval if he performs poorly.

It seems clear that achievement training contributes more to the development of *n* Achievement than does independence training. Indeed, the role of independence training in generating achievement motivation can only be understood in the context of what appears to be a division of labor between the fathers and mothers of high *n* Achievement boys.

Fathers and mothers both provide achievement training and independence training, but the fathers seem to contribute much more to the latter than do the mothers. Fathers tend to let their sons develop some self-reliance by giving hints (N) rather than always telling "how to do it" (S). They are less likely to push (P) and more likely to give the boy a greater degree of autonomy in making his own decisions. Fathers of high *n* Achievement boys often appear to be competent men who are willing to take a back seat while their sons are performing. They tend to beckon from ahead rather than push from behind.

The mothers of boys with high achievement motivation tend to stress achievement training rather than independence training. In fact, they are likely to be more dominant and to expect less self-reliance than the mothers of boys with low *n* Achievement. But their aspirations for their sons are higher and their concern over success greater. Thus, they expect the boys to build higher towers and place them farther away from the peg in the Ring Toss experiment. As a boy works his mother tends to become emotionally involved. Not only is she more likely to reward him with approval (Warmth) but also to punish him with hostility (Rejection). *In a way, it is this factor of involvement that most clearly sets the mothers of high* n *Achievement boys apart from the mothers of low* n *Achievement boys:* the former score higher on every variable, expect specific directions. And although these mothers are likely to give their sons more option as to exactly (fewer Specifics) what to do, they give them less option about doing something and doing it well. Observers report that the mothers of high *n* Achievement boys tend to be striving, competent persons. Apparently they expect their sons to be the same.

The different emphasis which the fathers and mothers of high *n* Achievement boys place upon achievement and independence training suggests that the training practices of father and mother affect the boy in different ways. Apparently, the boy can take and perhaps needs achievement training from both parents, but the effects of independence training and sanctions, in particular Autonomy and Rejection, are different depending upon whether they come from the father or mother. In order for high *n* Achievement to develop, the boy appears to need more autonomy from his father than from his mother. The father who gives the boy a relatively high degree of autonomy provides him with an opportunity to compete on his own ground, to test his skill, and to gain a

sense of confidence in his own competence. The dominating father may crush his son (and in so doing destroys the boy's achievement motive), perhaps because he views the boy as a competitor and is viewed as such by his son. On the other hand, the mother who dominates the decision-making process does not seem to have the same effect on the boy, possibly because she is perceived as *imposing her standards* on the boy, while a dominating father is perceived as *imposing himself* on the son. It may be that the mother-son relations are typically more secure than those between father and son, so that the boy is better able to accept higher levels of dominance and rejection from his mother than his father without adverse effect on his need to achieve. Relatively rejecting, dominating fathers, particularly those with less than average warmth—as tended to be the case with the fathers of low *n* Achievement boys—seem to be a threat to the boy[s] and a deterrent to the development of *n* Achievement. On the other hand, above-average dominance and rejection, coupled with above-average warmth, as tends to be the case with mothers of high *n* Achievement boys, appear to be a spur to achievement motivation. It will be remembered that the fathers of high *n* Achievement boys are on the average less Rejecting, less Pushing, and less Dominant—all of which points to their general hands-off policy.

It is unlikely that these variables operate separately, but the way in which they interact in the development of achievement motivation is not clear. Possibly the variables interact in a manner which produces cyclical effects roughly approximating the interaction that characterized the experimental task situations of this study. The cycle begins with the parents imposing standards of excellence upon a task and setting a high goal for the boy to achieve (e.g., Ring Toss, estimates and choices in Block Stacking and Patterns). As the boy engages in the task, they reinforce acceptable behavior by expressions of warmth (both parents) or by evidences of disapproval (primarily mother). The boy's performance improves, in part because of previous experience and in part because of the greater concern shown by his parents and expressed through affective reaction to his performance and greater attention to his training. With improved performance, the parents grant the boy greater autonomy and interfere less with his performance (primarily father). Goals are then reset at a higher level and the cycle continues.

REFERENCES

Bales, R. F. *Interaction process analysis.* Reading, Mass.: Addison-Wesley, 1951.

Child, I. L., Storm, T., & Veroff, J. Achievement themes in folk tales related to socialization practice. In J. W. Atkinson, *Motives in fantasy, action, and society.* Princeton, N.J.: Van Nostrand, 1958.

Ericson, Martha C. Social status and child-rearing practices. In T. M. Newcomb & E. L. Hartley (Eds.), *Readings in social psychology.* New York: Holt, 1947.

Havighurst, R. J., & Davis, A. Social class differences in child-rearing. *Amer. sociol. Rev.* 1955, 20, 438–442.

Hollingshead, A. B., & Redlich, F. C. Social stratification and psychiatric disorders. *Amer. sociol. Rev.* 1953, 18, 163–169.

McClelland, D. C., & Friedman, G. A. A cross-cultural study of the relationship between child-training practices and achievement motivation, appearing in folk tales. In G. E. Swanson, T. M. Newcomb, & E. L. Hartley (Eds.), *Readings in social psychology.* New York: Holt, 1952.

McClelland, D. C., Atkinson, J. W., Clark, R. A., & Lowell, E. L. *The achievement motive.* New York: Appleton-Century-Crofts, 1953.

McClelland, D. C., Rindlisbacher, A., & de Charms, R. Religious and other sources of parental attitudes toward independence training. In D. C. McClelland *et al.* (Eds.), *Studies in motivation.* New York: Appleton-Century-Crofts, 1955.

Rosen, B. C. The achievement syndrome: a psychocultural dimension of social stratification. *Amer. sociol. Rev.* 1956, 21, 203–211.

Rosen, B. C. Race, ethnicity, and the achievement syndrome. *Amer. sociol. Rev.* 1959, 24, 47–60.

Sakoda, J. M. Directions for a multiple-group method of factor analysis. Univer. of Connecticut, June, 1955. (Mimeographed.)

Sears, R. R., Maccoby, Eleanor E., & Levin, H. *Patterns of child rearing.* New York: Row, Peterson, 1957.

Strodtbeck, F. L. Family interaction, values, and achievement. In D. C. McClelland, A. L. Baldwin, U. Bronfenbrenner, & F. L. Strodtbeck, *Talent and society.* Princeton, N.J.: Van Nostrand, 1958.

Tryon, R. C. *Cluster analysis.* Ann Arbor, Mich.: Edwards Brothers, 1939.

Winterbottom, M. R. The relation of need for achievement to learning experiences in independence and mastery. In J. W. Atkinson, *Motives in fantasy, action, and society.* Princeton, N.J.: Van Nostrand, 1958.

PART SIX

SOCIALIZING AGENTS: THE HOME, THE SCHOOL, AND THE PEER GROUP

The thesis of the editors of this anthology has been that the child acquires knowledge, develops a unique personality, and becomes a member of society as he interacts with significant others from infancy on. "Significant others" include mother, father, and other caretakers; and siblings, peers, and teachers. In this section we deal chiefly with the parents, the school, and peers as socializing agents. One could argue that television should be included here. We have already mentioned in Part 4 the role the "tube" plays in providing models for the child to imitate, but unfortunately we cannot do much more, for the influence of television-viewing on child development and behavior has yet to be assessed adequately.

THE PARENTS, THE CHILD, AND CHILD-REARING PRACTICES

In any discussion of socializing agents, the mother or mother-substitute is first in importance. Man is unique among animals in that his adaptation depends on his assimilation of the cultural heritage of his people. Unless each infant assimilates that heritage, he will be no more capable of coping with his environment than his prehistoric ancestors (Lidz, 1963). Fortunately he is biologically endowed with a central nervous system that includes a brain with a large language center, which enables him to acquire what previous generations have to transmit. And fortunately he is born helpless, which makes him amenable to discipline and training while he is receiving the nurturance he needs for survival. It is typically the mother who provides that nurturance and who, along with giving physical care and love, shapes the infant's behavior to conform with societal norms. Even before he has learned to talk, the infant has learned a great deal about what society expects of him in the way of eating behavior, toilet habits, cleanliness, dependency, and postponement of the immediate gratification of needs.

The dimensions of the mother-child relationship as they affect behavior have received considerable attention in the literature. We have seen in the papers by Bell and Ainsworth in Part 3 how the quality of care in infancy can affect development of attachment behavior, and how the quality of infant-mother attachment can affect the development of the concept of object. And we have seen in the Bayley and Schaefer paper in Part 4 how maternal behavior correlates with the development of mental abilities. In this section we call attention to the *reciprocal* nature of the mother-child relationship. Not only does the parent modify the child's behavior, but the child also affects the parent's behavior. Both are participants in a social system. The paper by Bell included here considers the stimulus effects of the child on parent-child interactions.

The dimensions of maternal care have been studied systematically and a number of models have been developed to show the important factors and possible clusters of factors in parent-child relations. Some that show up repeatedly in different models are: permissiveness, restrictiveness, or democracy; warmth or hostility; purposiveness or aimlessness; protectiveness or lack of concern; punishment or non-punishment. The diagram on page 250 reproduces Schaefer's circumplex model. Such models are useful in investigating the antecedents of certain child behaviors. For example, the effects of the warmth-hostility dimension and the permissiveness-restrictiveness dimension on dependency (Maccoby and Masters, 1970) have been investigated in a number of studies. Both of these dimensions appear to be important not only to dependency, but to the development of aggression and impulse control.

Harmony and lack of harmony between parents have been studied as variables. Becker *et al.* (1959) found in their study of children referred to a psychological clinic that conduct problems (aggressiveness, uncontrollableness) in the child coincided with lack of harmony between parents in dealing with the child. Both parents of the problem children tended to be maladjusted, to give vent to unbridled emotions, and to be arbitrary with the child. In addition, the mother tended to be dictatorial and thwarting, whereas the father tended not to enforce regulations. However, since maladjustment of parents and disharmony are both factors in this study, it is difficult to assess the impact of lack of harmony alone upon the child. The report by Baumrind included here gives us a clearer picture of harmonious parents and their children. Eight families were pulled out of a larger sample and the effects of harmonious child-rearing on child development were discussed. The report is both interesting and timely since so many young people today are turning to communal living as a way of life.

The impact of absence of the father on the male child continues to be of interest, an interest fanned by the Moynihan Report (1965) characterizing black lower-class families as pathological due in large part to the absence of the father. However, presence of the father does not guarantee a stable family environment, and delinquent children, claim Moynihan's critics, are just as likely to come from intact families as father-absent families. Age of separation and the quality of the son's relationship with his mother are both important. Biller and Bahm (1971) found that if a boy lost his father for any reason after the age of five, the boy's masculine self-concept did not seem to be affected. But if the boy lost his father earlier, an interference with masculine identification was likely. However, the critical factor was the behavior of the mother. Where the boy perceived the mother as encouraging aggression, his self-concept was more likely to be masculine. Whether or not the boy perceived the mother as encouraging independent behavior was not significant. It would appear that, at least in the eyes of growing boys, aggression is the mark of masculinity.

THE TEACHER AS SOCIALIZING AGENT

That the teacher can effect changes in pupil behavior is fairly obvious. In nearly all but extreme cases a teacher can get children to conform to certain standards of classroom behavior and to carry out the learning tasks she assigns. In part this is because the school is a social institution with a highly stylized environment and well-established rituals which children are expected to learn and which they do learn or suffer the consequences. Studies such as Jackson's (1968) and Silberman's (1970) have emphasized the joylessness and drabness of much of school life. Jackson points out that classrooms are unique institutional settings. They require that the students learn to live in a crowd and, in fact, *alone* in a crowd, concentrating on work and not communicating with others; that they experience continual and public evaluation; that they learn to adjust to being "bossed around" by persons in positions of authority. To meet these requirements the students must acquire certain adaptive strategies that have relevance for other contexts and other life periods.

We have known since the late 1930's, and the classic study of classroom climates by Lewin, Lippitt, and White (1939), that a particular setting can induce the production of certain kinds of behavior. In that study, a boys' club was exposed to a democratic leader, a laissez-faire leader, and an authoritarian leader. Results indicated that such factors as group morale, sociability, and work habits were better under democratic leadership than under the other two types.

Teachers, as members of the middle class, try to instill a respect for the work ethic (not wasting time, working hard to get ahead), for property values (not wasting supplies), and for authority (obeying the teacher). The difficulty of establishing good teacher-pupil relationships in inner-city schools is evidence of the fact that teachers have a hard time imposing these norms on lower-class children. But whether the school really changes even middle-class children is also open to question. Middle-class students may conform by behaving in accordance with the institutional norms, but they may do so without being changed in any fundamental way. In fact, what knowledge there is of personality development tends to support the notion of stability of individual personality and behavior through time. Martin (1964) studied dependency, nurturance, aggression, control-dominance, autonomous achievement, avoidance-withdrawal, and friendship-affiliation in preschool children over a period of four semesters, and found that 80 percent of the children maintained a stable personality profile and exhibited a pattern of social behavior that was strikingly unchanged during the nursery-school years. Cultural support of certain traits helps; Kagan and Moss (1962) report sex differences with respect to stability of passive and dependent behaviors. Such behaviors were quite stable for women, less so for men. The investigators attribute the difference to the social acceptance of passive and dependent behavior in females.

There have also been studies focusing directly on the question of whether school does indeed influence certain aspects of personality and behavior. Ogle (1971) investigated the long-term effects of three different types of nursery-school curricula on anxiety level, self-esteem, and internal versus external controls (willingness to accept responsibility for one's actions). One group of children had been exposed for two years to a highly structured, rote-type curriculum with certain harsh and punitive features (the original Bereiter-Engelmann Program); a second group was also exposed to a structured curriculum, but with nonpunitive teachers; the third group was a traditional nursery school emphasizing social-emotional development. Although one might hypothesize that a setting that was often harsh and demanding might make children more anxious and might lower self-esteem, Ogle found no significant differences in children at the second-grade level in the variables that he studied.

Several explanations might be offered for the negative findings. One is that children's basic character and personality are formed by what has been experienced in the family during the very early years, and that this basic character tends to persist. The school can mold school behavior, as the Bronfenbrenner study of Soviet schools (included here) illustrates for the U.S.S.R. and which the behavior modification school (represented here by the Becker *et al.* study) illustrates for the United States. But each child enters the classroom with a set of preformed attitudes including feelings about one's self and one's ability to perform competently, feelings about being evaluated, feelings about authority figures. A harsh, demanding setting may have only temporary, if any, effects on such preformed attitudes.

School phobia, or morbid dread of school, results from feelings the child brings with him to school. In school phobia, the child's morbid fears of, for example, losing a parent or of injury to himself, are displaced onto the school (Sarason *et al.*, 1960). These fears may manifest themselves in active resistance to going to school, but in less extreme cases they are expressed as anxiety about specific aspects of the school situation—the teacher, peers, learning to read, recess. The Waldfogel *et al.* paper included here analyzes the development of school phobia. The process of adjusting to school may bring conflicts into the open, and the teacher's way of handling the conflict may damage the child's ability to adjust, but rarely does she effect a profound change. By serving as a model, by meting out rewards and punishments, she can weaken or strengthen behaviors already present, but generally she does not change the personality of the child in any significant way.

THE PEER GROUP

The influence of his peers on the American child has generally been recognized to be a pervasive and important one. Beginning with the young child in nursery school, investigators have explored several facets of that influence and described the process by which peers become an important influence on the child.

Several studies show the influence of modeling on the behavior of the young child. Hartup and Coates (1967) found that preschool subjects who observed sharing behaviors of another child exhibited more such altruistic behaviors than subjects who had not. And in a modeling study by Bandura, Grusec, and Menlove (1967), children rated as fearful of dogs showed a reduction in avoidance behavior, even after a month's interval, after having observed a brave child interacting with a dog. Teachers and parents both can attest to the fact that nursery-school children often change their food preferences, their personal hygiene habits, their daily routines, and even their playtime activities as a result of nursery-school attendance.

But such changes can occur at a rather superficial level and need not reflect the strength of the peer group as a socializing agent. Cross-cultural investigations, however, where responsiveness of children of different nationalities to peers has been studied, help to evaluate the relative strength of the American peer group. The kibbutz-reared child who from infancy on spends the major portion of each day with his peers looks to peers for praise and for good behavior models (Spiro, 1958), although whether he does so to a greater extent than the child reared in the family is not clear from the research. Bronfenbrenner and others (Devereux *et al.,* 1965) compared sixth-grade children in England, Germany, the Soviet Union, and the United States on a "dilemmas test" where subjects chose between an adult-endorsed norm and peer pressure to deviate from the norm in thirty conflict situations. Interestingly enough, though we think of American children as most peer-oriented, the English children showed the most orientation to peers, and the American and German children less; the Soviet children were the least peer-oriented of all. However, ratings changed when subjects were told on a second test that their responses would be seen by teachers and parents and on a third test by their classmates. The amount of shift was greater under conditions of classmate-exposure for American children than for the Soviet and the shift was in a different direction. When they thought classmates were going to see their responses, Soviet children increased their choice of adult-endorsed values, while American children moved in the direction of peer values.

Both the amount of time children spend with their parents and how much value parents place on peer opinion appear to be factors in determining the strength of the peer group. Middle-class English children go to boarding schools at an early age, and parental influence is weakened. In the United States, getting along well with others is stressed in middle-class families, and there may be some training for conformity to peer pressure in connection with this emphasis. The child who is told, "Johnny won't want to play with you if you keep on doing that" may indirectly learn that what Johnny thinks of him is important to his parents. Also, because the school day is shorter, and school assignments less demanding in time, American children have more free time than Soviet children to spend with peers after school hours. Much of that time is spent in organized groups with leaders who emphasize the importance of other people's opinion of oneself. Peer pressure increases in the junior-high and high-school years, and a youth culture, discussed in the Keniston paper in Part 2, emerges, distinguished by dress, music, dance, language, and rituals. One finds youth cultures in other countries, although nowhere as strong as in the United States.

REFERENCES

Bandura, A.; Grusec, J.; and Menlove, F., "Vicarious extinction of avoidance behavior." *Journal of Personality and Social Psychology*, 1967, 5, 16–23.

Becker, W. C.; Peterson, D. B.; Hellmer, L. A.; Shoemaker, D. J.; and Quay, H. C., "Factors in parental behavior and personality as related to problem behavior in children." *Journal of Consulting Psychology*, 1959, 23, 107–18.

Biller, H., and Bahm, R., "Father absence, perceived maternal behavior, and masculinity of self-concept among junior high school boys." *Developmental Psychology*, 1971, 4, 178–81.

Devereux, E.; Bronfenbrenner, U.; and Rodgers, R., "Child-rearing in England and the United States: a cross-national comparison." Unpublished manuscript, 1965.

Hartup, W., and Coates, B., "Imitation of a peer as function of reinforcement from the peer group and rewardingness of the model." *Child Development*, 1967, 38, 1003–16.

Jackson, P., *Life in classrooms* (New York: Holt, Rinehart and Winston, 1968).

Kagan, J., and Moss, H., *Birth to maturity: a study in psychological development* (New York: Wiley, 1962).

Lewin, K.; Lippitt, R.; and White, R. K., "Patterns of aggressive behavior in experimentally created 'social climates.'" *Journal of Social Psychology*, 1939, 10, 271–99.

Lidz, T., *The family and human adaptation* (New York: International Universities Press, 1963).

Maccoby, E., and Masters, J., "Attachment and dependency." In P. Mussen, ed., *Carmichael's Manual of Child Psychology*, vol. II (New York: Wiley, 1970).

Martin, W. E., "Singularity and stability of profiles of social behavior." In C. B. Stendler, ed., *Readings in Child Behavior and Development*, 2nd ed. (New York: Harcourt Brace Jovanovich, 1964).

Moynihan, D., *The Negro family: the case for national action* (Washington, D.C.: Office of Policy Planning and Research, U.S. Department of Labor, 1965).

Ogle, R., "Long term effects of highly structured preschool intervention programs on children's personality development." Unpublished doctoral thesis, Graduate School, University of Illinois, 1971.

Sarason, S.; Davidson, K.; Lighthall, F.; Waite, R.; and Ruebaush, B., *Anxiety in elementary school children* (New York: Wiley, 1960).

Silberman, C., *Crisis in the classroom* (New York: Random House, 1970).

Spiro, M., *Children of the kibbutz* (Cambridge, Mass.: Harvard University Press, 1958).

STIMULUS CONTROL OF PARENT OR CARETAKER BEHAVIOR BY OFFSPRING

RICHARD Q. BELL

Since 1961 eight different investigators have commented on the oddity that the child's contribution to parent-child interaction is overlooked (Bell, 1968; Gewirtz, 1961; Kessen, 1963; Korner, 1965; Rheingold, 1969; Stott, 1966; Wenar & Wenar, 1963). Child behavior is seldom an independent variable, parent behavior a dependent variable, even if the child is acknowledged by a formal place in theories. Until very recently we have had no hypotheses concerning the child's stimulating effects on the parent. Accordingly data are not gathered so that the effects of the child can be identified, and most of the relevant findings are accidents generated by research directed to other purposes. Parent and child are clearly a social system and in such systems we expect each participant's responses to be stimuli for the other. Why, then, is the child's own contribution to an interaction overlooked by social scientists, and what can be done about the problem?

HISTORICAL DETERMINANTS

One possible historical determinant is our American political and social philosophy which emphasized egalitarianism and opportunity, as a reaction to hereditary determination of position in European societies. If one is committed too zealously to our philosophy it is difficult to admit the diversity of human existence contributed by the individual's own nature. Thus the general climate of our American political and social philosophy seems, at first glance, to provide an answer to the question of historical

determinants. Closer examination of this possibility, however, reveals that considerable fluctuations in the views of social scientists have occurred in periods when major changes in the general climate of opinion have not been identified.

Clausen (1967) has pointed out changes in the views of sociologists. An overeager and uncritical acceptance of the theory of evolution in the formative years of sociology, around the end of the last century, led to an equally strong counterreaction. When instinct theory and the search for innate differences between social classes and national groups was abandoned, it became unfashionable to hold or express views on biological contributors to development. To hold such views was to be a conservative. The liberal sociologist believed in educability and thus turned his attention to society's values, institutions, and child-rearing techniques. This shift in perspective led to overlooking the child's contribution to the interaction in socialization theory; then, as today, the contribution of the child was equated with the operation of genetic or congenital factors.

Some of the same factors which affected sociology also affected psychology, but there were additional elements. The backlash of behaviorist reaction to introspection negated consideration of the child as a source of stimuli. Here again, as in sociology, the contribution of the child to development was equated with genetic and congenital factors and dismissed with them.

From the historical review it is evident that, for both sociology and psychology, the importance accorded the child's contribution to behavior development was linked with the value placed on biological factors during any given

Reprinted by permission of the author and the American Psychological Association from *Developmental Psychology*, 1971, **4**, 63–72.

era. The equation of the child's contribution with biological factors led to a fundamental error in socialization theory. The possibility has been overlooked that the child could process and integrate experience during one period, and subsequently manifest to the parent new products of this integration at a later period, even if there were no maturational contributions to changes in behavior and no individual differences on congenital or genetic grounds. It seems evident that the child, after exposure to parent behavior, can present the parent with emergent behaviors which, in turn, modify subsequent parent behaviors. Thus, it is necessary to assert the view that stimulus effects of children on parents deserve treatment regardless of the question of genetic, congenital, or experiential contributors and their differential weights. We may study child behavior directly without necessarily being concerned with its origins; we may observe it, manipulate it, and thus move toward specifying its effects on the parent in various developmental periods.

PRESENT STATUS OF SOCIALIZATION RESEARCH

Since it is difficult to identify the operation of biological factors, let alone experimentally manipulate their contribution, it is quite understandable that even investigators who recognized the importance of the child in socialization (Nowlis, 1952; Sears, Maccoby, & Levin, 1957) simply proceeded with their studies, hoping the omission of the child's effects on the parent would not be overly damaging. If a substantial body of dependable findings had emerged from the study of socialization over the last 28 years, the omission of the child's stimulating effects could be overlooked, along with the shortcomings of the interview and questionnaire approaches used. However, several reviewers have noted that the approach has been barren of results (Becker & Krug, 1965; Caldwell, 1964; Orlansky, 1949; Sewell, 1963; Yarrow, Campbell, & Burton, 1968). Authors of the last mentioned review concluded that the case for positive findings can only be maintained by relying on studies in which both parent and child behavior was reported by the same informant, by interpreting consistency in nonsignificant correlations, or by ignoring contradictory data.

Even if we accept some of the disputed findings, it is possible to provide quite plausible interpretations in terms of effects of children on parents. This is because in almost all cases the findings are based on a simple correlation between parent and child characteristics, and a correlation does not indicate direction of effects. Too often it has been assumed that it is most parsimonious to interpret correlations between parent and child characteristics in terms of a unidirectional effect from parent to child in spite of Sears et al.'s (1957) original caveats on this issue. To counter this tendency, explanations in terms of child effects on parents have been offered for major findings of socialization studies (Bell, 1968). Furthermore, if the criterion for explanation is to be parsimony, it should be noted that the explanations based on child effects on parents were developed from a single set of propositions which is not overly complicated or difficult to defend. This alternative system of explaining correlations between parent and child characteristics is detailed later in this article and expanded into a system for dealing with ongoing interactions.

DISENTANGLING THE DIRECTION OF EFFECTS

It is difficult to discriminate child and parent effects when each participant is reacting in turn to the other in an ongoing process, and the process is not subjected to an experimental intervention. It does not follow, however, that we are limited to a purely descriptive approach such as simply recording the event sequences. For example, predictions concerning interaction contingencies differ, depending on whether we expect it to be the child or the parent who initiates interactions. Data bearing on these different predictions are reported later. In addition, logical systems applicable to a wide variety of research problems, have been developed for making inferences about causal relations in naturally occurring sequences. The underlying concept is that a change by one participant, in the direction of the other's base line, supports the influence of the other. The bases for conclusions about causation are not as firm as would be the case with direct manipulation of the behavior of participants, but there is an increase in the confidence which can be attached to conclusions. A review of statistical techniques appropriate to this approach is available (Yee & Gage, 1968). A related approach has been used by Hinde and Spencer-Booth (1968) in analyzing changes in rhesus mother-infant pairs over a period of several weeks.

Better control over possible unrecognized contributors can be achieved by manipulating behavior of one of the participants and noting the effect on the other. A previous article has listed studies which have isolated effects of experimentally manipulated adult behavior on children and vice versa (Bell, 1968). In some the experimenter altered the mother's attitude toward her child's performance, then noted the shift. The most recent example is a study by Hilton (1967), who experimentally altered the mother's attitude and produced dramatic shifts in the interaction characteristics of mothers of first- and later-born children. In other studies, children with different behavioral capabilities were brought into interaction with adults with whom they had had no previous experience: The effects on the adults of the behavior of these children were measured.

White (1969) and McCall and Kagan (1967) have carried out sustained manipulations of infant behavior by changing (or having mothers change) their environment for several weeks. If the subsequent impact on the caretakers of the infant's changed behavior had been measured, we would have had the necessary elements for identifying stimulus effects of the infant on the parent.

A more complete form of the research approach advocated occurred serendipitously in a learning study carried out by Etzel and Gewirtz (1967). Levels of crying and smiling were manipulated in the case of two 6- to 20-week-old infants by removing them each day from a boarding nursery to an experimental room for a short training session, then returning them to the nursery. Informal observations indicated that the increased level of smiling shown in the nursery by one infant affected the behavior of several caretakers. This change in the infant resulted from reinforcement produced in the ex-

perimental room. The caretakers who previously spent little time with the infant now spent considerable time responding to his smiles.

To recapitulate, several studies have been described to document the point that the inclusion of the offspring in our theories of socialization need no longer be held up for lack of available research approaches. Stimulus effects of both the young and their caretakers can be differentiated.

A BIDIRECTIONAL MODEL APPLIED TO ONGOING INTERACTIONS

Up to the present point in this article very general points have been made concerning history, previous theory, and methods. If these points have served to provide perspective, a state of discontent with our hypotheses, and reassurance that new kinds of data can be gathered, the next task is to provide a way of thinking about interaction in terms of stimulus effects of both participants. First, some of the usual ways in which we think about stimuli, responses, and participants in social interactions are reviewed, then to these are added two special propositions which have proved useful in accounting for correlations between parent and child characteristics reported in studies of socialization (Bell, 1968). Two samples of mother-infant interaction are then interpreted with the concepts at hand to provide concrete illustrations in actual ongoing sequences. Following this, hypotheses developed from these concepts are tested against available quantitative data from interaction sequences. Sooner or later all theories of parent or child effects, all extrapolations from laboratory manipulations of child or parent behavior, must be tested against these minute-to-minute interactions occurring in their natural context—the kinds of interactions which Wright (1967) pointed out were the basis for less than 8% of 1,409 empirical studies of childhood and adolescence.

Were it not for our history of slighting the child's contribution to parent-child interactions, it would seem superfluous to note, first of all, that we should consider these interactions as comprising a social system. Sears (1951) has described the properties of a simple dyadic social unit in which mutual expectancies make the behavior of the participants interdependent. Parsons and Bales (1955) elaborated the view of the family as a social system. Brim (1957) further spelled out the implications of this conceptual approach, including the need for investigators to make a number of distinctions called for by role theory, and to consider the reciprocal nature of parent and child roles. Glidewell (1961) followed the same line of thinking and pointed out the applicability of the basic paradigm in which a unit of behavior is both a response of one participant and a stimulus for the other. If we treat each response of the caretaker as a possible stimulus for the young, we should also look for all the ways in which stimuli from the young may affect the caretaker.

Marler and Hamilton (1966) have provided a classification of stimulus effects at a level of generality which should prove helpful in the initial stages of developing a theory of parent and child effects. Generally, stimuli are facilitating or inhibiting. More specifically, they orient, elicit, produce decrement or increment (sensitization, learning, habituation), and check or arrest behavior.

Next, it is necessary to select a level of complexity at which responses will be defined. Most investigators of parent-child interaction have set a minimum level which is appropriate to a social system, the discrete actions of each participant being at least of sufficient complexity to be recognized by the other and perceived as relevant. As Wright (1967) has pointed out in connection with the Midwest studies of behavior ecology, crying might be recorded, but not expiration and setting the vocal cords.

Most investigators also attempt conceptual organization above the level of discrete, molar acts. In the present approach it is assumed that actions or responses may occur in subsets called repertoires. An example is fussing, crying, grimacing, and threshing shown by infants and comprising, in effect, an "alerting and proximity maintaining" repertoire. The several acts a mother uses in soothing also constitute a repertoire. Items in a repertoire are interdependent in the sense that given one response to a stimulus, others in the same set are more likely to occur than those in another set.

Further organization within the set may also exist. The various responses may be graded relative to which one is most likely, given various levels of stimulation which activate the repertoire. The several responses may be released in a certain order; that is, a sequentially ordered repertoire may exist.

It should be noted that although the repertoires have been labelled in terms of their likely effect on the other participant, they should be demonstrable from interaction data without reference to the stimulating effects of their component responses on the other. All that is required is that there be a temporal association of certain elements within the one participant's total set of responses occurring during the interaction.

It is expected that differences in repertoires will be found. For example, the young should have fewer, more sparse, and less well organized and differentiated repertoires than their caretakers.

An additional assumption is that each participant has upper and lower limits relative to the intensity, frequency, or situational appropriateness of behavior shown by the other. When the upper limit is reached, the reaction of the other is of a kind likely to redirect or reduce the excessive or inappropriate behavior (upper limit control reaction). When the lower limit is not reached, the reaction is to stimulate, prime, or in other ways increase the insufficient or nonexistent behavior (lower limit control reaction).

The limits and control reactions would vary with the participants, but by way of illustration, one could say that a characteristically high level of parent control reaction would be expected in response to excessive and sustained crying in infants or to impulsive, precocious, or overly assertive children. Parent lower limit control behavior would be elicited by lethargy in infants, by low activity, overly inhibited behavior, shyness, and lack of competence in the young child. These widely different child behaviors are assumed to be similar only with respect to their effects on the appropriate parent control pattern.

The conceptual system is now applied to one sequence of mother-infant interaction which primarily involves caretaking, and to another consisting of more purely social interaction. Both were extracted from a continuous 3-hour observation by Howard Moss of the National Institute of Mental Health, for a 3-month-old male infant and its mother. The case selected was simply the first from a series of 14 for which an analysis had been completed for the contingencies of several maternal and infant behaviors. The sequence is presented while interweaving propositions from the conceptual system, using such terms as reinforcement descriptively, since to provide evidence for the interpretive use of such a term would require data from rather sustained units, or across several units.

Caretaking Sequence

The infant had been alone in his crib, awake and quiet for a 13-minute period in which there was no interaction. The interaction was initiated by a $3\frac{1}{2}$-minute period in which he changed to an awake fussing state. This oriented the mother to the infant but did not at that time disrupt other ongoing activities or elicit approach. Presumably, the level of fussing was below a level which activates her soothing repertoire. This period was followed by $1\frac{1}{2}$ minutes during which fussing progressed to full cyclic crying, and the latter did elicit the mother's approach. She looked and presumably saw grimacing and threshing—further stimuli from the infant which had the effect of keeping the mother in the immediate vicinity. The mother stood over him, since he continued to thresh and cry. She then talked. The crying continued. The mother then picked him up and cradled him in her arms. This part of her repertoire was reinforced by the infant, who reduced motor movement but continued crying. After about 8 seconds the mother again talked, but the crying continued, and another element was introduced from the maternal repertoire—she stressed his musculature by holding him so his weight was partially on his arms and legs. The crying was maintained, however, and the mother then showed another behavior: holding the infant up in the air in front and above her. The crying continued. She then held him against her shoulder and relieved ingested air. This was followed by rather massive tactile stimulation,

jiggling, rubbing, and patting, but, after a pause, the infant resumed crying. Continuation of the tactile stimulation by the mother was followed by a reduction of the crying to fussing. However, the infant started crying again. Then the infant opened his eyes and was quiet for several seconds. The mother talked again, and the infant provided reinforcement for this behavior by continuing to remain quietly awake for several seconds, then emitting a noncrying vocalization. This elicited responsive talking by the mother, who then placed her baby in an infant seat. He remained quiet and awake in his seat, smiled, and the mother left a few seconds later. The state of the infant apparently terminated the interaction sequence. The smile could have differentiated this unit into a reciprocal social interchange, but the mother at this time was apparently only set to quiet the infant. Eighteen minutes in which the infant remained quiet and awake elapsed before another unit of interaction.

To recapitulate, in the absence of a change in stimulation from the mother the infant showed a sequential repertoire in that he progressed from fussing through alternating fussing and crying to full crying. The fussing oriented the mother toward the infant, then the crying activated what is best described as a sequentially ordered quieting repertoire. The mother talked to the infant first, then, after trying different methods, including stressing the infant's musculature and relieving air, she finally reached the stage of jiggling, rubbing, and patting. She reverted to talking when the infant quieted, and his resumption of crying was followed by a recycling of her ordered repertoire, though in shortened form. She proceeded directly to points in the repertoire that were later in the order when first presented.

Social Interaction Sequence

The next illustrative sequence is from the record of the same mother-infant pair 1 hour and 50 minutes later. The baby had been placed in a seat after he was fed, and ingested air had been relieved. Throughout this period the mother had talked to him, held him in different positions, and wiped his face. He either looked directly at her, smiled, or both, when being wiped. There followed an essentially social interaction sequence, lasting 6 minutes, in which infant vocalized and mother talked alternately eight times during the first 3½ minutes. The infant then smiled for the first time in 4 minutes, and the mother's rate of talking increased from one utterance in the ½-minute period before, to one every 3 seconds in the ½-minute afterward. The infant's rate of vocalization in turn increased from one per 17 seconds to one every 4 seconds for the same periods. There followed an interval of 2½ minutes in which the infant smiled no more and there were six alternations of infant vocalizing and mother talking. The infant maintained his rate of vocalization, though introducing no novel responses, while the mother's rate of talking declined to one every 6 seconds. This last rate of decline was superimposed on a more general response decrement for maternal talking over the entire 6 minutes. Finally, the mother abruptly picked up the infant, held him close upright, then at a distance, tickled him, and turned her attention away. This burst of maternal activity reduced the infant's vocalizations, but the mother's cessation of responding was followed by fussing, then crying. She repeated the physical contact, but the infant continued to cry, and the sequence was terminated by the mother leaving the immediate vicinity of the infant and remaining away for nearly 3 minutes.

Sequentially ordered repertoires are not evident in the social interaction period of this sequence as in the previous caretaking sequence. Rather, the interaction has the qualities of a well-practiced game, each participant alternating in providing a response which serves as a stimulus to the other's response. While the infant dependably provides his phase of the alternation, the lack of novelty in his response is a likely basis for the general maternal response decrement. This is evidenced both in the general reduction in the mother's rate of talking, but also in the fact that a brief introduction by the infant of novelty, the smile (novel relative to this segment of the interaction), is followed by an increase in the maternal rate.

The effect of the novelty of the smile within this sequence raises the question of infant stimulus effects operating to prevent maternal re-

sponse decrement across episodes. It is possible that a decrement in maternal attachment would occur were it not for general changes in infant behavior, particularly eye-to-eye contact and smiles, that engender a feeling of reciprocal relations. It can be surmised that in the previous example the gradual emergence of "the game" was an exhilarating experience to the mother, especially in contrast with the drudgery of caretaking that primarily prevented the appearance of aversive stimuli. From normative data in other studies it is readily apparent that such a mother could hardly fail to note a procession of other changes, and these are of interest in themselves. She could have observed that the infant was more "choosey," ceasing to respond when her own behavior was repetitive (Lewis, Goldberg, & Rausch, 1967); that his visual attention had shown a steady increase, and that it was accompanied by qualitative changes—early motor quieting, then scanning and excitation, then particular attention to her face, with smiling and soft cooing rather than mouth and head movements (Carpenter & Stechler, 1967). She could have seen a progression from mere swiping at objects after the second month, through to ability to open the hand in anticipation of contact with the object (White, Castle, & Held, 1964).

The origin of the changes just listed is a very complex matter, but at least we can say that there is no simple and straightforward support from White's (1969) series of enrichment studies for the notion that the changes are simple creations of the mother's stimulation as such. Some enrichment disturbed and upset the infant, actually reduced the level of functioning; some functions were unaltered; others altered in very unpredictable fashion. It should be noted, however, that these enrichment studies did not use behavior contingencies provided by a caretaker.

Returning to the system of thinking about caretaker-young interactions and to the illustrative sequences, the latter exemplify content in which we can expect to find answers as to how infants develop. Sequences such as these are going on during these periods, and we know that infant and maternal behavior progress during the same time. The system of interaction analysis which was applied is a general model, but the infant's contribution was emphasized in the selection and description of the sequences because, in the past, the mother's contribution has been belabored at the expense of the infant. The purpose of the conceptual system is to open up for consideration, along with parental effects, a wide variety of ways in which stimuli coming from the young may control and guide parental behavior. These sources of control by the young are not now represented in customary ways of looking at parent-child interactions. If we can begin to think of interactions in this way, the necessary empirical work will follow.

Quantitative Data from Interaction Sequences

It has been possible to locate only two published reports from the period of infancy through early childhood which were based on analyses preserving natural sequences. In the material to follow, these will be supplemented with unpublished results from ongoing analysis of Moss' data already mentioned. More data are available in the files of various investigators, but informal communication indicates that analyses have been held down by the mass of such information resulting from only a few hours of observation on a single case, as well as the difficulties of hand, and even computer analysis. The absence of a method of conceptualizing sequences so that the contribution of both participants is identified lies at the heart of the problem of analysis.

The data which are available, however, can be brought to bear in a crude way on the question of whether it is necessary to consider the infant or young child's response as a stimulus preceding the caretaker's. Reasoning from the old model of training being carried out by an agent of culture, we would expect parents to start interactions, and any infant or child behavior which might be found occasionally preceding parent behavior would not be specific to that which followed. This expectation follows from the assumption that what the object of socialization is doing does not matter, only the fact that at a given moment the training agent elected to transfer a bit of culture. If this latter assumption appears to make a straw man of socialization theory, it is nonetheless justified in effect by the following: (*a*) the small num-

ber of studies concerned with effects of children on parents (Bell, 1968), (*b*) the equally small number which record parent and child behavior as mutually contingent (Hoffman, 1957), (*c*) in Brim's (1957) survey of research on parent-child relations, the number of studies primarily concerned with child behavior only approached those for parents in the case of role *prescriptions*—what children should do, while in the category of role *performance,* there were four times as many studies concentrated on the parent.

The assumption of the irrelevance of behavior shown by the young finds little support in the available data. Lawrence Harper of the author's laboratory analyzed discrete behaviors in the 3-hour interaction sequence from which the first illustrative sequence was chosen. No interaction units were imposed. Of 29 instances of the mother looking at the infant, 15 were preceded by the crying of the infant. Of 13 instances of the mother holding the infant in the close-upright position, 9 were preceded by the infant crying or fussing. One other category accounted for all other preceding infant events (infant awake). The state of an infant is a very obvious kind of control over maternal behavior.

The previous data were from an intensive analysis of several categories for a single case. Moss and Robson (1968) have reported maternal response contingencies for a single category of infant behavior in 54 mother-infant pairs studied during two 6-hour home observations at 1 month, and one 6-hour observation at 3 months. The question was whether maternal contacts preceded or followed episodes of continuous crying or fussing. An episode was considered terminated if 1 minute or more elapsed without crying or fussing. The mean number of episodes preceding maternal contact was 21.3 at 1 month, 11.0 at 3 months, in contrast with means of 4.1 and 2.5 for episodes following maternal contacts for the same time periods. The mean differences at each point were not only significant ($p < .001$), there was only 1 mother-infant pair at 1 month, and 4 at 3 months which did not show the same direction of differences as the means. The potency of crying and fussing in eliciting maternal behavior has been the subject of much comment based on casual observation, but here is rather strong evidence from systematic direct observation.

Moving to a later period of development, Gewirtz and Gewirtz (1965) have reported caretaker-infant contingencies based on full-day home observation of two 32-week-old infants. Frequencies of four kinds of interaction sequences were sufficient to permit a statistical test by the present author from tabular data. For one infant, three-event sequences initiated and terminated by the infant, with one intervening response from the mother, were more frequent than the converse, those in which the mother initiated and terminated sequences with one intervening infant response (23 versus 10; $\chi^2 = 5.12$, $p < .05$).

For the same infant, differences in frequencies between two-event sequences were not significant, being 61 for those initiated by the infant and terminated by the mother, versus 67 for the converse. For the other infant, there was no significant difference in frequencies between the infant- versus mother-initiated three-event sequences (37 versus 48), but there were significantly more mother-initiated two-event sequences than the converse (148 versus 115; $\chi^2 = 4.14$, $p < .05$).

The data from the two infants show no preponderance of interactions initiated and terminated by the mother, as we would expect from the dominant role accorded the mother in most socialization studies. Instead, one infant appears to control one kind of interaction, one mother another kind, while mothers and infants play an equivalent role for the other two types of interaction.

Schoggen (1963) has reported a special analysis of 18 specimen records available from the Midwest study for three mother-toddler pairs, the shortest of the 18 covering over 11 hours. Interactions were coded into environmental force units. This unit is an action of the child or parent which is directed toward a recognizable end state and is identified as such by the other. These characterizations of the data were made years ago without reference to the problem of direction of effects. Because of the method of analysis, it is possible to answer the question of who starts interactions when the units are defined in this way. During this period of observation, for these particular pairs, from 49 to 61% of the units were initiated by behavior of the child.

This analysis was based on units of interaction; one can always argue with the units used. However, a different analysis into episodes resulted in very similar results for 11 children covering the age range from 1 year 2 months to 10 years 9 months. Children started approximately one-half of the episodes at all age periods (Wright, 1967). There was no significant change in age in this basic division of initiating exchanges, although many other interaction parameters showed considerable change with age.

Schoggen commented on the surprising fact that the most frequent judged goal of the mothers in all but 1 of the 18 records was that of getting the toddler to cease his demands on her (i.e., to quit bothering her, not to question her further, to leave her alone, not to press a request, not to attack). And these are passive, impressionable children! The intensity of the toddler's behavior, and the nature of the mother's reactions, makes it possible to see the value of one feature in the conceptual scheme just applied to interaction sequences. The mothers may be described as showing upper limit control behavior, the toddlers, lower limit control behavior. Characterizing the toddlers as showing lower limit control behavior means that the mothers' behavior was perceived by the toddlers as generally insufficient in intensity, frequency, or variety.

To return to the primary question asked in this portion of the article, do the available data on interaction support the concept of the irrelevance of behavior of the young? The answer is negative. That is, if any inferences about dynamic action can be drawn from a knowledge of which participant's behavior came first and the specificity of antecedent-consequent behaviors, the young must be given considerable credit for impelling action.

CONCLUSION

The propriety of hereditary determination of position in society was discredited long ago, as was the notion of innate ideas and the view that children are just little adults who don't need education. More recently, but certainly long enough in the past that it is no longer necessary to pay scientific penance, we ceased looking for instincts in every human behavior pattern and for evidences of the doctrine of the survival of the fittest in national, ethnic, and individual differences.

While for the better part of this century social scientists have considered it necessary to deny these views, proclaiming the malleability of man, at this time some unfortunate consequences of the denial may be safely considered.

It is now no longer necessary to assert the child's educability with such vehemence that we deny his contribution, whatever may be its origins. A way of restoring his contribution to our basic view of the process of parent-child interaction has been offered in this report. If we can come out from under the shadow of old ideological conflicts, the child can be recognized as a very lively educator himself. To quote Peter De Vries (1954), "The value of marriage is not that adults produce children but that children produce adults [p. 98]."

REFERENCES

Becker, W. C., & Krug, R. S. The parent attitude research instrument—a research review. *Child Development,* 1965, 36, 329–365.

Bell, R. Q. A reinterpretation of the direction of effects in studies of socialization. *Psychological Review,* 1968, 75, 81–95.

Brim, O. G. The parent-child relation as a social system: I. Parent and child roles. *Child Development,* 1957, 28, 343–364.

Caldwell, B. The effects of infant care. In M. L. Hoffman & L. W. Hoffman (Eds.), *Review of child development research.* Vol. 1. New York: Russell Sage Foundation, 1964.

Carpenter, G. C., & Stechler, G. Selective attention to mother's face from week 1 through week 8. *Proceedings of the 75th Annual Convention of the American Psychological Association,* 1967, 2, 153–154. (Summary)

Clausen, J. A. The organism and socialization. *Journal of Health and Social Behavior,* 1967, 8, 243–252.

Etzel, B. D., & Gewirtz, J. L. Experimental modification of caretaker-maintained high-rate operant crying in a 6- and a 20-week-old infant (Infans tyrannotearus): Extinction of crying with reinforcement of eye contact and smiling. *Journal of Experimental Child Psychology,* 1967, 5, 303–317.

De Vries, P. *The tunnel of love.* Boston: Little, Brown, 1954.

Gewirtz, J. L. A learning analysis of the effects of normal stimulation, privation, and deprivation on the acquisition of social motivation and attachment. In B. M. Foss (Ed.), *Determinants of infant behavior.* New York: Wiley, 1961.

Gewirtz, J. L., & Gewirtz, H. B. Stimulus conditions, infant behaviors, and social learning in four Israeli child-rearing environments: A preliminary report illustrating differences in environment and behavior between the "only" and the "youngest" child. In B. M. Foss (Ed.), *Determi-*

nants of infant behavior. Vol. 3. New York: Wiley, 1965.

Glidewell, J. C. On the analysis of social intervention. In J. C. Glidewell (Ed.), *Parental attitudes and child behavior.* Springfield, Ill.: Charles C Thomas, 1961.

Hilton, I. Differences in the behavior of mothers toward first- and later-born children. *Journal of Personality and Social Psychology,* 1967, 7, 282–290.

Hinde, R. A., & Spencer-Booth, Y. The study of mother-infant interaction in captive group-living rhesus monkeys. *Proceedings of the Royal Society (Ser. B),* 1968, 169, 177–201.

Hoffman, M. L. An interview method for obtaining descriptions of parent-child interaction. *Merrill-Palmer Quarterly,* 1957, 3, 76–83.

Kessen, W. Research in the psychological development of infants: An overview. *Merrill-Palmer Quarterly,* 1963, 9, 83–94.

Korner, A. F. Mother-child interaction: One- or two-way street? *Social Work,* 1965, 10, 47–51.

Lewis, M., Goldberg. S., & Rausch, M. Attention distribution as a function of novelty and familiarity. *Psychonomic Science,* 1967, 7, 227–228.

Marler, P., & Hamilton, W. J. *Mechanisms of animal behavior.* New York: Wiley, 1966.

McCall, R. B., & Kagan, J. Stimulus-schema discrepancy and attention in the infant. *Journal of Experimental Child Psychology,* 1967, 5, 381–390.

Moss, H. A., & Robson, K. S. The role of protest behavior in the development of the mother-infant attachment. In J. L Gewirtz (Chm.), Attachment behaviors in humans and animals. Symposium presented at the meeting of the American Psychological Association, San Francisco, September 1968.

Nowlis, V. The search for significant concepts in a study of parent-child relationships. *American Journal of Orthopsychiatry,* 1952, 22, 286–299.

Orlansky, H. Infant care and personality. *Psychological Bulletin,* 1949, **46,** 1–48.

Parsons, T., & Bales, R. F. *Family socialization and interaction process.* Glencoe, Ill.: Free Press, 1955.

Rheingold, H. L. The social and socializing infant. In D. Goslin (Ed.), *Handbook of socialization theory and research.* Chicago: Rand McNally, 1969.

Schoggen, P. Environmental forces in the everyday lives of children. In R. G. Barker (Ed.), *The stream of behavior: Explorations of its structure and content.* New York: Appleton-Century-Crofts, 1963.

Sears, R. R. A theoretical framework for personality and social behavior. *American Psychologist,* 1951, **6,** 476–482.

Sears, R. R., Maccoby, E. E., & Levin, H. *Patterns of child rearing.* Evanston, Ill.: Row, Peterson, 1957.

Stott, D. H. *Studies of troublesome children.* New York: Humanities Press, 1966.

Sewell, W. H. Some recent developments in socialization theory and research. *Annals of the American Academy of Political and Social Science,* 1963, **349,** 163–181.

Wenar, C., & Wenar, S. C. The short term prospective model, the illusion of time, and the tabula rasa child. *Child Development,* 1963, **34,** 697–708.

White, B. L. Child development research: An edifice without a foundation. *Merrill-Palmer Quarterly,* 1969, **15,** 49–79.

White, B. L., Castle, P., & Held, R. M. Observations on the development of visually-directed reaching. *Child Development,* 1964, **35,** 349–364.

Wright, M. F. *Recording and analyzing child behavior.* New York: Harper & Row, 1967.

Yarrow, M. R., Campbell, J. D., & Burton, R. V. *Child rearing: An inquiry into research and methods.* San Francisco: Jossey-Bass, 1968.

Yee, A. H., & Gage, N. L. Techniques for estimating the source and direction of causal influence in panel data. *Psychological Bulletin,* 1968, **70,** 115–126.

HARMONIOUS PARENTS
AND THEIR PRESCHOOL CHILDREN

DIANA BAUMRIND

The purpose of this article is to describe a particularly interesting pattern of child rearing which came to the author's attention during a study of current patterns of parental authority and their effects on the behavior of preschool children. In that study, as in two previous studies, data concerning the children were obtained after a period of 3 months of observation in the nursery school setting and in a structured situation; and data for parental behavior were obtained during two home visits of 3 hours each, followed by a structured interview with the mother and the father. The results of these studies have been reported in some detail (Baumrind, 1967, 1971; Baumrind & Black, 1967). The data to be presented here, while of great interest because of their novelty and relevance to social changes taking place in this country, must be viewed as speculative because of the manner in which the group members were identified.

While in the study proper, pattern membership was determined by multiple criteria, defined theoretically and then operationally by standard scores, the eight families placed in this pattern had but one identifying characteristic in common. The observer assigned to study each of these families would not rate the family for the construct designated firm enforcement and for at least two of the five items which operationally defined that construct. In each case, the observer stated that any rating on these items would be misleading since the parent, while he or she almost never *exercised control,* seemed to *have control* in the sense that the

Reprinted by permission of the author and the American Psychological Association from *Developmental Psychology,* 1971, **4,** 63–72.

child generally took pains to intuit what the parent wanted and to do it.

The atmosphere in these families was characterized by harmony, equanimity, and rationality.

While Permissive parents avoided exercising control but were angry about not having control, and Authoritarian and Authoritative parents exercised control willingly, Harmonious parents seemed neither to exercise control, nor to avoid the exercise of control. Instead, they focused upon achieving a quality of harmony in the home, and upon developing principles for resolving differences and for right living. Often they lost interest in actually resolving a difference once agreement upon principles of resolution had been reached. These parents brought the child up to their level in an interaction but did not reverse roles by acting childishly, as did some Permissive and Nonconforming parents. Harmonious parents were equalitarian in that they recognized differences based upon knowledge and personality, and tried to create an environment in which all family members could operate from the same vantage point, one in which the recognized differences in power did not put the child at a disadvantage. They lived parallel to the mainstream rather than in opposition to it. In their hierarchy of values honesty, harmony, justice, and rationality in human relations took precedence over power, achievement, control, and order, although they also saw the practical importance of the latter values [Baumrind, 1971, p. 10].

Specifically, on the parent behavior rating clusters (with a mean standard score of 50, $SD = 10$), both mother and father in all cases were rated very high on a cluster designated encourages independence and individuality (mean standard score of 61 for mothers and

TABLE I

Individual Scores and Summary Statistics for IQ and Preschool Behavior Q-Sort Clusters in Children of Harmonious Parents

Score	IQ	Q-Sort Clusters						
		Hostile–friendly	Resistive–cooperative	Domineering–tractable	Dominant–submissive	Purposive–aimless	Achievement oriented–not achievement oriented	Independent–suggestible
Girls								
a	143	38.09	50.85	42.19	56.69	56.48	60.50	58.41
b	125	41.32	45.40	52.85	56.36	56.21	62.14	53.74
c	124	39.81	38.81	52.80	53.02	54.84	59.94	51.32
d	142	35.76	40.69	48.96	49.33	41.93	50.88	59.77
e	134	44.58	40.85	46.92	60.47	58.13	56.95	59.62
f	147	42.47	52.15	42.87	47.12	61.83	53.38	50.28
M	135.83	40.34	44.79	47.76	53.83	54.90	57.63	55.52
SD	9.75	3.16	5.65	4.65	4.99	6.80	4.12	4.28
Boys								
g	116	47.64	36.39	32.88	28.09	36.85	44.15	29.26
h	117	56.68	51.12	42.71	40.68	23.86	27.56	41.78
M	116.50	52.16	43.75	37.79	34.38	30.35	35.85	35.52
SD	0.71	4.52	7.37	4.92	6.30	6.49	8.30	6.23

Note. These scores are based on a standardized score with a mean of 50 and standard deviation of 10.

56 for fathers) and enrichment of child's environment (mean joint rating for families of 59); rather high on passive-acceptant (58 for mothers and 55 for fathers); rather low on rejecting (45 for mothers and 47 for fathers); and fathers were rated very high on promotes nonconformity (59) and low on authoritarianism (43). Parents were generally drawn from the highest educational levels and were either very well-to-do, or, as was true of two families, had "dropped out" of that class.

The effects of harmonious child-rearing patterns on children appeared sex related. The six daughters of harmonious parents were extraordinarily competent and very similar in their scores on the child behavior measures. Their average Stanford-Binet IQ was 136 (that of the entire sample was also high, 128). On clusters derived from scores on the Preschool Behavior *Q* sort, when compared to others, these girls were achievement-oriented (.05), friendly (.05), and independent (*ns*). By contrast, the two boys whose parents were classified as harmonious, while cooperative, were notably submissive, aimless, not achievement-oriented, and dependent. The harmonious pattern of child rearing seemed to produce an effeminate orientation in boys (if one can say much about two cases), while the effect in girls was entirely positive. In girls, high achievement and independence resulted, without loss of a feminine (i.e., cooperative and tractable) disposition.

An excerpt from an interview with a harmonious mother of a 4-year-old girl exemplifies the values and practices of parents placed in this pattern.

Interviewer: Describe Nina.

Mother: She's strong-tempered, which comes up because she's always been taught that her opinions are valid. So if you disagree with her, she'll stand there and argue all day if she feels differently. But all of the things that make her hard to deal with are again the same things that make her very appealing. She's a very individualistic person. She tries very hard to please people and to communicate with people and to amuse them, but she's not a follower, really. And she doesn't need other people—she's not dependent,

really. Psychologically she's not dependent on other people—I don't think she feels so, although she knows she couldn't do a number of things herself.

Interviewer: How do you feel when she disobeys?

Mother: If you use the term disobeys, that sort of conjures up a negative feeling. Oftentimes she just doesn't *think* the way I do. It's just a difference of opinion. But I figure to a certain amount that I've been here longer—walked around on the earth longer, so I know more. Which isn't particularly valid either.

Interviewer: Does Nina ever downright refuse to obey?

Mother: Oh yeah.

Interviewer: What do you do?

Mother: It depends on what is in question. If I really feel it's not all that important, I'll just give up—just walk off. Say forget it. If from my point of view it's important, I'll pursue it. . . . There have been times when we've sat for hours and hours and yelled at each other—just incredible—really stubborn, both of us. But most of the time, if I really feel it's not important, I'll drop it.

Interviewer: Do you reason with Nina?

Mother: Oh yeah. She tries to reason with me too, from her point of view. What I consider reasonable, I'll throw at her. We just had a big discussion of reason the other day. Reason—I'd never thought about it as much as the other night. It's a very charged word also —it only means that the person who's saying it thinks it fair, or, quote, 'reasonable.' But it doesn't mean that in some huge all-over sense it's just or anything. As far as I'm concerned it doesn't mean that at all.

Interviewer: What do you do when Nina disobeys?

Mother: I don't know. I don't ask her to do a heck of a lot, really. Usually it gets done. We go and do it together, or—if she's really dead-set against it, she won't do it completely on her own. If she feels that from her standpoint it's not something she's required to do, whether it makes sense to me for her to do it, she won't do it. I really dislike punishing her. Punishing her comes down to—most of the time—doing physical things. And I have a strong distaste for that so I conk out. That's probably why she's so headstrong too.

Interviewer: What do you think about the importance of children obeying parents?

Mother: We discuss general philosophies. . . . There's a lot of discussion now. Terry [older sister] is exposed to a lot of my philosophy, but she's also been exposed to the fact that it's just the way *I* feel—that it's not particularly the way she has to feel, or the way she should feel. Or the way anybody else feels.

Interviewer: What do you think of respect for parents as a reason for obedience?

Mother: Being Japanese has a bearing on this. I've always felt that you owe a certain cognizance of the fact that your parents are your parents and they more than likely raised you and clothed you and fed you and saw that you didn't get sick and die. So the degree of respect would be how much they'd earned. There would be a certain amount of respect just because of the things I mentioned. But past that, it would be how much you earned as an individual.

Interviewer: Is it to her best interest in the long run that Nina learn to obey?

Mother: No.

Interviewer: Why not?

Mother: I only think that obedience is practical.

I've taught my kids to do whatever you want to do, but you're responsible for your actions and therefore also suffer the consequences or whatever you want to say. For instance, in the sense of society, if you break a law and are cognizant of the fact, and you know that if you're going to go out and play the game, if you break the rules, you're going to have to take the consequences.

Interviewer: What decisions does Nina make for herself?

Mother: She makes all her own decisions and then we argue about them. She really does. She decides all her own things. She decides her clothes, what she'll eat; but they're sort of in the context of what's happening. She goes to the store and she decides what she'll wear by what she'll see. Or if she gets dressed in the morning, she'll decide what she'll wear by what she can see around her.

Many of these harmonious families were preparing themselves for communal living, and indeed their interpersonal attributes seem ideally adapted to some type of extended family organization. It would be of interest to identify more families like these and to study the long-range effects upon children of what may be newly developing forms of family organization based upon antinomian values.

REFERENCES

Baumrind, D. Child care practices anteceding three patterns of preschool behavior. *Genetic Psychology Monographs*, 1967, 75, 43–88.

Baumrind, D. Current patterns of parental authority. *Developmental Psychology*, 1971, 4, 1–103.

Baumrind, D., & Black, A. E. Socialization practices associated with dimensions of competence in preschool boys and girls. *Child Development*, 1967, 38, 291–327.

Journal editor's note: Dr. Baumrind's material about the six girls and two boys described herein is interesting and timely to a degree that it seemed to me it should be pulled out from her more formal report . . . and reported in some detail. Dr. Baumrind clearly recognizes and states that the sample is small and its selection unusual. Her scientific caution was such that she made only a brief mention of these eight children in the first draft of her monograph, and the present fuller treatment resulted from my encouraging her to report her results in more detail, even though they are not the last word on the matter.

PARENTS AS TEACHERS: HOW LOWER CLASS AND MIDDLE CLASS MOTHERS TEACH

ROBERT HESS   VIRGINIA SHIPMAN

In most American families, the mother is the major socializing agent for her preschool child. Consequently, she continually functions as a teacher in their everyday interactions, whether or not she is aware of her teaching role. Much of the implicit curriculum to which the child is exposed in his preschool years is conveyed by the communications he receives from his mother.

Mothers react differently to comparable socialization situations, attaching different meanings to them and consequently contrasting with one another in their responses to their children. However, even when two mothers react in the same way in attempting to communicate the same message to their children, they may still differ in their communication behavior and consequently have differential effects upon their children. They may teach the same content but differ in their methods. They may be said to have different maternal teaching styles. Research was designed at the University of Chicago Early Education Research Center to study differences in teaching styles. Mothers and children were brought to the laboratory, where each mother was to teach the same content to her child. The teaching situations were structured so that the information to be conveyed to the child was constant for all subjects, but each mother was free to use any means or techniques she desired in attempting to convey it.

The interactions revealed striking differences in the way mothers attempted to teach the same basic message or skill to their children and in their relative success in doing so. In attempting to account for these differences, we have examined a number of maternal teaching variables including language (variety, organization, and relevance), motivation techniques (methods used in attempting to get the child to want to learn or to be prepared to learn), ability to interpret the child's responses, and success in giving appropriate feedback in reaction to those responses. Effects observed in the children were also measured and were analyzed in relationship to the various maternal variables.

Differences among mothers in these teaching variables not only affect the degree to which the children learn the intended message or meaning, but also affect their motivation in the learning situation and the kinds of learning strategies or habits they develop. Although some of the latter kinds of effects may be extraneous or even antithetical to a mother's intent as she teaches her child, they may occur as direct reactions to the way in which she teaches.

Mothers attempting to teach their children in deliberate instruction situations differ considerably from one another in the kind of techniques that they use and the degree of success they achieve. This variety is partially due to differences in education, intelligence, and general experience which cause the mothers to differ in their repertoire of abilities in communication skills. These general factors tend to limit the range of techniques available to each mother, although many other factors are involved in determining the specific behavior which she uses in a given interaction with her child.

Many of the maternal communication variables studied are aspects of the *information transmission* or teaching. This aspect of mother-child communication has been given relatively

Reprinted with abridgment by permission of the authors from mimeographed Document ED 025-301 (Urbana: ERIC Clearinghouse on Early Childhood Education, University of Illinois, 1967).

little attention in previous research, but it is a primary focus of the present investigation. Consequently the mothers were coded on such variables as language specificity, completeness and clarity of presentation, and the sequential ordering of messages and concepts presented. Other aspects of information transmission involve the mothers' attempt to obtain feedback from the children and their own subsequent confirmatory or corrective feedback responses to the child.

In addition to the information transmission aspects just described, the behavior of mothers in interaction with their children will also differ in the affective sphere. Previous studies have ordinarily been based on mother-child interaction in an unstructured, free play situation. Our mother-child interactions were deliberate instruction situations in which the mother had to exercise considerable control over the child's behavior and in which the constant face-to-face interaction was likely to increase the general intensity of affect. Consequently the *warmth* and *control* in these interaction situations do not have quite the same meaning as they do when applied to general parental behavior in the home. The second major consideration differentiating the present research from earlier ones is our emphasis on the information transmission aspects of the mothers' communication. In effect we are adding a third major dimension in our factor of maternal behavior, studying it not only in its own right but in its interaction with the other two. Thus maternal control is not merely a matter of permissiveness vs. strictness. It is approached as a complex factor which includes both quantitative (to what degree does the mother obtain compliance with her wishes?) and qualitative (what methods does she use in attempting to do so?) aspects. In the teaching situation, in fact, the mother must usually do more than obtain compliance by controlling the child in the usual sense of the word; she must instill a positive attitude of cooperation and interest in learning in the child. She must *motivate* rather than merely *control* the child, and much of this is accomplished through behavior more closely identified with information transmission and warmth than through control as it is traditionally used. In the realm of maternal warmth, the deliberate instruction situation raises the question of the degree to which

the mother ties in her affective responses to the child's achievement in learning the task. The affective responses of some mothers toward their children may vary little from situation to situation, while other mothers may vary their affective response to the child according to his success and cooperation. Affective responses may also have information transmission aspects, since a given expression of warmth or hostility may also provide information (feedback) and reinforcement when it follows the task response of the child.

Important differences also occur among the children. Factors such as intelligence, interest in learning, and attention span make for differences among the children in their readiness for the task, and other factors appearing during the task itself affect the speed and completeness with which the child is able to learn it. Three separate situations were used. These included a relatively easy cognitive sorting task, a more difficult sorting task, and a task involving the copying of geometric designs. The tasks required each mother to teach the same content but allowed the mother complete freedom of time and method.

Prior to teaching, the mothers were familiarized with the task in an informal, somewhat redundant approach designed to make certain that they clearly understood the task but at the same time designed to avoid giving them any specific model to copy in teaching their child. Once the mother had learned the task she was asked to teach it to her child, and was specifically instructed to use any method and to take as much time as she desired.

In the two cognitive sorting tasks the mothers were asked to teach their children to sort objects in specific ways and to explain the sorting principles or reasons for the resultant groupings. The first was a toy sorting task involving three kinds of toys (trucks, spoons, and chairs) represented in each of three colors (red, yellow, and green). The mother's task was to teach her child to divide the toys into three groups by each criterion, *kind* of toy and *color,* and to be able to verbalize the reasons for these groupings ("These are all chairs," "These are the same color," etc.).

The next task was a more difficult block sorting task in which the mothers had to teach the children how to sort blocks into four groups using two criteria simultaneously. The blocks differed according to four attributes: color (red, yellow, green, and blue), shape (rectangular or circular cross section), height (tall or short), and mark (X or O painted on top of the block). The children were to learn to group together blocks which were the same height and were marked with the same mark and to explain the reasons for these groupings. This required the formation of four groups of blocks, each of which was internally consistent on the two criterion variables but not on the other two variables. The four groups were composed of tall blocks marked X, short blocks marked X, tall blocks marked O, and short blocks marked O, respectively.

The mother was taught each of the sorting tasks while the child was out of the room and then, after she had learned it, was instructed to teach the child to sort the blocks correctly and to verbalize the sorting principle. The mothers were oriented to the task with a method developed to avoid suggesting particular teaching methods or terminology. They were allowed to use whatever labels for the variables that they verbalized spontaneously while being taught the task ("O," "circle," "zero," "goose-egg," etc.). Task teaching was continued to overlearning criteria to insure that the mother knew the task and was not likely to become confused later when teaching the child.

The difficulty levels of the tasks were such that appropriate and useful interaction could be obtained from the entire range of subjects. Although there were differences among the children in their degree of familiarity with the task materials and in their repertoire of labels for the attributes involved, the tasks themselves, sorting into groups and explaining the sorting principles, were unfamiliar to all subjects.

The task facing each mother was the same, that is, to teach the child to sort the toys appropriately and to explain the reasons behind the sorting. However, each mother entered the situation with her own unique background and approach to the task and with a particular history of interaction with her own child. The instructions given to the mother served only to set her goal—to tell her what she was to achieve. The means of achieving that goal, the way in which she taught the task to the child, was left entirely up to her.

The mother's ability to communicate specific meanings was crucial in these two tasks, since the child knew nothing about them and had to depend entirely upon the messages he received from her. This placed a considerable burden on the mothers since their task was clearly defined but the way in which they were supposed to go about it was not, and since they could expect little help from their children, at least in the beginning. It was clearly up to the mother to engage the child's interest in the task and to impart the information that he needed to know in order for him to participate more actively. Because the child could not participate actively and intelligently until he had acquired a certain amount of task-relevant information from the mother, the mother's communication skills were of crucial importance in the cognitive sorting tasks.

The teaching of many mothers was poorly organized or incomplete during this crucial period of introduction of basic information, so that their children participated only in a passive way or else began to resist the task early. In these dyads the interaction was for the most part one-way—from mother to child. The mother kept attempting to get desired responses from the child but met with little or no success. Other mothers who were able to transmit the necessary basic information to their children early in the task usually settled into a more balanced or complementary interaction in which the child participated more actively, asked questions, made relevant comments, and generally showed evidence of self-motivation over and above that provided by the mother.

The information transmission aspects of maternal teaching were evaluated for specificity (clarity and precision in specifying the intended meaning). Specificity is construed as a continuous variable, having both verbal and nonverbal aspects, which is present in all communication. Different degrees of specificity in both verbal and nonverbal aspects are shown in the following series of examples, all of which are possible maternal responses to a mistake in block placement by the child:

1. "That's not right."
2. "What about the mark?"
3. "No, those are O and that's an X."

4. (Mother retrieves block and points to mark:) "No, this has an *O* . . . see? You have to find some more with *O*."

5. (Mother points back and forth between the erroneously placed block and the other blocks in the group:) "No, see . . . this one is an *O* and those have *X*."

6. (Mother points back and forth between the erroneously placed block and the other blocks in the group:) "No, see, this has *O* and these have *X*. We don't want to mix up the *O*'s and the *X*'s, so you have to put this block where there are some other blocks that have *O* on them, too."

The data in the Chicago study clearly show that the more successful mothers, in addition to being more specific in their teaching, tended to rely on praise and engagement rather than coercion as their means of motivating the children. Although an equivalent amount of regulation of the child's overt behavior can be achieved through either method, differences in method may be expected to have contrasting effects upon the child's internal subjective state. The

mother who motivates through praise and engagement provides an inducement for the child to participate in the task and follows this up with encouragement and praise which tend to make the task a pleasant experience for him. In contrast, the mother who confines herself to criticism and coercive control encourages the development of an avoidance orientation in the child and in effect makes the task itself a punishment.

. . . Mothers who attempt to motivate the child through engagement and presentation of information are usually person-oriented in their appeal, and their statements are usually instructive as well as motivating. Mothers who rely on coercive control, on the other hand, are usually confined to imperative commands appealing to status-normative rationales. Illustrations of these differences are provided in the examples below. Each pair of examples represents contrasting maternal behavior in response to the same antecedent situation. The examples in the left column involve the use of engagement and presentation of information, while those on the right are confined to coercive control and criticism.

1a. "I've got another game to teach you."

2a. "Now listen to Mommy carefully and watch what I do because I'm going to show you how we play the game."

3a. "No, Johnny. That's a big one. Remember we're going to keep the big ones separate from the little ones."

4a. "Wait a minute, Johnny. You have to look at the block first before you try to find where it goes. Now pick it up again and look at it—is it big or small? . . . Now put it where it goes."

5a. "No, we can't stop now, Johnny. Mrs. Smith wants me to show you how to do this so you can do it for her. Now if you pay close attention and let Mommy teach you, you can learn how to do it and show her, and then you'll have some time to play."

1b. "There's another thing you have to learn here, so sit down and pay attention."

2b. "Pay attention now and get it right, 'cause you're gonna have to show the lady how to do it later."

3b. "No, that's not what I showed you! Put that with the big ones where it belongs."

4b. "That doesn't go there—you're just guessing. I'm trying to show you how to do this and you're just putting them any old place. Now pick it up and do it again and this time don't mess up."

5b. "Now you're playing around and you don't even know how to do this. You want me to call the lady? You better listen to what I'm saying and quit playing around or I'm gonna call the lady in on you and see how you like that."

The above examples are typical of the maternal statements observed in the interaction tasks. They were chosen to represent contrasting maternal reactions to the same basic stimulus

on the part of the child. The difference in appeal (instructive vs. imperative; person vs. status) is one of degree, being sometimes quite obvious and sometimes very subtle. For each pair of examples, however, the statement in the left column is superior to the one in the right column in one or more of the following ways:

1. It is more conducive to the consideration of alternatives for thought and action.
2. It represents an appeal to logical contingencies or personal considerations rather than an arbitrary exercise of power.
3. It presents the task as desirable, either as an end in itself or as a means to a desired end, rather than as a chore or an arbitrary demand made upon the child.
4. It places the mother in the role of a supportive sponsor or helper rather than an impersonal or punitive authority figure.
5. It defines the situation as a cooperative venture in which the mother has some responsibility rather than as something that involves the child alone.
6. It specifies immediate means rather than merely repeat ultimate goals.
7. It connotes cooperation, affiliation, and positive expectation of success, as opposed to conflict, withdrawal of positive regard, and emphasis on failure.

Despite the desirable effects that these techniques might be expected to have upon the children, most of the mothers made relatively little use of praise and engagement. Mothers of different education and background differed very little in their relative use of coercive control, but the middle-class mothers were the only social status group to praise their children or attempt to engage their interest in the tasks with regularity. In all four social status groups the use of coercive control exceeded the use of engagement techniques. However, among middle-class mothers the difference was very slight, while among lower-class mothers the frequency of engagement was far below that of coercion.

The data on maternal motivation techniques appear to provide part of the explanation for the high rate of teaching difficulty and undesirable child behaviors observed in the interactions. The majority of mothers made relatively little attempt to elicit the child's interest through positive engagement, but instead were apt to react to problems by attempting to force

compliance through coercion. In view of this it is easy to see how any initial positive feelings about the task that the child may have had would become quickly dissipated and replaced by a failure-avoidance orientation, especially if coercive control were combined with poor teaching so that successful learning was made difficult.

In a few extreme cases observed in our sample, attention was confined almost entirely to the physical or block-placement aspects of the task, with little or no emphasis given to the sorting principle. In such cases the mother's method was to demonstrate block placement for the child and then to ask him to do it himself, giving feedback and continuing this practice until the child had learned where each block went. Specific labels in the feedback, when they occurred at all, tended to be given in an off-hand manner which did not clearly indicate the importance or relevance of the attribute. For example:

"I have some blocks here and you have to learn how to put them where they go. Watch me now so you'll learn how to do it. See, this one goes here, and this one goes here, and this one goes here with the big ones, and this one goes here. See how they go now? These are all the same, these are all the same, these are all the same, and these are all the same. Can you do that now for Mommy? Let's see you do it for me. . . . That's right. . . . No. . . . No. . . . That ain't right. It goes here with the big ones. . . . No, over here. . . . Ok. Can you do that again?"

The preceding example demonstrates the kind of teaching that resulted when the mother made no attempt to specify the relationship between the attributes of the blocks and the physical act of sorting them into separate groups. This is comparable to the situation in which a programmer would ask the machine to divide a deck of cards into subgroups without telling it which columns to scan as the basis for separation into groups. The machine would be unable to interpret such instructions and would not act on them. Children, however, can and do react, at least to that portion of the instructions which they can understand. To a degree this is an advantage for a mother with a primarily reactive teaching style, for if the child begins responding and making errors, the mother may see that he does not understand the task and may try to correct him. In the process of correction she often may fill in the gaps in her teaching program so that the child can make the connection between the attributes of the blocks and the sorting principle and conceivably learn the task, although by a long and disorganized trial and error method.

This "do as I do" approach, however, with its emphasis on the placement responses at the expense of discussion of the sorting principle, can cause the child to view the task as a guessing game or a rote memory exercise. Problems also arise if the child is successful in learning where to place the blocks, since this may cause the mother to assume mistakenly that he has mastered the sorting principle and will be able to generalize it to new blocks. Even where this does not happen, a mother who starts out with this reactive style may en-

counter difficulties later when she tries to teach the sorting principle.

Optimal maternal communication implied high levels of specificity in all areas previously discussed, in both labeling and focusing behavior. This included not only orientation and feedback but also pre-response instructions, where specificity occurred least frequently. It also implied a preference for eliciting the child's interest in the task through engagement and for maintaining it through encouragement and praise. An additional element, not specifically discussed previously, was sequential organization. Ideally the mother would proceed in a step-by-step process, introducing subparts of the task first before requiring the child to make responses which assumed prior knowledge of those subparts. An idealized example of this kind of teaching is presented below, along with interpretative comments analyzing the functions of each step.

Maternal Behavior	*Interpretation*
"Hi, Johnny. Sit down here by Mommy because I've got something to show you. It's a game that you play using these blocks here. There's a special way that you can put blocks together in different groups here on the board. I'll show you how to do it, and then you can show Mrs. Smith [the tester] when she comes back.	With these few brief remarks, the mother manages to: (1) greet the child warmly; (2) give the child a general overview of what is to come without getting into specific details; (3) describe the task ("game") in a positive manner, connoting that the child will enjoy it; (4) refer to the post-task test in a way that suggests that it is an opportunity for the child to show off his knowledge to a known person, rather than picture it as an arduous trial conducted by a feared authority figure; and (5) subtly but consistently stress the importance of the sorting rationale (that is, the task involves learning a method which will tell *how* to sort the blocks, as opposed to a task requiring the child to learn *where* to put the blocks).
"Ok?	This simple pause in the teaching has several functions: (1) It provides a check on the child's attention and cooperation. (2) It allows the child to express any objection to the task itself or interests in non-task activities which are competing with his willingness to attend to the mother. If the child does have objections or competing interests, it is important for the mother to deal with them at this point, before the introduction of formal teaching, since teaching will proceed more smoothly if the

Maternal Behavior

Interpretation

child is interested and cooperative. (3) It allows the child to ask questions which will enable the mother to clarify or expand on some part of her remarks.

"All right, now there are two things about the blocks that you have to remember. You have to look at the size of the block to see whether it's tall or short, and you have to see what kind of mark the block has on it. Now look at these two blocks [placing a tall and a short next to each other]. This one is bigger than this one, isn't it? This one is tall, and this one is short [putting hands over tops of the two blocks and moving hand back and forth]. Now look at the other blocks. Some of them are tall like this one, and some of them are short like this one. What about this block? Is it tall or short? . . . Right. And this one? . . . Fine.

[Replacing the other two blocks and getting two blocks of contrasting mark:] "Now the second thing we have to look at is the mark on the blocks. Notice each of these blocks has a white mark on each end [showing each end of the blocks to the child]. Now this block has those two crossed lines there [tracing with finger], see? Now what do we call that mark? We call that an *X*. That's an *X*. Now this block has a round mark on it [tracing], and we call that an *O*. That's an *O*. So this one is *X* and that one is *O*. What are they now? . . . Right. And what's the mark on this one here? . . . Ok, and this one? . . . Right.

This example represents a highly organized presentation of the relevant attributes, with high specificity both in verbal labeling and in focusing behavior. The mother begins by stating the relevance of what is to come to the ultimate goal of the task, that is, that the child needs to know the two things that she is about to teach him in order to know how to group the blocks. However, she avoids overwhelming the child by trying to put them all together at once, and instead confines herself to introducing the relevant attributes.

To further simplify the presentation she introduces the attributes one at a time rather than in combination, and she presents each term with specificity and a certain amount of redundancy before requiring the child to use it himself. She does, however, require the child to produce labels, getting specific feedback from him rather than simply assuming that he has understood, and she affirms each correct response as it appears.

To make sure that the child is attending to the appropriate aspects of the blocks, his mother asks him to label blocks that she has not already discussed. Her periodic seeking of feedback allows the child to assume the role of an active participant rather than of a passive listener. The order and specificity in the presentation maximizes the child's chances of learning quickly and easily, which in turn maximizes the likelihood of successful response and positive reinforcement rather than failure and negative reinforcement.

"Now when we divide up the blocks into groups, we have to see whether they're tall or short and whether they have *X* or *O*. The blocks in each separate group should be the same size and should have the same mark on top of them. Now look at this group. Both of the blocks are tall, not little like these other ones here and here—they're both tall and they both have the same mark on top. See [pointing]—they both have *X*. Now that's why they go together, because they're both tall and they both have *X* on top. Now look at this group; these blocks are both tall, too, but they both have *O* on top, so they go by themselves—they're tall with *O* [pointing].

In this sequence the mother first shows how the blocks in each group already formed on the board have the same height and mark, and then goes on to demonstrate the method of placing the blocks. Throughout the presentation she consistently emphasizes both similarities and differences among the blocks and carefully specifies the relationship between the attributes of height and mark and the basis upon which the groups are formed. In demonstrating sorting she operationally describes each step so the child sees that the actual placement is the end result of a series of decisions based on evaluation of the similarities and differences among the blocks.

Maternal Behavior

"Now the blocks in this group go together because they're both short and because they both have [showing the ends of the blocks to the child]? . . . X, right. And the blocks in the last group go together because they're both [holding hand over tops of blocks]? . . . short, and they both have [showing ends of blocks to child]? . . . O, right.

"Now that's what we have to know when we put these extra blocks into their groups on the board. The blocks in each group should be the same size and they should have the same mark on top. Now this block is tall and has an X on top, so I want to find some other blocks that are tall and have X on top to put it with. This group has tall blocks and both have X [pointing] just like the block in my hand, so that's where it goes.

"Now look at this block. It's a short one and it has an O on top [pointing]. Now we want to find the group that has the same size and the same mark on top. [Placing block with tall O's:] Now these blocks have O on top, but they're big ones and this one is a little one, so it couldn't go there. [Placing with small X's:] These blocks are the same size—they're both small—but they have X's on top, so the marks aren't the same [pointing], so it can't go there either. [Placing with short O's:] But these blocks are both short and they both have O on top, just like the one in my hand. So that's where it goes—it goes with other blocks that are short and have O on top. [Mother continues in similar fashion for the other two blocks.]

"Now do you want to try it? . . . Ok, I'll take a block out of each group and we'll let you put them back where they go. [Mother removes a block from each group and hands one block to the child:] Now remember, we want to fix them so that the blocks in each group are the same size and have the same mark on top.

"Now look at this block—is it tall or short? . . . Ok, and does it have an X or an O on it? . . . Right, so we want to put it in the group that has short blocks with O on them. Can you find that group? [Child places block with short X's.] Well, those are short, all right, but what about the marks? Look at them—is the mark on this block the same as the mark on those two blocks? No—those are X's. So you have to find the group that has short blocks with O on top. . . . That's right—fine. Now the blocks

Interpretation

By thus operationalizing the sorting process, the mother can help the child to see the end result as a natural outcome following a series of understandable, goal-oriented steps, and not simply as a *fait accompli* to be accepted but not understood. This is an important consideration, because Piaget has shown that a child of this age will not ordinarily ask how an adult is able to do such a thing, or seek a logical, operational explanation. He may, however, accept the assertion that the block does indeed belong in the group that the mother says it belongs in, taking this as a fact which requires no explanation or which is ascribed to magical properties thought to reside in the mother or the stimuli themselves. Mothers who failed to verbalize the logical operations behind the sorting process often unwittingly encouraged this kind of response in the children, especially if in addition they neglected to ask the child to explain the reasons for placement on his own.

This sequence represents a continuation and extension of the same principles illustrated in the earlier ones. Before definitively concluding her demonstration and moving on to the first placement response, the mother consults the child regarding his willingness to try placing the blocks himself. This provides a check on the child's motivational state and in addition gives him an opportunity to express confusion or to seek further information or demonstration.

After eliciting the child's consent, the mother then moves on to the placement unit, although not without giving him considerable additional help before allowing him to actually place a block. She first restates the sorting principle in the form of a global description of the task, and then follows through with specific instructions concerning the first block. All of this helps the child to respond correctly, but more

Maternal Behavior

in that group are all short and they all have
O on top.

"Now how about this block. Is it tall or
short? . . . Ok, and what mark is that? . . .
Fine, now can you find the group that has tall
blocks with *X* on top? . . . Good. Now why
does that go there, Johnny? It goes there because these blocks are all tall and have what
on top? . . . Right." [Mother continues in a
similar vein, although as the child's knowledge
becomes more secure, she gradually reduces
the frequency of prompting in specific instructions and gradually increases her attempts to
elicit this material by questioning the child
until eventually he is able to sort and to verbalize the sorting principle correctly on each
trial.]

Interpretation

importantly it stresses the cognitive operations
which the child is to pursue. The emphasis
throughout is on processing of the blocks before placement and verbalization of the sorting
principle after placement. The demands made
upon the child are gradually increased at a rate
corresponding to his increasing ability to cope
with them.

The mother regularly provides immediate af-
firmation or negation after each response, although her responses to errors are problem-
centered and informative rather than critical.
Her general role is that of a friendly helper
rather than an impersonal or critical evaluator.

The preceding example of maternal teaching,
particularly if read from beginning to end
without attention to the interpretative comments, may not seem particularly noteworthy
or impressive. It has a natural, almost familiar
quality which tempts the reader to think, "Well,
that's about how I would explain it myself." In
a sense this reaction is perfectly valid, since
the presentation appeals to common sense as a
straightforward way of presenting the block
sorting task which involves no unusual didactic
techniques or specially prepared equipment.
Most, if not all, of the principles discussed and
illustrated are well known, appearing routinely
in works on teaching and learning. This sim-
plicity is more apparent than real, however,
since teaching which approached the ideal outlined above was very rarely observed in this
research. Paradoxically, the example seems simple partly because of its high clarity, specificity,
and organization. It is so easy to follow that it
makes the learning of the task itself seem easy.
However, for the mothers in our study, who
had to teach it to their children without benefit
of previous discussion and analysis, the task
proved to be quite difficult. Despite the fact
that no time limit on teaching was imposed,
only 10 of 162 children received perfect scores
on the post-task test.

Since each of the mothers knew the task herself, at least well enough to meet our criteria,

why were there such gross differences among
the mothers in their ability to communicate it
to their children? Part of the answer, of course,
is that mothers differed in general intelligence,
academic education, and breadth of experience
which made them relatively more or less well-
prepared for the task. The past history of interaction between the mother and her particular
child was also important, since the mothers
presumably differed in their experience in teaching children and the children differed in the
degree to which they would be willing to cooperate in such a task. Two additional factors
which appear to be related to the observed differences are the mothers' abilities to abstract
the essentials of the task and encode them in
language, and to interpret and respond to the
behavior of the children. The best teaching was
distinguished from that which was adequate but
less ideal primarily in the careful organization
and sequencing of the presentation. It is likely
that mothers who taught this way were able to
make an implicit or even explicit task-analysis
of the situation, abstracting the essentials into
an orderly sequence of subparts leading to an
ultimate goal. Many mothers presented all the
essentials in adequately specific language but
lacked this kind of organization, so that they
frequently had to backtrack or present new information as it became evident that the child
did not completely understand them.

The teaching of some mothers reflected a failure to understand the child's needs and limitations. This was evident in many ways, such as in failures to give orientation to the child or to attempt to gain his positive interest in the task, in failures to explain terminology or to supplement verbal presentation with nonverbal focusing, and in failures to properly interpret the actions of the child. The latter difficulty is inferred from observation of maternal reactions to behavior such as nonmeaningful and spuriously successful placement, which often were not recognized as such by the mothers. Some mothers allowed the children to establish a pattern of going from group to group until they reached the right one, or of placing the blocks quickly without giving any verbal labels, and made no observable attempt to break it. Such mothers seemed to simply project their view of the task onto the child or to assume that he was following the presentation and conceptualizing the task the same way they were without attempting to test out this assumption.

Sometimes the mothers provided direct evidence of their own failure to properly interpret the children's behavior. Examples include those mothers who were surprised and dismayed to find during the test period that their children (previously coded for spuriously successful placement) were unable to place test blocks correctly. Other mothers handled inhibition poorly because they were unable to accept the child's protestations of ignorance, apparently believing instead that the child really knew how to put the blocks where they went but for some reason was unwilling to do so. Failure to distinguish between process and performance in block placement was often evident in mothers whose children were coded for nonmeaningful placement, as when the mothers made comments such as, "Now I thought you knew that one, Johnny—you got it right the last time."

Before discussing differences among the social status groups, some additional comments about the mothers should be made. In discussing failures in communication in the mothers' teaching, it has been stated or implied that poor teaching has undesirable effects on the children. It is important, however, to carefully distinguish between the mother's motives and intentions on the one hand and her actual behavior or performaance on the other. The differences among mothers were primarily differences in means rather than ends or goals, since presumably the major goal of every mother in the interactions was to teach the task as we had requested her to do. It is also assumed that every mother, if questioned about the matter, would have stated her intention to make the task pleasant and enjoyable for her child in addition to making it a learning experience. Under these assumptions, then, the frequency of learning difficulties and undesirable reactions on the part of the children are considered unintended and unwanted by the mothers, resulting from inadequate communication skills rather than from any deliberate callousness or rejection of the child. Omissions and inadequacies are felt to have resulted from the fact that more desirable and effective methods simply did not occur to the mothers (limited repertoire in the proactive aspects of communication), or that the need for them was not perceived (inadequate reactive responses due to failure to recognize or interpret the process aspects of the children's responses). The net result of such communication, however, is that the ineffective mother not only fails to implement her goals but also unwittingly creates undesirable side effects.

SOVIET METHODS OF CHARACTER EDUCATION: SOME IMPLICATIONS FOR RESEARCH

URIE BRONFENBRENNER

Every society faces the problem of the moral training of its youth. This is no less true of Communist society than of our own. Indeed, Communist authorities view as the primary objective of education not the learning of subject matter but the development of what they call "socialist morality." It is instructive for us in the West to examine the nature of this "socialist morality" and the manner in which it is inculcated, for to do so brings to light important differences in the ends and means of character education in the two cultures. For research workers in the field of personality development, such an examination is especially valuable, since it lays bare unrecognized assumptions and variations in approach. Accordingly, it is the purpose of this paper to provide a much-condensed account of Soviet methods of character education and to examine some of the provocative research questions that emerge from the contrast between the Soviet approach and our own.

THE WORK AND IDEAS OF A. S. MAKARENKO

To examine Soviet methods of character training is to become acquainted with the thinking and technology developed primarily by one man —Anton Semyonovich Makarenko. Makarenko's name is virtually a household word in the Soviet Union. His popularity and influence are roughly comparable to those of Dr. Spock in the United States, but his primary concern is not with the child's physical health but with his moral upbringing. Makarenko's influence

Reprinted with abridgment from the Research Supplement to *Religious Education*, July–August 1962, 845–61, by permission of the author and the publisher, The Religious Education Association, New York City.

extends far beyond his own voluminous writings since there is scarcely a manual for the guidance of Communist parents, teachers, or youth workers that does not draw heavily on his methods and ideas. His works have been translated into many languages and are apparently widely read not only in the Soviet Union but throughout the Communist bloc countries, notably East Germany and Communist China. Excellent English translations of a number of his works have been published in Moscow (1949, 1953, 1959) but they are not readily available in this country.

Makarenko developed his ideas and methods over the course of a lifetime of practical work with young people. In the early 1920's, as a young school teacher and devout Communist, Makarenko was handed the assignment of setting up a rehabilitation program for some of the hundreds of homeless children who were roaming the Soviet Union after the civil wars. The first group of such children assigned to Makarenko's school, a ramshackle building far out of town, turned out to be a group of boys about 18 years of age with extensive court records of housebreaking, armed robbery, and manslaughter. For the first few months, Makarenko's school served simply as the headquarters for the band of highwaymen who were his legal wards. But gradually, through the development of his group-oriented discipline techniques, and through what can only be called the compelling power of his own moral convictions, Makarenko was able to develop a sense of group responsibility and commitment to the work program and code of conduct that he had laid out for the collective. In the end, the Gorky Commune became known throughout the Soviet Union for its high morale, discipline, and for the productivity of its fields, farms, and shops. Indeed, Makarenko's methods proved so successful that he was selected to head a new commune set up by the ministry of Internal Affairs (then the Cheka, later to become the GPU and NKVD). In the years which followed, Makarenko's theories and techniques became widely adopted throughout the USSR and now constitute the central core of Soviet educational practice.

To turn to the ideas themselves, we may begin with an excerpt from what is possibly the most widely read of Makarenko's works, *A Book for Parents* (1959).

But our [Soviet] family is not an accidental combination of members of society. The family is a natural collective body and, like everything natural, healthy, and normal, it can only blossom forth in socialist society, freed of those very curses from which both mankind as a whole and the individual are freeing themselves.

The family becomes the natural primary cell of society, the place where the delight of human life is realized, where the triumphant forces of man are refreshed, where children—the chief joy of life—live and grow.

Our parents are not without authority either, but this authority is only the reflection of societal authority. The duty of a father in our country towards his children is a particular form of his duty towards society. It is as if our society says to parents:

You have joined together in good will and love, rejoice in your children and expect to go on rejoicing in them. That is your personal affair and concerns your own personal happiness. Within the course of this happy process you have given birth to new human beings. A time will come when these beings will cease to be solely the instruments of your happiness, and will step forth as independent members of society. For society, it is by no means a matter of indifference what kind of people they will become. In delegating to you a certain measure of societal authority the Soviet State demands from you the correct upbringing of its future citizens. Particularly it relies on you to provide certain conditions arising naturally out of your union; namely, your parental love.

If you wish to give birth to a citizen while dispensing with parental love, then be so kind as to warn society that you intend to do such a rotten thing. Human beings who are brought up without parental love are often deformed human beings [Makarenko, 1959, p. 29].

Characteristic of Makarenko's thought is the view that the parent's authority over the child is delegated to him by the state and that duty to one's children is merely a particular instance of one's broader duty towards society. A little later in his book for parents, the author makes this point even more emphatically. After telling the story of a boy who ran away from home after some differences with his mother, he concludes by affirming: "I am a great admirer of optimism and I like very much young lads who have so much faith in the Soviet State that they are carried away and will not trust even their own mothers" (Makarenko, 1959, pp. 37–38). In other words, when the needs and values of the family conflict with those of society, there is no question about who gets priority. And society receives its concrete manifestation and embodiment in the *collective,* which is an organized group engaged in some socially useful enterprise.

This brings us to Makarenko's basic thesis that optimal personality development can occur only through productive activity in a social collective. The first collective is the family, but this must be supplemented early in life by other collectives specially organized in schools, neighborhoods, and other community settings. The primary function of the collective is to develop socialist morality. This aim is accomplished through an explicit regimen of activity mediated by group criticism, self-criticism, and group-oriented punishments and rewards.

Makarenko's ideas are elaborated at length in his semibiographical, semifictional accounts of life in the collective (1949, 1953). It is in these works that he describes the principles and procedures to be employed for building the collective and using it as an instrument of character education. More relevant to our purposes, however, is the manner in which these methods are applied in school settings, for it is in this form that they have become most systematized and widely used.

SOCIALIZATION IN THE SCHOOL COLLECTIVE

The account which follows is taken from a manual (Novikova, 1959) for the training and guidance of "school directors, supervisors, teachers, and Young Pioneer leaders." The manual was written by staff members of the Institute on the Theory and History of Pedagogy at the Academy of Pedagogical Sciences and is typical of several others prepared under the same auspices and widely distributed throughout the USSR.

This particular volume carries the instructive title: *Socialist Competition in the School*. The same theme is echoed in the titles of individual chapters: "Competition in the Classroom," "Competition between Classrooms," "Competition between Schools," and so on. It is not difficult to see how Russians arrive at the notion, with which they have made us so familiar, of competition between nations and between social systems. Moreover, in the chapter titles we see already reflected the influence of dialectical materialism: Conflict at one level is resolved through synthesis at the next higher level, always in the service of the Communist collective.

Let us examine the process of collective socialization as it is initiated in the very first grade. Conveniently enough, the manual starts us off on the first day of school with the teacher standing before the newly assembled class. What should her first words be? Our text tells us:

It is not difficult to see that a direct approach to the class with the command "All sit straight" often doesn't bring the desired effect since a demand in this form does not reach the sensibilities of the pupils and does not activate them.

How does one "reach the sensibilities of the pupils" and "activate them"? According to the manual, here is what the teacher should say: "Let's see which row can sit the straightest." This approach, we are told, has certain important psychological advantages. In response,

The children not only try to do everything as well as possible themselves, but also take an evaluative attitude toward those who are undermining the achievement of the row. If similar measures arousing the spirit of competition in the children are systematically applied by experienced teachers in the primary classes, then gradually the children themselves begin to monitor the behavior of their comrades and remind those of them who forget

about the rules set by the teacher, who forget what needs to be done and what should not be done. The teacher soon has helpers.

The manual then goes on to describe how records are kept for each row from day to day for different types of tasks so that the young children can develop a concept of group excellence over time and over a variety of activities, including personal cleanliness, condition of notebooks, conduct in passing from one room to the other, quality of recitations in each subject matter, and so on. In these activities considerable emphasis is placed on the externals of behavior in dress, manner, and speech. There must be no spots on shirt or collar, shoes must be shined, pupils must never pass by a teacher without stopping to give greeting, there must be no talking without permission, and the like. Great charts are kept in all the schools showing the performance of each row unit in every type of activity together with their total overall standing. "Who is best?" the charts ask, but the entries are not individuals but social units—rows, and later the "cells" of the Communist youth organization which reaches down to the primary grades.

At first it is the teacher who sets the standards. But soon, still in the first grade, a new wrinkle is introduced: Responsible monitors are designated in each row for each activity. In the beginning their job is only to keep track of the merits and demerits assigned each row by the teacher. Different children act as monitors for different activities and, if one is to believe what the manual says, the monitors become very involved in the progress of their row. Then, too, group achievement is not without its rewards. From time to time the winning row gets to be photographed "in parade uniforms" (all Soviet children must wear uniforms in school), and this photograph is published in that pervasive Soviet institution, the wall newspaper. The significance of the achievements is still further enhanced, however, by the introduction of competition between *classes* so that the winning class and the winning row are visited by delegates from other classrooms in order to learn how to attain the same standard of excellence.

Now let us look more closely at this teacher-mediated monitoring process. In the beginning, we are told, the teacher attempts to focus the attention of children on the achievements of the group; that is, in our familiar phrase, she accentuates the positive. But gradually, "it becomes necessary to take account of negative facts which interfere with the activity of the class." As an example we are given the instance of a child who despite warnings continues to enter the classroom a few minutes after the bell has rung. The teacher decides that the time has come to evoke the group process in correcting such behavior. Accordingly, the next time that Serezha is late, the teacher stops him at the door and turns to the class with this question: "Children, is it helpful or not helpful to us to have Serezha come in late?" The answers are quick in coming. "It interferes, one shouldn't be late, he ought to come on time." "Well," says the teacher, "how can we help Serezha with this problem?" There are many suggestions: get together to buy him a watch, exile him from the classroom, send him to the director's office, or even to exile him from the school. But apparently these suggestions are either not appropriate or too extreme. The teacher, our text tells us, "helps the children find the right answer." She asks for a volunteer to stop by and pick Serezha up on the way to school. Many children offer to help in this mission.

But tragedy stalks. The next day it turns out that not only Serezha is late, but also the boy who promised to pick him up. Since they are both from the same group, their unit receives two sets of demerits and falls to lowest place. Group members are keenly disappointed. "Serezha especially suffered much and felt himself responsible, but equal blame was felt by his companion who had forgotten to stop in for him."

In this way, both through concrete action and explanation, the teacher seeks to forge a spirit of group unity and responsibility. From time to time, she explains to the children the significance of what they are doing, the fact "that they have to learn to live together as one friendly family, since they will have to be learning together for all of the next ten years, and that for this reason one must learn how to help one's companions and to treat them decently."

By the time the children are in the second grade, the responsibilities expected of them are increased in complexity. For example, instead of simply recording the evaluations made by the teacher, the monitors are taught how to make the evaluations themselves. Since this is rather difficult, especially in judging homework assignments, in the beginning two monitors are assigned to every task. In this way, our text tells us, they can help each other in doing a good job of evaluation.

Here is a third grade classroom:

Class 3-B is just an ordinary class; it's not especially well disciplined nor is it outstandingly industrious. It has its lazy members and its responsible ones, quiet ones and active ones, daring, shy, and immodest ones.

The teacher has led this class now for three years, and she has earned the affection, respect, and acceptance as an authority from her pupils. Her word is law for them.

The bell has rung, but the teacher has not yet arrived. She has delayed deliberately in order to check how the class will conduct itself.

In the class all is quiet. After the noisy class break, it isn't so easy to mobilize yourself and to quell the restlessness within you! Two monitors at the desk silently observe the class. On their faces is reflected the full importance and seriousness of the job they are performing. But there is no need for them to make any reprimands: the youngsters with pleasure and pride maintain scrupulous discipline; they are proud of the fact that their class conducts itself in a manner that merits the confidence of the teacher. And when the teacher enters and quietly says be seated, all understand that she deliberately refrains from praising them for the quiet and order, since in their class it could not be otherwise.

During the lesson, the teacher gives an exceptional amount of attention to collective competition between "links." (The links are the smallest unit of the Communist youth organization at this age level.) Throughout the entire lesson the youngsters are constantly hearing which link has best prepared its lesson, which link has done the best at numbers, which is the most disciplined, which has turned in the best work.

The best link not only gets a verbal positive evaluation but receives the right to leave the classroom first during the break and to have its notebooks checked before the others. As a result the links receive the benefit of collective education, common responsibility, and mutual aid.

"What are you fooling around for? You're holding up the whole link," whispers Kolya to his neighbor during the preparation period for the lesson. And during the break he teaches her how better to organize her books and pads in her knapsack.

"Count more carefully," says Olya to her girl friend. "See, on account of you our link got behind today. You come to me and we'll count together at home."

In the third grade still another innovation is introduced. The monitors are taught not only to evaluate but to state their criticisms publicly.

Here is a typical picture. It is the beginning of the lesson. In the first row the link leader reports basing his comments on information submitted by the sanitarian and other responsible monitors: "Today Valadya did the wrong problem. Masha didn't write neatly and forgot to underline the right words in her lesson. Alyoshi had a dirty shirt collar."

The other link leaders make similar reports (the Pioneers are sitting by rows).

The youngsters are not offended by this procedure: they understand that the link leaders are not just tattle-telling but simply fulfilling their duty. It doesn't even occur to the monitors and sanitarians to conceal the shortcomings of their comrades. They feel that they are doing their job well precisely when they notice one or another defect.

Also in the third grade, the teacher introduces still another procedure. She now proposes that the children enter into competition with the monitors, and see if they can beat the monitor at his own game by criticizing themselves. "The results were spectacular: if the monitor was able to talk only about four or five members of the row, there would be supplementary reports about their own shortcomings from as many as eight or ten pupils."

To what extent is this picture overdrawn? Although I have no direct evidence, the accounts I heard from participants in the process lend credence to the descriptions in the manual. For example, I recall a conversation with three elementary school teachers, all men, whom I had met by chance in a restaurant. They were curious about discipline techniques used in American schools. After I had given several examples, I was interrupted: "But how do you use the collective?" When I replied that we

really did not use the classroom group in any systematic way, my three companions were puzzled. "But how do you keep discipline?"

Now it was my turn to ask for examples. "All right," came the answer. "Let us suppose that 10-year-old Vanya is pulling Anya's curls. If he doesn't stop the first time I speak to him, all I need do is mention it again in the group's presence; then I can be reasonably sure that before the class meets again the boy will be talked to by the officers of his Pioneer link. They will remind him that his behavior reflects on the reputation of the link."

"And what if he persists?"

"Then he may have to appear before his link—or even the entire collective—who will explain his misbehavior to him and determine his punishment."

"What punishment?"

"Various measures. He may just be censured, or if his conduct is regarded as serious, he may be expelled from membership. Very often he himself will acknowledge his faults before the group."

Nor does the process of social criticism and control stop with the school. Our manual tells us, for example, that parents submit periodic reports to the school collective on the behavior of the child at home. One may wonder how parents can be depended on to turn in truthful accounts. Part of the answer was supplied to me in a conversation with a Soviet agricultural expert. In response to my questions, he explained that, no matter what a person's job, the collective at his place of work always took an active interest in his family life. Thus a representative would come to the worker's home to observe and talk with his wife and children. And if any undesirable features were noted, these would be reported back to the collective.

I asked for an example.

"Well, suppose the representative were to notice that my wife and I quarreled in front of the children [my companion shook his head]. That would be bad. They would speak to me about it and remind me of my responsibilities for training my children to be good citizens."

I pointed out how different the situation was in America where a man's home was considered a private sanctuary so that, for example, psychologists like myself often had a great deal of difficulty in getting into homes to talk with parents or to observe children.

"Yes," my companion responded. "That's one of the strange things about your system in the West. The family is separated from the rest of society. That's not good. It's bad for the family and bad for society." He paused for a moment, lost in thought. "I suppose," he went on, "if my wife didn't want to let the representative in, she could ask him to leave. But then at work, I should feel ashamed." (He hung his head to emphasize the point.) "Ivanov," they would say, "has an uncultured wife."

But it would be a mistake to conclude that Soviet methods of character education and social control are based primarily on negative criticism. On the contrary, in their approach there is as much of the carrot as the stick. But the carrot is given not merely as a reward for individual performance but explicitly for the child's contribution to group achievement. The great charts emblazoned "Who IS Best?" which bedeck the halls and walls of every classroom have as entries the names not of individual pupils but of rows and links (the link is the smallest unit of Communist youth organization, which of course reaches into every classroom, from the first grade on). It is the winning unit that gets rewarded by a pennant, a special privilege, or by having their picture taken in "parade uniforms." And when praise is given, as it frequently is, to an individual child, the group referent is always there: "Today Peter helped Kate and as a result his unit did not get behind the rest."

Helping other members of one's collective and appreciating their contributions—themes that are much stressed in Soviet character training—become matters of enlightened self-interest, since the grade that each person receives depends on the overall performance of his unit. Thus the good student finds it to his advantage to help the poor one. The same principle is carried over to the group level with champion rows and classes being made responsible for the performance of poorer ones.

Here, then, are the procedures employed in Soviet character education. As a result of Khrushchev's educational reforms, they may be expected to receive even wider application in the years to come, for, in connection with these reforms, several new types of educational institutions are to be developed on a massive scale. The most important of these is the "internat," or boarding school, in which youngsters are to be entered as early as three months of age with parents visiting only on weekends. The internat is described in the theses announcing the reforms as the kind of school which "creates the most favorable conditions for the education and communist upbringing of the rising generation" (Communist Party of Soviet Russia, 1958). The number of boarding schools in the USSR is to be increased during the current seven-year plan from a 1958 level of 180,000 to 250,000 in 1965 (figures cited in *Pravda,* November 18, 1958), and according to I. A. Kairov, head of the Academy of Pedagogical Sciences, "No one can doubt that, as material conditions are created, the usual general educational school will be supplanted by the boarding school" (Kairov, 1960).

If this prophecy is fulfilled, we may expect that in the years to come the great majority of Soviet children (and children in some other countries of the Communist bloc as well) will from the first year of life onward be spending their formative period in collective settings and will be exposed daily to the techniques of collective socialization we have been describing. It is therefore a matter of considerable practical and scientific interest to identify the salient features of these techniques and subject them to research study, in so far as this becomes possible within the framework of our own society.

GUIDING PRINCIPLES OF THE SOVIET APPROACH TO CHARACTER TRAINING

As a first approximation, we may list the following as distinguishing characteristics or guiding principles of Communist methods of character education.

1. The peer collective (under adult leadership) rivals and early surpasses the family as the principal agent of socialization.

2. Competition between groups is utilized as the principal mechanism for motivating achievement of behavior norms.

3. The behavior of the individual is evaluated primarily in terms of its relevance to the goals and achievements of the collective.

4. Rewards and punishments are frequently given on a group basis; that is to say, the entire group benefits or suffers as a consequence of the conduct of individual members.

5. As soon as possible, the tasks of evaluating the behavior of individuals and of dispensing rewards and sanctions is delegated to the members of the collective.

6. The principal methods of social control are public recognition and public criticism, with explicit training and practice being given in these activities. Specifically, each member of the collective is encouraged to observe deviant behavior by his fellows and is given opportunity to report his observations to the group. Reporting on one's peers is esteemed and rewarded as a civic duty.

7. Group criticism becomes the vehicle for training in self-criticism in the presence of one's peers. Such public self-criticism is regarded as a powerful mechanism for maintaining and enhancing commitment to approved standards of behavior, as well as the method of choice for bringing deviants back into line.

There are of course many other important features of the Soviet approach to socialization, but the seven listed above are those which present the greatest contrast to the patterns we employ in the West. It is for this reason that they are selected for special consideration here. We shall now proceed to examine each feature in greater detail with particular attention to the research ideas which it may generate. . . .[1]

GROUP CRITICISM AND SELF-CRITICISM

The feature of Soviet socialization practices which clashes most sharply with the American pattern is the Russians' widespread resort to the procedure of criticizing others and one's self in public. The practice is common throughout all levels of Soviet society from school, farm, and factory to the highest echelons of the

[1] Sections in the original report, "The Family Versus the Collective" and "Group Incentives," have been deleted here, together with references therein. [Eds.]

party. Thus by being taught these techniques in early childhood, Soviet youths are being prepared in patterns of response that will be expected and even required of them throughout their life span. Since such practices are uncommon in American society, it is not surprising that they have not been subjected to research study in any direct way. As already noted, however, the work of Asch and others (Asch, 1956; Berenda, 1950) testifies to the power of an overwhelming majority forcing the deviant member of the group to conform to majority opinion. In these experiments members of the majority do not engage in criticism but simply give responses which conflict with the reality perceptions of the experimental subject. The effect on the subject is to lead him, in an appreciable number of instances, to change his own response in the direction of the majority. In a sense, such alteration represents a confession of his own previous "error." Obviously, the experiments cannot be said to reproduce explicit features of Soviet group criticism and self-criticism, but the fit could be made much closer by instructing confederates to engage in criticism and by asking the subject to admit that his previous responses had not been correct. Such variations would of course make even more salient questions of scientific ethics that invariably arise when experiments of this kind are viewed from the perspective of the Western Judeo-Christian moral tradition. (It is doubtful, incidentally, that such questions would ever be raised in a Communist society.) Still ways can probably be found to conduct experiments on the processes of group criticism and self-criticism without doing serious violence to our own ethical traditions.

The fact remains, however, that such socialization procedures as group criticism and self-criticism have moral implications and hence may be expected to have moral consequences; that is to say, they are likely to influence the moral attitudes, actions, and character structure of the individuals on whom they are employed. Moreover, it is doubtful whether such consequences are fully or even adequately reflected by the measures of conscience and guilt currently employed in research on moral development. Certainly it would be important to know about the nature of conscience and guilt in the "new Soviet men" who have been exposed to a lifetime of experience in group criticism and self-criticism. But in building "socialist morality" Soviet educators are less concerned with such questions as whether the individual tends to blame others or himself than with his sense of commitment to the collective, especially in the face of competing individualistic values and preferences.

Accordingly, perhaps the most important research implication to be drawn from our examination of Soviet methods of character education is the necessity of expanding the spectrum of what we conceive as moral development beyond the characteristically Judeo-Christian concern with personal responsibility and guilt to a consideration of the broader moral issues inherent in the relation of man to man and of the individual to his society.

We have tried to take some beginning steps in this direction in the research on character development being conducted at Cornell by Bronfenbrenner, Devereux, and Suci. Specifically, as a point of departure we have distinguished five hypothetical extreme types of character structure representing the presumed products of five divergent patterns of socialization and moral development in children and adolescents. These five are tentatively designated as self-oriented, adult-oriented, peer-oriented, collective-oriented, and objectively-principled character structures.[2]

The self-oriented child is motivated primarily by impulses of self-gratification without regard to the desires or expectations of others or to internalized standards. Such an asocial and amoral orientation is presumed to arise when the child's parents are so permissive, indifferent, inconsistent, or indulgent that immediate self-indulgence becomes the practicable and, in the long run, most rewarding course of action for the child. The development of this personality type is further facilitated by participation in peer groups which encourage self-indulgence and exact neither loyalty nor discipline from their members.

The adult-oriented child is one who accepts parental strictures and values as final and im-

mutable. He is completely submissive to parental authority and the moral standards imposed by the parent. This orientation generalizes to adult authority outside the home in school and community. In other words, here is the over-socialized "good child," already a little adult, who causes no trouble but is relatively incapable of initiative and leadership. He is presumed to be the product of intensive socialization within the nuclear family but with minimal experience outside the home.

In contrast, the peer-oriented child is an adaptive conformist who goes along with the group and readily accepts every shift in group opinion or conduct. This is the "other-directed" character type of Riesman's (1950) typology or the future "organization man" described by Whyte (1956). His values and preferences reflect the momentary sentiments of his social set. The optimal circumstances for the development of this personality type involve a combination of parents who are either permissive or actively encourage conformity to group norms, accompanied by early and extensive participation in peer groups requiring such conformity as the price of acceptance. The norms of such groups, however, are ephemeral in character and imply no consistent standards or goals.

The prototype of the collective-oriented personality is of course the "new Soviet man" —a person committed to a firm and enduring set of values centering around the achievement of enduring group standards and goals. These group values take precedence over individual desires or obligations of particular interpersonal relationships. Such an orientation presumably springs from a developmental history in which from the very outset the parents place the needs and demands of the collective above those of the child or of particular family members. Affection and discipline are bestowed in the name and interests of the social group and the child spends most of his formative years in collective settings under the guidance of adults and leaders who train him in the skills and values of collective living.

Finally, the behavior of the objectively-principled child is guided by values which, although learned through experience in the family and in peer groups, do not bind him to undeviating conformity to the standards of the one or the

---

[2] A similar typology, but unlinked to particular patterns and agents of socialization, has recently been proposed by Peck and Havighurst (1960).

other. This is the "inner-directed" personality of Riesman's (1950) typology. On one occasion he may act in accordance with the standards of his parents, on another with the mores of the peer group, or in still a third instance he may take a path which deviates from the preferences of both parents and peers. There is, however, a consistency in pattern of response from one situation to the next which reflects the child's own now autonomous standards of conduct. The developmental history posited for this type of character structure assumes a strong, differentiated family organization with high levels of affection and discipline but at the same time considerable opportunity granted to the child to participate in selected but varied peer-group experiences both with and without adult supervision. These peer groups, in turn, are also characterized by high levels of affectional involvement and their own particular disciplinary codes. The hypothesis implicit in this developmental sequence is that an autonomous set of moral standards is developed from having to cope with different types of discipline in a variety of basically accepting social contexts, so that the child is forced to compare and come to terms with different codes of behavior imposed by different persons or groups each of whom is supportive and wins his liking and respect. This hypothesis, though highly speculative, derives in part from some of our research results (Bronfenbrenner, 1961a, 1961b, 1961c) which suggested that children who are rated by teachers and peers as high in social responsibility and initiative tend to come from families where parental affection and discipline are relatively strong, parental roles are moderately differentiated (e.g., one parent tends to exercise authority slightly more than the other), but

the child also participates in many group activities outside the home. Unfortunately, in these initial studies very little information was obtained about the child's experiences in peer-group settings.

We are currently in the process of devising instruments for measuring the five types of character structure outlined above as these are manifested both in attitudes and behavior. Several of our instruments have yielded promising results in pilot studies but have also brought to light shortcomings in theory and method. The principal value of the approach in its present stage of development is its capacity to generate fruitful hypotheses and research designs for the investigation of character development as a social process.

The last consideration brings us back to the main objective of this paper. Its primary purpose is not to argue for a particular theoretical orientation or methodology; the sole and central aim is to encourage and assist behavioral scientists and educators to give careful attention to the problems and processes implicit in collective methods of character education such as those employed in the Soviet Union and elsewhere in the Communist bloc. We have tried to show that these problems and processes have considerable social relevance and theoretical importance far beyond their immediate social context. We have also attempted to demonstrate that they can be made amenable to empirical investigation. This paper will have served its purpose if it contributes to a renewal of research interest in the study of extrafamilial groups as socializing agents, for such scientific study should do much to enhance our understanding of intriguing social processes through which human character is formed.

REFERENCES

Asch, S. E. Studies of independence and conformity: a minority of one against a unanimous majority. *Psychol. Monogr.,* 1956, 70, No. 9 (Whole No. 416).

Berenda, R. W. *The influence of the group on the judgments of children.* New York: King's Crown Press, 1950.

Bronfenbrenner, U. The changing American child. In E. Ginsberg (Ed.), *Values and ideals of American youth.* New York: Columbia Univer.

Press, 1961. Pp. 71–84. (Also in *Merrill-Palmer Quart.,* 1961, 7, 73–84.) (a)

Bronfenbrenner, U. Some familial antecedents of responsibility and leadership in adolescents. In L. Petrullo & B. M. Bass (Eds.), *Leadership and interpersonal behavior.* New York: Holt, Rinehart & Winston, 1961. Pp. 239–272. (b)

Bronfenbrenner, U. Toward a theoretical model for the analysis of parent-child relationships in a social context. In J. C. Glidewell (Ed.), *Pa-*

rental attitudes and child behavior. Springfield, Ill.: Charles C Thomas, 1961. Pp. 90–109. (c)

Communist Party of the Soviet Union. *Ob ukreplenii svyazi shkoli s zhiznyu i o dalneishem razvitii sistemi naraodnogo obrazovaniya b strane* [On the strengthening of ties between school and life and the further development of the system of public education in the country]. (Theses of the Central Committee of the Communist Party of the Soviet Union.) Moscow: Gospolitizdat, 1958.

Kairov, I. A. [Long range plans for the development of pedagogical sciences and coordination of the work of the Academy and Chairs of Pedagogy of Pedagogical Institutes, U.S.S.R.] (Translation of an article in *Sovetsk. Pedag.,* 1960, **24,** 16–44.) New York: United States Joint Publications Research Service, 1960.

Makarenko, A. S. *Pedagogicheskaya poema* [A pedagogical poem]. (Available in English under the title *The road to life,* translated by Ivy and Tatiana Litvinov. Moscow: Foreign Languages Publishing House, 1951.) Leningrad: Leningradskoye gazetno-zhurnalnoye i knizhnoye iz-

datelstvo [Leningrad Newspaper-Periodical and Book Publishing House], 1949.

Makarenko, A. S. *Learning to live.* Moscow: Foreign Languages Publishing House, 1953.

Makarenko, A. S. *Knigda dlya roditelei* [A book for parents]. (Available in English, Moscow: Foreign Languages Publishing House, undated.) Petrozavodsk: Gosudarstvennoye Izadatelstov Karel'skoi A.S.S.R. [State Publishing House of the Karelian Autonomous Soviet Socialist Republic], 1959.

Miller, D. R., & Swanson, G. E. *Inner conflict and defense.* New York: Holt, Rinehart & Winston, 1960.

Novikova, L. E. (Ed.) *Sotsialisticheskoye sorevnovaniye b shkole* [Socialist competition in the school]. Moscow: Uchpedgiz, 1950.

Peck, R. F., & Havighurst, R. J. *The psychology of character development.* New York: Wiley, 1960.

Riesman, D. (with N. Glazer & R. Denney). *The lonely crowd: a study of the changing American character.* New Haven: Yale Univer. Press, 1950.

Whyte, W. H. *The organization man.* New York: Doubleday, 1956.

THE CONTINGENT USE OF TEACHER ATTENTION AND PRAISE IN REDUCING CLASSROOM BEHAVIOR PROBLEMS

WESLEY C. BECKER   CHARLES H. MADSEN, JR.
CAROLE REVELLE ARNOLD   DON R. THOMAS

The importance of attention, praise, nearness, and other social stimuli produced by the behavior of adults in maintaining both deviant and prosocial behavior of children has been repeatedly demonstrated with preschool children (e.g., Allen, Hart, Buell, Harris, & Wolf, 1964; Harris, Johnston, Kelley, & Wolf, 1964). The basis for assuming that attention in most any form may maintain deviant behaviors lies in the high probability that attentional responses from adults will be repeatedly followed by relief from aversive stimulation or the presentation of positive reinforcers in the history of most children. With such a history, stimuli produced by attentional responses are likely to become positive conditioned reinforcers and function to strengthen responses which are followed by such attentional stimuli. The establishment of the effectiveness of praise comments as conditioned reinforcers involves an essentially similar process, whereby initially neutral words such as "good boy," "that's fine," "you're doing great" acquire conditioned reinforcement value through their repeated pairing with positively reinforcing stimuli.

The differential use of attention by nursery school teachers has been used to modify such behaviors as "regressive" crawling, isolate behavior, excessive orientation to adults, "aggressive" rather than cooperate peer interactions, lethargy or passivity, and many other behaviors. In addition, a similar procedure has been used

to train mothers to modify the demanding-aggressive behavior of their children (Hawkins, Peterson, Schweid, & Bijou, 1966). There is little question in the face of the extensive research produced by Sidney Bijou, Donald Baer, and their students, that a powerful principle for influencing the development of social behaviors has been isolated.

The series of studies to be reported here demonstrate how the differential contingent use of teacher attention and praise can be effectively applied in elementary classrooms. The studies also involve an exploration of ways of training teachers to be more effective in managing classroom behavior problems.

THE SETTING

The studies were carried out in Urbana, Illinois, in an elementary school whose population was 95% Negro. Our research group was invited into the school because it was believed we could provide a service and they would provide us with a research laboratory. Seven teachers (50% of those invited) agreed to participate in a workshop and seminar on applications of behavioral principles in the classroom. The present report covers studies carried out between February and June, 1966, involving five of these teachers. . . .

Because of the need to initially sell ourselves and to maintain close contact with the teachers, the seminar-workshop was initiated at the beginning of the second semester. Simultaneously,

Reprinted with abridgment by permission of Wesley C. Becker and *Journal of Special Education* from *Journal of Special Education*, 1967, **1**, 287–305.

training of observers, selection of target children, and baseline recordings of children's behavior were proceeding. This sequence of events is not ideal, since, even though instructed otherwise, the teachers were likely to try out the procedures being learned in the workshop before we wished them to do so. Some evidence that they did this is suggested by an occasional decreasing baseline of problem behavior for a target child. However, most changes were dramatic enough that this potential loss in demonstrating an experimental effect did not grossly distort possible conclusions.

Most similar work in this area has used designs of the ABAB type. After baseline (A), an experimental effect is introduced (B), withdrawn (A), and reintroduced (B). This design was not used (though we have an accidental counterpart to such a design in one room where the second A condition was provided by a student teacher) because: (a) we were afraid it might jeopardize the support of the teachers; (b) the nature of the experimental processes involved has been repeatedly confirmed; (c) "accidental" influences which might have produced changes in child behavior would not likely happen to 10 children at the same time in five different classrooms; (d) we are unimpressed by the argument that the weather or time alone is causative in view of *b* and *c* above. By not using an ABAB design we were also able to show the persistence of effects maintained by conditioned reinforcers over a longer period of time than is usually the case (nine weeks). As a result of our caution and our success, we are now in a position where other teachers and administrators are permitting us to establish controlled designs, in return for our helping them with their problem children.

PROCEDURES

Selection of Target Children

The authors initially spent time observing in the classrooms of teachers who had volunteered for the project. This was followed by discussion with the teachers of possible problem children. After tentative selection of two children in each class, explicit behavior coding categories were evolved and tested. Final selec-

tion of children was contingent upon demonstration that problem behavior did occur frequently enough to constitute a problem and could be reliably rated.

Rating Categories

During the first four weeks the rating categories were repeatedly revised as reliability data demanded. Where it was not possible to get rater agreement for a category above 80%, a new definition was sought or a category abandoned. For example, in three classes (A, B, & C) inappropriate talking and vocal noise were rated as separate categories (see Table 1). In two classes (D and E) the behavior patterns made it difficult to discriminate these behaviors, so they were combined. The general rules followed in establishing categories were as follows:

a. They should reflect behaviors which interfere with classroom learning (time on task), and/or,

b. They should involve behaviors which violate the rules established by the teacher as to permissible behavior, and/or,

c. They should reflect particular behaviors a teacher wants to change (e.g., thumbsucking).

d. The classes should be constituted by behaviors which are topographically similar in some important way.

e. The classes should be mutually exclusive.

f. The definitions must refer to observables and not involve inferences.

g. The number of classes should not exceed 10.

As Table 1 indicates, some codes were usable with all 10 target children; others were devised especially for a particular child. For convenience we will speak of the A and B categories of Table 1 as "deviant behaviors."

Observer Training and Reliabilities

Observers were obtained from undergraduate classes in psychology and education and were paid $1.50 an hour. Initially they worked in pairs, often with one of the authors also rating. After each rating session of 40 minutes, ratings were compared and discussed, and reliability examined by category. Definitions were clarified and changes made when necessary. Reliabilities

TABLE I

Coding Categories for Children with Teachers A, B, and C

Symbols	Class Label	Class Definitions
	A. Behaviors Incompatible with Learning: General Categories	
X	(Gross motor behaviors)	Getting out of seat; standing up; running; hopping; skipping; jumping; walking around; rocking in chair; disruptive movement without noise; moves chair to neighbor.
N	(Disruptive noise with objects)	Tapping pencil or other objects; clapping; tapping feet; rattling or tearing paper. (Be conservative, only rate if could hear noise when eyes closed. Do not include accidental dropping of objects or if noise made while performing X above.)
∧	(Disturbing others directly and aggression)	Grabbing objects or work; knocking neighbor's book off desk; destroying another's property; hitting; kicking; shoving; pinching; slapping; striking with object; throwing object at another person; poking with object; attempts to strike; biting; pulling hair.
⌒↓	(Orienting responses)	Turning head or head and body to look at another person; showing objects to another child; attending to another child. (Must be of 4 seconds duration to be rated. Not rated unless seated.)
!	(Blurting out, commenting and vocal noise)	Answers teacher without raising hand or without being called on; making comments or calling out remarks when no question has been asked; calling teacher's name to get her attention; crying; screaming; singing; whistling; laughing loudly; coughing loudly. (Must be undirected to another particular child, but may be directed to teacher.)
T	(Talking)	Carrying on conversations with other children when it is not permitted. (Must be directed to a particular child or children.)
//	(Other)	Ignores teacher's question or command; does something different from that directed to do (includes minor motor behavior such as playing with pencil when supposed to be writing)—to be rated only when other ratings not appropriate.
B. Special Categories for Children with Teachers A, B, and C (to be Rated Only for Children Indicated)		
+	(Improper position) Carole and Alice	Not sitting with body and head oriented toward the front with feet on the floor, e.g., sitting on feet; standing at desk rather than sitting; sitting with body sideways but head facing front. (Do not rate if chair sideways but head and body both oriented toward the front with feet on the floor.)
S	(Sucking) Alice and Betty	Sucking fingers or other objects.
B	(Bossing) Carole	Reading story out loud to self or other children (do not rate ! in this case); acting as teacher to other children, as showing flash cards.

TABLE I (cont.)

Symbols	Class Label	Class Definitions
//	(Ignoring) Charley	This category expanded to include playing with scissors, pencils, or crayons instead of doing something more constructive during free time—only for Elmer.
	C. Relevant Behavior	
———	(Relevant behavior)	Time on task, e.g., answers question, listening, raises hand, writing assignment. (Must include whole 20 seconds except for orienting responses of less than 4 seconds duration.)

were above 80% before the baseline period was begun. Several reliability checks were made each week throughout baseline, and periodically thereafter. As indicated in Figures 1 to 5, only occasionally did reliability fall below 80% when calculated by dividing the smaller estimate by the larger. The observers were carefully trained not to respond to the children in the classes. They were to "fade into the walls." This procedure quickly extinguished the children's responses to the observers. Several incidents were reported where children were surprised to see the observers respond to a request from the teacher to move. After a while it was possible for other visitors to come into the class without distracting the children as they had in the past.

Rating Procedure

In most cases target children were observed 20 minutes a day, four days a week. A few exceptions occurred due to absences. In the experimental phase of the study frequency of reliability checks was reduced so that ratings of teacher behavior could also be obtained. Each observer had a clipboard with a stop watch taped to it. Observers would start their watches together and check for synchronization every five minutes (end of a row). They would observe for 20 seconds and then take 10 seconds to record the classes of behavior which occurred during the 20 second period. All child data are reported as percentage intervals during which deviant behavior is observed to occur. The activity in which the children were involved varied considerably from day to day, and con-

tributes to daily fluctuation. For this reason only weekly averages are reported.

Ratings of Teacher Behavior

At the beginning of the experimental phase for 4 teachers, and for a week prior to the experimental phase for teacher E, a 20 minute sample of teacher's behavior was also obtained. The rating categories are given in Table 2. The main purpose of the ratings was to insure that the experimental program was being followed.

Experimental Phase Instructions

Following a five-week baseline period (for most children) teachers were given instructions to follow for the nine-week experimental period. In all classes the teachers were given general rules for classroom management as follows (typed on a 5″ × 8″ card to be kept on their desks):

GENERAL RULES FOR TEACHERS

1. Make rules for each period explicit as to what is expected of children. (Remind of rules when needed.)

2. *Ignore* (do not attend to) behaviors which interfere with learning or teaching, unless a child is being hurt by another. Use punishment which seems appropriate, preferably withdrawal of some positive reinforcement.

3. Give *praise* and *attention* to behaviors

TABLE 2

Teacher Coding Categories

Symbols	Class Label	Class Definitions
C	Positive contact	Positive physical contact must be included. Such behaviors as embracing, kissing, patting (on head), holding arm, taking hand, sitting on lap, etc. are to be included.
P	Verbal praise	This category includes paying attention to appropriate behavior with verbal comments indicating approval, commendation or achievement such as, "that's good," "you're studying well," "fine job," "I like you."
R	(Recognition in academic sense)	Calling on child when hand is raised. (Do not rate if child calls teacher's name or makes noises to get her attention.)
F	(Facial attention)	Looking at child when smiling. (Teacher might nod her head or other indication of approval—while smiling.)
A	(Attention to undesirable behavior)	This category includes the teacher verbally calling attention to undesirable behavior and may be of high intensity (yelling, screaming, scolding, or raising the voice) or of low intensity ("go to the office," "you know what you are supposed to be doing," etc.). Calling the child to the desk to talk things over should also be included, as well as threats of consequences. Score the following responses to deviant behavior separately:
L	(Lights)	Turning off the lights to achieve control.
W	(Withdrawal of positive reinforcement)	Keeping in for recess, sending to office, depriving child in the classroom.
/	(Physical restraint)	Holding the child, pulling out into hall, grabbing, hitting, pushing, shaking are included.

which facilitate learning. Tell child what he is being praised for. Try to reinforce behaviors incompatible with those you wish to decrease.

Examples of how to praise:

"I like the way you're working quietly."

"That's the way I like to see you work."

"Good job, you are doing fine."

(transition period) "I see Johnny is ready to work."

"I'm calling on you because you raised your hand." "I wish everyone were working as nicely as X." etc. Use variety and expression.

In general, give praise for achievement, prosocial behavior, and following the group rules.

In addition to these general rules, teachers in classes A to D were given specific instructions with respect to their target children. An example follows:

SPECIAL RULES FOR ALICE

Attempt to follow the general rules above, try to give extra attention to Alice for the behavior noted below, but try not to overdo it to the extent she is singled out by other children. Spread your attention around.

1. Praise sitting straight in chair with both feet and chair legs on floor and concentrating on own work.

2. Praise using hands for other things than sucking.

3. Praise attention to directions given by teacher or talks made by students.

4. Specify behavior you expect from her at beginning of day and new activity, such as, sitting in chair facing front with feet on floor, attention to teacher, and class members where

appropriate, what she may do after assigned work is finished, raising hand to answer questions or get your attention.

The fifth teacher was given the general rules only and instructed not to give the target children any more special attention than was given the rest of the class. This procedure was decided upon because our observers felt that general classroom management was a problem for Mrs. E. She relied heavily on negative control procedures and the general level of disruptive behaviors was high in the room. In view of this, we decided to see if the two target children in her class might not be used as barometers of a more general effect on the class of a change in control procedures.

When we first initiated the experimental phase of the study, we attempted to give the teachers hand signals to help them learn when to ignore and when to praise. This procedure was abandoned after the first week in favor of explicit instructions, as given above, and daily feedback on their progress. While hand signals and lights have been found to be effective in helping parents learn to discriminate when to respond or ignore (Hawkins, et al., 1966), the procedure is too disruptive when the teacher is in the middle of a lesson and is placed in conflict about which response to emit next.

At this point, the seminar was used to discuss and practice various ways of delivering positive comments. For some teachers, delivery of positive comments was difficult, and their initial attempts came out in stilted, stereotyped form. With time, even our most negative teacher was smiling and more spontaneous in her praise (and enjoying her class more). Shortly after the experimental phase began, one teacher commented, "I have at least 15 minutes more every morning and afternoon in which to do other things."

The experimental phase was initiated March 30th and ended May 27th. A breakdown in the heating plant in part of the building for the week of April 8th (week 7) accounts for the loss of data for some children that week.

RESULTS

The main results are presented in Figures 1 to 5. The average "deviant" behavior for 10 chil-

dren in five classes was 62.13% during baseline and 29.19% during the experimental period. The *t*-test for the differences between correlated means was significant well beyond the .001 level. All children showed less deviant behavior during the experimental phase. However, differential teacher attention and praise were not very effective with Carole and did not produce much change in Dan until his reading skills were improved. Each child and class will be discussed in more detail and a breakdown of the behaviors which changed will be examined.

Teacher A

Mrs. A is an anxious, sensitive person who expressed many doubts about her ability to learn to use "the approach" and about whether it would work with her middle-primary adjustment class. Both of the children on whom data were collected (Figure 1) changed remarkably, as did Mrs. A and other members of her class. The teachers' views of what happened to themselves and to members of their classes are very instructive and will be presented elsewhere.

Albert (age 7-8) tested average on the Stanford-Binet, but was still on first-grade materials during his second year in school. He was selected because he showed many behaviors which made learning difficult. He talked, made other noises, did not attend to teacher, and got in and out of his seat a lot. He loved to be "cute" and make his peers laugh. In Mrs. A's words:

"He was a very noisy, disruptive child. He fought with others, blurted out, could not stay in his seat, and did very little required work. I had to check constantly to see that the minimum work was finished. He sulked and responded negatively to everything suggested to him. In addition, he was certain that he could not read. If I had planned it, I could not have reinforced this negative behavior more, for I caught him in every deviant act possible and often before it occurred. I lectured him and, as might be expected, was making only backward motion. In November Albert came to me to tell me something and I was shocked by the intensity of his stuttering. He simply could not express his thought because his stuttering was so bad. I declared an 'I Like Albert Week.' I gave him a great deal of attention, bragged on his efforts and was beginning to make some prog-

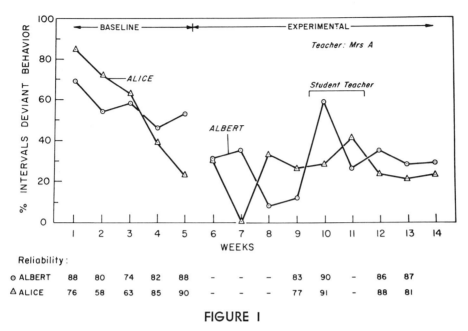

FIGURE I

Percentages of deviant behavior for two children in class A.

ress. This turned out to be the basis upon which an 'ignore and praise' technique could be established. When the class began, I could see quickly what had happened to my relationship with Albert and had to fight to keep up my negative remarks until the baseline was established. Finally, I was free to use the technique. He quickly responded and his deviant behavior decreased to 10%, the lowest recorded. Along with the praising and ignoring, I attempted to establish a calmer atmosphere in which to work, and carefully reviewed class behavior rules. A good technique with Albert was to have him repeat the rule because 'he was following it.' "

During weeks 8 and 9 Albert showed less than 12% deviant behavior on the average. His worst performance out of seven observation days was 18.77% and he was under 5% deviant four out of seven days. Then an unplanned experimental reversal occurred.

Mrs. A relates what happened: "As my student teacher gradually assumed more and more of the teaching load, the deviant behavior increased again. She made the same mistakes that I had. I deliberately planned her work so that I would be working with Albert most of the time. She felt the efficiency of the direct command, but she also realized that this was not

modifying Albert's behavior in a lasting way. Gradually, she accepted the positive approach and in the last week or two of her work the deviant behavior began again to decrease. She had learned that with so negative a child as Albert, only building a rapport by using positive reinforcement would succeed.

"Albert has improved delightfully. He still blurts out, but makes an effort to stop this. He is often seen holding his hand in the air, biting his lips. He completes his work on time, and it is done well. Often, when he has to re-do a paper, he takes it cheerfully and says, 'I can do this myself.' No sulking. He still finds it difficult to sit for a long period of time, but time on task has increased. He works very hard on his reading and has stated that he can read. His stuttering has decreased almost to zero. When the observers were questioned concerning this, they had detected little, if any, stuttering. Most important to me, Albert has become a delightful child and an enthusiastic member of our class who feels his ideas are accepted and have merit."

Examination of the separate categories of behavior for Albert only serves to confirm the teacher's reports about which behaviors were most frequent and which changed the most.

The record of Mrs. A's behavior showed that she attended to and praised positive behaviors over 90% of the time during the experimental period. Similar effective following of procedures was demonstrated for all five teachers.

Alice (age 7-8) scored 90 on the Stanford-Binet and was doing low first grade work. The data on Alice are less clear than for Albert since her average deviant behavior showed a decline prior to the experimental phase. Mrs. A considered Alice a "sulking child." She would withdraw at times and not talk. She was observed to sit inappropriately in her chair, suck her thumb, and make frequent movements of her hands and legs. Mrs. A said that Alice would report headaches after being scolded.

Mrs. A also indicated that two weeks before the end of baseline she told Alice she was "disgusted with her sulking and would she please stop it." Mrs. A felt that this instruction in part accounted for the drop in deviant behavior prior to the experimental phase. Analysis of Alice's separate classes of behavior indicates, however, that the motor category declined from 45% to 25% to 8% the first three weeks of baseline and remained under 12% the rest of the experiment. Following this decline in "getting out of seat," frequency of odd sitting positions rose from 0% to 25% to 18% over the first three weeks of baseline and declined to zero over the next two weeks. There was also a decline in talking during the first two weeks of baseline. In other words Mrs. A got Alice to stay in her seat, sit properly, and talk less prior to the experimental change. The behaviors which show a correlation with the experimental change are decreases in *orienting, sucking,* and *other* (ignoring teacher) response categories.

It is probable that the maintenance of Alice's improvement, except for the short lapse when the student teacher took over the class, can be attributed to the experimental program. Mrs. A reported at the end of the year as follows:

"Alice is a responsible, hard-working student who now smiles, makes jokes, and plays with others. When a bad day comes, or when she doesn't get her way and chooses to sulk, I simply ignore her until she shows signs of pleasantness. Through Alice I have learned a far simpler method of working with sulking behavior, the one most disagreeable kind of behavior to me. Alice is a child who responds well to physi-

cal contact. Often a squeeze, a pat, or an arm around her would keep her working for a long while. This is not enough, however. Alice is very anxious about problems at home. She must have opportunity to discuss these problems. Again through the class suggestions, I found it more profitable to discuss what she could do to improve her problems than to dwell on what went wrong. Alice's behavior is a good example of the effects of a calm, secure environment. Her time on task has lengthened and her academic work has improved."

Teacher B

Mrs. B had a lower intermediate class of 26 children. She tended to control her class through the use of sharp commands, physical punishment, and loss of privileges prior to the experimental phase of the study. The two children on whom observations were made (Figure 2) showed considerable change over the period of the experiment. Observers' comments indicate that Mrs. B was very effective in following the instructions of the experimental program. Only occasionally did she revert to a sharp command or a hand slap.

Betty (age 9-7) scored average on various assessments of intelligence and was doing middle third-grade work. Her initial problem behaviors included "pestering" other children, blurting out, sucking her thumb, making other noises. She also occasionally hit other children. Often she said or did things which were followed by laughter from others. As Figure 2 shows, many of her problem behaviors showed a reduction during the baseline period (as happened with Alice), but thumbsucking did not. The experimental program brought thumbsucking under control for a while, but it increased markedly the last week of the experiment. Betty's other problem behaviors showed continued improvement over the experimental period and remained at a level far below baseline for the last five weeks of the experimental period.

Boyd (age 9-7) was of average IQ. His achievement test placements varied between second- and third-grade levels. During baseline he was high on getting out of seat and other gross movements, talking out of turn, and making noises. Mrs. B also reported Boyd to

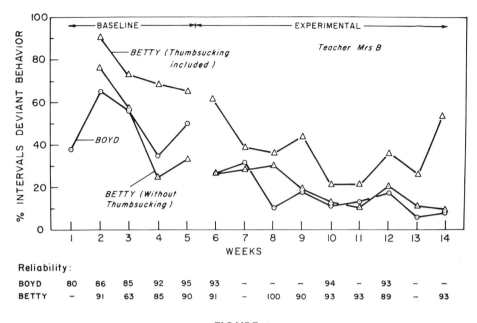

FIGURE 2

Percentages of deviant behavior for two children in class B.

have difficulty "saying words he knows," to giggle a lot, and not to try doing things alone. He very much liked to be praised and tried not to do things which led to scolding. During this period Boyd was getting a great deal of teacher attention, but much of the attention was for the very behaviors Mrs. B wished to eliminate. Boyd was able to readily learn to sit in his seat for longer periods of time working on task through a gradual shaping process. He has learned to work longer by himself before asking for help. Mrs. B reports he is less anxious and emotional, although we have no measure of this. Blurting out was not stopped entirely, but now he usually raises his hand and waits to be called on in full class activities and waits for his turn in reading.

Teacher C

Our biggest failure occurred in Mrs. C's middle primary class of about 20 children. Mrs. C was one of our most positive teachers and we underestimated the severity of the many problems she was facing. With our present knowledge, we would likely have gone directly to a more potent token economy system for the whole class (see O'Leary & Becker, 1967). Given the above, the experiment reported below is still of considerable value in pointing to one of the limits of "the approach," as our teachers came to call it. Besides focusing on Carole and Charley, as described below, we assisted Mrs. C in extinguishing tantrums in Donna (beginning week 8), and in reducing swearing and hitting by Hope. The work with Donna was very successful.

Carole (age 7-5) scored from 78 to 106 on various intelligence tests. She was working at the mid first-grade level. Carole is an incessant beehive of activity. She scored high on response categories which indicate that she spent much time talking out of turn, turning in her seat, getting out of her seat, bossing other children, and hitting others. Her most frequent behavior was talking when she should have been quiet. She was very responsive to peer attention. At times she would stand at the back of the room and read out loud to everyone. She liked to play teacher. She was also described as good at lying, cheating, stealing, and smoking. Like most of the children in the study, Carole came from a deprived, unstable home. Descriptions of home backgrounds for most of the children in this

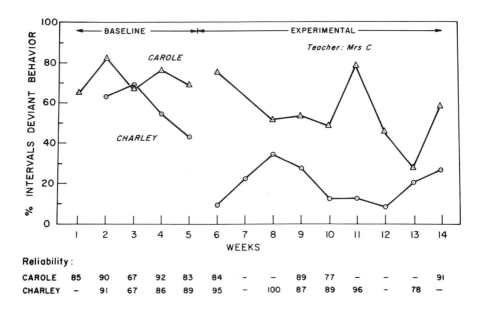

Reliability:

CAROLE	85	90	67	92	83	84	–	–	89	77	–	–	–	91
CHARLEY	–	91	67	86	89	95	–	100	87	89	96	–	78	–

FIGURE 3

Percentages of deviant behavior for two children in class C.

study consist of sequences of tragic events (see Mrs. D).

The experimental phase of the program reduced Carole's average deviant behavior from about 75% during baseline to 55% for weeks 7 to 9. A detailed analysis of Carole's responses shows that talking out of turn and blurting out still constituted over 30% of her deviant responses during weeks 7 to 9. However Carole was in her seat more, sitting properly, responding more relevantly to teacher, and was on task 50% of the time. We were not satisfied with her improvement and felt that Charley (our other target child) while doing well, could also do better.

On April 25th (week 9) we instituted a program in which ten-cent notebooks were taped to Carole and Charley's desks. Mrs. C instructed the children that every 30 minutes she would put from one to ten points in their notebooks, depending on how hard they worked and how well they followed the class rules. At the end of the day if they had "so many" points they could exchange the points for a treat. The reinforcer initially was candy. During this phase the rest of the class could earn a candy treat

by helping Carole and Charley earn points. In this way they were not left out. The number of points required was based on a shifting criterion geared to Carole and Charley's progress. As noted below and in Figure 3, Charley responded well to this added incentive and was gradually shifted to saving points over two, then three, then five days to earn puzzles. Carole still resisted. She worked for points for several days, but on May 3rd (week 10) she announced she was not going to work for points today, and she didn't. She was a hellion all day. Over the following two weeks Carole worked for a ring and then the components of a make-up kit. We were seeking stronger reinforcers, and were stretching the delay of reinforcement.

On May 17th Mrs. C reported that Carole had earned points for three days in a row and was entitled to a component of the make-up kit. The 20% deviant behavior of that week showed that Carole could behave and work. The last week of May, Carole was back to talking and blurting out again. While some of our reinforcers were effective, Carole still needs a classroom where the structure would require her to depend on the teacher for praise and attention and where peer attention to her deviant behavior could be controlled.

Charley was presumed to be age 8-2 at the start of the study, but in fact he was 2 years older. His IQ was given at 91, but with a proper CA was 73. He was doing mid first-grade work in most subjects. Charley "picked on" the girls, hit others and bullied them (he was larger), got loud and angry if reprimanded, and "sulked" and withdrew at times. No one was going to force him to do anything. Our ratings showed him highest in categories labeled *motor activities* (out of seat), *ignoring* teacher's requests, *turning in seat,* and *talking* to peers.

Initially Charley responded very effectively to rules and praise. He loved to receive praise from Mrs. C. However, praise was not enough to keep him on task. Also he was still fighting with Donna at recess. As noted above, a point system was initiated April 25th (week 9) which worked well for the rest of the semester, while the delay of reinforcement was gradually extended to five days. On April 25th Charley was also informed that further fighting with Donna would lead to a loss of the following recess.

Comments on May 10th: "Charley is great. He ignores others who bother him as well as keeping busy all the time." May 26th: "Charley seems much more interested in school work and has been getting help with reading from his sister at home."

It is not possible to evaluate whether the point system was necessary for Charley. At best we know that social reinforcement helped considerably and that the point system did help to maintain good classroom behavior for Charley.

Teacher D

Mrs. D teaches a lower intermediate class of about 25 children. One group of her children had been in a slow class where the teacher allowed them "to do what they wanted." A brighter group had been taught by a strict teacher who enforced her rules. Since September the class has been divided and subdivided six times and has had seven different teachers.

Mrs. D describes the families of her two target children [Don and Danny] as follows: "Don has average ability and achieves below the average of the class. The father works late afternoons and evenings. The mother, a possible alcoholic, has been known to do some petty shoplifting. She is frequently away from home in the evening. One older brother drowned at the age of seven. An older sister with above average ability left home at the age of fifteen. She later married. Her husband was killed this spring in an automobile accident. Another older sister lost an arm at a very early age and is an unwed mother at the age of fourteen. Another sister attends Junior High School.

"Danny's mother is of mixed parentage and has been in the hospital this year. The mother is divorced. The father remarried and it appears that there is a good relationship between the two families; however, the father has been in prison because of 'dope.' "

Mrs. D was initially quite bothered about being observed, but quickly learned to look more carefully at the way in which her behavior affected that of her class.

Don was 10 years and 4 months old at the start of the study. In April of 1961 he was recommended for EMH placement. Since kindergarten his performance on intelligence tests has risen from 75 to 102. He was obviously of at least average ability. His level of school achievement was between grades two and three, except for arithmetic reasoning (4.3). Observations revealed a high frequency of moving around the room and talking when he should have been working. He was called "hyperactive" and said to have poor "attention." His talking to other children was quite annoying to his teacher and interfered with class work. Don appeared to respond to teacher attention, but obtained such attention most often when he was acting up.

The experimental procedures quickly brought Don's level of deviant behavior down from about 40% to under 20%. Don was particularly good at working when the task was specifically assigned. When he was left to his own devices (no stimulus control) he would start to play around. These observations suggest that Don would greatly profit from more individualized programming of activities. Don was reported to show improved behavior in his afternoon classes involving several different teachers.

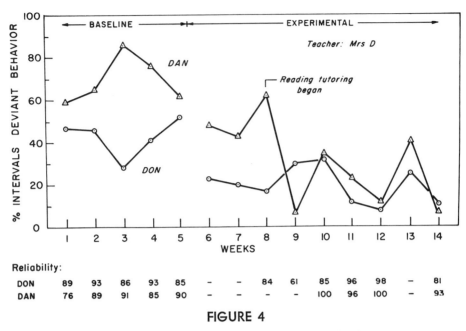

Reliability:													
DON	89	93	86	93	85	–	–	84	61	85	96	98	–	81
DAN	76	89	91	85	90	–	–	–	–	100	96	100	–	93

FIGURE 4

Percentages of deviant behavior for two children in class D.

Danny was age 10-6 at the start of the study. He measured near 85 on several IQ tests. His classroom behavior was described as being generally disruptive and aggressive. During baseline he scored high on *motor, talking, orienting, ignoring,* and *noise.* By all standards Danny was a serious behavior problem. He seldom completed work assignments and was in the slowest reading group. Because of the severity of Danny's behavior and difficulty staying on task, an educational diagnosis was requested during the early part of baseline. The staffing on 3-1-66 indicated a two-year reading deficit and a one-year arithmetic deficit. The following comments from the psychological report which followed the staffing are of interest:

"Danny's lack of conscience development and other intrinsic controls still present a serious problem in controlling his behavior. His immediate impulsive aggressive reaction to threatening situations may hamper any educational remediation efforts. The evidence presented still suggests that Danny, in light of increasing accumulation of family difficulties, lack of consistent masculine identification, his irascible and changeable nature, and educational pressures will have a difficult time adjusting to the educational situation.

"It is our opinion that unless further action is implemented, i.e., school officials should attempt to refer this boy to an appropriate agency (Mental Health, Institute for Juvenile Research) for additional help and correction, he is likely to become a potentially serious acting out youngster."

The data presented in Figure 4 on Danny are most interesting. They show a small improvement in Danny's behavior the first two weeks of the experimental phase. Generally, the observers felt the whole class was quieter and better behaved. Danny especially stayed in his seat more of the time. However, a most dramatic change occurs when tutoring sessions in reading were begun (weeks 8 to 9). It would appear that unless the child is capable of following the assigned activity, social reinforcement for "on task" behavior is not enough. In Danny's data this point is supported by an analysis of the kinds of activities where he showed the most improvement. Danny was averaging 80% deviant behavior when the activity was workbook assignments related to reading and language. In reading group where the teacher was there to help and direct activity he averaged only 40% deviant behaviors. By early May the amount of deviant behavior during "seat work" activities had dropped to an average of 15%, with only an occasional bad day.

Well into April, Danny had not shown much improvement in his afternoon classes (with teachers not in our program). Several observations suggested that he would still show high rates of deviant behaviors on days when he was otherwise on task, if the activity shifted to something he could not do. For example, May 5th showed 25% deviant behavior during a period of seat work (*reading*), 30% during *spelling,* and 55% an hour later during *grammar* and *composition*. Danny was just beginning to move in reading, but was not ready for composition. The increase during week 13 is due to one day where he was rated 40% off task. The rater comments indicate the basis for the "deviant" rating: "Danny should have been sitting quietly after doing his work, but, instead of just waiting for the next assignment, he was playing with clay with another child. However, he was very quiet." Comments from May 9th and 10th give some flavor of the changes which occurred.

May 9th: "Mrs. D reported that Danny, after he finished reading, immediately started on spelling. This is a highly unusual occurrence. Until now Danny has avoided spelling activities until made to work on them."

May 10th: "Danny completely surprised the observer when he was on task the whole observation period, except for one minor talking to neighbor."

In view of the rather dramatic changes Danny has made in classroom behavior through a combination of remediation and social reinforcement, perhaps it is necessary to question the assumptions implicit in the quotation from Danny's psychological report given earlier. It should be noted that no attempt was made to work on family problems, his conscience, his masculine identification, or his "irascible nature" in changing his adjustment to school.

Teacher E

We have saved until last the most dramatic of all the changes produced in teachers and children. Mrs. E had a lower primary class of 23 children.

Observation of February 1, 1966: "Six chil-
dren were in a reading group and 15 were working on individual projects. The noise level for the entire classroom was extremely high and went higher just before recess. Some behaviors noted included whistling, running around the room (5 occasions), yelling at another child (many times), loud incessant talk, hitting other children (7 times), pushing, shoving, and getting in front of each other in recess line. Mrs. E would re-establish quiet by counting to 10, after giving a threat."

Observations suggested that control was obtained mainly by shouting, scolding, and the like, in an attempt to suppress unwanted behaviors. This approach would work for a while, but there was then a gradual build-up in noise until quiet was again demanded. Figure 5 shows that Mrs. E's responses on three days prior to a shift to positive reinforcement, contained very few positive statements. Essentially, there was nothing to maintain appropriate classroom behaviors. The focus was on what not to do rather than what to do. There is a good possibility that the attention given deviant behavior in fact served to reinforce it.

Edward and Elmer were selected as barometers which might reflect changes for the whole class. Mrs. E was given the general instructions presented above, but no special instructions were given for Edward and Elmer. They were not to receive more attention than other members of the class. She was to make her rules clear, repeat these as needed, ignore deviant behavior, and give praise and attention to behavior which facilitates learning. We wanted to see if a general approach to classroom management would be effective on children showing a high level of deviant behavior. The rating of Mrs. E's behavior before and after the change clearly shows an effect of the experimental instructions and training on her behavior.

Edward (age 6-8) tested 95 on the Stanford-Binet. Mrs. E considered him to be "distractable," to have poor work habits, show poor attention, and not to comprehend what he read. He never finished assignments. He could sight read and spell first-grade words. The baseline observations showed high frequencies of wandering about the room, turning around in his seat, talking at the wrong time, and making odd noises. He also showed little peer play. A psychological examination of

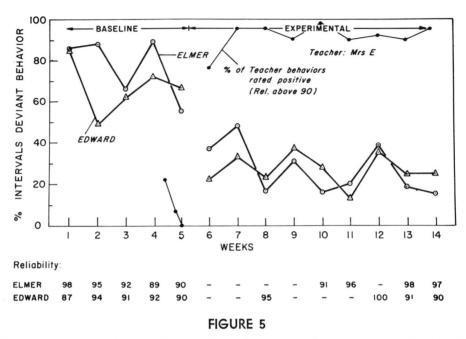

Reliability:														
ELMER	98	95	92	89	90	–	–	–	–	91	96	–	98	97
EDWARD	87	94	91	92	90	–	–	95	–	–	–	100	91	90

FIGURE 5

Percentages of deviant behavior for two children in class E, and change in teacher E's behavior.

1-17-66 stressed Edward's poor social history (his parents have not talked to each other for three years), his lack of enthusiasm and emotional responsiveness, the apparent restriction on his peer interaction by his mother, and the need to train better listening skills and language skills. Edward received speech therapy while in kindergarten. Throughout the baseline and experimental phase of this study, Edward was seen by a social worker and continued in speech therapy. In view of the fact that his behavioral changes (and those of Elmer) are found to be directly associated with the change in classroom procedures, rather than time per se, these other treatments do not offer convincing alternative explanations for the data.

Edward greatly reduced the time he spent in aimless wandering, twisting in his seat, and talking. Edward responded well to praise in both the reading group and class activities. Mrs. E reports that he began to complete assignments. He also showed better give and take with his peers, and would laugh, cry, and make jokes. While still "distractable" he has learned to work independently for longer periods of time.

Elmer (age 6-10) scored 97 on a group IQ test. He apparently started out the school year working well, but this deteriorated. He seemed "nervous," hyperactive, and would not work. He also threw several tantrums and would cry if his work was criticized. His twin sister was also in the class and doing well. By comparison Elmer often lost out. The parents expected as much of Elmer as his sister. During baseline he was rated as showing inappropriate gross motor behaviors as much as 70% of the time. *Talking* was as high as 50% at times. *Noise* and *turning* in seat were at about 10% each. He was a hyperactive child. Initially our observers thought he was brain-damaged.

Elmer's rapid response to positive reinforcement and a better structured classroom made it possible for him to stay on task longer. However, he did not improve greatly in his reading group. When the children were silent reading, he would make noises and clown at times. More work on reading will be necessary for academic progress.

Elmer's father came to work as a teacher's aid in one of our other classes just after the shift off baseline. His work with Mrs. C and changes in Elmer led slowly to his accepting the value of a positive rather than a punitive approach. Very likely father's attempt to be more rewarding with Elmer contributed to the maintenance of Elmer's improved classroom behavior. More to the point, however, is the fact that Elmer's improved classroom behavior (we showed father the graph during week 9) served to reinforce father's acceptance of a positive approach.

In her report at the end of the semester Mrs. E felt that 12 of 23 children in her class definitely profited from her change in behavior, that 6 children were unchanged, 3 improved some, and 2 were more deviant. The children who were reported unchanged tended to be the quiet and submissive ones who escape Mrs. E's attention much of the time. From her own comments, it is likely that those reported to be more deviant are so only because they stand out from the group more now that Elmer and Edward are not such big problems.

IMPLICATIONS

The results of these investigations demonstrate that quite different kinds of teachers can all learn to effectively apply behavioral principles to modify the behavior of problem children. These results extend to the elementary classroom, with normal teacher-pupil ratios, the importance of *differential* social reinforcement in developing effective social behaviors in children. Work now in progress suggests that rules alone do nothing, and that ignoring deviant behavior by itself increases deviant behavior. The combination of ignoring deviant behavior and reinforcing an incompatible behavior seems critical. Nearly all of our teachers found that the technique of praising a child who was showing an incompatible appropriate behavior, when another child was misbehaving, was especially effective. This action keeps the teacher from attending to the deviant act and at the same time provides vicarious reinforcement for an incompatible behavior. In the future we hope to bring together a group of techniques which various teachers found effective in implementing the general strategy of this project.

The findings of this research add support to the proposition that much can be done by the classroom teacher to eliminate behaviors which interfere with learning without having to rely on massive changes in the home, or intensive therapy.

REFERENCES

Allen, K. Eileen; Hart, Betty M.; Buell, Joan S.; Harris, Florence R.; & Wolf, M. M. Effects of social reinforcement on isolate behavior of a nursery school child. *Child Development,* 1964, 35, 511–518.

Harris, Florence R.; Johnston, Margaret K.; Kelley, C. Susan; & Wolf, M. M. Effects of positive social reinforcement on regressed crawling of a nursery school child. *Journal of Educational Psychology,* 1964, 55, 35–41.

Hawkins, R. P.; Peterson, R. F.; Schweid, Edda; & Bijou, S. W. Behavior therapy in the home: Amelioration of problem parent-child relations with the parent in a therapeutic role. *Journal of Experimental Child Psychology,* 1966, 4, 99–107.

O'Leary, K. D., & Becker, W. C. Behavior modification of an adjustment class: A token reinforcement program. Mimeographed report, Urbana, Ill.: University of Illinois, September, 1966.

Wahler, R. G.; Winkel, G. H.; Peterson, R. E.; & Morrison, D. C. Mothers as behaviour therapists for their own children. *Behaviour Research and Therapy,* 1965, 3(2), 113–124.

AN EXPERIMENT IN GROUP UPBRINGING

ANNA FREUD with the collaboration of SOPHIE DANN

INTRODUCTION

The experiment to which the following notes refer is not the outcome of an artificial and deliberate laboratory setup but of a combination of fateful outside circumstances. The six young children who are involved in it are German-Jewish orphans, victims of the Hitler regime, whose parents, soon after their birth, were deported to Poland and killed in the gas chambers. During their first year of life, the children's experiences differed; they were handed on from one refuge to another, until they arrived individually, at ages varying from approximately six to twelve months, in the concentration camp of Tereszin.[1] There they became inmates of the Ward for Motherless Children, were conscientiously cared for and medically supervised, within the limits of the current restrictions of food and living space. They had no toys and their only facility for outdoor life was a bare yard. The Ward was staffed by nurses and helpers, themselves inmates of the concentration camp and, as such, undernourished and overworked. Since Tereszin was a transit camp, deportations were frequent. Approximately two to three years after arrival, in the spring of 1945, when liberated by the Russians, the six children, with others, were taken to a Czech castle where they were given special care and were lavishly fed. After one month's stay, the 6 were included in a transport of 300 older children and adolescents, all of them survivors from concentration camps, the first of 1000 children for whom the British Home Office had granted permits of entry.

Reprinted with abridgment from pp. 127-68 of *The Psychoanalytic Study of the Child*, Vol. VI, edited by Ruth S. Eissler *et al.*, by permission of Anna Freud, Sophie Dann, and International Universities Press, Inc. Copyright 1951 by International Universities Press.
[1] Theresienstadt in Moravia.

They were flown to England in bombers and arrived in August 1945 in a carefully set-up reception camp in Windermere, Westmorland, where they remained for two months. When this reception camp was cleared and the older children distributed to various hostels and training places, it was thought wise to leave the six youngest together, to remove them from the commotion which is inseparable from the life of a large children's community and to provide them with peaceful, quiet surroundings where, for a year at least, they could adapt themselves gradually to a new country, a new language, and the altered circumstances of their lives.

This ambitious plan was realized through the combined efforts of a number of people. A friend of the former Hampstead Nurseries, Mrs. Ralph Clarke, wife of the Member of Parliament for East Grinstead, Sussex, gave the children a year's tenancy of a country house with field and adjoining woodland, "Bulldogs Bank" in West Hoathly, Sussex, containing two bedrooms for the children, with adjoining bathrooms, a large day nursery, the necessary staff rooms, a veranda running the whole length of the house and a sun terrace.

The Foster Parents' Plan for War Children, Inc., New York, who had sponsored the Hampstead Nurseries during the war years 1940–1945, took the six children into their plan and adopted Bulldogs Bank as one of their colonies. They provided the necessary equipment as well as the financial upkeep.

The new Nursery was staffed by Sisters Sophie and Gertrud Dann, formerly the head nurses of the Baby Department and Junior Nursery Department of the Hampstead Nurseries respectively. A young assistant, Miss Maureen Wolfison, who had accompanied the children from Windermere was replaced after several weeks by Miss Judith Gaulton, a relief worker. Cooking and housework were shared between the staff, with occasional outside help.

The children arrived in Bulldogs Bank on October 15, 1945. The personal data of the six, so far as they could be ascertained, are given in Table 1.

Meager as these scraps of information are, they establish certain relevant facts concerning the early history of this group of children:

(i) That four of them (Ruth, Leah, Miriam, Peter) lost their mothers at birth or immediately afterward; one (Paul) before the age of twelve months, one (John) at an unspecified date;

(ii) that after the loss of their mothers all the children wandered for some time from one place to another, with several complete changes of adult environment (Bulldogs Bank was the sixth station in life for Peter, the fifth for Miriam, etc.

TABLE I

Name	Date and Place of Birth	Family History	Age at Arrival in Tereszin	Age at Arrival in Bulldogs Bank
John	18.12.1941 Vienna	Orthodox Jewish working-class parents. Deported to Poland and killed.	Presumably under 12 months	3 years, 10 months
Ruth	21.4.1942 Vienna	Parents, a brother of 7 and a sister of 4 years were deported and killed when Ruth was a few months old. She was cared for in a Jewish Nursery in Vienna, sent to Tereszin with the Nursery.	Several months	3 years, 6 months
Leah	23.4.1942 Berlin	Leah and a brother were illegitimate, hidden from birth. Fate of mother and brother unknown. Brother presumed killed.	Several months	3 years, 5 months. Arrived 6 weeks after the others, owing to a ring-worm infection
Paul	21.5.1942 Berlin	Unknown.	12 months	3 years, 5 months
Miriam	18.8.1942 Berlin	Upper middle-class family. Father died in concentration camp, mother went insane, was cared for first in a mental hospital in Vienna, later in a mental ward in Tereszin where she died.	6 months	3 years, 2 months
Peter	22.10.1942	Parents deported and killed when Peter was a few days old. Child was found abandoned in public park, cared for first in a convent, later, when found to be Jewish, was taken to the Jewish hospital in Berlin, then brought to Tereszin.	Under 12 months	3 years

John's and Leah's and Paul's wanderings before arrival in Tereszin are not recorded.) ;

(iii) that none of the children had known any other circumstances of life than those of a group setting. They were ignorant of the meaning of a "family";

(iv) that none of the children had experience of normal life outside a camp or big institution.

BEHAVIOR TOWARD ADULTS ON ARRIVAL

On leaving the reception camp in Windermere, the children reacted badly to the renewed change in their surroundings. They showed no pleasure in the arrangements which had been made for them and behaved in a wild, restless, and uncontrollably noisy manner. During the first days after arrival they destroyed all the toys and damaged much of the furniture. Toward the staff they behaved either with cold indifference or with active hostility, making no exception for the young assistant Maureen who had accompanied them from Windermere and was their only link with the immediate past. At times they ignored the adults so completely that they would not look up when one of them entered the room. They would turn to an adult when in some immediate need, but treat the same person as nonexistent once more when the need was fulfilled. In anger, they would hit the adults, bite or spit. Above all, they would shout, scream, and use bad language. Their speech, at the time, was German with an admixture of Czech words, and a gradual increase of English words. In a good mood, they called the staff members indiscriminately *Tante* (auntie), as they had done in Tereszin; in bad moods this changed to *blöde Tante* (silly, stupid auntie). Their favorite swear-word was *blöder Ochs* (the equivalent of "stupid fool"), a German term which they retained longer than any other.

GROUP REACTIONS

Clinging to the Group

The children's positive feelings were centered exclusively in their own group. It was evident that they cared greatly for each other and not at all for anybody or anything else. They had no other wish than to be together and became upset when they were separated from each other, even for short moments. No child would consent to remain upstairs while the others were downstairs, or vice versa, and no child would be taken for a walk or on an errand without the others. If anything of the kind happened, the single child would constantly ask for the other children while the group would fret for the missing child.

This insistence on being inseparable made it impossible in the beginning to treat the children as individuals or to vary their lives according to their special needs. Ruth, for instance, did not like going for walks, while the others greatly preferred walks to indoor play. But it was very difficult to induce the others to go out and let Ruth stay at home. One day, they actually left without her, but kept asking for her until, after approximately twenty minutes, John could bear it no longer and turned back to fetch her. The others joined him, they all returned home, greeted Ruth as if they had been separated for a long time and then took her for a walk, paying a great deal of special attention to her.

It was equally difficult to carry out measures for the children's health, so far as they did not apply to everybody. When the children arrived, they were in fairly good physical condition, though somewhat pale, flabby, with protruding stomachs and dry, stringy hair, cuts and scratches on their skin tending to go septic. All the children were given cod-liver oil and other vitamins which were taken easily and liked by everybody. But it was nearly impossible to keep individual children in bed for small ailments, or for instance to give Miriam and Peter, who needed it, an afternoon nap while the others had no wish to rest. Sometimes those two children would fall asleep exhaustedly in the middle of the noise made by the others. At night, all children were restless sleepers, Ruth being unable to fall asleep, Paul and Peter waking up in the night crying. Whoever was awake, naturally disturbed the sleep of the others. The upset about separation was so great that, finally, children with colds were no longer kept upstairs. The only child who was in bed once, for two days with a slight bronchitis, was Paul.

Another time three children had to be isolated for several days with stomatitis. The only other child in need of individual physical treatment was Leah. She had a bad squint, her eyes were treated daily but the operation was postponed for six months to give her time for better adjustment to a renewed separation.

Inability to be separated from the group showed up most glaringly in those instances where individual children were singled out for a special treat, a situation for which children crave under normal circumstances. Paul, for example, cried for the other children when he was taken as the only one for a ride in the pony cart, although at other times such rides were a special thrill to him as well as to the others. On another, later, occasion the whole group of children was invited to visit another nursery in the neighborhood. Since the car was not large enough to take everybody, Paul and Miriam were taken earlier by bus. The other four, in the car, inquired constantly about them and could not enjoy the trip nor the pleasures prepared for them, until they were reunited.

Type of Group Formation

When together, the children were a closely knit group of members with equal status, no child assuming leadership for any length of time, but each one exerting a strong influence on the others by virtue of individual qualities, peculiarities, or by the mere fact of belonging. At the beginning, John, as the oldest, seemed to be the undisputed leader at mealtimes. He only needed to push away his plate, for everybody else to cease eating. Peter, though the youngest, was the most imaginative of all and assumed leadership in games, which he would invent and organize. Miriam too played a major role, in a peculiar way. She was a pretty, plump child, with ginger hair, freckles and a ready smile. She behaved toward the other children as if she were a superior being, and let herself be served and spoiled by them as a matter of course. She would sometimes smile at the boys in return for their services, while accepting Leah's helpfulness toward herself without acknowledgment. But she, too, did not guide or govern the group. The position was rather that she needed a special kind of attention to be paid

to her and that the other children sensed this need and did their best to fulfill it. The following are some recorded examples of this interplay between Miriam and the group:

November 1945.—Miriam, on a walk, has found a tiny pink flower, carries it in her hand but loses it soon. She calls out "flower!" and John and Paul hurry to pick it up for her, a difficult task since they wear thick gloves. Miriam drops the flower again and again, never makes an attempt to pick it up herself, merely calls "flower!" and the boys hurry to find it.

March 1946.—From the beginning Miriam liked to sit in comfortable chairs. In the winter she would drag such a chair to the fireplace, put her feet on the fire guard and play in that position. When outdoor life began again, Miriam had a chair in the sandbox. She even helped weed the garden while sitting in a chair. But it did not happen often that she had to fetch a chair herself, usually the other children carried it into the garden for her. One day, Miriam and Paul played in the sandbox after supper. Suddenly Paul appears in the house to fetch Miriam's chair. When told that the evening was too cold already for outdoor play and that they had better both come in, he merely looks bewildered and says: "But Miriam wants chair, open door quickly."

May 1946.—Miriam drops her towel, turns around and says: "Pick it up, somebody." Leah picks it up for her.

August 1946.—Ruth is found in Miriam's bed in the morning and is asked to get up. Miriam replies instead of Ruth: "Oh, no, she much better stays here. She has to wait to fasten Miriam's buttons."

August 1946.—Miriam bangs her hand on the table and says to John: "Can't you be quiet when I want to talk?" John stops talking.

The children's sensitiveness to each other's attitudes and feelings was equally striking where Leah was concerned. Leah was the only backward child among the six, of slow, lower average intelligence, with no outstanding qualities to give her a special status in the group. As mentioned before, Leah's arrival in Bulldogs

Bank was delayed for six weeks owing to a ringworm infection. During this period the five other children had made their first adaptation to the new place, had learned some English, had established some contact with the staff and dropped some of their former restlessness. With Leah's coming, the whole group, in identification with her, behaved once more as if they were all newcomers. They used the impersonal *Tante* again instead of first names for the members of staff. They reverted to talking German only, shouted and screamed and were again out of control. This regression lasted approximately a week, evidently for the length of time which Leah herself needed to feel more comfortable in her new surroundings.

*Positive Relations Within the Group:
Absence of Envy, Jealousy, Rivalry,
Competition*

The children's unusual emotional dependence on each other was borne out further by the almost complete absence of jealousy, rivalry and competition, such as normally develop between brothers and sisters or in a group of contemporaries who come from normal families. There was no occasion to urge the children to "take turns"; they did it spontaneously since they were eager that everybody should have his share. Since the adults played no part in their emotional lives at the time, they did not compete with each other for favors or for recognition. They did not tell on each other and they stood up for each other automatically whenever they felt that a member of the group was unjustly treated or otherwise threatened by an outsider. They were extremely considerate of each other's feelings. They did not grudge each other their possessions (with one exception to be mentioned later), on the contrary lending them to each other with pleasure. When one of them received a present from a shopkeeper, they demanded the same for each of the other children, even in their absence. On walks they were concerned for each other's safety in traffic, looked after children who lagged behind, helped each other over ditches, turned aside branches for each other to clear the passage in the woods, and carried each other's coats. In the nursery they picked up each other's toys. After they had

learned to play, they assisted each other silently in building and admired each other's productions. At mealtimes handing food to the neighbor was of greater importance than eating oneself.

Behavior of this kind was the rule, not the exception. The following examples merely serve the purpose of illustration and are in no way outstanding. They are chosen at random from the first seven months of the children's stay in Bulldogs Bank:

October 1945.—John, daydreaming while walking, nearly bumps into a passing child. Paul immediately sides with him and shouts at the passer-by: "Blöder Ochs, mein John, blöder Ochs Du!" ("Stupid fool, my John, you stupid fool!")

November 1945.—John refuses to get up in the morning, lies in his bed, screams and kicks. Ruth brings his clothes and asks: "Willst Du anziehen?" ("Don't you want to put them on?") Miriam offers him her doll with a very sweet smile. John calms down at once and gets up.

November 1945.—John cries when there is no cake left for a second helping for him. Ruth and Miriam offer him what is left of their portions. While John eats their pieces of cake, they pet him and comment contentedly on what they have given him.

December 1945.—Paul has a plate full of cake crumbs. When he begins to eat them, the other children want them too. Paul gives the two biggest crumbs to Miriam, the three middle-sized ones to the other children, and eats the smallest one himself.

December 1945.—Paul loses his gloves during a walk. John gives him his own gloves, and never complains that his hands are cold.

January 1946.—A visitor gives sweets to the children in the kitchen. Peter and Leah immediately demand a sweet for Miriam who is alone in the nursery.

March 1946.—Sister Gertrud opens a door and knocks it against John who stands behind it. When she enters the room next time, Ruth and Peter throw bricks at her and shout: "You naughty boy hit John!"

March 1946.—John has a temper tantrum

when a ladybird, which he has caught, flies away. Leah hurries to him, strokes his hair, picks up his basket and all the carrots which he dropped out. She carries both John's and her own full baskets on the way home.

March 1946.—A dog approaches the children who are terrified. Ruth, though badly frightened herself, walks bravely to Peter who is screaming and gives him her toy rabbit to comfort him. She comforts John next by lending him her necklace.

April 1946.—On the beach in Brighton, Ruth throws pebbles into the water. Peter is afraid of waves and does not dare to approach them. In spite of his fear, he suddenly rushes to Ruth, calls out: "Water coming, water coming," and drags her back to safety.

Discrimination Between Group Members: Antipathies and Friendships

Although the positive reactions of the children extended to all members of the group, individual preferences or their opposite were not lacking. There was a certain discrimination against Leah on the part of the other girls, as the following recordings indicate:

February 1946.—When Miriam cries, Leah runs immediately to comfort her, although Miriam each time screams: "Not Leah," and then accepts comfort from the other children.

April 1946.—Ruth is very helpful toward Leah, looks after her on walks and helps her to dress and undress. But her behavior indicates that these actions are duties, imposed by Leah's comparative clumsiness, rather than acts of friendship.

There were, further, close and intimate friendships between individual children, as for example between Paul and Miriam.

October 1945.—On his first evening in Bulldogs Bank, Paul goes to bed, saying with a deep sigh: "My Miriam."

October 1945.—Paul is very fond of Miriam. He gives her toys and serves her at mealtimes. Sometimes he takes her doll,

walks with it around the room and returns it to her.

October 1945.—Paul loves eating corn flakes. He has just started eating when Miriam—who is not sitting next to him—drops her spoon. Paul at once stops eating and picks up the spoon for her before continuing.

November 1945.—On her third day in Bulldogs Bank, Miriam had been given a doll from which she became inseparable in day- and nighttime. No other child was allowed to touch it except Paul who sometimes took it for a walk around the room.

On November 11, Miriam gives the doll to Paul when saying good night and goes to sleep without it.

On November 12, she gives him the doll again in the evening but later cries in her bed. Paul, who has the doll in bed with him, gets up and calls through the closed door: "Miriam, dolly!" Miriam gets her doll and Paul goes to sleep without it.

December 1945.—After having had Miriam's doll for a few evenings and twice for a whole night, Paul takes it as his own possession. Now he is inseparable from the doll as Miriam has been before. The children call it now "Paul's dolly."

Aggressive Reactions Within the Group

With the exception of one child the children did not hurt or attack each other in the first months. The only aggressiveness to which they gave vent within the group was verbal. They quarreled endlessly at mealtimes and on walks, mostly without any visible provocation. The following is a sample of these word battles, as they raged between October and January:

December 1945.—
John: "Is hot."
Ruth: "Is nicht (not) hot."
John: "Is hot."
Ruth (shouting): "Is nis hot."
John (triumphantly): "Is hot."
Paul: "Is nis hot, blöder Ochs" ("Stupid fool").

John: "Blöder Ochs, Paul."

Paul: "Nicht blöder Ochs Paul, blöder Ochs John."

John (shouting): "Blöder Ochs, Paul!"

John shouts so loud that the other children begin to laugh; he joins in the laugh.

The disputes ended sometimes in a general uproar, sometimes in a concerted attack on any adult who had tried to interfere and appease the quarrel; mostly the quarrel merely petered out when some new event distracted the children's attention.

After the children had entered into more normal emotional relationships with the adults and had become more independent of each other, word battles diminished and were replaced to some degree by the fights normal for this age. This second phase lasted approximately from January to July, when the relations between the children became peaceful again on a new basis.

The only child whose reactions did not fit in with the general behavior of the group was Ruth. She behaved like the others so far as being inseparable from the group was concerned, did not want to be left alone and worried about absent children. She also did her share of comforting others or of helping Leah, the latter especially after Leah began to call her "my Ruth." But apart from these reactions, she was moved by feelings of envy, jealousy and competition, which were lacking in the other children and which made her actions stand out as isolated instances of maliciousness or spitefulness. In this connection it is interesting to remember that Ruth is the only child among the group who has a recorded history of passionate attachment to a mother substitute. The evidence is not sufficient to establish with certainty that it is this past mother relationship which prevented her from merging completely with the group, and which aroused normal sibling rivalry in her. On the other hand, the difference between her and the other children's behavior together with the difference in their emotional histories seems too striking to be a mere coincidence.

The following are instances of Ruth's negative behavior in the group. Between October and January these instances were daily events. They lessened considerably after she had formed a new attachment to Sister Gertrud and they disappeared almost altogether after June.

October 1945.—Ruth hurts other children secretly, by kicking or pinching them underneath the table.

October 1945.—Ruth takes other children's toys, shows a very pleased, triumphant expression.

October 1945.—Peter has to wear a bonnet to protect a bandage where he has cut his head. Ruth takes off his bonnet repeatedly.

November 1945.—Peter gets soap in his eyes at bathtime and cries. Ruth watches him. When he has almost ceased crying, her watchful expression changes suddenly to a malicious one. She snatches the piece of soap and tries to put it into Peter's eye.

November 1945.—Ruth takes Paul's plate away while he is eating.

November 1945.—Each child receives a sweet. Ruth keeps hers until the others have finished eating theirs. Then she offers her sweet to one child after the other, withdrawing it as soon as the child touches it. Repeats this for twenty minutes and again later until the children stop paying attention to her.

November 1945.—Paul and Peter have fun at lunch by pretending to bite each other. When they stop, Ruth encourages them to continue and while they do so, she eats Peter's lunch with her fingers, although her own plate is still full.

December 1945.—Ruth breaks everybody's colored pencils.

January 1946.—Ruth kicks Peter under the table. This had not happened for some time.

January 1946.—John, Miriam and Peter are isolated with stomatitis. Ruth cannot stand the extra care given to them and takes out her jealousy on Paul and Leah by hitting and biting them. Her aggressiveness ceases again when the patients recover.

May 1946.—Ruth cries for her doll which Peter has taken and refuses to return. Leah takes it from Peter and hands it back to Ruth. Ruth, with a malicious expression, gives it once more to Peter and immediately begins to cry for it.

May 1946.—The children pick flowers which grow behind high nettles. They are warned to avoid being stung. John continues but moves and picks carefully. After a while he cries out as he gets stung: "Die Ruth, die Ruth push." Ruth stands behind him, pushing him into the nettles with a malicious expression on her face.

AGGRESSIVENESS TOWARD THE ADULTS

As reported above, the children behaved with strong and uncontrolled aggression toward the adults from their arrival. This aggression was impersonal in its character, not directed against any individual and not to be taken as a sign of interest in the adult world. The children merely reacted defensively against an environment which they experienced as strange, hostile and interfering.

On arriving it was striking that the form of aggressive expression used by the children was far below that normal for their age. They used biting as a weapon, in the manner in which toddlers use it between eighteen and twenty-four months. Biting reached its peak with Peter, who would bite anybody and on all occasions when angry; it was least pronounced with Leah who showed very little aggression altogether. For several weeks John and Ruth would spit at the adults, Ruth also spitting on the table, on plates, on toys, looking at the adults in defiance. Similarly, Peter, when defying the staff, urinated into the brick box, on the slide, into the toy scullery, or wetted his knickers.

After a few weeks, the children hit and smacked the adults when angry. This happened especially on walks where they resented the restrictions imposed on them in traffic.

Shouting and noisy behavior were used deliberately as an outlet for aggression against the adults, even though the children themselves disliked the noise.

Toward spring these very infantile modes of aggressiveness gave way to the usual verbal aggressions used by children between three and four years. Instead of hitting out, the child would threaten to do so, or would say: "Naughty boy, I make noise at you," and then shout at the top of their voices. Other threats used by the children were: "Doggy bite you." Paul once used: "Froggy bite you." After a visit to Brighton in April, where Peter had been frightened of the waves, a new threat was used by them: "You go in a water." They sometimes tried to find a water so as to carry out the threat.

From the summer of 1946 onward, the children used phrases copied from the adults to express disapproval: "I am not pleased with you."

The following samples of aggressive behavior are chosen from a multitude of examples of similar or identical nature during the first three months.

October 1945.—Mrs. X from the village returns the clean laundry. Both John and Peter spit at her when she enters the nursery.

October 1945.—A painter works in the nursery with a high ladder. Peter, who climbs on the ladder, is lifted down by Sister Gertrud. He spits at her and shouts "Blöde Tante, blöder Ochs!" ("Stupid auntie, stupid fool.")

October 1945.—John hits Mrs. Clarke repeatedly.

November 1945.—Paul does not like the sweet given by Sister Sophie in the evening, but does not ask for a different one. He wakes up in the night and without seeing Sister Sophie says: "Blöde Sophie." He says it again when waking up in the morning.

November 1945.—Sister Gertrud polishes shoes and tells Ruth not to play with the shoe polish. Ruth spits at her, throws the box with polish down the stairs and runs through the house, shouting: "Blöder Ochs, Gertrud."

FIRST POSITIVE RELATIONS WITH THE ADULTS

The children's first positive approaches to the adults were made on the basis of their group feelings and differed in quality from the usual demanding, possessive behavior which young children show toward their mothers or mother substitutes. The children began to insist that the members of the staff should have their turn or share; they became sensitive to their feelings, identified with their needs, and considerate of their comfort. They wanted to help the adults with their occupations and, in return, expected to be helped by them. They disliked it when any member of staff was absent and wanted to know where the adults had been and what they had had done during their absence. In short, they ceased to regard the adults as outsiders, included them in their group and, as the examples show, began to treat them in some ways as they treated each other.

Sharing with the Adults

Christmas 1945.—The children are invited to a Christmas party in Mrs. Clarke's house. They receive their presents with great excitement. They are equally thrilled when they are handed presents for the staff, they call out: "For Gertrud," "For Sophie" with great pleasure, and run back to Mrs. Clarke to fetch more presents for them.

December 1945.—The children are given sweets in the shop and demand a "sweet for Sophie." After leaving the shop, they want to make sure that she has received the sweet. Sister Sophie opens her mouth for inspection and, in so doing, loses her sweet. The children are as upset as if they had lost one of their own sweets. John offers his but Sister Sophie suggests that she can wait to get another on returning home. When they reach home after an hour's walk with many distracting events, Peter runs immediately to the box of sweets to fetch one for Sophie.

Considerateness for the Adults

November 1945.—When the children are told that one of the staff has a day off and can sleep longer in the morning, they try to be quiet. If one or the other forgets, the others shout: "You quiet, Gertrud fast asleep."

November 1945.—Sister Sophie has told the children that the doctor has forbidden her to lift heavy weights. Paul asks: "Not too heavy?" whenever he sees her with a tray or bucket.

May 1946.—Leah, though a noisy child, tries hard to keep quiet when her Judith is tired.

Equality with the Adults: Helpfulness

December 1945.—The children become keen on fetching from the kitchen what is needed. They carry logs, set chairs and tables. They help to dress and undress themselves and to tidy up.

January 1946.—Ruth sees a woman with a shopping bag in the street. She approaches her and takes one handle silently to help carry it.

April 1946.—The children are alone in the nursery after breakfast. Ruth and Peter each take a broom and sweep up the rubbish. When Sister Sophie enters, they call to her: "We tidy up nicely."

May 1946.—Miriam begins to help Sister Sophie in the kitchen when the latter is called away. When she returns Miriam has dried four big dishes, twelve bowls, sixteen spoons and has placed them tidily on a tray.

On a similar occasion Miriam is found on a chair in front of the sink, her arms up to the elbows in soapy water, with most of the washing-up done.

Sensitiveness to Adults: Identification

March 1946.—Ruth and John lag far behind on a walk. When they reach the others eventually, Peter calls to them: "You naughty boys, you dragging behind; Sophie calling and calling and calling. You not coming, Sophie cross and sad!" Then he turns to Sister Sophie and says in a low voice: "You still cross and sad?" When she nods, he repeats his speech.

May 1946.—While the children are picking bluebells, Sister Sophie listens intently to the calling of birds. Paul suddenly puts his hand into hers and says: "You cross with everybody?" Though she assures him that she is not cross, merely absent-minded, he leaves his hand in hers to comfort her.

SECOND PHASE OF POSITIVE RELATIONS WITH ADULTS: PERSONAL RELATIONSHIPS

Several weeks after arrival in Bulldogs Bank the first signs of individual personal attachments to adults appeared, alongside with and superimposed on the relationships based on community feelings. These new attachments had many of the qualities which are well known from the relationship of young children to their mothers or mother substitutes. Attitudes such as possessiveness, the wish to be owned, exclusive clinging, appeared, but they lacked the intensity and inexorability which is one of the main characteristics of the emotional life at that age. During the year's stay at Bulldogs Bank these ties of the children to the adults in no way reached the strength of their ties to each other. The children went, as it were, through the motions and attitudes of mother relationships, but without the full libidinal cathexis of the objects whom they had chosen for the purpose.

Examples of Owning and Being Owned

Miriam was the first to say "Meine Sophie, my Sophie" at the end of October.

Peter, the youngest, was the next to show a personal attachment. At the end of November he cried on several occasions when Sister Gertrud left the room. He began to say: "Meine Gertrud" and shortly afterward called himself "Gertrud's Peter." He picked flowers for her and liked her to bathe him. But his attachment was in no way exclusive and he did not mind being with somebody else. He was fond of Sister Sophie too and disliked her going away.

Ruth very soon afterward showed a first preference for Mrs. Clarke. She began showing pleasure in seeing her, kissed her once spontaneously and said on another occasion: "Is bin (I am) Mrs. Clarke's Ruth."

Leah was a clinging child who made advances to every visitor and even to people passing in the street. She became attached to the assistant Judith, would hold her hand on walks, picked flowers for her and sang sometimes all day long: "My Judith bathes me all the time!" But the apparent warmth of this relationship was belied by the fact that she continued to attach herself to every stranger.

John called the young assistant "his" Maureen. His attachment showed more warmth than those of the others but was broken again, unluckily, by Maureen's leaving.

Examples of Conflicting Relationships

Several children had considerable difficulties in choosing their mother substitutes, their positive feelings wavering uncertainly between the adult figures. John, after being left by Maureen, attached himself to Sister Gertrud, and shortly afterward became fond of Sister Sophie. Neither relationship was exclusive or very passionate and consequently he seemed to have no difficulties in maintaining both simultaneously. In contrast to this, Miriam, who was attached equally to Sisters Sophie and Gertrud, suffered badly from the consequent conflict of feeling. She lived in a constant state of tension without finding relief and satisfaction in her relationships. During Sister Sophie's absence, she "wrote" and dictated long letters to her and she was full of happiness on Sister Sophie's return. But the preference for Sister Sophie, which seemed established at the time, gave way once more to a preference for Sister Gertrud in the course of a few weeks.

Examples of Resentment of Separations

Even though the children's attachments to their mother substitutes took second place in their emotional lives, they deeply resented the absences or the leaving of the adults.

January 1946.—Sister Sophie has left the house together with Mrs. Clarke. When she returns a few hours later, Peter refuses to say goodnight to her. He turns to the other side and says: "You go, you go to a Mrs. Clarke."

March 1946.—When Sister Sophie returned to Bulldogs Bank after an absence of two months, Peter refused to let her do anything for him for a week, would not even take bread or sweets from her. Whenever she left the house, he asked: "You go in a London?"

He regained his affection for her through a process of identification with her interests. Five weeks after her return the children played that they took a bus ride to London. When asked what they wanted to do there, Peter said: "Go in a Miss X's house." Peter saying: "Miss X all better?" From then onward, he called the patient "Peter's Miss X," cuddled and kissed Sister Sophie and held her hand on walks although the children usually preferred to walk on their own.

Example of Full Cathexis of a Mother Substitute

The only child to choose a real mother substitute was Ruth, an exception which is easily explainable on the basis of her former attachment to the superintendent of the Children's Ward in Tereszin. She chose as her object Sister Gertrud, and developed toward her the same demandingness, aggressive possessiveness and wish for exclusive attention which had characterized her earlier relationship, a mixture of emotions which is well known from children in the toddler stage and at later ages from those who have gone through the experience of loss, separation, rejection and disappointments in their earliest object relationships. Ruth's lack of satisfaction and insecurity expressed itself with regard to Sister Gertrud in the constantly repeated phrase: "And Ruth? And Ruth?"

Example of a Passionate Father Relationship

The only child to form a passionate relationship to a father figure was Miriam. Since Miriam arrived in Tereszin at the age of six months, her father having been killed sometime previously, it cannot be presumed that what she went through was a past father relationship transferred to a new object, rather that it was the need for a father which found a first outlet in this manner:

January 1946.—Mr. E., a neighbor, visits the Nursery for a whole afternoon and teaches the children songs. At the time, Miriam seems more interested in his picture book than in his person. But in the evening she begins to cry for him. She wakes up in the night twice and cries for him and keeps asking for him during the next two days.

March 1946.—Miriam has seen Mr. E. more often lately. He has brushed her hair once in the evening and she insists on his doing it again. On evenings when he does not come, her hair is not brushed at all since she will not allow anybody else to touch it.

She blushes whenever she sees him. About twenty times a day she says: "Mein Mr. E. —meine Sophie."

March 1946.—Mr. E. says about Miriam: "I have never seen anything like her. That girl is puffing and panting with passion."

ORAL EROTISM, MASTURBATION

There was a further factor which accounted for the children's diminished capability to form new object relationships. As children for whom the object world had proved disappointing, and who had experienced the severest deprivations from the oral phase onward they had had to fall back to a large degree on their own bodies to find comfort and reassurance. Therefore oral-erotic gratifications persisted with each child in one form or another. Ruth, besides, had a habit of scratching herself rhythmically until she bled, and of smearing with the blood. One child, Paul, suffered from compulsive masturbation.

Peter, Ruth, John and Leah were all inveterate thumb-suckers, Peter and Ruth noisily and incessantly during the whole day, John and Leah more moderately, gradually reducing it to bedtime only. Miriam sucked the tip of her tongue, manipulating it with her teeth until she fell asleep. With Peter, sucking changed in spring to "smoking" carried out with match sticks, twigs, grass blades, then again to sucking his thumb when cross, angry, or at bedtime only. With Ruth sucking persisted even while she was carrying out interesting activities such as threading beads or playing with plasticene.

Since the children's sucking was noisy and obvious they often heard remarks from passers-by or in shops that they should stop or that "their thumbs would be cut off." Contrary to their usual oversensitiveness they remained completely indifferent on such occasions, not even needing reassurance. Sucking was such an integral and indispensable part of their libidinal life that they had not developed any guilt feelings or conflicting attitudes concerning it.

That the excess of sucking was in direct proportion to the instability of their object relationships was confirmed at the end of the year, when the children knew that they were due to leave Bulldogs Bank and when sucking in daytime once more became very prevalent with all of them.

This persistence of oral gratifications, more or less normal under the circumstances, which fluctuated according to the children's relations with the environment, contrasted strongly with Paul's behavior, where compulsive sucking and masturbation manifested themselves as a complicated and, at the time, inaccessible symptom.

Paul, in his good periods, was an excellent member of the group, friendly, attentive and helpful toward children and adults, and capable of friendship. Though not aggressive himself, he was always ready to come to another child's rescue and take up arms against an aggressor. But when he went through one of his phases of compulsive sucking or masturbating, the whole environment, including the other children, lost their significance for him. He ceased to care about them, just as he ceased to eat or play himself. He did not bother to take part in his favorite communal activities such as sorting the laundry or lighting fires. He did not defend himself, or anybody else, merely cried passively when something or somebody made him unhappy. These spells attacked him at any time of the day, while playing, when eating at the table, and during work. He was only free of masturbation on walks, when he sometimes sucked his thumb but otherwise showed a completely changed, cheerful and interested attitude.

In masturbating Paul used his hands, soft toys, picture books, a spoon; or rubbed himself against furniture or against other people. When sucking, his whole passion was concentrated on face flannels or towels which he sucked while they were hanging on their hooks. He also used a corner of his dungarees, of his coat and the arms of a doll, which he sucked while it was hanging from his mouth. For a period of several weeks he treated the children's used bibs or feeders as so many fetishes, rubbing them rhythmically up and down his nose while sucking, treasuring all six feeders in his arms, or pressing one or more between his legs. When on a walk, he sometimes looked forward to these ecstasies with passionate excitement, rushing into the nursery on coming home with the joyous exclamation "Feeder—feeder!" Since he was indifferent to the same feeders when they were freshly laundered, it may be concluded that his erotic excitation was connected with the smell belonging to a feeding situation. . . .

TOILET HABITS

According to the report from Tereszin, all the children had undergone, and successfully completed, an elaborate process of toilet training while in the Ward for Motherless Children. Martha Wenger attributed the length and difficulty of this procedure, which included taking up some of the children two or three times every night, to the "watery diet." The present authors recognize this protracted battle for cleanliness as characteristic for institutional children who do not acquire bowel and bladder control on the basis of an exclusive relationship with their mothers or with a stable mother substitute. According to Martha Wenger, the six children were finally completely and reliably clean and dry during day and night from the spring of 1945 until their liberation.

It bears witness to the disturbing effect of their subsequent changes of environment that with four of the children the result of this toilet training was wholly or partially undone. As usual, there was no simple direct correspondence between the extent of emotional disturbance and the loss of cleanliness. The two most deeply disturbed children, Paul and Ruth, remained clean, without relapses, manifesting their conflicts and abnormalities through other channels. John, Leah and Peter wetted regularly at night with frequent accidents in daytime; Leah and Peter even regressed to soiling for short periods. Miriam merely lost her reliability in toilet matters and had frequent accidents.

The close connection of wetting with the relationship to the adult world was demonstrated most convincingly by Peter's behavior. He used urination quite deliberately in defense against and in defiance of the staff, and as the expression of emotions such as anger, or a feeling of frustration. Characteristically enough for children with this type of wetting, a decisive turn in his toilet habits followed a present of new trousers with braces from his American foster parents. He was very excited about this personal gift, was very careful not to wet these trousers and, on the basis of these positive feelings, reacquired his lost bladder control.

DEVIATIONS FROM THE NORM IN EGO ATTITUDES

In Tereszin, i.e., up to the ages of three to three and one half, the children had led the existence of inmates of a Ward, within a restricted space, with few or no toys, with no opportunities for moving about freely, for contact with animals, for observing nature. They had not shared or observed the lives of ordinary people and, in the absence of strong emotional ties to the people who looked after them, they had lacked the normal incentives for imitating the adults and for identifying with them. Consequently, their knowledge of the external world, their ability to understand and to deal with it, were far below the level of their ages and of their intelligence.

Indoor and Outdoor Activities

During their first weeks in Bulldogs Bank, the children were unable to use play material. The only toys which attracted their attention from the start were the soft toys, dolls and teddy bears which were adopted as personal possessions and not so much played with as used for autoerotic gratification (sucking, masturbation), or in replacement of it. All the children without exception, took their dolls or teddy bears to bed with them. When a child failed to do so in the evening, it would invariably wake up in the middle of the night, crying for the missing object.

The first play activity, which the children carried out with passionate eagerness, was the pushing of furniture, the usual favorite occupation of toddlers who have just learned to walk. They began their day in the morning with pushing chairs in the nursery and returned to this activity at intervals during the day, whenever they were free to do so. After they had learned to play in the sandpit, they used sand for the same purpose, pushing a supply of it along the whole front of the veranda by means of an inverted chair. They would revert to pushing furniture even on coming home from long walks, or when tired.

Gradual progress in their physical ability to handle objects and to manage their own possessions coincided with the growth of the children's emotional interest in the adult world. This led to the wish to "help," to share the work of the adults and, as described above, to fetch and carry, to set chairs and tables, etc., activities which were carried out surprisingly well. For a short while, the wish to be equal to the adults in these matters led to a frenzy of independence, as the following example shows:

> In November, the children are taken for their first bus ride. The situation has been explained to them beforehand, also that the ride will be short and that they will have to get out quickly at the bus stop. They have promised to co-operate, and they leave their seats without protest at the appointed time. But when the conductor and a passenger try very kindly to help them down the steps, they push them away, and shout and scream that they want to do it alone. Finally Miriam lies on the road, her face almost blue with fury, Paul sits next to her, kicking and screaming, the others cry and sob.

While such a phase of independence brought marked increases in the skill and range of the children's activities, in periods of an opposite emotional nature the advances seemed to be lost once more. In January all the children went through a phase of complete passivity, and dependence on the adults, corresponding to the change of their relationships with them from the more impersonal community feelings to warmer personal attachments. During this time they refused to do anything for themselves, wanted to be fed, dressed, etc., and did not co-operate in work. Their ambivalent attitude toward the adults, the outgoing and withdrawal of emotion toward them, was reflected in the sphere of activities by violent demands to be helped and looked after like a helpless infant, coupled with an equally violent refusal to accept the care. In such moods the children would run away from being dressed, push the tables and chairs away when they had been set for a meal, refuse to carry even their own belongings, etc.

After approximately six months' stay in Bulldogs Bank, these violent upheavals gave way to more ordinary and stable modes of progress.

In March 1946 the children began to lose interest in their soft toys and took picture books to bed with them for "reading." For some time each child was content to have any book. From April onward the children demanded books in which they were particularly interested.

When Miriam received her postcard from Mr. E. and "wrote" her answer on it before going to sleep in the evening, "reading" came to an end and "writing" took its place. Several children had received letters and parcels from their American foster parents and "wrote" to them in bed. At first they used pencils indiscriminately, after a while they chose their colors. The imaginary letters written at that time dealt with matters such as Sister Sophie's absence, news about animals, flowers, etc., i.e., interests in the external world which had taken the place of the exclusive autoerotic activities of the bedtime hour.

In the second half of their year in Bulldogs Bank, the children became increasingly interested in the usual nursery school occupations. At the end of the year they had become able to concentrate on an occupation for as much as an hour. They had become able to handle scissors, pencils, paint brushes, blunt needles, and enjoyed painting, cutting out, doing puzzles and threading beads. Even then they preferred "grownup work" to nursery occupations and carried it out very efficiently.

After the beginnings, which had showed the children to be backward in their play by as much as eighteen months or two years, it was all the more impressive to watch the speed with which they passed through consecutive stages of play activity making up for development which had been missed.[2]

Absence of adequate experience with conse-

quent backwardness in understanding and behavior was even more striking outdoors than indoors. The children lacked both the city child's knowledge of traffic, shops, busy streets, etc., and the country child's familiarity with animals, trees, flowers and all types of work. They knew no animals except dogs, which were objects of terror. They did not know the name of a single plant and had never picked or handled flowers. They seemed to know no vehicles and were completely oblivious of the dangers of the road. Consequently their walks on the country road, through the village or the lanes and paths, were exciting events during which innumerable new impressions crowded in on them.

Parallel to the speed of their development in the sphere of play, the children passed rapidly through the various stages of experience and behavior with regard to outdoor events, which are usually gone through between the ages of two and four. Their interest in animals, once awakened, was accompanied by the usual animal play, identification with animals and observations of animals. Interest in cars went from an initial terror of being "made too-too by a car" to a pride in being able to manage crossings, to admonish others to do so, and to distinguish between the types of car. Before they left Bulldogs Bank the children had acquired the experience normal for country children of their age. They knew most trees and practically all the common flowers by name and asked for information when meeting new specimens. They distinguished weeds from plants; they picked flowers with long stems instead of tearing their heads off as at first. They were greatly helped in making up for lost time by the interest of the village people who showed them their animals, permitted them to come into their gardens, gave them flowers, explained their tools, allowed them to look inside their vans or behind counters, all of it new experiences of unique importance for the children.

Retardation in Modes of Thinking

In dealing with the mass of experience which crowded in on them, the children revealed, during the first weeks, some characteristic peculiarities which are worth noting in individuals of their ages.

[2] See in this respect the paper by Lotte Danzinger and Lieselotte Frankl (1934) on the test results with Albanian infants who, according to custom, spend their first year tied down in their cradle. The authors watched some of these infants being taken out of the cradle and allowed to play with toys. While they at first appeared extremely backward in comparison with other children, they nearly caught up with them (though not completely), when they had played with the toys for some hours only. As explanation, the authors suggest that inner processes of maturation had taken place and progressed in spite of deprivations.

See also Phyllis Greenacre's comprehensive article on "Infant Reactions to Restraint" (1948).

A first perception of an object, or the experiencing of an event, together with the naming of it, left an impression on their minds far overriding all later ones in strength and forcefulness. This was clearly demonstrated on several occasions.

A pony in the field had been introduced to the children as a donkey by mistake, and the first ducks which they met had been misnamed geese. In both cases it took several weeks to undo the wrong connection between object and word. In spite of repeated efforts at correction, the children clung to the names connected with their first image of the animal.

The first leaf shown to the children was an ivy leaf. For a whole month every green leaf was called ivy leaf.

When the children noticed a plane overhead for the first time and asked where it was going, they were told that it was going to France. "Going to France" remained a fixed attribute of every plane from then onward. During the whole year they called out: "Aeroplane going to France," whenever they heard a plane overhead.

The first time that letter writing had come into the children's lives was on the occasion of Sister Sophie's absence. All later letters, imagined or dictated by them, retained the opening phrases which they had used then: "Dear Sophie in a London in a Miss X's house. Miss X all better," regardless of the fact that Sister Sophie had returned long ago and that the letters were addressed to other people.

The first English song which the children learned in Bulldogs Bank was "Baa, baa, black sheep." Though they learned and sang many other nursery rhymes during their stay, "Baa, baa, black sheep" remained in a class of its own. They would sing it when cheerful or as a treat for somebody on special occasions.

When talking of people the children would name them according to their most interesting attribute or possession, or would name these objects after them. Mrs. Clarke, for example, had two small dogs which were the first friendly dogs known to the children and played an important role in helping them to overcome their terror of dogs. In December all children called Mrs. Clarke: "Miss Clarke's doggies." Objects given by her to the children were called by the same name. A big electric stove which came from her house was called by Peter: "Miss Clarke's doggies." Green porridge bowls given by her as a Christmas present were called Mrs. Clarke by everybody.

December 1945.—When washing up, John says: "You wash Mrs. Clarke. I dry Mrs. Clarke. Look at that, Mrs. Clarke all dry."

January 1946.—Ruth throws Peter's green bowl on the floor. Three children shout: "Mrs. Clarke kaputt, poor Mrs. Clarke all kaputt."

The examples quoted in this chapter reveal primitive modes of thinking which are shown by children in their second year of life. The overwhelming strength of a first link between an object or event and its name is characteristic for the time when children first learn to speak, or—to express it in metapsychological terms—when word representations are first added to the images (object representations) in the child's mind. The inability to distinguish between essential and nonessential attributes of an object belongs to the same age (see example of aeroplanes). Instances of naming where this is directed not to a single limited object but to a whole idea related to it (see example of "Miss Clarke's doggies") are forms of "condensation," well known from the primary processes which reveal themselves normally in dream activity, and continue in the second year of life as a mode of waking thought.

That these infantilisms in the sphere of thinking were not based on a general mental retardation with the children under observation was borne out by their adequate, adapted reasoning and behavior in situations with which they felt familiar (such as household tasks, community affairs, etc.); that they were not merely a function of the reversal in their emotional development is suggested by the fact that they overcame them before their libidinal attachments had changed decisively. That the rapid growth of life experience brought about an equally rapid advance in the modes of dealing with it mentally, suggests rather that it was the extreme dearth of new perceptions and varied impressions in their most impressionable years which deprived the children of the opportunity to exercise their mental functions to a normal degree and consequently brought about a stunting of thought development. . . .

CONCLUSION

"Experiments" of this kind, which are provided by fate, lack the satisfying neatness and circumscription of an artificial setup. It is difficult, or impossible, to distinguish the action of the variables from each other, as is demonstrated in our case by the intermingled effects of three main factors: the absence of a mother or parent relationship; the abundance of community influence; and the reduced amount of gratification of all needs, from the oral stage onward. It is, of course, impossible to vary the experiment. In our case, further, it proved impossible to obtain knowledge of all the factors which have influenced development. There remained dark periods in the life of each child, and guesswork, conclusions and inferences had to be used to fill the gaps.

Under such circumstances, no claim to exactitude can be made for the material which is presented here and it offers no basis for statistical considerations. Though an experiment staged by fate, in the sense that it accentuates the action of certain factors in the child's life (demonstrated through their absence or their exaggerated presence), it has little or nothing to offer to the experimental psychologist. What it helps to do is to create impressions which either confirm or refute the analyst's assumptions concerning infantile development—impressions which can be tested and in their turn confirmed or rejected in detailed analytic work with single individuals.

According to the results of child analysis and reconstruction from the analyses of adults, the child's relationship to his brothers and sisters is subordinated to his relationship to the parents, is, in fact, a function of it. Siblings are normally accessories to the parents, the relations to them being governed by attitudes of rivalry, envy, jealousy, and competition for the love of the parents. Aggression, which is inhibited toward the parents, is expressed freely toward brothers and sisters; sexual wishes, which cannot become manifest in the oedipal relationship, are lived out, passively or actively, with elder or younger brothers and sisters. The underlying relationship with siblings is thus a negative one (dating from infancy when all siblings were merely rivals for the mother's love), with an overlay of positive feelings when siblings are used for the discharge of libidinal trends deflected from the parents. Where the relations between the children of one family become finally manifestly positive, they do so according to the principles of group formation, on the basis of their common identification with the parents. The rival brother is tolerated as belonging to the mother; in special cases the rival brother even becomes an object of identification as the mother's favorite. The child's first approach to the idea of justice is made during these developments of the brother-sister relationship, when the claim to be favored oneself is changed to the demand that no one should be favored, i.e., that there should be equal rights for everybody. Since contemporaries outside the family are treated like the siblings, these first relationships to the brothers and sisters become important factors in determining the individual's social attitudes.

It is well in line with these views when our material shows that the relations of the Bulldogs Bank children to each other were totally different from ordinary sibling attitudes. The children were without parents in the fullest sense of the word, i.e., not merely orphaned at the time of observation, but most of them without an early mother or father image in their unconscious minds to which their earliest libidinal strivings might have been attached. Consequently, their companions of the same age were their real love objects and their libidinal relations with them of a direct nature, not merely the products of laborious reaction formation and defenses against hostility. This explains why the feelings of the six children toward each other show a warmth and spontaneity which is unheard of in ordinary relations between young contemporaries.

It merely bears out this theory to find that attachments to a mother figure in single instances disturb these positive relations, such as in Ruth's case. Or when John, in his mourning for Maureen, turned against his companions and began to hurt them. In these instances the positive libidinal attachment was directed toward the adult; the other children were thereby changed from the position of friends and love objects to that of enemies and rivals.

When working with the children of the Hampstead Nurseries (Freud & Burlingham, 1944), one of the authors has described certain attitudes of helpfulness, co-operation, identification and friendship which appeared in a group of toddlers (between fifteen months and two and one half years of age) who had been temporarily deprived of their mothers' care. The six Bulldogs Bank children, as the observations prove, show these attitudes in excess, the quantitative difference between them and the Hampstead Nursery group corresponding to the difference between total and partial absence of a parent relationship.

The high degree of identification with each other's needs is known from one other relationship in early years, that of identical twins to each other. In a recent study of the subject, Dorothy Burlingham (1951) demonstrates the emotional importance of twins to each other, the way in which the twin is treated as an extension of the self, cathected with narcissistic as well as object love. Identification with the twin prospers on the basis of common needs, common anxieties, common wishes, in short, on the similar reactions of two beings of the same age living in close proximity under the same external conditions. While in the case of twins the twin relationship conflicts with and has to adapt itself to the parent relationship, the attitude to the companion within our age group of orphans reigned supreme.

That the children were able to attach their libido to their companions and the group as such, bypassing as it were the parent relationship which is the normal way to social attitudes, deserves interest in relation to certain analytic assumptions. In recent analytic work the experiences of the first year of life, the importance of the relationship to the mother during the oral phase and the linking of these experiences with the beginnings of ego development have assumed great significance. Explorations in these directions have led to the belief, held by many authors, that every disturbance of the mother relationship during this vital phase is invariably a pathogenic factor of specific value. Grave defects in ego development, lack or loss of speech in the first years, withdrawnness, apathy, self-destructive attitudes, psychotic manifestations, have all been ascribed to the so-called "rejection" by the mother, a comprehensive term which includes every disturbance within the mother relationship from loss of the mother through death, permanent or temporary separation, cruel or neglectful treatment, down to lack of understanding, ambivalence, preoccupation or lack of warmth on the mother's part.

The six Bulldogs Bank children are, without doubt, "rejected" infants in this sense of the term. They were deprived of mother love, oral satisfactions, stability in their relationships and their surroundings. They were passed from one hand to another during their first year, lived in an age group instead of a family during their second and third years, and were uprooted again three times during their fourth year. A description of the anomalies which this fate produced in their emotional life and of the retardations in certain ego attitudes[3] is contained in the material. The children were hypersensitive, restless, aggressive, difficult to handle. They showed a heightened autoerotism and some of them the beginning of neurotic symptoms. But they were neither deficient, delinquent nor psychotic. They had found an alternative placement for their libido and, on the strength of this, had mastered some of their anxieties, and developed social attitudes. That they were able to acquire a new language in the midst of their upheavals, bears witness to a basically unharmed contact with their environment.

The authors hope that further contact with these children, or those of similar experience, will give indications as to how such emotional anomalies of early life influence the shaping of the Oedipus phase, superego development, adolescence and the chances for a normal adult love life.

3 —though much of these have to be ascribed to the additional material deprivations—

REFERENCES

Burlingham, Dorothy T. *Twins*. London: Imago, 1951.

Danzinger, Lotte, & Frankl, Lieselotte. Zum Problem der Funktionsreifung, *Z. f. Kinderforschung,* 1934, 43.

Freud, Anna, & Burlingham, Dorothy T. *Infants without families*. New York: International Universities Press, 1944.

Greenacre, Phyllis. Infant reactions to restraint. In C. Kluckhohn & H. A. Murray (Eds.), *Personality in nature, society, and culture*. New York: Knopf, 1948.

THE DEVELOPMENT, MEANING
AND MANAGEMENT OF SCHOOL PHOBIA

SAMUEL WALDFOGEL   JOHN C. COOLIDGE

PAULINE B. HAHN

FAMILY RELATIONS IN THE DEVELOPMENT OF SCHOOL PHOBIA

DR. WALDFOGEL: While school phobia has been recognized as a distinct disturbance of childhood for several decades, relatively little discussion of this problem has appeared in the literature. In most published reports the number of cases described has been small, and there seems to be some disagreement among the various authors regarding both its course and treatment. Although school phobia in its acute form does not occur very commonly in children, it can, once entrenched, become one of the most crippling disorders of childhood, with the principal symptom persisting indefinitely.

Our desire to increase our clinical effectiveness in dealing with this acute problem was one of the principal reasons for undertaking the present investigation. While our central purpose has been to explore possibilities for more effective treatment and management through closer cooperation of the school and clinic, we have not confined ourselves to therapeutic considerations alone. We have also been interested in learning more about both the etiology and epidemiology of this disturbance, particularly as they shed light on such basic theoretical issues as the specificity of symptom choice, the relation between the structure of personality and symptom formation, and the dynamics of parent-child relationships in the development of neurosis.

The term school phobia refers to reluctance to go to school as a result of a morbid dread of some aspect of the school situation. The fear may be attached to the teacher, the other children, the janitor, eating in the lunchroom, or almost any detail of school life. It is invariably accompanied by somatic symptoms, usually involving the gastrointestinal tract, but sometimes including such diverse symptoms as sore throat, headache, or leg pains. The somatic complaints are used as a device to remain at home, and often disappear once the child is assured that he does not have to attend school. The most typical picture is that of a child nauseated and vomiting at breakfast or complaining of abdominal pain, resisting all attempts at reassurance, reasoning, or coercion to get him to school. Often other phobic symptoms may accompany the fear of school—fear of animals, fear of noises, night terrors, etc.

During the period of this study, 53 cases of school phobia of varying degrees of severity have been referred. The distribution of these cases according to age and sex is given in Table 1. The frequency of boys and girls is approximately the same. This contradicts our previous impression, shared by many earlier authors, that school phobia was more commonly found among girls.

The age distribution clearly indicates that school phobia is a disorder that occurs most commonly in the lower elementary school grades. Even where the acute symptom developed later, there is evidence that its precur-

Reprinted with abridgment by permission of John C. Coolidge from the *American Journal of Orthopsychiatry*, 1957, **27**, 754–80. Copyright © 1957, the American Orthopsychiatric Association, Inc. Reproduced by permission. [The original paper included a section on follow-up by Pauline Hahn which is not reproduced here.]

TABLE I

Sex and Age Distribution of Total Group

	Age			
Sex	*5–7*	*8–10*	*11 +*	*Total*
Boys	15	10	3	28
Girls	12	9	4	25
Total	27	19	7	53

sors were usually present from the beginning of school. This has implications for early detection and treatment that will be discussed in more detail in the third section of this paper.

While our cases were all selected on the basis of their primary presenting complaint, namely, fear associated with school attendance, they were by no means a homogeneous group. The majority presented a typically neurotic picture in which displacement of anxiety appeared as the main mechanism of symptom formation, and in which either obsessive or hysterical personality traits were often present. This description seemed in general to fit the younger children in our study. Among the older children, however, we were more apt to find depressive or paranoid features, with projection playing a more prominent part in their symptom, as evidenced by mistrust, hypersensitivity, and ideas of reference. With the younger age group, the symptom represented an acute regressive reaction accompanying a panic state. In the older age group, the symptom was a part of a widespread character disturbance in which there had been fixation of infantile conflicts that finally emerged in the phobic symptom.

Accordingly, we have distinguished these groups as *neurotic* and *characterological* types of school phobia. While a simple dichotomy of this kind obscures the fact that we are probably dealing with a continuum, it has proved useful to us in terms of prognosis and treatment. Again, the fuller implications of this distinction will be made clear later in the discussion.

Childhood phobias are of such common occurrence that mild and transient ones are regarded as a part of early normal development. Nevertheless, in their severe forms they can be

one of the really disabling emotional disturbances of childhood. Before the dynamics of childhood phobia were elucidated in Freud's study of Little Hans, it was generally assumed that such exaggerated fears stemmed either from a frightening past experience or from the child's inability to comprehend the lack of realistic danger in the phobic situation; to understand, for example, that wild animals are no longer to be found in cities. However, Freud presented convincing evidence that the child's phobia was derived not from the fearfulness of the object itself, but from his own frightening impulses that had been externalized and displaced onto the phobic object.

School phobia is in this respect like the other phobias of childhood, the anxiety in this instance being shifted from its basic source to the school. When we trace the anxiety to its source, it is invariably found to originate in the child's fear of being separated from his mother. This root is often discernible in overt behavior, the mother being an obligatory companion in many instances. The child will attend school only if she accompanies him, and often her continued presence is required in the classroom. Frequently, the fear of separation from mother applies to other situations as well, so that she becomes a virtual prisoner of the child. The significance of the mother-child relationship is thus projected into the foreground in school phobia, making its importance in the genesis of this disturbance difficult to overlook.

The importance of this relationship was first noted by Adelaide Johnson and her co-workers. It was their feeling that the basis of the problem lay in the hostile dependent relationship between the mother and child. In the main, our findings are in agreement with those of Johnson et al., but on the basis of more extensive observation, we are in a position to make certain emendations that both clarify the dynamics of the mother-child relationship and account more directly for the choice of symptom. The description that follows is a composite one, and as with any generalized description, fits some cases better than others. However, we feel that these cases show such a remarkable degree of similarity that dealing with them in generalities does not do serious injustice to the individual case.

As Johnson and her co-workers had previously observed, the typical mother in this group is closely identified with her child, and the child is used excessively as a means of vicarious gratification, although not necessarily or exclusively for the mother's dependency longings. Thus, there may also be narcissistic gratifications which she seeks through her child, especially if the child is a girl, by identifying with her physical attractiveness, intelligence, or achievement. More directly, we have seen instances of the mother's expressing her sexual needs in disguised form in relation to the child. The male child, for example, may be used by the mother for erotic gratification, the mother often becoming involved in bodily contact under the guise of maternal affection and innocent playfulness. One of our mothers, who had strong voyeuristic impulses based on a need to deny sexual differences, encouraged unnecessary displays of nudity on her husband's part on the grounds that she didn't want her daughter to grow up in ignorance of male anatomy or with guilt about sexuality.

The mother's identification with her child is rooted in a strong affectionate attachment toward him or her. Her affection appears primary and spontaneous and is not simply an attempt to deny her hostility. Even when she is angry, she does not withdraw her affection from her child but is more apt to "reason" with him, a procedure which usually consists of a mixture of nagging and pleading. She resorts to physical punishment only rarely and then anxiously undoes this as a means of atonement. Her anger derives from her feelings of exasperation and helplessness, and physical punishment is used in desperation, not in order to express brutal or sadistic impulses.

The entire pattern of child rearing in this group reflects the mother's subservience to her child. She is determined that there shall be no deprivation of either his physical or emotional needs and constantly sacrifices her own comfort and convenience to his. Thus, one mother, who had to sit with her son every day in kindergarten, stated resignedly that she did not mind as long as it was for his good.

Despite her subordination to the child, the mother is not necessarily overpermissive. Her anxiety cannot permit her to indulge the child too freely. On the contrary, she tries to be restrictive and controlling, but her great anxiety about creating fear or rage in the child causes her to vacillate between strictness and leniency. When a clash between her wishes and the child's does occur, she usually yields in the end, but will feel overwhelming rage at being exploited.

Overprotectiveness is another characteristic way in which the typical mother of this group handles her anxiety regarding the child. She adopts an "antiseptic" attitude toward him and tries to protect him from pain, shock, and frustration. She goes to considerable trouble and planning to prevent his coming in contact with anything unpleasant, this category usually including the "painful" facts of life, e.g., sex, childbirth, illness, and death.

Lurking behind the mother's wish to do everything possible for her child is her deep-felt uncertainty about her competence as a mother. This was perhaps most clearly expressed by one mother who reported that she had to give up breast feeding after a week because of anxiety that the child was not getting enough to eat, despite encouragement by her physician and her knowledge that the baby's gain in weight was adequate. It is this feeling of inadequacy in her maternal role which is basic to the mother's own anxiety at separation. Added to this is her resentment at the child's demands which she feels incapable of fulfilling. There can be little doubt that the mother's problem around separation antedates the problem in the child, and a careful case history will invariably disclose evidence of it.

One mother described her first attempts to leave her daughter of just under a year with a baby sitter. She had decided to get away at least one afternoon a week on the advice of her pediatrician, who felt she was "too close" to the child. When she left for the first time, the baby cried, and it took all her resolve to stay at the nearby shopping center for three quarters of an hour. During the following weeks, she gradually decreased the time she spent out of the house until by the end of the month she abandoned the attempt entirely.

By her excessive preoccupation with her child's welfare and her inability to set limits effectively, the mother feeds the child's narcissism and omnipotent fantasies. The nature of their relationship is such that the child becomes increasingly dependent upon her for gratifications and she consequently becomes an active partner in his neurosis.

We usually find that the fathers also play a significant role in this pathological constellation. Here our information is more limited, but the central fact that emerges is that the father, because of his own uncertain sexual identification, is unable to define clearly his paternal position. He shares the mother's anxious concern for the child and often vies subtly with her for the maternal role. At times, it is as though the child had two anxious mothers to contend with instead of one. The father is usually very much involved in the problems of child care and rearing, and by trying to prove that he can handle the children better than his wife, undermines the shaky foundations of her own feelings of maternal adequacy. Actually, the mother and the father are both looking to each other for gratification of their own dependency needs.

Thus, we hear one father saying, "When I come home from work, all my wife wants to tell me is how much trouble the kids have given her, and how her legs and back have been killing her. I think her physical complaints are mostly emotional anyhow, and I can't feel too much sympathy for them. I have plenty of pressure at work, too, and I would like to be able to talk about my troubles. If I try to get sympathy from her, she just complains all the more about her problems."

In relation to the child, the father's search for dependent gratification usually takes the form of overidentification with the child, but sometimes we see him competing as a sibling for mother's affection.

The lack of clear differentiation between the parental roles presents difficulties for the child, in establishing his own sexual identity, and in case after case we find bisexual conflicts in the patient. These are magnified during the oedipal period, the impact of which is especially heightened because of the parents' strong emotional attachment to the child and their competition for his favor.

The child growing up with this kind of relationship to his parents develops certain deficiencies in his character structure that constitute the substratum of his neurosis. Autonomy of ego development is hampered by the oppressive proximity of the parents. The child rarely has occasion to master a difficult situation, the parents always being at hand to protect him from the pain of an emotional crisis. It is significant that we do not encounter traumatic events in the lives of these children very frequently. Their anxiety stems not so much from earlier external traumata as from the lack of opportunity to test the real consequences of distressing emotions. The feelings of fear and rage come to assume overwhelming proportions and are associated with catastrophic expectations. There is no inner sense of being able to cope with these dangerous emotions independently, and when the child experiences these feelings, his inadequate ego requires the presence and support of his parents.

Coupled with his deficiency of autonomous ego functioning is the inflated need for narcissistic gratifications, which he achieves mainly through the continuous exploitation of his subservient parents. Their inability to limit his demands, which at times assume tyrannical proportions, nurtures his omnipotent fantasies, supporting the tendency toward magical thinking, where the wish becomes equivalent to its realization.

The prolongation of the child's infantile position in regard to parental gratification has still an additional consequence, namely, the impairment of the repressive process. Thus, although the children in our study were observed predominantly during the latency period, we quite commonly found the conscious expression of oedipal and even preoedipal fantasies that by this age are ordinarily repressed. This is associated with the child's inability to inhibit successfully his regressive dependent tendencies. This is not to say that these impulses can be indulged without guilt. As in any neurosis, there is an abundance of guilt, but the superego can be temporarily set aside because of the feeling that the parents really condone his regressive tendencies. This makes it difficult for him to resist the temptation of his infantile wishes, but having indulged them he then suffers the pain of his transgressions.

His incapacity in this respect is a direct reflection of the parents' own shortcomings where the gratification of his wishes is concerned. Too often when they would like to say "no" to his demands, they yield grudgingly, so that he feels the full onslaught of their resentment. Thus, the parents, by their own vacillation in regard to his impulses, fail to provide the child with any basis for a stable system of inner controls. At the same time, he internalizes their rage at his parasitical demands, and is left without any substantial source of narcissistic support except even greater reliance on his parents to bolster his self-esteem.

The intensity of the child's demanding attachment and the parent's desperate rage was expressed most clearly by one mother. In referring to her daughter, she would repeatedly use the expression, "She eats me up alive. At times I feel I could kill her." Here she may be expressing the formula in its most fundamental form: the omnivorous child fastened onto a mother, who, doubting her capacity to satisfy even a more limited hunger and fearing that she will be devoured, can only hope for the child's destruction. Perhaps it is the unconscious representation of this basic conflict at the oral level that accounts for the frequency with which nausea and vomiting accompany the anxiety of children with school phobia and explains the central position of the mother in this disturbance.

In order to comprehend the relationship between the deficiencies in character development we have mentioned and the symptom itself, it will be necessary to reflect briefly on the dynamics of the phobic process. There are at least three mechanisms involved in the development of a phobia. One is the *displacement* of the anxiety from its original source to a substitute object; e.g., fear of mother may be displaced to a fear of teacher. Second, there is *projection* of intolerable impulses. Thus, oral aggressive

fantasies may be transformed into a fear of being bitten by dangerous animals. Finally, there is the mechanism of *externalization* of punishment, the process by which guilt is transformed into fear of being injured or annihilated by some dangerous object in the environment. This process is perhaps best exemplified by the ubiquitous bogeyman of childhood.

To a certain extent, all children utilize these mechanisms, and to a degree, all have phobic experiences. The presence of a clinical phobia implies a greater reliance on such mechanisms than is ordinarily the case. If we inquire further into the purpose they serve, we perhaps can understand why the family constellation we have described should bring these mechanisms actively into play.

If we assume that in the phobias of childhood it is the function of displacement to split off the hostile aspect of the parent that the child cannot incorporate as part of his total image, then it follows that in situations of intense ambivalence, where the child is greatly dependent upon the parent, the feared and hated aspects will have to be separated from the rest. Here again, the child mirrors the parent's example. We have seen how the mothers in particular deny their hostility toward the child by using overcompensatory devices and presenting themselves as being zealously devoted to the child's welfare. This is the only image of themselves that is tolerable. Since they are so terrified of their own angry image, it is hardly any wonder that the child shares their fear, and needs to protect himself from the full realization of the mother's anger by shifting it to another object.

The child, however, must not only deny his mother's anger, but his own as well. In an atmosphere where rage always carries with it a destructive connotation, and where he is so totally dependent upon his mother for support and protection, he is left little alternative but to displace his anger onto some other object or person. Thus, by displacing his anger, he protects himself from the terrifying prospect of being alone and helpless.

Finally, the child must relieve himself of the enormous burden of guilt which any situation of unresolved ambivalence inevitably creates. The transformation of guilt feelings into fear of external punishment by the phobic object not only reduces his objective anguish, but justifies his wish for making even greater claims on his parents for protective support.

It is our belief that the preceding formulations apply not only to school phobia, but to childhood phobias in general. The distinguishing feature of school phobia is the child's greater reliance on his mother's presence to control his anxiety. This derives from the long history of dependency, and is thrust into the fore when a dangerous situation arises. School is such a situation in that it represents the first major obligatory separation from the mother. At the same time, it deals the child a severe narcissistic blow, since he must relinquish his favored position in the family for the anonymity of the classroom. When dangerous fantasies arise either in the school or as a result of some crisis in the family, the child seeks to return to his mother's protective presence. Usually such precipitating factors can be found, but they only trigger off the deep regressive urges that underlie the symptom. In clinging to mother the child is able to assure himself that his own hostile wishes will not come true. He has to protect himself not only from the pain of guilt for his death wishes, but more fundamentally from the state of lonely helplessness that would ensue if the wishes were realized. By prolonging the position of the dependent child in relation to mother, he also protects himself against the full implication of his oedipal wishes. At the same time, his clinging satisfies the mother's own unconscious desire to be indispensable, making her an unwitting accomplice in the perpetuation of his neurosis, despite her conscious feelings of bewilderment and distress.

THE CLINICAL TREATMENT OF SCHOOL PHOBIA

DR. COOLIDGE: The treatment of school phobic children and their parents does not differ to any great degree from that of other children and parents who show approximately the same ego strength and character structure. Certain reaction patterns have manifested themselves with such regularity during treatment, however,

that it seems worth while to highlight their presence.

The main technical problem in the treatment of the mother is dealing with her unresolved dependency conflicts. The mother presents herself as eager for help. For the most part she is poised, has a demeanor of grown-up sophistication, and shows in matters other than child raising considerable independence of thought. However, when she talks about her child, she shows herself to be a frightened and frustrated little girl who feels she cannot cope with being a mother. It is as if she had been pretending to be a grownup and this pretense was destroyed when she was faced with the task of raising her own children. This is illustrated from the intake interview with Mrs. W.

Mrs. W unfolded a quite complete story of her 7½-year-old daughter's school troubles and developmental history. Throughout the material ran the theme of an anxious relationship between mother and daughter with a mutual struggle for control. The parents' frustration and bewilderment led to overindulgence, time and again, with increasing attempts to placate Elizabeth by giving in to her increasing demands. Alternating with this were occasional anxious and hostile attempts to get Elizabeth to conform, many of which ended in further frustration.

This mother's opening statement, "I do not know whether I did right or wrong," is directly stated or implied by almost every mother in her first contact with the clinic. It expresses her obsessional doubt that she is a good mother, as though she had never been taught by maternal grandmother how to be a mother. This craving to be led by the hand in the maternal role comes up repeatedly. One frequently has the impression that not being able to "feel" the role of a mother spontaneously, the mothers compensate by needing to "know."

From the manner in which the material is presented about the child, the worker can quickly deduce that the mother is also presenting the two sides of her own personality: the grown-up, mature and rather sophisticated person who has done so well in so many ways; and the helpless little girl with great, unresolved dependency yearnings, caught and confused in the relationship to her own child. With the loss of her sense of adequacy and self-esteem, there has been a rise both in her dependency yearnings, and in her defenses against them. The mother comes to the clinic searching to find what she has done "wrong," yet simultaneously rationalizing and projecting blame to others. This sense of guilt is augmented by entering treatment, and the mother expects to be blamed or scolded by the worker. The worker finds herself dealing with a person who feels both guilty and not guilty, who wishes to be told, yet is fearful of dependency. Deeper down lie painful frustration and anger with herself for having fallen short of her exacting standards. Although the mother may seem to want the worker to do so, it is therapeutically undesirable for her to accept the mother's defensive maneuvers at face value, to sound critical of her attempts to deal with her difficulties, or to become involved in giving asked-for advice. It is necessary instead to help the mother face the fact that there is an emotional problem in which she is involved and that she is to be an important participant in the treatment of her child. At the same time it is imperative to gauge whether the mother is at her wit's end and needs more than just understanding. This is especially true at the beginning of treatment, when there is a high degree of tension and when firm support and encouragement are often needed. With this sympathetic and flexible approach, the mother is helped to sense that she herself has assets and strengths, on the one hand, and yet that her real needs for help as a mother are also recognized and will be met.

As described earlier, prior to treatment, the mother's sporadic attempts to be firm were often unreasonably rigid. The child had naturally reacted with hostility and attempts at countercontrol. Our experience indicates that even from the initial interview the mother can generally make constructive use of support from her worker in subsequent dealings with the child. She interprets the support as permission to assume a mother's role and feels that she is no longer alone in the struggle with her child. As the mother's anxiety is reduced, her comfort and certainty increase. Her handling of the child is quieter, more effective and more consistent, and therefore more meaningful. Mrs. W, in her second interview, reported that

she had felt a great deal of support and thereafter made it quite plain to Elizabeth, in a quiet way, that "home would not be a welcome place" for her during school hours. Elizabeth returned to school.

One problem in treatment arises when the mother is reluctant to take a parental stand in situations in which she anticipates that the child will be anxious or resentful. Visits to the dentist, the clinic, the doctor, are handled by bargaining with the child or asking him to make the decision and thereby free her of the responsibility. It is frequently necessary to tell the mother quite directly that the child should not have to be faced with such decisions, clarifying with her the confusion and anxiety that arise in the child's mind when the decision is left to him. Although the mother can often use this kind of help, the worker must be prepared to deal later with the ambivalence that such direct advice will arouse.

The support and advice that are offered will inevitably arouse the mother's dependency yearnings and her fears that if she gives in to these, she will become helpless. The worker can encourage the mother to realize that it is possible to express some of her dependency needs without total surrender. It is equally important, however, not to permit the mother to become so dependent that the anxiety and hostility associated with this dependency impel her to discontinue treatment or to withhold emotionally in treatment.

The prevailing personality characteristic of the helpless little girl who needs to be taught may serve as resistance in treatment. The worker taking this aspect at face value will be lured into undue guiding and answering of questions, and dealing exclusively with the immediate problems and anxieties aroused by the child's refusal to go to school. She will find herself giving in to increasing demands and being controlled in such a way that deeper dynamic material is being avoided. If this be the case, the worker should scrutinize her own countertransference feelings to ascertain if she has been lured unwittingly into believing that she must be most cautious lest too much anxiety be aroused in the mother. This only re-creates the same relationship with the mother that she had had with her child. We have found repeatedly that when properly timed, gentle firmness in focusing with mother on her own past and present emotional life is effective. Leads offered by the mother herself, by the child in his treatment, or from our experience with other cases provide the pathway into this area. Such refocusing is usually readily accepted, often with much relief to the mother, who can then proceed to break down the barriers and construct a truer dynamic picture of herself and the relationship to her child.

The second year of casework with Mrs. W again illustrates such a phase in treatment.

In her treatment, Elizabeth plunged into the seductive relationship with her father, and her pleasure in taking mother's place, and gave indications of being under a high degree of strain. The mother, who was still dealing in her interviews with the daily tribulations about school, was confronted quite directly with our belief that Elizabeth was under considerable sexual tension. With this as an aid and with implicit permission, mother proceeded to deal with this area and gradually revealed an important part of her own past and present. It quickly became apparent to her that Elizabeth's difficulty in falling asleep seemed related to father's early bed hours. Elizabeth remained awake until father retired and then, complaining of being lonely, would climb into bed with him, where she was readily received. Mother, sitting downstairs alone, also felt lonely. She felt her husband could stay downstairs a little longer with her, but was powerless to express her wishes. She heard Elizabeth and her father laugh and giggle upstairs but could recognize neither the seductive relationship between them nor the mounting sexual tension in her daughter, who at just under nine was already undergoing definite pubertal changes. Finally she recalled how lonely her own nights as a child had been. For several years her mother "ordered her" to bed with her older brother, who had night terrors, and though consciously feeling she did not like this, she felt compelled to comply in order to please her mother. Later she tried sleeping with her older sister, and felt rejected when this sister refused to sleep with her. She added, "I guess children aren't comfortable to sleep with. I know it isn't comfortable to sleep with Elizabeth. She is so restless." She recalled a persistent desire to sleep with somebody, and she herself occasionally slept in bed between her parents. It appeared as if, consciously, she felt that age or sex made no difference; and as if, having suppressed her own infantile, sexual tensions, she now could not see them in Elizabeth.

There were indications of disturbances in mother's own sexual life; she hinted that her feelings had changed and she no longer liked to share the same bed with her husband.

Although mother could discuss sexual matters with adults in a matter-of-fact way, she felt confused and anxious with Elizabeth and was unable to give her any sex education. Once having recognized what was taking place and how sexually aroused Elizabeth became, she began to assume more authority as a mother and effectively put a stop to the acting out in which all three were involved.

The worker often feels pressed by family and school to help "get the child back to school." If she identifies with the mother too much, she will react to such pressure and lose sight of more basic problems. For example, the client, after discussing some aspects of her life, may add: "That may be well and good but what has it got to do with my child's fears about school?" If the worker can help the mother realize that the child's return to school, although an important achievement in itself, is in reality only the relief of the symptom, and that the real therapeutic aim is to correct the disturbances in the family relationships, then the mother herself will feel less pressed and concerned about immediate results and more willing to explore other emotionally significant but apparently unrelated areas.

With this judicious mixture of guidance, yielding, clarification and firmness, the relationship between the worker and the mother becomes a mutually respecting and confident one, a fertile field in which the mother feels really understood, and in which the majority show a remarkable capacity for growth.

In the treatment of the school phobic children, as with their mothers, certain problems recur. One of the most troubling of these is the waiting period that ordinarily intervenes between the onset of the symptoms and the beginning of clinic treatment. Acute symptom formation represents a psychiatric emergency and should be dealt with as such. Within the framework of the current research project, it has been possible to reduce the waiting period to a minimum. When treatment was initiated quickly, before the symptom had a chance to crystallize and secondary complications in the child's relationship to mother and school developed, rapid symptomatic improvement resulted. In those children who had withdrawn completely from school, a quick return, often in a matter of four to six weeks, was accomplished. In those children who had not completely withdrawn from school, but whose attendance was erratic, precarious and deteriorating, a complete withdrawal was often forestalled. This was not generally true when treatment had been delayed. . . .

It is usually possible and therapeutically profitable to focus early with these children on the major symptom and on such ancillary phobic or physical symptoms as may be present. These children, keenly aware of the alien quality of their symptoms and consciously desirous of freeing themselves of them, usually talk quite freely about them even in the first hour. In many youngsters it is also possible to use their clinic behavior to translate the fear of going to school into the fear of separation from the mother. Since these children relate to the therapist quickly and warmly, there is some temptation to move into this area too rapidly, overlooking the child's need to protect himself by symptom formation. We have found that while a discussion of the onset of the referral symptom is possible from the start, it is better to reserve interpretations for some little while, until the child's relationship to the therapist has been solidified. . . .

In many of the children the symptom abates as a result of the therapeutic relationship and the opportunity it offers for discharge and clarification. Even though the central unconscious conflicts remain uninterpreted, the fantasies within the hour begin to change, indicating spontaneous resolution of the conflicts. The clinical evidence suggests that the bisexuality is being appropriately resolved, and symptoms of anxiety and suppressed hostility wane. This is accompanied by encouraging reports from parents and school. The treatment of these children is terminated when the therapist and the parents agree that the child has embarked along a fairly healthy path of normal development. The length of treatment of these children varies from six months to one year.

While the two phases of treatment outlined above, symptom focus and fantasy focus, appear almost invariably, the third phase of treatment, interpretation—working through and actual integration of symptom and fantasy with unconscious conflicts—is not as consistently present. In a few children, before the conflicts are laid to rest, the process of therapy demands the linking of these fantasies with the symptom. These are the children in whom fear of being apart from the mother has usually been increasingly specified until it has become verbalized as a fear that harm may befall her. This, in turn, must be translated into the wish behind the fear, that the child under certain circumstances actively wishes harm or death upon his mother. It then becomes possible to link this wish with the child's conscious fear of being separated from mother. In this process of dealing with the child's ambivalence toward his mother, the therapist can often help the child to become specifically aware of the inner stress that ensues when feelings of anger and resentment against a mother upon whom he is necessarily dependent become strong. The therapist can also help the child delve into the sources of the anxiety—for instance, in the case of the girls, the feelings of rivalry that lie at the root of the hostility. We are not yet certain whether the fears of reprisal or the reality perception of the abandonment and helplessness which would take place if the hostile wishes came true is more important.

An example of the integration of symptom and fantasy life can be given from the treatment of Elizabeth. Although previously material of an oedipal nature had been present and anxiety on separation from mother had been constantly manifest, the two themes had never been satisfactorily integrated. The following interviews demonstrate the first successful attempt to do so.

Miss Gray, Elizabeth's unsympathetic teacher, openly blamed Elizabeth and another girl for making her sick with a skin rash. Elizabeth told how upsetting this had been and mentioned how furious she often had felt toward Miss Gray. Although she could not accept the interpretation that she had been fearful that Miss Gray's illness could have resulted from her thoughts, she did concede that she sometimes wished mother to be the victim of a minor catastrophe, such as breaking her ankle. It was suggested that this was why, then, she needed to remain close to mother, so that she could be sure nothing would happen to her as a consequence of her hostile thoughts. Elizabeth again denied this connection but immediately changed the subject, the new topic itself obviously associated with the root of her hostility toward mother. "There is something going through my mind. It was a trick I played on father. I sneaked up and unfastened his suspenders. He chased me and we had a lot of excitement and a lot of fun." She finally agreed with the therapist that she and her father were sweethearts, but hastened to add that he could get angry, too, and she wasn't sure she preferred father to mother.

The next week Elizabeth was reluctant to come and needed to be reassured by her therapist before she would join him in the interview room. She then reported a dream. The atom bomb dropped in bed. She woke terrified, calling for mother. She felt afraid of being alone and mother quickly came into her single bed. It was crowded. Elizabeth complained to mother, who reportedly told her she could take mother's place in father's bed. This Elizabeth did. "Father and I talked and did all sorts of things and had a real good time." The doctor echoed her frequent wish to exchange places with her mother. Elizabeth agreed, "Oh yes, I would tell her," and gesticulating violently with his fists, "and when I have children, I'll make them go to school. If they don't, I'll march them there and make them stay." It was interpreted that she was angry at mother for not being firmer, as well as for standing in her way. The theme that something might happen to mother as a consequence of these thoughts was again broached. The next week Elizabeth proudly announced she had returned to school.

In termination of treatment certain considerations are of prime importance. For these children, termination represents a vitally significant phase of treatment, re-evoking as it does their core problem, that of separation from an intensely and ambivalently loved person. Thus, it affords a second opportunity for a therapeutic experience, one which should be grasped and utilized to the fullest. For this reason, termination should be anticipated with the child well in advance of its actual date, and the feelings about it should be thoroughly explored. The positive feelings derived from the child's wish to grow and be independent should be supported and encouraged. The negative ones deriving from his hostility and fears should be interpreted and allayed. It has seemed well founded to permit the child a voice in making the decision to terminate and in setting the date, and to give him opportunity to experiment with independence by increasing the interval between treatment appointments before regular contacts have finally been discontinued.

Partly in the interests of our research, we have maintained a continued though irregular contact with the cases which have been terminated. This contact preserves in the child a sense of the availability of the helping person and softens the finality of the separation. The follow-up seems to undermine residual tendencies to associate disappearances with the magical effects of hostile feelings and provides opportunities for the child to obtain gratification and appreciation by being able to report the positive steps he has taken.

EARLY EDUCATION:
A COGNITIVE-DEVELOPMENTAL VIEW

LAWRENCE KOHLBERG

A glance over the field of early education in America at the time of Jean Piaget's seventieth birthday reveals a curious contrast. While Piaget's ideas are salient wherever research is done on early cognitive development, their salience in formulations of goals and processes in early education is much less widespread. Enthusiasts for early cognitive stimulation often make reference to Piaget's ideas but adapt them to a viewpoint different than that held by him. Bruner (1960, 1966), Bruner, Olver, and Greenfield (1966), and Hunt (1961, 1964) interpret Piaget's ideas as consistent with the notion that intelligence is a set of acquired information-processing skills and that any intellectual content can be taught early if the teaching is adapted to the child's cognitive level. On the opposite pole, the "child-development" tradition of preschool education has appealed to Piaget's ideas as part of a body of maturational theory including Freud (in Kessen, 1965), Gesell (1954), Isaacs (1933), and Spearman (1930). In this context, Piaget's ideas have been viewed as consistent with the notion that preschool educators should just let cognitive abilities grow and that the educator should concentrate upon helping the child to adjust and develop emotionally.

This ambiguity is not surprising in light of the fact that "if one looks carefully through Piaget's writings, one seldom, if ever, finds an attempt to deal with concrete problems of pedagogy or childrearing" (Elkind in Piaget, 1967, p. xvi). More fundamentally, however,

the ambiguity is due to Piaget's rejection of traditional dichotomies implicit in much controversy about early cognitive learning. In the first place, Piaget discards the dichotomy between maturation and environmentally determined learning. He insists that cognitive processes emerge through a process of development which is neither direct biological maturation nor direct learning in the usual sense, since it is a reorganization of psychological structures resulting from organism-environment interactions (Elkind, 1967; Flavell, 1963; Hooper, 1968; Piaget, 1964; Wallace, 1965). In the second place, Piaget discards the dichotomy between the cognitive (usually considered as a set of intellectual skills) and the social emotional. According to Piaget, social development, play, and art all have large cognitive-structural components and contribute to, and are contributed to by, cognitive development in the narrower sense. . . .

As we elaborate in the following sections, there are three broad streams of educational thought which vary from generation to generation in their statement, but which are each continuous in starting from the same assumptions. The first stream of thought commences with Rousseau (in Kessen, 1965) and is contemporarily represented in the ideas of followers of Freud and Gesell. This maturationist stream of thought holds that what is most important in the development of the child is that which comes from within him and that the pedagogical environment should be one which creates a climate to allow inner "goods" (abilities and social virtues) to unfold and the inner "bad" to come under the control of the inner good, rather than to be fixated by adult cultural pressures. The extreme of this view is presented by Neill (1960). The second "cultural training" stream of thought assumes that what is important in the development of the child is his learning of the cognitive and moral knowledge and rules of the culture and that education's business is the teaching of such information and rules to the child through direct instruction. This stream of thought can be traced from John Locke to Thorndike and Skinner (cf. Kessen, 1965). The clearest and most thoughtful contemporary elaboration of this view in relation to preschool education is to be found in the writing of Bereiter and Engelmann (1966).

The third stream of thought, the "cognitive-developmental" or "interactional" view is based on the premise that the cognitive and affective structures which education should nourish are natural emergents from the interaction between the child and the environment under conditions where such interaction is allowed or fostered. More specifically, the basic postulates of this approach are:

1. The terms "cognition," "thought," or "intelligence" basically refer to adaptive actions upon objects or internalizations of such actions. Mature or adequate cognition is defined by an equilibrium or reciprocity between action and object. Cognition is defined as function (as modes of action) rather than as content (as sets of words, "verbal responses," associations, memories, etc.) or as a faculty or ability (a power of producing words, memories, etc.). The encouragement of cognitive development, then, is the provision of opportunities for activities of an organized or equilibrated form.

2. Cognition proceeds through stages of structural reorganization. While cognitive functions are present from birth, cognitive structures are radically different from one stage to the next.

3. The implication of structural reorganization in development is that the source of cognitive structure and of cognitive development is to be found neither in the structure and maturation of the organism nor in the teaching structures of the environment but in the structure of the interaction between organism and environment.

4. The optimal conditions for such structural organization entail some optimal balance of discrepancy and match between the behavior structures of the child and the structure of his psychological environment.

5. From birth, there are inherent motives for cognitive activities, but these motives too undergo structural change in development.

6. Both the "cognitive" and the "affective" are functions, not psychic contents or structures. Cognitive and affective development are parallel aspects of the structural transformations undergone in development.

While all of the above ideas are common to all writers in the cognitive-developmental tradition, Piaget's work has been the first to apply these assumptions to children's behavior in logically precise and empirically specified form. The implication of Piaget's work for education, then, may best be understood as giving greater precision to the general functional-genetic approach to education, presented in its most comprehensive form by Dewey (1913, 1930, 1938, 1965).

In the present paper, we shall first summarize the Piagetian (or cognitive-developmental) position and some exemplary research as it bears upon two related topics central to preschool education: first, the general role of experience in cognitive development, and, second, the issue of whether preschool cognitive experience defines a special or "critical" period in intellectual development. In the course of this discussion, we shall attempt to consider its implications for the introduction of various types of cognitive "curricula" into the preschool. In a forthcoming book (Kohlberg & Lesser, in press) we use this viewpoint to analyze the contributions of play, art, and social interaction to the child's development.

Part of the purpose of this paper is to examine some of the implications of Piaget's rather difficult notions of cognitive development for the concrete concerns of the preschool educator, because it may be of some practical use for educational policy. In part, it also seems of use for the clarification of theory itself. Piagetian theory must take account of research on early education as well as "pure" research on cognitive development if it is to undergo the elaboration and refinement required of a viable theory. Accordingly, this paper attempts to both elaborate the position and to review some of the findings which make it plausible. Such a review of a broad range of findings somewhat tangentially related to Piaget's ideas is bound to be somewhat cursory and superficial, but it will at least suggest areas where current findings and Piagetian theory must confront one another.

THE COGNITIVE-DEVELOPMENTAL APPROACH AND THE CONCEPT OF STAGE

We have suggested that the basic characteristics of the cognitive-developmental approach may be best grasped by contrasting them with theories of innate patterning and maturation on the one hand and theories of environmental associationistic learning on the other. As opposed to either set of theories, cognitive-developmental theories are "interactional," that is, they assume that basic mental structure is the product of the patterning of the interaction beween the organism and the environment rather than directly reflecting innate patterns or patterns of event-structures (stimulus contingencies) in the environment.

The distinction between theories stressing the innate and theories stressing the acquired has often been thought of as a contrast in quantitative emphasis on hereditary biological factors as opposed to environmental stimulation factors in causing individual differences. When the problem is posed in such a fashion, one can be led to nothing but a piously eclectic "interactionism" which asserts that all concrete behavior is quantitatively affected by both hereditary and environmental factors. The theoretical issues are quite different, however. They are issues as to type of theory, that is, between conceptions of basic mental structure and the location of the principles producing this structure within or without the organism.

The statement just made presupposes a distinction between behavior differences in general and mental structure. Structure refers to the general characteristics of shape, pattern, or organization of response rather than to the rate or intensity of response or its pairing with particular stimuli. According to cognitive-developmental theory, all mental structure has a cognitive component (and all cognition involves structure). Many cognitive theories do not employ structural concepts. As an example, Baldwin (1968) terms a number of theories (including his own) "cognitive" because (*a*) they postulate a coding or representational process intervening between stimulus and response, and (*b*) they postulate that the learning of representations or maps may occur without any overt response and without any definite reinforcement for this learning. In addition to these more general assumptions, cognitive-developmental theory assumes that "cognitions" are internally organized wholes or systems of internal relations, that is, structure. Cognitive structures are rules for processing information or for connecting experienced events. Cognition (as most clearly reflected in thinking) means putting things together, relating events, and in cognitive theories this relating is assumed to be an active connecting process, not a passive connecting of events through external association and repetition. The process of relating events depends upon general categories which represent the modes of relating common to any experienced events, for example, causality, substantiality, space, time, quantity, and logic (i.e., the identities, inclusions, or implications of classes and propositions).

The awareness that the child's behavior has a cognitive structure or organizational pattern of its own which needs description independently of the degree of its correspondence to the adult culture is as old as Rousseau, but this awareness has only recently pervaded the actual study of cognitive development. Two examples of the revolution resulting from defining the structure of the child's mind in its own terms may be cited. The first is that of Piaget, whose first psychological effort was to classify types of wrong answers on the Binet test. By moving beyond an analysis of intellectual development in terms of number of right answers to an analysis in terms of differences in structure, Piaget transformed the study of cognitive development. The second example comes from the study of children's language, which was for a generation based on counting nouns and verbs as defined by conventional adult grammar. In the last decade, psychologists have approached children's grammar with the methods of structural linguistics, as if the child's language were that of an exotic tribe. While the implications of the Piagetian revolution in cognition and the structuralist revolution in language are far from clear, they have made the conception of mental structure a reality accepted even by associationistic S-R psychologists of cognition (cf. Berlyne, 1965).

It is evident, then, that general questions as to the origins and development of mental structure are not the same as questions regarding the origins of individual differences in behavior. As an example, the fact that one 6-year-old child may pass all the 6-year items on the Binet test and another fail them all might be attributed purely to hereditary differences in general intelligence, while the patterns of behavior involved in the child's actual test performance (knowing the word "envelope") may be purely culturally learned behavior. Because many American psychologists have been peculiarly concerned with individual differences rather than developmental universals, and because they have failed to understand the distinction between behavior differences in general and behavior structure, they have frequently misinterpreted European theories of development. It is because of this confusion that some American writers have misinterpreted Piaget's stages as "maturational" and have thought that he claimed intelligence is unaffected by environment, while others have correctly interpreted Piaget's stages as being based on the assumption of organism-environment interactions, but take this assumption as indicating that individual differences in intellectual performance are less hereditary than was long believed. In fact, there is nothing in Piaget's theory which suggests that individual differences in speed of development through his stages is not largely due to the hereditary factors which seem to account for at least half of the variance in the usual IQ tests.

Maturational theories, then, are not theories based on quantitative assumptions about the role of heredity. In terms of quantitative role, maturational or nativistic theories, like those of Gesell (1954) or Lorenz (1965), recognize the importance of environmental stimulation in modifying genetically grounded behavior patterns. In a similar sense, associationistic learning theorists, like Hull (1943) or Pavlov (1928), recognize the quantitative role of hereditary traits of temperament and ability in causing individual differences in personality and in rate and type of learning. The difference between the two types of theories is not in the recognition of both innate and environmental causal factors in development but in the belief about which set of factors are the source of basic patterning.

The contrast between the quantitative and structural roles awarded to experience becomes clear with regard to the issue of critical periods. Most research on the effects of experience upon development has postulated "critical periods" in which the individual is especially sensitive to environmental influence in a given domain. Yet this notion of extreme quantitative sensitivity depends upon a maturational or nativistic theory. The existence of a fixed time period, during which a certain amount of stimulation is required to avoid irreversible developmental deficits, presupposes an innate process of growth with an inner time schedule and an inner pattern which can be arrested or distorted by deficits of stimulation.

In the nativistic view, stimulation may be needed to elicit, support, and maintain behavior patterns, but the stimulation does not create these patterns, which are given by templates in the genotype. In fact, learning or environmental influence itself is seen as basically patterned by genetically determined structures. Learning occurs in certain interstices or open places in genetic patterns, and the structuring of what is learned is given by these patterns (Lorenz, 1965). As an example, "imprinting" represents a type of learning, a determination of response by environmental stimulation. However, the "learning" involved represents a specific sensitivity or open spot in a genetically patterned social-sexual response, phylogenetically determined to produce a tie to others of the species. As another example, an insect or bird may learn a specific "map" of the geography of its home place, but this map is structured by an innate organization of space in general (Lorenz, 1965).

In dealing with developmental changes, nativistic theories such as Gesell's (1954) have stressed the notion of unfolding maturational stages. The patterning of these age-specific behavioral forms, their order and timing, is believed to be "wired into" the organism. The organism grows as a whole so that the effort to teach or force early maturation in one area will either be ineffective or will disrupt the child's total pattern and equilibrium of growth.

In contrast to nativistic theories, learning theories may allow for genetic factors in personality and in ease of learning of a complex response, but they assume that the basic structure of complex responses results from the structure of the child's environment. Both specific concepts and general cognitive structures, like the categories of space, time, and causality, are believed to be reflections of structures existing outside the child, structurings given by the physical and social world.

Almost of necessity, the view that structure of the external world is the source of the child's cognitive structure has led to an account of the development of structure in associationistic terms. From John Locke to J. B. Watson and B. F. Skinner (Kessen, 1965), environmentalists have viewed the structure of behavior as the result of the association of discrete stimuli with one another, with responses of the child, and with experiences of pleasure and pain.

At its extreme, this conception of mental structure has the following implications for early education:

1. Mind or personality is a set of specific responses to specific stimuli in the environment. Cognitive development is the result of guided learning, of recurrent associations between specific discriminative stimuli in the environment, specific responses of the child, and specific reinforcements following these responses.

2. "Cognition" is a matter of discrimination and generalization learning. Conceptual development occurs through learning overt or covert verbal labeling responses to discriminated and generalized classes of stimuli. Training in discrimination of the stimulus attributes implied by cultural concepts and generalization of response to these attributes lead to concept learning.

3. The child is born with very little patterning of personality or of mind. Accordingly, it is possible to teach a child almost any behavior pattern, provided one teaches in terms of the laws of association learning and provided one starts at an early age before competing response patterns have been learned.

4. It is important to start education early because early learnings, if appropriate, facilitate later learnings, while if they are inappropriate they impede later learnings.

It is important to recognize that all these educational postulates of environmentalist theories of learning are not inconsistent with the innate determination of IQ or other traits of ability or temperament. These postulates do, however, suggest that teaching can go on without much prior understanding of the structure of a given desired behavior pattern as it "naturally" develops and as it relates to prior organismic behavior structures. Teaching instead requires primarily a careful statement of a behavior pattern considered desirable (e.g., a skill such as reading or arithmetic) in terms of specific responses. This pattern is then to be taught in accordance with general laws of learning believed applicable to the learning of all organisms (old or young, human or nonhuman) and to the learning of all behavior patterns.

In general, such a program implies a plan for shaping the child's behavior by successive approximation from responses he is now making to the desired end responses. At every step, immediate feedback or reward is desirable and immediate repetition and elaboration of the correct response is used. A careful detailed programing of learning is required to make sure that (*a*) each response builds on the preceding, (*b*) incorrect responses are not made since once made they persist and interfere with correct responses, and (*c*) feedback and reward are immediate.

We have contrasted the maturationist assumption that basic mental structure results from an innate patterning with the learning theory assumption that basic mental structure is the result of the patterning or association of events in the outside world. In contrast, the cognitive-developmental assumption is that basic mental structure is the result of an interaction between certain organismic structuring tendencies and the structure of the outside world, rather than reflecting either one directly.

This interaction leads to cognitive stages, which represent the transformations of simple early cognitive structures as they are applied to (or assimilate) the external world and as they are accommodated to or restructured by the external world in the course of being applied to it.

The core of the cognitive-development position, then, is the doctrine of cognitive stages. Cognitive stages have the following general characteristics (Piaget, 1960):

1. Stages imply distinct or qualitative differences in children's modes of thinking or of solving the same problem at different ages.

2. These different modes of thought form an invariant sequence, order, or succession in individual development. While cultural factors may speed up, slow down, or stop development, they do not change its sequence.

3. Each of these different and sequential modes of thought forms a "structured whole." A given stage-response on a task does not just represent a specific response determined by knowledge and familiarity with that task or tasks similar to it; rather it represents an underlying thought-organization. An example is the stage of "concrete operations," which determine responses to many tasks which are not manifestly similar to one another on the "ordinary" dimensions of stimulus generalization. According to Piaget, at the stage of concrete operations, the child has a general tendency to maintain that a physical object conserves its properties on various physical dimensions in spite of apparent perceptual changes. This tendency is structural; it is not a specific belief about a specific object. The implication is that both conservation and other aspects of logical operations should appear as a consistent cluster of responses in development.

4. Cognitive stages are hierarchical integrations. Stages form an order of increasingly differentiated and integrated *structures* to fulfill a common function. The general adaptational functions of cognitive structures are always the same (for Piaget the maintenance of an equilibrium between the organism defined as a balance of assimilation and accommodation). Accordingly, higher stages displace (or rather reintegrate) the structures found at lower stages. As an example, formal operational thought includes all the structural features of concrete operational thought but at a new level of organization. Concrete operational thought

or even sensorimotor thought does not disappear when formal thought arises but continues to be used in concrete situations where it is adequate or when efforts at solution by formal thought have failed. However, there is a hierarchical preference within the individual, that is, a disposition to prefer a solution of a problem at the highest level available to him. It is this disposition which partially accounts for the consistency postulated as our third criterion.

The question of whether cognitive stages "exist" in the sense just defined is an empirically testable question. It has been held by Kaplan (1966) and others that stages are theoretical constructions and that their theoretical value holds independently of whether or not they define empirical sequences in ontogeny. Every theoretical set of structural stages are defined in such a way that a higher stage is more differentiated and integrated than a lower stage. In this logical sense, a set of structural stages form a valid hierarchy regardless of whether or not the stages define an ontogenetic sequence.

In spite of this fact, it is extremely important to test whether a set of theoretical stages does meet the empirical criteria just listed. If a logical hierarchy of levels did not define an empirical sequence, the hierarchy would tell us little about the process of development nor would it justify our notion that the sequence is interactional in nature. If empirical sequence was not found, one would argue that the "stages" simply constituted alternative types of organization of varying complexity, each of which might develop independently of the other. In such a case, the "stages" could represent alternative expressions of maturation or they could equally well represent alternative cultures to which the child is exposed. It would hardly be surprising to find that adult physical concepts are more complex, more differentiated and integrated in educated Western culture than in a jungle tribe. The fact that the Western and tribal patterns are at different levels of structural organization, however, in itself tells us little about ontogenesis in either culture and leaves open the possibility that ontogenesis in either culture is simply a process of learning cultural content.

In contrast, if structural stages do define general ontogenetic sequences, then an interactional type of theory of developmental process must be used to explain ontogeny. If the child goes through qualitatively different stages of thought, his basic modes of organizing experience cannot be the direct result of adult teaching or they would be copies of adult thought from the start. If the child's cognitive responses differed from the adult's only in revealing less information and less complication of structure, it would be possible to view them as incomplete learnings of the external structure of the world, whether that structure is defined in terms of the adult culture or in terms of the laws of the physical world. If the child's responses indicate a different structure or organization than the adult's, rather than a less complete one, and if this structure is similar in all children, it is extremely difficult to view the child's mental structure as a direct learning of the external structure. Furthermore, if the adult's mental structure depends upon sequential transformations of the child's mental structure, it too cannot directly reflect the current structure of the outer cultural or physical world.

If stages cannot be accounted for by direct learning of the structure of the outer world, neither can they be explained as the result of innate patterning. If children have their own logic, adult logic or mental structure cannot be derived from innate neurological patterning because such patterning should hold also in childhood. It is hardly plausible to view a whole succession of logics as an evolutionary and functional program of innate wiring.

It has just been claimed that it is implausible to view a succession of cognitive stages as innate. This claim is based on an epistemological assumption, the assumption that there is a reality to which psychology may and must refer, that is, that cognition or knowing must be studied in relation to an object known.

The invariant sequences found in motor development (Ames, 1937; Shirley, 1931, 1931–1933) may well be directly wired into the nervous system. The fact that the postural-motor development of chimpanzees and man proceed through the same sequence suggests such a maturational base (Riesen & Kinder, 1952). The existence of invariant sequence in ⁀ognition is quite a different matter, however,

since cognitions are defined by reference to a world. One cannot speak of the development of a child's conception of an animal without assuming that the child has experience with animals. Things become somewhat more complicated when we are dealing with the development of categories, that is, the most general modes of relating objects such as causality, substance, space, time, quantity, and logic. These categories differ from more specific concepts, for example, the concept of "animal," in that they are not defined by specific objects to which they refer but by modes of relating any object to any other object. Every experienced event is located in space and time, implies or causes other events, etc. Because these categories or structures are independent of specific experiences with specific objects, it has been plausible for philosophers like Kant to assume that they are innate molds into which specific experiences are fitted. If structures or categories like space and time were Kantian innate forms, it is difficult to understand how these structures could undergo transformation in development, however.

The interactional account assumes that structural change in these categories depends upon experience. The effects of experience, however, are not conceived of as learning in the ordinary sense, in which learning implies training by pairing of specific objects and specific responses, by instruction, by modeling, or by specific practices of responses. Indeed, the effects of training are determined by the child's cognitive categories rather than the reverse. If two events which follow one another in time are cognitively connected in the child's mind, it implies that he relates them by means of a category such as causality, for example, he perceives his operant behavior as causing the reinforcer to occur. A program of reinforcement, then, cannot directly change the child's causal structures since it is assimilated to it.

If cognitive development occurs in terms of stages, then, an understanding of the effect of experience upon it requires three types of conceptual analysis customarily omitted in discussions of learning.

In the first place, it requires an analysis of universal structural features of the environment. While depending on structural and functional invariants of the nervous system, cognitive stages also depend upon universal structures of experience for their shape. Stages of physical concepts depend upon a universal structure of experience in the physical world, a structure which underlies the diversity of physical arrangements in which men live and which underlies the diversity of formal physical theories held in various cultures at various periods.

In the second place, understanding cognitive stages depends upon a logical analysis of orderings inherent in given concepts. The invariance of sequence in the development of a concept or category is not dependent upon a prepatterned unfolding of neural patterns; it must depend upon a logical analysis of the concept itself. As an example, Piaget postulates a sequence of spaces or geometrics moving from the topological to the projective of the Euclidean. This sequence is plausible in terms of a logical analysis of the mathematical structures involved.

In the third place, an understanding of sequential stages depends upon analysis of the relation of the structure of a specific experience of the child to the behavior structure. Piaget (1964) has termed such an analysis as "equilibration" rather than a "learning" analysis. Such an analysis employs such notions as "optimal match," "cognitive conflict," "assimilation," and "accommodation." Whatever terms are used, such analyses focus upon discrepancies between the child's action system or expectancies and the experienced event, and hypothesize some moderate or optimal degree of discrepancy as constituting the most effective experience for structural change in the organism.

In summary, an interactional conception of stages differs from a maturational one in that it assumes that experience is necessary for the stages to take the shape they do as well as assuming that generally more or richer stimulation will lead to faster advances through the series involved. It proposes that an understanding of the role of experience requires (*a*) analyses of universal features of experienced objects (physical or social), (*b*) analysis of logical sequences of differentiation and integration in concepts of such objects, and (*c*) analysis of structural relations between experi-

ence-inputs and the relevant behavior organizations. While these three modes of analysis are foreign to the habits of associationistic learning theorists, they are not totally incompatible in principle with them. While associationistic concepts are clumsy to apply to universal objects of experience or to the logical structures of concepts and to the problem of match, it can be done, as Berlyne (1961, 1965) has demonstrated. As yet, however, such associationistic analyses have not led to the formulation of new hypotheses going beyond translations of cognitive-developmental concepts into a different language. . . .

RESISTANCE OF SEQUENTIAL COGNITIVE DEVELOPMENTS TO SPECIFIC TEACHING: EXPERIMENTS ON CONSERVATION

In the preceding section, we outlined an interactional theory of the role of experience which shares with maturationism a pessimism about the effect of specific teaching on cognitive-structural development. In a practical sense, the interactional view suggests that limited specific training experiences cannot replace the massive general types of experience accruing with age. Both views then agree in the factual importance of age-readiness but disagree in their interpretation of this fact. An example of evidence used for the maturational view is the finding of Gesell and Thompson (Gesell, 1954) that an untrained twin became as adept at tower building and stair climbing after a week of practice as was the trained twin who had been given practice in tower building and stair climbing over many weeks. As Hunt (1964) convincingly argues, while this finding shows the limited value of *specific training,* it does not show that the function in question does not depend upon *general experience.* The untrained twin was not just "maturing," he was walking and climbing on other objects than stairs; he was placing and manipulating other objects than block towers, etc. While the developmental and the maturational view may practically agree on the relative futility of early specific training of a function, the developmental view sees specific training as failing primarily because it cannot make up for the age-linked general experiential lacks of the young child rather than because it cannot make up for his neurological immaturity.

As an example, preschool children advanced in verbal knowledge and information are still almost as immature in level of development of the dream concept as are less verbally knowledgeable preschool children. Thus, Jack, a bright verbal child (Stanford-Binet MA = 6 yr., 10 mo.), age 5 years, 2 months, responds as follows to the dream task: "Dreams come from God. God makes the dreams and puts them in balloons. The balloons float down from heaven and enter a dream bag under your stomach. In the dream bag there are some little men and a sergeant. They have a cannon that shoots the dream-balloons up into your head where they burst into pictures outside your head."

Jack here is much closer in developmental level to his chronological age-mates than to his mental age-mates. Yet his creative thinking and his possession of verbal concepts are high. Ongoing research by DeVries (in preparation) and others (Goodnow & Bethon, 1966) suggests that in general mildly retarded children are more advanced in Piaget concepts than younger average children of the same psychometric mental age and that average children are in turn more advanced than younger bright children of the same psychometric mental age. Our interpretation is not that Piaget stages represent age-fixed maturational unfoldings independent of psychometric ability but that cognitive-structural development depends upon massive general experience, a requirement which the "innately" bright child cannot short circuit. The psychometrically bright child is adept at organizing or "educing relations and correlates" in a cognitive field (Spearman, 1930), but the logical structure of the relations which are induced demands massive experience for its reorganization.

Much more comprehensive evidence to support the notion that specific training cannot substitute for age-linked general experience comes from the numerous experiments designed to teach conservation of mass, weight, or number to young children (Sigel & Hooper, 1968). These studies suggest that direct teaching of ~rvation through verbal instruction and reinforcement or through provision of observations of examples of conservation (e.g., weighing masses changed in shape on a balance) does not lead to the formation of a general or stable concept of conservation. Little change is induced by such methods.

If specific experimental teaching seems to have only limited value for the attainment of conservation, general formal schooling appears to have no influence at all upon conservation. Conservation of number, mass, weight, and volume appears at the same age in schooled and unschooled subjects when other relevant variables are controlled. Probably the most definitive study on this question is that of Mermelstein (Mermelstein, 1964; Mermelstein & Shulman, 1967). Mermelstein compared the conservation responses on a number of tasks (including number) of 6- and 9-year-old Negro children of Prince Edward County who had been deprived of schooling with northern urban Negro children who had attended school. No significant differences were found between the two groups. An equally careful study by Goodnow showed no difference between unschooled Hong Kong children and comparable IQ schooled children in various types of conservation (Goodnow & Bethon, 1966). Price-Williams (1961) found that African Tiv children without schooling attained conservation on several tasks including number at about the same age Western children achieve conservation. Greenfield (1966) found some retardation on conservation in nonschooled Senegalese children, but this retardation disappeared when an appropriate form of the conservation task was used which eliminated set effects due to beliefs about magical attributes of white authorities. Kohlberg (1968a) hypothesized that Montessori schooling for young children might accelerate conservation and transitivity because the Montessori training tasks are directed at sensorimotor experiences of quantitative measurement and comparison. While Montessori schooling over 9 months did significantly raise Stanford-Binet IQ, it failed to have any effects upon Piaget conservation tasks.

While the resistance of conservation to specific instruction is noteworthy, it is more significant to note that the conditions under which instruction does change conservation are those expected by cognitive-developmental theory.

In the first place, the approach distinguishes between reversible situational learning and structural development. An associationistic theory of learning typically assumes that any learning is situation-specific (i.e., under the control of situational discriminative stimuli and reinforcers) and is reversible (i.e., can be extinguished). In the operant conditioning paradigm, the demonstration of reversibility (extinction and subsequent relearning) is part of the demonstration that the researcher has isolated the variables controlling behavior change. In contrast, both common sense and cognitive-developmental theory hold that cognitive development is generalized and irreversible. This constitutes the root meaning of the notion of cognitive structure. If the child has developed a concept of conservation, we expect that he will not lose it even in the face of contrary stimulation or social pressure. We also expect that he will invoke or apply the concept under conditions appropriate to the meaning of the concept rather than in terms of situational and sensory parameters extraneous to its meaning. It is obvious that insofar as structural change can be induced such change should take precedence over reversible situational learning as a focus of educational effort. There is no particular reason to expect that preschool teaching of a reversible situation-specific type can have any lasting effect upon the child.

There is ample evidence that "naturally" developing conservation concepts have the structural properties mentioned. They typically cannot be reversed by trick demonstrations of nonconservation nor by social pressure from the experimenter (Kohlberg, 1963; Smedslund, 1961a). While some forms of conservation are more difficult than others, the order of difficulty tends to be regular (constituting a Guttman-scaled "horizontal decalage," e.g., conservation of mass, weight, and volume), and children showing conservation on a given task are likely to show it on others, that is, to generalize or transpose the concept in comparison to children of the same chronological or mental age who do not show conservation on that given task (Uzgiris, 1968).

In contrast, most of the effects of specific instruction in inducing conservation do not have the structural properties mentioned. Artificial acceleration of conservation seems to be limited in generalization. While generalizing across specific objects, training of number conservation does not seem to lead to acceleration of other forms of conservation (Gruen, 1968). Apparent attainment of conservation so obtained seems to be partly or wholly reversible. Exposure to trick conditions suggesting nonconservation leads to loss of belief in conservation where conservation has been taught rather than developing naturally (Smedslund, 1961b).

We have stated that conservation responses are resistant to direct instruction and that often when they are not resistant (i.e., where conservation is induced) the response changes do not represent a genuine acquisition of conservation in the sense of an irreversible generalized belief in conservation. However, it also appears that some genuine acceleration of conservation may be induced if the instruction methods used follow from the conceptions of cognitive structure and of conflict and match implied by Piaget's theory. In the first place, successful induction of conservation is contingent upon the match in the sense that the child must already be near the level of attainment of conservation in terms of chronological and mental age. In the second place, some successful induction of conservation is achieved through stimulation of the development of the logical prerequisites of conservation defined by Piaget (e.g., the ability to make double classifications or to consider two dimensions simultaneously [Sigel, Roeper, & Hooper, 1968] or the stimulation of imaginative reversal [Wallach & Sprott, 1964]). In the third place, some successful induction of conservation results from creation of experiences in which nonconserving expectations lead to certain conditions of conflict (Langer, 1967; Smedslund, 1961a, 1961b).

In addition to the experimental findings mentioned, naturalistic studies support the notion that acquisition of conservation is contingent upon a background of general experience, as we have already discussed for the dream concept. Some degree of retardation in conservation appears in some semiliterate non-Western cultures, regardless of schooling (Greenfield, 1966; Hyde, 1959; Kohlberg, unpublished data on the Taiwan Atayal). Preliminary findings indicate that lower social class and "culturally disadvantaged" (Aid to Dependent Children) groups matched with middle-class subjects on Stanford-Binet mental age do more poorly on conservation tasks (Kohn, in preparation).

It seems unlikely that the "general experience" effects of social class and culture upon conservation are primarily or directly linguistic. The fact that conservation development is not directly contingent on language development is indicated by findings on the deaf (Furth, 1966). While these findings indicate some retardation of conservation among the deaf, this retardation is not marked, in spite of the fact that most of the deaf children studied have almost no facility with verbal language in any form. Much more marked deficits have been found in blind children of normal verbal IQ who do not appear to attain most forms of conservation reached by normal children at ages 5 to 7 until ages 9 to 11 (Nordan, 1967). The findings seem to be in line with Piaget's notions of the visual-motor roots of "concrete operations."

In summary, the conservation findings, like the dream-concept findings, clearly demonstrate that conservation is not a strict maturational product but is the product of interactional experience between organismic structure and environment. On the practical side, however, they do not give much support to the notion that development on basic Piaget-type cognitive functions can be markedly accelerated by deliberate intervention of a schooling variety, since such acceleration tends to be limited, specific, and contingent upon a narrow time gap between the intervention experience and the child's natural readiness. This readiness is determined by age, IQ, and the richness of the child's general background of stimulation. . . .

[The author goes on at this point to analyze critically various approaches to preschool curricula, including specific intellectual instruction and language stimulation. His conclusions follow. (Eds.)]

CONCLUSIONS AS TO PRESCHOOL COGNITIVE OBJECTIVES

This paper has elaborated a view of preschool intellectual development as one of sequential structural change equipotentially responsive to a variety of specific types of experience but reflecting differences in the effects of general amount and continuity of organized experiences in the preschool age range. I have argued that specific types of preschool academic and linguistic training, even if immediately successful, are unlikely to have long-run general beneficial effects and that programs directed toward raising general psychometric intelligence are unlikely to have marked success. I have claimed that a Piagetian conception of methods of accelerating intellectual development (employing cognitive conflict, match, and sequential ordering of experience), a Piagetian focus upon basic intellectual operations, and a Piagetian procedure of assessment of general intellectual development might generate somewhat more general and long-range cognitive effects than would other approaches.

Basically, however, the Piaget approach does not generate great optimism as to the possibility of preschool acceleration of cognitive development (or of compensation for its retardation) nor does it lead to a rationale in which such acceleration (or compensation) is especially critical during the preschool years.

The cognitive-developmental approach suggests both modesty in the hopes of creators of preschool stimulation programs and modesty in the claims that one program of stimulation will differ markedly from another in its general impact upon the child. Cognitive-developmental theory, itself, is broadly compatible with a diversity of specific cognitive-stimulation programs, ranging from Moore to Montessori, insofar as all these programs define their cognitive goals developmentally and center on relatively active and self-selective forms of cognitive stimulation for the child (Kohlberg, 1968). The compatibility of the cognitive-developmental view with a variety of programs is based first on its definition of cognitive advance in terms of natural lines of development rather than in terms of specifically taught "content." Second, this compatibility is based upon a concern with general forms of active experience, in terms of which a variety of specific types of stimulation are more or less functionally equivalent for cognitive development.

More generally, cognitive-developmental theory does less to suggest or support radical new preschool cognitive stimulation programs than it does to clarify the child-centered developmental approach to education expressed in its broadest form by John Dewey. The approach departs more from traditional child development concerns in providing a systematic analysis of the cognitive-structural and cognitive-interest implications of the play, aesthetic, constructive, and social activities which form the heart of the preschool than in suggesting narrowly "cognitive" activities in the preschool. Recent American Piagetian research on the preschool child has focused almost exclusively

on children's quantitative and logical classificatory concepts, as indicated by Sigel and Hooper's (1968) anthology. It should be recalled, however, that Piaget and his followers have systematically studied the development of preschool children's play, their conversations with one another, their conceptions of life, of death, of reality, of sexual identity, of good and evil. The implications of these and other themes for the broader definition of preschool objectives are taken up elsewhere (Kohlberg & Lesser, in preparation).

REFERENCES

Ames, L. B. The sequential patterning of prone progression in the human infant. *Genetic Psychology Monograph,* 1937, 19, 409–460.

Baldwin, J. M. *Thoughts and things or genetic logic.* Vol. 3. New York: Macmillan, 1906–1915.

Bereiter, C., & Engelmann, S. *Teaching disadvantaged children in the preschool.* Englewood Cliffs, N.J.: Prentice-Hall, 1966.

Berlyne, D. *Conflict, arousal and curiosity.* New York: McGraw-Hill, 1961.

Berlyne, D. *Structure and direction in thinking.* New York: Wiley, 1965.

Bruner, J. *The process of education.* Cambridge, Mass.: Harvard University Press, 1960.

Bruner, J. *Toward a theory of instruction.* Cambridge, Mass.: Harvard University Press, 1966.

Bruner, J., Olver, R., & Greenfield, P. *Studies in cognitive growth.* New York: Wiley, 1966.

DeVries, R. Performance of bright, average, and retarded children on Piagetian concrete operation tasks. Unpublished monograph, University of Chicago, Early Educational Research Center, in preparation.

Dewey, J. *Interest and effort in education.* Boston: Houghton Mifflin, 1913.

Dewey, J. Experience and conduct. In C. Murchison (Ed.), *Psychologies of 1930.* Worcester, Mass.: Clark University Press, 1930.

Dewey, J. *Experience and Education.* New York: Collier, 1963 (originally written in 1938).

Dewey, J. In R. Archambault (Ed.), *Dewey on education, a selection.* New York: Modern Library, 1965.

Elkind, D. Piaget and Montessori. *Harvard Educational Review,* 1967, 37, No. 4.

Flavell, J. *The developmental psychology of Jean Piaget.* New York: Van Nostrand, 1963.

Furth, H. *Thinking without language; psychological implications of deafness.* New York: Free Press, 1966.

Gesell, A. The ontogenesis of infant behavior. In L. Carmichael (Ed.), *Manual of child psychology.* New York: Wiley, 1954.

Goodnow, J., & Bethon, G. Piaget's tasks: The effects of schooling and intelligence. *Child Development,* 1966, 37, 573–582.

Greenfield, P. On culture and conservation. In J. Bruner et al. *Studies in cognitive growth.* New York: Wiley, 1966.

Gruen, G. E. Experience affecting the development of number conservation in children. In I. Sigel & F. Hooper (Eds.), *Logical thinking in children: research based on Piaget's theory.* New York: Holt, Rinehart & Winston, 1968.

Hooper, F. Piagetian research and education. In I. Sigel & F. Hooper (Eds.), *Logical thinking in children: research based on Piaget's theory.* New York: Holt, Rinehart & Winston, 1968.

Hull, C. *Principles of behavior.* New York: Appleton-Century, 1943.

Hunt, J. McV. *Intelligence and experience.* New York: Ronald, 1961.

Hunt, J. McV. The psychological basis for using pre-school enrichment as antidote for cultural deprivation. *Merrill-Palmer Quarterly,* 1964, 10, 209–248.

Hyde, D. M. An investigation of Piaget's theories of the development of number. Unpublished doctoral dissertation, University of London, 1959.

Isaacs, S. *Social development in young children.* London: Routledge, 1933.

Kaplan, B. The study of language in psychiatry. In S. Arieti (Ed.), *American handbook of psychiatry.* Vol. 3. New York: Basic Books, 1966.

Kessen, W. (Ed.) *The child.* New York: Wiley, 1965.

Kohlberg, L. Stages in children's conceptions of physical and social objects in the years 4 to 8—a study of developmental theory. Unpublished monograph, 1963, multigraphed (in preparation for publication).

Kohlberg, L. The Montessori approach to cultural deprivation. A cognitive-development interpretation and some research findings. In R. Hess & R. Bear (Eds.), *Preschool education, theory, research and action.* Chicago: Aldine, 1968.

Kohlberg, L., & Lesser, G. *What preschools can do: theories and programs.* Chicago: Scott, Foresman, in press.

Kohn, N. The development of culturally disadvantaged and middle class Negro children on Piagetian tests of concrete operational thought. Doctoral dissertation, University of Chicago, in preparation.

Langer, J. The role of cognitive conflict in development. Paper delivered at meetings of Society for Research in Child Development. New York, March 21, 1967.

Lorenz, K. *Evolution and the modification of behavior.* Chicago: University of Chicago Press, 1965.

Mermelstein, E. The effect of lack of formal schooling on number development, a test of Piaget's theory and methodology. Unpublished doctoral dissertation, Michigan State University, 1964.

Mermelstein, E., & Shulman, L. S. Lack of formal schooling and the acquisition of conservation. *Child Development,* 1967, 38, 39–52.

Neill, A. S. *Summerhill.* New York: Hart, 1960.

Nordan, R. The development of conservation in the blind. Unpublished minor research paper, University of Chicago, 1967.

Pavlov, I. P. *Lectures on conditioned reflexes.* New York: Liveright, 1928.

Piaget, J. The general problem of the psychobiological development of the child. In J. M. Tanner & B. Inhelder (Eds.), *Discussions on Child Development.* Vol. 4. New York: International Universities Press, 1960.

Piaget, J. Cognitive development in children. In R. Ripple & V. Rockcastle (Eds.), *Piaget rediscovered, a report on cognitive studies and curriculum development.* Ithaca, N.Y.: Cornell University, School of Education, 1964.

Piaget, J. *Six psychological studies.* D. Elkind (Ed.). New York: Random House, 1967.

Price-Williams, D. R. A study concerning concepts of conservation of quantity among primitive children. *Acta Psychologica,* 1961, 18, 297–305.

Riesen, A., & Kinder, E. *The postural development of infant chimpanzees.* New Haven, Conn.: Yale University Press, 1952.

Shirley, Mary M. The sequential method for the study of maturing behavior patterns. *Psychological Review,* 1931, 38, 501–528.

Shirley, Mary M. *The first two years, a study of twenty-five babies.* Minneapolis: University of Minnesota Press, 1931–1933. 2 vols.

Sigel, I., & Hooper, F. (Eds.), *Logical thinking in children: research based on Piaget's theory.* New York: Holt, Rinehart & Winston, 1968.

Sigel, I. E., Roeper, A., & Hooper, F. H. A training of procedure acquisition of Piaget's conservation of quantity. In I. Sigel & F. Hooper (Eds.), *Logical thinking in children: research based on Piaget's theory.* New York: Holt, Rinehart & Winston, 1968.

Smedslund, J. The acquisition of conservation of substance and weight in children, III: Extinction of conservation of weight acquired normally by means of empirical control as a balance. *Scandinavian Journal of Psychology,* 1961, 2, 85–87 (reprinted in Sigel & Hooper, 1968). (a)

Smedslund, J. The acquisition of conservation of substance and weight in children, V: Practice in conflict situations without external reinforcement. *Scandinavian Journal of Psychology,* 1961, 2, 156–160, 203–210 (reprinted in Sigel & Hooper, 1968). (b)

Spearman, C. The psychology of "g." In C. Murchison (Ed.), *Psychologies of 1930.* Worcester, Mass.: Clark University Press, 1930.

Uzgiris, I. Situational generality of conservation. In I. Sigel & F. Hooper (Eds.), *Logical thinking in children: research based on Piaget's theory.* New York: Holt, Rinehart & Winston, 1968.

Wallace, J. G. *Concept growth and the education of the child.* The Mears, Upton Park, Slough, Bucks: National Foundation for Education Research in England and Wales, 1965.

Wallach, L., & Sprott, R. Inducing number conservation in children. *Child Development,* 1964, 35, 1057–1071.

RESPONSE TO PRESSURE FROM PEERS VERSUS ADULTS AMONG SOVIET AND AMERICAN SCHOOL CHILDREN

URIE BRONFENBRENNER

PROBLEM

The experiment to be reported here is part of a more extensive research project investigating the differential impact of adults and peers on the behavior and personality development of children in different cultural contexts. Our earlier studies had pointed to important differences from culture to culture in the part taken by peers *vis-a-vis* adults in the socialization process. For example, in Germany the family appears to play a more central and exclusive role in upbringing than it does in the United States, where children spend a substantially greater proportion of their time outside the family in peer group settings (Devereux, Bronfenbrenner and Suci, 1960). The influence of peers emerged as even stronger, however, among English children, who were far more ready than their American age-mates to follow the lead of their companions in socially disapproved activities rather than adhere to values and behaviors approved by parents and other adults (Devereux, Bronfenbrenner and Rodgers, 1965). In other words, the evidence suggested that in both these Western countries, especially in England, peers often stood in opposition to adults in influencing the child to engage in anti-social behavior.

In contrast, field observations in the Soviet Union (Bronfenbrenner, 1963) indicated a rather different pattern. In that country, in keeping with the educational principles and methods developed by Makarenko (1952) and others, an explicit effort is made to utilize the peer group as an agent for socializing the child and bringing about an identification with the values of the adult society (Bronfenbrenner, 1962). Accordingly we were led to the hypothesis that in the Soviet Union, in contrast to America or England, children are less likely to experience peer pressure as conflicting with adult values and hence can identify more strongly with adult standards for behavior.

RESEARCH DESIGN AND PROCEDURES

An opportunity to investigate this hypothesis was provided during the author's visits as an exchange scientist at the Institute of Psychology in Moscow in 1963 and 1964. With the cooperation of Soviet colleagues, it was possible to carry out a comparative study of reaction to pressure from peers *vs* adults in six American (N = 158) and six Soviet (N = 188) classrooms at comparable age and grade levels (average age of 12 years in both countries, 6th graders in US, 5th graders in USSR, where school entrance occurs one year later).

To measure the child's responsiveness to pressure from adult *vs* peers we employed the following experimental procedure.[1] Children were asked to respond to a series of conflict

[1] This procedure was developed by the author in collaboration with the other principal investigators for the project as a whole: E. C. Devereux, Jr., G. J. Suci, and R. R. Rodgers, who also carried out the American phase of the experiment.

Reprinted from the *International Journal of Psychology*, 1967, **2**, 199–207, by permission of the author and the International Union of Psychological Science and Dunod, Publisher, France.

situations under three different conditions: 1) a *base* or *neutral* condition, in which they were told that no one would see their responses except the investigators conducting the research; 2) an *adult* condition in which they were informed that the responses of everyone in the class would be posted on a chart and shown to parents and teachers at a special meeting scheduled for the following week; and 3) a *peer* condition, in which the children were notified that the chart would be prepared and shown a week later to the class itself. The conflict situations consisted of 30 hypothetical dilemmas such as the following:

The Lost Test

You and your friends accidentally find a sheet of paper which the teacher must have lost. On this sheet are the questions and answers for a quiz that you are going to have tomorrow. Some of the kids suggest that you not say anything to the teacher about it, so that all of you can get better marks. What would you *really* do? Suppose your friends decide to go ahead. Would you go along with them or refuse?

REFUSE TO GO ALONG
WITH MY FRIENDS

absolutely certain	fairly certain	I guess so

GO ALONG WITH MY FRIENDS

I guess so	fairly certain	absolutely certain

Other items dealt with such situations as going to a movie recommended by friends but disapproved by parents, neglecting homework to join friends, standing guard while friends put a rubber snake in the teacher's desk, leaving a sick friend to go to a movie with the gang, joining friends in pilfering fruit from an orchard with a "no trespassing" sign, wearing styles approved by peers but not by parents, running away after breaking a window accidentally while playing ball, etc.

A Russian-language version of the same thirty items was prepared, with minor variations to adapt to the Soviet cultural context. Each response was scored on a scale from −2.5 to +2.5, a negative value being assigned

to the behavior urged by age mates. To control for a positional response set, scale direction was reversed in half of the items. The situations were divided into three alternate forms of 10 items each, with a different form being used for each experimental condition. Thus under any one condition a child could obtain a score ranging from −25 to +25 with zero representing equal division between behavior urged by peers and adults. Split-half reliabilities for the ten-item forms ranged from .75 to .86 under different experimental conditions; the reliability of the total score (*i.e.,* sum across all three conditions) was .94. All reliability coefficients are corrected for length of test by the Spearman-Brown formula.

The basic research design involved a double Latin square with experimental treatments constituting the three rows, classrooms appearing in the columns, and forms distributed randomly, with the restriction that each form appear only once in each column and twice in each row. This basic pattern was repeated twice in each culture, once for boys and once for girls, for a total of four sets of double Latin squares (three conditions by six classrooms in four sex-culture combinations). In order to equate for varying numbers of boys and girls in each classroom, the individual cell entries used for the primary analysis of variance were the mean scores obtained by all boys or girls in a given classroom under a particular experimental condition. In this model, classrooms and forms were treated as random variables, and culture, experimental treatment, and sex of child as fixed effects. It is, of course, the latter three which constitute the primary focus of interest in the experiment.

RESULTS

Mean values obtained by boys and girls in each culture under the three experimental conditions are shown in Table 1, relevant mean differences and corresponding significance levels in Table 2. Several findings emerge from this analysis. First of all, there is clear evidence that Soviet children are far less willing than their American age mates to say that they will engage in socially disapproved behavior. The

TABLE I

Mean Scores Obtained by Boys and Girls in the US and the USSR Under Three Experimental Conditions

Subjects	I Base	II Adult	III Peer	IV M across Conditions
Boys				
Soviet	12.54	14.21	13.18	13.30
American	1.02	1.57	.16	.92
Difference	11.52	12.64	13.02	12.38
Girls				
Soviet	15.13	17.02	16.90	16.33
American	3.83	4.35	2.38	3.52
Difference	11.30	12.67	14.52	12.82
Both sexes				
Soviet	13.84	15.62	15.04	14.82
American	2.43	2.96	1.27	2.22

TABLE 2

Differences in Total Score and Experimental Effects by Culture and Sex

	I Soviet	II American	III Effect across both cultures (Sov. + Amer.)	IV Cultural Difference (Soviet — Amer.)
Total scores				
1. Both sexes (Girls + Boys)	14.82	2.22	—	12.60**
2. Sex differ. (Girls — Boys)	3.03	2.60	5.63**	.43 ns
Shift scores (Girls + Boys)[1]				
3. Ad[2]-peer conflict (Ad — Peer)	.58	1.69	2.27**	−1.11 ns
4. Ad shift (Ad — Base)	1.78	.53	2.31	1.25
5. Peer shift (Base — Peer)	−1.20	1.16	−.04	−2.36
6. Ad shift — Peer shift	2.90	−.63	2.35 ns	3.61*

* significant at .05.
** significant at .01.
[1] None of the shift effects showed a significant interaction by sex.
[2] Ad = Adult.

mean scores for Russian boys and girls (Table 1, Col. IV) average about 13 and 16 respectively, values that are clearly on the adult side of the continuum. The corresponding American averages of approximately 1 and 3.5 are barely over the dividing line, indicating that the children are almost as ready to follow the prompting of peers to deviant behavior as to adhere to adult-approved standards of con-

duct. The above cultural difference is highly significant across both sexes (Table 2, Line 1).

Second, the data indicate that both in the USSR and in the United States, boys are more inclined to engage in socially undesirable activity than girls. The absence of a reliable sex by culture interaction (Table 2, Col. IV) indicates that the sex difference was no larger in one country than in the other. It is noteworthy that despite the differing conceptions of the role of women in the two societies, females in the Soviet Union as in the United States lay greater claim to virtuous behavior, at least up to the age of twelve!

Third, turning to the experimental effects, we learn (Table 2, Line 3) that in both countries children gave more socially approved responses when told that their answers would be seen by adults than when faced wtih the prospect of having their statements shown to classmates. Although American youngsters exhibited a greater shift than their Soviet counterparts, a fact which suggests stronger conflict between peer and adult influences in the United States, this cultural difference is not statistically significant (Table 2, Line 3, Col. IV). A reliable difference does appear, however, for the remaining independent degree of freedom which measures whether the two shifts from base condition differed from each other; that is, whether there was any difference in direction or degree between the shift from base to adult condition and that from base to peer condition. As indicated in Table 2 (Line 6), Soviet children shifted more when subjected to pressure from grown-ups, whereas Americans were slightly more responsive to pressure from peers. The components entering into this difference are shown in Lines 4 and 5 of the same table. Although the cultural differences cannot be subjected to an independent statistical test, since they are incorporated in the single degree of freedom tested in Line 6, they do provide a more detailed picture of the differing reactions of children in the two countries to pressure from grown-ups *vs* age mates. Thus we see from Line 4 that although both Russian and American youngsters gave more socially acceptable responses in moving from the neutral to the adult condition, this shift was more pronounced for the Soviet children. Moreover, under pressure from peers (Line 5), there was a difference in direction as well as degree. When told that classmates would see their answers, American pupils indicated greater readiness to engage in socially-disapproved behavior, whereas Soviet children exhibited increased to adult standards. In other words, as against the United States, the

influence of peers operated in the same direction as that of adults.

DISCUSSION

Our original hypothesis has been sustained in a number of respects. First, in contrast both to American and English children, Russian youngsters showed less inclination to engage in anti-social activity. Second, although pressure from adults induced greater commitment to socially approved behavior in both cultures, Soviet children were more responsive to the influence of grown-ups than of peers, whereas their American age mates showed a trend in the opposite direction. Putting it another way, pressure from peers operated differently in the two countries. In the USSR, it strengthened commitment to adult-approved behavior; in the United States it increased deviance from adult standards of conduct.

If, as our data strongly suggest, the social context is a powerful determinant of behavior, then we should expect difference in responses to be associated not only with molar social structures like cultures but also smaller units such as classroom groups. This expectation can be tested from our data by determining whether, in each culture, there were significant classroom effects; the error term used for this comparison was the mean square for individual differences within classrooms. Table 3 shows the variance of class-

TABLE 3

Variances Among Classroom Means Under Three Experimental Conditions

	American	Soviet
Base	36.01**	43.40**
Adult	13.43	9.25
Peer	45.77**	17.01

** *F* significant at .01.

room means in each country under each of the three experimental conditions. The accompanying significance levels reveal that there are reliable classroom differences in both countries, but only under base or peer conditions, never in the adult condition. It would appear that the tendency to conform to peer group norms operates only in the absence of monitoring by parents and teachers, and threat of exposure to adults has the effect of dissolving pressure to conform to peer standards. Although the pattern of classroom variances under the three experimental conditions differs in the two countries—the highest mean square occurs under peer condition in the United States and base condition in the USSR—this cultural variation was not significant. Nor were there any reliable classroom differences associated with the sex of the child.

What about individual differences within classrooms? Is there a greater tendency for children to conform to classroom norms in one country than in the other? The data of Table 4

TABLE 4

Average Variance of Individuals Within Classrooms

	American	Soviet	Ratio US/USSR
Boys	$df = 75$	$df = 103$	
Base	5.70	5.03	1.13
Adult	6.10	5.23	1.17
Peer	6.05	5.71	1.06
Total	14.07	11.55	1.22
Girls	$df = 71$	$df = 73$	
Base	4.28	2.08	2.06**
Adult	4.98	1.73	2.88**
Peer	5.36	2.03	2.64**
Total	11.31	3.02	3.74**

** *F* significant at .01.

reveal that there is such a cultural difference, but for one sex only. Although American boys show slightly higher individual variation than either Soviet boys or American girls, these differences are not significant. Soviet girls, however, show a surprisingly strong tendency to respond as a classroom group, with little individual deviance. The variances are about half the size of those for any other group, and

significantly smaller. Finally, individual differences for the Russian girls were smallest when exposed to pressure from adults. It will be recalled that the Soviet girls were the most adult-oriented of the four groups of subjects. Under all those conditions, including peer pressure, their mean scores were above 15, closer to the maximum possible 25 than to the borderline of anti-social behavior represented by zero on the scale. Given this combination of especially high means with extremely low variances, we may conclude that it is Soviet girls in particular who support adult standards of behavior and, both as individuals and as a classroom collective, experience and exert social pressure to conform to these standards.

The finding that in both societies adult pressure dissolved group solidarity suggests some opposition between adult values and peer interests in the Soviet Union as well as in the United States. The fact remains, however, that at least in our data, readiness to resist promptings to anti-social behavior, and responsiveness to adult influence, were greater among Russian than among American children. In addition, the results showed that in the USSR peer groups exerted some influence in support of adult standards, whereas in America they encouraged deviance from adult norms.

Although these results are in accord with our original hypothesis, and indeed perhaps for this very reason, it is important to stress the limitations of the study. To begin with, our samples were rather small, only six classrooms, comprising less than 200 cases, in each culture. Second, both samples were essentially accidental, the American classrooms being drawn from two schools in a small city in upstate New York, the Russian from three *internats*, or boarding schools, in Moscow. The latter fact is especially important since one of the reasons for the widespread introduction of boarding schools in connection with the educational reform carried out in the Soviet Union during the past decade was to make possible more effective character education in the school environment. It is therefore possible that pupils in the internats are more strongly identified with adult values than those attending day schools. For this reason, the experiment here described is currently being carried out, through the collaboration of the Institute of Psychology, in six other Moscow classrooms in schools of the more conventional type where the students live at home. At the same time, the experiment is also being repeated in a series of classrooms in a large American city more comparable to Moscow.

Even if these further and more relevant replications confirm the trends revealed by the present data, two additional questions remain. First there is the matter of the generalizability of the results outside the experimental setting. Although carried out in school classrooms, the research remains in effect a laboratory study dealing with hypothetical situations rather than behavior in real life. What evidence is there that in fact American children are more likely than their Soviet age mates to engage in antisocial behavior? None in the present study. The present investigator has reported elsewhere, however, some field observations of Soviet children which described a pattern quite in accord with the findings of the present research. For example, "In their external actions they are well-mannered, attentive, and industrious. In informal conversations, they reveal strong motivation to learn, a readiness to serve their society. . . . Instances of aggressiveness, violation of rules, or other anti-social behavior appear to be genuinely rare" (Bronfenbrenner, 1963).

Finally, we must bear in mind that both the earlier observations and present experimental study were carried out with children at a particular age level, namely late childhood and early adolescence. We are therefore left with the all important question, unanswered by our data, as to how these same youngsters will behave as adults. Do children who at the age of 12 or 13 yield to peer pressures toward antisocial behavior continue to show such reactions

in later years? Does early commitment to the values of the adult society endure? Does the presence of such a commitment in adulthood require that the norms of behavior among children be fully compatible with those of grown-ups, or does some conflict of interest further the development of capacities for independent thought and responsible social action? Our results shed little light on these important questions.

Despite the acknowledged limitations of the study, it permits several inferences, both theoretical and practical. With respect to the former, the experiment demonstrates that social pressure has appreciable effects in such differing social systems as those of the Soviet Union and the United States. At the same time, the research indicates that these effects can vary significantly as a function of the larger social context. Where the peer group is to a large extent autonomous, as it often is in the United States, it can exert influence in opposition to values held by the adult society. In other types of social systems, such as the USSR, the peer group, and its power to affect the attitudes and actions of its members, can be harnessed by the adult society for the furtherance of its own values and objectives. This fact carries with it important educational and social implications. Thus it is clear that in the Soviet Union the role of the peer group is in large part the result of explicit policy and practice. This is hardly the case in the United States. In the light of the increasing evidence for the influence of the peer group on the behavior and psychological development of children and adolescents, it is questionable whether any society, whatever its social system, can afford to leave largely to chance the direction of this influence, and realization of its high potential for fostering constructive development both for the child and his society.

REFERENCES

~brenner, U. Soviet methods of character
. *American Psychologist*, 1962, 17,

~r, U. Upbringing in collective set-

tings in Switzerland and the USSR. Paper presented at the XVIIth International Congress of Psychology, Washington, D.C., 1963.
Devereux, E. C., Jr., Bronfenbrenner, U. & Suci,

G. J. Patterns of parent behavior in the United States of America and the Federal Republic of Germany: A cross-national comparison. *International Social Science Journal* (UNESCO), 1962, 14, 488–506.

Devereux, E. C., Jr., Bronfenbrenner, U. & Rodgers, R. R. Child-rearing in England and the United States: A cross-national comparison. Unpublished manuscript.

Makarenko, A. S. *O Kommunisticheskom Vospitanii* (On Communist Upbringing). Moscow: Gosudarstvennoe Uchebno-pedagogicheskoye Izdatel'stvo, 1952.

INDEX OF NAMES

For authors who are discussed in selections or introductions and cited in reference lists, page numbers are given for the discussions only; for authors who are cited in reference lists, with no accompanying discussion, page numbers of the citations are given.

Page numbers in *italics* indicate selections included in this book.

INDEX OF SUBJECTS

Page numbers in *italics* indicate illustrative material.

phase of, 3; phallic phase of, 3–4

Shame, 21–22

Socialization processes, 309–15; in Soviet culture, 447–55; in Temne and Eskimo cultures, 99–100

Social learning theory, 16, 310, 341–42

Socioeconomic status, effect of: on achievement motivation, 407, 409; on attention focus of infant, 158–60; on health and education, 127–35; on in-

fant behavior, 79–87; on intelligence of child, 92, 212, 218, 246–48; on parents as teachers, 437–46; on student dissent, 108–09

Stages: in ego development, 20–29; in Piagetian theory, 10–12, 168–72, 504–07; in psychoanalytic theory, 2–5

Stimulus-response theory, 15–16; Piaget's view of, 43–46. *See also* Behaviorism

Sublimation, 6

Superego, 8, 22–24, 54–59, 315

Tactual discrimination, 222–30

Teachers: and behavior problems, 457–71; as socializing agents, 419–20, 459–71; in Soviet culture, 448–51. *See also* School phobia

Temptation, resistance to, 374–80

Trust (infant), 19–21

Visual perception, in infants, 147–51; improvement of, 222–30; of objects, 239–42; of space, 235–39

A 2
B 3
C 4
D 5
E 6
F 7
G 8
H 9
I 0
J 1